THE LONG SHADOW

THE
LONG
SHADOW

*The Lutcher-Stark
Lumber Dynasty*

Ellen Walker Rienstra
Jo Ann Stiles

The H.J. Lutcher Stark Center for Physical Culture and Sports
The University of Texas at Austin
Distributed by Tower Books, an Imprint of the University of Texas Press

Requests for permission to reproduce material from this work should be sent to:
   Permissions
   University of Texas Press
   P.O. Box 7819
   Austin, TX 78713-7819
   http://utpress.utexas.edu/index.php/rp-form

♾ The paper used in this book meets the minimum requirements of
ANSI/NISO Z39.48-1992 (R1997) (Permanence of Paper).

LIBRARY OF CONGRESS CATALOGING-IN-PUBLICATION DATA

Names: Rienstra, Ellen Walker, author.
Title: The long shadow : the Lutcher-Stark lumber dynasty / Ellen Walker Rienstra, Jo Ann
   Stiles.
Description: First edition. | Austin : Tower Books, an imprint of the University of Texas
   Press, 2016. | Includes bibliographical references and index.
Identifiers: LCCN 2016024820
   ISBN 978-1-4773-0871-4 (cloth : alk. paper)
Subjects: LCSH: Stark family. | Stark, Henry Jacob Lutcher, 1887–1965. | Stark, Nelda, 1909–
   1999. | Lutcher and Moore Lumber Company.
Classification: LCC CS71 .S795 2016 | DDC 929.20973—dc23
LC record available at https://lccn.loc.gov/2016024820

Frontispiece: A figure thought to be William Henry Stark surveys the site of The Lutcher
& Moore Lumber Company's new Lower Mill on the Sabine River in Orange, Texas, 1915.
Stark Foundation Archives.

★

For our families
Judy, Tom, Miles, Sean, John, David, Allen, Carol, Dan (1963–1996)
Trey, Ruth Ann, David, Joseph
And the people of Southeast Texas

Contents

Acknowledgments

It is rare indeed for historians to be given the chance to research a historically significant but as-yet-unexplored body of material, as was the case for our work on the Lutcher and Stark business and family papers. For allowing us this once-in-a-lifetime opportunity, we remain deeply grateful to the Nelda C. and H.J. Lutcher Stark Foundation and to its president and chief executive officer, Walter G. Riedel III. From start to finish, he afforded us constant support and granted us much additional time to complete this project, which grew exponentially in scope, far beyond anyone's initial imaginings, as more valuable primary material was discovered and brought to us almost daily.

Many other individuals have rendered us invaluable assistance, willingly given, and to them we also extend our sincere thanks. Through their contributions of time, expertise, reminiscences, photos, letters, diaries, and other historical material, the story of the Lutcher and Stark family dynasty has taken shape, and its principals have again been brought to life as the vital human beings they were.

We can never sufficiently express our profound gratitude to the late Roy Stephen Wingate, lifelong Orange resident, former Orange County district attorney, and Stark Foundation Board Member Emeritus, our "walking encyclopedia" who spent every day with us for many years, patiently and knowledgeably guiding us through the vast maze of material comprising the Foundation's records and serving as our "go-to" source for all of Orange County history and background information. "Let's ask Roy" became our daily mantra during the time we were fortunate enough to work with him and for a time afterward, as his illness permitted, before his death on January 12, 2014.

We extend our heartfelt thanks to Beth Turley, vice president–chief compliance officer and general counsel of the Stark Foundation, who generously gave us many hours of her time and the benefit of her considerable editorial skills, as well as much technical and moral support.

We are also immensely grateful to John Cash "Jack" Smith, longtime Orange resident, attorney, and former Stark Foundation board member, who initially recommended us to the Stark Foundation for this project and shared with us his personal reminiscences of Lutcher Stark. Without Jack's introduction, we would never have had the chance to work with this material.

Our hearty gratitude also goes to Judith Walker Linsley, our longtime colleague (and Rienstra's sister), who joined us in working on this project; without her dedication, long hours spent reading and rereading, and exemplary editing, we could not have succeeded in completing it.

The late Eunice Robinson Benckenstein and her niece, the late Anita Cowan, shared invaluable insights and reminiscences of the daily lives of Nelda and Lutcher Stark. The late Dr. Howard Williams, Orange's premier historian, established and published a broad body of local history that proved invaluable to us. He also encouraged us in this project and furnished historical materials.

Our colleague and friend Patsy Herrington, the former director of The W.H. Stark House (the restored home of Miriam and William Stark and the childhood home of Lutcher Stark), furnished many details of the Starks' everyday lives and accompanied us on our research trips to Williamsport, Pennsylvania, the former home of the Lutcher family. Jeffry Harris, the present curator of The W.H. Stark House, shared newfound historical treasures with us, as did Samantha Hoag, former collections and exhibitions manager, and Drew Whatley, assistant site manager/educator.

Clyde V. "Tad" McKee III, vice president–chief financial officer of the Stark Foundation, furnished several items of historic value as well as moral support; and his mother, Mary Louise Bevil McKee, who personally knew many of the principals in the history, graciously served as an unofficial historical consultant.

Sarah Boehme, curator of the Stark Museum of Art, willingly gave us much-needed information, background, and sources on the Stark family's extensive art collections; and Allison Evans, collections manager and registrar at the museum, lent us assistance on references.

The late Michael Hoke, former director of Shangri La Botanical Gardens and Nature Center in Orange, furnished us invaluable information about the flora, fauna, and history of the gardens in Lutcher Stark's time, as well as many personal stories of the Stark family. Joseph Johnson, director of horticulture at the gardens, gave us information on the Stark family's greenhouses. Horticulture/epiphyte specialist Jennifer Buckner assisted us in understanding the culture of the orchids that Frances Ann Lutcher, nicknamed "the Orchid Lady," loved to grow.

Terry and Jan Todd, director and co-director, respectively, of the

H.J. Lutcher Stark Center for Physical Culture and Sports, provided support, information, historical material, and personal stories of Lutcher Stark's dedication to weight lifting and physical fitness. Kyle Hood shared her stories of Frances Ann Lutcher and her extensive knowledge of the art and history of the Lutcher Memorial Building of Orange's First Presbyterian Church. Cynthia Carter Leedy Horn furnished us much valuable information and many delightful personal stories of her lifetime association with the Brown family and relayed to us her mother's reminiscences of Frances Ann Lutcher.

Phyllis Woodford lent us the benefit of her considerable computer skills, saving us on many occasions from our own "electronically challenged" state, and offered invaluable assistance in organizing images. Jenniffer Hudson Connors, library and archive manager, provided references and shared information and historical treasures, and Claire Smith, library and archive administrative assistant, gave us much-needed help in locating various items in the archives. In addition, both Claire and Jenniffer afforded many hours of help in locating and scanning images. Mike Brister, the Foundation's technology manager, also offered assistance in working with the technical properties of the images. Richard H. "Dick" Dickerson, the Foundation's retired archivist, assisted us in locating archival documents and images, and Kaycee Spears offered her help during her stints as summer intern at the archives.

Robert and Jeannette Lutcher of Williamsport, Pennsylvania, graciously took us into their home and shared invaluable information and family stories of the Lutcher family in Williamsport. Robert Lutcher showed us the lot in South Williamsport where the home of Frances Ann and Henry Jacob Lutcher had once stood, as well as the nearby location of the Lutcher & Moore mill. They also shared some priceless treasures: the family Bible belonging to Henry Lutcher's parents, Lewis and Mary Barbara Beerweiler Lutscher, containing a tintype of them; and the huge, lethal-looking meat cleaver from Lutcher Brothers, the family's Williamsport butcher shop. The Lutchers have since donated these precious items to the Stark Foundation.

The late Dr. Jeremiah Stark of Woodville, a former Lamar University professor and a much-younger cousin of Lutcher Stark's, inherited many of the John Thomas Stark family archives on the death of Lily Rose Stark, John Thomas's last surviving child, and donated much of the material to the Stark Foundation, adding greatly to our knowledge of that nineteenth-century family.

Sawmill owner Dan Elder and his family of Kirbyville, Texas, placed on permanent loan with the Stark Foundation a century-old cypress "sinker" log, bearing the Lutcher & Moore Star and Crescent brand, which he himself had retrieved from the Sabine River bottom. Patty Renfro, administrative associate senior in the Lamar University History Department, transcribed the eighty-plus interviews we conducted for the Foundation's oral history program; and Mary Charlotte Carroll, a student at Rice University, assisted in proofreading the interviews. Jean Bell Moncla and Patrick L. Bell shared memorabilia of their grandfather, 1920s University of Texas football star C.L. "Ox" Higgins, a protégé and good friend of Lutcher Stark.

Thanks to Larry Manley; the late Alton Laird; Ryan Smith, director of the Texas Energy Museum; and the Tyrrell Historical Library, where we acquired previously undiscovered information pertaining to Frances Ann Lutcher's travels with her chauffeur, Herbert W. Fiedler, donated to the Tyrrell Historical Library by Manley, Fiedler's nephew. Theresa King, Darrell Duchene, and the staff at InFocus Camera and Imaging in Orange patiently assisted us with our requests for images and accomplished amazing restorations of historic photographs. John A. Watson volunteered his knowledge of the life and Interscholastic League activities of longtime UIL Director Roy Bedichek, as did Paul Prosperie on the life of Beaumont newspaper columnist Florence Stratton.

Scott Sagar and the staff at the Thomas T. Taber Museum of Lycoming County, Williamsport, Pennsylvania, furnished us much assistance in finding material pertaining to the lives of the Lutcher family and several rare images of early-day Williamsport. The staff at Lycoming College, formerly Dickinson Seminary, Henry Lutcher's alma mater, delved into their records to find not only Lutcher's registration at the school but also his scholastic marks and other pertinent information, as well as the records of G. Bedell Moore, Lutcher's business partner, who also attended the school. The staff at Messiah Lutheran Church in Williamsport allowed us access to church records—the Lutcher family's births, baptisms, marriages, deaths—unavailable from any other source, and Williamsport historian Thad Stephen Meckley gave his time to share much of the city's sights and history with us.

Thanks, too, are due the staff members of the Austin History Center, the Dolph Briscoe Center for American History, and the Nettie Lee Benson Latin American Collection at the University of Texas at Austin; the Lorenzo de Zavala State Library and Archives; and the Legislative Reference Library of Texas. For East Texas historical sources, we were greatly assisted by the staff at the Tyrrell Historical Library in Beaumont, the Mary and John Gray Library at Lamar University in Beaumont, the Lamar State College–Orange Library, the Orange Public Library, and the Heritage House Museum and Archives in Orange. The Newton County Historical Society granted us access to their publications, archives, and museum and referred us to the Woodville Pioneer House Museum with its family archives on the Adams and Blewitt families.

Stiles owes personal thanks to her sister, Carol Pankratz, who, with her friend Robert Ligon, detoured to Lincoln, Kansas, to find the gravesites of Frances Ann Lutcher's father, David Robinson; her stepmother, Matilda Robinson; and his family. Carole and Peter Jackson introduced Stiles to Canadian Bonnie Sitter and a friend, who conducted additional research on David Robinson's family, turning up other family members (but not, unfortunately, Frances Ann's mother).

We also extend our fervent thanks to all the interviewees of our oral history program, too numerous to name here, who so willingly shared their time, memories, and in many cases their memorabilia with us. Their interviews will eventually be made available to the public as a part of the Nelda C. and H.J. Lutcher Stark Foundation Archives.

And last but certainly not least, our continuing gratitude goes to our families—for their unflagging support, their ongoing patience with our years'-long and total absorption in this project, and their faith that somehow, someday, we would finish it.

Ellen Walker Rienstra
Jo Ann Stiles
Orange, Texas

Prologue

For the tree of the field is man's life.
—DEUTERONOMY 20:19

In the twilight of his life, Henry Jacob Lutcher Stark often walked in an Eden of his own creation, huge gardens he had carved from woods and wetlands on his family's property near his hometown of Orange, Texas. The gardens were the fruit of years of the hard labor of many, including himself. Lutcher Stark, as he was called, had named his Southeast Texas paradise "Shangri-La" after the mythic land high in the Himalayas featured in the 1933 best-selling novel *Lost Horizon*. At the pinnacle of his physical, mental, and financial power and influence, he had created his own climate, much like that other icon of the Himalayas, Mount Everest. But in his later years, he increasingly took refuge here, in Shangri-La, his private garden kingdom.

He particularly enjoyed contemplating a huge, gnarled old pond cypress brooding at the water's edge of Adams Bayou, deep in the heart of the gardens, its myriad knees clustered like beggars at its base. He had placed a bench near it, and when he took his walks in Shangri-La, he settled himself on the bench and gazed by the hour at the natural scene around him. The tree was an anomaly, since pond cypresses did not ordinarily grow in Southeast Texas, but here it thrived, having defied natural law in this foreign spot for twelve hundred years. On Christmas Day in AD 800, near the time the tree had begun to grow, Charlemagne had been crowned emperor of the Romans in the old St. Peter's Basilica in Rome.

In fact, the story of Lutcher Stark's family had begun with trees—at first with the white pine and hemlock of Pennsylvania's Susquehanna River Valley and later with the vast virgin forests of cypress and longleaf yellow pine of Southeast Texas and Louisiana. With the trees grew the history of three illustrious generations of the Lutcher-Stark lumber dynasty, three regimes marked by singular achievement:

- Stark's grandfather, Henry Jacob Lutcher, the visionary, who foresaw the boundless potential of the Texas and Louisiana timber forests and reaped their bounty
- Stark's father, William Henry Stark, the genius capitalist, who expanded and diversified the lumber kingdom into a complex network of interrelated enterprises
- Lutcher Stark, the philanthropist and the last of the triumvirate, who channeled his inheritance into largesse for uncounted charities, particularly toward his alma mater, the University of Texas

He served the university for many years as chairman of its Board of Regents, but his rock-hard traditional beliefs and values eventually collided with elemental changes in the world and at his beloved university, and he ultimately saw his power and influence wane amid acrimony and a series of personal crises and major losses of his own. In bitter disillusionment, he returned his attention to his native Southeast Texas, where he continued his philanthropies in his home territory.

Now he was nearing the end of his own prodigious life. After years of estrangement, he had accepted the university's invitation to join the Longhorn Hall of Honor. And with his third wife, he created a lasting legacy: Orange's Nelda C. and H.J. Lutcher Stark Foundation, its aim to improve and enrich the quality of life in the Southeast Texas region, where the family made their fortune—and their home. In the course of their lives, separately and together, these three generations significantly altered the course of the economic and cultural history of Orange, Southeast Texas, and the University of Texas. Just as the old tree still lived, so would the legacy of this extraordinary family.

Our goal in writing this history has been to discover the truth about the Lutcher and Stark families and to write accurately from that body of facts, divesting them of accrued myth. In telling their story, we hope to capture their essence, to remain true to their spirits, and to place them squarely within the framework of the times and places in which they lived.

Spelling and punctuation in all correspondence in the early sources have been left intact.

PART I

THE

VISIONARY

CHAPTER ONE

Williamsport . . . the Beginning

May his shadow never grow less and good luck always be his portion.
—"LUMBERING IN THE LONE STAR STATE," WILLIAMSPORT
DAILY SUN AND BANNER, OCTOBER 13, 1881
(ARTICLE ON HENRY JACOB LUTCHER)

In the frigid Pennsylvania winter in January 1877, two young lumbermen, Henry Jacob Lutcher and his business partner, Gregory Bedell Moore, set out from their hometown of Williamsport to "cruise for timber," as they called it in the industry.[1] The handwriting stood plainly on the wall, and Lutcher and Moore had read it: timber, especially white pine, was growing scarce in the Susquehanna River Valley, and indeed in all of Pennsylvania. Lutcher and Moore had been successful in Williamsport. The rapid growth of the young republic of the United States, followed by the added demands of the Civil War, had prompted ever-increasing needs for lumber and other building materials, and the wealth of white pine and eastern hemlock in Pennsylvania's forests served as a plentiful source, fostering a lumber boom in the Susquehanna Valley beginning in the 1850s. Williamsport, Lycoming County, lying in north-central Pennsylvania on the West Branch of the Susquehanna and surrounded by these forests of prime softwood, was situated in an optimal spot to profit enormously from the new urgency.[2]

This was the town and the world in which Henry Jacob Lutcher and Bedell Moore had first formed their business association, then flourished. Lutcher, older by four years and the visionary and dominant personality of the two, was a native of Pennsylvania. He was of German stock, the third child and elder son of Maria Barbara Beerweiler and Ludwig Friedrich Lutscher and the second of their children to be born on American soil.[3] Pennsylvania was a haven for German settlers, and the young couple and their two-year-old daughter, Rosina Dorothea (later Americanized to Rosanna, or Rosa), had emigrated in 1833 from Degerloch, a village near

Figure 1.1. Henry Jacob Lutcher, undated. Stark Foundation Archives.

Stuttgart, Wurttemberg, via Holland to settle briefly in the borough of Mill Hall, Centre County (present-day Clinton County), in the Nittany Valley. Here their second daughter, Maria Barbara (Mary), arrived August 2, 1834, followed two years later by a son, Jacob Heinrich (Henry Jacob), born November 4, 1836.[4] Soon thereafter, the family relocated to the nearby town of Williamsport and settled in a house on William Street.[5]

Figure 1.2. Mary Barbara Beerweiler and Lewis Frederick Lutscher, undated. Courtesy of Robert Lutcher.

Most of the German immigrants coming into Pennsylvania during that period were of the middle class—merchants, farmers, laborers. Lutscher was a butcher by trade, and at some point he opened a shop in the "city market" in Williamsport, near the city's Market Square.[6] The Lutschers eventually had five more children: Christiana (Christina), Louisa, Henriette (Henrietta), Albert William (probably originally Albrecht Wilhelm, although there is no record), and Amalia Elisabeth (Amelia). The Lutschers Americanized their own first names, becoming "Lewis Frederick" and "Mary Barbara," although, unlike their children, they retained the German spelling of their last name throughout their lives.[7] On February 3, 1841, Lewis Lutscher filed his intention in the Lycoming County Court of Common Pleas to become a citizen of the United States, and on February 13, 1844, the court granted his citizenship.[8]

At the time of the Lutschers' arrival in Williamsport, a lumber boom was as-yet unimagined. The little town of less than a thousand inhabitants nestled comfortably in the heart of the beautiful Susquehanna River Valley on the north bank of the wide, slow-moving river, among gently rolling hills. Game abounded in the dense stands of hardwood, hemlock, and white pine surrounding the town, and trout swam thickly in the rocky, tumbling streams. Farms dotted the surrounding countryside, farming and home industry being the two main occupations. The 1796 log-built Russell's Inn and Tavern, the first structure in Williamsport, served as the hub of the town, which also boasted a post office, a newspaper, a courthouse, a few shops, and a jail, as well as blacksmiths, doctors, lawyers, and others employed in trades and crafts.[9] In August 1831, the town acquired a cultural amenity: a band, consisting of flutes, clarinets, a piccolo, and one French horn. It later named itself the Repasz Band, after one of its conductors.[10] In 1834, the year following the Lutschers' arrival, the first mule-drawn packet boats plied the waters of the newly opened West Branch Canal, hauling freight and later passengers, and in May 1835, the first public schools opened in town.[11]

In 1836, the year of Henry Jacob Lutscher's birth, another occurred, far to the southwest. On April 21, with a decisive victory by General Sam Houston's Texas Army over Mexican forces at the Battle of San Jacinto, a certain vast territory in northern Mexico was reborn on the battlefield as the infant Republic of Texas. And in Texas would lie Henry Lutscher's future.

In the late 1840s and early 1850s, the Pennsylvania lumber industry, engendered before the American Revolution in the eastern part of the future state and growing exponentially as it furnished wood for dwellings,

Figure 1.3. The great Susquehanna Boom, Williamsport. Henry Lutcher utilized
the idea for this innovation when he moved his lumber operations to Texas.
Collection of the Lycoming County Historical Society and Thomas T. Taber Museum.

barns, ships, furniture, charcoal, barrels, and other needs of the burgeoning young nation, began moving into the interior toward Williamsport.

Other factors were also working to Williamsport's advantage. The twin
innovations of steam-driven machinery and the circular saw blade had rev-
olutionized the entire lumber industry by improving and accelerating production.[12] And two New England business tycoons named James H. Perkins and John Leighton saw a new opportunity to expand their business
horizons when they realized that the slow-moving West Branch Susquehanna at Williamsport was ideal for construction of a log boom. Perkins,
Leighton, and others formed a boom company in 1849, and by 1851 they
had completed the great Susquehanna Boom, a seven-mile system of four
hundred sunken wood-and-stone "cribs" connected by chained-together
logs, designed so the river's natural currents would trap the timber that
had been cut upriver, branded, and then floated downstream to be milled
into lumber. The milled lumber, nailed into log rafts, was then conveyed
to market via the West Branch Canal, and later the railroads.[13]

Almost overnight, Williamsport exploded into undreamed-of prosperity. In 1850, the town's population was 1,615; by 1860, it had jumped to
5,664.[14] Sawmills and furniture factories sprang up on both the north
and south banks of the Susquehanna. During spring thaws, the river was

WEST FOURTH STREET, LOOKING WEST FROM ELMIRA ST.
WILLIAMSPORT, PA.

Figure 1.4. West Fourth Street, Millionaires' Row, Williamsport. G. Bedell Moore
lived on this street before his move to Texas. Stark Foundation Archives.

crowded from shore to shore with myriad logs caught by the Susquehanna
Boom, waiting to be fed into the hungry maws of the city's mills. Workers—so-called boom rats—swarmed over the log jams, wielding pikes,
cant hooks, or peaveys to break up the jams and keep the logs moving.[15]
Stacks belched smoke and steam, and the air was rife with sawdust and
the earsplitting scream of the mill whistles. At the peak of the boom in the
1870s, Williamsport boasted more mills than any other city in the country
and produced 350 million board feet per day, which, at that time, was the
highest level of production in the world and led the city to style itself the
Lumber Capital of the World.[16]

Williamsport blossomed into a thriving metropolis, with a good public school system, numerous commercial establishments, and a cultural
scene, eventually including two opera houses and a music academy.[17] In
fact, during its Golden Age, Williamsport hosted more millionaires per
capita than anywhere else in the United States.[18] Beginning in the 1850s,
these new lumber barons began to construct Victorian mansions in fan-
ciful architectural styles—Eastlake Queen Anne, Richardsonian Roman-
esque, Italianate, Gothic, French Renaissance—along West Third and
West Fourth Streets, dubbed "Millionaires' Row."[19] The town's abrupt
new direction, with its resulting development, would irrevocably change
the course of its history and affect the lives of many of its individuals, including that of Henry Lutscher—or Lutcher, as he and his siblings later
spelled their name.

Figure 1.5. Winter view from Dickinson Seminary toward the Susquehanna River, Williamsport, ca. 1917. Stark Foundation Archives.

Most of Williamsport's large German contingent belonged to the Lutheran denomination. In 1852, several members of the German Lutheran church in Williamsport founded a new congregation, the First English Evangelical Lutheran Church (later St. Mark's Lutheran Church), and in 1854, they erected the first church building at 14 Market Street.[20] The Lutcher family became staunch members of this congregation.[21] On May 14, 1854, as a seventeen-year-old, Henry Lutcher was awarded a small Bible for bringing the largest number of children into the Sabbath School.[22]

Young Henry received what he later described as "a good English education" in Williamsport's public schools,[23] and at seventeen, he entered Dickinson Seminary, Williamsport's respected preparatory school. The seminary advertised itself as "organized on the most approved plan, of the best Institutions of New York and New England," and its course of study as "systematical and extensive, embracing the Common English, Scientific, Classical, and Ornamental branches."[24]

Henry, by his own account, attended the seminary for two years, but the school's records show his enrollment only for the academic year of June 1854–55.[25] (He could possibly have attended part of another year, but his name does not appear anywhere else on the other years' registers.) On the school's rolls, his last name is spelled "Lutcher"; it is unknown whether a school official or Henry Lutcher himself was responsible for the Americanized spelling.[26] During his time in the seminary, he studied in the Common English Department, Class Two, Section A. The school set certain goals for its students: "the cultivation of a cheerful and amiable disposition—in the formation of good habits and manners,—in ardent devotion to study,—and in the attainment of high moral character."[27] Henry Lutcher must have taken the rules to heart, at least most of them; he received a deportment grade of 7 out of 8.[28]

Henry, along with the rest of his siblings, undoubtedly would have been required to work in his family's butcher shop after school and during vacations. Beginning in 1853 as a sixteen-year-old, he also worked at another job—picking edging in the Ellis Schnabel Mill,[29] an old water-powered, or "thundergust," mill (so called because the water rose to a depth sufficient to operate the mill only after a thunderstorm or melting snow[30]). The mill stood in Armstrong Township on the south bank of the Susquehanna, just east of the Market Street Bridge, where a small, clear stream called Hagerman's Run crossed the Linden Branch of the Philadelphia and Erie Railroad. Henry later bought that mill.[31]

The first bridge across the Susquehanna, a toll bridge, had been constructed in 1849, extending Market Street across the river to the south bank.[32] A decade later, August 5, 1859, Henry's father, Lewis Lutscher, paid $225 for two lots on the south bank of the river in Rocktown, a modest neighborhood in Armstrong Township (later the Borough of South Williamsport), near the old Schnabel mill.[33] This property later became the senior Lutschers' family home, and some of their children also bought property in this neighborhood, which hosted Lutcher family homes and businesses for the next century and a half.[34]

Even though he henceforth lived in Rocktown, Lewis Lutscher continued to operate his meat market across the river in Williamsport proper; the 1866–67 Boyd's Williamsport City Directory listed his shop at 10–11 Market House on Market Street between Third and Fourth Streets. The 1869–70 and 1871–72 directories noted that his home was in Rocktown but still listed his shop in the "city market," or "Market House"—Williamsport's Market Square,[35] a well-established curbstone market that constituted a major part of the city's economy. In Market Square, farmers, merchants, peddlers, butchers, flower sellers, and all manner of vendors brought in their wares on Wednesdays and Saturdays to Market Day, where one could buy any of life's essentials.[36]

A postcard written from Williamsport offers a clue to Lewis Lutscher's operation: "Those [vendors] that come regular have a regular place in front of a regular store, paying the city $3.00 per month and 50 [cents] each Market Day they come. Butchers mostly use those frame houses on 4 wheels, storing them on vacant lots other days."[37] Lutscher might indeed have utilized one of these movable buildings to house his shop. In any event, he

Figure 1.6. Curbstone market in Market Square, Williamsport, ca. 1880s.
The Lutcher family would have visited this market many times.
Courtesy of Robin van Auken and Louis E. Hunsinger.

became well known throughout the city and county, supplying "not only the town with meat, but much of the surrounding country."[38]

According to a later account by his grandson, H.J. Lutcher Stark, Henry Lutcher took over his father's work in the butcher shop as a boy of seventeen, freeing Lewis Lutscher to "walk . . . around the streets [of Williamsport] . . . in true Prussian style . . . entertain[ing] himself conversing with people such as he deigned to notice, carrying a gold-headed cane."[39] In 1857, as a twenty-one-year-old already exhibiting an exemplary work ethic, Henry went into business for himself as a butcher and farmer, and at that time, his destiny seemed clear.[40]

Sometime during the year 1857, however, Henry Lutcher encountered his real fate—in the person of a young woman named Frances Ann Robinson. Frances Ann, little more than a girl, had come to Williamsport with her family that year from Jersey Shore, Pennsylvania, a borough on the Susquehanna a few miles west, or upstream, from Williamsport.[41] She

Figure 1.7. Frances Ann Robinson Lutcher, undated. Stark Foundation Archives.

was actually a native of Canada, born in Windsor, Ontario, October 17, 1840,[42] to a French Canadian named David Robinson, nicknamed "Pap," who hailed originally from nearby Amherstburg, also in Ontario.[43] Either at Frances Ann's birth or during her early childhood, her mother died, but the circumstances of her death and even her name so far remain unknown.

In 1841, when Frances Ann was a year old, David Robinson immigrated to Pennsylvania,[44] relocating himself and his daughter to Jersey Shore, where he met a young widow, Matilda Roulon Wilson, thirteen years his junior. Born in Gloucester County, New Jersey, Matilda had moved with her family to Jersey Shore, where she met and married Samuel T. Wilson in 1843.[45] They had a son, George H., and Samuel Wilson died in 1849. Matilda and David married in 1852, making her stepmother to eleven- or twelve-year-old Frances Ann,[46] who apparently came to regard Matilda as her real mother.[47]

The Robinson family lived in Jersey Shore for another five years, then moved eastward into Williamsport sometime in 1857, where David Robinson pursued his lifelong occupation of tailoring.[48] The family moved to 143 Hepburn Street, and he opened a tailoring concern at 97 Pine Street at the corner of West Fourth, probably renting these spaces, since no record exists of his having bought them.[49] Several years later, on May 16, 1869, David Robinson bought property at the southwest corner of West Fourth Street and Pine Alley, where the family lived in a two-story frame building that served as their tailor shop and dwelling.[50]

At the time of the Robinsons' arrival in Williamsport, Frances Ann was possibly still sixteen. The earliest photograph of her shows a young woman, no beauty but already exhibiting the seriousness, independence, and strength of character that would define her throughout her life. A later passport describes her as gray-eyed, standing five feet in height.[51]

In that day, downtown Williamsport comprised a small area of only a few blocks, and the homes and businesses of the Lutchers and the Robinsons stood in close proximity to one another. Somewhere along the way— with a group of friends, in Market Square, in her father's tailor shop, the Lutchers' butcher shop—Frances Ann Robinson inevitably encountered a handsome young butcher named Henry Jacob Lutcher.

It must have been a whirlwind courtship; on January 23, 1858, within a year of her move to Williamsport, they married.[52] She was barely seventeen, and he was just twenty-one. A fragile handwritten poem, "How Henry Lutcher Courted His Bride," found in one of the Lutcher family Bibles and probably composed, if not written, by Frances Ann herself, tells the story of their courtship and elopement:

Oh listen to the story I will tell
It will please you to death I know very well
It's of a Henry Lutcher,[53] a butcher by trade
Who inveigled the affections of a young fair maid.

This gallant young butcher was fair to see
And quite spruce in his uniform blue
He was born in Pennsylvania, was a sweet-spoke boy
And became a young woman's joy.

After her parents had both gone to bed
Out of the house as still as a mouse she would tread
All for to see this young man who had loved her full well
And listen to the stories he would tell.

This gallant young butcher he soon won her heart
And she vowed that from him she never would part
On her sweet lips the contract was sealed
And they went to be married by a Mr. Hatfield.

The fair bride as a servant was dressed
While the gallant H. Lutscher was dressed up at his best.
The knot was soon tied without other losses
And she went right home and he looked to his horse.

When the morning came the fair young woman
Resolved to live with her gallant young man
So she went to her mother and told her outright
What she and the butcher had just been about.[54]

The rhymed tale reveals two facets of Frances Ann's personality that remained dominant throughout her life: her independence and her resolve, extraordinary in a female of her time. Even at seventeen, she knew what she wanted, and she set about accomplishing it. But the poem also illustrates her sense of propriety: after they had eloped, she did not spend a night with her new husband until she had told her mother.[55]

The young couple's whereabouts immediately following the marriage remain unknown, but chances are they lived with relatives, either in Rocktown or across the river with Frances Ann's family in Williamsport. Their circumstances were apparently modest in the extreme; according to a story told by their grandson, Lutcher Stark, they "pooled their resources on their marriage, found they had $2.69, bought a calf and went into the butcher business in competition with the groom's father."[56] Two later entries in the *Williamsport Directory* seem to bear out Stark's statement: "Lewis Lutscher, butcher, shop located at 10-11 Market House on Market Street between Third and Fourth Streets," and "Henry J. Lutscher, butcher, shop located at 1-2-3 Market House." Apparently Henry Lutcher and his father not only were in competition with each other; their shops were only a few doors apart.[57]

On their first wedding anniversary, Henry and Frances Ann's daughter, Miriam Melissa, was born, followed by another daughter, Carrie Launa, September 14, 1861.[58] In the early days, Frances Ann—as well as Miriam and Carrie, as they grew old enough—worked in the butcher shop, and Lutcher Stark later reported that all three "cleaned tripe and chitterlings for spending and education money."[59]

With the passing days, the young Lutchers found themselves living in increasingly troubled times. A crescendo of ominous events was inexorably propelling the nation toward civil war—or, as the citizens of Lycoming County called it, the War of the Rebellion. The prevailing sentiment among Pennsylvanians was in support of the Union, and Lycoming County was no exception. As an early historian put it, "Patriotism found prompt and appropriate expression in the county when the safety of the Union seemed to be imperiled."[60]

As tensions had increased during the 1850s, many abolitionists in Williamsport and Lycoming County had begun acting as "conductors" and "agents" with the Underground Railroad, assisting slaves to their freedom.[61] On August 23, 1856, a group of Lycoming County's young men, called by one historian "the best young men of the city," formed an artillery company, naming themselves the Woodward Guards of Williamsport after one of the town's prominent citizens, and nineteen-year-old Henry Lutcher was listed among them.[62] The group, which boasted ownership of a twelve-pound Napoleon gun, took part in exhibition drills and parades.

In 1858, the year that began so joyously for the young Lutchers with their marriage, a rising young Republican politician named Abraham Lincoln prophetically observed that a house divided against itself could not stand, and his words would soon grow into terrible reality. The year of Miriam's birth, 1859, saw the bloody events at Harpers Ferry. Lincoln's election to the presidency in November 1860 ignited the final fuse, and through the next months, it hissed and crackled its way toward the inevitable detonation. The following April 1861, Carrie's birth year, Confederate cannon fired on the Federal garrison at Fort Sumter in Charleston Harbor; Federal troops surrendered to Confederate forces April 14, and the nation exploded into full-blown war. The next day, Lincoln called for seventy-five thousand volunteers to quell the "rebellion."[63]

In Williamsport, enthusiasm "broke forth in a flame. Monster war meetings were held and the citizens demonstrated in the most unmistakable manner that they were solid for the Union."[64] Actually, support for the war was not quite as solid as it seemed; a good number of Germans living in the rural eastern counties of Pennsylvania refused to enlist at all, believing the war was "at once a vast Republican hoodwink designed to ignore the constitutional rights of fellow Democrats in the southern states and a scheme to interfere with [the Germans'] sequestered, autonomous, and conservative way of life."[65] There is evidence that Henry Lutcher's sentiments echoed these last; one source reported that he was said to have been "an ardent Democrat, but with his father was bitterly opposed to the late war. He believed that it was brought on by scheming and reckless demagogues, indifferent to the long train of miseries they heaped upon their distracted country."[66] Lutcher Stark later stated that "Grandfather Lutcher was called a Copperhead in Yankee Pennsylvania because he thought the South was right."[67]

Nevertheless, Henry Lutcher did not decline to participate in military action. Lycoming County was proud of the promptness with which, in response to Lincoln's call, it sent the first three companies to serve in the Union army. Among the three were the Woodward Guards, mobilized with the Williamsport Rifles on April 23, 1861, but by that time the composition of the membership had changed, and Henry Lutcher's name no longer appeared among them.[68] He did serve, this time as a corporal, enlisting in the militia in September 1862, 3rd Regiment, Company K.[69]

Briefly leaving Frances Ann, three-year-old Miriam, and one-year-old Carrie at home, he saw combat in one of the major battles of the Civil War: Antietam (Sharpsburg), the bloodiest single day in American military history, fought September 17, 1862, when Union general George B. McClellan confronted Confederate general Robert E. Lee at Sharpsburg, Maryland.[70] Lutcher apparently survived the battle unscathed. According to Lutcher Stark, "he fought against Lee at Antietam" and brought home a scabbard and bayonet from the battlefield as a souvenir.[71]

The Battle of Antietam marked the end of Lee's first offensive into Union territory; thereafter he withdrew the Army of Northern Virginia south across the Potomac. McClellan failed to pursue his advantage, and the battle was officially considered a draw, although Lincoln and the Union claimed a moral victory that paved the way for his Emancipation Proclamation on January 1, 1863. Lee attempted a second invasion of the North, culminating in the Battle of Gettysburg on July 1–3, 1863; the Union victory there marked the turning point of the war, and thereafter the South headed toward gradual but certain defeat.

Henry Lutcher was mustered out September 25, 1862, after the Battle of Antietam.[72] His unit had been composed of approximately ninety men from Lycoming County. Lutcher probably knew all, or most, of them and may already have met one of them who was serving as a private, since they had both attended Dickinson Seminary, although in different years.[73] This young man, Gregory Bedell Moore, would play a major role in Lutcher's future.

CHAPTER TWO

Lutcher & Moore

The pine forests are simply magnificent. . . . You can drive through them with a horse and buggy as the ground is as level as a floor, and no underbrush whatever.
—HENRY JACOB LUTCHER, "LUMBERING IN THE LONE STAR STATE"[1]

Around 4:00 p.m. on Palm Sunday, April 9, 1865, in the parlor of a two-story brick house near the small settlement of Appomattox Court House, Virginia, Confederate general Robert E. Lee signed the terms surrendering the Army of Northern Virginia to Union forces under the command of Gen. Ulysses S. Grant. After 630,000 deaths of the finest young men of a generation, many more wounded, civilian casualties, vast loss of property, and unimaginable agony and grief, the American Civil War was passing into history.[2]

Williamsport's Repasz Band, which had become a part of the 8th Pennsylvania Cavalry, and a Confederate band were present at Appomattox with the assembled troops of both armies, and the two groups engaged in a musical "duel." As General Lee emerged from the house, the Confederate band played "Dixie"; not to be outdone, the Repasz Band played "The Star-Spangled Banner" upon the appearance of General Grant. The two bands continued to alternate playing their respective patriotic songs for some time.[3]

Despite the wartime turmoil, the fortunes of the young Lutcher family—Henry, Frances Ann, six-year-old Miriam, and three-year-old Carrie—had been rapidly improving; Henry, already employing the foresight and shrewd business sense that characterized him in later years, had managed to accumulate between $15,000 and $16,000 during his years as a farmer and butcher.[4]

On May 3, 1865, Lutcher paid $150 for a house and lot in Rocktown near his extended family on the southeast corner of Main and Henry Streets.[5] (A condition was inserted into the deed, doubtless in view of his occupation: "The said Henry Lutscher will not erect or build any slaughter house stable or other building that may become when occupied offensive on account of offensive or unpleasant smells arising therefrom.") On January 4, 1866, he bought another lot near their homestead from his sister Rosanna and her husband, Jacob Weis, for $500.[6]

Lutcher was about to make another move, this one determining the course of his meteoric career and the remainder of his life. In the mid-1860s, the lumber boom in Williamsport was at its height, and the ambitious young butcher must have spotted his chance. Armed with the capital he had earned, he went into partnership with John Waltman, forming the firm of Lutcher & Waltman "for the manufacture of white pine and Eastern hemlock." On January 7, 1867, they leased from H.B. Packer, a Lycoming County associate judge,[7] a tract of land on the south bank of the Susquehanna just east of the Market Street Bridge. The property was bisected by Hagerman's Run, a small stream, or "crick," as it was locally known.[8] They leased the property for ten years, paying yearly rent of "one hundred and fifty dollars—half yearly in advance." They were granted the right to remove any mills or other buildings they might erect during the term of the lease, and Packer retained the right "to get driftwood and haul lumber or materials for fencing from the river at the mouth of Hagerman's Run."[9]

On this land, near the spot where Hagerman's Run crossed the Linden Branch of the Philadelphia and Erie Railroad, stood the old water-powered "thundergust" Schnabel Mill, where Lutcher had spent his school vacations picking edging.[10] A March 1880 article in the St. Louis Lumberman, "Henry J. Lutcher, Esq.," called this mill "a quaint and curious old affair of which [Lutcher] delights to speak," describing it as "a water mill, with an overshot wheel, a sash gate, or as it was called in that locality, an English gate. . . . The operators, we are informed, would usually start the saw into a log when preparing to leave for dinner and upon returning would find the cut unfinished—unless the log was a 'mighty short one.'"

Lutcher and Waltman continued to operate the old mill on the property they had leased from Packer, but in the autumn of 1867, they also built a new mill, "quite substantial," according to a Williamsport newspaper, this one located north of the existing mill and nearer the river, between the mouth of Hagerman's Run on the east and the foot of the Market Street Bridge on the west. This new mill measured 56 by 144 feet and contained "one circular saw and one muley saw" and an engine of about forty horsepower.[11]

In January 1868, Lutcher made a second significant move: for reasons unknown, John Waltman sold out his share in Lutcher & Waltman

Figure 2.1. Henry Jacob ("H.J.") Lutcher, who went into business with Gregory Bedell Moore to form the Lutcher & Moore Lumber Company. Stark Foundation Archives.

to Gregory Bedell Moore, who had also attended Dickinson Academy and who was Lutcher's comrade-in-arms at the Battle of Antietam.[12]

The respective backgrounds of the two men lay at opposite poles. Lutcher was the product of working-class German immigrants; Moore, the issue of Anglo-American Episcopal clergy, a long line of "noble and

Figure 2.2. Gregory Bedell Moore. Stark Foundation Archives.

godly ancestors." He was born in Elizabeth, New Jersey, October 20, 1840, the second child of Rev. Richard Channing Moore, the rector of St. John's Episcopal Church, and the grandson of Rt. Rev. Richard Channing Moore, bishop of Virginia. His mother was Julia Grant, the daughter of wealthy New York merchant Samuel Grant, and "a woman of education, culture and refinement." Moore was christened "Gregory Townsend Bedell Moore" after his father's cousin, clergyman Gregory Townsend Bedell of Philadelphia.[13]

The Moore family lived in Elizabeth until 1857, when Reverend Moore was transferred to Christ Episcopal Church in Williamsport,[14] where he served as rector from 1858 until 1868.[15] Young Bedell Moore had attended Dickinson Seminary in Williamsport, but his and Lutcher's terms do not appear to have overlapped; Lutcher attended only during the 1854–55 term, while Moore was enrolled for the terms of 1855–56 and 1856–57.[16] Unlike Lutcher, who had studied in the Common English Department, Moore, the product of a religious and scholarly tradition, was taught courses in the Higher English Department, designed for students who were college bound.[17]

Moore's family was large—seven children—and his father's income as rector of Christ Church quite meager; thus, when Moore was seventeen, he decided to cut short his education to help with the family finances. Menial work at the sawmills was plentiful in Williamsport during that lumbering era, and he soon found a job hauling sawdust at the Taylor & Endsworth Company. He was promoted to the task of marking logs with a heavy-duty sledgehammer, but his employers speedily discovered his skill with numbers and put him to work in the offices as a bookkeeper.[18] *Boyd's Williamsport City Directory* for 1866–67 listed Moore, then around age twenty-six, as a lumber dealer for Taylor & Endsworth.[19] By working in the various departments of the company, Moore thoroughly familiarized himself with every aspect of the lumbering trade. Ultimately, he went into business for himself, operating a small sawmill in Williamsport.[20]

Toward the end of the Civil War, Moore married Alice Clements, a native of Virginia described as "a young woman of splendid character, talented and cultured, a woman of many philanthropies and charities."[21] The Moores had three children: a daughter, Alice, born August 31, 1865, but living only a day; a daughter, Julia Grant, born in March 1868; and a son, Hilgard, born in December 1869. Tragically, both these children died within a few weeks of each other from "malignant diphtheria," Hilgard in December 1875 and Julia in January 1876.[22]

The young Moores boarded for several years on Millionaires' Row— West Fourth Street—on an upper floor of the palatial Italian Villa–style mansion of Peter Herdic, Williamsport's greatest lumber tycoon and builder.[23] Herdic would have served as a good connection for the fledgling lumberman. By 1875, Moore was listed in that year's *Directory* as being at home at 292 West Fourth Street in an impressive two-story Victorian house of his own.[24]

During those early years in the lumber industry, Moore apparently

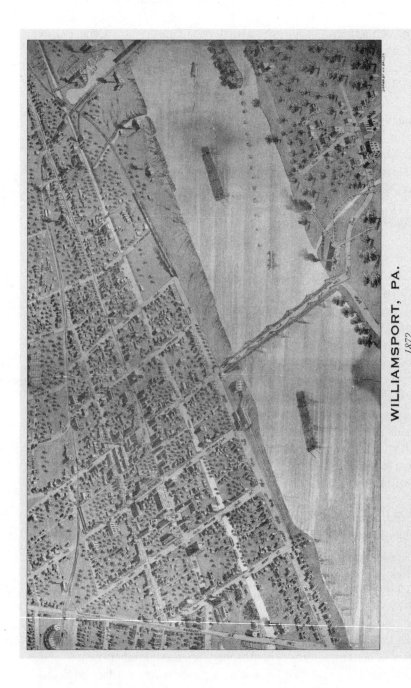

WILLIAMSPORT, PA.
1872

Figure 2.3. Williamsport, 1872. The Lutcher & Moore mill is pictured on the south bank of the Susquehanna, just east of the bridge. Collection of the Lycoming County Historical Society and Thomas T. Taber Museum.

accumulated a fair amount of capital, at least enough to buy out John Waltman's share in the Lutcher & Waltman mill in 1868.[25] Thus, the Lutcher & Moore Lumber Company was born. No details of the transaction survive—it could have been sealed with a handshake—but on April 22 of that year, as proof of their association, Lutcher and Moore together purchased eight hundred acres in Susquehanna Township (just west of Armstrong Township), probably as a timber source.[26] They established an office across the river in Williamsport proper at 19 West Third Street, on the second floor of Williamsport's First National Bank, and began advertising their product: "Lutcher & Moore, Dealers in Lumber. Hemlock a specialty. Roofing Lath, Pickets, Lath, &c, &c, Pine and Hemlock Bills cut to Order."[27]

A family story, probably apocryphal, is told regarding the spelling of the Lutscher/Lutcher surname: as Lutcher and Moore were ordering a sign for their new concern, the painter they had hired informed them that the name "Lutscher & Moore" was too long to fit on the selected board—by one letter. To make the names fit, the painter instructed them, they would be required to delete a letter from one name or the other. Lutcher and Moore somehow arrived at the decision that the "s" in "Lutscher" was more expendable than an "o" in "Moore" would be; thus, ever after, the sign read "Lutcher & Moore." As a result, the entire first American generation of the family spelled the name without the "s." Or so the story goes. (Henry Lutcher and all of his siblings did in fact adopt the Americanized spelling of "Lutcher.")[28]

On March 1, 1871, Lutcher and Moore paid $400 for a tract of land adjacent to the mill site they had been leasing, and on June 1, exactly three months later, they purchased the mill site itself for $13,000. Their terms: $8,000 to be paid as down payment, "stipulating for the execution a good and sufficient deed on or before the first day of June A.D. 1874, with interest payable semi-annually," and the balance to be paid in five equal annual payments beginning June 1, 1874.[29] The mill was barely four years old when the partners encountered a setback. Because of the lethal proximity of combustible materials—logs, lumber, sawdust—to sparks from boilers, flues, or smokestacks, the specter of fire lurked constantly in the sawmills, and the first of Lutcher & Moore's encounters with the lumber industry's most-feared menace occurred on April 16, 1871, when the mill caught fire and burned. Williamsport's *Daily Gazette and Bulletin* described the conflagration:

> Fire was communicated to the woodwork of the boiler room from smouldering ashes that had been removed from the furnaces on Saturday evening, and bursting out suddenly, soon wrapped the entire building in flames. A strong

wind springing up at the time, fanned the flames to such an extent that it was found impossible to save any of the contents of the mill, and in less than one hour the entire building and machinery were completely destroyed. The loss sustained by the young firm amounted to fully ten thousand dollars, and many feared that they would not be able to recover from the blow. But they were young men of energy and pluck, and at once resolved to rebuild their mill and try their luck once more.[30]

The company justified the newspaper's kind words by rebounding quickly.

The embers had not ceased smoking when they commenced clearing away the debris and making preparations to erect a better and more substantial mill than the old one. Work was pushed forward with remarkable energy. New and heavy timbers were purchased and hauled to the spot—the carpenters worked like beavers to get the frame ready, and the millwrights labored with equal energy to have the machinery ready to be set up the moment the building was raised and had a roof. So well did all parties succeed that in just six weeks from the time the old mill was destroyed the new one was completed and in running order.[31]

The new building measured 70 by 114 feet, "the fire room separated from the main building by a solid brick wall, and every precaution taken to ensure safety from the devouring element."[32] Lutcher and Moore were taking no chances. The new mill, "one of the best and most solidly constructed of its size in this part of the state," now boasted a sixty-inch circular saw, a muley saw, a gang edger with five saws, and a lath and picket mill, the machinery "all of the latest and most approved kind, [working] with remarkable smoothness and precision" with a seventy-five-horsepower engine and steam supplied by two horizontal boilers with fifty-eight flues each, not to mention a "patent log turner." The mill cut forty thousand feet of lumber a day, and the firm kept on hand a full line of building material so that orders could be filled at a moment's notice. Lutcher & Moore shipped to the mining regions, Philadelphia, and New Jersey and supplied much of the home trade.[33] The firm continued to "prosper quite well," according to the *Daily Gazette and Bulletin*, "steadily building up an excellent trade not only at home but abroad, and were hard pushed at times to fill the orders that were beginning to pour in upon them."[34]

Lutcher & Moore seemed generally to avoid various other difficulties endemic to the industry. Lumber companies were not immune to labor troubles; lumbering and sawmill work were dangerous, and workers put in long hours for poor pay. A case in point occurred in the summer of 1872 with the so-called Sawdust War, when workers in Williamsport's sawmills struck and ultimately rioted. The strike was settled but not before the military was called out. Twenty-one workers were convicted but finally pardoned by the governor of Pennsylvania, John W. Geary. Workmen at Lutcher & Moore possibly took part, although there is no record of their participation.[35]

Some situations at the Lutcher & Moore mill were unintentionally hilarious, as in this incident involving a one-horse wagon as its driver headed toward the Market Street Bridge with a load of produce:

> Just as [the driver] was passing the sawmill of Lutcher & Moore the horse suddenly took fright at the escaping steam, and making a dash forward and a sharp turn into the bridge, upset the wagon and ran furiously. In addition to the driver the wagon contained two small girls and another man, besides . . . four bushels of huckleberries. The occupants and contents were thrown out . . . [but] neither the children or the man were injured.
>
> [The driver] . . . held on firmly to the lines as the horse dashed madly forward, and was dragged some distance. He was finally compelled to relinquish his hold, and the animal tore furiously through the bridge, dragging the overturned wagon after him, which occasionally struck the railings . . . shivering them into splinters. As the horse ran, the bridge commenced vibrating, the iron rods creaked, the timbers groaned, and the noise soon became terrific.
>
> To increase the danger two teams and several pedestrians were some distance ahead. The drivers, noticing the danger behind, put their horses to the trot, the women commenced shrieking and the children screaming, and the bridge swaying and snapping as they all madly dashed forward [toward] the toll gate. The teams in front managed to keep out of the way of the runaway horse, and had just reached the toll gate, when with a bound he cleared the end of the bridge . . . [took] the plank walk which leads to the toll house . . . and rushed madly forward. Several children had just passed the house to cross the bridge when they observed the danger in front of them and ran screaming back. . . . The toll gatherer had barely time to . . . drag them into the house. . . . The frightened horse was seized and secured. . . . The huckleberries . . . were scattered along the road. Some . . . were gathered up, but as they were mixed with dirt they were in a manner worthless.[36]

Throughout the 1870s and even into the 1880s, Henry Lutcher and Bedell Moore continued to buy and sell property in Lycoming County, probably as timber sources, sometimes turning a handsome profit when they resold it.[37] By good fortune, Lutcher had also retained his interest in butchering and the livestock trade, and sometime during his early years in the partnership with Moore he earned between $50,000 and $60,000—a huge sum of money in that era—by buying a large number of cattle on the hoof, shipping them into Williamsport via the Philadelphia & Erie Railroad, and selling them to local butchers.[38] This capital would prove invaluable in his and Moore's subsequent ventures.

In the meantime, Miriam and Carrie Lutcher were growing up in Rocktown among the grandparents, aunts, uncles, and cousins in their extended family. Their mother, Frances Ann, without a large family of her own, apparently became like another sister to her siblings-in-law, and in the future, the Pennsylvania and Texas branches of the Lutcher family retained close ties, visiting one another regularly throughout their lives.

Even though their circumstances had been extremely modest, at least at the beginning of their marriage, Henry and Frances Ann Lutcher nevertheless imbued their family life with a significant dimension of gentility.[39] An interview with Miriam as an adult revealed that the Lutcher home, "even in its days of simplicity, was permeated by an atmosphere of good taste and culture," adding that she acquired her love for literature and her taste in art from her parents in the home environment and that, "as a child, she delighted to hear her father read voluminously" from Byron, Shakespeare, and other classics.[40]

As the Lutchers' financial situation continued to improve, they were able to offer Miriam and Carrie additional advantages, sending them to Miss Wilson's School on Pine Street in Williamsport, a seminary "for Young Ladies and Children," where they received "the best education possible for girls during that time."[41] They probably studied in the school's Literary Course, which included composition, grammar, English literature, and ancient and modern history as well as French and German, two languages Miriam learned early and later employed on her travels. (She must also have acquired some German from her extended family in Williamsport.)[42]

According to the interview, Miriam also inherited from her father "an exacting sense of order; she would tolerate no compromise. Anything she did must be right."[43] Her handwritten notebook, dating from November 1, 1870, to January 17, 1878, containing poems, quotations, and essays she copied from the time she was eleven years old until she was eighteen, reveals a high level of intelligence and an awareness of the material's content and significance. (Of note is her use of the German spelling of her surname, written on the cover: "Miriam Lutscher, Rocktown, Pa.")[44] After the family's move to Texas, Miriam and Carrie were sent back periodically to Williamsport for their schooling.[45]

During that era of its phenomenal growth, Williamsport was acquiring more and more amenities. In view of their family's educational and cultural bent and improving financial situation, Miriam and Carrie in all probability crossed the Market Street Bridge to Williamsport proper to at-

Figure 2.4. Miriam Melissa (*left*) and Carrie Launa Lutcher as young girls,
Williamsport, 1870s. Stark Foundation Archives.

tend concerts by the Repasz Band or performances at the Ulman Opera
House, where the likes of Mark Twain had performed, or to view the exquisite still-life paintings of Severin Roesen, Williamsport's resident artist.[46] They would certainly have gone, alone or with one or both of their
parents, to Market Square on market days to buy meat, fish, fresh produce,
dry goods, or notions for the family's needs. Possibly, on fine April days,
they strolled Williamsport's streets and savored the spring air, enjoying

the profusion of flowering trees—apple, cherry, mulberry, dogwood—and in the last two years of their residence there, hearing the quarter hours sounded by the Cambridge chimes of Trinity Episcopal Church on Fourth Street, near the Lutcher & Moore offices. In 1875, Bedell Moore had helped build this church, where he served terms as junior warden and president of the Sunday School.[47]

Worship occupied a central place in the lives of the Lutcher family as well. They had belonged to the English Lutheran Church across the Susquehanna in Williamsport, but in the 1860s members who were residents of Rocktown had begun to feel that the church's formal order of service was ill adapted to a working-class community. And during winter weather, crossing the Susquehanna on the Market Street Bridge to attend Sunday services was risking not only hardship but outright danger:

> Rising before dawn on a winter Sunday, housewives heated bricks for the sleigh, warmed caps and mittens in the oven, and with their families started across the bridge with the horse and cutter. They arrived at the church with frost-bitten fingers, chilled to the bone from sleet and wind, only to shiver through the service with one ear attuned to the sermon and the other to the champing of the half-frozen horses standing before the church door. Warmed neither in body nor in spirit, a small group of people from the south bank of the river regretfully gave farewell to [the English Lutheran Church in Williamsport] and . . . met for worship in their own struggling community [of Rocktown].[48]

They first met in homes, later moving services to a schoolhouse. In January 1868, five families met together to organize the new church, among them two of Henry Lutcher's sisters and brothers-in-law, Rosanna and Jacob Weis and John and Christina Reinhart. On June 28, 1869, the new congregation bought a tract of land adjacent to a tavern in Rocktown and planned to build their church there.[49] Reinhart and Henry Lutcher's father, Lewis Lutscher, were among those named in the deed as trustees.[50]

Henry Lutcher himself played a major part in building the new Rocktown church, christened "Messiah's Evangelical Lutheran Church."[51] Both he and Jacob Weis served on the building committee, at one point advancing funds "from their own personal resources"—Lutcher headed the subscription list with a gift of $100.[52] The annals of the church note Miriam Lutcher's first communion on May 12, 1872, at the age of fourteen and Carrie's "baptism" (probably her first communion) on February 23, 1875, at the same age. The names of Henry Lutcher's parents, Lewis and Mary Barbara Lutscher, appear regularly in the records as attending communion

English Lutheran Church
Williamsport Pa

Figure 2.5. English (later St. Mark's) Lutheran Church, Williamsport,
the church the Lutcher family first attended. Image found in a prayer book
belonging to Mary and Lewis Lutscher. Stark Foundation Archives.

from April 12, 1868, shortly after the church was founded, until April 9,
1882, just before their deaths in 1883.[53]

However successful Henry Lutcher and Bedell Moore found themselves, they still stood ready for new opportunity—and remained sensitive to currents and aberrations in the lumber industry. Global financial
failures, an unstable economy, unregulated business growth in the United
States, and the failure of Jay Cooke and Co., the country's premier investment bank, triggered the Panic of 1873, sending the American economy
into a downward spiral and triggering widespread social unrest. In Williamsport, business suffered and the area lost population.[54] Although the
depression seemed to have had little, if any, effect on Lutcher & Moore's

concerns, it might have served as a warning sign to the partners that their good fortunes could be temporary.

In the meantime, a more compelling warning signaled the partners to reassess their circumstances. As the decade of the 1870s wore on, it became increasingly obvious that the once-vast timber forests in the Susquehanna River Valley—in particular the huge stands of white pine—were rapidly being depleted. Hemlock was still in comparatively plentiful supply, but anyone could predict that it would eventually suffer the same fate.[55] Lutcher and Moore surely saw enticing advertisements and articles in the local newspapers such as this one in the Williamsport Sun and Banner:

> According to the census bulletins there are 122,675,500,000 feet of merchantable pine timber in the States of Alabama, Mississippi and Texas, enough to supply the demand of the whole country for at least 60 years. On the other hand, Minnesota, which is one of the most important lumber States in the North, has only 6,100,000,000 feet of this timber. The total cut in the three Southern States enumerated is only 638,541,000 feet, or about one-half of 1 percent, considerably less than the usual growth of the forest.[56]

The market was undeniably expanding westward and southward, and although white pine was considered to be the most desirable softwood in the Northeast, it was the longleaf yellow pine of the vast southern Piney Woods—southwestern Arkansas, southeastern Oklahoma, East Texas, and southwestern Louisiana—that was proving to be the stronger and more durable wood, "possibly the finest of the softwoods," according to one account.[57] With the modest capital Lutcher and Moore had accumulated, they decided to continue their operation in Williamsport for the time being but to look for a fresh timber source in the South—before it was too late.

On January 11, 1877, they left Williamsport via rail to begin their odyssey to the "Empire of Trees," as one writer dubbed the southern timber forests.[58] Fortunately for posterity, Moore kept a detailed diary of their entire journey, noting the physical terrain of every place they visited—depths and flows of rivers, species and growth habits of trees, and so forth—as well as collecting information on volume of lumber production, types of lumber sold, and marketing statistics.[59]

The first leg of the trip took them through Pittsburgh and Indianapolis to St. Louis, Missouri, where they obtained information and letters of contact to business associates in Texas—Palestine, Houston, and Galveston. They continued their way south through Poplar Bluff and Ash Hill, Missouri, and Little Rock, Arkansas, then plunged into the great timber forests of the Piney Woods, striking a southwestern route through

Figure 2.6. Henry Lutcher's "magnificent" virgin forests of longleaf yellow pine (*Pinus palustris*) of the southern Piney Woods of Texas. Stark Foundation Archives.

Arkansas into East Texas, always on the lookout for mills to inspect and new information to glean on costs, prices, and machinery. They traveled through Texarkana, Texas, and stopped for dinner in Marshall on the way to Longview, seeing mills "scattered" along the way, then crossed the upper Neches River, arriving at Palestine the evening of January 18.[60]

At Palestine they met Col. J.T. Wood, who informed them that he owned seventy-two thousand acres of timberland farther south in Hardin and Tyler Counties, mainly consisting of "what is known as Long Leaf Pine," as Moore noted in his diary. Such was Henry Lutcher's and Bedell Moore's first direct introduction to longleaf yellow pine (*Pinus palustris*), the wood that would make their fortunes in the forests of Texas and Louisiana. Colonel Wood was asking $1.50 per acre for the entire tract, or from $2.00 to $5.00 per acre for smaller portions. Another lumberman they met in Palestine, W. S. Peters, owned five mills in the area, sawing "pine called 'loblolly,'" Moore observed, "a species similar to what we call yellow sap pine on our Penna. Mountains."[61]

From Palestine they traveled through Crockett, Texas, then caught a southbound passenger train to Houston, to Moore's amazement passing through a Texas prairie, the first they had ever seen, just outside town. (Moore observed that the only game they saw were prairie chickens.) They finally arrived in Houston, where they stayed at the Hutchins Hotel, "a very comfortable and commodious house," Moore noted, "price $3 a day."[62]

They left Houston January 22 on the Texas and New Orleans Railroad, headed for Beaumont, a small Texas lumber town on the west bank of the Neches River, where they obtained rooms at Wilson's Hotel and began inspecting the mills—two shingle mills and three sawmills—which were cutting cypress shingles and pine lumber. Moore observed that the Neches River at Beaumont was 150 yards wide and 20 to 30 feet deep, with a current that ordinarily ran slow, and that the pine logs were floated to Beaumont from a distance of 50 to 250 miles upstream down the Neches and Angelina Rivers.

The two men learned the local method of harvesting the great cypress trees growing in the nearby river bottoms: in the fall, the trees were "girdled"—cut through bark and cambium around the entire circumference—to kill them. Several months later, when the river overflowed, flooding the swamps, they were cut down and towed to the river, then floated down to the mills. Lutcher and Moore presented letters of recommendation to several community leaders in Beaumont, including attorney, newspaper editor, and Civil War veteran Capt. George W. O'Brien, "who treated us kindly," Moore reported. They rented horses and engaged local farmer James Ingalls Jr. as a guide for a journey up the Neches River by horseback, into the thick of the Piney Woods.[63]

On the first afternoon of the "six days' hardship in the Woods," as Moore later described their trek, they rode nine miles north of Beaumont and ferried across the Pine Island Bayou to the little settlement of Concord, then forged into the most impenetrable part of the Piney Woods—that shadowed, trackless green region traditionally known as the Big Thicket, where outlaws and miscreants lurked, tales of murders and attendant ghosts abounded, and the quirks and eccentricities of its denizens, animal and human, would become the stuff of legend. Lutcher and Moore had their own adventures with the Big Thicket populace. Staying overnight that first night at the home of farmer William Hooks and his family, they were given supper "of a poor quality"—corn bread, bacon, coffee, and sweet potatoes—and a breakfast the next morning of almost the same fare. But Moore approved the sleeping arrangements, at least: "four of us were quartered in one room, in two quite comfortable beds."[64] A day later, they rode north to the house of Isham Sheffield, "a deaf old man," as Moore described him.

When we informed him that we wanted to stay with him all night, [he] replied: "If you can put up with our fare, you can." Mr. Lutcher responded with a loud voice, "If you can stand it we can . . ." so we dismounted & after seeing our horses well cared for we went into the house. This edifice had no windows but like most of the houses in the woods, when you wanted light you opened the door. . . . Supper was announced, it consisted of corn dodgers (corn meal & water mixed & baked), bacon and cold turnips, tops and all mashed up together, a most palatable dish? And very poor coffee without sugar or milk, our breakfast the next morning was eased by leaving out the turnips.

For this miserable fare and poor dirty beds, we were charged $1.25 each, 25 cts more than we were charged anywhere that we stayed in the woods. Moral,—avoid all Isham Sheffields.[65]

Moore noted yet another new phenomenon: "The houses through all this district are built with two wings and an open hallway between & one story in height." He and Lutcher were seeing their first East Texas "dogtrot" house.[66]

The two continued northward to Spurger and crossed to the east bank of the Neches at Town Bluff, riding out of the Big Thicket's solid wall of vegetation through fine stands of hardwood—oak and ash—"the trees and vines [meeting] across the road [to form] a bower for many miles." With the Hamilton family, living a mile east of Town Bluff, Lutcher and Moore enjoyed "the best accommodations and the first wheat bread since leaving Beaumont."[67] They traveled to the west bank of the Angelina River at Bevilport, where they spotted the stern-wheeler *Laura* loading cotton, then ten miles north between the two rivers, recrossing the Angelina and riding eastward to Jasper, where they gleaned an important bit of information: the pine timber stands in East Texas extended eastward across the Sabine River, on the same latitude, into Louisiana.[68]

Leaving Jasper January 26, they stayed overnight at the home of seventy-year-old John Bevil, two miles east of Jasper.[69] (Moore, civilized Easterner that he was, noted with a tinge of awe that Bevil "was said to have killed several men during the past twenty years.") Before the Civil War, Bevil had owned twenty-three slaves; he now opined to Lutcher and Moore that he had no quarrel with Emancipation but thought the government should have paid him something for them when they were freed, "even if it was a moderate sum."[70]

The men returned southward down the east side of the Neches, arriving back in Beaumont on January 28 after having traveled 175 miles by horseback, "more than one half this distance having been through 'Long Leaf Pine' timber," Moore reported, "the weather having been all the time very fair, days bright & nights beautiful moonlight."[71] Of the East Texas timber stands they saw, Lutcher later declared, "The pine forests are simply *magnificent*. You can drive through them with a horse and buggy as the ground is as level as a floor, and no underbrush whatever."[72]

On January 29, the travelers left Beaumont by rail, headed twenty-three miles east through thick woods to the small town of Orange, Texas, on the west bank of the Sabine River. Here they found a settlement of one thousand to fifteen hundred inhabitants, with three sawmills, two shingle mills, and two mills under construction. They found Orange a pleasant prospect, said to be for the most part "healthy," Moore observed, with "flowers, verbenas, violets, etc. in bloom in several gardens." Moore reported that they met several Orange merchants, Dennis Call and Col. Hugh Ochiltree, as well as sawmill owner David R. Wingate, whom Moore described as "an old gentleman who has been engaged in manufacturing lumber at Orange for the past twenty years and shipping it by vessel to Galveston, Houston and along the Gulf Coast."[73]

Wingate and others informed them that the Sabine River at Orange was 250 yards wide and from 20 to 50 feet deep, wider and deeper than the Neches at Beaumont. They also learned that the distance downriver from Orange to Sabine Lake—the large saltwater lake into which both the Sabine and Neches Rivers emptied—was only twelve miles, while the stretch from Beaumont down the Neches to the lake was approximately eighteen miles; moreover, the depth over the bar at the mouth of the Sabine was supposedly a foot deeper than that at the mouth of the Neches. In Orange, more timber could be obtained closer to the mills and the river's edge than in Beaumont, and less timber on both the Texas and Louisiana sides of the Sabine had been cut than on the Neches.[74] Just south of Orange, cypress, valued primarily for shingles, lined the edges of the streams and flourished in the swamplands. And land in the entire region was plentiful—and cheap.[75]

The lumbermen left Orange early in the morning of January 30 via the Texas and New Orleans Railroad for Houston and Galveston, where they priced engines, boilers, and other necessities. As they traveled, they continued to collect all possible information regarding the Texas lumber industry: how many million feet of lumber could be sold annually; types of wood most in demand; prices of lumber, siding, flooring, laths, pickets, and shingles. In Galveston, they strolled the beaches and stood in awe "upon the shore of the Gulf of Mexico, a place we had often heard & read about but never before had seen."[76]

Along the way, Moore continued to marvel at unfamiliar sights. As they traveled west to San Antonio, the men saw "the first Jackass Rabbit running wild, nearly as large as a small goat," he reported in wonder. They also caught their first glimpse of a Texas prairie sunset. "It was grand," he enthused; "nothing similar have we ever seen in the East. We were out on the platform of the rear car until the last light faded away. . . . Such sunsets . . . we hope may be our privilege to see again, it cannot be described, language fails, it must be seen to be appreciated." In San Antonio they toured the Alamo, "the fortress where the Texas band perished in 1836 at the hands of Santa Anna."[77]

From San Antonio they returned to Houston on a construction train, on the way crossing the Guadalupe River on a low-water bridge, another wonder to Moore:

> A bridge laid on piles driven in the bed of the river . . . mostly on a level with the water. . . . The approach . . . was a steep downgrade to the edge of the river, and the track rose to a corresponding height on the opposite side, the impetus gained by going downhill took us up on the other side. Such a fearful plunge for our engine and train to make to keep the rails I never saw, we sped like lightning down the hill, shot across the bridge and up the track on the other side & [I] gave a sigh of relief when we were safe again on the level.[78]

From Houston, they departed for Austin, "a fine city . . . [the] capitol of the state," where they called on Gov. Richard B. Hubbard, who extended them a cordial welcome. Hubbard pronounced himself to be "incensed at the frauds perpetrated by individuals styling themselves 'agents' of the state" for the sale of Texas' public lands and warned them against those who "publish circulars in reference to towns which have no existence & getting up RR excursions & colonies for such points."[79] (The warnings were unnecessary; Lutcher and Moore, no novices in the business, knew well to steer clear of "speculative purchases.")[80]

The two lumbermen traveled on to Dallas, which Moore described as a city having "a great many cheap buildings," where they again checked markets and gathered statistics. Prominent Dallas lumberman William Cameron gave them much statistical information and an optimistic view of the future of Texas lumbering: annual consumption far exceeded production.[81] Thus encouraged, they made their way northeastward to Chicago and thence home to Williamsport, arriving on February 13, 1877, after an absence of nearly five weeks.[82]

From the tone of Moore's diary, their decision was all but made. They evaluated their discoveries, particularly the advantages at Orange: a vast abundance of cypress and longleaf yellow pine timber, possibly the strongest softwood known; advantageous physical conditions, including the superior width and depth of the Sabine River and its close proximity to the Gulf of Mexico; and hundreds of thousands of acres of available, inexpensive timberland, theirs for the purchase. As it happened, their timing was impeccable; since the Southern Homestead Act restricting acquisition of public lands had been repealed just the year before, they would be able to buy large tracts of US public lands in Louisiana—just across the river from the mill.[83] (The act had not applied to Texas; no federal public lands lay within its borders.)[84] Utilizing their accumulated capital, they could buy substantial tracts of timberland and build a mill on the Sabine River at Orange. The matter was settled; Lutcher and Moore would extend their operations to the Sabine River and the Gulf Coast of Texas.

The final determination must have been made quickly; a brief squib appeared in the *Daily Gazette and Bulletin* under a "Personal and Particular" column on February 22, 1877, only eight days after the partners' return: "H. J. Lutcher of the firm of Lutcher & Moore will leave for Texas today, where he will engage in lumbering." In spite of the amused jeers of some of the local lumbermen at their supposed folly in seeking their fortunes so far from home, they proceeded with their plan: Lutcher would relocate to Orange, build a mill, and buy as much timberland as they could possibly afford; Moore would remain at home to operate their Williamsport mill.[85]

W hen Henry Lutcher returned to Orange and Southeast Texas after so short an absence, he probably soon realized that he now inhabited a new world, in many ways alien to his prior life in the East. The veneer of civilization could wear perilously thin in this land of dangerous animals; poisonous snakes; yellow fever that menaced during the hot, steamy summers; fearsome storms; and casual violence that erupted in the muddy streets as an everyday occurrence. And a breed of individuals lived here who did not readily brook authority, their lineage and character forged by the terrain and the region's rich, checkered history, where for centuries warring cultures had vied for supremacy.

Lutcher's new domain lay at the convergence of diverse ecosystems, rich in natural resources, bounded by the vast virgin pine and hardwood forests lying to the north, the cypress-studded streams and swamplands to the south, and the rich blackland coastal prairies to the southwest, roamed alike by Spanish explorers and French traders.

In 1685, French explorer René Robert Cavelier, Sieur de La Salle, established the French presence east of the Sabine River in what would become the Louisiana Territory.[86] By the first quarter of the eighteenth century, French traders were crossing the Sabine River into Spanish Texas, making incursions into woods and waterways to barter with the American Indians there.[87] In 1803, when Napoleon sold the Louisiana Territory to the United States through the Louisiana Purchase, Spanish Texas found itself with a new neighbor: the burgeoning young American republic.[88]

Spain and the United States were unable to agree on the border between the two countries, but finally, the military commanders of each nation forged an understanding: the region between the Sabine River on the west and the Arroyo Hondo (Spanish term for "deep stream") on the east would be designated as the so-called Neutral Ground. Although settlers were officially forbidden to enter, they promptly defied the agreement and flocked to the area in droves. It was inevitable that this forbidden territory would become a pesthole of lawlessness for thieves, debtors, gamblers, murderers, and fugitives from the law of every kind as they fled from Spanish and American rule alike.[89]

When Mexico won its independence from Spain in 1821, hordes of American settlers swarmed in earnest over the Sabine into Mexican Texas, their objective to acquire cheap land.[90] Many came in from Louisiana by the old Atascocito Road, or Opelousas Trail, just upriver from present-day Orange, and their first sight on crossing the Sabine would have been the fertile green region on the river's west bank, then a part of the Mexican Municipality of Liberty. Some stayed to settle in this spot, first known as Green's Bluff.[91] Conflict between this self-reliant group, resistant to authority of any kind, and the faraway, authoritarian Mexican government was inevitable, and tensions began to simmer that eventually boiled over into open hostilities. In November 1835, Texians, as they were known, formed a provisional government, and on March 2, 1836, Texas declared its independence from Mexico.[92] The war was on. Green's Bluff and Cow Bayou, a settlement just to the west, sent sixty volunteers to fight.[93]

The commander of the Mexican forces, Gen. Antonio Lopez de Santa Anna, personally led an invasion of Texas, taking the Alamo on March 6, 1836, and massacring Texian troops at Goliad on March 27. General Sam Houston, commander of the Texian army, began a long retreat toward the Sabine River, now the eastern boundary of Texas, with Santa Anna hounding their trail. Before them, frightened settlers fled their homes and headed eastward toward the United States and safety in what became known as the "Runaway Scrape." As the crowds of refugees attempted to cross the rain-swollen Sabine at Green's Bluff, word came of Houston's defeat of Santa Anna at San Jacinto on April 21.[94] With that victory, won just over six months before Henry Lutcher's birth in far-off Pennsylvania, Texas became a new republic. Less than ten years later, however, on December 29, 1845, it became the twenty-eighth state in the Union, and on February 19, 1846, the last president of the Texas Republic, Anson Jones, lowered the Texas flag and in its place raised the Star-Spangled Banner.[95]

In 1842, the Republic of Texas legislature had changed the name of Green's Bluff to Madison, after the nation's fourth president. On February 5, 1852, the Texas State Legislature carved a new county from the eastern portion of the existing Jefferson County, its boundary stretching from the east bank of the Neches River to the west bank of the Sabine. It was christened Orange County, and six years later, on February 6, 1858, the citizens of the existing town of Madison successfully requested that the town be renamed Orange.[96]

During this time, the inevitable course of the settlement's future was set as the fledgling lumber industry began to develop. Settlers were well aware of the commercial potential of the surrounding timber forests; the first mill of record had been an 1835 water mill situated on Adams Bayou, a few miles northwest of Green's Bluff. The first steam sawmill was built in 1841, utilizing "parts of an old, wrecked steamboat" to process cypress. Other mills were built throughout the 1850s, and by January 1, 1861, track for the Texas and New Orleans Railroad for the 106 miles from Houston to Orange was completed for the express purpose of delivering East Texas lumber products to the shipping center of Galveston.[97]

But cataclysm loomed on the horizon amid escalating hostilities between North and South. The sympathies of Orange County residents, the majority southern-born, lay predominantly and irrevocably with the South; on February 23, 1861, by a vote of 142 to 3, they ratified an ordinance in favor of Texas' secession from the Union. In the first few months of the Civil War, Orange County, like its counterpart in Pennsylvania, Lycoming County, sent three companies of soldiers to serve—but in the Confederate military.[98]

On October 4, 1862, Union forces captured Galveston.[99] The city was recaptured by the Confederates on New Year's Eve of 1863, but by that time most industry in Orange County had ceased.[100] Military action came closest to Orange in the early morning of September 8, 1863, when Federal gunboats fired on Fort Griffin, the earthen Confederate garrison guarding Sabine Pass, the outlet from Sabine Lake into the Gulf of Mexico. When the Union ships came into range, the Confederates opened fire, defeating them in a forty-five-minute battle, although the victory failed to alter the ultimate course of the war.[101]

In September 1865, a few months after the war's end, nature delivered an unrelated reminder of the hazards of living on the Gulf Coast: a monster hurricane struck Orange County, leaving almost total destruction in its wake. According to an eyewitness, Orange resident Robert E. Russell, "There was not a leaf left on a tree or weed and grass was torn out of the ground by its roots. Trees that were not blown down, some of them two or three feet in diameter, were broken off a few feet above ground." Every boat in the Sabine at Orange was wrecked save one, and only three houses in town withstood the blast.[102] Years passed before Orange recovered— both from the storm and the war.

Only twelve years after the Southern surrender at Appomattox and a mere seven after Texas had rejoined the Union, Henry Jacob Lutcher came to live and work in Orange. Doubtless, he soon discovered that Confederate sympathies still ran dangerously high and postwar feelings remained raw; yet, extraordinarily, he experienced little conflict with his new neighbors. Although he had been called a "Copperhead" north of the Mason-Dixon line, he was probably saved a great deal of grief south of it by being a Democrat who had opposed the war. Even though it was necessary for him to overcome some initial regional dislike, it spoke well for his character that he was able to meld so seamlessly into his new environment.[103] Besides, his new neighbors were surely aware that the Lutcher & Moore Lumber Company mills and lumbering operations meant much-needed capital and jobs for the area's struggling economy.

When Lutcher reached Orange, he lost no time. On March 17, 1877, a little over three weeks after he had left Williamsport, he purchased a tract of land on the Sabine River in the Alexander Calder Survey, just downriver from the settlement of Orange. He then promptly bought two adjoining tracts and at once began preparations to go into operation.[104] His letters to Moore, back in Williamsport, offer a glimpse into the scope of his mental acumen and the rare combination of vision, organizational ability, drive, and practicality that would bring him such extraordinary success. The letters also confirm that, in addition to being compatible business associates, Lutcher and Moore regarded each other as personal friends.

Always addressing Moore as "Friend Bedell," Lutcher first wrote from Orange March 19, providing details of his land purchases for the mill site and informing him that he had already contracted to buy pine and cypress logs to process in the mill. "I had to take the ship yard and . . . four acres this side and five acres behind it," he reported. "That is the only adjoining lands I could get a good title for."[105] He had negotiated terms—some for cash, some for down payment and a note.[106] Enclosing a sketch "of how the mill would stand," he asked Moore to obtain advice on construction of its "brick house" from one of his brothers-in-law in Williamsport, bricklayer John Reinhart (the husband of his sister Christina).[107]

Lutcher also requested that Moore send him materials for construction of the mill: edger, pulleys, gang saws, circular saws, belts, engines, a log timber press, picket headers, "good" cant hooks with picks, boilers. He himself found an old steam engine from the Trinity River steamboat *Josiah H. Bell*, which had been transformed into a cotton-clad gunboat during the Civil War; when the *Bell* was scuttled after the war, the engine was salvaged, and Lutcher discovered it at an Orange shipyard.[108]

A mill whistle was paramount. "I think Sands [someone in Williamsport] ought to give us a mill whistle," Lutcher wrote. "If he don't," he instructed, "get one [from] Snyder and have Sands to tap a hole in the boiler for it." Moore apparently found one: an enormous brass whistle, said to have come from Williamsport, was mounted at the new mill. (For decades, its governing blasts marked its operating hours and became an alarm clock for the town and the entire countryside.)[109] "We want to hurry everything," Lutcher urged, "as we are losing $100 per day for every day we lose in getting our mill up." He and Moore agreed to ship supplies by water into Galveston, which was the quickest and least expensive method.[110]

Skilled workers were difficult to find. "If you can spare Geo. Britenbach [a worker from the Williamsport mill] . . . send him," Lutcher requested, "—and if there is any more good men that wish to come, send them along as I have to pay these common laborers $1.25 per day, and I know our men are worth $1.50 per day as well as those men here are worth $1.00." "I would not care if I had a whole crew of our Wmsport men," he declared. "George Britenbach I can use any time." Moore duly sent Britenbach to Orange, where he became Lutcher's second-in-command. Other workers from Williamsport came down, including the mason, Reinhart. "It will cost us $5.00 per day for a man from Houston, and he won't do half as much work in a day as John," Lutcher wrote. "And he knows how to do it. But don't send John til I telegraph you, for the boilers might get here before I get the brick." "Now, in regard to a filer," he wrote, "it is very hard to get a man that we can depend on that can file both gang and circular [saws]. . . . [But] get a good man anyhow, Bedell," he urged.[111]

Lutcher added a short but portentous postscript to his March 26 letter to Moore: "Frances," he wrote, "is at Houston. Will leave tomorrow night."[112] Whether he intended to travel to Houston to collect Frances Ann or to await her arrival in Orange is unclear, and the letter fails to mention their daughters, Miriam and Carrie; they might either have come with their mother or temporarily remained in Williamsport with relatives.

In the midst of the green East Texas spring, Lutcher's spirits soared. "Bedell," he wrote, "I have much to write you, but I have a great deal to contend with here in the way of facilities, but I feel equal to it. My health was never better. Hurry everything along, as I want to make sawdust by June 1st ." "The weather here is splendid," he enthused. "We are getting along first rate."[113] (He had yet to suffer through an East Texas summer.)

A little later, his spirits were not quite so high. "Friend Bedell," he complained, "no letter tonight from you. What is the matter? It is eleven P.M. o'clock now, and my head aches some." He repeatedly requested monies necessary for mill construction, payroll, and other expenses. "They come for me like a pack of hungry wolves," he grumbled, "if they have a cent coming to them." In the matter of insuring the mill, however, he allowed himself a moment of pardonable pride: "Lumber 150 ft from mill, boiler house separate from mill. It is a safer mill than any I know at Wmsport." He ordered another engine from St. Louis, which was placed on two railroad cars and shipped to Orange.[114]

In his May 16 communication, Lutcher made a personal allusion to what must have been an ongoing family problem. "Mr. Robinson

Figure 2.7. Lutcher & Moore's first mill in Orange, constructed in 1877,
at that time the largest mill in Texas, undated. Stark Foundation Archives.

[Lutcher's father-in-law, David Robinson] has written me that he was going
to send [Frances Ann's stepbrother] George Wilson out," he wrote Moore,
"and that if George drank one drop I should let him know and he would
send the money out to send him home with." Lutcher responded to Robinson summarily: "I wrote him if he came that the first drop would settle
it. It is late," he added, "and I have the headache," apparently a recurring
problem.[115]

By late May, Lutcher was getting his first real taste of East Texas heat:
"11 o'clock P.M. and mosquitoes biting," he complained; "98 [degrees]
in the shade." The mill itself arrived in Galveston May 28 via the Mallory Steamship Line,[116] and as soon as it was discharged from the vessel,
they would forward it to Orange.[117] The final letter was written June 1 to
Moore from George Britenbach in the absence of Lutcher, who had gone
to Galveston to order steam pipe. Britenbach reported that the circular
mill had arrived. "It has been very warm today," he added. "Thermometer
105 [degrees] in the shade."[118]

Lutcher apparently failed to "make sawdust" by June 1, as had been his
original aim, but he came "mighty close," as his new East Texas neighbors would have said. In July 1877 they fired up the saws, and the new
Lutcher & Moore Lumber Company mill commenced operations.[119] The
much-anticipated new mill, the first large, modern mill to be built in the
state, boasted four times the producing capacity of other local mills and
the largest engine in the Southwest, and was predicted to be capable of

turning out fifty thousand to one hundred thousand board feet of lumber (accounts differ) every twenty-four hours.[120]

Lutcher had no way of knowing that a young sawyer, William Henry Stark, who had skillfully ridden the cable-pulled carriage to cut the lumber for the framework of the new mill, would become his business partner—and his son-in-law.[121]

PART II

THE

CAPITALIST

CHAPTER THREE

The Quiet Man

They came to this new land with boundless dreams,
They often felt the keen-edged blade of grief,
But even this could not dim hope's bright flame.
—UNKNOWN, EXCERPT FROM CLIPPING FOUND
IN STARK FAMILY PAPERS[1]

In the shadowed reaches of the great East Texas Piney Woods, another family was carving out an existence among the same towering pines that held such prosperous potential for the Lutcher clan. Jeremiah Stark, the grandfather of that strong, quick young sawyer, William Henry Stark, was the first member of his particular branch of the Stark family to come to Texas, bringing his wife and children from Ohio in 1837, shortly after Texas had become a republic.

Jeremiah and his son, John Thomas Stark, struggled with life in a frontier republic, a secession crisis, a brutal civil war, and a harsh postwar period. But the third Stark generation, William Stark and his siblings, lived in a Texas once more under the Stars and Stripes, with an economy stable enough to allow William's talents as an entrepreneur to bloom. And bloom they did; a man of quiet, even disposition and thoughtful, deliberative action, William Stark was also blessed with an enviable work ethic and a gift for developing business concerns that would serve him well indeed. A fortuitous marriage set his feet on the path to extraordinary material success for himself, his family, and the entire East Texas region, but those intrinsic qualities that enabled him to such achievement were rooted in his family history and personal experiences in the forests of East Texas, especially during the Civil War.

William Stark's ancestors entered the British royal colony of New Hampshire from Scotland and Ireland in the early eighteenth century. Three brothers immigrated: Archibald, James, and John, the sons of Glasgow merchant John Stark and the grandsons of another John Stark, a Glasgow bishop. Little is known about John, the youngest of the three. The oldest, Archibald, emigrated with his family from Scotland to Londonderry, Ireland, where he trained as a carpenter, but after King James II of England laid siege to Londonderry during religious turmoil in 1688–1689, he and his extended family moved to another Londonderry in New Hampshire in 1719–1720.[2] He lived in that area for the rest of his life, working as a carpenter and farmer.[3] A strong Stark presence remains there today.

One of Archibald's sons, yet another John Stark, served in the colonial military before and during the French and Indian War, engaged primarily in fighting Indians. When the American Revolution broke out, Stark led a force of New Hampshire troops at the Battle of Bunker Hill and participated in other engagements, including Trenton, Princeton (both under Gen. George Washington), and Bennington, a part of the successful campaign against British general "Gentleman Johnny" Burgoyne (who was defeated by Continental troops at Saratoga two months later). This John Stark emerged from the Revolution a brigadier general and the best known of the early Stark settlers in New Hampshire.[4]

The Jeremiah Stark who eventually moved to Texas was a descendant of the second Stark brother, James (born 1695 in Scotland). At some point James immigrated to the Colonies,[5] appearing in colonial records in Stafford County, Virginia, where, at the time of his death in 1754, he owned six slaves and a small "plantation."[6] In 1783, some of his descendants followed the promise of new land with the Daniel Boone migration from Virginia to Bourbon County, Kentucky, where, several generations later, Jeremiah was born in 1800.[7] A land grant given to an uncle as a veteran of the War of 1812 led Jeremiah and his family, along with other Stark relations, to move to the Midwest, and various family members spread to Indiana, Illinois, Missouri, and Ohio. Jeremiah's oldest son, John Thomas, was born in Preble County, Ohio, in 1821.[8]

And it was once more that glittering jewel, the promise of free land, that lured the Jeremiah Stark family from Ohio to the Republic of Texas in 1837. At this time the sparsely populated new nation, damaged by invasion and war, burdened by debt from the recent Revolution, and lacking a decent transportation system or a reliable money supply, was also haunted by the effects of a major depression in the United States that continued in some areas until the mid-1840s. The United States served as the major market for Texas goods, and if there was little money in circulation in the States, there was even less in Texas; thus, the Starks and the other settlers struggled in an economy that was elemental at best, based largely on barter.[9]

When Jeremiah Stark and his family arrived in San Augustine County

Figure 3.1. Brig. Gen. John Stark, who fought in the Revolutionary War's Battle of Bennington, August 16, 1777. He led a force of two thousand men to victory over British troops. Source: John Spargo, *The Bennington Battle Monument* (Rutland, VT: Tuttle, 1925).

in September 1837, they claimed 1,280 acres of land "by donation" on Ayish Bayou near the site of Nuestra Señora de los Dolores de los Ais, one of the oldest Spanish missions in Texas.[10] This property served as their base of operations from 1837 to 1853. Here Jeremiah opened a store, and John Thomas, often called "Thomas," or "Tom," worked with his father—

Figure 3.2. Jeremiah Stark, father of John Thomas Stark, undated.
Stark Foundation Archives.

farming, helping operate the store, and delivering goods to the community.[11] On July 21, 1847, he married Martha Ann Skidmore from San Augustine County, and the young couple started a family.[12] Their first child,
Susan Ellen, was born July 8, 1848, but lived only two days. Almost exactly
a year later, July 10, 1849, another daughter, Eugenia Rebecca, made her
appearance. Their first son, William Henry, nicknamed "Bud," was born

Figure 3.3. John Thomas Stark, father of William Henry Stark,
prior to the onset of the Civil War. Stark Foundation Archives.

Figure 3.4. Martha Ann Skidmore Stark, wife of John Thomas Stark and
mother of William Henry Stark, with the Starks' oldest child, Eugenia Rebecca, undated.
Stark Foundation Archives.

March 19, 1851, followed by his brother Jeremiah, or "Jerry," December 22,
1852.[13] In the coming years, other children were born with regularity.

In the 1840s, San Augustine County had been crippled by the so-called
Regulator-Moderator War, vicious battles fought between two vigilante
factions over land frauds, many originating in the days of the old Neutral Ground. Land values dropped, and the trade route from San Augustine to Natchitoches, Louisiana (part of the ancient Spanish Camino Real,
or King's Highway, stretching from San Antonio eastward into the United
States), was effectively rendered unusable by the violence, hampering San

Augustine's commerce. Its economy, apparently unable to adapt to other methods of transportation (such as shipping goods down the Sabine River to Galveston), began to stagnate.[14]

In 1853, perhaps in part because of those conditions, John Thomas, Martha, and their three children struck out on their own. They stopped briefly at the settlements of Wiess Bluff and Belgrade before heading toward Burkeville and Newton, two towns laid out in 1844 and 1853, respectively, in Newton County.[15] They traveled by wagon through the East Texas countryside—gentle rolling hills laced with spring-fed creeks, rife with game, and thick with virgin hardwood and pine timber, so lofty and thick that the trees shaded out undergrowth, enabling easy travel across the forest floor (as William Henry Stark's future father-in-law, Henry Jacob Lutcher, would later find so remarkable).

John Thomas Stark kept a home in Burkeville, owning land for farming, home sites in town for speculation purposes, and a store and blacksmith shop, but he also maintained businesses in Newton, located about twenty miles south by southwest, recently established as the Newton County seat.[16] Because he was away from Burkeville for lengthy periods of time, much of the responsibility for the store and farm fell on Martha and his two oldest children, Eugenia and Bud. Fortunately, Martha's mother, Rebecca Wofford, whose husband had joined the California Gold Rush and had never returned, stayed with her daughter to help with her growing family.[17]

Family letters surviving from the 1850s and 1860s increasingly reveal John Thomas Stark's fractious personality. By 1859, he was justice of the peace in Newton County, performing marriages and settling local controversies.[18] He also served as Burkeville's postmaster, and it was the latter position that led him to provoke what was, in his own view, the area's greatest dispute—with the possible exception of the Civil War itself. The opening salvo of the altercation was fired by an unidentified person or persons who complained to the US postmaster general about Stark's service as postmaster. A form letter from US First Assistant Postmaster General Horatio King, dated July 12, 1860, specified the charges, which alleged Stark to be irresponsible and unfit for office; the mystery complainants had declared that *"nearly every* mail from your [Stark's] office to Newton contains mail matter which should have been kept at Burkeville."[19]

Stark took instant umbrage. He wrote to Washington, D.C., lawyer A.H. Evans and demanded his help in ascertaining his accusers' identities.[20] "I beg to say it is impossible to get the names you desire," Evans replied. "Department will not let me have them—Nor could you recover in libel suit as you could prove no injury, *the Department having sustained you, and ignored all your accusers.* The names are Kept secret, & can not be seen."[21] But even with Evans's assurance that the government had held in

Figure 3.5. The John Thomas Stark house in Burkeville, Texas, ca. 1920.
Stark Foundation Archives.

Figure 3.6. William Henry Stark as a boy. Stark Foundation Archives.

his favor, the contentious Stark refused to relinquish the matter and continued trying to obtain the names of the complainants.

Later that year, Evans wrote that yet another complaint had been leveled against Stark, this time charging him "with offences enough to hang him": a draft for $1,000 had been taken from a letter sent to his post office for mailing; some letters had been opened before they were sent through the post office; and mail had been unnecessarily held.[22] The complainants even recommended a postmaster to replace Stark, who instantly shot back a letter in his own support, signed by sixty-seven local residents he had presumably recruited. Evans duly reported in January 1861 that once more Stark had been vindicated: "I am authorized to say that after full inquiry and investigation, the case is decided in your favor, and your integrity is sustained by the official action of the Government."[23]

Even then, Stark still believed that his honor had been impugned and refused to allow the situation to die; he repeatedly fired off letters to the US postmaster general, demanding his accusers' names, even after Texas' secession from the Union.

> The Dep[artment] ha[s] suffered charges to be filed against me as false un-founded & malicious as Hell itself could devise, ha[s] called on me to disprove them, which I have done although it was like fighting in the dark and now refuse[s] my repeated and urgent entreaties to give me the names of my ac-cusers. . . . You may now understand me as wishing to resign, for the manner in which I have been treated by the [US Post Office] Dep[artment] ever since I have accepted the appointment is anything but fair, and *has tended as much as any other one thing to increase the secession feeling in this vicinity.*[24]

As Stark saw it, his treatment had actually influenced the area's vote to secede from the Union! After the war, his attackers finally identified themselves and recanted some of their charges.[25] He promptly sued them. The case dragged on for years, and in 1873, as one of the men, David Ford (incidentally, the father-in-law of Stark's daughter Eugenia), lay dying, Stark wrote him a letter, astonishing in its singularity. There is no record of Ford's reply, if any.

> Let me beg of you not to face the *Beyond* without having made all the repara-tion in your power. . . . Think of this and think of it *now* for there is no repen-tance, no reparation, no doing justice to the wronged one in the cold grave to which we haste. . . . Think how much better your mind would feel, how much better prepared you would feel if this breach were healed and all of us at peace. . . . Let God judge between us, and may he forgive you is my earnest prayer and incline your heart to do right before it is too late.[26]

A soldier criticizing Stark's leadership summed up his captain's trouble-some trait: "I do not think this malign influence proceeded so much from evil intention as from 'a contentious and fractious spirit.'"[27] (Fortunately for posterity, Stark's son Bud did *not* inherit this particular characteristic from his father.)

However, John Thomas's personality harbored a softer side. Music was of great importance to him; he loved its soothing and pleasurable effect. He played violin all of his life, as had his father, Jeremiah. This love of music was also shared by many of his children, especially Eugenia, Bud, Jerry (both the latter two played violin as well[28]), and later, two of his younger children, Hobby and Lilly. Eugenia later remembered that, in her childhood, their grandfather Jeremiah frequently rode the thirty miles by horseback to visit the family, always bringing his own violin. After supper, father and son, Jeremiah and John Thomas, played late into the night after the rest of the family except Eugenia went to bed. Eugenia described herself as

> a little thin, big-eyed girl, sitting by the big fireplace listening with all my soul while those two men played on and on, until after midnight, too much absorbed in their music to notice me and make me go to bed. I never heard but one violin like that of my father's, and it was in the last chautauqua here. . . . When I go to heaven, I know I will hear music like that![29]

When John Thomas went off to war, he took his violin with him and it was still in his possession at his death in 1893.[30] A Stark family story holds that John Thomas acquired the violin as he was traveling by horseback through a rural area of East Texas when he saw a group of children playing in the sand with an old, battered violin, pretending it was a toy sled. Recognizing its fine workmanship, he bought it at a reasonable price and had it repaired, and it was this instrument that he played for the rest of his life. At his death, the executor of his estate placed the violin in a group of other items to be sold, fixing its price at $10. His widow (his third wife, Donna Jerusha Smith Stark) bought it for their son A.M.H. "Hobby" Stark, who loved to play. When the violin was appraised after Hobby's death, it was found to be an Amati,[31] worth $5,000. Or so the story went.[32]

When the Republic of Texas joined the Union in 1845 as a slaveholding state, Texans had hoped statehood would help resolve several serious issues. Some of the problems—dispute over the state's boundaries and payment of debts incurred during the Texas Revolution and the time of the republic—had been settled with the 1848 Treaty of Guadalupe Hidalgo (ending the Mexican War) and the subsequent Compromise of 1850.

The other issues dashed Texans' hopes against a wall of reality.[33] One was state related: as the population of Texas had grown and settlement had expanded, American Indians' land and way of life were threatened, and their acts of violence against settlers had increased.[34] Two remaining problems—the slavery question and states' rights—were national in scope; in their attempts to protect the underlying issue of slaveholding within their individual state boundaries, Southern slave owners raised the related one of states' rights.[35] These two obstacles also proved insurmountable and were resolved only by the Civil War.[36]

Immediately following the 1860 election of antislavery, pro-Union Republican Abraham Lincoln to the nation's presidency, the states of the Deep South seceded from the Union, but states such as Texas that bordered US-held territory moved more slowly. (Texas was the last of the first seven to secede before the Confederate attack on Fort Sumter on April 12, 1861.) After holding a secession convention, Texas conducted a statewide popular vote (the only state to do so) that proved to be a landslide in favor of secession.[37] The state left the Union March 2, 1861—exactly twenty-five years after Texans had declared their independence from Mexico—and quickly joined the Confederacy.[38]

With the notable exception of John Thomas Stark's accusations against the US Post Office, not one of the extant letters to or from the members of his family mentions these political issues prior to the outbreak of the Civil War. The Starks were not slave owners, although they rented slaves when they needed them to help in the house or in the fields, but the onset of hostilities in April 1861 did indeed force the lives of the family members in unexpected directions.[39] With secession, the US Postal Service closed down in the South and was replaced by a new one under the purview of the infant Confederate States of America. John Thomas Stark's service as the Burkeville postmaster officially came to an end when the new postmaster of the Confederacy, John Reagan of Texas, sent a request for an inventory of all items in the Burkeville office in preparation for creating a Confederate postal system.[40]

It would not be long before the war reached Texas, and most Texans knew it was coming. In Newton, a neighbor passed by the Stark property as John Thomas was applying beeswax and tallow to a tent. The neighbor asked him what would happen to his large family if he went to war. "Why," he replied in honest surprise, "I have a boy ten years old." As far as he was concerned, that was the end of the matter; he figured that Bud was perfectly capable of acting as man of the house and taking care of the family.[41] In the spring of 1862, John Thomas enlisted in the Confederate Army, and Bud watched his father ride away to war, leaving him, his older sister Eugenia, his mother, and his grandmother in charge at home.[42] "Bud," his father told him as he departed, "you've got to be a man."[43]

John Thomas joined the self-named Newton County "Dreadnaughts," shortly to be placed as Company H in the recently formed 13th Texas Cavalry Regiment, attached to Gen. John G. Walker's Texas Division.[44] (It had been organized with approximately twelve thousand men, all Texans, the only division in either the Union or Confederate armies made up entirely of soldiers from one state.)[45] Walker's Division was sent to Little Rock, Arkansas, to defend against a threatened Union invasion and, long term, to prevent Union forces from cutting the flow of supplies from Mexico and Texas to the rest of the Confederacy. Soon after his regiment was established, John Thomas's company marched with them to Little Rock to reinforce the defenses. He traveled far from home and into the face of a terrible winter in the Arkansas hills.[46]

To the Texas soldiers' outrage, in the division's first campaign in Arkansas their unit was retrained and reclassified as infantry. This was done for several reasons: their horses were costly to maintain, locals could not spare fodder for them, and some of the animals were also needed to pull wagons and heavy artillery. But none of the Texans wanted to walk, and in their eyes, the change in status was an indignity. As one writer observed, "To say they were upset is to put it in the mildest possible terms for a near mutiny." To the end of the war, they persisted in referring to themselves as "Dismounted Cavalry."[47]

The overall Union strategy lay in isolating the Confederacy with a blockade, then dividing it internally and striking at Southern industry, the North's target being the Mississippi River (which Union forces captured in the summer of 1863). In the spring of 1864, Gen. Nathaniel P. Banks began a campaign to control the Red River and divide the western Confederacy. Beginning the following November, Gen. William Tecumseh Sherman marched through Georgia to the sea to split the eastern Confederacy. John Thomas's company did a great deal of walking and very little fighting from the spring of 1862 to the spring of 1864, suffering more from disease, miserable weather, exhaustion, sore feet, difficult terrain, and a shortage of supplies; still, they served their purpose of checking Union maneuvers west of the Mississippi.[48]

John Thomas's family members were all strong defenders of the Confederacy (especially Eugenia, who wrote her father asking him to send her a lock of hair from the first Yankee soldier he killed).[49] But loyal to the Southern cause though she might have been, Martha Stark could not refrain from complaining to her soldier husband about many personal concerns; she was facing the necessity of running a home, a farm, and several businesses without the presence of an adult male in the family. Money was scarce during wartime, and although schools were set up from time to time by various individuals, the Starks could not always find the ready cash to keep the children enrolled. John Thomas insisted that they remain in school "to prepare themselves for their respective roles in society," but if that was not possible, he wrote, he would simply be forced to return to take care of his family.[50]

His words were probably an empty threat; in reality, coming home was not an honorable option unless a soldier was wounded or seriously ill, and in spite of the hopes and expectations on both sides of the conflict, it was becoming increasingly apparent to all factions that the war was not destined for an early end. Even so, Martha's protestations of loneliness and her entreaties to her husband to come home formed a constant litany in her letters.[51]

Times would grow worse for the Stark family, but they met the new challenges as best they could. Bud was already proving himself to be a capable farmer. (Later in life, he was fond of remarking that he became a farmer at ten years of age.)[52] Eugenia helped her mother and grandmother in spinning and weaving homespun to make clothes for John Thomas, the rest of the family, and other soldiers who needed them. Although Martha complained that, during the East Texas winters, their home was much too drafty and smoky to endure, it offered more amenities than most, and she dealt with the chores and problems of their home existence well enough.

Still, she worried. She heard that a measles epidemic had struck John Thomas's regiment—no small problem for adults. Typhoid also made its deadly appearance in the soldiers' ranks. Sickness was prevalent at home as well: "Bud is verry sick with congestive fever," Martha wrote John Thomas. "He was taken Tuesday night with a very bad pain in his head and high fever. . . . He is a little better but very sick yet." Later, Bud himself wrote his father that he was recovering from mumps.[53]

Martha, lonely, anxious, and exhausted, was also rearing a greatly enlarged family. Since their arrival in Burkeville in 1853, five more children had arrived: another girl, Elizabeth Sarah, born in 1855 (who had died at three years of age in 1858); John Thomas Jr., born in 1857; Martha Ann, or "Mattie," in 1858; and Mary Virginia, or "Molly," in 1860. Martha's last child, Benjamin McCullough Stark, was born in May 1862, shortly after John Thomas left for the war.[54] She wrote to tell him that he was once again a father. "I was confined on the 13th of this mont, oh how I did miss you Thomas at such a trying time I felt scared and uneasy."[55]

She had worried for nothing. "I had a verry good time as it happened," she reported afterward, "and I feel verry smart I have a pretty little boy oh how I wish you could see him." When Martha wrote two months later, once again to "encourage" John Thomas to come home, either for a visit or for good, she was holding the infant Benny in her arms, her hands literally full. Fortunately, Rebecca was there to assist in caring for the children, and in August 1862 a neighbor, William Blackshear, lent Martha one of his slaves and the woman's three children for two months for room and board, freeing her to spin and weave.[56] In all, she was probably better circumstanced than the wives of most soldiers, gray or blue.

But Martha Stark suffered an additional concern. It surfaced in a letter she wrote to John Thomas July 6, 1862, informing him that she was aware that he harbored romantic feelings for another woman and that she was sensing his increasing withdrawal. "I know that I am getting old and care worn and cannot blame you for placing your affections on one younger and handsomer than I am," she wrote in anguish. "As to beauty I was not blest with that but there beats as warm and loveing heart in my bosom as ever beat in the breast of another.[57] Oh Thomas this is like taking my verry life." She added that her suspicions about her husband and the unnamed woman made being apart from him even more difficult for her, and to make the situation even less bearable, he had not even been required to go to war; it had been his choice. (The draft age for the Confederate army extended only to age thirty-five, and at the time he joined, he was forty-one.) He had volunteered, leaving her at home, not only with myriad responsibilities but, worse, doubts about her place in her husband's heart.[58]

Every time a letter from their father arrived, the children clamored to hear every word of its contents; thus, Martha warned her husband to refrain from writing anything in a letter that he did not want the whole family to know. But in an undated reply that he had marked "Private," he wrote fervently:

> Perhaps some would think me foolish, but I cannot restrain my feelings. O if you knew what a warm loving heart your old man has and how deeply and devotedly he loves you, you would never, never suffer yourself to doubt again. I have dreamt of seeing you almost nightly. O if I had these fond arms around my sweet girl again it would be sometime before I would let you go again. . . . I have to do without those sweet kisses and fond embraces now but I will make it up when I return home again. My own sweetest best dearest girl only love me as you did in the first years of our happy marriage and I ask no more. How my heart bounds to think that you will at last restore your sining long mourning husband to that warm place in your heart again.[59]

After that revealing exchange, Martha never again mentioned doubts about his love for her (in any extant letter, at least), but the fact remained that she wanted him to come home.

Eleven-year-old Bud also carried a huge load of responsibility for the family, manfully tackling his assigned role as farmer. He wrote his father in April 1862, shortly after John Thomas had gone to war, that "corn has come up we tried to work our pony the other day and he wouldn't work and we had to go down to Mr. Woodses and borrow a yoke of his oxen." A letter he wrote that August details conditions on the farm:

> Dear farther I take my pen in hand to let you know that we are all well at the Present but marry [Mary] she had the fever last night but she is up and playing about we have cut up pretty neare all of the new ground corn and shocked

it up we have sowed our turnips and the grass or potatoes looks very well the ground is covered with vines our mules foot got sore and the screwworms got in it but it is getting well now the hogs about here got in the doctors lot and eat up nearly all of the corn and we turned our hogs in it and let them eat up the balance. We have all started to school we are looking for you home for clothing and you must be shore and come ma and granny is spinning weaving very hard to get the clothing done time you come ma says if you come across any cotton cards you must be certain and buy her a pair and save them for her till you come home and get her some indigo to color her some dresses. Benny is Just as fat as a pig. I planted your plum seads we had to give 20 dollars for a sack of salt and we haven't got it home yet. Charily macmahon [Charlie McMahon] got his leg shot of in the battle of Richmond and harison ford was in to feet of him. Jim Mac has gone after charly but has not got back yet we turned bill out yesterday and got him up to day and they was a gash about an inch and a half long cut on his leg and about an inch deep. We planted out onions yesterday.[60]

Quite a descriptive letter for an eleven-and-a-half-year-old, erratically educated boy to write—but he failed to mention the persistent drought in East Texas during the war years that made life even more difficult, both at home and on the battlefield, for obtaining an adequate food supply and for keeping prices in check.[61] (He must have studied diligently over the next year; another letter to his father, written a year later, showed that his grammar and spelling had vastly improved.)[62]

By necessity, Bud was growing up fast, and he took his family responsibilities seriously. "Bud has gone to see the Jasper shoemaker," Martha wrote John Thomas in August 1863, "to get some shoes made for all the children." Bud received a high compliment from a local doctor, N.P. West, who wrote John Thomas: "Bud braggs mightily about his crop, and is without any exception the most manly boy [with whom] I am acquainted. I would give a great deal if Nat [presumably his son] was only half as much so."[63]

Newton and Jasper County citizens received a great deal of war news from throughout the country. Martha wrote to John Thomas that she had heard word of the threatened Federal invasion of Sabine Pass September 25, 1862 (thwarted only by a local yellow fever epidemic); the Union capture of Galveston that October; and the battles at Corinth, Mississippi, April 6–7, 1862, and the following September 17 at Sharpsburg, Virginia (Antietam, as it was known in the North, the same battle in which Henry Jacob Lutcher fought as a Union soldier). Units from the Newton and Jasper area participated in both the latter battles. Martha wrote that she had heard they had been "cut all to pieces" and that "the whole land seems to be in mourning."[64]

Figure 3.7. William Blewett, commander of the Newton County Dreadnaughts until his death in 1862. John Thomas Stark eventually married Blewett's widow, Nancy. Stark Foundation Archives.

John Thomas Stark's Company H remained west of the Mississippi for the entire war, moving from Little Rock into southwestern Louisiana, then back toward Little Rock, depending on where they were needed. The company saw fighting throughout, but more casualties resulted from disease than from combat. When Capt. William H. Blewett, the original commander of Company H, died of "a hemorrhage of the bowels" outside Little Rock in September 1862, John Thomas Stark was promoted to captain and leader of the company.[65] In the summer of 1863, after Union victories at Vicksburg and Port Hudson, Louisiana, had cut the Confederacy in half along the Mississippi River, Company H was relocated south from Arkansas to the Louisiana-Texas border, and John Thomas's unit was sent to Camp Texas, near Alexandria, Louisiana.[66]

Martha Stark was herself a casualty of the war as surely as any soldier killed in battle. Since John Thomas was now much nearer home, he and Martha were able to communicate more quickly, but they still did not see each other, much to Martha's dismay. The distance between Burkeville and Camp Texas was short enough to make a journey feasible, and she decided to take the opportunity to visit her husband, as many East Texas relatives and friends of the soldiers were doing.

John Thomas did not discourage her; he merely asked for enough advance notice to give him time to arrange housing. She responded that she would come if the company would remain in that location for any length of time—and if he still wanted her. "I will bring my knitting and stay untill you get tired of me," she wrote. She, Bud, and the baby, Benny, started for Camp Texas by horse-drawn wagon sometime after August 21, 1863 (the date of Bud's last letter to his father before they left), while Rebecca Wofford stayed in Burkeville to care for the younger children.[67]

After their arrival at Camp Texas, according to a Stark family story, the soldiers in the camp, enchanted to have a child among them, took Benny and walked him across a stretch of sand, then built a little fence around his footprints to remind them of home.[68] But disaster soon struck. John Thomas wrote to Rebecca on August 26:

We are all or have been sick. I was taken the same day Martha got here with a bad attack of Neuralgia. Before I got well Martha was taken with something like flux [dysentery] though not a bad attack. Doctor Hollis has been attending on her. The disease is checked but leaves her very weak and sore. Bud has been having light chills but does not seem to affect him much. I did intend for Martha to return with Mr. Smith but she will not be able to travel for some days yet. I do not want her to start until she is entirely recovered for fear of a relapse. I am sorry that I could not have got to a house but we are pretty comfortably fixed we have a very large tent and a good mattress for Martha. . . . Every house near here is filled with soldiers sick or convalescent. We are camped off to one side of the Regiment in a retired place and two other ladies from Jasper close by us Mrs William Seals and Mrs Morris.[69]

No written account of the next few days' events survives, but Martha obviously took a turn for the worse. Six days later, September 1, 1863, she died. There was no quick means to transport her body; in the Louisiana heat, necessity dictated that she be buried near the camp.[70] No marker was immediately placed on her grave, but when John Thomas's command left the Alexandria area the following November, he wrote to Rebecca, asking her "to try and get a pair of those largest size tombstones for the dear one that is lying so far from home, if they are not all gone. I can not bear the idea of leaving her there without any mark to show who it is."[71] He wrote that her grave could be found by "inquiring at Loyd's Mills [south of Alexandria, near Cheneyville, Louisiana] for the Springhill Church burying ground, and any of the neighbors then can show the grave."[72] (The location was later corroborated by Eugenia Stark Ford.)[73] Rebecca replied that all of the tombstones had indeed been sold, and to date, no evidence has been found that a marker was ever placed on Martha's grave.[74]

Bud, then only twelve years old, helped bury his mother, then assumed the care of the fifteen-month-old Benny. Holding the infant on the wagon seat beside him, Bud took his brother safely home to Burkeville, leaving his mother in that unmarked grave in Louisiana. (According to Eugenia, Benny was also ill and after his recovery had to learn to walk again.)[75] Those terrible days remained seared into William's memory throughout his life; in later years he would recount them but always insisted that he was not embittered by them.[76]

Rebecca Wofford stayed on with the family to care for her deceased daughter's children. After her husband's disappearance and her daughter's death, she considered obtaining a divorce, but the procedure was too costly—around $150. She asked John Thomas to fund the divorce, but there is no record of his response, if any.[77] Even so, she received at least two marriage proposals, the first from an unnamed professor of religion and an "excellent phisition" who was willing to help her rear the Stark children, but lack of funds in the middle of a war doomed their chances.[78]

Eugenia described her grandmother's second proposal to John Thomas. "Oh!" she wrote, "don't you think Granny has got a beau right at this minute. He is a Russian by the name of Posener[,] rich as can be." Posener, "as rich as Creosus," Eugenia declared, had called on her grandmother, bringing papers to show his worth, claiming to have $100,000 in Confederate money and $20,000 in gold and silver. "I have pretty near killed myself laughing at him—the way he talks and everything," Eugenia reported. "[He said] he had plenties of horses and cattle and sheep and chickens and turkeys and gooses and everyt'ing," she mimicked. Her grandmother had responded in eerily modern parlance that the marriage was "no go." According to Eugenia, Posener departed that same day.[79]

John Thomas Stark remained in Walker's Division, retaining the command of Company H, Newton County's Dreadnaughts, from September 1862 until November 1864. During the war, the division had become known as "Walker's Greyhounds" for their ability to make long forced marches from one point to another in the Trans-Mississippi territory, some units marching as much as a total of thirty-five hundred miles.[80] Walker's Greyhounds successfully discharged their main responsibility to assist in protecting the western Confederacy from Union general Banks's expected land invasion. In April 1864, during the Red River campaign, John Thomas led his Dreadnaughts in their most important battlefield operation, fighting in one of the bloodiest battles of the Trans-Mississippi West.

Just before the campaign started, however, he was given a welcome leave of absence—from January 14 to February 25, 1864—and during his leave he enjoyed a bit of social life. A poem written to him February 1, 1864, by his neighbor and close friend William "Bill" Blackshear, indicates that John Thomas, by now a widower of a mere five months, was already cutting a swath among the ladies—and encroaching on territory Blackshear considered his own. "I see by the tone of your note, Tom," Blackshear wrote,

No signs of Contrition or Sorrow
Look out for a Squall in the night from
My pistol, my sword, or my arrow.

I have two guns in my house, Tom,
Well loaded and primed for the flurry
If you bother My Widows or Maids, Tom
I'll send you off home in a hurry.

Keep on your own side of Jorden, Tom
Where Widows and gals are so plenty
Or if you cross over that Stream, Tom,
Be sure you take one under twenty.

If I had any Widows to Spare, Tom,
I would freely divide with a Major,[81]
But you grab at the fairest I have, Tom,
Nor ask the old man for the favor.

Hands off, be patient and wait, Tom.
No Major should be an intruder.
If you bother my Martha's or Ellen's, Tom,
I'le Send you to Genl McGruder.[82]
      As ever, the Widows friend
        W. R. B.
        Yellow Bayo.

THE QUIET MAN ★ 65

Stark replied in like verse:

I see by your note No 2 Bill
You expect me to express great sorrow
Else in body I shall fare very ill
From your pistol your sword or your arrow.

Let your guns rest quiet in your house Bill
And to use them don't be in a hurry
Be certain I've bothered your widows or maids Bill
Before you get up such a flurry.

For one who has had the run of the County Bill
Where Widows and maids are so plenty
I think you are certainly selfish & ill
To Restrict me to one under twenty.

If you had any widows to spare Bill
You say you would be willing to divide
Then why are you so captious and ill
And bent all my claims to deride.

Then let me enjoy my furlough Bill
In the society of the Widows so fair
For if I should get one to accept still
There would be enough and to spare.

You know my leave will soon be out Bill
And I to the camp must repair
Then both on Jordan and Cat Creek Bill
You freely can roam with the fair.

Then no longer with sword and with sash Bill
Will you find the Soldier an intruder
No more will he bother your Martha's or Ellen's Bill
In the District of Genl Magruder.[83]

The two old friends had their fun, but when Stark returned to duty, little time remained for writing verse. He reported back to winter quarters at Camp Rogers in Marksville, Louisiana, on February 25, 1864, and within three weeks the Union forces landed at Simmesport, Louisiana, and began marching toward Alexandria.[84]

That spring, panic spread throughout western Louisiana and East Texas as the long-feared Union land invasion, forty thousand strong, struck from both north and south along the Mississippi toward its confluence with the Red River. The objective was to cut the Trans-Mississippi Confederacy in half, destroying its industrial capacity and confiscating its cotton for Northern mills.[85] The Southern defenders totaled only about twenty thousand, and it was feared that the Union invasion would succeed. But because the Red River was shallow, a result of the East Texas drought, Banks's plan to move soldiers and equipment upriver by boat proved difficult or sometimes impossible, giving the Confederate troops in the Trans-Mississippi region time to rally their defenses.

In the meantime, Union troops moved closer to their immediate target of Alexandria and their ultimate one of Shreveport (the capital of Louisiana, since Union forces had taken Baton Rouge, and the center for military planning for the Confederacy in the West).[86] The Confederate military waited until Banks committed to one of three possible routes to Shreveport before they set up fixed defenses to defend the city—then, beyond it, East Texas. Confederate preparations included weeks of strategic retreat, and local citizens were forced to flee their homes ahead of the advancing Union soldiers. Western Louisianans grew almost as angry with their own troops, who, they believed, should have been defending them, as they were with the Union army that, as it advanced, was stripping their homes and land of all they possessed.[87]

Ultimately, Banks chose the stage road through Pleasant Hill and Mansfield to reach Shreveport. The maneuvering on both sides came down to a two-day battle, fought on April 8, 1864, outside Mansfield and on the following day, April 9, at Pleasant Hill, culminating in a bloody Confederate victory and the retreat of Union forces. On both days, Company H was in the thick of the fray. John Thomas Stark described the scene on the field as troops lined up before the first battle: "Scenery on our right, Cavalry on the extreme right, infantry, artillery and cavalry as far as I can see. The sun shining brightly over all—All of God's creatures seem to be rejoycing in the beautiful spring day except man. And he only bent on destroying his kind."[88] His bitter introspection was pardonable; when Confederate general Richard Taylor delivered orders for the coming battle, Walker's Division was placed second in line, directly behind Gen. Alfred Mouton's two brigades, one of Texans and the other of Louisianans.

The order to advance reached Walker's Division at 5:30 p.m. They began moving forward through an area scattered with dead soldiers and horses and approached the crest of the hill. General Walker rode up in front of the line, shouting, "Aim low, boys, and trust in God!" "With a wild yell we dashed down the slope," Stark wrote. "Here one poor wounded Texan raised on his elbow waving his hat over his head. [He] said, 'Crowd them, boys, crowd them!' and well was he obeyed." Nightfall and Federal reinforcements brought an end to the fighting, with both sides withdrawing from the field.[89] Mouton lost his life that day, but his men, backed by Walker's "Greyhounds," forced Banks's troops to withdraw to Pleasant Hill during the night. The number of casualties for both sides on that first day stood very high.

The sun rose April 9, 1864, with surprises in store for both sides; during the night, each had received reinforcements of which the other knew nothing. Banks's forces were swelled by eight thousand additional men under Gen. Andrew Jackson Smith, while Taylor's were augmented by four thousand Missouri and Arkansas troops. Both armies endured another day of bloody fighting, neither with adequate water or rations.[90] Finally, Banks ordered a withdrawal of Union forces, and Smith, employing Sherman's hated tactics, laid waste to the country between Pleasant Hill and Grand Ecore on the Red River.[91] (In large part because of these depredations, angry Louisianans remained unwilling to cooperate with the victorious Union.)[92]

And East Texans were safe—for a while, at least. Although many had been killed at Mansfield and Pleasant Hill, East Texas itself was spared the trauma of an invasion; the drastically low water level in the Red River and decisions to deploy Federal troops to other areas precluded it. Over six weeks lapsed before John Thomas Stark's children received a letter from him, giving them the news that he was alive, along with his own version of the Mansfield–Pleasant Hill battles.[93] Even though he sustained no injuries, he had reached his mid-forties and had lived for two years under harsh conditions; thus, his health had been jeopardized. He took part in several other battles, but his effectiveness continued to diminish. After one engagement he was actually forced to ride in an ambulance rather than on horseback or marching with his men.[94]

In the midst of it all, ever mindful of the ladies, he launched a search for a new wife. He pressed Eugenia, Rebecca, and his sister, Eliza Stark Wooderson, to recommend possible candidates, and they in turn volunteered suggestions.[95] Eugenia wrote him of a "little French widow," a Mrs. George Swift, who had moved from Louisiana to the safety of East Texas. She also mentioned a "Miss Ann," a "Miss Bragg," and a "Widow Collins," along with indirect references to other ladies. In a letter to Rebecca, John Thomas mentioned Nancy Blewett, the well-to-do widow of Capt. William Blewett, who had perished in Arkansas in 1862. He respected her, he wrote, but added that it did not seem possible that a lady in her position could take a liking to a man of whom, he presumed, she had heard so much evil said. He had spoken to her only once in his life, he went on, adding somewhat obscurely that he suspected her reported afflu-

Figure 3.8. John Thomas Stark in later life in Confederate uniform,
with sword and Dreadnaughts battle flag, undated. Stark Foundation Archives.

ence might be more of a problem to their relationship than an asset. The
matter became moot when Bud Stark wrote his father in late October that
"Mr. Bill Snell married the Widow Bluette."[96]

About this time an issue of another nature reared its head. In the summer of 1864, John Thomas was passed over for a promotion to the rank of

THE QUIET MAN ★ 69

major in favor of a Jasper businessman, Elias T. Seale, a slight that predictably kindled the former's infamous ire.[97] He protested, writing an appeal to the Confederacy's secretary of war, claiming that Seale had been on duty only fifty-three days and had "never done any service and perhaps never will and displacing one who has ever been at the post of duty . . . [I am] made to stand aside for one who has done comparatively nothing."[98] Seale's tenure in the Confederate army was actually of longer duration than the fifty-three days John Thomas had claimed; he first served as captain of the 13th Regiment, Company F from March 1862 to early 1863, when he obtained medical leave, then reentered in August 1864, again as captain.[99] Thus, he had served almost a year before he had obtained his medical leave.

In a hearing on November 13 regarding John Thomas's qualifications for the promotion, held before the Retiring Board of Forney's Division, 13th Regiment, Company H, several men in his company provided statements, mainly positive; all agreed that John Thomas's bravery in battle was beyond reproach. That same day twelve officers of the 13th Regiment filed a document with the Retiring Board supporting him and recommending him "for appointment to any office to which he may aspire."[100] But two criticized him as an administrator and leader, among them Col. Anderson F. Crawford, then commander of the 13th Texas Cavalry, who testified that "[Stark's] influence on other companies I considered unworthy of an Officer[; he] had a bad influence on the men."[101] To John Thomas's fury, Elias Seale was allowed to retain the appointment.

A few days later, John Thomas resigned from the Confederate army. (Ironically, Gen. John Stark of Revolutionary War fame had resigned from the Continental army after Bunker Hill, Trenton, and Princeton and had gone into retirement, piqued because he had been passed over for a promotion.[102] Perhaps John Thomas was carrying on a family tradition.) His resignation was accepted by Gen. Edmund Kirby Smith, effective November 26, 1864.[103]

Shortly afterward, the resignation was changed to a medical leave; in February 1865, N.P. West, the Burkeville physician who had earlier praised Bud's manliness, issued a statement that John Thomas had left the army in late 1864 on a Surgeon's Certificate, listing the medical problems he had developed after three years of active service and requesting that he be given an exemption from active duty.[104] Receiving it, he was then appointed enrolling officer for Hardin County. (In a March 1865 letter that probably rubbed salt into John Thomas's wounded feelings, his sister Eliza commiserated with him over an unnamed lady's rejection of his marriage proposal, suggesting that the reason for the rebuff might have been that he had given up "high office for a little office.")[105]

John Thomas's Hardin County appointment came late in the day; by that time, the war was nearing its end.[106] The Confederate army was disintegrating; soldiers simply left for home. Eliza's March 8 letter added a poignant postscript: "Tis the general opinion of the People we are badly whipt."[107] Lee's surrender at Appomattox on April 9, 1865, effectively ending the Confederate war effort, and the assassination of President Lincoln five days later threw the nation into profound shock and the government into confusion. Over the next weeks, the war in Texas ground to a halt amid sinking morale, desertions, and mutinies. Federal troops occupied the state, instituting Reconstruction under guidelines set by newly sworn-in president Andrew Johnson. General Gordon Granger landed in Galveston on June 19, 1865, to announce the emancipation of slaves in Texas—a prelude to radical changes in the state's economic and social fabric.[108]

The harsh Reconstruction years from 1865 to 1874 brought a total restructuring of the Texas economy. Tenant farming, the new labor system, actually trapped many emancipated African Americans, as well as poor white farmers, in a cycle of poverty because they owned no land. John Thomas, Bud, and Jerry Stark, with Rebecca's help, continued to work some of his farmland, first aided in the fields by a slave rented from a neighbor, David Ford; then, after the slaves were freed on "Juneteenth," as it came to be known, they contracted with them to tenant-farm and plant crops on some of his land.[109] John Thomas struggled, along with his neighbors. His business letters reflect his obvious problems—he had no cash, but neither did anyone else. Money was difficult to come by, and businesses he had dealt with for many years found it too risky to extend credit.[110] By the time the Panic of 1873 hit the national economy, the whole country was suffering—as it would for years to come.

The political transition was equally painful. Texas was occupied by the US military; John Thomas spotted the first "Yankie" troops, as he called them, in Burkeville on August 13, 1865.[111] The state's residual resistance to the new order (along with that of the rest of the South) spurred the Republican US Congress to reject Texas' proposed new government and first constitution. This time, Texans would be required to meet new, more stringent congressional guidelines, among them granting African American males the right to vote.[112]

Military occupation did not end until 1870, and Texas finally returned to the Union with full rights of statehood.[113] By 1874, a white Democratic majority replaced Reconstruction Republican power in state offices. This change, along with the waning of the depression following the Panic of 1873, smoothed a path for the Industrial Revolution gathering momentum across the country. However, it spelled the beginning of a new era of oppression for African Americans.[114]

Figure 3.9. Nancy Adams Snell Blewett Stark, John Thomas Stark's second wife, undated. Stark Foundation Archives.

At war's end, John Thomas, still a widower, had already launched himself on a new career: during his sojourn in Hardin County in the last months of war, he had begun to read the law.[115] By the end of 1865, he was also remarried—to Nancy Adams Blewett Snell, once again a widow.

Nancy Adams had moved to Jasper, Texas, with her parents, Abel and Nancy Adams, from Thomas County, Georgia, in the 1840s. They traveled with the large wagon train of their relatives, the wealthy John Blewett family, who were transporting much of their Georgia plantation to Texas, including twenty-one slaves.[116] In 1852, Nancy married a scion of the family, William Blewett. In their ten years together, they had six children (only two lived to adulthood).[117] In 1858 the Blewetts moved to Newton, where William became a storeowner and befriended John Thomas Stark, and the two men simultaneously entered the 13th Texas Cavalry. During the war years, Nancy suffered multiple family losses: the deaths of William Blewett near Little Rock in September 1862 and of their young son in July 1863, then their eight-year-old daughter in August 1864, leaving her with only two surviving children, four and six years of age.[118]

As Bud Stark had written his father, Nancy Blewett married for a second time in October 1864 to William D. Snell, a thirty-five-year-old farmer and Confederate private.[119] He and Nancy had one son, Albert Adams Snell, born July 25, 1865, but tragedy struck yet again with William Snell's death within the year. Now, with three small children, her second husband deceased, and her slaves newly freed, Nancy Adams Blewett Snell must have felt the need for a helpmate.[120]

Nancy married John Thomas Stark on November 12, 1865. At the time of the marriage, Eugenia was sixteen years old; Bud, fourteen; and Jerry, thirteen; the others—Johnny, Mattie, and Molly—ranged in between, down to the youngest, Benny, then three. Eugenia and Rebecca had been running the house in Burkeville and caring for the younger children, but after John Thomas's marriage, the entire family apparently moved to the Blewett house outside Newton to live with him and Nancy.[121] Ultimately, the children would number an even dozen: John Thomas's seven, Nancy's three, and the two they had together: Sarah Elizabeth, known as Sallie, born October 9, 1867; and James Boroughs, born February 16, 1870.[122]

Nancy herself survived James's birth by only four days, succumbing to puerperal fever. She was buried at Zion Hill Cemetery in Jasper County near the graves of her young Blewett children. Curiously, her tombstone identified her as Nancy Blewett.[123] A Stark family story offers an explanation: Her Blewett relatives had wanted her to be buried there, beside her deceased children, but John Thomas had at first refused. A dispute ensued without a resolution, and he lost patience, finally instructing them to "just come and get her." They duly fetched her body and buried her with her children at Zion Hill—as a Blewett.[124] It was thus doubly ironic that, shortly before her death, Nancy had actually been the first of the Stark family to invest in the sawmill business in Orange; the previous year, John Thomas had purchased a one-third interest in four acres of land, a steam boiler, and a small mill on the Sabine just north of Orange in the name of his wife—Nancy Stark.[125]

On July 5, 1870, four months after Nancy's death, Rebecca Wofford died, to the end of her life still caring for her former son-in-law's large brood.[126] Eugenia and Bud—William—had emerged from the war years as independent, self-reliant, responsible young people, and when John Thomas returned from the war, they continued to work for and with him. In 1866, John Thomas attempted to enter politics with a run for a seat in the Texas House of Representatives, but he and the other candidate in the race, Henry Harrison Ford, were defeated by Randolph Doom of Jasper.[127] In 1867, Ford married Eugenia Stark, who was the first of the Stark children to leave home.[128]

When John Thomas received a government contract in 1869 to deliver mail by horseback from Burkeville to Orange, William and Jerry, then both working for their father, rode the eighty-mile route through the thick East Texas woods to Orange and back, beginning that August, after the corn and cotton crops were put by; John Thomas would not have released them from their farm work to run the mail route until late summer.[129]

William made the first trip by himself. "I can't give you exact directions," John Thomas told him, "but bear to the south and stay on that course."[130] He gently slapped the horse's rump, and William was off to Orange—and new horizons. He did not know the way, but he remembered seeing a small signboard nailed high on the corner of the general store in Newton: "Eighty Miles to Orange."[131] He did not lose his way until he reached a point about five miles north of Orange. "Somehow or other I confused my directions," he remembered, "and for a long time after I came to Orange, north never seemed to be in the right place for me." The trip required two days of hard riding through thickets, over creeks, and among vast stands of virgin longleaf pine—land and resources that he could never have imagined would someday be his. To the end of his life, William could recall every creek he crossed—Cow, Nichols, Big Cypress, Caney, Quicksand, Little Cow—and the name of every settler whose house he passed.[132] When the creeks reached flood stage, he hefted the mailbag to his shoulders and swam his horse across.[133]

After that first trip, William and Jerry took turns carrying the mail.[134] Later that month, John Thomas's nephew, Henry Hardy, joined them on the routes.[135] With the addition of a third rider, one of them was able to stay in Orange for five days, then take the next delivery back to Burkeville. This arrangement allowed the young men time to acquaint themselves with the developing port town and sawmilling center on the Sabine, where eventually all three made their home.

Within a month of Nancy's death, John Thomas Stark began yet another search for a new wife. On March 17, 1870, he wrote to one of his previous flames, Susannah Mitchell. "Can I say Dear Susie, for you were ever dear to me and ever will be," he coaxed, "I write to you because I am again

Figure 3.10. Donna Jerusha Smith Stark, John Thomas Stark's third wife, undated.
Stark Foundation Archives.

alone in the world. . . . If you are still single and are willing to listen to my defense say the word and I will be there as quick as I can ride. Susie dear Susie I want you I know I could make you happy as my wife."[136] He enclosed a picture of himself with his plea.

"Susie's" response cut straight to the point. "I am surprised at you," she replied. "I thought you had forgotten there was such a creature in existence as I, and as you have forgotten me this long I am willing to remain forgotten. . . . I am still single and no prospect of marrying but that is no reason why I should encourage you, you have disappointed me once and I think that is enough."[137] With her reply, she returned John Thomas's photograph. His reaction is not recorded, but her response must have severely wounded his ego.

He married for the third and final time February 23, 1871, to Donna Jerusha Smith, the daughter of Samuel Hoy Smith, an Ohio surveyor, and Elizabeth Jane (Victor) Smith. Born in Venice, Ohio, in June 1842, Donna had moved to Texas with her family, who settled in Newton, where Smith continued surveying. When she married John Thomas, he was forty-nine; she, twenty-eight. The newlyweds set up housekeeping in the Blewett Place outside Newton, where John Thomas had continued to live after Nancy's death.

John Thomas and Donna Stark had seven children: Victor Hoy, Alfred Marmaduke Hobby, Ida Jane, Donna Jerusha, Oran Milo Roberts, Byron DeWitt Clinton, and Lilly Rose. Their first two were born at the Blewett Place, but the other five made their appearance after the family moved to Orange in 1874. (By the time John Thomas died in 1893, he had fathered a total of eighteen children with his three wives, as well as becoming stepfather to the three children that Nancy had brought into the family. At the time of his death, his youngest child, Lilly Rose Stark, was eight years old, and he was seventy-two.)[138]

During the arduous years of Reconstruction, William had acquired some debt. Several months after John Thomas's marriage to Donna, William asked his father to allow him to go to Orange to work out the amount he owed. John Thomas refused, but on the morning of October 19, 1871, he ignored his father's dictate and left for Orange, calmly and quietly bidding John Thomas good-bye and informing him that he would return "in a month or two." Predictably, John Thomas exploded with anger. In a multipage tirade written to William just hours after his departure, he savagely accused his son of "cool unfeeling ungrateful conduct. . . . If I should give way to my feelings," he raged, "I could curse the hour you were born; to think how I have nursed you and led you by the hand when you could not help yourself, and now . . . to return all my care with the basest ingratitude, it is almost more than I can bear."[139]

My own son has deserted me . . . life is but little worth to me[.] Your Mother in her far off grave in Louisiana is happy for she died when she thought you good and obedient while I live to wish I were dead. . . . You have convinced me by your conduct this morning that you have no feeling nor respect for me or my wishes. . . . I again say come right home[.] If you do not I shall be compeled to take steps to make you and if you put me to it the farthest corner of the globe shall not hide you. You must come. But no stay. I am nearly crazy this morning. Stay and never come unless you can say you are sorry for the anguish you have caused . . . your only remaining parent. Your deserted father, John T. Stark.[140]

Understandably, William did not take his father's horse; instead, he chose one that he could keep with him in Orange. He rode away through the woods toward a new life, perhaps the wiser for having learned from his experiences with his volcanic father that the most effective course in dealing with fractious, egocentric personalities would lie in pursuing a steady, reasoned, independent course of his own. In the future, he and his father would mend their fences, and soon most of his family joined him in Orange, prospering from its opportunities. Although he never lost his love for his native Piney Woods, William Henry Stark had carried his last mailbag.[141]

CHAPTER FOUR

Romance and the "Empire of Trees"

*Wait until you come home to give me that scolding. I can tell better then how
mad you are and you will have more to scold me about. It would do me good
to hear you scold a while. I have not had a quarrel for so long that don't know
whether I could conduct one properly or not. . . . As ever, whether you like it
or not.*

—WILLIAM STARK IN ORANGE TO MIRIAM LUTCHER
IN WILLIAMSPORT, APRIL 13, 1879

In October 1871, William Stark rode south through the Piney Woods of
East Texas, heading toward a life he could not have predicted. Although
only twenty years old, he had proved himself from his earliest years
to be bright, conscientious, hardworking, and reliable, and within a few
weeks he found employment in Orange, working at a job that would today
be classified as entry-level—"jacking" (lifting and moving) logs and pitching out tree bark and other debris at the R.B. Russell and Son Sawmill.[1]

Several weeks after his arrival, the still-irate John Thomas Stark wrote
to William's employer, mill owner Robert B. Russell, to enlist his assistance in persuading his son to return to Newton. Russell's efforts were unsuccessful. "I received your letter in regard to William and tried to get him
to go home but to no purpose," he responded politely. "He Says that [he] is
willing to Stay here and if you wanted his wages that you were welcome to
them[.] I shall therefore withhold his wages subject to your order as long
as he works for us."[2] John Thomas Stark's response, if there was one, does
not survive, but apparently he relinquished any claim he might have made
on his son's earnings. William continued to work for Russell and later became a sawyer—a job requiring strength, coordination, and quick wits.

The availability of work for William depended entirely on his employer's decisions either to run the mill or, for a number of reasons, to
shut it down; thus, the work was not always steady.[3] While sawmills were

Figure 4.1. William Henry Stark, ca. 1870s. Stark Foundation Archives.

unquestionably a major source of employment in Orange and paid fairly well when they were operating, the industry in the early 1870s did not furnish a particularly reliable source of income for either workers or owners. Floods or droughts could disrupt the downriver course of logs; broken machinery or fires, not uncommon occurrences, could shut down production. At such times, employees were on their own. (During one such shutdown in 1873, William's brother Jerry moved his family to Louisiana in an effort to save money on living expenses.)[4] The vagaries of weather and mill breakdowns notwithstanding, lumber was quickly joining cattle and cotton as a dominant industry in late nineteenth-century East Texas and Louisiana. And construction of an infant railroad system in Texas greatly increased possibilities for lumber concerns seeking larger markets.

At some point, perhaps simply with the passage of time, William and his father mended their quarrel. By December 1872 they had even entered into a joint mercantile venture, J.T. Stark & Son, in Orange, although for the time being John Thomas continued to live and practice law in Newton, handling the paperwork for their new concern.[5] But as early as 1873, he wrote to ask a fellow attorney and longtime friend Dan Triplett, living in Orange, what he thought of the town. "I think Orange the best place in Southeast Texas," Triplett answered.

> If a man wishes to farm we have the land. . . . [If] you wish to go in to the lumber bus[iness] . . . there is plenty of openings in either the lumber or mercantile bus[iness]— In fact for a man with VIM there is an open field and as fair play as a *business* man expects— Legally there is a good local practice, & at present I play a lone hand[,] tho in Dist Court outside Attys get the *other* side of my cases.[6]

He suggested land and housing but finally urged John Thomas to visit Orange and take a look for himself. He ended by congratulating John Thomas and Donna on the birth of their newest son, Alfred Marmaduke Hobby Stark, John Thomas's thirteenth child. "I told H.T. Davis about the number the new comer bore, & he told me to tell You to *Quit*," Triplett wrote, then added as an afterthought, "Davis ain't never."[7]

John Thomas apparently took Triplett's advice regarding Orange, at least; on November 12, 1874, he, Donna, and their growing family loaded four wagons with possessions and supplies and "commenced moving to Orange," as his notebook entry termed it, to a house they called "Pleasant View," located on tree-shaded property on the west bank of Adams Bayou.[8] He continued to conduct an active practice in the Newton courts but by 1875 had relocated his law office to Orange. Perhaps his decision to move the office resulted partially from difficulties with his own father,

Figure 4.2. John Thomas Stark's Orange, Texas, home, "Pleasant View,"
west bank of Adams Bayou, after 1874. Stark Foundation Archives.

Jeremiah, by that time also a resident of Newton County. In December of
that year, Jeremiah wrote angrily to his son, accusing him of dishonesty
with the family business, particularly taking "estate money from the Sheriff without any authority whatever." Jeremiah's letter, unpleasantly reminiscent of John Thomas's scorching letter to William, was probably a re-
flection of his own lifelong relationship with his son. He ended his letter
on a more conciliatory note than had John Thomas in 1871, adding "I did
not mean to lecture."[9]

He might have saved his ink. With the mercurial ire typical of him,
John Thomas fired off a vitriolic response to his father, vehemently denying the older man's charges. "I never took a dollar of your money . . . without authority in my life," he asserted furiously. "You seem to think that
the only rights I [illegible] is to labor for you and take nothing for it. I did
that a long time & would be willing to do so yet if I got anything except
blame for it."[10] The father-son exchange underscores the personality differences between John Thomas and his own son William; even though both
reacted to the trouble with their respective fathers by relocating permanently to Orange, William had left quietly and with purpose.

While his father's family was settling into their new home, William
was working to establish himself in various enterprises in Orange, but
the financial Panic of 1873 and the subsequent depression created difficulties for both of them. They continued to operate their mercantile busi-

ness, J. T. Stark & Son, but credit was hard to find.[11] Donna Stark assisted with the business and operated several small ones of her own—selling and delivering butter, eggs, and garden vegetables around Orange as well as offering magazine subscriptions and selling such patent medicines as Dr. Peck's Liver Pills—but still they struggled.[12] William could not yet afford to break away from his work in the Russell Mill, but as the Panic eased, he began to diversify his economic situation with the purchase of a livery service, Bee Wilson's Livery Stable.[13] He also entered into a silent partnership—or so he intended it to be—with his brother Jerry in a saloon on Main Street, near the drugstore of a local physician, Dr. Samuel Brown.[14]

By the mid-1870s, economic conditions in Orange were beginning to improve, especially compared to those in more isolated parts of East Texas, which suffered from expensive or inadequate transportation. Railroads and steamboats now connected Orange to the rest of the world. John Thomas wrote his sister Eliza Wooderson on April 29, 1877, that the Texas and New Orleans Railroad stood in "fair view" of their house, the lines having been completed from Houston, with three trains a week leaving at six o'clock in the morning, bound for Orange. From its vantage point on the Sabine, Orange also enjoyed access to the Gulf of Mexico (though navigation was still problematic). The region's huge timber resources stood ripe for development, and the arrival of entrepreneurs and investment capital lay on the near horizon.

John Thomas seemed happy with the family's new location. He described their new "Prairie home" to Eliza and brought her up-to-date on family members:

> Ford & Genie—and Mattie & her old man [Ped Ferguson] live in and near Jasper. Wm is still single . . . a Sawyer at a steam mill in Town. Jerry is married and lives in Town. Mary is with Sue Russel in Town. John & Ben are going to school [in Jasper] . . . also Sally & Jimmy [Nancy's two]. Donna has four . . . two boys & two girls . . . Victor Hoy [&] A. M. Hobby—Ida Jane and Donna J. You see, we still have a house full. . . . I am County Judge of this County and am practicing law in the District Courts. . . . We have a beautiful situation here [with] timber on the North and east of us and prairie South and West, with but little timber to Sabine Bay & the Gulph.[15]

The previous winter, word had sped like a grass fire through the territory that two lumbermen from Pennsylvania were coming to build a great sawmill; and on February 29, 1877, as William was riding the cable-pulled carriage amid flying sawdust and the searing whine of the saws, he spotted the two Pennsylvanians—his future father-in-law, Henry Lutcher, and

Lutcher's partner, Bedell Moore—as they looked over operations at the Russell mill. That spring, William would saw the lumber for the framework of the new Lutcher & Moore mill at Orange.[16]

Writing Eliza the following August, John Thomas reported the economic decline in upper East Texas, while Orange was growing rapidly in size and prosperity, he allowed, and investment capital was coming in from distant places. "I meet strange faces on the street every day almost and men from all parts of the U.S.," he declared. "There are mill men and lumber men here from Michigan, Illinois and even from Pennsylvania . . . some building mills and some running timber down the river."[17] One of the Pennsylvania mill men he mentioned was Henry Lutcher.

Henry Jacob Lutcher moved to Orange in March 1877 to live and work, and his family followed shortly. But his brief reconnaissance in Southeast Texas in January would have scarcely prepared any of them for the surprises that still awaited them in Orange, some of them unwelcome—summer heat and humidity, yellow fever, mosquitoes, hurricanes. It is likely that the entire family experienced some degree of culture shock. Since Lutcher himself faced all-consuming work and could not afford to dwell on lurking thoughts of being a stranger in a strange land, his own adjustment hardly compared to any that his family had to make.

Frances Ann Lutcher reached Houston in late March, only a short time after her husband's move,[18] and Lutcher probably traveled to Houston to meet her at the train, accompanying her on the last leg of the journey. Although Lutcher did not say so, Miriam and Carrie probably arrived with their mother or soon thereafter. Frances Ann, at thirty-seven years of age, had already proved herself equal to anything life might throw her way; she surely took the radical move in stride, dealing with each new problem with her characteristic aplomb and practicality. It was possibly the girls— Miriam at eighteen and Carrie at fifteen—who felt the impact of the move more acutely than either parent; they had left home, friends, and relatives, not only for another town but another world.

Documents and photographs from Orange and Williamsport in the late 1870s highlight a few similarities between the two towns—but many more differences. Both were lumber towns located on navigable rivers, thus faced the same problem of floods and waterlogged streets. But Williamsport afforded a larger, infinitely more sophisticated milieu than Orange, which, its growth notwithstanding, still remained essentially a frontier town—wooden houses, churches, and stores; an abundance of saloons; dirt streets that became seas of mud during rainy seasons; shootings; even the occasional hanging.[19] Williamsport, hosting an established lumber industry; huge, modern sawmills; and a major market, enjoyed

Figure 4.3. Fifth Street, Orange, looking north, 1885. After the swamp was drained, Main Street was built through. University of North Texas Libraries, Portal to Texas History, crediting Heritage House Museum, Orange, Texas.

Figure 4.4. Hanging on Front Street in Orange, undated. University of North Texas Libraries, Portal to Texas History, crediting Heritage House Museum, Orange, Texas.

Figure 4.5. Orange jail, 1888. University of North Texas Libraries,
Portal to Texas History, crediting Heritage House Museum, Orange, Texas.

a complex industrial and transportation network, while Orange housed
fewer, smaller, more primitive sawmills and a railroad that reached an
abrupt dead end at the Sabine River. Williamsport, on the Susquehanna,
lay among scenic, heavily timbered hills; Orange, on the muddy Sabine,
stood squarely between the southern edge of the East Texas Piney Woods
and the flat, mosquito-plagued Southeast Texas Gulf Coast plain. Though
both locales enjoyed lush vegetation, the contrast between the two physical environments must have struck the Lutcher family forcibly. The differences in the social and cultural scene must have necessitated adjust-
ments as well, but at least in Pennsylvania the Lutcher family had lived
in Rocktown, a smaller, less sophisticated community than Williamsport,
and were possibly accustomed to more modest surroundings.

In March, Texas weather is notoriously erratic. Even though they arrived late in the month, Frances Ann and her daughters could still have
faced raw Texas "northers"—cold temperatures, rain, or even rarely sleet
or snow—or they could have enjoyed sunshine and balmy temperatures.
But whatever the weather, the East Texas woods would already have been
transforming into a mass of young green leaves, alight here and there
with the delicate pink of flowering redbuds or starred with the white blossoms of haw and dogwood. For the Lutchers, springtime would have been

the loveliest season to arrive in East Texas and the most reminiscent of home; a few weeks later in the year, Williamsport and its surrounding terrain would look much the same, though with different varieties of trees. And East Texas enjoyed one advantage over Pennsylvania—milder winters. Perhaps for Miriam and Carrie, at least, the major change came from the absence of their friends and large extended family group, so much a part of their life in Williamsport.

In the meantime, "Papa" was moving quickly and aggressively into the region's lumbering world (in spite of the weather, which seemed to have been his major complaint), armed with investment capital critically needed in the region and, just as important, knowledge of the modern technology and internal workings of Eastern lumber milling. In the months and years to come, Henry Lutcher rapidly became known for fairness, honesty, and innovation in business practices, and he was soon on his way to becoming one of the strongest moving forces in the town of Orange and the region. His influence eventually spread to state and national levels in the lumber industry.

Lutcher himself seemed to feel that their move had been the right decision, reinforced by the emerging truth that the days of the Lutcher & Moore mill in Williamsport were numbered. In July 1879, just two years after the family's relocation to Orange, he wrote Lewis Lutscher:

Dear Father, We are all well the girls are contented, So am I because I am doing well. . . . I am Sorry that the Mill at Home isn't doing More But profits are very Small there so it don't make so much difference after all. . . . Frances Sends her Regards as well as the Children. I am going to pay you a visit Next Spring. I hope the Lord will give us all good Health till We meet again. Your son Henry Lutcher[20]

In 1880, only three years after his move to Orange, Henry Lutcher was elected president of the Southwestern Lumber Manufacturers' Association, in recognition of his creativity and leadership in the region.[21]

This enterprising businessman was also the father of two attractive—and unattached—daughters. While Lutcher was building mills, contracting for timber, and buying land throughout East Texas and Louisiana, the young bachelors in Orange were eyeing his offspring. The first to show signs of success was William Stark. One day, as he walked with a friend past the Lutcher home, he spotted Miriam and Carrie in the front yard. He turned to the friend and bet him that he could make a date with one of them,[22] and he won that bet. He most likely met the Lutcher sisters formally that summer or fall of 1877 and soon became better acquainted with them at social gatherings organized by the Orange youth. He was drawn

Figure 4.6. Miriam Lutcher Stark, undated but probably sometime before the turn of the twentieth century. Stark Foundation Archives.

to the serious, sweet-natured Miriam, and by the late summer of 1878, only a little over a year after the Lutcher family had arrived, his relationship with her was beginning to bloom into full-blown love.[23]

At first glance, William Stark would have seemed an unlikely beau for Miriam Melissa Lutcher, the educated and cultured daughter of the owner of the largest sawmill in the territory. William had grown up with very little education or resources; by his own account, he had entered adulthood without a penny, and he was still far from being a wealthy man.[24] At the time he met Miriam, he was a twenty-six-year-old small-scale entrepreneur who was supplementing his modest resources by working at a local sawmill. Miriam was eight years younger than he, and her parents might understandably have harbored reservations about her growing relationship with this hardworking, genial young East Texan—about whom they knew almost nothing.

The relationship was put to an early test in August 1878, when Miriam and Carrie returned to Williamsport for a ten-month stay. The nineteen-year-old Miriam was planning to teach there,[25] and Carrie, at sixteen, almost surely intended to study art, music, and voice—"accomplishments" that every young lady was expected to acquire and instruction in which would not have been readily available in Orange. Whether Frances Ann and Henry Lutcher also wished to put physical distance between William and Miriam is a matter of conjecture, but it is tempting to speculate that they did.

During that first visit to Williamsport and again in 1881, on a second visit, Miriam and William continued to exchange letters. Unfortunately, her letters to him do not survive, but she saved twenty of his letters to her, and they often provide clues to the content of her own. From the correspondence of 1878 and 1879, it is evident that Miriam expended a great deal of paper, ink, and postage in an attempt to keep William at an emotional distance, but he was equally determined to maintain their friendship, at least, and to deepen it if possible. Though her letters arrived only about once a month, he always answered them promptly, and in them, his essential human qualities—humor, kindness, intelligence, common sense—emerge clearly.

"After anyone finds out another's ways, they can get along if they want to," he wrote on one occasion. And in another letter: "I don't like to tease anyone about anything when I think that it hurts." Glimpses of his underlying ambition occasionally surface as well: "If I thought there was no chance for me to ever get ahead in this world I would rather die than live," he declared. "But I expect if I was put to the test, that I would . . . rather live."[26]

His letters mirror everyday life in Orange and East Texas in the late

1870s and early 1880s. He reported on horseback-riding parties on the prairie, trips to a fair in Houston, weddings, "BlackBerrying" expeditions, picnics, fishing and boating excursions on the river and Sabine Lake, concerts, masquerade balls, and farces and other amateur theater productions. He and Miriam enjoyed a wide circle of young singles and married couples who frequently gathered at homes in the evenings to socialize, sing, and dance—polkas, waltzes, schottisches, quadrilles—and once he expressed the fear that, with all the youth leaving town for the new "coledge" in Jasper, too few ladies would be left in town to "have a little social dance to pass the time away." (There seemed to be plenty, after all.) He enlivened his descriptions with chatty comments about their mutual friends, especially the relationships—who was "keeping company" with whom—and kept up a running commentary on the activities of Miriam's friends, among them Jessie Latchem and Lilly and Ollie Ochiltree. Margaret Smith, the "Miss Mug" in William's letters, who married Eugene Bancroft, a member of a local mill-owning family, seemed to be a favorite of all who knew her.[27]

William's news was not always about the social scene. Winter brought pneumonia, and summer and early fall, yellow fever, which remained the Gulf Coast plague it had always been. He wrote in September 1878 that when the fever appeared, Galveston quarantined all ships from Orange and at one point even refused mail deliveries. In his next letter, he reported that Jessie Latchem had contracted the "fever" again: "It has helped her looks," he observed, his droll East Texas wit surfacing irresistibly. "I think if she keeps on she will get real pretty." Some of the young men had planned to give a ball, he wrote, but had failed: "There is too much excitement about Yellow Fever to talk about dancing now. . . . The social Club meets tomorrow night to try and raise funds for the sufferers."[28] In late October cooler weather arrived; he rejoiced that he had not heard a mosquito for three days and was "in hopes that I won't again this winter."[29] A few months later, his tone grew more serious when he mentioned several deaths from pneumonia, including those of some of their friends.[30]

The summer months also brought the menace of that other scourge of the Gulf Coast—hurricanes. In October 1881 William reported that everyone had been expecting a "blow," as he called it, but September, the deadliest month for hurricanes, had passed "without creating any disturbance on this part of the gulf coast." That year, Orange escaped a hurricane, though an exceptionally high tide, "the highest tide that we have ever had here except in time of a blow," William remarked, drove salt water up the Sabine River some distance north of Orange. But nature did provide its compensations; in the spring of 1879 a lonely William wrote, "I wish you were here. This evening everything is in full bloom. Mrs. Thompson's yard looks splendid. . . . We get out on the river these moon shining nights and drift along with the tide and inhale the perfume from these locust trees."[31]

He kept Miriam informed about church activities, if not precisely in a way she might have appreciated. She remained a lifelong churchgoer who, with Carrie and eight others, had successfully petitioned the Presbytery of Eastern Texas in April 1878, less than a year after their arrival in Orange, to send an evangelist for the purpose of organizing a Presbyterian church.[32] William viewed church activities from a more humorous perspective, giving her descriptions of events he had attended at various local churches, particularly fund-raisers featuring tables loaded with food. He regaled her with accounts of several revivals; he observed dryly of the sparse crowd that had attended such a gathering held in August 1878, "I don't suppose that there was many that had new hats or dresses, therefore listeners were few."[33]

In the 1870s, Orange Methodists were still served by a ministry of circuit riders who traveled from town to town in East Texas, preaching at a different church each Sunday, and William believed that preachers who lasted a year on this route (known widely as the "Alligator Circuit" for the reptilian denizens they often encountered) had proved their faith. Even so, he derided one Methodist circuit rider, Rev. Lacy Boon, who seemed to him to be concerned only about the size of the collection plate: "Boon says that he has but little hope for the People of Orange but that he intends to stick to them, and I think that it is the worst thing that he could do for them. He never looks as though he meant what he said until he says Bro. Street, take up a collection." In January 1879 a new circuit rider, a Reverend Burke, appeared on the religious scene, and William deemed him a much better preacher. Burke soon organized a Sunday School on his biweekly trips to Orange.[34]

Ironically, at the same time he was writing Miriam regarding the growth of Orange churches, William was also reporting on increased incidents of lawlessness, particularly during the year 1881. A long history of disregard for the law on both sides of the Sabine River had existed since the days of Spanish Texas and the old Neutral Ground, where neither the laws of Spain nor those of the United States had been enforced.[35] The Mexican Republic had allowed American citizens to settle in Mexican Texas but had required them to move into the interior, at least sixty miles west of the Sabine and thirty miles from the Gulf of Mexico,[36] thus curtailing settlement in the region that would become Orange County (until the policy was eased in the early 1830s). But Americans had settled there in defiance of the law, and in the absence of a system of justice, they created their own, employing violence if they deemed it necessary. This tradition of aggressive self-protection had been exacerbated by the turmoil of the Civil War and Reconstruction, and along the Sabine, recurrent lawlessness had become a way of life.

William's letters to Miriam indicated that both churches and legal institutions in Orange faced an uphill task in establishing reform. Sometimes violence actually began at church affairs, as with one "baptizing" held at the Upper Lake on Adams Bayou in October 1878, where the church ceremony became a skirmish between two families, the Harrises and the Jetts. William added laconically that one of the Jett boys was "likely to die."[37]

Even Henry Lutcher was forced to deal with local lawlessness. William described the event to Miriam in the summer of 1881:

> The night that you left, somebody shot in to one of those German's houses . . . the place where the child was sick, and struck one of the men in the eye or near the eye and scared them all nearly to death. The child died. Your Pa got them all a gun a piece the next day to protect themselves with, but I am afraid that they will all leave. They seem to be very much dissatisfied or some of them do. One family tried to leave last night, but your pa would not let them.[38]

William did not give a reason for the shooting, but it might have been a "work-and-pay" issue; Lutcher had earlier written Bedell Moore to send skilled workers from Pennsylvania to Orange to work in the best-paying jobs in the Lutcher & Moore mill, and local mill workers possibly resented the outsiders.[39]

William wrote of other violent incidents that year. That August, a gang of local men attempted to assassinate Orange's sheriff, George Michael, and when the attempt failed, they precipitated a riot that lasted several days and resulted in a declaration of martial law in the town.[40] In early October, he reported a killing in a neighboring town: "Tis reported here that [Deputy Marshal] Billy Paterson was killed in Beaumont last week. He arrested a young lad and started to the calaboose with him, and the Boy pulled out a revolver and shot him four times. . . . The report here is that Pat is dead. That is three men shot in Beaumont in one week." (The "young lad" who shot Marshal William Patterson that night happened to be a youthful ruffian named Pattillo Higgins, who was charged with murder but acquitted by a local jury. He later underwent religious conversion and ultimately gained another kind of fame in the discovery of oil at Spindletop, near Beaumont.)[41]

During that violent summer and fall of 1881, politics posed touchy issues as well; Orange citizens stood deeply divided over the issue of reincorporating the town.[42] They ultimately voted in favor of it, but feelings still ran high. As William put it to Miriam, "Orange is pretty lively now

. . . at least growlers is plentiful. Nearly every man you meet has got something to say about the incorporation. There is considerable talk of starting a petition to vote it out but I have not seen any yet. There has been several convictions for obstructing the sidewalks and two for drunkenness." Later in the fall, whether it was settlement of the incorporation issue or the onset of cooler weather that exercised a soothing effect on the citizenry, the mood in town became less restive; that October 8, in his last letter to Miriam before her return to Orange, William mentioned that the streets were so quiet it seemed "like Sunday" every day. "You can hardly ever hear a gun fired now." (He did concede that "once in a while somebody goes over in Louisiana and shoots off their pistol.") "I don't know how long it will last," he observed.[43]

He was not the only one who wondered how long Orange would remain quiet. By the time Miriam received his last letter, Henry and Frances Ann Lutcher had already arrived in Williamsport to visit their families and to accompany Miriam and Carrie back to Orange. A newspaper reporter for the *Weekly Sun and Banner* found Lutcher in Williamsport's police headquarters, examining regulations. When questioned, Lutcher responded that, as a member of Orange's city council, he hoped to find ideas for new codes that would assist them in keeping peace on the "western frontier," as the reporter termed it.[44]

William Stark's gossipy news notwithstanding, his primary goal in writing lay in reminding Miriam that he cared for her, but their road to romance was a rough and circuitous one, their tiffs sometimes seeming willful. From the content of his first letter to her in August 1878, it is apparent that he had already declared his feeling for her and that his jealousy had flared at the attentions paid to her by other young men. It is equally apparent that Miriam had not welcomed such possessiveness, her distance possibly reinforced by her parents' reservations. When she had left for Williamsport, the young couple had parted with their differences unresolved, and William worked diligently to mend fences. "I think that I will reform to some extent before you come back," he promised; "in twelve months or two years, I can school myself to hide my feelings a little better."[45]

Beyond conveying his good intentions, William attempted to allay Miriam's doubts, allowing her to set the pace of their relationship. She had apparently indicated cautiously that she thought of him only as a friend. "So long as you are single," he returned, "you may know in me you have a friend that loves you and who you can safely trust. . . . You need not give yourself any uneasiness about my showing you too much attention when you come back for I don't intend to get in anybody's way . . . that is if you ever come back," he could not resist adding. "It looks a little unreasonable to think that I would tell you that I loved you if I doubted your truth," he riposted to Miriam's suggestion that he did not trust her. "I never met anybody in my life that I would put more confidence in than you." "[I] like for you to be plain," he gently chided her. "The trouble has always been that you have not been plain enough quite."[46]

In spite of his disclaimers, relationships, love, and marriage were frequent topics in William's letters, and he managed to interject comments about single young women and widows he found attractive. "She is pretty and no mistake, the prettiest eyes I ever seen," he said of one young Orange belle but hastened to add, "excepting your own." He might have hoped to make Miriam jealous, but he was also unable to resist finding the humor in any situation. "I fell in love with two girls and one widow," he reported after going on an excursion to Sabine Pass, "and it [has] taken me nearly all day to get over it."[47]

He frequently chided her for failing to write often enough to suit him. "I know that I ought not to expect letters verry often . . . but I do want you to write when you have time." As usual, after promising in one letter that he would not again complain, he allowed his sense of humor to get the better of him: "If it becomes really necessary for me to grumble at anybody I will go over and scrape up a little row with Miss Jessie. . . . At any rate," he added, "there will be a cessation of hostilities between you and I until I can see you again."[48]

In a probable effort to disarm her, he insisted that he was not hunting a wife. "Those people who tell you that I never go out are terribly behind the excitement," he maintained. "It is true that I don't wait on any young Lady, but the reason is simply because there is none for me to wait on that I care to." A mutual friend had told him that a man should "not get uneasy" about finding a wife until he was sixty. "All that bothers me is I neglected asking her whether bald-headed ones were included or not."[49] (He was sensitive about the loss of his hair, which was rapidly disappearing.)

At the same time he was working to overcome Miriam's reservations, William was cultivating a closer acquaintance with her parents. During her absence, he frequently visited them, thus allowing him to give her news about them; he was hoping to allay their doubts, as well. Writing on October 5, 1878, he dropped by to visit Henry Lutcher, who was recovering from an unspecified but evidently serious illness. Frances Ann confided to William that she had been very worried about her husband and had sat up with him all night by herself. She "could hardly keep from crying," she confessed, thinking of "what a fix she would be in if anything was to happen." If she had had even one of "the girls"—Miriam and Carrie—with her, she declared to William, she would have been "better satisfied." He seemed to have gained the senior Lutchers' trust; in any case, as time

passed, they would certainly have become aware of his growing good reputation in town. In January 1879 he reported that Frances Ann had sent
a mince pie to the "Ranch," as he called the bachelors' quarters where he
and his roommates lived, and that they all had had a "big time."[50]

For a short while that spring, however, all his careful efforts seemed
in danger of coming to naught; he heard around town that his silent partnership in the saloon venture had incurred Frances Ann's disapproval.
"I didn't know whether to write again or not," he began. "Miss Jessie
[Latchem] told me that she heard that your Ma said that I would not be allowed to visit you when you came home. Don't know whether she said it
or not. I thought if I had become so disgraced as not to be allowed to call
on you that you would not care to write to me."[51] He explained that he had
only provided funds for the saloon so that his brother Jerry could leave the
sawmill, where he was not making a sufficient living. "I did not intend
to be known in it at all," he wrote, "but it got out before we started fairly."
He hastened to assure her that he was not directly involved with the saloon and in fact was now running the livery stable as his primary livelihood. (About that time he also became a representative for a Houston
grain firm, an even more respectable enterprise.)[52] No one mentioned the
saloon again—at least in existing records—and the situation obviously resolved itself.

A potential obstacle to their relationship beyond his control was that he
believed that Miriam still thought of Williamsport as her real home. She
must have indicated that she did not want to return to Orange. "I hope you
may never have to come back since you hate to leave home [Williamsport]
so bad," he wrote solicitously, "but if you do, I for one will do everything
that I can to make it pleasant for you." Judging from subsequent events, he
made good on his promise. Miriam and Carrie duly returned to Orange
in late spring or summer of 1879, and during the next two years, Miriam and William saw a great deal of each other, including quiet evenings
spent sitting on the porch of her parents' house after Henry and Frances
Ann Lutcher had gone to bed, and in that time their relationship evolved
into an engagement. In the summer of 1881 Miriam and Carrie returned
to Williamsport for a three-month visit, and the tone of William's letters to
her was now considerably different. He addressed Miriam as "Miss Mina,"
or simply "Mina" (his variation of "Minie," a pet name for Miriam used by
family and friends), and the young couple were planning their wedding.
"Dear Mina," his first letter read, "I am that lonesome that I hardly know
what to do with myself."[53]

He gave her periodic updates on the progress of two family homes being constructed in Orange by Albert Robinson, a local skilled craftsman.[54]
That September and October, carpenters and painters were reaching the

Figure 4.7. "Holly Home," the home of Frances Ann and Henry Lutcher on the Sabine River in Orange. The flower bed is formed in the shape of a star and crescent, symbol of the Lutcher & Moore Lumber Company. Stark Foundation Archives.

final stages of construction on "Holly Home," the Lutchers' palatial new Victorian mansion being built on the west bank of the Sabine River just north of the Lutcher & Moore mill, on four acres framed by Georgia and Water Streets. The house had been designed in the Queen Anne style by Fred Wilbur, one of Henry Lutcher's brothers-in-law, utilizing elements from some of the mansions in Williamsport.[55]

The other was the house that William was having built for himself and Miriam on the southwest corner of Main and Sixth Streets.[56] Actual construction had not yet begun as of September 1, the date of his letter, but he duly reported that the lumber had been sawn and was being delivered and the kiln to fire the bricks was ready. "It will take eight days to burn the brick," he estimated, "and then the work commences."[57] The house would be a two-story frame dwelling, much like other new homes in Orange at that time, and William assured her that the site was "the prettiest place on the side of the marsh."[58] (He knew that she had her doubts; at that time the best-developed area of Orange lay south of the marsh and along the river, where her parents' new home was located.)[59]

Miriam must have written him that she did not want to marry until their house was completed, in order that, as newlyweds, they could move directly into their own home. "I did not know before that Robinson's building of the house had anything to do with our getting married," he answered in surprise, citing a scarcity of timber and "dry" lumber. "If you propose to wait until he finishes the house we are not apt to get married this year; that is certain."[60] Ultimately, they decided not to wait. In spite of freezing weather, they celebrated their wedding at her parents' Holly Home, which had recently been completed, on December 22, 1881,[61] with Carrie serving as her attendant and Will Loving of Bunn's Bluff, a some-time admirer of Carrie's, as groomsman.[62] Their ceremony was performed by Rev. T.H. Hensley, then serving as pastor of the First Presbyterian Church of Orange.[63] The monogram on their wedding invitation depicted the union of the Lutcher and Stark families: an "L" fashioned to resemble a pine log, an "S" intertwined around it.[64]

They must have made a handsome couple. A photographic portrait made in Miriam's youth presents an attractive young woman, tending toward plumpness, with "the prettiest brown eyes," as William himself had described them,[65] and dark hair curled and piled high in the style of the time. William's photographs show expressive dark eyes and features marked by strength and humor.[66] In his youth he had boasted a full head of dark brown hair, but much to his chagrin, at thirty, he was dealing with a rapidly receding hairline. "The summit of my cranium I think will show up butifully by the time you get home," he wrote Miriam shortly before the wedding. "But you don't care, do you?" he added hopefully. "Carrie should "not worry her self about the capillary substance on the summit of my cranium," he wrote a little later, "for if she stays [in Williamsport] very long there won't be much for her to pull."[67]

In his letters to Miriam, William regularly mentioned Carrie, a mischievous, lively teenager who enjoyed teasing him about his hair—or the lack thereof—and he chaffed her constantly about her beaux. Carrie and Miriam differed in temperament—Miriam placid and generally compliant, Carrie individualistic and possibly a bit headstrong, more like her mother. Even their looks were dissimilar—Carrie slender, with a defined, classic beauty inherited through her French-Irish mother, and Miriam with soft features more resembling those in her German father's family. And Carrie was already showing an artistic bent; William commented admiringly on a sketch that she had drawn in the margin of a letter she had written to Albert Robinson, hinting that he would like one for himself.[68]

While she was visiting in Williamsport in the fall of 1878, the sixteen-year-old Carrie had corresponded with several young people in Orange, especially Jessie Latchem, a friend of Miriam and William's who boarded with the R.B. Russell family.[69] And as William had noted, Carrie attracted admirers aplenty. He speculated on a possible marriage between her and

Figure 4.8. Carrie Lutcher, Chicago World's Fair, 1893. Stark Foundation Archives.

Benjamin Franklin "Frank" Hewson, the operator of a family drugstore in Orange.[70] She also corresponded with a young man named only as Will, who was interested in her, and apparently, she in him. In his letters to Miriam, William kept Carrie up-to-date on "Will's" activities, never giving his last name, but he could have been the Will Loving who served as William's best man.[71]

Carrie finally married at the age of twenty-seven to yet another local youth, Edgar William Brown, who with his brother Walter attended many of the social events in town.[72] They and their sister, Georgia Augusta, were

Figure 4.9. Edgar William Brown, ca. 1890s. Stark Foundation Archives.

the children of physician Samuel Brown, a descendant of a wealthy, influential South Carolina family, and his wife, née Georgia Malone. Brown had received his degree from the medical college of Louisville, Kentucky, in 1857 and had begun practicing in Ringgold, Georgia (where his son Edgar was born November 22, 1859).[73] When the Civil War erupted, Brown became a surgeon with the Army of Northern Virginia, serving under Stonewall Jackson and Robert E. Lee.[74]

After the war the Brown family moved to Mississippi, then in 1866 to Texas, first to Jasper and then on to Orange.[75] Brown practiced medicine and also owned a mercantile store, pharmacy, and office on the southwest corner of Fifth and Front Streets,[76] as well as an opera house, known informally as "Dr. Brown's Hall," the scene of many local social events.[77] He died tragically on March 1, 1887, while attempting to pull two young girls from the path of an onrushing locomotive.[78]

His sons, Edgar and Walter, tried their hands at a number of occupations before both settled on medicine (the 1880 census lists Edgar as a store clerk). "Walter and Edgar Brown have got back to Orange," William wrote Miriam in September 1881. "[They] Sold out their Sheep Ranch. The boys say that there was no Billiard Tables out west or they would of stayed one year."[79] By 1882 Edgar was a licensed physician, recently graduated from Tulane Medical School in New Orleans, and Walter soon followed suit. Edgar set up a medical practice in Orange, where he courted and ultimately married Carrie Lutcher on November 29, 1888.[80]

Miriam and William, once they were wed, entered into the intricacies and challenges of married life, though, as he had predicted, their home was not yet finished. Most likely they lived with the Lutchers until it was completed, which fortunately was not long. Within a month or two, Miriam became pregnant, and a baby daughter, Frances Ann Lutcher Stark, named for her maternal grandmother, was born November 29, 1882.

Tragically, the much-loved child died July 2, 1884, at the age of nineteen months.[81] That year was a "year of high water" at Orange, as happened frequently when heavy rains flooded the streets and sent the surrounding bodies of water out of their banks, and according to one local settler, a "spell of sickness" descended on the town.[82] It is unknown if this sickness, possibly yellow fever, killed young Frances Ann or she died of any one of a number of other childhood diseases; many afflictions prevalent in nineteenth-century East Texas proved deadly for children. William's stepmother, Donna, wrote: "After all the bad luck in his family, the loss of his little babe."[83] She was probably buried first in the City (later named Evergreen in 1898 or 1899) Cemetery; then her casket was transferred to the Lutcher mausoleum sometime after its construction in 1908.[84]

For her bereaved parents, her memory never dimmed; the image of the little girl, tiny and fine featured, gazes ethereally from the few images made of her, multiple copies of which were kept by the Lutcher and Stark families throughout their lives. It would be three years before another baby brightened the Starks' lives: their son and only surviving child, Henry Jacob Lutcher Stark, born December 8, 1887.[85]

The "bad luck" to which Donna Stark referred could have been Miriam's loss of both her paternal grandparents in 1883, the year before the baby Frances Ann died. Mary Barbara Lutscher, Miriam's grandmother,

Figure 4.10. Frances Ann Lutcher Stark, daughter of Miriam and William Stark.
Stark Foundation Archives.

had died in Williamsport on March 21 after a long illness, followed exactly two weeks later, on April 4, by her grandfather, Lewis Lutscher.[86]
Mary Barbara was seventy-one years of age; Lewis, eighty. Six years prior
to his death, Lewis had relinquished the butchering trade to become a gardener and had continued working until his wife became so ill that she required all of his time and energy. His obituary in Williamsport's *Daily Ga-*

Figure 4.11. Henry Jacob Lutcher Stark, son of Miriam and William Stark.
Stark Foundation Archives.

zette and Bulletin judged that "the terrible strain upon him for the last two years no doubt greatly shortened his life, as he was taken down immediately after her burial. . . . His life had been a useful one although checkered—sometimes by success and then again by heavy losses—but he has been able to look the world squarely in the face, having done his duty faithfully and well. Peace to his ashes."[87] Services for both Lutschers were held in the Rocktown home of their daughter and son-in-law, Rosanna and Jacob Weis,[88] followed by burials in Wildwood Cemetery, a wooded tract in the hills north of Williamsport.[89] The German spelling of their name is carved onto their tombstones (leaving some Lutcher descendants to wonder who they were and if they were even related).[90]

Miriam's maternal grandparents, David and Matilda Robinson, lived into the 1890s. By 1876, the Robinsons, like so many Americans in the aftermath of the Panic of 1873 and the subsequent depression, were losing their business—and their home. In early 1878, the sheriff of Lycoming County, John G. Bastian, confiscated the tailor shop and dwelling and sold it at auction, designating a substantial part of the proceeds to go to a creditor of Robinson's—Henry Lutcher, who had probably lent his parents-in-law the money for the purchase in the first place.[91] (Regardless of their financial transactions, Henry Lutcher and David Robinson seemed to remain on decent terms, judging from their subsequent correspondence.)[92]

In 1878, a year after the Lutcher family had migrated to Texas, the Robinsons left Williamsport. They first moved to Battle Creek, a few miles outside the central Kansas town of Lincoln; in 1883, they moved into Lincoln itself to a stone house on Lincoln Avenue, where David set up a tailor shop.[93] Between that time and his death eleven years later, Frances Ann and her daughters visited them at least once, probably more.[94] David Robinson died at the age of eighty-three on June 22, 1894. Shortly after his death, Matilda developed an unidentified malady that left her an invalid, and she died February 5, 1898.[95] Almost exactly a year later, her son, George Wilson, died, and all three family members were buried in Lincoln.[96]

With the exception of her daughters and their children, the passing of the Robinsons marked the end of Frances Ann's immediate kin, but Miriam and William still enjoyed a sizable extended family, counting their numerous Stark relations in Orange and their Lutcher kin in Williamsport. In time, Carrie and Edgar Brown added their own progeny: Fannie, born September 14, 1889; Edgar William Brown Jr., born February 10, 1894; and Henry Lutcher Brown, born July 6, 1899.[97]

While his daughters were settling their futures, Henry Lutcher and his partner, Bedell Moore, were busily proving the fortuitous timing of their move to the South, making inroads into the vast untapped forests of East Texas and Louisiana. During the 1870s and 1880s, the two men continued working from their respective locations, Lutcher running the mill in Orange and Moore remaining in charge of the Williamsport operations. In the company's earliest stages in Orange, the two had entered into a one-year partnership with P.B. Watson, possibly for financial reasons,

Figure 4.12. The first office building of Lutcher & Moore in Orange, undated.
Stark Foundation Archives.

but on May 1, 1878, Lutcher and Moore bought out Watson's one-third interest, making the company a two-way partnership, and so it remained for several years.[98]

The Orange business grew rapidly from the start, and the new Lutcher & Moore mill on the Sabine was a wonder to all who beheld it. "At the extreme southern edge of the town [of Orange] rises the grand pile of machinery," rhapsodized the *Galveston Daily News*.[99] According to the *St. Louis Lumberman*, the mill was "one of the most complete and perfect of the kind in the world":

> Power is furnished by a double battery of three boilers each, aggregating 580 horsepower. Steam is taken from these by a 24 × 34-inch engine driving the planing mill, and an 8 × 10-inch engine running their electric light plant. In the saw mill they have a double rotary slabbing gang, flat gang, double edger, trimmer, slab slasher, cut-off saws, live rolls, lath mills and all kinds of labor-saving devices. In the rear of the saw mill is a lately-invented Hoyt planer that will plane a stick at one operation 10 inches thick by 30 inches wide and 50 feet long. This machine has a capacity of 100,000 feet a day. The present capacity of the saw mill is 125,000 feet of lumber and 50,000 lath, but the output of the former will be increased to 250,000 feet when the intentions of the firm are carried out.[100]

Simultaneously with construction of the mill, another necessity lay in acquisition of timber. This was accomplished in several ways: purchasing already-harvested logs, buying or leasing stumpage rights,[101] and acquiring timberlands outright. At first, because of an incomplete supply of logs and an incompetent contractor, the mill did not operate full time, but Lutcher had immediately begun contracting with other logging operations in Louisiana and Texas to buy already-harvested pine and cypress logs to process in the new mill, and soon it was performing at capacity.[102]

At the same time, the firm was working to hire its own loggers and was always seeking new customers. Utilizing modern equipment and innovative methods the company brought from the East, it was able to produce lumber at a third of the cost incurred by other local mills, thus enormously increasing the profit margin.[103] In one practice new to East Texas lumbering, Lutcher formed a boom company, directing the construction of a boom on the Sabine River four miles upstream from the mill to trap logs floating from upriver and then hold them until they were fed into the mill.[104] He modeled the boom, which was capable of storing several million board feet of lumber, after Williamsport's great Susquehanna Boom.[105]

Meanwhile, the partners pursued their never-ending search for land. Both Lutcher and Moore recognized the deceptively simple formula for success: to own or control as much timberland as was humanly possible. Soon they began buying all the acreage they could possibly afford. Financing was a constant worry, but they had their sources; they frequently made arrangements with the First National Bank of Houston to "take their paper,"[106] and in at least one instance Lutcher journeyed to Williamsport to see his old friend Abraham Updegraff, president of the First National Bank in Williamsport, for a loan.[107] Frederick Henry Farwell, later vice president and general manager of Lutcher & Moore, described Lutcher's modus operandi in making the business work: "Mr. Lutcher traveled in a cycle. He ran the operations, sold the lumber, borrowed the money with which to buy more timber land from which to cut more lumber." Farwell added, "He was always broke."[108]

Although cypress had been the mainstay of the region, Lutcher believed that the future of its lumbering industry lay with the longleaf yellow pine, and from the beginning, he poured all the partnership's financial resources into acquiring pine acreage, both in Texas and Louisiana.[109] At first, they purchased lands in Louisiana. In 1866, in the wake of the Civil War, a Republican Congress had passed the Southern Homestead Act, which had reserved public lands in five southern states, including Louisiana, exclusively for "legitimate" settlers. The law, designed to aid freed slaves and other poor Southerners in making a start after the war and to prevent exploitation by either Northern or Southern speculators, was part of the congressional Reconstruction program so hated by many white Southern businessmen.

When the southern states returned to the Union, their congressional representatives sought to repeal the law, which they saw as a hindrance to industrial development, especially the southern lumber industry; and in 1876, the year before Lutcher and Moore moved their operations southward, they succeeded.[110] The sudden availability of these vast federally owned public timberlands played an important part in paving the way for the large-scale southern lumber boom that ensued, and Lutcher and Moore's timely relocation the very next year enabled them to lay claim to their choice of timberlands in Louisiana, fortuitously the southern state with the largest quantity of uncut timber. They bought thousands of acres of pinelands in Vernon and Calcasieu Parishes from the US General Land Office.[111]

Eventually, Louisiana's public lands began to dwindle, and the federal government removed what remained from the market.[112] Undeterred, Lutcher and Moore continued to acquire small, privately owned pieces in Louisiana but began buying large tracts of pinelands in Newton, Jasper, and Sabine Counties in Texas, where the Southern Homestead Act did not apply, since, at the time of its annexation in 1845, the Lone Star State had retained its public lands. In Texas, the partners' search for forestland worked in their favor; much of the timber acreage was too poor for farming, thus virtually worthless to the owners, who sometimes offered it to the two men for as little as twenty-five cents an acre, privately thinking the two Yankees were fools even to pay that much.[113] Such offers, far too advantageous to forgo, spurred the partners to beat the brush for the investment capital to pay for them.[114]

Their intense buying campaign paid off; Lutcher & Moore was soon on its way to becoming the largest lumbering operation in East and Southeast Texas and southwestern Louisiana. In 1880, the St. Louis Lumberman reported that "the extent of their operations may be inferred that last year their shipments from Orange were 36,316,283 feet; shipments from other points 25,105,431, making the total amount of lumber sold and shipped during the year 61,421,714 feet."[115]

Whatever their origins, Lutcher & Moore logs carried unmistakable credentials. To avoid confusion on the log-jammed rivers and to deter log "rustlers," each lumber company operating in Texas or controlled by Texas law adopted a brand that was burned, pounded, or cut into each log that floated down the river. The brands, like those used with livestock, were registered with each county or parish.[116] Lutcher & Moore registered a

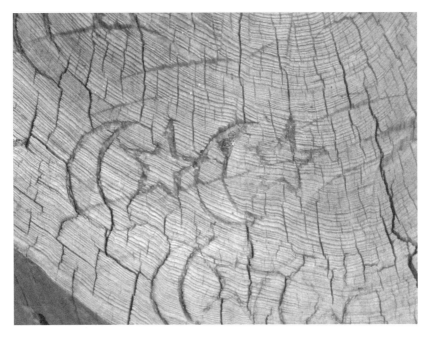

Figure 4.13. The Lutcher & Moore "Star and Crescent" log brand,
stamped on a century-old cypress "sinker" log. Courtesy of Dan Elder,
who retrieved the log from the bottom of the Sabine River.

number of brands for their trees, but the one most often identified with
the company depicted a vertical crescent moon, its horns pointed toward
the right and enclosing a five-pointed star—the so-called Star and Crescent brand.

The symbol itself, used by various cultures since antiquity, had held
many meanings throughout the years, among them "new beginnings."
What Lutcher and Moore might have had in mind when they chose it is
anyone's guess; perhaps, since they first used it soon after their move to
Orange, "new beginnings" seems the most likely choice. (No evidence has
been found to indicate that it was ever used by the company in Williamsport, either before or after their move.)[117] Or they could have chosen it simply because their first southern mill stood near a crescent-shaped bow in
the Sabine River.

The Star and Crescent icon came to symbolize Lutcher & Moore. In fact,
the partners so named that first mill on the Sabine River; "Star & Crescent Saw and Planing Mills" appeared on the company's letterhead in the
1880s and 1890s, along with a precursor of the later image—a star with
a crescent moon curving across its top, horns pointed downward.[118] The
symbol could also be found in many places associated with the company,

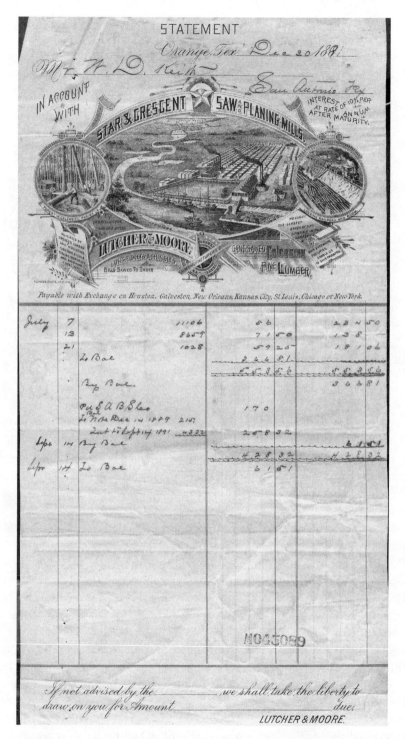

Figure 4.14. Lutcher & Moore statement of account of the 1880s and 1890s, depicting the first image of the Star and Crescent logo. Stark Foundation Archives.

Figure 4.15. Lutcher & Moore mule and ox teams pulling logs out of the pine forests of either East Texas or Louisiana, undated. Stark Foundation Archives.

including the front lawn of the Lutchers' mansion, in which was planted a star-and-crescent-shaped bed of shrubs and flowers, and the Lutcher & Moore office stationery, as a watermark.

Later, the company sent wreaths in the shape of the Star and Crescent to its officers' funeral services, and it subsequently served as part of the decor for William Stark's birthday celebration on March 19, 1929. It also graced the tip of the cupola spire of the second Lutcher & Moore Lumber Company office building and later appeared in many places on the third (and still existing) office building.[119] Not one of the other brands registered by Lutcher & Moore came to so epitomize the company as a whole.[120]

As operations moved deeper into the pine forests of the newly purchased timberland in Louisiana and thus farther from the Sabine River, Lutcher & Moore built spur railroad lines, or trams, to access them. The first tram—built in 1883 and christened the Gulf, Sabine, and Red River Railroad—eventually extended twenty-five miles northeastward into the Louisiana forests from its terminus at Niblett's Bluff on the Sabine River, facilitating movement of the cut timber.[121] As the logs were harvested, they were loaded onto flatbed railroad cars, conveyed to the riverbank, and from there unloaded into the water.[122] In another of the innovations the partners brought from the East, the company, instead of continuing the local

Figure 4.16. Lutcher & Moore log skidder and locomotive, undated.
Stark Foundation Archives.

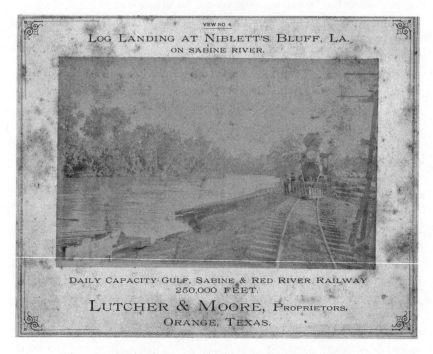

VIEW NO 4

LOG LANDING AT NIBLETT'S BLUFF, LA.
ON SABINE RIVER.

DAILY CAPACITY GULF, SABINE & RED RIVER RAILWAY
250,000 FEET.

LUTCHER & MOORE, PROPRIETORS,
ORANGE, TEXAS.

Figure 4.17. Lutcher & Moore log landing at Niblett's Bluff, Louisiana,
on the Sabine River, undated. Stark Foundation Archives.

practice of building the logs into rafts to float them downriver, drove the logs singly down the river "like cattle" some fifteen miles into the waiting boom above the Lutcher & Moore mill, thus enabling the company to hold logs sufficient to operate the mill at or near full capacity at all times.[123] In the 1890s the company constructed another tram, the Orange and Northwestern Railroad, to develop the timber acreage that Lutcher & Moore owned in Jasper, Newton, and Sabine Counties in Texas.[124]

The tram roads facilitated operations, created new jobs, and increased production, but they also accelerated the decimation of the pine forests of East Texas and Louisiana. The farseeing Henry Lutcher, well aware of the consequences of uncontrolled cutting, made efforts at conservation in the early stages of his operations, instructing his loggers, when working an area, to remove only trees that were "larger than 10 inches in diameter at a height of 24 feet from the ground." This selective cutting allowed smaller trees to survive and mature before being revisited by later logging operations, thus ensuring a constant supply of timber. At least, that was Lutcher's intent. But the intense competition in the industry ultimately "forced Lutcher and Moore to operate at full capacity," as one historian put it[125]—in other words, to clear-cut their timber or fall behind in the market. Lutcher's conservation program soon fell by the wayside—along with all of the first-growth trees.

In 1886, Lutcher, by now fully acquainted with William Stark's capabilities, invited his son-in-law to buy into Lutcher & Moore as a partner, at the same time bringing in Frank Jacob Drick, a promising young Williamsport man. In an agreement dated May 19, Henry Lutcher and Bedell Moore sold them an undivided one-sixteenth of the properties in Orange for $5,000 each, paid over time. The agreement further stated that Stark and Drick should "give their whole and individual attention to the said business and the furtherance of its interests, and that the said H.J. Lutcher and G. Bedell Moore though they will at all times have the interests of the Company and the welfare of the business in view, shall not be expected to devote their whole time to the same."[126] In short, Henry Lutcher and Bedell Moore were bringing in reinforcements. The new association marked the beginning of a long and fruitful relationship for both the company and for William Stark, but Frank Drick died unexpectedly only four years later, March 18, 1890, at the young age of twenty-eight, leaving a wife and a thirteen-month-old baby. With his death, "[Lutcher & Moore] lost a treasure," declared a writer for the *Northwestern Lumberman*, adding with unintended irony that "devotion to business was the cause."[127]

While the Lutcher & Moore Lumber Company was growing and prospering in Texas and Louisiana, it was continuing to decline in Pennsylvania, as Henry Lutcher had known it must. Profit from the Williamsport mill had been dwindling for years, and it became increasingly clear that the company's future lay in the South. In 1886 Lutcher and Moore closed their mill at Williamsport, and it remained vacant and idle until February 1888, when they signed a lease with a Williamsport lumberman, R.M. Foresman, who intended his son, Frank, to operate the mill.[128] The younger Foresman might never have had the chance because a colossal Susquehanna River flood in 1889 swept the mill downriver and deposited it against the Philadelphia and Erie Railroad Bridge.

> Between the island [west of the railroad bridge] and the mainland is a pile of wreckage twenty feet high. The pile of wreckage . . . is as interesting as an old curiosity shop. . . . The Lutcher & Moore saw mill forms a prominent part, and it was deposited there so gently that the accumulated dust of its years of idleness was not shaken from the rafters. Apparently not a thing in the mill was disturbed. The tools, machinery, etc. are all intact, and the mill might be propped up and put in operation where it stands. . . . Remains of fences, chicken coops, barns and many other things are mixed up together with logs and lumber, the whole forming a mixture the heterogenicity of which can scarcely be described.[129]

The Williamsport mill was gone for good. In the late 1880s Bedell Moore and his wife relocated to Orange, enabling him to participate actively in the Texas and Louisiana operations, but the hot, humid Southeast Texas climate seemed detrimental to Alice Moore's health. The couple began spending more and more of their time in San Antonio, where Henry Lutcher had already established subsidiary company concerns, and Moore entered into Lutcher & Moore affairs there.[130] By 1893 the couple decided to make the old Spanish city their permanent residence, building a beautiful home, "Laurelia," in Laurel Heights, an upscale subdivision in town.[131] Alice Moore became involved in church, civic, and social activities in her new surroundings, while her husband pursued various business interests. But for the next eight years, Bedell Moore also commuted to Orange to work with Lutcher & Moore, dividing his time between the two locales.

By 1888, Lutcher & Moore had acquired several barges and tugs, had purchased a schooner, and was carrying "more manufactured lumber than any firm this side of Chicago."[132] In 1890, in view of their growing operations, the partners—Lutcher, Moore, and William Stark—incorporated the company, with Lutcher as president, Moore as vice president, Stark as secretary-treasurer, and the three serving as directors.[133] During the 1890s the company expanded its reach every year, marketing not only in Texas and Louisiana but also in New Mexico, Colorado, Kansas, Nebraska, Iowa, Wyoming, Minnesota, Missouri, Illinois, Indiana, and Indian Territory (later the state of Oklahoma).[134] The company brought about this new commerce by utilizing the railroad system that had expanded and unified so quickly throughout the country.

To protect Lutcher & Moore from fluctuations in the US economy during this period of rapid growth and industrialization, Henry Lutcher increasingly explored and emphasized the overseas market, negotiating contracts in the West Indies, Mexico, and other Central and South American countries, particularly for railroad ties, as the railroad industry was rapidly developing in those countries as well.[135]

In 1891 Lutcher & Moore extended even farther into Louisiana and greatly expanded its timber holdings with a major land purchase, this time of cypress timberlands on the east bank of the Mississippi River, about forty miles north and west of New Orleans. On July 13, the principals—Lutcher, Moore, and Stark (along with J.H. McEwen)—formed a new company, the Lutcher & Moore Cypress Lumber Company, building a sawmill at a cost of $750,000—"one of the largest and best appointed sawmills in the United States," according to a contemporary source—and establishing the company town of Lutcher, Louisiana, in St. James Parish on the Mississippi.[136] Henry Lutcher then acquired considerable cypress acreage on the west bank of the river across from the new mill.[137]

In 1900, his sons-in-law, William Stark and Edgar Brown, with New Orleans lumberman John Dibert,[138] invested in approximately twenty-five thousand acres southwest of Lutcher, constructing yet another mill at Donner, Louisiana, under the name of the Dibert, Stark, and Brown Cypress Lumber Company.[139] These related companies eventually owned cypress acreage in St. James, Terrebonne, Assumption, LaFourche, and St. Martin Parishes.[140] The new eastern Louisiana holdings offered access to railroad transport and the Mississippi River waterway, which provided a reliable water route for cypress lumber and shingles from the mills to the Gulf of Mexico, thence to national and international markets.

However, the mills in Southeast Texas and southwestern Louisiana on the Sabine River faced a potentially ruinous shipping problem. To travel from inland locations on the Neches or Sabine Rivers through Sabine Lake and Sabine Pass to the Gulf of Mexico, vessels were forced to overcome a series of often-insurmountable obstacles. The depth of Sabine Lake, into which both the Neches and Sabine emptied, was a uniform seven to eight feet—too shallow for large, deep-draft vessels. Moreover, a mud bar at the mouth of Sabine Pass lay only six or seven feet below the surface at high tide, and at low tide, vessels frequently "dragged bottom."

To further complicate matters for Sabine River shipping, at Southwest Pass, the point below Orange at which the Sabine River flowed into Sabine Lake, the water in some places stood only *four* feet deep at low tide.

The only way to move lumber from Orange mills to the Gulf lay in loading it onto shallow-draft barges for transport through Southwest Pass, Sabine Lake, and Sabine Pass, then, once safely in the open waters of the Gulf, transferring it to larger vessels.[141] But this course of action brought its own set of problems; depending on weather and other conditions, Gulf waters could be extremely rough, making cargo transfers difficult to dangerous. Henry Lutcher had immediately spotted the problem when he arrived in Orange and, not surprisingly, became an early supporter of bringing deep water to the town—a huge, complex project that would require local, state, and federal support. Later, he also pushed for federal development of the Intracoastal Canal from the Mexican border all the way to New Orleans to facilitate the movement of goods; but the first order of business lay in deepening the entry from Sabine Pass into the Gulf.[142]

Beginning in the mid-1880s, Lutcher and other interested Southeast Texans traveled a number of times to Washington, D.C., sometimes at Lutcher's expense, in an attempt to convince Congress of the necessity to create a deepwater port at the town (and harbor) of Sabine Pass. In the earliest attempt of record, tugboats dragged a "massive steel harrow" through the pass to break up the shoal bottom and allow the current to deepen the channel. But the harrow failed to accomplish its purpose, and the experiment was soon abandoned.[143]

The first positive result came soon after 1885, when Charles Stewart of Houston, who represented Southeast Texas in Congress and served on the House Committee on Rivers and Harbors, assisted in passage of a bill to build jetties to protect the Sabine Pass entrance. This method was successful; the jetties, constructed of brush mattresses weighed down by large stones, caused a change in the outward wash of the currents, which gradually deepened the channel.[144] In 1888, the schooner *Comet*, with a ten-foot draft, was able to anchor at the Sabine Pass harbor and take on a load of crossties shipped from Lutcher & Moore by the steamer USS *Nicaragua*; and by 1893, the outward wash had deepened the channel to seventeen feet, enabling vessels of even deeper draft to navigate through the pass. In 1890, Henry Lutcher and others again journeyed to Washington to request funds to make Sabine Pass into "a permanent deepwater port." The committee approved the request and appropriated money for the port's regular maintenance and improvement.[145]

It was likely on this 1890 trip to Washington that Henry Lutcher traveled with Beaumonters William Fletcher, William Wiess, and W.C. Averill and Orange residents Sam Swinford and Alexander "Sandy" Gilmer. The group chose Lutcher to speak for the East Texas constituents before the Rivers and Harbors Committee. In a letter to the editor of the *Beau-*

Figure 4.18. The USS *Nicaragua,* the first steamer ever loaded at
the Lutcher & Moore mill wharves in Orange. Stark Foundation Archives.

mont Enterprise, Averill painted a vivid word portrait of Lutcher's impassioned plea:

> Mr. Lutcher in his close fitting Prince Albert coat, fully primed with statistical matter, arose to make his talk. Sam Swinford and I were seated on either side of him, and, fearing he might talk too long, had arranged to make him quit at the proper time, by force if necessary. He made a good impression . . . showing maps giving the geographical location of Sabine Pass . . . making it very plain to the committee which seemed much interested, and then came the climax: Straightening up, he said: "Now gentlemen . . . I could go on and give you in absolutely correct figures the number of billion feet in standing timber, board measure, contiguous to, and susceptible of being shipped from Sabine Pass. . . . None of you could form any idea of its bulk so, for your benefit, I have made a little calculation which you can rely on as correct. If there could be assembled at Sabine Pass a sufficient number of vessels each with a carrying capacity of 800,000 feet, board measure, enough of them could be loaded, stem to stern, to reach around the world and lap over at Sabine Pass, 1200 miles." It was a corker and "brought down the house." Swinford and I both whispered to

him to stop, realizing he had said all that was necessary, but he was "rarin" to go and was, as he said, just getting wound up. We finally pulled him down by the coat tails.[146]

Making Sabine Pass a deepwater port was only the first step; the rapid increase in the amount of lumber cut in East Texas and Louisiana was creating an ever-growing need for a deepwater channel that would course all the way from Orange to the Gulf of Mexico. The shallowest barrier on the route lay at the shoal at Southwest Pass, but the problem was solved comparatively easily when a federal government dredge deepened it.[147] The next step was obvious but more formidable: dredging a channel through Sabine Lake itself. But the project hit an unexpected snag: because of the danger from sudden squalls to ships crossing the open water of the lake, delegates from Beaumont demanded that a separate channel be dug around the perimeter of the lake, bypassing it completely. Federal officials rejected Beaumont's plan, and the project deadlocked for nearly a decade.

By the time proceedings were revived in 1899, the recently established town and port of Port Arthur boasted its own ship channel, the Port Arthur Canal, and in 1901 Congress allocated $325,000 to dredge a ten-and-a-half-foot channel from the mouths of both the Sabine and Neches Rivers through Sabine Lake to the canal. Unfortunately, this first channel was still of insufficient depth to accommodate vessels drawing deeper draft than barges and tugs, and during the lengthy negotiations to deepen it further, Henry Lutcher's health began to decline. Although he was listed as a member of the delegation that made several trips to Washington during the first decade of the twentieth century to request federal funds to work on the channel, it is doubtful that he was even able to attend.[148]

During the 1890s, however, Henry Lutcher was still able to pursue other matters. It was probably his lobbying efforts in Washington that had piqued his interest in the American political system, showing him firsthand how Congress worked—or did not. Whatever his reasons, in those years he increasingly slackened his previously intense focus on his business interests, immersed himself in his extensive library, and directed his thoughts to the study and contemplation of American politics—and to the country's past and future.

An especially controversial political issue during that decade lay in the changing race relations in the South, particularly voting rights for African American males, granted in the Fifteenth Amendment to the US Constitution during Reconstruction. Lutcher spoke out frankly on that topic on a visit to Williamsport in late June in the presidential election year of 1892, rising in a Democratic Party meeting to make what the local *Gazette and*

Bulletin titled "A Southern Speech."[149] The unnamed reporter identified Lutcher as "thoroughly southernized," and his speech doubtless mirrored the feelings of many southern whites; at that time, all-white legislatures in the South were limiting the black male vote with poll taxes, white primaries, literacy tests, and any other means they could employ.[150]

According to the newspaper, Lutcher attacked the proposed passage of the Lodge Bill (known derisively among white southerners as the "Force Act"), designed to protect the black male's right to vote. Its passage would pose no problem in the Pennsylvania area, Lutcher reasoned, but in the South, with its large numbers of free blacks, "the passage of the Lodge bill would mean that the white man had lost self government. It would mean that we are to be governed by a people inferior. . . . When the Republican Party put [the Lodge Act] on their platform, it made the Democracy [Democratic Party] of the south as solid as the Rocky Mountains." With this speech, Lutcher was expressing the prevailing attitude in the white South, but in Williamsport, he faced amused mockery and outright ridicule: "Mr. Lutcher was followed by Rep. Walter F. Ritter, who endeavored to explain away some of the utterances of the southern gentleman concerning the Lodge Bill."[151] Pennsylvanians might deride him, but Lutcher was correct on one point. A short five months later, a columnist for the rival *Daily Sun* of Williamsport recapped "the much-maligned" Lutcher's speech and dubbed him a "prophet," because, as he had predicted, the Democratic Party was solidifying in the South and the Republican Party was fading. Even though a Republican, Benjamin Harrison, then occupied the presidency, the Lodge Bill failed in the Senate by one vote, and in the presidential election that year, Grover Cleveland, a Democrat, solidly defeated Harrison.[152]

Other aspects of the national situation gave Lutcher plenty to ponder. In the late nineteenth century, the country was undergoing major economic change and accelerated industrialization, by the 1890s becoming the world's largest economy. The growth—rapid, uncontrolled, and rife with overexpansion and reckless investment—resulted in serious depressions in the 1870s and 1890s. Toward the turn of the century, both the Republican and Democratic Parties stood pro-business on major issues and were almost identical in size. Various protest groups—such as debt-ridden farmers, laborers, urban dwellers, immigrants, and social reformers—demanded constraints on the adverse results of uncontrolled industrialization; but if either party had run on reform issues, it would have lost some voters and gained others, the outcome unpredictable in any case. Thus, politicians in both parties avoided addressing the pressing new economic issues, and America faced a congressional gridlock.

Henry Lutcher simply saw a corrupt, inefficient government and, being who he was, launched into a serious study on how best to deal with the issues. While still actively running Lutcher & Moore, he wrote and printed a short treatise, entitled *A Stronger and More Permanent Union*, suggesting a plan to revitalize the national government and reduce political corruption. Focusing his study on the US Senate, whose members in the 1890s were still elected by the legislatures of the states they represented, Lutcher called for senators to be directly elected by the voters in each state,[153] laying out in great detail the manner in which he believed the elections should be conducted. (In fact, that reform was partially implemented in 1913, the year after his death, by passage of the Seventeenth Amendment, Section 1, Article 3, to the Constitution.)

Lutcher put forth a number of other suggestions that were never adopted. He sought a sixteen-year term for each senator with a limit of one term and proposed that when sworn in, senators would drop all political affiliations to better represent the entire populace of the United States. Senate elections should be held every eight years, Lutcher argued, staggering the terms of the two senators from each state, and after sixteen years of service each senator and immediate family members would draw a generous retirement pay, Lutcher's design being to encourage the most qualified candidates to enter the race without too much sacrifice for their families.[154] Finally, he expressed the hope that retired senators would serve Congress as advisers and that

> the mention of their names would be to inspire noble aspirations, and the effect of their influence would be *to elevate the Caucasian race*; they would weld their lives to the nation, and their best thoughts would always be at her command; in fact, their whole after existence would become one and an inseparable part of the country's welfare. Their ambition would be to emphasize the glory of our nation by ways peaceful, and at all times honorable; and when they passed to the great beyond, would leave behind them the record of a well spent life, one eminently fit for emulation by the growing youth of our country."[155]

As he had stated, Lutcher did indeed seek the reforms to "elevate the Caucasian race": well read, thoughtful, and farseeing though he was, he was also a man of his time—and by that point in his life, he was a thoroughgoing southerner. Another fifty years passed before America truly began to confront its contradictions regarding the race issue.

Unquestionably, however, Henry Lutcher could claim his own visionary spot in the rapidly developing industrial pantheon of the late nineteenth and early twentieth centuries. In choosing East Texas and Louisiana as the base of his operations, he brought a new level of prosperity to the entire region, irrevocably influencing its entire subsequent course of development.

As historian Donald R. Walker has phrased it, "The successes of [Henry Lutcher and Bedell Moore] . . . would . . . hasten the transformation of Texas from a predominantly rural, agricultural state into one in which industry and manufacturing could claim positions of equal, if not greater, importance in the state's economy."[156]

The anonymous author of "A Reminiscence," published in the *Northwestern Lumberman* in April 1896, portrayed Lutcher as his contemporaries saw him:

> Henry Lutcher was the Orange end of the business, and don't you think he was not a pusher. With his first advent into Texas he grasped the idea of the worth of the pine lands and he bent his energies toward acquiring as much of the timber land as he could. . . . He never took his eye from the goal. . . . He is one of the most aggressive business men I have ever met and so earnest and honest in his convictions that should you differ from him in politics or religion or be on the opposite side of a trade with him you could not help respecting his ideas and abilities.[157]

To all appearances, by the 1890s, Henry Jacob Lutcher and his formidable wife, Frances Ann, stood at the top of their world, a shared success in every respect. Throughout their ventures—and adventures—Frances Ann had stood as an equal beside him, and by his own admission, he owed her much of his success; "as they have journeyed down the stream of time," according to one interview, "she has steered him clear of many a dangerous snag."[158] And they evidently retained their affection for each other. "My own dear wife," he wrote her tenderly in 1894 from Lutcher, Louisiana, where he had traveled on business at Lutcher & Moore Cypress Lumber Company:

> I received your kind letter last night. I am very sorry to hear that you have had that neck trouble again. I wish I were there to bathe it again; you will recollect it relieved you very quickly. The next time I come over here I want you to come with me, as life is too short for us to be separated so much. Besides, I always feel so much happier when you are with me. . . . *Write soon.* Your own husband, H. J. Lutcher.[159]

Henry Lutcher, a self-made man in every sense, reigned superbly as the ruler of his vast and ever-growing web of enterprises, the lord of all he surveyed. But as it happened, as the family and their concerns stood poised at the cusp of the twentieth century, a new generation was emerging, and it would be led primarily by that affable, quietly shrewd gentleman from East Texas: William Henry Stark.

PART III

THE

PHILANTHROPIST

CHAPTER FIVE

The Heir

Fortunate indeed are Miss Fannie Brown and Master Lutcher Stark in having such a lovely grandmother as Mrs. H.J. Lutcher.
—"YESTERYEAR, SEVENTY YEARS AGO, 1903," *OPPORTUNITY VALLEY NEWS*, JUNE 27, 1973

The young male child with the weighty and prodigious name of Henry Jacob Lutcher Stark could be considered, by most reckoning, to be the most favored of children. Born into privilege after the death of a cherished baby girl, the only surviving child of doting parents and the oldest grandchild of maternal grandparents whose fortunes were increasing by the day, the long-awaited heir was indulged, protected, and idolized and remained his family's primary focus for his entire life. Given only the confines of the small East Texas lumber town in which he grew up, the young Lutcher Stark enjoyed every advantage his affluent family could offer him, including that added dimension that proved so significant in his later life: their cultural and philanthropic tradition.

Lutcher Stark was destined to become a star on the family stage. He arrived at adulthood equipped with a brilliant mind, an often-generous disposition, an inexhaustible store of energy, and a natural ability for leadership. He did not inherit his father's quiet nature; on the contrary, his was a multifaceted personality in which eccentricities and faults loomed large along with virtues. Not many have been blessed with resources sufficient to weave the insubstantial strands of their dreams into solid reality, as he did repeatedly throughout his life with a succession of all-consuming, visionary philanthropic interests. He boasted the imagination to conceive them, the mental acumen to execute them, the financial substance to pour into them, and the commitment to see them through. And because of their magnitude, these visions affected the lives of many, primarily for good, sometimes for ill.

Figure 5.1. Henry Jacob Lutcher Stark, called "Lutcher," at around five years old. Stark Foundation Archives.

Lutcher Stark called the Southeast Texas region his home for his entire life. He could have lived and worked anywhere in the world, but, except for a brief flirtation with living in the city of Austin, he preferred his hometown of Orange to more exotic locales. He grew up amid the rivers, bayous, creeks, and cypress groves of Southeast Texas as well as the giant pine forests of East Texas just to the north, where his family owned vast holdings, and undoubtedly his lifelong love of nature was born there, surrounded by the region's lush flora and abundant fauna.

His earliest existing letter, written June 2, 1897, to his mother, Miriam, reveals a nine-year-old child perfectly in his element, crawfishing in some unnamed bayou or slough in Lutcher, Louisiana. (Since the letter indicates that his father, William, was at home in Orange, he was probably taken to Lutcher either by his uncle Edgar Brown or his grandfather Henry Lutcher, both of whom traveled to Lutcher periodically to conduct

Figure 5.2. Lutcher Stark, around eight or nine years old. Stark Foundation Archives.

Figure 5.3. Lutcher Stark in nautical gear. He loved boats all his life.
Stark Foundation Archives.

business at the Lutcher & Moore Cypress Lumber Company mill.)[1] "Dear Mamma," the young Lutcher Stark wrote; "I have a good time crawfishing every morning[,] Mammy[,] Fanny and I. We have a shrimp net and we catch more than we can eat. . . . And Mamma . . . I hope that you are all well. Mamma when are you coming over hear Kiss Papa for me Good by Your loving boy Lutcher stark."

In those years of Lutcher & Moore's phenomenal growth, the spotlight fell early on Lutcher Stark as the oldest surviving offspring of Orange's most prominent family. A local editorial recounted his part in the launching ceremonies of a new barge belonging to Lutcher & Moore:

> On Wednesday last several hundred people assembled in and about the ship yard belonging to the Lutcher & Moore Lumber Company, to witness the launching of a new barge. . . . At 5:20 in the afternoon Master Lutcher Stark, the [seven]-year-old son of Mr. H. Stark [sic], mounted a platform near the stern, where hung suspended by a frial cord a quart bottle of Mumm's dry champaign. The handsome little fellow looked eager to strike, every inch a marine, in his pretty midshipman's uniform. With mallet in hand he waited anxiously until the word was given to let her go, when with all his energy he struck the bottle a savage blow that set the sparkling wine free and at the same time christened the new boat the "Sabine."[2]

As a child, Lutcher Stark was by his own description "sickly," suffering every known childhood ailment, including the feared *Cholera infantum,* or "summer complaint," a form of gastritis that killed many infants on the nineteenth-century frontiers.[3] As he told it, he became ill "every time I got my feet wet." His family sheltered him from the seamier aspects of life in the rough sawmill town by not allowing him to play football, baseball, or any other of the strenuous games for fear "I would be killed,"[4] but still he spent time outdoors; a 1903 newspaper squib noted that "Dr. E.W. Brown, Mr. W.H. Stark, and Master Lutcher Stark spent the cooler hours of Saturday afternoon fishing along the bank of the Sabine, near Lutcher & Moore Lumber Company. They caught several perch and a couple of large catfish and enjoyed the fishing trip."[5]

Even though Orange retained many vestiges of the frontier, its character was gradually acquiring a new dimension. Gracious homes were being constructed, congregations formed, churches and dance halls built. The lumber industry was now operating in full force, and several new industries, including rice farming and a foundry, were being developed. By 1891, Orange boasted a bank and a new newspaper, the *Orange Leader.* The town was also enjoying social gatherings—parades, ship launchings, band concerts, chautauquas, weddings—and the more well-to-do women hosted teas, wedding showers, and other gracious entertainments in their homes.[6] The civic- and social-minded Lutchers, Starks, and Browns took part in such events.

In 1893, Frances Ann and Henry Lutcher, Miriam and William Stark, and Carrie Brown traveled to the World's Fair Columbian Exposition, held in Chicago to celebrate the four-hundredth anniversary of Christopher Columbus's arrival in the New World.[7] (Don Cristóbal Colón, the fourteenth

Figure 5.4. Frances Ann and Henry Lutcher, Lutcher Stark, and Miriam and William Stark, undated, but probably around the turn of the twentieth century.
Stark Foundation Archives.

Duke of Veragua and Columbus's direct descendant, was an honored guest at the exposition and was presented the keys to the city.)[8] While attending the fair, Frances Ann purchased three medal-winning opalescent stained-glass windows "of heroic proportions" (approximately six by twelve feet), made by the J & R Lamb Studios of New York.[9] Possibly she had already intended to build a new sanctuary for the Presbyterian Church in Orange; finding the windows might have inspired her to move forward. She arranged for Lamb Studios to store them while she planned the new church, which, with the purchase of the windows, became a virtual certainty.[10] In the following years, she commissioned additional windows.

On September 29 of that year, Miriam Stark, carrying on her father's tradition of studying and reading the literary classics, joined a group of young women in forming a cultural study group, the Shakespeare Club.[11] Meetings were held in members' homes. Rules were strict: two unexcused absences forfeited membership, only out-of-town visitors were admitted, and members were required to respond to roll call with selected quotations. Each was assigned the part of a particular character in one of the plays to read aloud in the meetings (for *Coriolanus*, Miriam read the part of Tullus Aufidius, and for *The Comedy of Errors*, Adriana). The club next decided to study the history and culture of various countries, but the difficulty of the subject matter and the extensive reading required for the group's first selection—the entire history of Scotland from Celtic colonization to the present—convinced them to abandon the project. They reorganized their curriculum to study English history and the works of English writers (possibly fostering Miriam's later emphasis on collecting English literary works),[12] then progressed to the study of the history and literature of the United States, Texas, and the South.[13] In one of the group's later incarnations, the Ladies' Reading Club, Miriam was named to direct the studies, and Carrie occasionally appeared on the rolls.[14] (The club survives to the present date as the Woman's Club of Orange.)[15]

In 1904, Miriam established a reading and declamation contest for Orange students, offering them a cultural opportunity not otherwise available. (She possibly derived the idea from the literary contests held during her childhood in Williamsport, where prizes were given by the local newspaper for best essay, poem, and "original tale.")[16] The contest she established, presently named the Miriam Lutcher Stark Contest for Reading and Declamation and held annually for Orange County public high school students, has continued for more than a century and has become one of the longest-running reading contests in the nation.[17]

Both Miriam and Carrie played the piano,[18] but sometime in her young adulthood, Miriam began translating her stronger cultural interests—history, art, art objects, and literature—into collecting, taking the first steps toward accumulating what became a significant collection of the treasures she loved: art, art objects, and rare books and manuscripts. Carrie's artistic interests manifested themselves in active participation; she became an accomplished artist and musician, performing periodically as a harpist, pianist, and vocalist. Her paintings and other works adorned the homes of her family and friends, and her voice was said to be of operatic quality.[19] Thus, throughout his youth, Lutcher Stark was exposed to a cultural and artistic dimension rare in East Texas lumber towns, or, for that matter, anywhere on the "western frontier," as Williamsport's *Sun and Banner* had once described the town of Orange.[20]

As the new generation was emerging, the old began to fade from the scene. When young Lutcher Stark was almost six years of age, his paternal grandfather, John Thomas Stark—storekeeper, lawyer, judge, unreconstructed survivor of the Civil War—died September 24, 1893, at age seventy-two at his home in Orange.[21] Toward the end of his life he had lost his sight, but according to his third wife, Donna Stark, "seemed to hear and know all that was going on."[22] A family story holds that he contracted influenza by sitting by an open window as he was returning by rail from court in Newton. According to the story, when he walked in the door of his home, he told Donna, "Mother, I have come home to die." He began to hallucinate, and they put him to bed. He never got up again.[23] At his death, the *Orange Tribune* reported that "last Sunday night . . . Judge John Thomas Stark who had been identified with the interests of East Texas for more than fifty-three years answered to the last roll call at 11:10 o'clock and his soul was transferred from the army terrestial [*sic*] to the army celestial, to bask in the sunlight of God's glory."[24] The *Tribune* described his funeral service:

> A large number of old Confederates [were] in the assembly. Camp Walter P. Lane, United Confederate Veterans, took charge of the body at the First Baptist Church and escorted it to the grave. Over the casket was draped the old battle flag of his company under which he did such valiant service during the Civil War. The old flag was tattered and worn and the sight of it could but awaken sacred memories in the hearts of the old comrades who sat in solemn awe.[25]

Stark was survived by sixteen living children and three stepchildren. "Bless his old heart," Donna Stark wrote a nephew a little over two months after Stark's death. "We miss him so much."[26]

In 1894 Miriam and William Stark completed a magnificent new home on Green Avenue, a three-story frame mansion built in the ornate Queen Anne style with elements of Charles Locke Eastlake design, similar to that of Holly Home, the Sabine River mansion of Miriam's parents. Acting as architect and contractor for the project was Fred Wilbur, Henry Lutcher's brother-in-law, who had served in a similar capacity for the Lutchers.[27] An unnamed correspondent for the *Houston Post* described the Starks' new residence, still under construction:

> [Mr. W.H. Stark] is erecting one of the finest private residences in Orange. . . . Underneath the entire house is a large and commodious cellar. . . . The foundations are of cement and concrete. . . . The frame work of the house is very heavy and calculated to last. The floors are of hardwood and are laid diagonally. The inside finish will be entirely of native wood, carefully worked and will present a beautiful appearance. Noting the conveniences in this mansion . . . it will be thoroughly lighted by electricity, and that it has bath rooms on every floor and will also contain a large billiard hall. The heating and the ventilation will be perfect. Near by a fine stable and carriage house are in course of construction and cement drives and walks are being laid. When fully completed with all its ornamentation, it will stand [as] a palace of strength and incomparable beauty.[28]

In its entrance hall, the finished house boasted exquisite "floating" panels of curly longleaf yellow pine from the Lutcher & Moore mills. The

Figure 5.5. William, Miriam, and Lutcher Stark in the library of "The Elms," their new Green Avenue home in Orange, which remains intact and is now known as The W.H. Stark House. Stark Foundation Archives.

Figure 5.6. Lutcher, William, and Miriam Stark enjoying a musicale at home, undated. Lutcher and William are playing violins, and Miriam is accompanying on piano. An unidentified friend or family member plays the mandolin. Stark Foundation Archives.

Figure 5.7. Lutcher Stark, high school age, ca. 1901–1905. Stark Foundation Archives.

correspondent concluded that the house was "a graceful ornament to the city and a triumph to the modest, frank and manly owner, who is doing so much for the upbuilding of this city."[29] Lutcher Stark grew up in the house, and his parents lived there the rest of their lives.

During the time Fred Wilbur was supervising construction of the Starks' house, he was also completing a similar one for Carrie and Edgar Brown. The elegant mansions reflected the refined tastes of the Lutchers, and over the succeeding years the three women—Frances Ann, Miriam, and Carrie—filled their homes with beautiful objects of every description, dispensing "royal hospitality" to families, friends, and business associates.[30]

In planning the entertainments that had already made her hospitality legendary, Frances Ann Lutcher did not exclude her grandchildren; in the spring or early summer of 1903, she gave a lawn party in honor of Lutcher Stark, then sixteen, and his oldest cousin, Fannie Brown, age fourteen, entertaining them and thirty-five of their friends:

> Wednesday evening Mrs. Lutcher had her lawn beautifully decorated with Japanese lanterns and then added to these was the crowd of bright, pretty young misses and the manly lads gathered to enjoy themselves as only the young and light of heart can. By Mrs. Lutcher nothing had been left undone that would add to the pleasure of her young guests. Refreshments of ice cream and candy were served and all left declaring it a perfectly lovely party.[31]

Miriam followed her mother's example of lavish entertaining; in April 1904, during the Eighteenth Annual Convention of the Lumberman's Association of Texas held in Orange, she and William, "Colonel William Stark, one of nature's noblemen," as the account named him, hosted a "splendidly brilliant" reception for the visiting lumbermen and their wives, "the veritable cap sheaf of the . . . convention . . . where hundreds of electric bulbs flashed back the glint of diamonds and pearls worn by the ladies and reflected in prismatic splendor the sheen of silver and cut glass in the grand dining hall. . . . The Stark reception will live in the hearts and memories of the guests long after the convention itself has been forgotten."[32]

On January 6, 1898, Henry Lutcher assigned his power of attorney to William Stark, and on January 27, he made his will.[33] Several days later, he and Frances Ann embarked on the first stage of an extensive three-month trip to Europe, Africa, and the Middle East, possibly a long-time dream. Their extraordinary life journey together had led them a long way, in every sense, from that butcher shop in Williamsport.

Figure 5.8. Frances Ann and Henry Lutcher at home, ca. 1890s. Stark Foundation Archives.

Leaving from New York at noon on February 5, the Lutchers boarded the German steamer SS *Aller*, bound for Spain, Algiers, Italy, Malta, Egypt, the Holy Land, Lebanon, Syria, Turkey, and Greece. They traveled as members of a tour group of 327 passengers, including themselves. The *Aller* docked first at Gibraltar, then sailed through the Strait into the Mediterranean Sea.[34] On February 21, Frances Ann wrote to Miriam and her family from Naples that they had visited Mount Vesuvius and that the volcano was "red hot." She appended a chilling note, the first grim harbinger of Lutcher's oncoming illness: "I wanted your Papa to rite to you," she confided, "but he gets all befodde [befuddled] he semes to be wel but his mimery is not eny beter it is worse if any thing.[35]

Yet Henry Lutcher did write frequently throughout the trip, and his letters were far from befuddled. "Dear Children," he wrote from the ship only three days later, on February 24,

We will arrive at Alexandria Egypt in the Morning from there we will go to the Ruins of Karnack and Luxor will be there Eleven Days also take in Cairo on the way from there Will go to the Holy Land It is no use Trying to tell you everything as I would have to have a stenographer to describe one half of *What* we have Seen & Learned. . . . We have had an elegant trip. . . . Mama has Stood the trip splendidly.[36]

From Jerusalem, he wrote, "Mama says I should tell you that [the weather] is as cold as Greenlands Icy Mountains She is Correct." He noted, "We are in best of health."[37] The correspondence was by no means one-sided; from Cairo, Frances Ann wrote Miriam that they had received letters from the grandchildren—Lutcher Stark, then almost eleven, and Fannie Brown, the oldest child of Carrie and Edgar, almost nine. Frances Ann informed her family that they had ridden camels to the Pyramids and Sphinx at Giza, "but we did not go up on top as meny did . . . good by kiss the Childern for me," she added. "From your mother F. A. Lutcher."[38]

Frances Ann did not neglect to write Lutcher Stark, her oldest and ultimately her favorite grandchild, setting her pen to paper just before they were to visit Smyrna and Ephesus on March 19: "My one Sweet hart," she began, "we received your kind letter of the tenth. . . . It was so sweet and nise. . . . Grandpapa and I are both well we are having a good time." She signed the letter "From your own Mamoose" (her grandchildren's nickname for her).[39] In Rome by March 29, Henry Lutcher wrote that they had received two letters from Miriam, one from Carrie, and one each from Lutcher and William Stark. "I think Mama is a little *homesick*," Henry confided, "*yet She does not Admit it. It has been very Bad weather ever Since we Left the boat. If this kind of weather is the Soft Balmy Breeses* of Italy, I prefer the Texas Breezes."[40]

The Lutchers left their party at Munich to make a sentimental side jaunt to Stuttgart to visit the house in which Henry's parents, Lewis and Mary Barbara Lutscher, had lived before their immigration; Frances Ann reported that they visited three of Henry's cousins.[41] She never failed to offer her southern hospitality to all and sundry, even royalty; on April 21, Henry wrote from Berlin, not without a glimmer of amusement: "Will say we have been unfortunate here as we have seen neither Bismark or the Emperor [Wilhelm II.] We so far have only saw Queen Victoria & the King of Saxony[,] Mama has invited *Both* of them . . . on their next trip to Texas *to stop off and take dinner with us*."[42]

Even though the Lutchers had enjoyed "splendid health," as Frances Ann put it, throughout the journey, they were no longer young—Henry was sixty-two; Frances, fifty-eight. "It is hard worke," Frances Ann complained. "We get very tired running around."[43] In his last letter before they left for home, Henry ended, "Mama is going to bed and So will I in Just one minute."[44] For their return voyage, the Lutchers departed from Southampton, England, on May 11 on the ship *Kaiser Friedrich,* arriving back in New York May 18, 1898, then heading toward Southeast Texas after an absence of over three months. Their last idyll had been played out; at home, they would face a new century and profound changes, not least of which was the specter of Henry Lutcher's deteriorating mental health.

His decline must have been fairly rapid. Except for Frances Ann's single mention of his confusion during their travels abroad, his mental condition was never directly mentioned in other contemporary letters or documents—an omission in keeping with the custom of the times. Some blamed his intense, long-term, self-imposed workload for the breakdown in his health;[45] others indulged in darker speculations and rumors, inevitable relative to any town's premier citizen. In any event, Henry Lutcher soon became disabled and was obliged to relinquish all work. Bedell Moore's second wife, Elizabeth Blasdel Moore, later asserted that he became incapacitated "several years previously to 1901."[46]

That year, 1901, when the partners donated the north tract of their old mill site in Rocktown to the borough of South Williamsport for use as a park, it was William Stark who signed for Henry Lutcher as his attorney-in-fact, as he did again in 1907, when Lutcher and Moore gave the south tract to Williamsport's Episcopal Church on January 23.[47] Stark also signed for Lutcher when, on January 1, 1902, the latter resigned as president of the First National Bank of Orange, a position he had held since the bank's inception in 1889.[48] Unquestionably, Henry Lutcher's mental health was steadily deteriorating.

As custom dictated, Henry Lutcher's family first attempted to care for him at home, but as his dementia progressed, he sometimes became violent, once, according to one story, even backing Frances Ann into an unlighted fireplace with a knife. In September 1900, Frances Ann hired a young woman named Rosa Hamilton to keep house for them. As needed, Hamilton also looked after Henry Lutcher, sleeping in his room on a cot and fetching him if he wandered away.[49] His mental illness had a profound effect on his oldest grandson; Lutcher Stark retained a lifelong fear that in his older years he would become like his grandfather.[50]

Finally the situation worsened, and the family was forced to make the decision, undoubtedly difficult in the extreme, to place Henry Lutcher in an institution.[51] They chose the Cincinnati Sanitarium, a facility in College Hill, an affluent neighborhood in Cincinnati, Ohio, in all probability taking him there sometime in 1902.[52] The sanitarium was a vanguard psychiatric hospital, one of the largest west of the Alleghenies, "fully equipped for the scientific treatment of nervous and mental affections."[53] Among other amenities, the facility featured a billiard hall, a flower conservatory, flower and vegetable gardens, and a two-acre spring-fed lake that offered rowing and ice-skating opportunities.[54]

As Lutcher's health and reason ebbed, more responsibility naturally devolved on his sons-in-law, William Stark and Edgar Brown, and his business partner, Bedell Moore. Moore increased his workload with Lutcher & Moore, commuting periodically from his home in San Antonio, but his own health soon broke, "and [he] realized he must have complete rest."[55] In 1900, he sold his interests in the Lutcher & Moore Cypress Lumber Company to William Stark, Edgar Brown, and John Dibert for a reported $550,000.[56] (To add to Moore's woes, his wife, Alice Clements Moore, died September 28 of that year.)[57]

The next year, in a transaction dated April 1, 1901, Moore sold his entire interest in the Lutcher & Moore Lumber Company itself, part to Henry Lutcher, William Stark, and Edgar Brown and the remainder to the same three plus John Dibert and bookkeeper Frederick Henry Farwell.[58] At the meeting of the board of directors on this date, Henry Lutcher was listed as present, but William Stark, as secretary-treasurer of the company and Lutcher's attorney-in-fact, was authorized to conduct the proceedings of the sale and to sign all papers.[59]

For his share of the Lutcher & Moore properties, Moore was paid $1.625 million.[60] The minutes of July 2, 1901, showed that the 1,855 shares of stock that had belonged to Bedell Moore were canceled and then reissued proportionately to Lutcher, Stark, Brown, Dibert, and Farwell.[61] That July, Farwell was promoted to office manager,[62] and Brown was appointed vice president.[63] The buyout of Moore by the Lutcher-Stark interests involved such a vast number of properties that the record of the deed in the Orange County Courthouse occupied 102 pages.[64] The Williamsport *Gazette and Bulletin* labeled the transaction "the Mammoth Deal of G. Bedell Moore . . . the largest ever recorded in the history of lumber trade in the South," reporting that Moore retired as "one of the wealthiest and most successful men in lumbering."[65]

Even though Lutcher and Moore were forced by circumstance to relinquish their center-stage roles, their brainchild, the Lutcher & Moore Lumber Company, would continue to prosper beyond anyone's imagining. The company continued to bring Edgar Brown into the family interests; in 1900, in addition to his position at the Lutcher & Moore Cypress Lumber Company, Brown became a stockholder and president of the newest concern, the Dibert, Stark, & Brown Cypress Lumber Company, chartered in 1900 and headquartered in Donner, Louisiana. Over the next twelve years, Brown commuted weekly to Donner by train.[66]

The new plant at Donner proved to be a moneymaker, milling the enormous cypress forests in the Louisiana marshlands in Terrebonne, Lafourche, Assumption, and St. Martin Parishes, with an eventual production of thirty-five million board feet of cypress lumber per year.[67] Its success lay in part in Henry Lutcher's prior contacts in Pennsylvania;

much of the cypress was sold to operators in the Pennsylvania oil fields for use in building storage tanks.[68]

In 1900, as the old century drew to a close, Lutcher & Moore lost their first office building, a small frame structure consisting of "what appeared to be two wooden houses joined together," to their old enemy, fire. They replaced it with a handsome octagonal Victorian structure "of unique construction," trimmed with "gingerbread"—elaborate wooden ornamentation—and sporting a tall, slender spire topped with the company's emblem, the Star and Crescent.[69]

After this initial loss, the new century began to unfold auspiciously, and 1901 proved to be a banner year for the company. That year, in addition to the buyout of Moore, the concern also purchased the L. Miller Lumber and Shingle Company mill in Orange, located just downriver from the original Lutcher & Moore mill. The mill, newly dubbed the "Lower Mill," increased the company's production to a full one hundred million board feet a year and furnished work for a thousand men.[70]

Lutcher & Moore expanded its markets overseas, and in the summer of 1901, it began "trademarking" its export products—stamping them with the name of the company that manufactured them and their place of origin—a pioneer practice in the lumber industry. From that time until the company ceased production, the "Lutcher-Orange" brand would become "the best-known yellow pine in the consuming world" and could be spotted on wharves in the far corners of the globe, including Mexico, England, Rotterdam, Le Havre, Antwerp, Amsterdam, and Genoa, as well as ports "from Cape Town to Cairo," as one account put it (although World War I briefly interrupted the company's European and African trade). [71]

Lutcher & Moore eventually purchased "a regular fleet of vessels," as the *Orange Leader* termed it, including three steam tugboats; six barges; *El Capitan*, a "magnificent" yacht built entirely of native woods; three gasoline launches; and several lumber schooners, one named the *Martha*, undoubtedly for William Stark's long-deceased mother.[72] At the apex of its operations, the Lutcher & Moore Lumber Company owned more than five hundred thousand acres of pine and cypress timberlands in Texas and Louisiana, and it was said that one could travel from Orange to New Orleans without ever losing sight of Lutcher & Moore land.[73] The company entered the twentieth century as one of the greatest lumber concerns in the South[74]—and in fact, the entire nation. By 1905, the company was shipping over 125 million board feet of lumber per year.[75] By 1906, the estimated worth of Lutcher & Moore enterprises was between $9 million and $10 million, the mill at Orange alone paying over $100,000 per month for labor, cutting three hundred thousand board feet per day and producing seventy-five million board feet of lumber per year.[76]

Figure 5.9. Lutcher & Moore, ca. 1900–1912. In the background stands the company's octagonal, Victorian-style office building, built when the first office building was destroyed by fire in 1900. Stark Foundation Archives.

Figure 5.10. Lutcher & Moore personnel in front of the octagonal office building, including William Stark (*bottom row, second from left*) and F.H. Farwell (*top row, left*). Sidney Mouton, the young African American man sitting on the steps, accompanied Lutcher Stark as his valet at the University of Texas. Stark Foundation Archives.

During the remainder of Henry Lutcher's life, William Stark's official title was secretary-treasurer, but when Lutcher became ill, his sons-in-law, William and Edgar, shared responsibility for overall supervision of Lutcher & Moore's increasingly complex concerns. Edgar Brown even relinquished his medical practice in 1900 to devote his full time and attention to the family's business interests (although he did serve two terms as mayor of Orange from 1908 to 1911).[77]

William Stark eventually emerged at the helm of the giant company and its many offshoots, and in guiding that vast realm of rapidly expanding ventures lay his particular genius. His early experience in lumbering served him well; he was "the moving spirit of the company," the *Beaumont Enterprise* proclaimed in 1905. "He is thoroughly familiar with all the details of the manufacture of lumber, is a fine organizer, and understands the handling of men,"[78] said David Rogers (Dave) Nelson, who later managed cattle and land for the family interests. "I believe that he can see through, around, and over a business proposition more clearly than any man . . . I ever knew."[79]

The parent company continued to diversify into a kaleidoscope of business concerns, not necessarily related to the lumber industry but nearly always formed by the Lutcher & Moore principals and their families, friends, and business associates. And according to some, their motives were altruistic in many instances; in establishing the new business entities, they were attempting to furnish jobs to the local populace.[80] The first of these interests was the Orange Rice Mill Company. Although the pine and hardwood forests in the north of Orange County were inhospitable to rice growing, the marshy lands to the south offered more favorable conditions, and at century's end, the advent of the canal system was transforming rice into a money crop.[81] The company was actually incorporated February 18, 1901, by Bedell Moore and several others, Moore being the only one of the partners with any overt connection to the Lutcher, Stark, and Brown families.[82] However, in the next two decades, the company's board of directors would include William Stark, Lutcher Stark, and Rucie A. Moore (no relation to Bedell Moore), the son-in-law of Carrie and Edgar Brown (married to the Browns' daughter, Fannie).[83]

A related company, the Orange County Irrigation Company, William Stark and Edgar Brown as two of the shareholders, began constructing rice canals that same year.[84] Other businesses followed, William Stark serving as a director and as president of many of them. In 1902, the group of investors inspected a Pensacola, Florida, plant that produced paper from longleaf pine fiber, with the idea that they might utilize the refuse from the Orange lumber mills for that purpose.[85] They purchased the en-

Figure 5.11. The Orange Ice, Light & Water Company improved life
for Orange residents from 1905 to 1925. Stark Foundation Archives.

tire plant and shipped it by rail to Orange, where they formed a new corporation in 1904, the Yellow Pine Paper Mill Company, described as "the
most interesting industrial plant in the South, the only plant in the world
making high-grade wrapping paper from yellow pine shavings."[86] William
Stark, Edgar Brown, and F.H. Farwell of Lutcher & Moore and Leopold
Miller and J.W. Link of the Miller-Link Lumber Company served as stockholders, and Stark was named as president.[87]

In 1905 the Orange Ice, Light & Water Company was founded by William Stark and other business partners to manufacture and sell ice and
to operate an electric light plant and system of water supply in Orange.
As well as furnishing light service, the plant pumped artesian water to
the city, which "has done more for the health and general good of the city
than any other one thing," proclaimed an advertisement.[88] William Stark
served on the first board of directors. The following year, he, George W.
Bancroft, Leopold Miller, F.W. Hustmyre, and F.H. Farwell formed the Orange Grocery Company, first located on Front Street, then at the corner of
Division and Market Streets. Stark served on the board of directors and as
first vice president of the company. And by 1911, William Stark and Edgar
Brown had begun accumulating small amounts of stock in a new venture,
the Vinton Petroleum Company, acquiring mineral interests and drilling
for oil and gas. This was the first of several such enterprises that would
prove extremely profitable.[89] The family's business interests were growing
exponentially.

By the time Lutcher Stark reached school age, a public school system had come into existence.[90] In 1884, a group of Orange citizens, including John Thomas Stark and Henry Jacob Lutcher, had raised a cash fund to build the first school, a one-story wooden building on Henderson Street,[91] and it is possible that Lutcher Stark attended grade school at the Henderson School. But, given his childhood health problems, it is possible he was taught at home. His composition book of childish riddles survives, written in his as-yet-unformed hand. ("Why is a hat like a king? Because it has a crown.")[92]

He attended Orange High School, then located in the old Henderson Street building. In a tenth-grade essay on Oliver Goldsmith, he wrote: "[Goldsmith's family's] hearts were in the right places but their heads often [led] them into many strange adventures."[93] (The same might well be said of Lutcher Stark himself.) He graduated May 19, 1905, as salutatorian of his class.[94] A draft of his speech, with many of his corrections, survives. "All is finished!" he wrote. "Today the vessel shall be launched! . . . She represents the labor of many years. . . . With the beginning when her 'keel of oak' was laid 'so straight and strong' deep care was taken that no imperfect piece of timber should be used. . . . Day by day the vessel grew / With timbers fashioned strong and true." "Come prepared to see the launching," he urged the assembled families and friends. "I now in the name of the graduating class of 1905 give you welcome with the earnest desire that you may depart tonight feeling well repaid for the time spent with us this evening."[95]

That fall of 1905, Lutcher Stark, not quite eighteen years old, left the Southeast Texas woods and bayous to enter a wondrous new world—the Texas Hill Country—as he matriculated as a freshman at the University of Texas in Austin. Enchanted with the university and all it offered, he immersed himself in it completely. As one writer later declared, "In such an atmosphere, Henry Jacob Lutcher Stark really found life."[96] He arrived on campus as a shy, bespectacled, overprotected, overweight teenager, bringing with him his own valet, Sidney Mouton,[97] and his own automobile, the first student-owned auto on campus. One writer described his debut:

> When Freshman Henry Jacob Lutcher Stark drove up to the main entrance that beautiful October morning in his very own Pope-Hartford, the astonishment, speculation, and chagrin which spread through the corridors may well be imagined. . . . These emotions were not unpunctuated with sniffs of disdain and sneers of derision at this supposed affront to our democracy. . . . Freshman Stark continued on his way without so much as returning sniff for sniff.[98]

Figure 5.12. Lutcher Stark and friends in his Pope-Toledo, ready for a parade, Austin, 1905–1910. Stark Foundation Archives.

Another account of Lutcher's grand entrance is accompanied by a photograph, supposedly taken in 1907, of Lutcher Stark at the wheel of a Pope-Toledo. It is possible that when he arrived in Austin in 1905, he owned a Pope-Hartford, as the article states, and by 1907 had switched to a Pope-Toledo. More likely, the Pope-Toledo was the original auto, and the written account of his debut is inaccurate.[99]

Lutcher Stark's room at the boarding house at 1903 Whitis Avenue also reflected his privileged state; it was richly furnished in Mission oak furniture (ultimately his favorite style), festooned with college and fraternity banners, and topped with a huge Japanese-style parasol suspended from the ceiling. Stacked guns formed a tepee against one wall, and an upright piano stood in a corner. On the floor lay Navajo rugs, a sign of the beginning of his lifelong penchant for collecting southwestern art. He acquired his first paintings—by living Texas artists, to avoid being fooled by fakes and forgeries—while he was a student at the university.[100]

His course of study that first year included physics, English history and literature, Spanish, and Greek. His notes were detailed, conscientious, and orderly, with no doodling or personal comments in the margins. He made acceptable grades (an A+ in Greek and mediocre marks in Spanish).

Figure 5.13. Lutcher Stark's room in an off-campus boardinghouse on Whitis Avenue when he attended the University of Texas in Austin. Stark Foundation Archives.

One of his college essays, "Being Up-to-Date," not only reflects his attitude toward academics but possibly affords a glimpse of his awakening view of life in general:

> We see a "grind," as he is commonly called, sitting at a desk laboring hard over his books. . . . He is trying to be up to date in his lessons. To be prompt with the preparation of his studies, does it necessarily require one to be a "grind"? There has been a great number who have kept up their work, and who [also] have indulged in the pleasures of life. These people may not make as good grades as the student who toils from one hour to the next . . . , yet the former have been up to date and have had pleasures that the latter does not know how to enjoy.[101]

He protested that "I am not fully capable of writing on being up to date in either a sociable or studious way, as I have never striven to be in such a condition."[102] In spite of his protestations, it is clear from the essay that neither did he want to be a "grind." And he proceeded to prove himself to be the direct opposite.

"In spite of the valet," as one wag put it, Lutcher Stark began gaining personal popularity on campus.[103] According to one account, "his gener-ous, frank, and open-hearted ways won him scores of friends from the ranks of those whose eyesight had once been darkened by the dust from his tires."[104] A story was told that, during one Sunday dinner at his board-inghouse, a young woman knocked over her glass of water. To save her embarrassment, he not only turned over his own glass but also everyone else's within reach, and the girl forgot her embarrassment amid the result-ing hilarity.[105]

At the beginning of his sophomore year, he pledged Tau Deuteron chap-ter of Phi Gamma Delta fraternity—the "Phi Gams," or "Fijis," as they were popularly known.[106] Characteristically, he entered into the new ex-perience with an energy and concentration that marked his thoughts and actions throughout his life, and he eventually became head of the chap-ter.[107] When the group purchased their chapter house in 1908, Lutcher

Figure 5.14. Lutcher Stark, in driving gear, posing in a child's toy car, Austin, ca. 1905–1910. Stark Foundation Archives.

Figure 5.15. Lutcher Stark as manager of the 1910 University of Texas football team, sitting on the bench with the team during a game. Stark Foundation Archives.

Stark served as vice president of the corporation formed to buy the house, owning ninety of the total two hundred shares. He also prevailed on his mother to assume the corporation's notes as they came due, and Miriam Stark eventually held them all. (He himself canceled the debt in 1937, when the chapter met his challenge to improve its scholarship record.)[108]

He served as assistant manager of the university's 1909 football team and as "graduate" manager of the 1910 team,[109] handling bookings, banquets, and travel accommodations as well as many additional amenities. He excelled at the job, exhibiting a personality trait that formed a lifelong pattern: anticipating and minutely controlling every detail and contingency and doubtless contributing his own (or at first, his family's) funds to effect the desired result. A contemporary journalist sang his praises: "Never before were the Orange and White athletes so well trained and cared for; seldom had so diversified or so representative a schedule been arranged. . . . Every necessity and comfort for a championship team [was] provided by the manager. . . . The season was one of the most successful, both financially and from the standpoint of clean, hard-fought games that the University has ever had," the writer concluded.[110] The chairman of the Athletic Council, E.C.H. Bantel, wrote him at the conclusion of the 1910 season: "Your administration has been honest, efficient, businesslike and satisfactory in every way. I cannot permit you to depart . . . without expressing to you my appreciation of your conscientious and painstaking labors, to which the happy situation, outlined above, is so largely due. . . . Your conduct and management has been all that could be desired, and I congratulate you on your unqualified success."[111]

Figure 5.16. University of Texas football team, 1910. Lutcher Stark is on the second row from top, far right. Stark Foundation Archives.

Lutcher Stark's experiences with the football teams produced a two-fold result: it kindled in him a lifelong obsession with sports, particularly those of the University of Texas, as well as a desire to improve his own physical state; during or immediately after his college years, he embarked on serious programs of weight training and physical fitness.[112] A tale was circulated of one of his weight-lifting stunts during a bull session in the Phi Gamma Delta house:

> A bunch of the boys got to telling whoppers one night in the fraternity house. Strong arm stunts. One about a fellow who could juggle a piano.
> "Believe I can do that," said young Stark. "Fact is, think I can go him one better." So Lutcher Stark laid down on the floor, while the other students hoisted the piano over his body. He not only braced and held the piano there, but sustained another student on the piano stool while he knocked off a ragtime tune.[113]

The incident might not have occurred during Lutcher's college years; a snapshot of him made as football manager in 1910 shows him as still being decidedly overweight.[114] Another, perhaps more plausible, version of the tale held that he performed the feat in front of an Orange recruiting station during World War I, and the tune the pianist played was "Yankee Doodle."[115] Stark employee Felix Anderson remembered that Lutcher himself later corroborated a slightly different story: "I decided I wanted to lift weights," Lutcher told Anderson. "I wanted to be muscular. I went into it with full intensity. You [can] believe it or not, but I lifted a seven-hundred-pound piano with a woman playing it."[116]

A tantalizing scrap of information appeared in an Austin newspaper on October 29, 1910. "Aeroplane to Fly from Clark Field [the football stadium]," trumpeted the headline. "Mgr. Stark's Machine Will Make Short Flight before Game—News Leaked Out. Will Be a Novel Sight." According to the article, Stark had purchased a "man-bird," variously named a "Farnham Monoplane" and a "Wright Biplane." "The daring and popular young man" intended to "spring a surprise upon the student body and the citizens of Austin," the article continued, by taking the plane on "at least a few evolutions" from Clark Field before the upcoming game with Auburn University the following Saturday.[117] No further mention of the occasion survives, and it is doubtful it took place; perhaps university officials, or his own parents, quashed it.

Thus, at the university Lutcher Stark formed friendships, found acceptance, and took a new direction in his life. Equally important, while still a student, he first gained his footing as a philanthropist,[118] a role that escalated on an increasingly extensive scale throughout his life. With these beginnings, he embarked on a monumental course of action concerning his alma mater, a combination of philanthropy and service that continued, for good or ill, for the next forty years, one of the major achievements of his life. Perhaps most important, he also found an enduring love. Lutcher Stark in a later interview for the *Saturday Evening Post* told the story that the first morning he arrived on campus, he spotted a beautiful, blue-eyed, fourteen-year-old girl sitting at a second-story window and combing out her "flaxen curls" to dry in the September sunshine. Making it his business to discover her identity, he found out that her name was Nita Hill.[119]

Nita Hill was almost exactly three years his junior, having been born December 5, 1890, in Austin, the only surviving child of Austin physician Homer Barksdale Hill and his wife, Ella Rankin "Granny" Hill.[120] Dr. Hill's roots had grown deep in Texas since the days of Mexican dominion; his father, James Monroe Hill, was an authentic Texas hero, having fought April 21, 1836, at the Battle of San Jacinto, the culminating battle in Texas' revolt against Mexico.[121] Homer Hill graduated from Tulane University Medical School with highest honors and came back to practice in Texas. In 1881 he married Ella Rankin, the orphaned daughter of Mary Cole and Dr. Calvin Patton Rankin.[122] The young couple first lived at Gay Hill in Washington County, where two children were born: Mary Creola, born July 26, 1884, who lived for only three weeks; and Herbert, born July 28, 1885, who died August 27, 1889.[123] Homer and Ella Hill moved to Austin in 1889, where their second daughter, Nita, was born.

For many years, Dr. Hill had served as the Varsity football team's volunteer physician, and Ella Hill had earned the nickname of "Granny" by serving as protector, counselor, and unofficial dean of men, particularly to members of the team. According to a *Saturday Evening Post* interview, "Doctor Hill sat on the players' bench at every football game, with his little black kit beside him, patched up the university huskies, and never mailed a bill. . . . Granny . . . kept a boarding table largely for athletes, and . . . she didn't have much use for gal children, save her one [Nita], whom she worshiped. . . . When there were dances, Granny did the decorations; when athletes got drunk and down, Granny and Doctor Hill went after them."[124] Throughout the years, coaches and players had filled the chairs around the Hills' dining table, and many a boy found temporary haven in their home until his circumstances improved.[125] At the university the Hills were "an institution in themselves," personifying the Varsity spirit. And fortuitously, they lived at 2007 Whitis, just down the street from Lutcher Stark's room. He was said never to have dated another girl.[126]

In the summer of 1907, between his sophomore and junior years, he traveled abroad for the wealthy young man's requisite "Grand Tour" of Eu-

Figure 5.17. Lutcher Stark, about the time of his graduation from the University of Texas and subsequent marriage, 1910–1911. Stark Foundation Archives.

rope with Thornton Rogers Sampson, the pastor of the First Presbyterian Church in San Antonio, who had earlier promised Lutcher's parents that he would "show him Europe."[127] By this time, he and Nita Hill were already obviously more than friends, though they still treated each other warily. He sent her postcards from his travels—short, noncommittal messages commenting mainly on the subjects of the images, some with no message at all, signing himself familiarly, "Lutch." But occasionally his feelings came through: "I'd like to be with you for an auto ride. Sure do miss you and the rides," he added.[128] Throughout, he maintained a running tally of days before he came home. "Only 16 days now," he wrote. "Just think. Sail tomorrow. Be in Austin about [September] 20–25th."[129] On a card he sent from Fontainebleau Forest bearing a picture of "Le Pharamond," one of its ancient oaks, he commented, "The oldest tree in the forest. H.J.L.S." The son and grandson of lumbermen would certainly have taken due note of the trees.[130]

Nita's correspondence with him—letters instead of postcards—furnishes a more complete picture of their budding relationship and its ups and downs and also offers a first glimpse of the Lutcher Stark temper, which in time became legendary. Nita apparently boasted a bit of temper of her own; during his Grand Tour, she wrote an angry response to a letter she had received from him, which, unfortunately, does not survive: "There was never a more unjust one written. Lutcher, I am getting mighty tired of being bawled out on every occasion without any foundation. . . . *You* whom I trusted as a gentleman and my friend have made me out a falsehood and insinuated things that I trust I may never have an enemy who hates me bad enough to think of me as it seems you have."[131] She proceeded to justify the actions that had apparently precipitated his tirade and delivered a spirited one of her own:

> Lutcher I never do one thing that is not open and above board. . . . You are unfortunately constituted. . . . It seems strange to me if you love me as you say you do (you certainly seemed to love [me] in Houston) and you so far away [that] you would feel like bawling me out. With such letters as you wrote you will never make me think any more of you. . . . Well I reckon I have bored you long enough so goodby Nita.[132]

It is possible that she never mailed this letter; the envelope shows only his name, with a stamp but without address or postmark. In any event, what was clear from the letter was that he had already declared his feelings for her. She scolded him further in a later letter, this one with postmark and addressed to him in Paris:

> Well Lutcher I am surprised at you in writing to me of the ladies' form and the remarks you make on the subject. You have always said you were very proud of my being a "modest girl." It seems to me you ought to think enough of me to appreciate it. . . . I can't think the same of you . . . to save me, when you do that way. And if you want to write that kind of letters you must find a *girl that it interests*. I will not stand for *any boy* to talk to *me that way*.

"Amen!" she added, for good measure.[133] The sixteen-year-old Nita Hill was proving that she could give as good as she got.

Notwithstanding hurdles, large and small, the romance flourished. In the summer of 1908, after Nita's graduation from Whitis Private School in Austin and just before she entered the university as a freshman, a new, more intimate tone appeared in her letters. That summer Lutcher remained in Orange for the first part of the summer but later traveled, this time within the United States: Toledo (where he left his automobile at the Pope Manufacturing Company), Buffalo, New York, and Boston.[134]

Nita, by then seventeen, wrote him in Orange on June 14 from Houston, where she was probably visiting with family or friends: "My Own Dear Lutcher . . . I surely miss you," she declared. "Can't you . . . run up someday to see me? . . . I would rather see you alone. Don't say *jealousy* for it is not. You might say *selfishness*. It is not that either. Can you guess what it is?" She closed with "lots of love and kisses, I am your devoted little girl, Nita." She wrote a day later: "I don't believe you could possibly love me as I love you. You are so dear and sweet to me."[135] Apparently, at that point, tiffs and scoldings were forgotten, and matters between them were serious indeed.

Beginning in the fall of 1908, she and Lutcher Stark attended the University of Texas together, where she pledged Pi Beta Phi sorority. On May 17, 1910, in her sophomore year, she was elected queen of the Varsity Circus.[136] The votes for the queen cost a penny each, and the major contributor to her campaign was undoubtedly Lutcher. The university's yearbook, the 1910 *Cactus*, proclaimed her "the Regnant Queen of Beauty," reporting that "at the last moment, Miss Nita Hill triumphantly swept the polls and was declared Queen of the Varsity's Fair." He had apparently made another such contribution earlier; an article in a 1911 California newspaper reported that, two years previously, he had contributed $500 to Nita's campaign in a campus contest for "the most popular girl," a benefit for the athletic fund. "His fiancée," the paper announced, "was finally elected."[137]

Even in the midst of his newfound obsession with the world of the University of Texas, Lutcher Stark did not lose touch with his powerful, all-pervading family roots. He stood at the front door to receive the guests at the home of his parents in Orange in December 1906 when Miriam and William Stark celebrated their twenty-fifth wedding anniversary with a gala party. The house—named "The Elms," according to a local newspaper—and gardens were decorated to a "fairy-like brilliancy." A double row of incandescent lights enclosed in multicolored Japanese "gloves" lined each side of the front walk from door to street, and the interior rooms were decorated with arrangements of pink roses, pink carnations, and white chrysanthemums. The veranda was enclosed with canvas and bedecked with palms, affording a retreat for smokers and "those who were fond of cozy corners." A harp ensemble played at the head of the stairs on the second floor, surrounded by a "bower of palms."[138]

In the parlor, the receiving party—Frances Ann Lutcher, Miriam and William Stark, and Carrie and Edgar Brown—greeted the hundreds of guests, who were served a "two-course luncheon" culminating with ice cream and cake, the ice cream molded into the shape of carnations. Each guest was given a souvenir: the women received a sterling silver bonbon spoon, and the men, a sterling silver pencil, each engraved with the dates of the marriage and anniversary and the monogram "S." Ida Achenbach's daughter, Helen, and Julia Russell Moss (the daughter of Robert B. Russell, William Stark's former employer) both sang to hearty applause and demands for encores.[139] Family friend Charles E. Keppler gave a rhymed toast, which read in part:

> Once on a time . . . a young man went on a lark,
> That the stamp of truth this tale doth bear
> We'll give his name as Stark.
> 'Tis told his forte was making love;
> I wasn't here, although
> It has been said by all the girls
> He made an ideal beau.
> With one fair lady he was bold
> And said: "I love you mucher";
> To doubly stamp this story true,
> We'll give her name as "Lutcher."
> 'Tis five and twenty years and more
> These two have plighted troth,
> And we have come with loving hearts
> To congratulate them both."[140]

Whatever the verses might have lacked in literary merit, their sentiments were beyond reproach.

Another of Lutcher Stark's college essays, this time with his father the subject, painted a vivid picture of William Stark:

> [My father] is a rather large, stout man. . . . He has a full, merry, brown face, whose lower portion is hidden by a long, raven beard and mustache, which part in the middle when he faces the wind, each part flying over his shoulders. He often laughingly threatens to either cut it off or to paste it together with tangle-foot,[141] but of course does neither. His steady brown eyes are large, laughing,

and well set, and really snap with the fire of determination when he is up against some hard problem. . . . He has a broad, high forehead which we, on account of his bald pate, tell him, extends to the back of his head. He has tried all manner of means to fill up this "vacant patch," as he calls it, but in vain. At last he has laughingly decided that the Lord didn't intend for him to have any hair on his head . . . from his hat to the shoes on his well shaped feet, he is scrupulously neat. And, with his good-humored but strong face and portly frame he makes quite a striking figure.[142]

No less eloquent was his description of his father's character:

As any one could tell you, and as his own life shows, his business ability is wonderful. He started out in life as a farmer's boy who, at ten years of age, made the living for his seventeen brothers and sisters, while his father was away in the war. [During that time, William Stark had only six siblings.] He then "road the mail," from that he became a lumber mill-hand. Next he kept store and a livery stable. . . . It was at this time that he married my mother, a Yankee girl, just come from the north. After some time as a store keeper, he returned to the lumber business with my grandfather, and worked up to what he is now.

One thing that has aided him in his career is his high standard of honor. It was this standard that put him and the firms [the business concerns] upon their high footing. . . . His slowness to anger and cool headedness has done him worlds of good. He does not fly up at the little things which happen everyday, but when he does get angry someone hears from him, though not as from a raging lion, but as from a clear-headed man. And when he has had his say, he is over it, with no hard feelings remaining.[143]

Lutcher Stark added a telling comment: "I don't know that I ever saw anyone who has more love for his family than he. Coupled with this is his *generosity* to them. Not a thing do they ask for, or even mention, that he does not procure for them. . . . [My father] is tender hearted," he went on, "but with all he can tell a deserving person at once, and frauds need never apply."[144] Lutcher's essay constituted a powerful, loving portrait of an admirable human being, who was also his father.

In the meantime, family dynamics were shifting with the passage of time, the development of the business interests, and Henry Lutcher's illness. Frances Ann Lutcher had always been a strong-minded individual who was thoroughly conversant with her husband's business affairs, and he had consulted her throughout their married life on matters of importance; now she was emerging as a dominant personality in her own

Figure 5.18. Frances Ann Lutcher (*second from left*) and Miriam Stark (*right*)
at Roslyn Ranch in Rand, Colorado, with family and friends. Stark Foundation Archives.

right, capable of making her own shrewd decisions and maintaining an
active role in the family's business interests. Even though the 1901 deed
donating Henry Lutcher's half interest in the northern portion of the old
Lutcher & Moore mill site to South Williamsport and the 1907 deed giving
his half interest in the southern portion to the Episcopal Church had been
conducted in Henry's name, it had been in name only; it had been William Stark who had signed as Lutcher's attorney-in-fact, and it must have
been Frances Ann who planned the gift with Bedell Moore.

During those years, Frances Ann became an inveterate—and intrepid—traveler. She showed an early preference for the mountainous
beauty of Colorado; a photograph of a group visiting Cheyenne Canyon,
near Colorado Springs, in August 1898 shows Frances Ann posing with a
ten-year-old Lutcher Stark, the rugged mountain vistas in the background.
She returned to Colorado the following year and frequently thereafter.[145]
She finally gratified her yen for the mountains on August 15, 1907, by concluding the purchase of Roslyn Ranch, a 560-acre tract of scenic terrain
in Rand, Colorado, north of Denver near Estes Park, and the Lutcher and

Figure 5.19. Lutcher Stark (*left*) and William Stark after a hunt at Roslyn Ranch.
Stark Foundation Archives.

Stark families began a tradition of summering at the ranch that continued
for many decades to come.[146]

The year 1908 saw two events of some significance for the family. Gregory Bedell Moore, Henry Lutcher's longtime friend and former partner and another giant of the lumber industry, died October 14 in Santa
Barbara, California, following complications from a long illness and
emergency hernia surgery.[147] After the Lutcher-Stark-Brown interests had
bought him out at the turn of the century, Moore had returned to his home
in San Antonio to recover his health and adjust to his new status as a widower. On recuperating, he had reentered the lumber business, purchasing a mill in Polk County, Texas, and renaming it the "Hilgard Lumber
Company" after his long-deceased son. In San Antonio, he had also built
a six-story office building, the Moore Building, "the handsomest and most
modern building in the city," and acquired ownership of another, the Riverside Building.[148] He had served as president and principal owner of the
Laredo Electric and Railway Company in Laredo and Nuevo Laredo and as
president and sole owner of the Val Verde Irrigation Company in Del Rio,
Texas. The latter innovation transformed thousands of acres of arid soil of

the South Texas brush country into productive farmland. As one editorial commented, "Inactivity does not suit [Mr. Moore's] temperament."[149]

Moore was also granted an added—and unexpected—measure of happiness. In September 1904, while on vacation in Lake Tahoe, he had the good fortune to meet Elizabeth Blasdel from San Jose, California, a secretary and music teacher at the State Normal School. She was thirty-one years his junior. At Tahoe they began to spend time together—boating, riding, walking, or sitting on the rocks overlooking the lake. In her third-person sketch of Moore's life, Elizabeth recounted the course of their May-December romance: "an *interest* more than mere friendship developed." After his return to San Antonio and Elizabeth's return to San Jose, correspondence followed and the *interest* quickly ripened into love. "Mr. Moore again came to California in Dec. 1904 & on Christmas Day, 1904, the engagement troth was plighted."[150]

Elizabeth Blasdel and Bedell Moore were married April 12, 1905, at the home of her sister in Sacramento, California. According to newspaper accounts, the bride wore a champagne-colored gown and orange blossoms in her hair. Her only ornament was Moore's gift to her, "an exquisite brooch of diamonds, representing a spray of lilies of the valley." On their honeymoon the newlyweds traveled to Niagara Falls and Quebec, but Bedell Moore grew ill toward the end of the trip, suffering from "a very weak heart & a peculiar fullness of the head." They cut the journey short, reaching home in San Antonio that October.[151]

Moore recovered sufficiently to organize the West Texas Bank and Trust Company of San Antonio and to serve as its first president, but he never fully regained his strength. In December 1907 Elizabeth gave birth to a son, Gregory Bedell Moore Jr. The senior Moore's health deteriorated steadily, and on doctor's orders, the Moore family traveled in 1908 to California, where his health continued to decline. Sometime in late summer or early fall of that year, he entered Miradero Sanitarium in Santa Barbara, where he died October 8.[152]

Moore's funeral service was held at St. Mark's Episcopal Church in San Antonio; Episcopal bishop J.S. Johnston gave the eulogy. William Stark was named as an honorary pallbearer.[153] Moore's body was then transported to Williamsport, where he was buried beside his first wife, Alice Clements Moore, and his children, Hilgard and Julia Grant "Pearlie" Moore, in Wildwood Cemetery. Serving as a pallbearer in Williamsport was Henry Lutcher's brother, Albert.[154] After the services were concluded, Moore's brother, S. Grant Moore, sent a telegram to his widow, Elizabeth, who had been too weak, presumably from grief, to make the trek to Williamsport: "Bedell rests in Wildwood."[155]

Moore left an estate worth $3 million and at least $70,000 to various charities, including Episcopal churches in San Antonio, Orange, and Williamsport as well as the Orphans' Home, the YMCA, and the West Texas Military Academy in San Antonio. At the time of his death, he was in the process of building a church in Williamsport as a memorial to his father, Rev. Richard Channing Moore, on the old mill site he and Henry Lutcher had given to Christ Episcopal Church.[156] A Williamsport newspaper named him "one of the most prominent churchmen and public benefactors in the history of the city."[157] And in San Antonio, members of the city's Associated Charities adopted a resolution that read, in part, "His generous nature and love of fellow man stamped him at once as a philanthropist and public-spirited citizen. . . . We mourn the death of one who was near and dear to all who knew and appreciated his generous and lovable nature."[158]

The second significant event of 1908 pertained not to the past but the future. On December 8, Lutcher Stark turned twenty-one. Under the protective sponsorship of his father and his maternal grandmother, he was already being groomed to take his place in the family business interests, and for his birthday that year, his Lutcher grandparents gave him $1,000, which they had promised him as a young boy if he refrained from using tobacco. William Stark wrote his son:

My Dear Boy . . . I wish you many happy returns of the birthday and enclose your deposit slip showing that your Grandpapa and Mamoosie had deposited in the First National Bank of Orange to your credit—the thousand dollars promised you when you were a little tot if you did not use tobaco, and we are proud to think you had will power enough to refrain from the use of it.—While your grandfather and myself both use it—and are hardly the ones to advise you not to do so it would please us all if you never used it.[159]

In spite of the family's hopes, Lutcher Stark became a lifelong cigarette smoker.

William appended a few words of caution, probably in view of Lutcher's serious relationship with Nita Hill and their extreme youth (in December 1908, Nita had just turned eighteen and Lutcher was twenty-one):

Now my son while you are of age and practically free you are all we have and we hope to have you with us for a good long time yet. You will never know until after you are married and have children of your own, and I hope you will not be in a hurry about this—how much a parent loves their child. Not that I don't approve of marriage I think every one should get married, but I think one should wait long enough to be sure of the love of his or her life partners love. I hope to love your wife when you do marry as I would my own daughter.[160]

William hinted that a larger gift was on the way:

As for your Mothers and my part of the contract we will reserve that until Christmas Morning as we hope to all be together then. . . . Your Mother and myself expect to fix you in that you will have money to have your own [illegible] from this time on. What we have accumulated will be yours some day, but I don't want you to have to start against the world as I had to and I don't want you to have to ask someone for money when you want to buy anything.[161]

He added a further word of caution, born of his own experience:

And above all I don't want you to be a spendthrift—I realize the fact that starting you out this way that you will not know so well the value of a dollar like you would if you started like I did without a penny. Still I give you credit of being levelheaded, and your travels over the country should of broadened you enough for you to be able to guard your own interests. With a heart full of love, I am your loving Dad W. H. Stark.[162]

William was as good as his word. "My Dear Boy," he wrote that Christmas Eve of 1908, "accept these stocks as a gift—from your Mother and Me if you keep a level head they will bring you enough in the way of dividends to Meet your wants and then some, with it—we wish you a long prosperous and happy life Mama and Papa."[163] Accompanying the letter was a substantial gift of various stocks, including forty shares of Lutcher & Moore Lumber Company.[164] Lutcher Stark would attain his majority financially well equipped for the future.

William Stark also influenced a major part of his son's life, this time by example: In January 1911, he accepted an appointment to the Board of Regents of the University of Texas.[165] He served only four years, but Lutcher Stark assumed a board position beginning in 1919 and served nearly twenty-four years, twelve of them as chairman.[166]

Lutcher Stark graduated from the University of Texas in 1910 with a bachelor of arts degree, and he and Nita Hill were married April 5, 1911, at the University Methodist Church in Austin.[167] He was twenty-three, and she was twenty. The invitation lists for wedding and reception included Texas' newly elected governor, Oscar Branch Colquitt; the Hogg siblings, Mike, Will, and Ima; US representative and Lake Charles lawyer Arsène P. Pujo and his wife, Augusta (the sister and brother-in-law of Edgar Brown);

Figure 5.20. Nita Hill as Lutcher Stark's bride, 1911. Stark Foundation Archives.

and lumbermen Leopold Miller of Orange and J. Frank Keith of Beaumont, as well as many other prominent families from all over the state.[168] Separate invitations were sent to Lutcher Stark's maternal grandparents, one to Frances Ann in Orange and another to Henry in care of "College Hill Sanitarium, Cincinnati, Ohio."[169]

According to Nita, Lutcher was late to his own wedding because of an

eccentricity of his—the habit, lifelong and apparently inviolable, of carrying a pair of pliers in his back pocket. At the church, he discovered that he
had forgotten the pliers and felt compelled to go back to retrieve them.[170]
He later quipped, "I got the habit when I was a kid and ran motor boats
on the Sabine River. . . . I have worn out more pants with pliers in the hip
pockets than with money in the side pockets."[171] The ceremony and reception duly took place, and the following May 8, his Mamoose, Frances
Ann, gave a gala reception and dance at the Holland Hotel for "Mr. and
Mrs. Lutcher Stark" to introduce the young couple to Orange.[172] With the
marriage to Nita and the resulting ties with the University of Texas' quin-
tessential family, the Hills, Lutcher Stark's immersion in the University of
Texas world was, for the time being, complete.

The year 1912 marked several milestones. The Stark interests constructed an imposing new two-story office building on Front Street
in downtown Orange as headquarters for their rapidly expanding business enterprises, while the Lutcher & Moore Lumber Company mills and
offices remained in their existing location a short distance downriver. In
many ways, the new building signified William Stark's assumption of the
reins.[173]

On December 22, the octagonal Victorian-style Lutcher & Moore office building burned to the ground. The *Enterprise* announced, "The
Lutcher & Moore Lumber Company's handsome two-story office building, together with the bulk of its contents, went up in smoke shortly after 5 o'clock this morning. . . . The company will rebuild its office where
the old one was burned down but in the meantime the company has established temporary offices in the second story of the new Stark Building on
Front Street."[174]

The loss of the offices necessitated construction of another landmark,
the new offices for Lutcher & Moore, "a remarkable Mission-style edifice," as noted modern-day architectural historian Peter Flagg Maxson described it, "featuring a tile hipped roof and curvilinear 'Alamotif' para-
pets reminiscent of the 1850s façade of the Alamo . . . more evocative of
large residences of the day than commercial buildings." The new building
fronted the Sabine River. Over the main entrance was placed a bronze me-
dallion bearing the company's emblem, the Star and Crescent. Except for
details, the new Lutcher & Moore office would be completed by September 1913.[175]

The other milestone of 1912 was the death of Henry Jacob Lutcher in
Cincinnati after an illness of more than a decade. His passing marked a
watershed, not only for his family but also for the Lutcher & Moore Lumber Company, the Southeast Texas business communities, and the en-

Figure 5.21. The 1912 Mission-style offices of Lutcher & Moore, built after
the octagonal office building burned. Stark Foundation Archives.

tire southern lumber industry. Sometime around September 22, Henry
Lutcher had suffered a "stroke of paralysis." His condition rapidly worsened, and members of his immediate family—Frances Ann, Miriam and
William Stark, and Carrie Brown—traveled to Cincinnati. They were gathered at his bedside when he died at 9:35 a.m. on October 2, a little over a
month shy of his seventy-sixth birthday.[176] The cause of death was listed
as "Cerebral Haemorrhage," and the contributory cause as *"Dementia
Senila."*[177]

On October 5, Lutcher's body was sent by train to his residence on the
Sabine River in his adopted home of Orange, there to lie overnight, visited
by family, friends, and employees.[178] The next morning at 10:30 a.m., he
was taken to the magnificent new Lutcher Memorial Presbyterian Church,
funded by Frances Ann, built under her loving personal supervision, and
dedicated the previous January 28.[179] There, "hundreds of friends looked
in the face of the man of great accomplishments for the last time."[180]

The funeral service, "perhaps the largest ever witnessed in Orange,"
was held in the Presbyterian Church at 4:00 p.m. on October 6. Reverend
E.T. Drake, long a family friend of the Lutchers, presided.[181] The casket
was then borne to the Lutcher mausoleum in Evergreen Cemetery, where

the Reverend Drake made closing remarks and the choir sang "Nearer, My God, to Thee."[182] More than eight hundred of his present and former employees and dozens of prominent lumbermen from Southeast Texas and across the state attended his services, and every business in Orange closed out of respect.[183]

Accolades for Henry Jacob Lutcher were legion. One account noted that he "left a colossal fortune, a wide reputation for probity of character and an unsullied name, which will stand for all time as an illustration of what can be accomplished by a combination of pluck, energy and perseverance." Another hailed him as "a proficient and interesting conversationalist upon all the varying themes of general knowledge."[184] The directors of the First National Bank of Orange composed a memorial to its founder and first president:

> The past comes back and in the mist, familiar forms appear; the forms we honored and the faces we had learned to love. Once more around the council table do they gather, these heroes of our struggles, our companions and our friends; and he is there; the form, the features, yea, the man—the man of yesterday; But the call of life knocks at the door, the day dream dies, the vision fades. We brush away a tear and bow to the way and will of God. The shaft we rear today, tomorrow falls; but deeds live on, and in the after years, when strangers come, on them will fall the influence of his life, a life well spent; a life to guide the yet unborn.[185]

According to Williamsport's *Gazette and Bulletin*, "the people of Williamsport in general and those of South Williamsport in particular learned with profound regret of the death of Henry Jacob Lutcher. Mr. Lutcher has done much for the South Side and will ever be held in grateful remembrance." The article added, "[Mr. Lutcher] and his family have always kept in close touch with this city and they frequently visited here."[186]

Perhaps Lutcher's friend and business associate Frederick Henry Farwell, by then general manager and later vice president of Lutcher & Moore, who served as one of Lutcher's pallbearers, said it best: "He was a lumberman of the highest caliber, was a wide traveler, a deep student, a logical reasoner, and a man with whom to associate was a liberal education. He possessed a fine library, of which he made frequent use, and with it all was a man who viewed his country and its interests as paramount to every other factor in life."[187] Later, Miriam commented sadly, "The poor Dear was much better off & out of his suffering."[188]

Henry Lutcher's will left to Frances Ann their homestead, furnishings, horses, cattle, buggies, carriages, and other household goods; she also retained her half of their community property. He left one-half of his community share of their Texas property to Miriam and one-half to Carrie, but he left the Louisiana property to all three—Frances Ann, Miriam, and Carrie—in equal thirds (apparently in error but never corrected).[189]

On October 15, 1912, thirteen days after his death, Frances Ann Lutcher, William and Miriam Stark, and Carrie and Edgar Brown all signed a document ratifying and validating the power of attorney Lutcher had given to William Stark on January 6, 1898; because "some question exists," the ratification stated,

> as to the extent of the powers conferred by said power of attorney and to the rights of the said W.H. Stark to execute all the instruments executed by him thereunder, and it is desired by the undersigned to forever set at rest and quiet and make valid and binding all things done under and by virtue of said power of attorney by the said W.H. Stark . . . each and every act of whatever kind or character done or performed by the said W.H. Stark as attorney in fact for H.J. Lutcher.[190]

At the January 20, 1913, board meeting of Lutcher & Moore, on Lutcher Stark's motion and Edgar Brown's second, William Stark was elected president of the company.[191] At that time, at least, Frances Ann and the Stark and Brown families stood in complete accord.

CHAPTER SIX

Over There

You all have been doing wonderful work "over there," and we are proud of all of you.
—FRANCES ANN LUTCHER TO CPL. MALCOLM W. PEARCE,
"SOMEWHERE IN FRANCE," OCTOBER 24, 1918

S oon after their wedding, Lutcher and Nita Stark came back to Orange to begin their lives together. Although still very young, they were already armed with ample financial means, thanks in large part to Miriam and William's generous Christmas gift in 1908. And since the family had begun early to bring Lutcher into its business interests, he had been a "director of a bank, a saw mill, a paper factory and several other industries" since his college days.[1] Nita found herself on the threshold of a new world. Even though her family had certainly not lacked for essentials, Nita, with her marriage into the Stark clan, entered the realm of the very wealthy. She dealt with her new circumstances with qualities apparently innate to her; she was reported to be "beautiful in person, gracious in manner, generous and loving in her family and her friends."[2]

When the young couple returned to Orange, Miriam and William Stark offered them "a city block" for a home site, according to one writer, but Lutcher declined, declaring to his parents that "we're not peacocks," and lent the land to the city for use as a park.[3] The young Starks chose to live in a large two-story, ten-room bungalow on the southeast corner of Tenth and Pine Streets, which they eventually furnished with treasures garnered through the years—antiques, paintings, Meissen and Dresden porcelain, miniatures, ornamental silver and glass, rare books, a Steinway grand piano, and Persian rugs.[4] Nita enjoyed a warm relationship with her in-laws, whom she adored and who seemed to return her affections wholeheartedly.[5]

Like most young couples, Nita and Lutcher hoped for children. In the spring of 1913 Nita traveled to New York with Frances Ann, lodging at the family's customary accommodation, the Waldorf Astoria. While there, Nita bought over $400 worth of baby clothes and accessories—gowns, shirts, bootees, diapers, wrappers—from Best & Company, a well-known children's clothing store.[6] She either suspected, or knew, that a baby was on the way, or perhaps her purchases merely represented her hopes, but she did become pregnant around that time. Predictably, the news gener-

Figure 6.1. Nita Hill Stark, young adulthood, undated. Stark Foundation Archives.

Figure 6.2. The house at Tenth and Pine Streets in Orange, where Nita and Lutcher Stark spent their entire married life. Stark Foundation Archives.

ated much excitement among the family and their friends. "Nita looks so well," an Austin acquaintance of Miriam's wrote, "and we all are so happy for her."[7] Elizabeth Howd (from whom Frances Ann had bought Roslyn Ranch in Colorado and who was still serving as the ranch's care-taker) wrote Frances Ann from the ranch: "I was awfully disappointed to hear Nita would not be at the ranch as she is always a pleasure to me but was delighted to hear the cause—no home is complete without those gifts of God children and I know too it will enrich Mrs. [Miriam] Stark's life. I dare say you remember how you felt when Lutcher and Mrs. [Fannie Brown] Moore were born."[8]

Nita, Lutcher, and Miriam traveled to Austin to be with her parents during the baby's birth, affording them the additional reassurance of Dr. Hill's medical expertise. "I am so sorry you were not able to come [to Austin] to-day but it is best as you think to have someone at the head of things at home," Miriam wrote William, at home in Orange. "I am afraid it will be some time before I can go home," she went on. "Mrs. H. [Nita's mother, Ella "Granny" Hill] seemed to think [the baby's birth] will be soon, but I think she is mistaken. Nita is looking so well," she added reas-suringly.[9] Noted poet and University of Texas scholar Jessie Andrews com-posed a short verse for Nita, "Little Mother Longing," made more poignant because of the pregnancy's sad denouement:[10]

Little mother longing for the child beneath thy heart,
Little mother waiting for the babe of thee a part,
Heavenly thoughts are thronging all about thy heart's deep longing,—
Heaven's holy angels guard thee, mother as thou art!

Little mother singing to the child beneath thy heart,
Lullabies are ringing for the babe of thee a part,
Heavenly songs thou'rt singing, all thy heart in love thou'rt bringing,—
God in heaven keep thee, bless thee, mother as thou art!

Little mother praying for the child beneath thy heart,
Little mother longing for thy babe of him a part,
Little mother praying heaven shall bring without delaying
Thine own child into thy arms, O mother as thou art![11]

Miriam had been right; the baby, a girl, was not born for another three weeks, arriving December 2 after a long, difficult labor.[12] Nita and Lutcher had chosen the name Frances Lutcher Stark. But they were to suffer grief and disappointment; the baby was stillborn. Nita again became pregnant in the last months of 1915, this time delivering a son on June 8, 1916.[13] This baby, whom they named Henry, lived only a few hours. Both babies were interred in the Lutcher mausoleum in Evergreen Cemetery in Orange. Their hopes buried with their infants, Nita and Lutcher would have no more biological children.

His grief notwithstanding, Lutcher Stark, now at the threshold of his adulthood, seemed to view the world as his proverbial oyster. Energetic, bright, self-confident, with a penchant for assuming command, he dreamed large, trying his wings in new ventures, some more successful than others and some outright failures. He continued to travel the path he had first struck during his college years, persisting in his sports interests and philanthropies to the University of Texas, for many years never missing a game played on Clark Field and very few anywhere else.[14]

One of his first significant gifts to his alma mater came soon after his graduation. In the early years, the university's teams had been called "Varsity," or "Steers," but in 1903, D.A. Frank, a writer for the *Daily Texan*, had informally coined the nickname "Longhorns." The moniker was informal, but in 1913, Lutcher made it official by donating orange blankets to the football team emblazoned in white with the words "Texas Longhorns" and a silhouette of the head of a Longhorn steer. His gift clinched the matter, ensuring the animal's enshrinement as the official mascot of the university.[15]

Figure 6.3. Lutcher Stark made official the University of Texas football team's nickname in 1913 by donating blankets with the words "Texas Longhorns" across the back. Courtesy of the H.J. Lutcher Stark Center for Physical Culture and Sports, University of Texas at Austin.

Lutcher Stark continued to give to the school on every level—gold baseballs and footballs for the "T Men" (athletes who lettered in university sports), benches and trophy cases for the gymnasium hall, individual lockers for the team members, mackinaws for the baseball team similar to those he had given the football squad, new uniforms for the Longhorn band (more than once).[16] He contributed substantially to the school's coaches' salaries, "thus enabl[ing] Texas to have the very best coaching system available," according to one sportswriter.[17] He helped send the tennis team to national tournaments. He was instrumental in building up the university's track program, awarding gold, silver, and bronze medals for the best work done in various events.[18] Ultimately, he assisted countless athletes and other students through college, finding them jobs in his family's business concerns or paying for their schooling outright.[19] He was eventually dubbed "the best little giver in the annals of the Varsity."[20] Once, when asked to list his gifts to the university, he refused—he had no intention of doing it, and in any event, such an inventory would have been impossible to compile.[21]

In that year of 1913, Lutcher also pursued another passion that had first been kindled during his college years: his own physical well-being. At a height of five feet eight inches,[22] he was not a tall man, and in adolescence and young adulthood he was overweight, at one point topping two hundred pounds. Now he traveled to Philadelphia to study with the leading expert in the field of weight lifting—or strength training, as it was also known—Alan Calvert, owner of the Milo Barbell Company.[23] Two months

Figure 6.4a. Lutcher Stark, showing weight gain during his young adulthood, undated. Stark Foundation Archives.

Figure 6.4b. Lutcher Stark, trim and muscular after undergoing a program in weight training and physical fitness. Stark Foundation Archives.

later, Lutcher returned, forty pounds lighter, much stronger, and with a new attitude toward the importance of physical fitness.[24]

The following year, he became the pupil of the world-renowned Lionel Strongfort (real name Max Unger), the founder of "Strongfortism," a worldwide mail-order strength-training course, and famed for his "Human Bridge" act—also known as the "Tomb of Hercules" position—which enabled a strong man to support great weights while positioned on his hands and knees.[25] (Lutcher was said to have employed the technique in performing his piano-supporting stunt.) "I welcome you now as my pupil on the Advanced Course and have pleasure in sending you herewith the first lesson," Strongfort wrote him November 28:

> I am starting you off with some strength building movements rather than feats of strength, for the purpose of preparing you for the actual feats of strength which you will get in your future lessons. These movements, of course, are to be taken with a barbell, and I would suggest a weight that you can handle without special difficulty, but which will be heavy enough to interest you intensely. That is to say, I do not wish you to strain yourself and yet I do not wish

to make the exercises too easy. In this way you will improve in strength. I think a weight of sixty pounds will be satisfactory to start with in your case.[26]

Lutcher Stark remained a devotee of physical fitness and athletics and continued strength training for most of his adult life. His long-term commitment eventually paid off; several years later, William's longtime private secretary and right-hand man, Douglas A. Pruter, wrote to William Stark in New York: "Lutcher reached home yesterday morning, it was necessary for me to look at him twice and hear him talk before I recognized him as he has reduced so much. Do not think he can reduce any more as there is nothing left but muscle which is as hard as steel."[27]

Somewhere around the time he began his weight-lifting program, Lutcher Stark met a young man named L. Theodore Bellmont, nicknamed "Theo," or "Ted," a native of Rochester, New York. Bellmont was an accomplished gymnast and athlete who had become the secretary of the Houston YMCA in 1908.[28] His capable work at the "Y" had attracted the attention of Sidney H. Mezes, then president of the University of Texas, and on Mezes's recommendation, the university's Board of Regents hired Bellmont in 1913 as the school's athletic director.[29] (William Stark was at that time serving as regent, and it is possible that, if Lutcher Stark had already met Bellmont, he had also recommended him to his father.)

As athletic director, Bellmont scored a series of impressive achievements, among them helping create the Southwest Conference in 1914 and 1915.[30] He also established the Department of Health and Physical Education at the university;[31] and in an era when the prevailing belief held that strength training would stiffen an athlete's muscles and consequently hamper movement—thus, becoming "muscle-bound"—he also incorporated the practice into the university's curriculum.[32] With their common interest in physical fitness, Theo Bellmont and Lutcher Stark enjoyed a long friendship; Lutcher took along his own barbells on his frequent trips to Austin in order to lift weights with Bellmont.[33] The two also became associates within the University of Texas realm, undertaking several extraordinary joint exploits to benefit the school. (Their friendship ultimately outlasted their university association.)[34]

Nor did Lutcher Stark neglect his home turf. In the early 1900s, Orange had hosted a baseball team called the Gray Eagles, and in the 1907 season no less a ball club than Connie Mack's Philadelphia Athletics had come to Orange to play the Eagles in West End Park, at the corner of Orange Avenue and Fifteenth Street.[35] (The outcome of the game is not recorded but was probably predictable.) Perhaps the arrival of the Philadelphia team inspired Lutcher to attempt a larger connection with big-league baseball; in 1914 he explored the possibility of establishing a major-league training

Figure 6.5. Lutcher Stark, young adulthood, undated. Stark Foundation Archives.

camp in Orange. Utilizing his prior experience as manager of the university teams, he wrote major-league ball clubs in New York, Cincinnati, Chicago, and St. Louis, among others, inviting them to establish training camps in Orange. He was met unanimously with courteous refusals. "Am not familiar with your town as a training quarter," the manager of the St. Louis Cardinals responded politely, "and in fact hardly think it is the intention of the Cardinals to go to Texas as we were in Florida last year and will probably return there next year."[36]

Undaunted, Lutcher benefited the teams of his own Orange High School several years later by building an athletic park with a baseball diamond, tennis court, and cinder track as well as allowing the teams the use of "his modern clubhouse situated on the grounds," which was "electrically lighted and equipped with hot and cold shower baths." The high school thanked him publicly for his generosity in its 1917 yearbook, the *Orange Peel.*

After the prescribed year of mourning for her husband, the indomitable Frances Ann Lutcher resumed her life, growing more independent by the year. Sometime in the first decade of the new century, she commissioned the noted Swiss portrait artist August Benziger, painter of such world figures as Theodore Roosevelt, Thomas Edison, Pope Leo XIII, and various figures of European royalty, to execute portraits of herself and members of her family.[37] (According to Benziger's daughter, Marieli, in her biography of her father, Frances Ann commissioned fourteen portraits in all, paying $2,500 each.)[38] Marieli reported that Frances Ann traveled to Cincinnati to meet him and was disappointed when he informed her that he would be unable to paint her portrait at that time, since he was about to leave for Europe and would not return for several months.[39] She then insisted that Benziger and his wife, Gertrude, visit her in Orange, and they finally accepted her invitation. Marieli described a hunting expedition Frances Ann staged there for their entertainment:

> In the back seat, flanked by her daughters, sat the elderly hostess, while [the daughters' husbands, William Stark and Edgar Brown,] sat forward with their guns in readiness to shoot. Never in his life had August seen so many pheasants and quail. In a very few hours the men had bagged hundreds. Protected by aprons, the women busily plucked the game in the back of the car while the hunt was in progress so that, when they all reached home, the feasting and celebration could begin at once.[40]

While in Orange, the Benzigers were shocked to learn that Frances Ann constantly received blackmail letters threatening to kidnap her, some demanding as much as $50,000; some, twice that amount. Benziger, believing that "this kindly old woman" needed a greater degree of protection in that untamed place, informed the "genial, placid" Miriam, as he referred to her, that if Frances Ann could afford to pay his portrait prices, she could certainly afford to hire private detectives to enhance her own safety. Miriam "listened passively" but did nothing, so Benziger resolved to take matters into his own hands if and when "Mamoose" (as her grandchildren, the Benzigers, and many others called her) ever came to Switzerland.[41]

According to Marieli, her father described Frances Ann as "this wrinkled little woman with snow-cap hair and with youthful agility," with a "remarkable wardrobe, planned especially for her and designed by a man from Texas named Neiman Marcus, a small-shop owner patronized solely by Texans."[42] Benziger often remarked that Frances Ann and her family were the best-dressed women he had ever seen,[43] and he marveled at her exquisite *point d'aguille* needlepoint dress, especially made for her in Belgium, which she chose to wear for her portrait.[44] She, Miriam, and William formed a close, lasting relationship with the Benzigers.[45] On his deathbed, Benziger named Frances Ann as one of his favorite clients: "Old Mrs. Lutcher, my greatest benefactress!" he declared. "She paid me my highest prices, never asking for discounts."[46]

Sometime around 1910, at seventy years of age, the energetic Frances Ann purchased a brown Pierce-Arrow touring car,[47] and that year she; her chauffeur, Herbert Fiedler; Ida Achenbach; and Ida's daughter Helen motored to Austin. The *Beaumont Journal* reported that "they figure to make the trip in three days."[48] She later acquired a second Pierce-Arrow, this one to travel behind the first, carrying "picks, poles, shovels, extra tires, 100 feet of wire cable and other incidentals which have heretofore proved necessary in emergencies." This second car was driven by one of Fiedler's brothers, while yet another brother accompanied the party as an emergency hand. Both cars were equipped to convert into tents if the travelers were caught on the road at nightfall. Frances Ann toured extensively in Europe, sometimes transporting her automobiles and her entire party across the Atlantic via steamship, other times traveling by rail, visiting England, France, Germany, Austria, Holland, Switzerland, and Italy, among other places, crossing the Alps a total of three times, and attending the Passion Play in Oberammergau, Germany.[49]

Fiedler later asserted that Frances Ann actually preferred travel in America; she toured most of the western and northwestern United States and crossed the Mojave Desert by automobile. The two-car caravan, the front vehicle sometimes doughtily flying Old Glory, survived many adventures: navigating high-altitude mountain roads and deep gulches; fording rivers and washouts; and being hauled, probably by oxen or mules, through miles of deep sand. Motoring in Oregon, they encountered roads two feet deep in dust, with holes ten feet across. The citizens of one town saw them approaching from a distance "and exclaimed at the appearance they made." Once the big passenger car slid down an embankment, causing a half-hour delay. ("No one was hurt and the car was not damaged," Fiedler reported.) Frances Ann even traveled to Nome, Alaska, by boat, leaving the cars in Seattle for the duration of her trip.[50]

Besides her treks to Roslyn Ranch every summer, Frances Ann traveled most often to New York, making the trip nearly every year, sometimes

Figure 6.6. Frances Ann Lutcher in front seat of her Pierce-Arrow touring car, driven by her chauffeur, Herbert Fiedler. Back seat from left: Ida and Helen Achenbach. Stark Foundation Archives.

Figure 6.7. Frances Ann Lutcher (*bottom row, fifth from left*) on a tour of Crystal Park, Colorado, July 1912. Stark Foundation Archives.

by automobile, sometimes by rail.[51] Miriam frequently traveled with her, as did Ida and Helen Achenbach. Miriam's letters to William during one such trip to New York in 1913 afford a glimpse of some intimate family dynamics. The correspondence reveals that both Frances Ann and Miriam were inveterate shoppers—in New York, Paris, Chicago, Philadelphia, and other cities. (When Miriam prepared for a trip, the staff at the Stark offices joked, "Get the money ready, boys. Mrs. W.H. is going to New York.")[52] Mother and daughter also got into occasional spats.[53] William might have been the master of a vast business domain, but it was apparently Miriam who commanded the home realm.

"My Dear William," she wrote from New York October 7, firing a rapid series of questions to him regarding current happenings in Orange: "Has Mr. Duffy finished [repairs to] the house? Have the trees grown much? . . . Are the rice and sweet potatoes all ruined [by a recent flood]? What is Mr. Duffy doing to Nita's & Lutcher's home? . . . Now if you have not written all about the things[,]" she added, "I ask you to do so at once." And in a reversal from their courtship, when William had scolded her for the infrequency of her letters, his occasional lapses in regular correspondence annoyed her. "You know of course that I sent a telegram to Mr. Farwell asking if he had heard from you," she fretted. "Why did you neglect to wire me that you were delayed?"[54] "Did they have no writing materials in Austin [where William was possibly attending to regents' business]?" she demanded in another letter. "I have had no letter for three days." "This is the fourth day without a letter," she complained in still another. "What is the matter? Have you no more paper down there?"[55]

In spite of the directives and scoldings she occasionally aimed at her husband, Miriam's letters reflect her enduring affection for him; as if to mitigate her imperative, sometimes petulant tone, she expressed her love at the end of every letter and telegram. "With much love from your loving wife, Miriam Stark," read a typical sign-off. She frequently ended them with a closing used by both of them through the years: "with oceans of love."[56] A card to him, "I hope it isn't foolish / Or breaking any laws, / To send a word of greeting / To you—well, just because," was signed simply, "I love you, Miriam."[57]

Miriam worried constantly about her weight and frequently went to fittings at corset-makers, and she was not free from those concerns even on vacation. "I have started a course of electric treatments to take that fat off my back," she wrote William from New York, "for with the new low corsets it just simply rolls over the top. The doctor thinks he can reduce me ten pounds in as many days." The doctor ordered a diet for her—predictably, dry toast, eggs, grapefruit, roast beef, chicken breasts, selected vegetables, saccharine instead of sugar. After a dinner party at the Benzigers' residence in New York, she wrote: "I of course did not enjoy the good things to

Figure 6.8. Miriam Lutcher Stark, prime of life, undated. Stark Foundation Archives.

eat so well for there are so few things I can eat. . . . I wonder if it is worth the self denial."[58]

Frances Ann, Miriam, and Ida habitually attended the theater while visiting New York, and Miriam filled her letters with news of the plays and musicals they were seeing, which starred many of the famous actors and actresses of the day. In her letter of October 7 Miriam wrote William that the next day they would attend a performance of *Hamlet*, starring Sir Johnston Forbes-Robertson in his most famous role, and later she informed him that they had seen popular opera singer Christie MacDonald in the operetta she had made popular, Victor Herbert's *Sweethearts*.[59]

Sometimes the indefatigable Frances Ann exhausted her daughter; Miriam complained that her mother wanted and expected to go to the theater every night, while she, Miriam, consequently "accomplished nothing." During a later automobile trip from the ranch through Nebraska, Iowa, Illinois, and Indiana, Miriam wrote in exasperation, "I am tired of going until dark every day. Mother talks of not being rushed but she can no more help it than breathing." In Austin awaiting Nita's confinement with her first pregnancy, Miriam perfectly captured Frances Ann's nature: "Do you know where Mother is?" she wrote William. "It seems to me that I ought to have had a letter from her."[60]

Throughout their travels, Frances Ann maintained her vaunted independence; the woman who had traversed mountain passes, forded rivers, and crossed the Mojave Desert in a touring car would not be thwarted by anyone. "Mother . . . is pouting," Miriam wrote William October 17, 1913:

> She has been riding in the front seat [of her Pierce-Arrow, with the chauffeur] & I asked her not to, telling her it looked strange when there was plenty room in the back for her to ride there. Of course it made her angry and she declared she would do as she pleased, so I told her I would go to another Hotel & not ride with her. She replied I could go if I wanted, she intended to do as she pleased.[61]

In spite of their periodic disagreements, Miriam loved travel as much as her mother did and the previous summer had realized a lifelong dream. She had crossed the Atlantic to make her first visit to Europe, traveling with William, Frances Ann, Ida Achenbach, and Gertrude and August Benziger and their children, who were returning from their New York residence to their home in Brunnen, Switzerland. The group also toured Holland, Germany, Austria, Italy, and France, remaining in Europe a full three months from May 27 until the latter part of August 1913.[62]

By virtue of her reading, study, and well-cultivated interests, Miriam was entering a world already familiar and natural to her, and she could scarcely contain her excitement. Aboard the SS *Rotterdam* en route to Holland, she and Ida spotted another ship headed back toward New York. "Aunt Ida [Achenbach] said [the ship] was going home," Miriam rhapsodized in her travel diary. "I replied 'Let it go I am . . . having the wish of my life I am going abroad. . . . Mother is a splendid sailor,' she added, 'never seeming to be lightheaded or sick at all.'" On their arrival in Rotterdam, her elation still bubbled over: "And now the one dream of my life has come true," she wrote again. "I am abroad and I intend to enjoy every minute of my trip."[63]

She wrote poetically, knowledgeably, and lovingly of all the beautiful things she was seeing—manuscripts and books, libraries, paintings, stained-glass windows, statuary, textiles, gardens, vistas, architecture, anything that appealed to her aesthetic sense—showing a deep insight and a breadth of scholarship regarding nature, history, art, and architecture unusual in an individual of her gender and era. Viewing manuscripts in a Zurich museum, she indulged the interest that would become closest to her heart: "I was especially interested in the old books," she wrote, "some of them beautifully illuminated." The performing arts also received due attention; in Munich, the group attended a performance of Wagner's *Die Walküre*, and later, when they reached Venice, they heard a duet from Verdi's *Rigoletto*, sung by a soprano and a tenor from a boat afloat on the Grand Canal.[64]

When they reached Switzerland, the travelers stopped briefly in Einsiedeln, August's birthplace and the ancestral home of the Benziger family,[65] and paid a longer visit to August and Gertrude when they all arrived in Brunnen, where August had built a luxury hotel on land that had belonged to his father.[66] The Grand Hotel, as it was called, attracted the rich, famous, and aristocratic from Europe and America, including the daughter of the maharajah of Lahore (who, while there, sat for her portrait by Benziger).[67] "I cannot fully describe the beauty of this place," Miriam declared, praising the hotel's gardens and the vistas of lakes and snowcapped mountains. "The hotel is all one could wish for," she went on, "everything perfectly clean and in perfect taste. . . . Altogether it would be hard to find a more comfortable place to spend a month or two."[68]

They established their base of operations in Brunnen, from which they made several short tours into Italy—Venice, Verona, Milan, Turin—and then returned to Brunnen before heading for France. On the way from Lucerne to Paris, Miriam found her language skills helpful. "This was the first time we had been alone since we arrived in Europe & we felt like veritable babes in the woods," she wrote. "Still we got along very well with my little knowledge of French and German."[69]

In August, the travelers returned to Brunnen for a last visit with the

Benzigers, who took them through the Great St. Bernard Pass to visit the ancient hospice, famed for its breed of rescue dogs. They arrived in pouring rain and were taken to a stone hall "that one would never hesitate one instant to know was the home of dogs," as Miriam delicately put it. They were then taken to an upper hall (where Miriam noted that the odor was somewhat less noticeable) and given a hot meal and a "very comfortable room & very well furnished," including beds with clean linen.[70] The next day they were taken to see the dogs, in particular one older dog that had assisted in saving a hundred lives, and afterward, to Miriam's great interest, viewed the monastery's twenty thousand–volume library. Although Miriam made no mention of it in her diary, Marieli Benziger related that her father made good his resolve by obtaining two St. Bernard puppies from the hospice "to guard the life of Mamoose." "Once [the dogs] arrived in Texas," Marieli reported, "their protective presence was felt immediately and the threats of the local terrorists ceased, although one wonders what terrors the dogs experienced in the transfer from the chill of the Alps to the heat and humidity of Texas."[71]

On August 19 they headed north to Berlin. In nearby Potsdam, at Sanssouci, the summer palace of Frederick the Great, Miriam saw the largest collection of Peter Paul Rubens paintings she had ever seen in one gallery. There, she also saw works by another artist: the seventeenth-century Dutch painter Gerrit Dou, who had been a student in Rembrandt's workshop. "There were some there by Dou, Rembrandt's master," she noted in her diary, "who painted the beautiful picture of R.'s mother in one of the Holland galleries."[72] The Stark family later acquired at least one work by Gerrit Dou.[73]

By journey's end, her cultural horizons must have been broadened considerably and her tastes sharpened and focused. These European influences proved to be at the heart of her collector's bent for the rest of her life. Her diary ended in Berlin on August 27, 1913, when the travelers made their way homeward to Texas. But on their way to Berlin, they made a short detour: a pilgrimage to the old village of Degerloch, "now one of the beautiful suburbs of Stuttgart," as Miriam described it, "from which place my father's parents went to America."[74]

William Stark continued to avail himself of new business ventures. One unforeseen opportunity came from the landmark oil discovery on January 10, 1901, at Spindletop, a salt dome just south of neighboring Beaumont, which had shown the world a previously unimagined quantity of oil, setting off a vast wave of exploration and resulting in the discovery of countless new oil fields. The sheer volume of the product opened up a new realm of demand for its uses—among the first, fuel oil for train and

Figure 6.9. William Henry Stark, prime of life, undated. Stark Foundation Archives.

steamship engines and gasoline for the infant automobile industry and the soon-to-be-invented airplane. But more would follow, and ultimately, the huge discoveries of oil in the wake of that 1901 discovery altered the development of modern civilization.[75]

On a local level, an unexpected aspect of these new developments benefited major landowners such as the Lutcher, Stark, and Brown families, who already knew the value of the surface of the lands they owned but who had not considered that the regions lying beneath those lands, also by law belonging to them, held treasures as well—and that, surprisingly, "surface interest" and "mineral interest" could offer separate, unrelated sources of revenue.

The first large field in the Orange area was discovered near Vinton, Louisiana, where local residents had long observed and speculated on the surface signs of oil to be found there: a low topographic mound, mineral springs, and oil and gas seeps. Predictably, the mound proved to be a salt dome, and the first well of the Vinton, or Ged, field, as it was also known, was drilled there shortly after the 1901 Spindletop discovery. But the field yielded only minor production; its major discovery well was not drilled until 1910,[76] when Leonard Frederick Benckenstein, an enterprising young businessman from Cincinnati, Ohio,[77] visited a cattle ranch near Vinton and observed the telltale signs of oil on the surfaces of the cattle ponds. Benckenstein, realizing the potential of the area, formed a drilling company—the Vinton Petroleum Company—and began securing leases. The Ged field proved to be a large one: a substantial gusher was brought in sometime in March 1913, flowing fifteen thousand barrels per day, and more wells followed.[78] In 1913, a gusher known as the Bland well was brought in six miles west of Orange, but another did not follow until 1922, establishing the Orange field (or, as it later became known, the town of Orangefield) as a major oil producer.[79]

Benckenstein recruited William Stark and Edgar Brown, among other investors, to join his drilling company venture, and Stark and Brown began acquiring stock in the company in 1911. By June of that year, the Starks—William, Miriam, and Lutcher—and Edgar Brown were listed as stockholders in the company, as well as L.F. Benckenstein and one of his sons, Charles H.; in 1914, William and Lutcher Stark and Edgar Brown were elected directors. The stockholders continued to increase their holdings, accumulating diverse mineral interests, and the company paid them regular dividends for many years.[80] William Stark and Edgar Brown also held interest in the Rescue Oil Company, another of the independent companies in the area.[81]

These new oil discoveries, and others like them, played a major role in events that were already being enacted on the global stage. Tensions in Europe were growing as the newly unified German Empire under Kaiser Wilhelm II increasingly threatened world domination. In the face of this menace, in 1911, only ten years after the discovery at Spindletop, young British home secretary Winston Churchill committed the British navy to converting to the use of oil-based fuel. His decision lay rooted in the abundance of Texas oil and the added mobility it would allow the British fleet.[82]

Figure 6.10. William Stark with Leonard F. Benckenstein, his business partner in several oil ventures. The impish William is standing on a rock to look eye to eye with the exceptionally tall Benckenstein. Stark Foundation Archives.

Figure 6.11. Lutcher & Moore's new Lower Mill in Orange, 1915.
Stark Foundation Archives.

On June 28, 1914, the assassination of Archduke Franz Ferdinand, heir-presumptive to the Austro-Hungarian throne, by a Serbian nationalist served as the spark that finally ignited the open hostilities of the Great War in Europe. Austria-Hungary and its allies, notably Imperial Germany, then declared war on Serbia, and, because of interlocking alliances, most of the major powers soon went to war. The Triple Entente of Russia, France, and Great Britain formed the Allied Powers, and both sides were soon joined by other nations as the war progressed. The conflict eventually spread throughout the world. The United States initially remained neutral amid the escalating hostilities, but the sympathies of most Americans already lay with the Allies,[83] and the shadow of war loomed perennially behind daily life in the States.

In the meantime, in Orange, fire paid its dreaded visit to the Lutcher & Moore interests for the last time: on August 1, 1915, flames destroyed the Lower Mill.[84] Lutcher Stark wired news of the disaster to William and Miriam, who were aboard the SS *Victoria* out of Seattle, Washington, then wrote them with more detail: "Dear Folks, As I wired you, we lost the lower mill and planer, saving the lumber and dry kiln. In fact, it was another miraculous escape, similar to the one in Lutcher. [On October 17,

1909, the Lutcher & Moore Cypress Lumber Company in Lutcher, Louisiana, had sustained a loss of $223,000 from a fire started by sparks from their own locomotive.[85] It [the Lower Mill fire] was a thing that as I have viewed it, could not have been helped," Lutcher continued, "and might have been a thousand per cent worse. . . . We intend to start the Upper Mill on a night and day run tomorrow. . . . Things seem to be turning over as nice as can be expected. . . . Mr. Trout will be here tomorrow with plans for the new mill."[86] Almost immediately, they began construction on the burned-out site of the old one. The new Lower Mill, with a much larger capacity, was "probably the most modern sawmill in the South," according to office manager Farwell.[87]

In 1916, four years after Henry Lutcher's death, a deepwater port for Orange became a reality at last. Congress had finally appropriated funds in 1911 to dredge a channel twenty-six feet deep on the lower Sabine and Neches Rivers, and as the New Year of 1916 approached, the project was nearing completion.[88] Although it had been Henry Lutcher's dream, most of the credit for pushing the project to fruition belongs to his sons-in-law, William Stark and Edgar Brown.[89]

That January 3, to underscore the drama of the situation, Lutcher & Moore brought five empty seagoing lumber schooners upriver to Orange, having received the promise of government engineers that the Sabine-Neches Channel would be opened for navigation before the ships loaded and were ready to sail back out to tidewater. If the channel were not finished to the projected depth, it would, of course, be impossible for the ships, once loaded, to leave Orange. But the engineers kept their promise: the laden ships sailed through the new channel "without trouble"—the first ones to navigate it. Orange celebrated the milestone with a banquet and telegrams to the outside world, "notifying shipping that [the city] was the first port on the channel open."[90]

Finally, the way stood clear: large seagoing vessels began to sail regularly from the Gulf of Mexico through Sabine Pass and the new channel across Sabine Lake, then all the way up the Sabine and Neches Rivers to Port Arthur, Orange, and Beaumont, where they could load their cargos and return to sea toward worldwide destinations.[91] At that time, William Stark and Edgar Brown deeded a tract of land adjoining the Lutcher & Moore Lumber Company to the city of Orange for use as a port. A three thousand–foot slip, twenty-six feet deep and two hundred feet wide, was then dredged, the upper portion to be occupied by Lutcher & Moore's private docks and the lower by city wharves and warehouses.[92] As Henry Lutcher had hoped, labored, and planned for the past three decades, Orange now boasted a deepwater port.

On February 12, 1917, the Lutcher, Stark, and Brown families entered into a contract with a Houston lumberman, Robert W. Wier, concerning approximately eighty-six thousand acres of pine timberlands in Jasper, Newton, and Sabine Counties that Henry Lutcher and Bedell Moore had bought when they first moved their operations to Texas. Through inheritance and various other transactions, Frances Ann Lutcher now owned one-third of this property, and Miriam, William, and Carrie and Edgar Brown owned one-sixth each.[93] The property was rich in longleaf yellow pine—perhaps the last great Texas stand—but it lay approximately eighty miles to the north of Orange, and transporting the logs to the Lutcher & Moore mills at Orange would not be economical.[94]

The contract provided that Wier would recruit investors, form a corporation with a capitalized stock of $400,000, build a mill on site, and harvest the timber from the property, cutting no less than forty million board feet per year.[95] The Wier Long Leaf Lumber Company would pay the landowners a monthly sum of $6.00 per thousand board feet plus 25 percent of all sales at prices over $13.50 per thousand board feet.[96] Lutcher Stark played a significant role in negotiating the contract, and he and Brown were named directors of the corporation, representing the timber owners.[97] This venture proved to be lucrative but in the future portended ill for family dynamics.

In Europe, the war to end all wars raged on, and unfamiliar names of foreign places sounded throughout America. The sinking of the British passenger liner *Lusitania* on May 7, 1915, by a German U-boat, the dead including 128 Americans, triggered a series of events that eventually eroded American neutrality. When the fearsome U-boats, the most formidable weapons in the German arsenal, sank several US merchant ships in the war zone surrounding the British Isles, Congress declared war on Germany on April 6, 1917, and the United States actively entered the conflict.[98]

Even though the US entry was belated, the war still affected every aspect of American life. In May 1917 Congress instituted the Selective Service System, and 24 million American males registered; some 2.8 million were actually called. US forces, sent to Europe to face the bloody, disease-ridden horrors of trench warfare, inevitably helped tip the scales in favor of the Allies. On the home front, the new Food Administration, headed by former mining engineer Herbert Hoover, instituted "wheatless" and "meatless" days.[99]

In Southeast Texas as elsewhere in the nation, households grew victory gardens and women knitted mufflers and socks and rolled bandages to be sent overseas for the troops. After an initial drastic drop in European lumber orders with the onset of the war in Europe, lumber prices had shot upward,[100] and shipbuilding, which had actually been a Southeast Texas regional industry for many decades, exploded in Orange in 1916, just before American involvement in the war, steering the city into an unanticipated but welcome boom. Fueled by the abundance and ready availability of oak, cypress, and longleaf yellow pine, new shipyards sprang up to lay the keels of ships, many far larger than the standard size of the ships of government construction,[101] and by March of that year, five shipyards were flourishing in Orange.[102]

For the war effort, the Joseph Weaver and Son Shipbuilders constructed three steamships and a four-masted schooner.[103] In 1916 the Capt. Fred Swailes and Co. Shipyards launched a five-masted wooden schooner named the *City of Orange*, said to be the largest ship ever built on the Gulf Coast—250 feet long and 43 feet wide and made of more than a million board feet of longleaf yellow pine.[104] In 1917, however, the National Ship Building Company built fourteen huge ships for the government, going the *City of Orange* one better by launching the mammoth five thousand–ton *War Mystery*, described as the "largest wooden ship that ever took water"—330 feet long with a 48-foot beam—on February 27, 1918.[105] National, located on the Sabine between the Lutcher & Moore Upper and Lower Mills, granted a contract to Lutcher & Moore to supply nearly all the lumber for its ships.[106]

Frances Ann Lutcher, in a preemptive strike, wrote the Orange County Draft Board on February 22, 1918, to request deferred classification for Lutcher Stark, then age thirty, asking that he be reclassified from Class I to Class IV, Divisions C and D, on the grounds that he was "a necessary sole managing, controlling, or directing head" of her properties.[107] Her petition stated that she was "77 years old, a woman, a widow, without sons of her own, and having no other person to manage her affairs and depending solely on the registrant for such management."[108] It went on to claim that

> she is unable to manage the same herself. . . . Registrant is affiant's grandson, and since his majority has managed her affairs more or less and during the last five years has had exclusive management of the same, and . . . he is the only person being familiar with her affairs, she not being familiar with same herself . . . his services are invaluable to her in that her affairs cannot be conducted in their present condition by any other person.[109]

Many among Frances Ann's family, friends, and business associates might have been surprised to learn that she claimed such helplessness and ignorance of her own affairs, but in any event, the Draft Board granted her request, thus ensuring that Lutcher Stark would remain at home and out of harm's way until war's end.

Nonetheless, members of the Lutcher, Stark, and Brown families variously involved themselves in the war effort. Miriam joined the Red Cross and helped assemble Christmas boxes for the troops.[110] Edgar Brown met in New Orleans with "Eastern capitalists" who were looking for a site on which to build wooden ships, then brought them to Orange, where Lutcher & Moore leased them a site on the Sabine River for one dollar per year and placed its timber production at the disposal of their shipyard.[111] Lutcher Stark received an urgent appeal from the deputy governor of the Federal Reserve to use his influence to ensure that workers covered the district selling Liberty Bonds.[112] (By October 1918, Orange had oversubscribed for the Fourth Liberty Loan, overshooting the $689,000 goal by $81,850.)[113] A blurb in the March 1918 *Alcalde*, the University of Texas alumni publication, reported that Lutcher had helped Orange adjust to "the new conditions arising from the sudden quintupling of her population" resulting from the shipbuilding boom by building fifty-two bungalows for the families of government employees in the shipyards.[114]

Frances Ann, who had begun to cultivate the hobby of growing orchids in the conservatories at her home,[115] gave away so many to local servicemen and those traveling by train through Orange en route to army camps that they began to call her "the Orchid Lady."[116] Later, she sent the exotic blooms to Presidents Woodrow Wilson and Warren G. Harding and their wives.

"My dear Mrs. Lutcher," Wilson wrote in response, "you must have known that orchids are our favorite flowers, and those you were so gracious to send me brought not only their own beauty but a very delightful message of friendship from you; and I thank you with all my heart."[117] Edith Bolling Wilson added her thanks: "You were lovely to think of me on Valentine's Day," she wrote, "and the house is filled with the exquisite flowers that give it a delicious breath of the Southland."[118] "Your wonderful box of orchids came just at the time of the last State dinner," declared Florence Kling Harding, "and so gave not only me but our many guests great pleasure. It seemed marvelous that such fragile, exquisite blooms could travel so far and arrive apparently as fresh as when they were cut."[119]

Frances Ann taught knitting to girls in her church and in the local Camp Fire group, seating the younger ones on her lap for greater ease in showing them the stitches, and patriotically resolved to write to all the "soldier boys" she knew in France. "I hear on every side how you all love to get letters, from *home* and *friends*," she wrote October 24, 1918, to Orange soldier Cpl. Malcolm W. Pearce, who was "somewhere in France," as she put it.[120] She also bought War Savings Certificates in 1919 and received a citation from the US Department of the Navy for serving in its "Eyes for the Navy" program—furnishing binoculars, telescopes, spyglasses, and

Figure 6.12. Frances Ann Lutcher, "the Orchid Lady," undated. Stark Foundation Archives.

navigation instruments for "the protection of our warships, transports and supply vessels against the submarine activities of the enemy during the Great War . . . in recognition of the sacrifice made for the safety of our ships and the assurance of final victory." The citation was signed by Assistant Secretary of the Navy Franklin D. Roosevelt.[121]

In an astounding new role, William Stark himself took up knitting for the soldiers' cause. "Am glad . . . you are getting along so nicely with your knitting," Miriam wrote him kindly in a letter from Chicago in October

Figure 6.13. Douglas A. "Doug" Pruter (*right*) as a soldier in World War I.
Pruter was William Stark's longtime private secretary and right-hand man.
Stark Foundation Archives.

Figure 6.14. The *Brownie* houseboat, named for an Austin club
of which Nita Stark was a member. Stark Foundation Archives.

1917. "I saw a little article in the paper in which men who are too old to go
to war are requested to learn to knit for the soldiers." At least William was
not alone in his endeavors.[122]

Nita Stark, too, seemingly emerging from the dark period of her late
losses, did her part for the war effort. The *Alcalde* noted:

> Mrs. Lutcher Stark . . . has become an expert in Red Cross work. Due largely to
> her energy and enthusiasm the Orange chapter is one of the largest and best
> organized in the State. She has made frequent visits to the New Orleans chap-
> ter to receive working instructions and has also visited St. Louis on the same
> mission. She has brought speakers and workers to Orange and has personally
> organized various auxiliaries . . . one among the Japanese women of the Japa-
> nese rice-growers' colony, seventeen miles from Orange.[123]

Nita also donated generously in 1918 to the Commission for Relief in Belgium and in 1920 sent $73 to the Fatherless Children of France toward the
support of two French war orphans, Emma and Jean Collet of Fontaine-
Denis, for a period of one year each.[124]

For Nita and Lutcher, life still held some pleasures. They had traveled to
Havana, Cuba, in February 1914, not quite three months after the loss of
their first child, with Frances Ann and the Farwells on Lutcher & Moore
business, and, by the tone of her letters, Nita had seemed to enjoy her-

self.[125] And the young couple spent a part of every summer on a houseboat on Sabine Lake, hosting a house party for the University of Texas Brownie Club, of which Nita was a member. At first they had rented the houseboat, but later they ordered one of their own, christened the *Brownie* and designed to their specifications; it was "commodious," with its own electric plant and a spacious living room on the upper floor, fitted with piano and ivory wicker furniture. "Mr. and Mrs. Stark possess to an extraordinary degree the happy faculty of knowing how to enjoy life to the fullest in a thoroughly wholesome way," the Austin periodical the *Gossip* reported, "and also how to make their friends enjoy it with them. In other words, they are never happier than when making others happy."[126] With the *Brownie* houseboat, an enduring tradition was born; Lutcher Stark owned houseboats for the remainder of his life.

The family—Carrie Brown in particular—experienced two grievous personal losses during those war years. After suffering for many months from cancer, Edgar Brown died in the early morning hours of June 16, 1917, at the Browns' home on Green Avenue in Orange and was buried later that day. He was just fifty-seven years of age.[127] In his lifetime, besides his primary commitments—to his medical practice, then to the Lutcher & Moore lumber interests—he had involved himself in diverse ventures, among them the Vinton Petroleum Company, the Yellow Pine Paper Mill, land development and management, and a hydroelectric project in West Texas. In addition to serving two terms as mayor of Orange, he had become in later life a gentleman farmer, taking great pride in his prize crops of rice, harvesting a record-setting crop of twenty thousand bags the year of his death. He devoted much of his time to supervising his farms, apparently a source of great enjoyment to him.[128]

Several months before he died, Brown's health began to fail in earnest, and, being a physician, he realized the gravity of his condition. He arranged his affairs "with splendid courage and manliness," according to one source,[129] writing a holographic will naming Carrie and his three children, Fannie Brown Moore, Edgar William Brown Jr., and Henry Lutcher Brown, as his executors. He made specific bequests to various family members, including $5,000 each to his son-in-law, Rucie Moore, and his daughter-in-law, Gladys Slade Brown, the wife of Edgar Brown Jr., and directed that the remainder be left intact for ten years to be administered by his executors, then divided equally among his three children.

He added three codicils to the will, the first a bequest of $5,000 to his granddaughter, Brownie Babette Moore; the second to correct an oversight: "I neglected to state," he wrote, "[that] I did not want the courts to have anything to do with [the will] only so far as necessary to comply with the law, I hereby . . . give my executors and administrators complete power to carry out my instructions without the courts and without bond." In the last codicil, dated only two weeks before he died, he bequeathed $5,000 to his newly acquired daughter-in-law, Emily Wells Brown, who had married his younger son, Henry Lutcher Brown, the previous April,[130] thus gifting her commensurate with his bequests to his other two children-in-law.

"[Dr. Edgar W. Brown] played a prominent part in the upbuilding of Orange," read one encomium. "He . . . was always among the first to act when the best interests of the city, district or state were at stake, and he built for himself a place in the hearts of the people of Orange for his kindness, high-mindedness and splendid citizenship. . . . [He] was one of the most widely known and highly esteemed lumber manufacturers in the entire South."[131] And the *Orange Leader* noted that "with all of his activities as physician and capitalist, Dr. Brown was always noted for his plain and unaffected manner, his democratic simplicity in dress and deportment, a quiet but powerful factor in all of his business associations, and concededly one of the most prominent and active figures in the great development of East Texas."[132]

A little over a year later, Carrie was dealt a second tragic blow with the loss of her only daughter. In the spring of 1918—ironically, just as world peace was looming as a real possibility—a profoundly virulent strain of influenza, the Spanish flu, sprang up around the world. Its name originated from Spanish news bulletins reporting the large numbers it killed in that country (since it was a neutral nation, Spain's news reports were more unbiased than those of countries actively engaged in the war, which were reluctant to publish correct accounts of influenza fatalities for fear of lowering morale). The Spanish flu began to take its deadly toll and ultimately threatened the population of the entire world.[133]

Modern epidemiological findings suggest that the disease actually originated in Haskell County, Kansas, and moved eastward across the state to a US Army camp,[134] then followed traveling soldiers, snaking like chain lightning along overcrowded rail and shipping lines and trade routes to every remote corner of the globe, by some estimates killing fifty million people worldwide. Compared by some historians to the Black Death of the Middle Ages, the scourge ultimately infected from 20 to 40 percent of the world's population, mainly killing young adults by turning their own healthy immune systems against them. In all, an estimated 675,000 Americans died.[135] It took a particularly heavy toll on the armed forces because of crowded conditions in encampments and on trains; by one estimate, more US soldiers died during the pandemic than were killed in battle.[136] "What is it like, this Spanish 'Flu'?" a contemporary verse queried:

Ask me, brother, for I've been through.
It is misery out of despair,
It pulls your teeth and curls your hair,
It thins your blood and bends your bones,
It fills your throat with moans and groans,
And, sometimes, maybe you get well—
Some call it "Flu," I call it Hell.[137]

Before long, the pandemic made its deadly presence known in South-east Texas. Twenty-nine-year-old Fannie Brown Moore, four months pregnant with her second child,[138] contracted the disease and died on October 12, 1918, at her mother's home of the particularly "viscuous"—and lethal—pneumonia that was its frequent aftermath.[139] Tragically, in a little over a year's time, Carrie Lutcher Brown had lost her husband, her only daughter, and her future grandchild.

Frances Ann, Miriam, and Ida Achenbach, in Denver after a sojourn at Roslyn Ranch, received a wire notifying them of Fannie's death and started immediately for home.[140] "She was only in bed 4 or 5 days," Frances Ann wrote sadly to Corporal Pearce (through Ida, acting as her amanuensis).[141] "They [in the Orange area] had a terrible time here, for 3 or 4 weeks . . . as they were all sick. I hope this terrible epidemic of Spanish influenza, as they call it, will not reach you soldiers, for it has killed them off over here, men women and children, almost faster than the Huns have mowed down you boys." She added that Lutcher Stark and the seven-year-old Babette, newly motherless, had also been quite ill with the flu but had survived.

"Conditions are improving fast now," Frances Ann continued. "All the picture shows were opened yesterday, and there are *some* shows. You wouldn't know Front St. with the new 'Liberty' and 'Strand' [movie theaters]; the last mentioned would do credit to a big city, from outside appearance, we haven't been inside yet, nor have no desire to go right now." She followed with news of Orange and words of praise for Pearce and the other "brave soldier boys":

All the other new buildings are going up slowly. I heard Mr. [William] Stark say it looked as if the bank and [the Frances Ann Lutcher] hospital would never be finished, it is so hard to get material. Well . . . Liberty Loan went "over the top" sailing, here in Orange, as well as almost everywhere, to keep you boys going, so you know how your home people feel about it, and how your country and its population is backing her brave soldier boys. You all have been doing wonderful work "over there," and we are proud of *all of you.* It is right amusing to see how Germany is trying to work up an armitice, to keep you boys from doing up their country, as they have France & Belgium.[142]

Figure 6.15. Four generations of the Lutcher-Brown family, 1911.
Left to right: Carrie Lutcher Brown, Frances Ann Lutcher, and Fannie Brown Moore,
who is holding her infant daughter, Brownie Babette Moore. Stark Foundation Archives.

"While I want to see the war ended, so that all this loss of life will be over with, yet I feel as though they ought to have to take a little of their own medicine," added the perennially feisty Frances Ann. "Well, my dear Malcolm," she concluded, "take as good care of yourself as you can, under existing circumstances, and remember that your country and her people are backing her boys."[143]

Figure 6.16. Frederick Henry ("F.H.") Farwell, longtime vice president and general manager of Lutcher & Moore, undated. Stark Foundation Archives.

On November 9, 1918, exactly four weeks after Fannie's death, Frances Ann, undoubtedly feeling her own mortality, gave her power of attorney to her oldest—and favorite—grandson, Lutcher Stark. And the following February 1919 she made her will.[144] On the very day that Frances Ann gave her power of attorney to Lutcher, Kaiser Wilhelm II abdicated his throne, and two days later, the fighting in the Great War ended when Germany signed an armistice with the Allied Forces. The country rejoiced, and Orange celebrated with a gala parade down Front Street.[145] A young Orange matron, Pearl Cottle Joiner, noted in her diary that "we were awakened about 5 o'clock by the firing of a gun, later bells and whistles blowing to announce the glad news of the signing of the armistice. . . . Everything in town declared a holiday, so great crowds thronged the streets and paraded and shouted."[146] The war would be formally concluded the following June 28, 1919, by the Treaty of Versailles.

At war's end, thanks in large part to the shipbuilding boom, the population of Orange had ballooned to an estimated eighteen to twenty thousand,[147] and Frances Ann's "soldier boys" were coming home. Hopes, plans, and energy turned once again to the home front—and to the future. With Edgar Brown's death, William Stark was left as the sole captain of the family interests, and he continued to expand and diversify them. In many cases, Lutcher Stark and Frederick Farwell joined him in these ventures, which, in addition to the already existing companies, soon included the San Jacinto Building in Beaumont, the San Jacinto Life Insurance Company, the Orange Car and Steel Company (an outgrowth of the old Southern Dry Dock & Ship Building Company, whose market had dissolved at the end of the war), and the ill-starred Hagan Coal Mines.[148] More followed, some more successful than others.

In 1919 Lutcher Stark embarked on two ventures that occupied huge segments of his life—his time, energy, ingenuity, and, not least, his wealth—for years to come, and he entered into them with the same obsessive focus and energy that already marked his personality. The first took place on the home front. A local chapter of a comparatively new men's service organization, the National Association of Rotary Clubs (later to become Rotary International), was organized May 2, 1919, in Orange and chartered that June 2. Lutcher and William Stark numbered among the twenty charter members of the Orange Rotary Club, and Lutcher Stark was elected its first president.[149] And in only the second year of his membership, he was elected governor of the Eighteenth Rotary District, then consisting of thirty-four clubs.[150]

Just a little over two weeks later, on June 19, 1919, he took the first step on a long road that altered not only the course of his own life but also the development of his alma mater: he accepted an appointment by Governor William Pettus Hobby to the Board of Regents of the University of Texas. At age thirty-one, Lutcher Stark became the youngest member yet named to the board.[151]

CHAPTER SEVEN

Mamoose

*Everyone, even the maidservants in the Henry Lutcher home, called
Mrs. Lutcher "Mamoose."*
—CYNTHIA CARTER LEEDY HORN[1]

Regardless of the preferences of grandparents, it is most often the oldest grandchild in a family who endows them with their nicknames.
The younger grandchildren follow suit, and thus the monikers ad-
here and become permanent. So it is probable that Frances Ann Lutcher's
oldest grandchild, Lutcher Stark, was the one who first called her "Mamoose." (Henry Lutcher was called the more conventional "Grandpapa.")[2]
In any event, Frances Ann eventually became "Mamoose" to practically
everyone. Even portrait artist August Benziger, reputedly an austere man
who held strict views on proper behavior, referred to Frances Ann by her
sobriquet. Marieli Benziger told this story regarding her parents' visit to
Frances Ann in Orange:

> When widowed, [Frances Ann] had been cared for by a "Negro mammy and
> her niece," and soon took on the cares and concerns of all those who lived
> about her. Mamoose, as she was called, generated only goodness and kindness;
> they radiated from her being, but it was her mammy who ruled the house. One
> oppressively hot day, she noticed August's beard and mustache which had been
> allowed to grow longer than usual. "Shucks, Mistah," she exclaimed, "Youse
> bettah go'n some uh dat dere hair afore Mamoose see yo'-all or youse shore
> gonna be vamoosed from heah, right quick!"[3]

According to Marieli, Benziger "vamoosed," presumably to trim his beard
and mustache.[4]

In the final quarter century of her life, Mamoose, diminutive in physical size but mighty in force of character, continued to reign supreme as

Figure 7.1. Frances Ann Lutcher, undated. Stark Foundation Archives.

Figure 7.2. The Lutcher Memorial Building of the First Presbyterian Church of Orange, Texas, Frances Ann Lutcher's creation, completed 1912. Stark Foundation Archives.

the matriarch and formidable personality she had become. At the time of the Benzigers' visit, a driver conveying them to her home refused to accept money for his services, declaring that it was an honor to take anyone to "that good soul." Without her, he explained, the town of Orange would have nothing—no school, no church, no library. "Why, she just plans everything, does everything, runs everything," he said proudly."[5]

Before Henry Lutcher's death, Frances Ann had already begun to assert her independence, undertaking several major philanthropic ventures in Orange. First, she brought to fruition her longtime plan to build a church for Orange's Presbyterian Congregation. In a venturesome departure from the prevailing neo-Gothic style so typical of churches of that era, she commissioned architect James Oliver Hogg of Kansas City, Missouri, to design a building in modified Greek Revival form—symmetrical construction, Ionic columns, and a wide front pediment, topped by a towering dome.[6] She herself pored over the plans and drawings and approved every minute element. Central to the church's design, of course, were the three opalescent stained-glass windows that she had purchased at the Chicago World's Fair Columbian Exposition and had since been stored at the New York studios of their creators, J & R Lamb.

Frances Ann also supervised every phase of the church's construction, which began in 1908 on a site at Green Avenue and Eighth Street. The exterior of the church was built of native Texas pink granite from a quarry at Granite Mountain, near Marble Falls (where the granite used to build the Texas State Capitol in Austin had also been quarried),[7] and the staircases were carved of Italian marble. She directed that the original three windows, symbolizing "The Church in Christianity" and depicting towering angelic figures representing "Religion," "The Church Militant," and "The Church Triumphant," be placed prominently in the foyer at the front of the church.

Every aspect of the building reflected Frances Ann's taste and vision, down to the smallest, finely wrought detail. She commissioned additional windows from J & R Lamb to be placed throughout the building, many copied from biblical scenes painted by contemporary artists such as Gustave Doré, Hans Hofmann, and William Holman Hunt.[8] The interior of the thirty-six-foot opalescent stained-glass dome, the only one of its kind

Figure 7.3. View from the second-floor foyer of the Lutcher Memorial Building, Orange. The mural in center depicts "Heavenly Justice." The window at right, representing "The Church Militant," is one of the J & R Lamb award-winning stained-glass windows that Frances Ann Lutcher purchased at the 1893 Chicago World's Fair. Stark Foundation Archives.

Figure 7.4. The dome of the Lutcher Memorial Building in Orange, the only opalescent
stained-glass dome in the United States. It depicts sixteen angelic figures
bearing various Christian symbols. Stark Foundation Archives.

in the United States, depicted sixteen angels, each holding a symbol of
Christianity—chalice, dove, cross, scepter, lamb, lily, and the stone tablets
of the Ten Commandments, among others.[9] World-famous artist and designer Louis Comfort Tiffany, a rival of J & R Lamb, visited the church in
1915 and pronounced himself pleased with the result, although he added
that he "would have placed a few precious stones on two of the windows."[10]

Frances Ann purchased a Hope-Jones organ and an altar and pews of
Honduran ribbon mahogany for the church and imbued the entire interior with Christian symbols, many overlaid with twenty-four-carat gold
leaf.[11] (She allowed no images of the crucified Christ in the church, although bare crosses figured in several of the windows.)[12] She also installed
a separate air-conditioning and heating system, making the church one
of the earliest climate-controlled buildings in the entire country. Because
the city of Orange at that time lacked sufficient power to operate the system, Frances Ann simply equipped the church with its own power plant—
as well as a full-time engineer to run it.[13] She shouldered the entire cost

Figure 7.5. Organ, Lutcher Memorial Building, First Presbyterian Church, Orange, undated. Stark Foundation Archives.

of construction herself and never divulged the cost of the building, supposedly destroying all records of expenditures of any kind.[14] To provide for "extraordinary" expenses in maintaining the church, she established the Frances Ann Lutcher Endowment. (In December 1942, Edgar Brown Jr. and Henry Lutcher Brown created a similar foundation to preserve and maintain the church property in memory of their mother, Carrie Lutcher Brown.)[15]

Frances Ann named the edifice the Lutcher Memorial Building in honor of her husband and his family and, by a general warranty deed dated January 27, 1912, formally conveyed the property and structure to the First Presbyterian Congregation of the Church in Orange, Texas.[16] Although it had been completed in 1910 and the congregation was already unofficially ensconced there,[17] a farewell service was held January 21, 1912, in the old white wooden church building on Polk and Market Streets, after which the congregation, in a body, walked the few blocks to the new building, where the services were concluded. It was dedicated January 28,[18] a little over eight months before Henry Lutcher's death the following October 2.

The church now finished, Frances Ann embarked on new ventures. A few mentions in the records indicate that, sometime around the year 1914, she opened a performance venue in Orange she christened the Henry Jacob Lutcher Opera House in honor of her late husband.[19] Around that time, she also began to implement another scheme she had planned for many years: a farm. The Lutcher Model Farm, as it was called, "would measure up to the standard in every particular, comparing favorably with the greatest achievements in the agricultural department of the nation's affairs," according to the *Beaumont Enterprise*.[20] Constructed at a cost of over $100,000, by one estimate, the farm was situated on an 859-acre tract of prairie land four miles west of Orange.[21]

Placed in charge of operations at the Lutcher Model Farm was Orange County native W.A. McDaniel, an experienced agricultural agent who had already spent a number of years with the US Department of Agriculture. The farm incorporated every possible innovation, its aim to demonstrate "the natural productiveness of the Orange County soil, aided by atmospheric conditions combined with skill and science," the *Enterprise* opined. The ten-room farmhouse was designed in a "correct and modern style of architecture in line with rural life," incorporating both beauty and comfort. The massive barn contained concrete floors and stalls with the name of each four-legged occupant displayed above each stall. Feed storage bins were located above the stalls, and a chute carried the feed from them to the mangers beneath.[22]

The farm housed animals of various kinds: Shropshire sheep, brought in from New York; "high-bred" chickens, who enjoyed cement water

Figure 7.6. Cabbage field at the Lutcher Model Farm, Orange, after 1912.
Photo by Farmer, Stark Foundation Archives.

troughs; Jersey cows; trotting and draft horses; "Scotch" collies, so well
trained that they were able to separate their owner's stock from those of
neighbors; and Chester White and black Hampshire hogs. A conveyer system transported waste from the barn to an outside compost pile, and "in
the hog stys there are automatic sanitary troughs which make hog growing more agreeable," the *Enterprise* noted euphemistically.[23]

The farm's apiary housed sixty hives of bees, and a combination pickle,
preserve, and canning factory processed produce grown on the farm. That
first year, under McDaniel's direction, truck patches of all kinds flourished. A hundred acres were planted in corn, forty in black-eyed peas, and
forty in sweet potatoes, and Irish potatoes were planted "in proportion."
Even though no fertilizer had yet been applied, "astonishingly fine crops
with fruitful yields have been grown, are growing and will grow."[24]

The final major charitable enterprise of Frances Ann's life was yet another of her abiding dreams, this one possibly of the longest standing.
Forced in the young years of Henry Lutcher's sawmilling career to witness terrible accidents and preventable deaths in the mills and logging operations with only rudimentary emergency treatment available, she had
resolved to see to it, if she were ever able, that someday more adequate

Figure 7.7. The Frances Ann Lutcher Hospital, Orange, dedicated in 1921.
Stark Foundation Archives.

medical treatment would be accessible in Orange.[25] She took the first step around 1916, when she purchased and donated a private home at the corner of Pine and Second Streets in Orange to be converted to a sixteen-patient hospital. "Orange Is to Have Its Own Hospital," the *Orange Leader* announced proudly. Before that time, patients had been required to travel to Galveston for major surgery. "This will save many lives," the article declared, "as the long trip has so weakened many patients that their last chance of life was lost."[26]

But the facility proved inadequate to the town's needs, and Frances Ann moved closer to her ultimate goal when she began construction of a larger hospital in 1918 on a city block of land bordered by Green Avenue and Second, Pine, and Third Streets in Orange.[27] She and other family members as well as the architect for the project, C.H. Page of Austin, and the physician in charge, Dr. Robert F. Miller, had visited leading hospitals throughout the country, adapting innovative ideas for use in the new Orange hospital that would "make for the comfort and well-being of the human race without stipulation as to color or creed" and sparing no expense to implement them.[28] Although the Frances Ann Lutcher Hospital was not a charity hospital as such, its charter specifically stated that she, as the owner, would never receive a penny's profit from the venture; all surplus funds would be returned to use for the institution's maintenance.[29] As was always the case with any of Frances Ann's enterprises, she painstakingly considered and approved every minuscule detail, and as always, hers was the final say-so.

The building afforded accommodations for sixty patients and provided facilities for both surgical and medical cases, a nurses' training school, and public education in disease prevention. It was built of fireproof materials with a pressed-brick exterior and an interior color scheme of gray ("more pleasing and restful than the monotonous white of most hospitals," sniffed a hospital brochure). Many of the rooms featured private baths, and every floor offered a glassed-in sun parlor. A suite was designated for surgery—two operating rooms and a dressing room each for surgeons and nurses, and skylights installed over the operating tables. The smaller of the two operating rooms was equipped with a circular overhead lighting fixture to offer maximum visibility for emergency surgery at night or on cloudy days.[30]

The hospital boasted an obstetrical room, a pathology laboratory, and three X-ray rooms, as well as a central system that controlled temperature and humidity throughout.[31] Frances Ann began buying trees and other plants in January 1920 from Griffing Nurseries in Beaumont, the largest nursery in the region,[32] and the completed landscape of the grounds featured palms and a sunken garden. The hospital's nursery was "the pride of Mrs. Lutcher's heart," the brochure declared, with "bassinets . . . soft as if lined with down . . . handmade pillowcases of the finest linen," and a Hess baby incubator, specified as essential by Frances Ann, since, according to her, a much-loved baby in her own family had died for lack of the device.[33] The sun parlor near the pediatric ward was "about all a child could ask for," with curtains in a French fabric portraying Mother Goose rhymes, walls painted a baby blue, toys for the older children, and "Kiddie Koops" to "confine the smaller child to his own territory."[34]

In keeping with the "separate but equal" segregation practices of the time, African Americans, or "colored," as the brochure called them, were housed separately in a department on the first floor, where, in addition to the wards, single rooms were available. Of the hospital's sixty beds, sixteen—fewer than half—were allotted to black patients, and linens were embroidered in red to distinguish them from those in areas reserved for white patients. Notwithstanding, the brochure maintained, "in every particular [the African American section] is furnished and equipped as well as the rest of the hospital"—in itself unusual for that day.[35]

The dedication of the Frances Ann Lutcher Hospital was held May 15, 1921, in the Lutcher Memorial Building that Frances Ann had previously given to the Presbyterian Congregation. Frances Ann was not present for

Figure 7.8. Frances Ann Lutcher (*left*) and Ida Roos, a.k.a. "Fraulein,"
in Williamsport, ca. 1914–1923. Stark Foundation Archives.

the ceremonies; she and her family had already left Orange in preparation
for a trip abroad, but Dr. Miller wrote her to describe the proceedings:

> The service was very beautiful, the music was wonderful, Mrs. Hart was in
> fine voice, Mr. Folsom ditto. . . . Mayor Lea made a good talk. Dr. Carrick was
> fine and Mr. Drake's prayer was a rare gem. Wish you could have been with us.
> All but Mrs. Hart went to Mount Zion and the crowded church full of Negroes
> said "*Amen*" and were loudest when your name was mentioned. . . . Yours and
> Mr. L[utcher's] pictures were surrounded by your orchids. . . . Everyone missed
> you. . . . Hope you are all well and have a happy trip. Drop me a card. Love from
> all of us.[36]

A little over a year before the hospital was dedicated, an event had
triggered a sea change in Lutcher, Stark, and Brown family rela-

tions: On June 30, 1919, Frances Ann deeded her entire one-third interest in the lucrative Wier Longleaf Lumber Company venture—approximately eighty-six thousand acres of pine timberlands in Newton, Jasper,
and Sabine Counties plus her part of the contract with Wier, the mill, her
stock in the company, and her percentage of its considerable income—to
Lutcher Stark.[37]

Hints of discord between the Stark and Brown branches of the family had first surfaced in August 1917. A few months after the family entered into the Wier contract and less than a month after Edgar Brown's
death, Lutcher Brown, doubtless on behalf of his mother, Carrie, wrote
to Orange attorney George Holland to inquire regarding her rights to audit the accounts of the Lutcher & Moore Lumber Company, including the
private ones of Frances Ann and Henry Lutcher. Holland advised that in
his opinion, Carrie, as a stockholder in the company, would indeed be entitled to demand an audit. He cautioned, however, that any such action
should be undertaken with mutual knowledge and consent, with full assistance given by all parties, "so that no errors will creep in or misunder-
standings arise."[38] His suggestions apparently were not heeded. The next
month, Miriam wrote William from New York: "I feel a little worried at
your not writing am afraid the other part of the family is trying to make
trouble again and you do not want to write us."[39]

Frances Ann had never made a secret of the fact that Lutcher was her
favorite grandchild,[40] although in their childhood she had treated her
older two grandchildren, Lutcher and Fannie, equally, at least with monetary gifts, giving them larger sums for Christmas, allowances, and other
occasions than she gave the younger two, Edgar and Lutcher Brown.[41] She
continued to favor Lutcher Stark, taking him on her travels from the time
he was an adolescent,[42] visiting him in Austin while he studied at the University of Texas, attending functions in which he participated, and shar-
ing his life at every opportunity, a connection he seemed to enjoy and
reciprocate. George S. Colburn, a longtime family friend and auditor of
both Lutcher & Moore's business accounts and Frances Ann's personal accounts, later stated for the record: "Mrs . . . Lutcher's attitude toward, and
personal feelings for, H. J. L. Stark . . . [were] deep affection and confidence. She always showed great pride in his activities and seemed to me
to show always a marked favoritism for him as among her kinfolks and
everyone else. She was absolutely devoted to him and would go to football
games, Rotary conventions, summer resorts and wherever his business
or pleasure called him."[43] Frances Ann confessed to her friend and confidante Ruth DeRieux Carter that she believed Lutcher paid her more attention, and loved her more, than did the others, and she began confiding to
Carter that she intended to change her will in his favor.[44]

By Lutcher's own account, his grandmother's pride in his election in 1919 to the presidencies of Orange's Rotary Club and Chamber of Commerce and his appointment to the Board of Regents of the University of Texas played a large part in her decision to deed the Wier property to him.[45] He was also being urged by his fellow Rotarians to stand for election as governor of the Eighteenth District of Rotary (to which post he was duly elected in 1920[46]). "My activities in connection with these matters, and some other public work, seemed to be pleasing to my grandmother," he stated, "and I believe influenced her to a certain extent in making the deed at that particular time, although she had stated her intention to do so on several occasions earlier."[47] He added:

> The part that I had taken in the negotiation of the contract with R. W. Wier, the fact that I was to be one of the Directors of the [Wier] corporation representing the timber owners, and the fact that this was one of the enterprises in which the family was interested, and in which my own initiative and experiences might be developed, the fact that my mother and aunt were already abundantly provided for, and that she desired that I might have this property as my own, because of her devotion to me, were the motives that prompted the transfer of the property to me, as far as I can interpret the words and acts of my grandmother.[48]

Other factors possibly played into the family scenario. As the years passed, Frances Ann had seemed naturally to grow closer to Miriam, traveling extensively with her and seeming to rely on her to a greater degree. Perhaps Carrie, deeply involved with her artistic pursuits—studying painting and sculpture in New Orleans (and winning acclaim for her work) and practicing and performing locally, giving piano, harp, and vocal recitals—was less involved with daily family affairs than her older sister. She was also occupied in administering the estate of her newly deceased husband and doubtless dealing with grief for him and for Fannie and the unborn child.[49] In any event, Frances Ann's gift to Lutcher Stark of her share of the Wier concern provided him with his own considerable independent means. But her actions exacted their toll: whether knowingly or not, she set the stage for a deep rift between the Stark and Brown branches of the family that would never quite heal.

The break was not long in coming. Five months later, on November 25, 1919, the Browns sold their interest in the Lutcher & Moore Lumber Company to Frances Ann, William and Miriam Stark, and F.H. Farwell (as individuals) for $2,914,600.[50] "Brown Estate Gets Millions for Holdings," trumpeted the *Beaumont Enterprise* on December 2: "By far the largest transaction ever made in Orange was consummated . . . when the interests of Mrs. Carrie L. Brown and the Dr. E. W. Brown estate in the Lutcher & Moore Lumber Company . . . was purchased by Mrs. F. A. Lutcher, Mr. and Mrs. W. H. Stark, and F. H. Farwell."

That December 30, the stockholders of Lutcher & Moore—now Frances Ann, Miriam and William Stark, F.H. Farwell, and Lutcher Stark—voted to restructure the company, increasing two-thirds of the capital stock from $1 million to $4 million, changing the authorized stock from four thousand to forty thousand shares, and slightly amending its purposes. They also authorized and instructed the new officers of Lutcher & Moore to buy the Brown properties from the Lutcher-Stark-Farwell individuals.[51]

In the early days of the new year, January 2, 1920, the directors of Lutcher & Moore duly authorized the amendment of the charter and the purchase of the Brown holdings for the original amount paid the Browns—$2,914,600.00—plus $100,000.00 in sale expenses and a further $2,725,599.29 for a like amount in dollars of the capital stock of Lutcher & Moore by virtue of its increased capital.[52] The amount paid by the Lutcher-Stark-Farwell group totaled $5,740,199.29.[53] Although the two separate branches of the family still owned some properties together, the Browns would no longer be a part of Lutcher & Moore.

On January 20, the directors voted in the new officers: president, William Stark; vice president and general manager, F.H. Farwell; and secretary, Lutcher Stark.[54] Lutcher, who had owned 50 shares of stock prior to the corporation's increase in capital, emerged from the reorganization of Lutcher & Moore owning 2,585 shares—151 additional shares as a result of the increase in value of his original shares and 2,384 shares an apparent gift from his mother.[55]

On November 9, 1920, Nita's mother, Ella Rankin "Granny" Hill, died in Austin at the age of sixty-one, a victim of many years' ill health.[56] The loss of this strong, loving, energetic, truly extraordinary woman was grievous not only to Nita but to the entire family.[57] Granny and Homer Hill had developed a close relationship with Miriam and William, and Granny had grown particularly close to Frances Ann.[58] A letter of Granny's written the year before her death to Frances Ann, who was then visiting in Williamsport, mirrors their friendship: "Dearest Mamoose," Granny wrote, "I certainly was more than *overjoyed* in getting your letter as I really was homesick for you. . . . I have not written as often as I would have loved to have done," she went on. "When I start to write I dread the hurting of my hands." She gave Frances Ann all the latest news of their mutual friends in Austin, then signed off, "Hurry home my dear little friend I miss you and need you. . . . Worlds of love, Dear from Granny."[59]

Granny Hill's death was also a great loss to the entire University of

Figure 7.9. Ella Rankin "Granny" Hill, mother of Nita Hill Stark.
Stark Foundation Archives.

Texas, particularly members of the sports teams, who felt it acutely and mourned deeply. The *Alcalde* dedicated an entire issue to her memory.[60] "When applying the term 'remarkable' to Granny Hill we are not indulging in rhetorical or sentimental exaggeration," one writer declared. "Each year for a quarter of a century and more she attracted to her sphere of influence a group of University boys who respected her counsel, were dominated by her judgment, and who loved her for her unselfish service."[61] As one of "Granny's Boys" put it, "She was disposed to mother every homeless or homesick boy whose path crossed hers." US Representative (and later Senator) Morris Sheppard wrote, "Always she prompted us to higher and better things. . . . That is why we look back to her hearth stone as to a holy shrine."[62] Granny Hill was buried in Oakwood Cemetery in Austin.[63]

After her mother's death, Nita received an anonymous verse by mail titled "Granny Hill":

Merchant of happiness, dealer in joys;
How they loved her, did Granny's boys . . .
Object of jokes; yet player of more,
They loved her each time more than before.
Comrade in fun; master as a scold;
When they seemed likely to lose steady hold . . .
Lover of merriment; dispenser of glee,
Absolute power of Granny's decree.[64]

Lutcher & Moore continued to flourish into the 1920s, furnishing jobs to over a thousand employees and remaining in operation during the 1920–1921 economic depression (caused partially by poor planning in the transition from wartime to peacetime economy), even though many other area mills shut down.[65] As of July 1, 1921, the net worth of the company totaled $9,011,197.35.[66] At that time Lutcher & Moore was operating the two mills at Orange, with a daily cut of four hundred thousand board feet, and a third mill at Lunita, Louisiana, which opened in 1921, "situated in the very center of its vast Louisiana timber holdings," cutting fifty thousand board feet a day.[67]

Even though the war had halted trade in Europe and Africa for a time, the familiar "Lutcher-Orange" trademark could be still be spotted on cargoes of sawn timber and lumber at various points in Mexico almost without interruption, not least because of the quality of the company's product—the famous Calcasieu longleaf yellow pine. Because Lutcher & Moore cultivated the export business, the Port of Orange at that time ranked eighth among the thirteen principal Gulf ports. Furthermore, pro-

Figure 7.10. Lutcher & Moore began grade-marking lumber in 1924,
an innovation later adopted by the entire lumber industry. Stark Foundation Archives.

claimed one publication, "there is not an industry of any magnitude in Orange that is not financed, wholly or in part, either by the Lutcher & Moore Lumber Co. as a company or by some one or more members of its board of directors."[68]

In 1924, Lutcher & Moore pioneered yet another, and perhaps its last, innovation in lumbering, this one of national import: it began grade-marking its product, beginning with a ninety-day trial, utilizing "just a common rubber stamp," according to Farwell in an open letter to the retail lumber trade.[69] On December 1 of that year, the first carload of grade-marked lumber left the company's mills. The process was so well received that not only did Lutcher & Moore adopt the practice, but the Southern Pine Association did so as well, and it quickly became universal throughout the industry.[70] "The grade marking of lumber . . . will tend not only toward a more economical distribution, but it is a big step toward bettering merchandising, and will directly benefit the manufacturer, middleman and consumer," wrote Herbert Hoover, by then US secretary of commerce. "It should be practical and beneficial for the domestic and export trade alike."[71]

In a brief foretaste of social changes to come, Orange was grazed by labor unrest in January 1919 when William Stark faced a threatened strike at the Lutcher & Moore sawmills. The Federal Labor Union Local No. 16124, an Orange union of approximately 1,250 "colored men," as they were called at the time, met with officials of the American Federation of Labor and received their approval for a proposed labor agreement seeking a closed shop, better wages, and shorter hours, to be presented to both the Lutcher & Moore and the Miller-Link lumber companies. On January 2, the local union duly delivered the proposal.[72] They requested a response by January 19, but it was not until January 21 that William Stark parried by sending a brief answer to the Central Labor Union in Orange asserting that the management of Lutcher & Moore knew of "no difficulty with our labor."[73]

The Central Labor Union insisted that the concerned parties hold a conference to discuss the unresolved issues arising from the proposed agreement,[74] requesting that consent to the meeting be given by noon on January 23. When they had received no answer from either company by January 28, local union members went on strike. That day's *Orange Daily Leader* quoted William Stark and Leopold Miller, a co-owner of the Miller-Link company, as saying that they "were at a loss as to the cause of the walkout."[75]

The mill owners finally consented to attend two meetings with committees from the central office of the American Federation of Labor. The two lumber companies insisted on conducting an "open shop," in which they would hire and employ both union and nonunion workers. (During one of the meetings, Miller declared that he "didn't care whether a man was a union man or a Baptist, so long as he delivered the goods.")[76]

Labor partisans did not prevail in that confrontation; the two Orange mill owners rejected all of the union's demands in spite of a gentlemen's agreement that had been negotiated the preceding weekend to raise wages to forty-two cents an hour and to drop the workday to nine hours. When the workers reported for work the Monday following the strike, they found that they were once again working at their original salary of thirty-six cents an hour for a ten- to eleven-hour day. (In a sign of the times, John Henry Kirby, president of the National Lumber Manufacturers Association, called their demand a violation of states' rights. "In the South," he asserted, "we tell negroes what to do; we do not counsel with them.")[77]

And one business endeavor would bode ill for the family interests. For once, William Stark's muse had failed him when, on August 4, 1920, he bought twenty-five thousand shares of stock in an investment that would haunt him: a coal mine in New Mexico—unfamiliar territory, to say the least, and a long way from home for the family in every way.[78] The Hagan

Figure 7.11. Hagan Coal Mines, near Bernalillo, New Mexico, a doomed 1920s Stark family venture a long way from the Piney Woods of East Texas. Stark Foundation Archives.

Coal Mines, Inc., deal was put together by Jean Justin "John" de Praslin, a physician and entrepreneur from Lake Charles, Louisiana, and his wife, Margaret, who floated an ambitious scheme to develop a defunct mine in Sandoval County, near Bernalillo, New Mexico. In conjunction with the mine, a railroad was to be built to connect with the nearest junction of the Atchison, Topeka, and Santa Fe Railway.[79] Initially, geologists estimated a reserve of seventy-five million tons of coal in the area, and de Praslin predicted that the mine could produce one thousand tons of coal per day.[80]

In 1922, William bought and received 85,000 additional shares from de Praslin, who expressed the hope that, with the aid of William's payment for the stock, he would be able to "paddle his own canoe." ("Here is hoping," Doug Pruter added wryly.)[81] The following year, William agreed to purchase $720,000 first mortgage bonds of Hagan Coal Mines at the price of eighty cents on the dollar, for which he would receive 720,000 shares of capital stock. Through the next few years, he continued to purchase more stock, ultimately accumulating at least 1,762,165 shares.[82]

Almost from the beginning, the Hagan Coal Mines venture went wrong. The coal turned out to be lignite, the lowest grade of coal, instead of the finest, anthracite;[83] the venture proved to be a consistent money drain; and as its financial footing deteriorated, the principals began to develop a growing distrust of de Praslin. "They seem to be going pretty strong when it comes to spending money," Pruter wrote William on August 8, 1924. "I advised Lutcher to insist on being furnished with a statement showing the amount of money it would take to complete construction."[84] With time, the situation only grew worse.[85]

The decade of the 1920s, arguably one of the most dynamic decades of Lutcher Stark's life, saw him blazing his own sizable—and highly visible—trail across the Texas horizon. Characteristically, he obsessively tackled his interests with every scrap of energy, mental and physical, at his command, and consequently began to effect an impressive list of triumphs. A contemporary newspaper account describes him in those years: "A well-built young man, whose hair is turning iron-gray around the edges, sat in the smoking room of a Pullman car as the Southern Pacific day train clicked over rail joints between New Orleans and Houston. He wore a snap brim hat, horn-rimmed glasses, and smoked an oddly shaped briar pipe."[86]

In a letter from the Samoset in Rockport, Maine (Miriam and William's favorite summer resort, where he enjoyed his daily golf game on their famed course[87]), to Frances Ann, Nita sketched a more intimate picture of her husband that allows a glimpse of his human side—and his temperament. "Lutcher took the car down to Springfield [Massachusetts] to see if everything was all right," she wrote Frances Ann:

> You know how cranky he is about a car. If anything ever goes wrong, he says [their chauffeur, I.B.] Murray is to blame. . . . On the way back he was driving through Methune [Methuen] Massachusetts when the cop told him he was going too fast. Lutcher says he was only going fifteen as he was lost and looking for the sign. Anyway the cop arrested him for stealing the car and put both him and Murray in jail. Lutcher phoned to the president of the Rolls factory to identify him also the mayor of Orange & sheriff, which all did and then that boob cop would not let him go as he did not have his registration papers. Lutcher said he was sorer than a boiled owl but dared not be anything but pleasant. Finally the cop told him unless he could get papers from the registrar in Boston, he would have to wait until papers came from Texas. Lutcher hired a taxi and beat it to Boston arriving just a few minutes after the office was closed but the girl let him in. The registrar gave him a N. E. licence & a reprimand to the cop. While [Lutcher was] in the custody of the police someone scratched the car and Lutcher said he was going to sue the town of Methune for a paint job. It is too funny to hear him tell it and when he tells it, he gets madder & madder.[88]

Lutcher took his place at Lutcher & Moore as its secretary-treasurer, and many of the commercial establishments in town counted him as an officer, director, or stockholder.[89] The year 1920 saw his election as governor of the Eighteenth District of Rotary,[90] and on May 24, 1921, he was

elected chairman of the University of Texas Board of Regents, the youngest ever to hold the office.[91] His early philanthropies on behalf of groups at
the university and in his hometown crystallized into a lifetime commitment to youth, and he began to utilize his high-ranking positions as a university regent and a Rotary officer for their benefit.[92] "Some men paint,
but I don't," he later declared. "Some men write, but I can't. And I won't
have anything to leave behind except the men I rear." "A one-man youth
movement," writer Kenneth Foree called him.[93] And Nita Stark later said
of him, "He gives of himself, his time, and his money unstintingly towards developing the most ideal situation that he can conceive of for the
education of the youth of this state."[94]

Almost simultaneously with his election as chairman of the regents,
Lutcher was also becoming active in Rotary International.[95] The Great War
had necessarily put a halt to the family's European travels, but in June
1921 the group—Frances Ann, Lutcher, Nita, William, Miriam, and Ida
Achenbach—as well as Ida Elisabeth Roos, a.k.a. "Fraulein," a young
Swiss woman who lived for several years with William and Miriam and
often traveled with them;[96] Byron Simmons, Lutcher's personal secretary,
who had come to work for the Stark interests the year before; and Nita's father, the newly widowed Homer Hill,[97] trekked across the Atlantic to Edinburgh, Scotland, where the annual Rotary International convention was
held, with plans to make another extended tour of Europe.[98] They sailed
June 1 from New York aboard the RMS *Caronia*,[99] Lutcher armed with letters of introduction from dignitaries at home, including US senator Morris Sheppard and Texas governor Pat M. Neff.[100]

In Edinburgh, the party enjoyed rounds of garden parties, pageants,
dances, meetings, speeches, and receptions.[101] "Lutcher is running for
Vice President [of Rotary International]," Nita wrote her cousins Raymond
and Frankie (Cochran) Hill,[102] "and [he] is all excitement. . . . Mamoose
does not know it so we dare not mention it as she blows up," she added
obscurely. But she later reported to the Hills that, in the election for vice
president, Lutcher had placed a disappointing third, making him Rotary's
third vice president. "Had Lutcher done as his Texas delegates wished,"
she went on, "he would have been first." She declined to elaborate on what
they had wanted him to do.[103]

They visited Melrose Abbey, described in Sir Walter Scott's poem "The
Lay of the Last Minstrel," and Dryburgh Abbey, his burial place, as well
as Abbottsford, his home. "Dear Old Scott," Nita wrote. "It was wonderful
to recall all his books and see the things he so romantically wrote about."
She described the Grand Ball at the convention, reflecting wryly that "all
Scotland turned out to visit the freaks (us)," but observing in turn, "when
these Scotch speak we need an interpreter."[104]

Figure 7.12. Lutcher Stark (*center*) at Rotary banquet in Edinburgh, Scotland, 1921, on his election as third vice president of Rotary International. Stark Foundation Archives.

The party moved on by train to London, where they enjoyed more rounds of social events, Lutcher sitting next to the Lord Mayor of the city at one dinner and being presented to King George V and Queen Mary at court. They saw the sights—the "magnificent grandeur" of Westminster Abbey as well as Windsor Castle and Hampton Court, where they were given tea in their honor by David Lindsay, the 27th Earl of Crawford. When Lutcher spoke at a luncheon in Nottingham, Nita noted, the assembly "came off their dignity enough to sing 'For He's a Jolly Good Fellow.'" She complained that she had never seen so much food in her life. "My poor gall bladder needs some repairs I can assure [you]," she wrote Raymond and Frankie Hill. The group visited Stratford-upon-Avon and "all the haunts of Shakespeare," where, Nita wrote, "we buried, reared, churched, schooled and married him." At the British Museum she viewed the Rosetta Stone with awe, marveling at the three forms of writing—Demotic, Greek, and the hitherto undecipherable Egyptian hieroglyphics—that first enabled scholars to translate the ancient pictographs.[105]

They crossed the English Channel at Calais and traveled through France, honoring Independence Day by visiting some of the battlefields of the Great War—Chateau Thierry, Belleau Wood, the Marne, Montigny—then enjoyed a taste of Paris night life before making more rounds of garden parties given by various members of the French nobility.[106] William left the group in mid-July to return home;[107] he actually preferred being at home—"a lover of his fireside," as one writer termed him.[108] "Your father was pleased to get home, being better satisfied here I suppose than anywhere else in the world," Farwell wrote Lutcher, who had remained abroad. "Still," he continued, "I do not believe he felt very easy about leaving all [you] folks over there."[109]

Although Nita made no further comment on the battlefields or the war beyond simply noting that they had visited them, Miriam wrote vividly to William, by then back in Orange, of the damage to the countryside wrought by the fighting and the progress the French had made toward recovery:

> You remember [the town of Montdidier, in Picardy] was entirely wiped out by the Germans. In fact that whole section was destroyed more or less. It is surprising how the people have recovered and are tilling the soil. . . . They are using American farming machinery. We came along miles of road where the trees have all been killed by being shot to pieces. You never saw such quantities of barbed wire as was along side of the road and wires hanging from the trees & many times wire netting with the camaflouge material hanging to it.[110]

After having toured the Argonne sector and the Saint-Mihiel battlefield, Miriam remarked on the beauty of the country. "What must it have been before the war," she exclaimed. "If you only had not been in such a great hurry to have gone home," she chided, "you could have seen it all in a week or two." She could not refrain from adding, "I hope pretty soon you will cultivate an inquiring mind."[111]

In spite of her scolding, she missed him. "I wish you were here with us," she wrote him wistfully later that July from Barcelona, Spain, where the group had traveled after they left France. "Somehow we must not allow ourselves to grow apart as we are doing. As we grow old it seems to me we should grow more chummy, don't you think so." (She had her priorities, however. "It seems to me we are too old to be so far apart," she wrote still later. "I would like to be with you, but Texas is too hot for me at this time of year.")[112]

In Valencia, Nita and Fraulein endured a frightening incident when "some kind of anarchist," as Nita called him, "attempted to end our erstwhile career" by throwing the remains of a bisque doll into their car. The doll did not explode, but they threw it out again as rapidly as possible, for, as Nita observed, "bomb throwing is the favorite stunt here." At Valencia Cathedral, Homer Hill, ever the physician and scientist, became outraged by what, in his view, constituted nothing more than schemes to hood-

Figure 7.13. From left, back row: Homer Barksdale Hill, Miriam Stark, Lutcher Stark. Front row: Nita Stark (*left*), Ida Roos (*right*). Photograph made in Barcelona during the family's 1921 European tour. Stark Foundation Archives.

wink the gullible: the display of the so-called Valencia Chalice, purporting to have been used by Christ at the Last Supper, and the large numbers of small gold articles fashioned in the shapes of various body parts that had been left at the altar, accompanying the pilgrims' prayers for healing. "Papa was so disgusted," Nita wrote, "that he could not refrain from showing his feelings at the fraud."[113]

In Madrid, the party saw a bullfight. "After the first bull was killed," Nita wrote, "I took a back seat, but got up twice too often to look. We saw the bull pick up . . . the toreador & pitch him in the air, goring him. They carried him out . . . [and] we fear he died. I also [saw] a poor horse gored to death. It is all barbarous & disgusting."[114] From Madrid they headed to Lisbon and other European destinations, including another visit to Brunnen, Switzerland, probably to pay a return visit to the Benzigers, then returned home in October.[115]

Lutcher's career in Rotary was still running at full throttle; in March 1922, in his official capacity as third vice president of Rotary International, he traveled with Nita to Havana, Cuba, to participate in the Twenty-Fifth District Conference.[116] (In the only recorded instance of any disapproval Frances Ann ever expressed of her favorite grandson, she "fussed" to Farwell about their flying from Havana back to Key West rather than traveling by boat.)[117] Lutcher harbored ambitions for even higher office; at the convention to be held June 4 in Los Angeles, he intended to run for president of Rotary International. He planned to attend with Nita, Frances Ann, Miriam, William, Ida Achenbach, and Fraulein—Ida Roos—then to make another extensive trip to Europe in the summer, embarking from New York on the steamship *Berengaria* on July 11 and remaining for several months to tour the British Isles, France, Italy, Holland, Belgium, Switzerland, Spain, and Germany.[118]

At the conference, Lutcher was nominated for president by Norman Black of Fargo, North Dakota. He held second place on the first and second ballots but then withdrew his name from the race and moved that election of the first-place candidate, Raymond M. Havens of Kansas City, be made unanimous.[119] Havens was duly elected. For unknown reasons, Lutcher and Nita apparently did not accompany the others to Europe. A squib appeared in the local newspaper the following October 21: "W. H. Stark, president of Lutcher & Moore Lumber Company, who, with Mrs. Stark, and her mother, Mrs. H. J. Lutcher, and others, toured in Europe this summer, will leave New York Sunday for Orange. Mr. Stark will arrive home alone, other members of the party remaining in the East for a few days."[120] No mention was made of Lutcher and Nita, and, although he remained active in Rotary on the local level, his defeat marked the end of his involvement on the international scene.

In March 1921 William Stark had marked his seventieth birthday, and Farwell could see that the years were beginning to take their toll on his employer and friend. That July, Farwell had written Lutcher, then on board the RMS *Berengaria* in Cherbourg, France, with a little fatherly advice and a gentle reminder that he was needed on the home front:

> I was interested . . . in asking . . . just what the duties of a Vice President were. Was glad to know that outside of attending board meetings you will be relieved of a goodly portion of that last-year high pressure traveling. While we are all delighted, Boy, that they recognized you over there, and while, personally, it goes without saying I knew you would climb, and, like your own folks, I am just about as anxious as you are that you make good higher up, still I think I have your feeling of wanting to get home and do some helping—and help is certainly needed. I am sensing that your father would like to have you offer to take some of his load, and I know you are going to do it.[121]

At some point, William began having eye problems of an unspecified nature that eventually led to his almost total blindness.[122] On April 9, 1922, he wired Doug Pruter from New York that he was entering the hospital the next day for surgery. "Don't know when can come home," he added.[123] Farwell wired Lutcher two days later: "Your father's left eye operated on yesterday successfully resting easy no fever stop letter from your father the other day said he was anxious to get it over with so he could see the golf ball better."[124] (William had become an avid golfer, and many of his letters contained accounts of his recent rounds and critiques of his own golf game—but never of anyone else's.)[125] In June, he wrote Pruter that the doctor had decided not to operate again at that time but had observed that the "blind spot" in the left eye had become larger, possibly necessitating further surgery in the future.[126] By that October, he still remained in New York for eye treatments, and as the years passed, the problems worsened.

Miriam telegraphed Pruter on June 27, 1923, from the Waldorf Astoria that William had entered Lenox Hill Sanitarium in New York for two weeks' treatment "same as he had before" and would not be able to go to Maine before mid-July.[127] "A message yesterday . . . said your father had gone to the sanitarium for rest and treatment," Farwell wrote Lutcher Stark. "Let's hope this rest, plus the summer in Maine, will be beneficial."[128] Writing Frances Ann in August, Lutcher reported optimistically that all seemed to be well with his parents: "Pop . . . has recovered his health & spirits and weighs 180," but he observed that "Mama is as heavy as her clothes will permit."[129]

On September 29, back in New York, William reported to Pruter that he was balancing his time between attending shows with Lutcher and seeing a dentist. He confessed: "My teeth were in terrible condition, and I have made up my mind that is the cause of my stomach trouble and maybe my eyes. Dr. Blum of [New Orleans] told me that he thought probably my teeth was augmenting that trouble. . . . I had five extractions day before yesterday in about five minutes. . . . I am eating soup," he added wryly.[130] The next year, he paid the dentist, Dr. Henry San, $10,000. "In reconditioning an entire dental structure [possibly for both William and Miriam]," Dr. San's bill read, "I make one original charge for the work done and thereafter make no charges . . . as I consider it then my responsibility to keep the patient's mouth fit."[131]

Inevitably, William's health problems recurred. "I have never seen Dad as contented as he is here," Nita, with William and Miriam at the Samoset, commented in a letter to Frances Ann, but added worriedly: "He seems much better but I think he is far from well."[132] On October 6, 1924, William wired Pruter, "am still going the rounds with the doctors." He wired later, "Reese [presumably one of his doctors] sending me to doctor in Philadelphia to pass on whether I have operation or not go there Wednesday."[133] His condition (he did not specify its nature) apparently required an operation; "I go under the knife this afternoon," he wired again on December 6.[134] Apparently, on that occasion, at least, he recovered fully. "It is certainly gratifying to learn of your rapid recovery from your operation," Pruter wrote on December 17. "I hope that it will be the last of your trouble."[135]

Even so, the following August, William wrote Doug from the Samoset, discussing various business issues, appending his usual critique on his golf game but adding a telling comment: "I do get beautiful drives but cannot yet control My approach shots *in fact I cannot see good enough.*"[136] And Miriam wrote Nita from the Samoset: "Dad has been quite sick since you left. Nothing serious but still it makes me feel anxious when he complains so much about the pain around his heart."[137]

Nita herself kept busy. In 1922 she was named chairman of the Settlement School in Gatlinburg, Tennessee, a school for disadvantaged children maintained by the national organization of Pi Beta Phi, and she for many years served as a national officer of the sorority, making periodic official visits to its various college chapters.[138] In 1923, Governor Pat Neff appointed her as a state delegate to the annual conference of the Illiteracy Commission of the National Education Association to be held that year in Little Rock, Arkansas.[139]

Lutcher Stark's affection for Nita apparently remained undiminished, as shown in a long, newsy letter in 1924 from him to his "little girl," who was staying at the Plaza Hotel in New York. "Dearest Girl," he began, then recounted gossip and news from home, including the current drought, progress on housecleaning and garden work, Nita's cousin's appendectomy, and politics—specifically the upcoming governor's race, in which Democrat Miriam "Ma" Ferguson was running against the former dean of the University of Texas Law School, George C. Butte, who headed the Republican ticket. (Ferguson won the race.) "It looks as if I always stay away from you when you need me," he added, possibly referring to a health issue, "but I assure you . . . such is not my intention. . . . You don't know how I miss you," he ended. "Lots of love to yourself. Lutch."[140] He later wrote Frances Ann, "Nita looks fine and weighs about 115."[141]

Nonetheless, in her photos from those years, a subtle sadness lurks behind Nita's eyes, and family letters contain the first mentions of her oncoming health problems. Although she herself made no reference to them in her letters during the 1921 trip, Farwell wrote to William in Brunnen that he hoped "the change, rest, and [unspecified] treatment will be beneficial to Nita."[142]

She sustained a terrible shock when her father died suddenly on July 18, 1923, at the age of seventy-two.[143] After Granny's death, Homer Hill had re-

Figure 7.14. Frances Ann Lutcher toward the end of her life, undated.
Stark Foundation Archives.

mained close to the family and visited frequently in Orange. That July 17, when he arrived for a short visit, he complained of feeling ill and retired to his room, informing Nita that he had been suffering from "neuralgia of the heart" but that she was not to be alarmed. When she went into his room a short time later, he asked that she call a doctor, who examined him but did not think his situation serious.[144]

Nita promptly called Lutcher, who was attending a Rotary luncheon, and asked him to return home. Dr. Hill's condition grew worse through the afternoon but by the next morning had improved slightly. Nonetheless, when Lutcher returned to the room a short time later, he found his father-in-law dead.[145] Funeral services were held at Nita and Lutcher's home; then his body was transported back to Austin for burial beside Granny in Oakwood Cemetery.[146]

His obituary read, in part: "His life was that of the highest type of southern gentleman, with high ideals distinctly drawn—right as opposed to wrong, charity and mercy as opposed to harshness."[147] As a friend said of him: "[He was] a man of rare and splendid qualities. . . . A Prince in Israel he certainly was, true, strong, gentle, and refined."[148] Until his death, Dr. Hill still served as an unpaid medical adviser to the athletic program at the University of Texas.[149]

The sudden blow struck Nita hard; she now found herself the last sur-

vivor of her immediate family. Lutcher, at the Samoset, wrote his grandmother, then in Colorado at the ranch:

> I'm sure everyone has written you about Doctor's passing. It was one of the
> greatest losses of my life and nearly killed Nita. If we had thought out every de-
> tail though we could not have wished it better. He was with her. He did not suf-
> fer long. He was active in his practice. And he was prepared to go. I'm sure he
> came to Orange prepared to die this time and he left everything in perfect or-
> der. Gradually we are recovering from the blow but his memory will linger al-
> ways growing sweeter as God gives us the realization of his many wonderful
> qualities. I don't know any man, except my father, who exerted so great an in-
> fluence upon my life.[150]

Nita wrote sadly to Frances Ann, "Somehow these days letter writing is
hard. My mind does not function clearly. . . . I am happy you had such a
lovely time at the ranch. There are very dear memories of that place, when
with all my dear ones seated in that lovely living room. How little did I
dream there that life was so short for those I loved most."[151]

That autumn, however, Nita and Lutcher Stark found just cause for celebration in the birth of fraternal twin boys, Frank Robert and William Patterson Mills.[152] They were born April 26, 1923, in Radford, Virginia,[153] to a twenty-eight-year-old single woman named Bertie Mills. The
father's name was listed as unknown.[154] Prior to the birth of the twins,
Mills had borne five other children, all with unknown fathers and all removed from her care and committed at various times to the Virginia State
Board of Public Welfare.[155] That September, the twins were also removed
from Mills's custody, committed to the State Board by the Juvenile and
Domestic Relations Court of Radford, and then to a state orphanage, the
Children's Home Society of Virginia.[156]

Nita and Lutcher found the infants through the services of a "baby
home finder," Osceola DeVault, who located the twins at the Children's
Home Society and began negotiations that October on the Starks' behalf.[157] They gained custody of the twins sometime in October or November 1923 and brought them to Orange.[158] The *Leader* reported that "they
are now nestled snugly at the Stark home . . . where they have both been
received as 'regular fellows' by their foster parents and friends. . . . Each
youngster now has a bank account which will grow until they become of
college age, and then an education will be theirs."[159]

The Starks questioned the Children's Home Society regarding the babies' family medical history and background. In reply the society sent them
a statement by the physician who had delivered them, Dr. J.A. Noblin, who

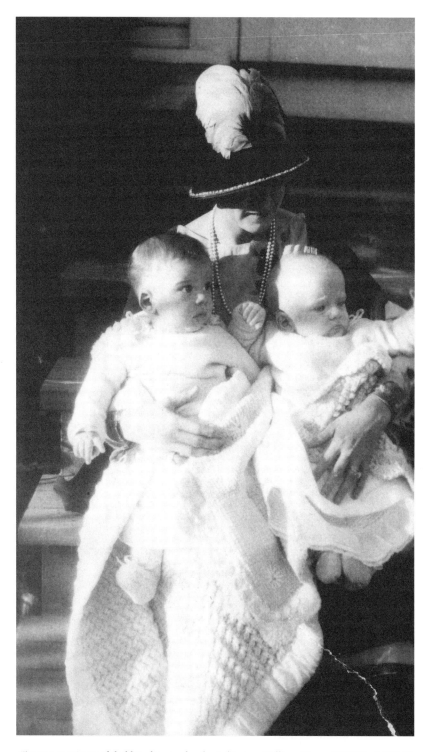

Figure 7.15. Nita Stark holding her newly adopted twins, William Henry "Bill" Stark II (*left*) and Homer Barksdale Hill Stark (*right*), 1923. Stark Foundation Archives.

Figure 7.16. William Stark, horseback, holding his namesake, Bill Stark, ca. 1924. Stark Foundation Archives.

Figure 7.17. William holding Homer Stark, ca. 1924, his amusement at Homer's tears apparent. Stark Foundation Archives.

asserted that the Mills family were "a very healthy and long lived people" with no insanity, venereal disease, cancer, or tuberculosis in their ranks (excepting one of Bertie's sisters, who had died of TB at age twelve) and that, except for the whooping cough that the twins had contracted in May and June of that year, they had enjoyed perfect health since their birth.[160]

"The mother is intelligent, but raised under bad environment,"

Dr. Noblin went on. He was obviously acquainted with the father as well, adding that "the father of the twins is intelligent."[161] The society appended a further bit of information: "The father of these twins is not living with the mother and the mother was not in a position to give the children any proper care and training."[162] Just over a year later, on January 29, 1925, the society issued certificates of consent to the twins' adoption.[163] The Starks signed the papers the following March, making them the legal parents.[164] They renamed the older twin Homer Barksdale Hill Stark for Nita's recently deceased father, and the younger, William Henry Stark II for Lutcher's father.

In the autumn of 1924, Frances Ann, still active and adventurous, launched herself on one of her frequent lengthy automobile tours, this one in the East.[165] (She traveled as she customarily did, driven in her Pierce-Arrow limousine by her chauffeur, Herbert Fiedler, the smaller Pierce-Arrow, loaded with luggage, supplies, and emergency equipment, following just behind.) She had reached New York, doubtless bent on making her regular rounds of shopping and theatergoing, when, on or around October 10 or 11, she suffered a massive stroke.[166]

Lutcher, Miriam, William, and Carrie rushed to New York.[167] On October 11 Doug Pruter wrote William there, prefacing his usual business report: "News of Mrs. Lutcher's condition was received with deep regret and we all hope that her strong constitution and will power will make this attack only temporary." The doctors, too, held out some hope that her iron will would prevail, but in the following days she developed pneumonia,[168] and ten days later, on October 21, 1924, surrounded by her family members, Frances Ann Lutcher—"wonder woman of the lumber industry," philanthropist, business executive, family matriarch, everyone's Mamoose— died at 10:43 p.m. She was four days past her eighty-fourth birthday.[169]

While the town stood by in mourning, Frances Ann's body arrived in Orange around 7:20 p.m. on October 24 by special funeral car. In love and respect for her, those from all walks of life, "thousands" according to one newspaper account, waited silently, men with heads uncovered, at the Southern Pacific passenger station in Orange as the funeral car was transferred on switch tracks to the Lutcher residence on Water Street. Her body was then borne inside, where she spent her last night in her old Sabine River home.[170] At 10:30 the next morning, she was conveyed to the Lutcher Memorial Building of the First Presbyterian Congregation, where she lay in state in the magnificent sanctuary, every detail of which she had so lovingly and carefully planned, until her funeral services commenced at 3:00 p.m. Until that time, a continuous stream of people filed past her open casket to pay their last respects.[171]

Figure 7.18. Frances Ann Lutcher holding Bill Stark, ca. 1923–1924.
Stark Foundation Archives.

Orange's mayor, S.M. White, issued a proclamation requesting that all city offices be closed from 2:00 p.m. to 5:00 p.m. and that all city employees stop their work. "I would appreciate it very much," he went on, "if the citizens of the city would join in paying respect to one we all loved and who will be missed exceedingly."[172] It had been intended that Orange businesses would remain closed from the time her death was announced until after her funeral, but the family suggested that only those concerns to which she was connected be closed, and for the day of the service only. Even so, they made up a large portion of the establishments in Orange.[173]

Appropriately for Frances Ann, floral tributes abounded, and her casket was covered with a blanket of lavender orchids and maidenhair fern from her own conservatories. "Flowers were never sent to one who loved them more than she," the *Leader* declared, "for wherever she was, at home or abroad, she had quantities of choice flowers around her."[174] A Williamsport newspaper noted that "her life will bloom in the memory of thousands of the citizens who knew and loved her."[175]

Reverend E.T. Drake conducted the service, simple and brief according to her wishes. Afterward, the congregation formed a procession, "the largest ever witnessed in Southeast Texas," according to the *Leader*, that included a full five hundred employees of Lutcher & Moore, who marched in the cortege to accompany the casket to the Lutcher mausoleum in Evergreen Cemetery. There, after twelve years as Henry Jacob Lutcher's widow, she joined him at last in death.[176]

"She was a philanthropist in the purest and deepest sense of the word," one newspaper declared, and another, "hers was the kindest, tenderest heart in the world with a ready sympathy when it was needed, and it was also the strongest, most courageous heart when righteous indignation was merited."[177] Another called her "the richest woman in the South, and one of the best loved."[178] Her former hometown of Williamsport paid its homage, too, with a memorial article and an editorial, describing her as "one of the grandest women in all of Southern Texas . . . a woman grand and good in generous deeds."[179] Amid the praise, one article probably came closest to expressing the feelings of her family: "And for those who were nearest and dearest, dear little 'Mamoosie's' place can never be filled."[180]

An envelope fragment, its letter missing, tells a poignant tale: it is addressed in Lutcher Stark's handwriting to "Mrs. H. J. Lutcher, Waldorf-Astoria, New York City," postmarked October 17, 1924, and marked "Special Delivery." It bears Nita Stark's handwritten note: "Bill's first letter to his Mamoose, three days before her death." The letter itself must have consisted of a few babyish marks on the page; Bill and his twin, Homer, would only have been a little over a year old when Frances Ann died.[181]

The contents of Frances Ann's will further exacerbated the already-strained family relations and plunged the Stark and Brown factions into a bitter wrangle that persisted for many years. She bequeathed portraits, art objects, and an astonishing array of jewelry of all kinds to various members of her family; her gifts to both Miriam and Carrie included pins, lavalieres, bracelets, earrings, and rings of all descriptions set with diamonds, sapphires, amethysts, opals, pearls, and other precious materials. She left to Lutcher a black diamond, a ruby, a large prayer rug, and a Satsuma vase, among other objects, and to Nita her diamond necklace and other pieces of jewelry, as well as a suit with chinchilla trim and a set of ermine furs.

She left her other grandsons, Edgar Brown Jr. and Lutcher Brown, a pear-shaped diamond each, and to her great-granddaughter Babette a pearl-and-diamond ring for her sixteenth birthday and a diamond ring for her seventeenth. For Babette's eighteenth, Frances Ann bequeathed her a diamond-and-emerald gold bracelet, a diamond ring, a miniature of Babette set with pearls, the Benziger portrait of herself with Babette, her rose point lace dress and fan, a chatelaine, and a box of trinkets.[182]

She left numerous cash bequests to various friends, relatives, and employees: monthly stipends to her lifelong friend Ida Achenbach (and a topaz ring and diamond bracelet to Ida's daughter, Helen Achenbach Fowler) and to her Lutcher sisters-in-law and cousins, and various cash gifts to her servants: Rosa Hamilton; Fannie Williams; her watchman, F.H. Clough; her gardener, Joseph Kastizenski; and her chauffeur, Herbert Fiedler.[183]

To Miriam and Carrie, she left the sum of $1 million each, and to her two younger grandsons, Edgar Brown Jr. and Lutcher Brown, $5,000 each. She named her oldest grandson, Lutcher Stark, as independent executor of her estate, directing him to pay her other bequests and to deliver the gifts she had assigned to others in the will. The entire residue of her estate, including all real property, stocks and bonds, personal property, her house in Orange, and Roslyn Ranch in Colorado, not to mention "one of America's finest collections of orchids," she left to Lutcher Stark.[184]

She added a final caveat:

> Should any person to whom a bequest is made herein contest this will or engage in any character of contest or attack thereon, or institute any litigation over my estate in contradiction of the terms of this will, such bequests to such person or persons shall immediately become null and void and the property or properties bequeathed to them shall become a part of the corpus of my estate as though no such bequest had ever been made.[185]

Ten days after her death, on October 31, 1924, Lutcher Stark applied to be appointed as its temporary administrator and was so named by County Judge E.S. McCarver on November 3.[186]

The backlash from the Brown side of the family came instantly. That same day, Fannie's widower, Rucie Moore, acting as guardian for their thirteen-year-old daughter, Babette, filed a contest of the will, alleging that the document presented for probate appeared to be an "altered and mutilated" instrument; that Frances Ann was "of unsound mind" when it was executed; that she did not have "sufficient mental capacity" to make a valid will; and that it was made as a result of "undue influence exercised . . . by those interested in the execution, including H. J. L. Stark, and is not the free will of the maker."[187]

Moore also filed an objection to Lutcher's appointment as temporary administrator of Frances Ann's estate. In place of Lutcher, who, he alleged, had exercised total control of her estate and who had misused her funds as his own, he petitioned the court to appoint a competent, disinterested administrator who could perform a complete audit of the estate and determine any debts it might owe to the estate of Henry Lutcher, since, he claimed, Frances Ann, as her husband's executrix, had never made a final settlement of her husband's estate, and that its condition was unknown to anyone. Charging that any conveyances from Frances Ann to Lutcher Stark were "fraudulent and void," Moore demanded that Lutcher be disqualified "by law and in morals" from acting as her temporary administrator.[188] Judge E.S. McCarver overruled Moore's objections, and Lutcher was duly sworn in November 4 as temporary administrator of Frances Ann's estate.[189]

A month later, Carrie Lutcher Brown filed a similar petition seeking that the court set aside Lutcher's appointment and name a disinterested temporary administrator with auditing authority. Carrie demanded an investigation of transferences from her estate to Lutcher, instituting suit for their recovery if they appeared to have been transferred for illegal purposes or were approved by Frances Ann without her understanding. She alleged that Frances Ann, as independent executrix of Henry Lutcher's will,

> had no actual control of the business and knew nothing about the affairs of either her own estate or the estate of her deceased husband: that she was in the habit of signing all instruments that were handed to her for her signature, and that most of her business either in the control of her own affairs or in administering the estate of her husband was conducted under a general power of attorney to H. J. Lutcher Stark, who has never accounted to her nor to any other person as to his administration thereof.[190]

Carrie further claimed that Lutcher Stark, William Stark, and F.H. Farwell actually controlled the affairs of both Frances Ann's and Henry Lutcher's estates and that her requests to have the accounts audited had so far been refused. She also expressed the fear that, since the will specified that the bequests be honored in order of their listing and since she was the last beneficiary named, she would never receive her bequest for reason that, under Lutcher's administration, it would be made to appear that sufficient funds would not be available to pay all bequests.[191]

Carrie, like Moore, charged that her father's estate had not been closed and that no final account had been given, and that Frances Ann's estate was heavily in debt to that of Henry Lutcher. She also took issue with Frances Ann's 1919 gift to Lutcher Stark of her one-third ownership in the Wier Long Leaf Lumber Company operation, claiming that her mother had acted "without knowledge or understanding" and alleging that Lutcher had engineered the gift as a means of avoiding estate and inheritance taxes. If the will were denied admission to probate, Carrie maintained, she would then be entitled to half her mother's estate, including Frances Ann's part of the Wier concern.[192] But she was doomed to disappointment; Judge McCarver overruled her motion and ruled that Lutcher's appointment continue in force.[193]

On January 12, 1925, following testimony by Orange jeweler Joe Lucas, a longtime business associate and friend, and Dr. A.G. Pearce, Frances Ann's personal physician, both of whom swore that at the time she signed the will she was "enjoying good health, and was of sound mind . . . vigorous in both mind and body,"[194] Judge DeWitt C. Bennett overruled Rucie Moore's contest, admitted Frances Ann's will to probate, and named

Lutcher Stark as executor of her estate.[195] Lutcher took the oath of office that same day.[196] But Moore gave notice of appeal, and *R.A. Moore, Guardian of Brownie Babette Moore, vs. H.J.L. Stark* was accordingly set for trial in the Orange County District Court on November 23, 1925.[197]

Judge Victor Hoy Stark, who was Lutcher Stark's uncle,[198] recused himself from the proceedings and exchanged districts with Judge J.D. Campbell of the Sixtieth Judicial District in Beaumont for the trial.[199] Judge Campbell affirmed the judgment of the Orange County Court, ruling that Moore had produced no evidence to prove Babette's interest in Frances Ann's estate and therefore had no right to contest her will. Moore again appealed, this time to the Court of Civil Appeals for the Ninth Judicial District of Texas, sitting in Beaumont.[200]

The Court of Appeals certified several questions to the Supreme Court of Texas, one regarding the will's possible violation of the rule against perpetuities, but the higher court ruled that the question was irrelevant, since in any case "the appellant [Moore] is not entitled to contest its [the will's] probate because his [ward is] shown to have no interest in the estate" and recommended that the motion for rehearing be overruled.[201] On November 21, 1929, the Court of Civil Appeals affirmed the judgment of the District Court and, by mandate dated February 22, 1930, so ordered it, directing Moore to pay all court costs, thus finally disposing of the case.[202]

In the meantime, on May 29, 1926, Carrie Brown also filed suit against Lutcher Stark in the Jasper County District Court, still seeking to set aside Frances Ann's gift to him of her one-third interest in the Wier operation. Carrie again charged that, when Frances Ann had made the gift, she was "without business experience, or knowledge, and not acquainted with her property or property rights," that she lacked the "mental capacity" to comprehend the effect of her actions, and further, that Lutcher "wrongfully took advantage of his confidential and trust relationship" with his "infirm and inexperienced" grandmother to exercise over her "such influence as to substitute his will for hers and deprive her of her own will in her acts . . . for his own selfish purposes and benefits."[203]

Carrie also alleged that Frances Ann's intent had been only to aid Lutcher in managing the property more effectively, not to convey it to him absolutely, and that, by virtue of being one of the only two actual heirs of the property (the other being her sister, Miriam Stark), she was the legal owner of half of Frances Ann's third of the property.[204] She petitioned the court that the deed be judged void, that she be declared the owner of half interest in the concern, and that the defendant—Lutcher Stark—be required to account for all income he had received from it. This suit languished in the Jasper County District Court until December 14, 1931, when it was finally dismissed,[205] marking an end to the lawsuits involving Frances Ann's estate a full seven years after her death.

Although it was true that, for her own purposes, Frances Ann herself had previously claimed in her February 22, 1918, letter to the Orange County Draft Board that Lutcher Stark was the "necessary sole managing, controlling, or directing head" of her properties, that she depended solely on him for their management, and that she herself was unable to manage them, not being familiar with them, many disagreed categorically with the plaintiffs' assessments of her capabilities. Her longtime housekeeper, Rosa Hamilton, stated that "Mrs. Lutcher did not need anyone to advise her in anything so far as my knowledge. . . . [She] would tell me what she wanted to and she was particular to keep things to herself."[206] A former chauffeur, Clint Glasgow, swore that Frances Ann was not controlled by anyone so far as he knew.[207] George Colburn, for years the auditor for Lutcher & Moore as well as Frances Ann's personal accounts, refuted some of the claims in a deposition taken during the litigation proceedings. "I know," he stated, "that Mrs. Frances A. Lutcher was at all times during my many years' acquaintance with her mentally sound and physically fit."[208] Colburn also directly refuted two of Rucie's and Carrie's charges: "I also know of my own knowledge that on April 26, 1917, there was a full and final settlement by Frances Ann Lutcher as Executrix of the estate of Henry Jacob Lutcher, deceased, with Mrs. Carrie L. Brown and Mrs. Miriam L. Stark, and that the estate of Mrs. Frances Ann Lutcher, deceased, is not indebted to the estate of Henry Jacob Lutcher, deceased, in any sums whatever." As Colburn also pointed out, Carrie had not hesitated to sell her part of Lutcher & Moore to Frances Ann in exchange for a seven-year promissory note for about five-sixths of the consideration, of which note Frances Ann was one of the makers.[209] Publicity from the trials even provoked gratuitous defense of Frances Ann from disinterested parties. San Antonio jeweler B.M. Hammond, who had done business with Frances Ann and was incensed by the implications that she was of unsound mind, wrote Lutcher Stark on June 14, 1926:

> I notice enclosed excerpt from a local paper here, that you are being sued. . . . I will be glad to go on the stand . . . to testify that Mrs. Lutcher was absolutely sound minded at, and after dates given, and that she had a remarkable business ability as well. As I am in no way interested in the affair, it may be a valuable testimony. My wife too remembers Mrs. Lutcher's remarkable memory. . . . I have never seen anyone exhibit more capable ability at any age.[210]

The legal tangle in which Frances Ann's estate was caught would necessarily preclude settlement until the lawsuits were resolved, but in March 1930, when it appeared that outcome of the litigation would be favorable to Lutcher Stark, he held a celebration in his home. Present were his legal team from the Houston law firm of Kennerly, Williams, Lee, Hill, and

Sears; friends and employees, including F.H. Farwell, Byron Simmons, George Colburn, Raymond Hill, Dave Nelson, C.L. Baker, D.A. Pruter, and others; and his father and mother, Miriam and William Stark. During the party that night, in the presence of Lutcher, Colburn, and Simmons, Miriam announced that she would disclaim her right to Frances Ann's $1 million bequest to her in favor of Lutcher. He thanked his mother, in his words "reaching over and kissing her." Thus he received a final gift, however indirectly, from his beloved Mamoose.[211]

For a full seven years after her death, Frances Ann's venerable Pierce-Arrow automobiles, the veterans of so many of her adventures, remained stored in a garage in New York, still in the location where she had taken them on her final arrival. Lutcher searched in vain for a buyer for the automobiles and finally instructed George Colburn to employ a junk dealer to dispose of them. In the spring of 1931, Leo Becker, a Stark family friend and a resident of New York, finally found a willing recipient and gave them away.[212]

CHAPTER EIGHT

The Longhorns

Willful, powerful men had attempted to mold the University to their vision before . . . and would do so in the future. . . . But no one, of whatever era, has wielded more actual power than H.J. Lutcher Stark did in the 1920s.
—RICHARD PENNINGTON, *"FOR TEXAS, I WILL": THE HISTORY OF MEMORIAL STADIUM*

Lutcher Stark's fingerprints are all over the Forty Acres. . . . He was the prototypical UT power broker, a larger-than-life force of nature and a wealthy visionary who was passionate about the advancement of the University in all areas.
—JENNA HAYS MCEACHERN, *100 THINGS LONGHORNS FANS SHOULD KNOW & DO BEFORE THEY DIE*

When Lutcher Stark took his seat in June 1919 on the Board of Regents of the University of Texas and entered its political arena, the move signified a logical extension and a strengthening of his long-standing bond with the university. His college years there had opened a new and fascinating world that had broadened his social and intellectual horizons and given him acceptance from his peers, and the school's mystique and lore had permeated his soul. For a time, the University of Texas had held a cherished spot at the center of his universe, and after graduation, he continued to seize every opportunity to make the school the chief recipient of his philanthropy. Now its Board of Regents offered him an ideal milieu in which to spread his wings even further.

His membership on the board, which required his regular presence in Austin, also broadened his relationship with the town, a link that had been forged with his marriage to Nita. When he entered the university in 1905, Austin had hosted a population of approximately twenty-five thou-

sand. Although, as the state capital, it was the center of political activity as well as a university town, it had still retained a definite flavor of
the countryside, affording residents and students alike such delights as
springtime excursions to nearby fields of bluebonnets and poppies, swims
in the crystal waters of Barton Springs, drives to view the expansive vistas
from Mount Bonnell, or picnics on the Colorado River, wending its way
through town.[1] As time passed, much of Austin's small-town atmosphere
remained, though the little city continued to grow; by 1920, the population
numbered nearly thirty-five thousand.[2] Austin was Nita's native world,
and she and Lutcher actively participated in its social life and also helped
establish the university's economic policy and political presence.

The University of Texas had first been envisioned in 1839 by the Congress of the Republic, but a lack of financial resources, followed by years of
political and financial upheaval, had prevented its becoming a reality. Not
until 1876 did a new Texas constitution make definite provision for a "university of the first class," and in 1881, the legislature passed a bill that established the university and initiated planning.[3] Texas governor Oran M.
Roberts named the first Board of Regents, who chose pioneer physician
and Republic of Texas official Ashbel Smith as their first president.[4] In the
fall of 1883 the University of Texas began holding classes in the temporary
state capitol, and by the spring of 1884, students were attending sessions
in the west wing of the first campus structure, the new Main Building.[5]

At the time Lutcher Stark began his first term in 1919, the Board of Regents and its chairman wielded a great deal of power at the university.
The 1881 bill establishing the school had held two controversial provisions:
First, the school would be coeducational. Second, there would be no office
of university president; instead, the legislators had followed the pattern set
at the University of Virginia under Thomas Jefferson: the University of
Texas would be administered by a governing board and an elected faculty
chairman. At Texas, the Board of Regents was originally given responsibilities that at other schools would have been assigned to a president.[6] For
the first twelve years of its existence, the university had operated without a
president, and even though its structure had been changed in 1895 to create the office, the tradition of a strong Board of Regents persisted.

It was this tradition from which Lutcher Stark derived his mandate during his chairmanship of the board, beginning in 1921 and continuing in-
termittently for nearly twelve of the almost twenty-four years he served as
regent.[7] Within its context, he regularly challenged the prerogatives of various presidents and asserted his right, as he saw it, to control every aspect
of the university's development, no matter how large or minute.[8]

Another long-standing tradition at the university, one that often worked
against Lutcher's aims, lay in the prickly independence of the student

Figure 8.1. The University of Texas Board of Regents, 1924. Lutcher Stark (*front row, center*) is chairman of the board. *Cactus,* 1924, yearly publication of Texas Student Publications (now Texas Student Media), University of Texas.

body. This collective trait had shown itself as early as 1897, when students had requested a holiday to celebrate the March 2 anniversary of the sign-ing of the Texas Declaration of Independence. The new president, George Tayloe Winston, fresh from the University of North Carolina and appar-ently unaware of his petitioners' mind-set, refused their request.[9] The stu-dents protested by firing a cannon they had "borrowed" from the Capitol grounds (or perhaps from Camp Mabry, a military installation near Aus-tin), breaking a few windows in the process. The demonstration then mi-grated to the football field, where President Winston, after first remon-strating with the students, finally surrendered and joined the celebration. "I was born in the land of liberty," he declared afterward, "rocked in the cradle of liberty, nursed on the bottle of liberty, and I've had liberty preached to me all of my life. But Texas University students take more lib-erty than anyone I've ever come in contact with."[10]

On a later occasion, a group of law students who had lately been work-ing as cowboys "ran off" a substitute lecturer because he was disparag-ing their absent professor. When he returned to his classroom, the pro-fessor asked the ex-cowboys what had happened. They confessed that they had informed the substitute that he was going to leave the campus "in one big hurry"—which the man did, by report, "as if the devil were after him." The professor apparently knew his students well. "You boys all had guns," he guessed. "No, Professor," they protested. "Not half of us toted guns. But that skunk would never have given us the chance to use them."[11]

This was the independent mind-set that had still prevailed during Lutcher Stark's attendance at the university. After his freshman year, his indulgent parents and doting grandmother had seen to it that he was lodged in the Phi Gamma Delta fraternity house with other privileged young men, but in the first decades of the century, the dominant force on campus was not the fraternity crowd but the many scrappy, independent young men who lived in Brackenridge Hall (affectionately known as "B Hall"), the dormitory built in 1890 by Austin businessman and university regent George W. Brackenridge to house students with limited incomes.[12] They negotiated successfully for the right to run the dormitory themselves, and the trials and benefits of living in B Hall forged many important Texas leaders.[13]

Later, as a regent, Lutcher encountered the same kinds of feisty, individualistic students—by that time neither cannon confiscators nor gun-toting former cowboys but, most often, the staff members of the *Daily Texan*, the university's supremely independent newspaper.

The years between William Stark's service as a regent, ending in 1915, and Lutcher's, beginning in 1919, were tumultuous ones, not only for the world but for the state of Texas and its university. In 1917, coinciding with the US entry into World War I, a different kind of war broke out on the home front. Early that year, Governor James E. "Farmer Jim" Ferguson had demanded the removal of the university's newly appointed president, Robert Vinson (whom the regents had chosen without consulting him), and several faculty members Ferguson disliked for various reasons. Vinson and the regents, backed by prominent alumni and supportive members of the Texas legislature, refused to comply with most of Ferguson's demands, although they removed a few of the faculty (later rehiring all but one).[14]

The governor retaliated by vetoing all but one provision of the entire itemized legislative appropriation for the university (the veto was later declared void on a technicality). For these transgressions and prior charges of irregularities dating from a previous election, Ferguson faced an investigation into his administration, leading to indictment, impeachment charges, a conviction, and his removal from the governorship, accompanied by the stricture that he never hold office in Texas again.[15] He was replaced by Lieutenant Governor William Pettus Hobby.

Ferguson's removal indirectly led to Lutcher Stark's appointment to the Board of Regents. The ousted governor, claiming that the prohibition against holding office did not apply to him since he had resigned the day before he was removed, ran against Hobby in the 1918 gubernatorial election but was defeated in a landslide. In 1919, the newly elected Hobby appointed Lutcher as a regent.

The country's entry into World War I brought trying times to the University of Texas. At the request of the federal government and the US military, the school began training pilots, radio operators, auto mechanics, and other personnel needed for wartime work. The medical school in Galveston furnished doctors and nurses for overseas service.[16] Numbers of students, staff, and faculty enlisted or were drafted, and ninety-one succumbed on the battlefield, either to combat injuries or disease. The lethal Spanish flu pandemic soon struck the university campus itself, forcing the dismissal of classes for approximately two-thirds of the 1918 fall semester.[17] At war's end, the regents, faculty, and students, wishing to remember those who had not returned, discussed establishing a memorial of some kind—such as a dormitory or student center—but given the school's limited financial resources, little was done.[18]

At the time Lutcher Stark began his service on the board in June 1919, the university was in the midst of scaling down its involvement in military affairs, and the Spanish flu that had stalked the campus was just beginning to subside. Most of those connected with the school who had survived their wartime service returned to campus, and suddenly it found itself bursting its boundaries, which in turn presented the regents with an added financial dilemma: legislative appropriations for the school were applied to salaries and maintenance needs but were barred by law from being used for building construction.

Some years previously, to alleviate the problem, the Texas legislature had endowed the university with over two million acres of West Texas land,[19] the income from which was earmarked to build the Permanent University Fund (PUF). The interest from this fund was to be channeled into another, the Available University Fund, and utilized for building physical plants and other necessities at both the University of Texas (including the Medical Branch at Galveston and the School of Mines and Metallurgy at El Paso) and the Texas Agricultural & Mechanical College in College Station, at that time a part of the University of Texas. (Texas A&M was not thus restricted and could receive legislative appropriations for buildings.)

Unfortunately, during World War I and into the early 1920s, the Available University Fund could never furnish sufficient monies to build many permanent buildings; hence the school, faced with the burgeoning postwar enrollment, was forced to construct a number of wooden "shacks,"[20] as they were derisively dubbed, to be used as classrooms and labs.[21] (It was said that a student could sit in one of them and hear three lectures simultaneously, and upperclassmen were quick to warn new students that they would need coats and umbrellas as often *inside* the shacks as outside them.)[22]

Lutcher Stark and his fellow regents found themselves faced with many other issues besides a critical shortage of funds. Another serious consequence of the war lay in the poisonous atmosphere of suspicion, paranoia, and fear running rife throughout the country, spawned not only by the war itself but by the emergence of the new Marxist government that had gained control of Russia following the 1917 Russian Revolution. Many Texans questioned the loyalty of the state's multitude of German immigrants and their descendants, especially those teaching in Texas colleges and its university.[23] Were they pro-American? Or were they preaching the "evils of socialism"? Rumors, nearly all false or exaggerated, harmed the reputations of those at whom the rumors were directed as well as, ultimately, that of the university itself—in academic circles, at least.

The first serious piece of regents' business in which Lutcher Stark participated involved such a situation. During the war, in the midst of rabid anti-German phobia, a professor of Germanic languages at the university, Bohemian-born Eduard Prokosch, had been targeted by rumors questioning his loyalty to the United States. In June 1918, a year before Lutcher's term commenced, President Vinson had appeared before the board in response to various accusations that "enemy aliens," as the rumor-mongers labeled them, were present on the campus, primarily in the person of Prokosch. But Vinson, after consulting first with the professor's colleagues in the German Department, second with a special university committee investigating charges of disloyalty, and finally with the US attorney general, reported to the board that, despite the frequent rumors, there were "at present, no enemy aliens in the employ of this institution"—so Prokosch had stayed on.[24]

Just over a year later, with Lutcher serving on the board and with national paranoia intensifying, the issue again arose. At hearings conducted by the Texas Senate's Finance Committee, held specifically to consider the question of Prokosch's loyalty, the professor vehemently denied such charges. (At the same time, as another symptom of the prevailing fears, the legislature was actually considering the abolition of German courses in all state-supported schools.) Ultimately, the Senate brought no charges against Prokosch. Though the regents never accused the professor of any specific questionable behavior, they concluded that the furor raised by the hearings and continual investigations was creating an atmosphere detrimental to the university.[25]

It fell to Vinson to suggest to Prokosch that it might be wise for him to resign rather than suffer dismissal. The professor requested that he be al-

lowed to remain on the payroll for work to be designated—perhaps trans-
lations in the twenty-one European languages in which he was fluent!—
while he tried to redeem his name.[26] "It is my candid belief," he added,
"that, after six years of service as a full professor, I have a moral right to
expect from the University a modification of the unusual suddenness of
this action against me." His plea was ignored. In a specially called meeting, the regents responded with a resolution stating that they "found it impossible, under the circumstances, to accede to Professor Prokosch's request, and . . . ordered his position vacated effective August 31, 1919."[27] The
regent who moved to adopt the resolution was Lutcher Stark, seconded by
George W. Littlefield.

Prokosch was dismissed with less than two months' notice. Ironically, by the same resolution, the regents retained the teaching of German
courses at the university—but Professor Prokosch would not be teaching
them.[28] Instead, he continued what proved to be a distinguished career.
He was quickly hired by Bryn Mawr, where he taught from 1919 to 1928.
He later taught at Yale University and headed the Department of German
at New York University.[29]

Lutcher Stark's consequence in the world of Longhorn sports might have
been indisputable, but even those at the university who cared exclusively about them could hardly ignore his immense impact on the university's library system, beginning with two major acquisitions in the 1920s
that greatly boosted the school's standing in the ranks of academically eminent institutions. By assisting the university to acquire these collections,
then augmenting them through the years, he would become a major force
in building the Rare Books and Latin American collections into world-
class libraries.[30]

The Latin American collection marked its beginnings in Mexico City.[31]
Serendipity reigned in December 1920 when Lutcher Stark and Professor
Charles Wilson Hackett, a Latin American historian with the university's
History Department, traveled to Mexico's capital to attend the inauguration of President Álvaro Obregón.[32] The two were enjoying an afternoon
stroll down Madero Street when Hackett, examining a display in a bookstore window, spotted a first edition of Bernal Díaz del Castillo's *Histo-
ria verdadera de la conquista de la Nueva España* (True history of the con-
quest of Mexico), published in Madrid in 1632. Recognizing its rarity, he
exclaimed to Lutcher that the book should be in the library of the University of Texas. On the spot, Lutcher committed to buying it.[33]

While still at the bookstore, the two discovered from an employee that
Genaro García, a Mexican bibliophile, senator, and historian, had recently
died and that his magnificent twenty-five thousand–volume library would

soon go on the market. The next year, Lutcher saw to it that the Board of Regents appropriated $100,000 for purchase of the García library, which became the nucleus of the university's Latin American collection.[34] Even though the library already housed other books on Latin America, the García collection was a prize of extraordinary magnitude. Lutcher continued to augment it by working toward the acquisition of other collections that would attract scholars throughout the world.[35]

The collection, now known as the Nettie Lee Benson Latin American Collection (named for its longtime librarian), remains one of the finest libraries in the world devoted wholly to Latin American works.[36] In 1964, less than a year before his death, Lutcher received a letter from the university's assistant to the chancellor, W.D. Blunk. "The Latin American Collection at the University of Texas continues to serve its vital scholarly purposes and I am sure you share our pride in knowing this," Blunk wrote. "We continue to be grateful for the prominent part you played in establishing the Latin American Collection at the University."[37]

The second acquisition, four years later, primarily concerned Lutcher Stark's mother. Miriam Lutcher Stark was an oddity for her time— a female book collector in a field traditionally occupied by men.[38] (Even though she operated in a traditionally masculine domain, she herself remained a modest, dignified female, with the Victorian ideas of propriety particular to her era. A family story is told that she ordered an especially beautiful set of *The Arabian Nights* but was horrified to discover that it was unexpurgated. She banished the volumes to "a high shelf in a locked closet," where they remained for the next quarter century until they were brought out to pack with the rest of her library to transfer to the university.)[39] Through the years, she had accumulated a significant collection of rare books, manuscripts, and historical documents, including works by Byron, Shelley, Keats, and other English Romantics; a page from the Gutenberg Bible; all four of the first folio editions of William Shakespeare; letters written by George Washington, Thomas Jefferson, and several English monarchs, notably Queen Elizabeth I; and the commission issued by Emperor Charles I to Hernán Cortés as captain-general of New Spain.[40]

On December 8, 1925, Miriam announced her gift of the corpus of her books and manuscripts as well as her extensive collection of paintings, bronzes, marbles, carved ivories, porcelains, tapestries, laces, and other rare and valuable items to the University of Texas.[41] At that time, the collection was valued at $500,000. Miriam donated an additional $150,000 in cash to build a museum on campus in which to house the collections, bringing her gift to a total of $650,000.[42] On that date, the Board of Regents formally—and gratefully—accepted "the richest gift yet made to the school by an individual."[43] Fannie Ratchford, the university's rare books librarian, wrote Nita Stark: "Let me say . . . that there is no exaggerating nor overstating the value of your mother's gift to the University. . . . Almost every book here is a crown jewel."[44] Miriam—and after her death, Lutcher—continued to add to the collection, periodically purchasing and donating items through Ratchford's assistance.[45]

At the time Lutcher Stark was elected chairman of the Board of Regents in May 1921,[46] a major conflict over the permanent location of the university was just drawing to its conclusion.[47] In 1910, former university regent George W. Brackenridge, concerned that the forty-acre campus originally given the school by the state of Texas would be insufficient to accommodate its steady growth, had given the university five hundred acres on the Colorado River southwest of Austin for the purpose of building a larger campus.[48] Several years later, he had proffered three hundred additional acres with the suggestion that the school create a fifteen hundred–acre campus by purchasing reasonably priced land in the less developed western part of Austin. President Vinson supported the offer, understandable since, in the years between 1914 and 1921, the university's student body had more than doubled.[49]

At that time, Brackenridge was one of two major benefactors of the university, the other being Texas cattleman, banker, and fellow regent George W. Littlefield.[50] Brackenridge, a Republican who had been a Union supporter during the Civil War, and Littlefield, a Democrat and Confederate veteran, clashed at every turn, and the campus location controversy afforded them yet another battleground. In 1920, Brackenridge began an active campaign to move the main part of the campus to the Colorado River site, but Littlefield threatened to withdraw his financial support if the campus did not remain on the original land grant.

The battle over the university's location did not end until after the deaths of both Brackenridge and Littlefield, six weeks apart, in late 1920. Before knowing the terms of either will, the Board of Regents actually decided to go with Brackenridge's offer, believing that he would bequeath the university the additional land as well as several million dollars in cash—worth the cost, they thought, of losing Littlefield's bequest, whatever it would be. On January 5, 1921, they adopted a "Memorial," signed by eight of the nine members of the board, including Lutcher Stark, urging support for the move to Brackenridge's land.[51]

But when the contents of both wills became known, their thinking abruptly reversed itself. Brackenridge, who had suffered major business reversals just before his death, had left no more to the university than the contributions he had already made; his will provided only for family members and dependents and for a foundation to administer student loans and

Figure 8.2. Littlefield Fountain, entrance to the campus of the University of Texas in the 1930s. Stark Foundation Archives.

scholarships.[52] Moreover, he had not previously disclosed the terms of the will—or his reduced financial circumstances—to the university. He had hinted to President Vinson that he was considering changing his will, but he apparently never did so; no subsequent will surfaced.[53]

However, if the university remained in its original location, per Little-field's stipulation, his will would provide over $1 million to the university—$500,000 for a new main building; $300,000 for a dormitory for women students, named for his wife, Alice Littlefield; $200,000 for a bronze arch over the southern entrance to the "Forty Acres," as the existing campus was known; and his home, located across Twenty-Fourth Street from the campus.[54]

With the regents now in favor of abiding by Littlefield's conditions, the Austin business community also rallied to oppose the move, and public and political opinion shifted toward leaving the campus in its original location. On March 12, 1921, a measure passed both the House and Senate, appropriating $135,000 to purchase 135 acres contiguous to the Forty Acres.[55] The dispute was finally settled; the university would remain in its original location, allowing the school to move forward with long-term plans for campus development.[56] With the controversy behind them, the regents, now under Lutcher Stark's chairmanship, moved to purchase the land needed for campus expansion and the construction of new facilities to house the growing student body. They also initiated efforts to separate the university from Texas A&M College (an institution equally interested in divesting itself of its connection with the university). But both schools were legal beneficiaries of the interest from the PUF, complicating any sort of settlement.[57]

These issues were soon profoundly affected by an event as electrifying as it was unexpected. In May 1923, to the astonishment of all concerned, oil—in huge quantities—was discovered on the West Texas property that, decades previously, the legislature had given the university for its future support. After the landmark 1901 discovery of the Spindletop field near Beaumont, oil had been found in many parts of the state, but as yet little exploration had been done amid the harsh isolation of West Texas. In fact, when George Brackenridge had first become a regent in 1886, no survey of the land had even existed. Brackenridge, using his own funds, had employed West Texas land managers to complete an abstract of the properties. His act was little appreciated at the time, and for years the acreage had only made the university "land poor"; however, the abstract emerged as one of the most important contributions he made to the university.[58]

As early as 1916, the director of the university's Bureau of Economic Geology, Johan A. Udden, informed Major Littlefield, then chairman of the Board of Regents, that he believed conditions indicated the possible presence of oil on the property. Udden published a paper suggesting the possibility, but no one acted on the prospect until late 1918, when Rupert P. Ricker, a West Texas rancher and war veteran, filed applications for permits to drill on university land.[59] He ran out of money, as happened so often in the oil industry, but the men to whom he sold out—one of them an army buddy, Frank T. Pickrell—brought in a gusher in Reagan County on

Figure 8.3. A windfall for the University of Texas—the Santa Rita No. 1, 1923, named for the patron saint of the impossible. Dolph Briscoe Center for American History, University of Texas at Austin, Prints and Photographs Collection, Santa Rita Oil Well, di_02265.

May 28, 1923. Pickrell christened the well the "Santa Rita," after the patron saint of the impossible. It proved to be the discovery well of the Big Lake oil field.[60]

From the production of the Santa Rita and subsequent wells in the field, revenue suddenly began pouring into the coffers of the PUF in quantities no one could have previously imagined. The new funds promised welcome financial relief for the school but created new issues—unprecedented and as yet unaddressed either by legislation or the state constitution. Despite Lutcher Stark's experience in his family's oil concerns, neither he nor the other regents had ever dealt with mineral interests administered through an endowment, and they knew very little about proper procedure to manage the income.[61]

In an effort to resolve the issue, the board petitioned the legislature to pass a bill that would allow the university to bypass the PUF and shunt the royalty income directly into the Available University Fund, thus making the entire windfall accessible for much-needed campus construction. The bill passed both houses of the legislature and was signed by Governor Miriam A. "Ma" Ferguson. "To the average man who sees the miserable-

Figure 8.4. University of Texas officials at the Santa Rita No. 1, 1923, including Lutcher Stark (*back row, left, in hat*) and university president Harry Yandell Benedict (*back row, second from right*). Dolph Briscoe Center for American History, University of Texas at Austin, Prints and Photographs Collection, Discovery Well of the Big Lake Pool, di_08203.

looking buildings at the University," she declared, "it would appear that the state is making an effort to store up hay instead of to store up knowledge." But she doubted the bill's constitutionality, and as she feared, it was later thrown out in the courts; the funds from the Big Lake field continued to go into the PUF, with only the interest going into the Available Fund.[62] Most of the major problems related to the oil monies were not solved until the late 1930s, when Maj. Jubal R. Parten and George D. Morgan, two oilmen appointed to the Board of Regents in 1935 by Governor James Allred, convinced the board to change its method of granting oil leases from receiving sealed bids to placing them in open auction, thus greatly increasing revenue.[63]

In the meantime, Chairman Stark and the board faced a related issue. The Available University Fund had been so small for such a long period of time that Texas A&M had not petitioned for its share, relying instead on the legislature to appropriate money for expenses, including building construction (legal for A&M but not for the University of Texas). With interest from the oil revenue in the PUF now coming into the Available University Fund at a radically increased rate, A&M's Board of Directors suddenly renewed their interest in the fund, reaffirming their status as a branch of the University of Texas and thus entitled to their share.[64]

In 1930 the university's Board of Regents and the directors of A&M settled the issue by a compromise: A&M would receive $200,000 per year for three years; beginning in 1933, it would receive a third of the revenue from the Available University Fund.[65] For a time, it would also remain a branch of the University of Texas, giving the university a powerful ally in protecting the fund from other Texas colleges.[66]

During the 1920s, the state's economy finally began moving toward prosperity, lumber and oil faring especially well, though farmers and ranchers remained victims of a slump throughout the decade. But the times saw rapid, dramatic social change as well. Texans continued to endure postwar backlash as the paranoia and fear spawned in the early years of the war, resulting in such injustices as the firing of Prokosch, lingered and actually intensified in 1919 and the early 1920s. Divisive issues such as race relations and national Prohibition, the former marked by strong resistance to change and the latter by deliberate flouting of the law, bitterly split public opinion.[67] Still other major worries—the prevailing phobia toward socialism and Marxism, a major recession in 1920 and 1921 resulting from the unsettled postwar economy, race relations in the form of the reemergence of the Ku Klux Klan, a growing labor union movement, and a youth-led rebellion in social customs—continued to trouble Texans' thoughts and lives. These and other elemental shifts were particularly disturbing to traditionalists such as Lutcher Stark.

Lutcher, never shy about plunging headlong into controversial situations, especially when he perceived his values to be threatened, did so many times during his four six-year terms on the Board of Regents. During his first term on the board, he had aggressively involved himself in most discussions, constantly making motions on various matters. From 1921 through 1931, as chairman, he made fewer motions but continued to involve himself in high-voltage campus issues.[68] Among them was his "aye" vote on a resolution that passed the board in the summer of 1923, imposing requirements regarding religion on all employees of the university.[69] Their "Resolution on Religion," passed that July 10, contained the following:

> Be it resolved by the Board of Regents that no infidel, atheist or agnostic be employed in any capacity in the University of Texas, and that while no sectarian qualification shall ever be required of persons now serving or who shall in future be elected or appointed to positions in this institution, no person who does not believe in God as the Supreme Being and the Ruler of the Universe shall hereafter be employed or at any time continue in or be elected or appointed to any office or position of any character in this University.[70]

The resolution directly countered the 1881 legislation that had originally established the University of Texas, which had stated that "no religious qualification shall be required for admission to any office or privilege in the university; nor shall any course of instruction of a sectarian character be taught therein."[71] The regents' substitution of the single word "sectarian" for the original "religious" negated the intent of the original legislation, clearing the way for enforcement of the remainder of the resolution, which required belief in a Supreme Being as a prerequisite for employment at the university.[72] With eight regents in favor, including Lutcher, and one "nay" vote cast by Regent Sam Cochran, the board adopted the policy—over the strong opposition of the recently appointed interim president of the university, William S. Sutton.[73]

Their action was reported in some newspapers but initially seemed to draw little public response. Coverage in the *Daily Texan* suggested that it might have been intended to "reassure the people of the state as to the University's position on religion."[74] Some believed it was designed to ward off the possible candidacy of Harry Yandell Benedict, dean of the College of Arts and Sciences, for the presidency. Benedict, known affectionately on campus as "Dean Benny," was a scientist by training—an astronomer and mathematician—with religious views that were difficult to categorize and a well-developed sense of humor. Shortly after the regents passed the resolution, they supposedly called him in for a conference. The stories, some undoubtedly apocryphal, ensuing from that meeting, in which he was allegedly questioned by Lutcher Stark, became the stuff of university legend. Writer Norman Brown presented one scenario, but the minutes contain no mention of the incident:

> As the story goes, Stark asked Benedict whether he believed in a deity. "Well," Benedict is said to have replied, "just recently I knew it would please my wife and I didn't think it would hurt our baby, so I consented to his being baptized." "Do you believe in God?" demanded Stark. "Do you mean an anthropomorphic God?" Benedict parried. The interrogation was adjourned until Stark could find a dictionary. It was never resumed.[75]

Although the veracity of this particular story is extremely doubtful (at least one other version, involving different participants, made the rounds of the university and the legislature), Lutcher still left no doubt in the minds of anyone where he stood on such matters.[76] "I will continue to oppose all those who are not God-fearing men," he later declared. "And we will not have any Socialists up there."[77] "[Lutcher Stark] is religious and a deep-dyed fundamentalist," one writer noted. "He got into a dispute a few years ago over the proposed teaching of evolution and 'modernism' in the state university."[78] R.R. "Railroad" Smith, an outspoken Texas alumnus who advocated a strict separation of church and state, dedicated a derogatory pamphlet, *A Little Preachment and a Short Epistle to the Bigots of Texas*, to "A Certain Rich Ruler," meaning Lutcher:

> Millionaire by lucky accident of birth, regent of a great university by a lucky accident of politics, hopeful of a lucky accident which may discount the impossible feat of the camel crawling through the needle's eye, who proclaims himself a "fundamentalist," whatever that is, and, still hoarding his riches, requires all those who serve the state under his regentcy to embrace his pet theology.

"Dean Benny" was ultimately named president of the university in 1927, four years after supposedly being questioned about his religious beliefs. One of the school's best-loved deans and presidents, he worked well with students, faculty, and regents alike and oversaw one of the largest physical expansions in the history of the school.

As the decade wore on, Lutcher became increasingly immersed in his "hobby," as he had once called the university.[79] He had been saluted in 1917 by one of the school's fiercest opponents, Texas A&M football coach Charlie Moran, in a comment to a writer for the *Alcalde*: "I don't envy you University people your big enrollment nor better location for staging your sports," Moran had declared, "but I do envy you Lutcher Stark."[80] During

Figure 8.5a. C.L. "Ox" Higgins, University of Texas star lineman on the 1925–1927 football teams, wears his "T" sweater, signifying that he is a member of the Order of the T. Courtesy of Jean Bell Moncla and Patrick L. Bell.

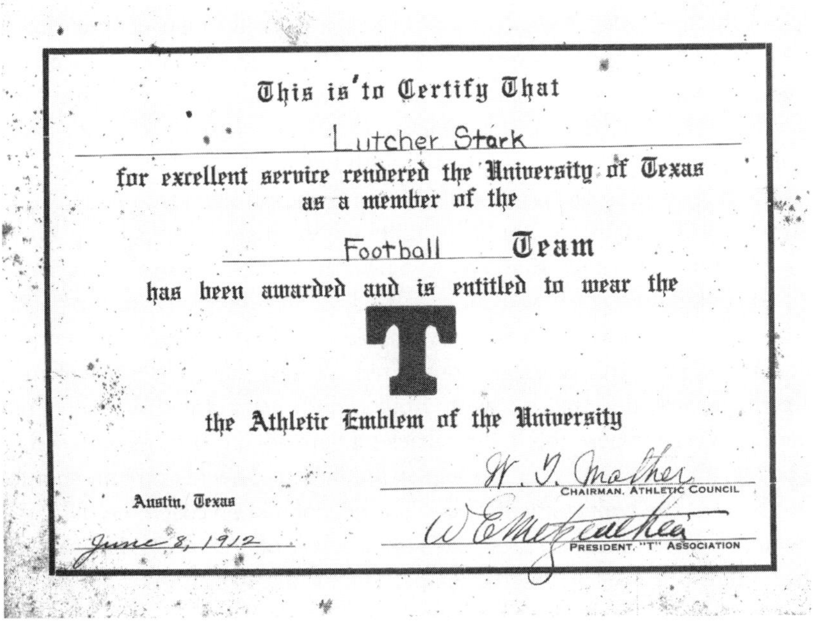

This is to Certify That

Lutcher Stark

for excellent service rendered the University of Texas as a member of the

Football Team

has been awarded and is entitled to wear the

T

the Athletic Emblem of the University

W. T. Mather
CHAIRMAN, ATHLETIC COUNCIL

Austin, Texas

June 8, 1912

W. E. Metcalfe
PRESIDENT, "T" ASSOCIATION

Figure 8.5b. Lutcher Stark was also made a member of the Order of the T for his contributions to University of Texas sports, especially football. Stark Foundation Archives.

his time as regent, Lutcher continued his gifts to the university in the athletic arena, its football program in particular, and his generosity to Texas sports continued to be felt for the next two decades.

From the time of his arrival as a student at the university, Lutcher's two overwhelming interests had been football and Nita Hill, and in fact, the two had come as a package, given the Hill family's total involvement in the sport. From her parents—Homer Hill, the much-loved team physician, and Granny Hill, the players' surrogate mother and unlicensed defense attorney—Nita had learned her love of the game, and during her life she maintained an ardor for, and sophisticated knowledge of, football.

She and Lutcher shared this passion for the sport throughout their marriage, both on the local and the college scenes, even when chronic illness prevented her from attending the games. She often wrote the sports editor of the *Houston Post*, Lloyd Gregory, a fellow university graduate and intercollegiate tennis player, to critique his various articles on high school and college games.[81] "I feel that after many years of observation," as she put it in one letter to him, "I know good football players when I see them." More than once she called him to account, writing him in 1933 to defend the playing ability of Orange football standout Bohn Hilliard, then a stellar member of the Longhorn team. "With all due respect to you, Mr. Gregory, I don't think that you are being fair to Bohn Hilliard, nor to the Texas supporters. Bohn has played like a fiend this year."[82]

"In the first place, I want you to understand [that] I respect your views on football," Gregory answered. "You know more football than any other lady with whom I have ever talked, and far more than most men (and this probably includes myself)."[83] Gregory rarely argued with her analyses, possibly because he felt that disagreeing with her would be impolitic (he enjoyed duck hunting on the Starks' Orange Cameron Land Company game preserve in Louisiana[84]). But he also seemed to relish their sparring. Or it could simply have been that Nita was usually correct in her observations.

When Lutcher Stark had matriculated at the university in 1905, UT football as a sport was only twelve years old. The first team had been organized in 1893 by two brothers from Laredo, Texas, Ray and Paul McLane, recently returned to the university from several years attending school on the East Coast, where football rivalries had already become established.[85] The McLane brothers, wanting to play football, had decided that it should be played at the University of Texas. The school had no coach, no field, no grandstand, a scarcity of rules, and a notable lack of opponents; few (if any) other Texas colleges sponsored teams. The brothers rounded up students who had been "cowboys and lumber-jacks," showed them a football, and began searching for other teams to play.[86] Since no intercollegiate games were being played that year, the McLanes scheduled two games each with so-called town teams from Dallas and San Antonio. When they won those games, the university's team members declared themselves to be the state champions.[87] (In 1893, the road to the championship was very short.)

The scarcity of regulations sometimes led to comical incidents. During one of the games with the Dallas team, Ray McLane decided that he was being excessively abused by the Dallas players. McLane, who had been reared on a military base on the Rio Grande, reverted to his lifelong solution to such situations. "Coming up through most of the Dallas team," the *Daily Texan* noted, "he let out a war-whoop and invited the visitors to pile on. . . . McLane dropped them as they came."[88] When he finished clarifying his point with the Dallas players, the game resumed.

For the first few years, the university's football games were played on a stretch of cow pasture owned by a local farmer, M.M. Shipe, located in today's Hyde Park neighborhood. Spectators were required to keep horse-and-buggy rigs off the field, but if they arrived on foot, they were allowed to move onto the field to watch the game. During one early contest, the father of Dave Furman, one of the UT players, stood on the field to watch his son, who took the ball for a good run toward the goal.[89] "The father lost control of himself completely," wrote student reporter Harry E. Moore for the *Daily Texan*. "Breaking through the opposing team in the wake of his son, he followed him down the field, brandishing a heavy cane that he carried and threatening to brain any man who dared tackle the boy."[90] "Verily, brother," Moore later added, "times have changed."

As early as December 1905, at the end of Lutcher's first semester at the university, President Theodore Roosevelt, concerned with growing violence on the playing field, had held two White House conferences on the issue that considered banning the sport on college campuses altogether.[91] Roosevelt's support for reducing the violence led directly to the creation of the Intercollegiate Athletic Association of the United States, which in 1910 changed its name to the National Collegiate Athletic Association (NCAA).[92] The NCAA was established not only to make the game of football safer but also to require it to operate within established guidelines.

By the time Lutcher Stark served as manager of the University of Texas team, new rules had been gradually transforming the game. One of the first goals of Athletic Director Theo Bellmont and T.W. Mather, head of the Faculty Athletic Committee when Bellmont came to the university in 1913, was the organization of the Southwest Conference to give structure to the football program. The university became a founding member of the conference. But the overhaul was just beginning, and during Lutcher's tenure on the Board of Regents, many of the practices later declared illegal— including gifts to athletes and athletic programs from individuals—still lay within the guidelines. "I have a pack of athletes camping on my trail for salaries," Bellmont wrote Lutcher on one occasion, "and I would therefore appreciate your forwarding a check for the receipts sent to you about a week ago." "In accordance with your suggestion," he wrote Lutcher later, "I am writing to request your favorable consideration in supplying an additional fund of $500.00 to be spent in a legitimate way for the benefit of our athletes . . . in order that some men at least may be saved for participation next year."[93] Through the years, there were innumerable such gifts and subsidies from Lutcher Stark.

Even though in the 1920s and 1930s it was not yet illegal under NCAA rules for athletes to receive such assistance, criticism of the practice was beginning to surface.[94] In the 1920s, the one request made by the university's Athletic Council of Lutcher was that he discontinue his custom of giving a monthly sum to Bellmont for use as needed in the athletic program. In 1927, after first agreeing that there had been no misuse of funds through the Athletic Department, the regents nevertheless adopted a recommendation that all funds, including private contributions, be deposited with the university auditor to provide controls over athletic program expenditures. On a related issue, they also discontinued using university money to pay for tutors for athletes, even though other schools in the Southwest Conference continued the practice.[95]

Lutcher duly stopped the payments for the sake of accountability, but he thought the policy the height of stupidity; in a later interview with a reporter from the *Daily Texan*, he defended a recommendation from the Faculty Athletic Committee to allow employment of the athletes and regulation of student athlete subsidization. "When a student has met those qualifications," he declared, "it's nobody's business if the chamber of commerce, the fire department, or some individual employs him."[96] The issue ultimately led to the creation of athletic scholarships.

Lutcher continued to make loans as an individual, however, and furnished summer jobs or gave money outright to a great number of university students, athletes and nonathletes alike, rarely keeping records or expecting to be repaid. He also aided students who attended other colleges, including African Americans, according to former Orange resident Elizabeth Johnson Washington, a recipient.[97] His generosity to students is best captured in the words of its beneficiaries: "Through your help I have been able to earn a part of my expenses in school this year," wrote one athlete. "Without this work I would have had to do outside work during the afternoons, thus preventing athletic activities on my part."[98]

"Mr. Stark truly changed the lives of so many young people," Orange resident Alexine Boudreaux Adams remembered.

> My older sister . . . was athletic, and we didn't have any girls' athletics in [Orange] High School at that time, so when she graduated, [he] told her if she would take a . . . course . . . to coach girls' basketball and girls' tennis, he would

send her to college. . . . When she finished school, she told him she was ready to pay him back, and he said, "You need to help Alexine go to school." He didn't say, "What's your sister's name?" He knew right off . . . who we were. So *I* went to school.[99]

"How about Dolores [their youngest sister]?" Lutcher asked when Alexine had earned her college degree. On learning that Dolores was bound for the altar instead of college, thus he would not be paying for a third college education, he remarked, "Two educations for the price of one should please anybody."[100]

In developing a football program, one of the early issues that the university was forced to face was the question of a playing field. As of 1896, the University of Texas owned no field, but at least the games had migrated from Shipe's cow pasture to a piece of land adjacent to the Forty Acres on the corner of Twenty-Fourth Street and Speedway. Initially, the landlord allowed free use of the area; then, three years into the arrangement, he demanded that the team buy the lot or vacate it. The university acquired the property over the next three years at $1,000 per year by an unusual means of purchase: students paid the first year's portion by donating library deposits refunded them if they owed no fines for overdue or lost books. Faculty and ex-students paid the second year with contributions, and the Board of Regents paid the final $1,000.

Thus, by 1901 UT football boasted the semblance of a permanent home. The new facility was christened Clark Field, after regent and university proctor James B. Clark. As the games became increasingly popular, law and engineering students, with a few helpers, periodically added more bleachers to accommodate the burgeoning number of fans.[101] Even so, space was seldom sufficient to hold the growing crowds, and the fear of collapsing bleachers was always present.

In the years following World War I, a new football stadium had been a repeatedly discussed dream, but it had been useless to pursue until the location of the campus had been settled. In the meantime, students and faculty members had continued to express support for designation of a monument of some sort on campus to honor those who had served in the war and to memorialize those who had given their lives, but the school's perennial shortage of funds had presented an almost insurmountable obstacle.

The Santa Rita No. 1 abruptly and drastically changed the picture, affording the university a financial security new in its existence. In the months after the discovery, two powerful campus figures—Lutcher Stark and his good friend Athletic Director Theo Bellmont, both dedicated supporters of intercollegiate sports—hatched the idea of building a "Memo-

Figure 8.6. The newly formed Texas Cowboys at Clark Field, before UT football game against Texas A&M, 1922. For many years, Lutcher Stark donated the chaps worn by the Cowboys. Note the Old Main Building in upper left corner. Dolph Briscoe Center for American History, University of Texas at Austin, Prints and Photographs Collection, UT-Football (1921–1922).

rial Stadium" as a way of accomplishing both goals at once. Although no funds could be forthcoming from the Available University Fund, since its monies could be applied only to construction of academic buildings, Stark and Bellmont initiated discussions. After a survey of new stadiums built through public fund-raising, they declared themselves ready to launch a drive to transform dream into reality.[102]

At an afternoon practice a week before the 1923 Thanksgiving Day game between UT and A&M, Bellmont casually let slip to Frank Kirksey, the sports editor of the *Daily Texan*, that a victory over A&M would provide an ideal occasion to launch a drive for a new stadium. Kirksey printed an article presenting the idea, UT won the game 6-0, and a large number of students enthusiastically endorsed it, their support vital to the effort. The first, and critical, meeting, held November 25, 1923, with twenty-eight of thirty invited students, brought together some of the campus leaders, who immediately committed themselves to building a stadium. Support grew swiftly; the initial meeting was followed on December 11 by convocation of a thousand students and faculty. Lutcher Stark, who spoke at the meeting, reminded those assembled that "the surest way to kill the stadium is to fight over the material, the cost or the location. The . . . details will be worked out by the experts and engineers."[103]

The goal was set for the stadium's completion in time for the UT-A&M game on Thanksgiving Day of 1924.[104] Lutcher assumed a highly visible role: when the regents endorsed the project on December 18, 1923, naming him their representative on the recently formed Central Stadium Committee (composed of a mix of businesspeople, faculty, ex-students, students, and regents), he was elected chairman of the committee. The board also commissioned Herbert M. Greene of Dallas, then serving as the university's architect, to draw up a plan. Greene's plan, completed by mid-January 1924, proposed a stadium with an ultimate seating capacity of forty thousand at a designated location: a wooded hillside to the east of the Forty Acres between Waller Creek and Red River Street and bounded by Twenty-First and Twenty-Third Streets.[105]

The mammoth scope of the stadium's construction required the Central Committee to raise approximately $500,000. The principals setting themselves to the landmark fund-raising task were Committee Chairman Stark, Athletic Director Theo Bellmont, and the manager of the university's student publications, William McGill. Their first target was the school's student body. Nay-sayers were convinced that the students would stand good for no more than $20,000 in pledges, and even supporters feared that with a poor showing on campus, the entire plan might disintegrate. But all of them underestimated the focused energy of Lutcher and Bellmont and the dedicated hard work of McGill. At a February 20 meeting, Lutcher warned student fund-raisers that "they cannot—they dare not—fail on this proposition."[106]

Five days later, amid near-blizzard conditions, over half the 4,465 students at the University of Texas slogged through freezing rain and snow to a convocation in the men's gymnasium (itself vastly in need of repair or, better, replacement) to hear Lutcher Stark make a major announcement: he promised to donate a dollar from his personal funds for every $10 collected by the students. "With good humor," Memorial Stadium historian Richard Pennington reports, "Stark urged them to make him dig deep in fulfilling his promise." The campus goal was set at $100,000, but the total finally pledged by students, faculty, staff, and some UT organizations was announced on May 5: $151,000. And as he had promised, Lutcher added another $15,000 to the total.[107]

Fund drives held in the city of Austin and among the Texas Exes—the alumni of the university—gained modest momentum. An option plan offering the purchase of either two or four "choice" tickets per game to donors of $50 or $100, respectively, for the following ten years served as a

Figure 8.7. By the summer of 1924, construction of UT's Memorial Stadium
was under way, as was the fund drive initiated by Lutcher Stark to build it.
Dolph Briscoe Center for American History, University of Texas at Austin,
Prints and Photographs Collection, Memorial Stadium, di_08343.

stimulus to the pledging.[108] Lutcher penned an article in the *Alcalde* issued April 24, 1924:

> If we are to meet successfully the first great call from our University for fi-
> nancial support, then we must all give of ourselves in the doing of the essen-
> tial things required. . . . The gift of money . . . will express an appreciation of
> the University's increasing importance in the work of building fine men and
> women to be citizens of the great state and nation. And, greater yet, it will ex-
> press affection for the men and women who served America with ardent patri-
> otism, some of them at the cost of their lives.[109]

The impressive figures merely represented the amount pledged; re-
deeming the pledges would be another matter entirely. At that point, only
$30,000 had been collected, and four more years were required to collect
most of them. Nevertheless, the groundbreaking ceremony took place on
April 4 at the designated location in the old East Woods, east of the Forty
Acres.[110]

However, the fund-raising in Austin and among Texas Exes around
the state did not meet the expectations of the Stadium Committee, par-

tially because another issue was diverting attention from the drive. This new problem—the choice of a permanent president for the University of Texas—also raised Lutcher Stark's profile on campus, but in a radically different light. The brewing storm over the selection process led to a bitter confrontation between Lutcher Stark and Texas Ex Will Hogg, a wealthy and powerful Houston lawyer and businessman and the oldest son of Texas' first native-born governor, James Stephen Hogg. Their personal feud ultimately threatened to derail the entire stadium project.

When Robert Vinson had resigned the presidency in 1923 to accept a position at another school, Texas governor Pat M. Neff, who would soon leave office, had been widely discussed as his replacement.[111] But the fact that Neff was a politician and that the majority of the board members were his appointees, not to mention his lack of academic qualifications, had aroused such active opposition, both on campus and among ex-students, that the issue had been dropped. "The *Post* can not believe," fumed an editorial in the *Houston Post* that April,

> that a board, two-thirds of whose members were appointed by Governor Neff, can hold the plain proprieties of the situation in such contempt as to entertain or execute any such purpose; it can not believe that Governor Neff . . . could be so forgetful of the delicacies and proprieties of his position, as to accept such an appointment at the hands of his own appointees. . . . Such action by the board and the acceptance of the office by the Governor would be such an outrage as upon good taste and public decency that it would grossly offend the finer sensibilities of the good people of Texas.[112]

After such outcry, William S. Sutton, dean of the School of Education, had stepped in as acting president.[113]

The following year the issue again arose during the fund-raising and early construction phases of the stadium when speculation surfaced that Neff was once again being considered for the presidency. Neff-appointed regents still dominated the board, and although Lutcher was not a Neff appointee, he supported the latter's candidacy. Rumors flew that in exchange, a deal had been cut to pave the way for Chairman Stark to win the governorship. Lutcher ignored the rumors, but whatever actually occurred, he and the majority of the regents handled the matter poorly.[114]

Many of the university's faculty, alumni, and students were already wary of politicians' involvement in its operation—with good reason. Political tampering in the internal operation of the school seemed to take place with regularity, the most recent, most blatant incident having occurred in 1917 with Governor James E. Ferguson's attack on its regents, faculty, and academic leadership. At that time, one of Ferguson's most implacable opponents had been Will Hogg, then secretary of the Ex-Students' Association. Hogg had set up anti-Ferguson campaign headquarters in Austin's Driskill Hotel, from which he had managed the successful opposition to the governor and had ultimately effected his impeachment and conviction.[115]

Hogg harbored a healthy suspicion of those he considered to be interfering politicians, especially regarding the university's internal affairs, and he had relentlessly opposed Neff's presidency from the first time his name had been mentioned in 1923. Now, with the issue's reemergence, he renewed his opposition—in company with a great number of the university's faculty, staff, students, and ex-students.

On the morning of May 16, the Board of Regents met in Austin to choose a permanent president for the university. Interim President Sutton expressed his wish to be released from the responsibilities of the office. Neff remained a possible candidate, having recently completed the last legislative session of his second term as governor. A group of ex-students actively opposing Neff named Will Hogg to attend the meeting as their spokesperson. Since Hogg was known for expressing his opinion aggressively, his younger brother Mike tried to dissuade him from attending. "You know there's a lady on the board of regents," Mike warned him, "and if you go in there, you're gonna start cussin' just as sure as fate. You shouldn't go." Will Hogg, finally promising Mike that he would not "raise hell," attended the meeting, but after speaking only a few minutes against Pat Neff as the choice of the regents, he "just let loose. . . . Cussed old Pat Neff and all of his cohorts. [One of the regents, Frank Jones,] promised then and there that morning that they would not elect Pat Neff president. [The ex-students' delegation] left with that assurance."[116]

When the meeting reconvened after lunch, the doors and windows of the room had been closed and no outsiders were present—at least so far as Chairman Stark and the regents knew—when they voted 7 to 2 to offer the presidency to Governor Neff. The two regents who voted "no," Frank Jones and Sam Cochran, promptly resigned from the board in protest. But unknown to any of them, an infiltrator in the person of a freshman reporter for the *Daily Texan* had eavesdropped on the meeting. Earlier in the day, so the story went, the reporter had overheard another student asking President Sutton how he could discover what was taking place inside the meeting room. Sutton jokingly replied that the only means lay in hiding under the table. While the young reporter did not follow Sutton's advice to the letter, he actually hid in a closet behind a large map collection and listened to the proceedings through a crack in the door. After the meeting, he duly reported what he had heard. (The full story of what had happened was not made public until the publication of the November 30, 1944, edition of the *Daily Texan*. But the identity of the student, whose sleuthing had caused a sensation, was never divulged, thus successfully protecting him—or her—from potential damage to his academic career.)[117]

Understandably, the regents' selection of Neff triggered resounding repercussions. Immediately upon resigning, Cochran and Jones issued a statement to the "People of Texas," expressing their objections to Neff's being named president:

> We believe it to be contrary to the best interests of the University and of the State, and wrong in principle, to select as the President of that institution the Governor of the State, who holds the appointive power with respect to the Board of Regents.
>
> The other members of the Board having seen fit to elect to that position the Honorable Pat M. Neff, Governor of the State, and being unable to concur in that action, we have this day placed our resignation as members of the Board in the Governor's hands.[118]

Within an hour of receiving the news of his election from Lutcher Stark, Neff sent back a wire, wisely declining the offer. The regents then offered the position to Guy Stanton Ford, dean of the graduate school of the University of Minnesota, but Ford also declined. After a failed attempt to convince former university history professor Herbert Eugene Bolton, by then teaching at the University of California, to accept the post, the board finally prevailed on Walter M.W. Splawn, a former member of the Economics Department who had become head of the Texas Railroad Commission. When Splawn heard that a member of the UT faculty had theorized that he was "Neff's man," he replied caustically that he did not believe that the governor "would in any way seek to put any friend of his on the faculty."[119]

An immediate aftershock of Neff's short-lived election came in a blast of rage from Will Hogg and a phalanx of Houston Texas Exes, who fired a telegram to Lutcher Stark sent at 6:30 p.m. the same evening of Neff's election, mere hours after the latter's rejection of the offer. The telegram, signed by sixteen Texas Exes, among them "the Hoggs" (surely Will and Mike), furiously attacked Lutcher and his fellow regent Joe Wooten, charging that by helping elect Neff, they, as the only ex-students on the Board of Regents, had failed "to defend the constitutional sanctity and tritest ideals of your Alma Mater by not resigning or at least registering a protest against that cheapening debasement of the position."[120] "If you truly desire to serve the university," the telegram went on, "you should at least resign from the Stadium Drive or complete it out of your own pocket as a trifling tribute from a contrite conscience for the shameful thing you have done."

Furthermore, the Exes swore, Lutcher Stark would not get a "sou marque" from the Houston alumni in support of the stadium project.[121]

Lutcher ignored Hogg's demand to vacate the Board of Regents. "I am not going to resign," he announced publicly. "The board is making no apology for . . . electing Gov. Neff president of the University, nor will the board back up on anything it has done. . . . Ex-students . . . should busy themselves with helping the board to select a president instead of spending their time in criticism."[122] Lutcher continued as chairman of the board and the Stadium Committee, but he did vacate the chairmanship of the Fundraising Committee. William McGill took over the unpaid position and performed commendably, but it seemed for a while that the Stark-Hogg feud might kill the stadium project in midstream.

Even though no direct connection existed between the Neff issue and the stadium drive, Hogg simply wanted Lutcher off the Board of Regents, and the drive became a lightning rod for his ire. He fired off letters and telegrams to ex-students around the state, demanding that they withhold their contributions to the stadium fund until Lutcher withdrew from both the stadium drive and the board.[123] He bolstered his argument by hurling derogatory epithets at Lutcher, on one occasion calling him a "rampant young ass with a rush of money to the head"; on another, an "ultraconservative neo-Klansman."[124] Few had ever dared to defy Hogg, according to folklorist and one-time Alumni Association secretary John A. Lomax, but in going against his wishes in the Neff matter, Lutcher had thwarted him with impunity. (Hogg's temper actually seems to have matched Lutcher's own; Lomax claimed that the Houston man's friends sometimes called him "William Combustible Hogg.")[125]

Even before the Neff issue had arisen, Hogg had not supported the stadium project; in fact, he had made no strong commitment to any intercollegiate sports on the university's campus. But his attack on Lutcher set him against a student body deeply committed to building the stadium; in fact, they had already raised a considerable amount of money among themselves, the faculty, and staff. The town of Austin had also made a major investment. Hogg's vitriolic letters and telegrams to the ex-students backfired, igniting an angry reaction—directed at himself.

A typical response came in a student statement in the *Daily Texan* of May 21, 1924. The manifesto, carrying twenty-five signatures, bypassed the Neff issue entirely to land in solid support of Lutcher and the stadium project: "The dynamic fact that concerns the student body of the University of Texas," it read, "is that the STADIUM MUST AND WILL BE BUILT and that Lutch is our friend and has proven it with his timeless endeavors in our behalf." The students refrained from naming Hogg but voiced their

Figure 8.8. Aerial view of Memorial Stadium at the University of Texas, Dedication Day, Thanksgiving Day, November 27, 1924. Construction was not completed until 1926. Dolph Briscoe Center for American History, University of Texas at Austin, Prints and Photographs Collection, UT Texas Memorial Stadium, di_05223.

scorn for "any who would throw a wrench into the wheels of the greatest project that the University of Texas has ever attempted."[126]

The statement seemed to take Will Hogg by surprise, and when it finally became obvious that the stadium project was in danger of being mortally wounded, he quickly reversed course and joined the drive, donating $10,000 to the campaign, as did his brother Mike, who also led the drive in Houston. But some damage was already done; although the effort was ultimately successful after the Hogg-Stark confrontation, it never quite recovered its earlier momentum.[127]

Still, Lutcher Stark remained the driving force behind the project, not only with his contributions of cash, which possibly totaled as much as $100,000, but also with his time and effort. In addition to his monetary gifts (as well as various loans he had made that were never repaid), he provided the stadium's lumber at cost from the Lutcher & Moore Lumber Company.[128] With him, Bellmont, and McGill at the helm, as well as an exemplary construction company—Walsh and Burney of San Antonio—

handling the actual building of the stadium, the 1924 Thanksgiving Day deadline was met.[129]

That game was actually the second played in the new facility; on November 8, Texas had been defeated by Baylor University. At that time the east grandstands were complete, but those on the west side were still under construction. By November 27, for the contest with A&M, all twenty-seven thousand seats in both the east and west stands stood ready for the overflow crowd of thirty thousand (by some estimates as many as thirty-seven thousand) who saw Texas defeat A&M 7-0 in the midst of pageantry Austin had not seen before. A lavish pregame parade launched the festival, followed by speeches by Governor Neff and assorted dignitaries; precision halftime shows by the Longhorn and Aggie bands; stunts performed by the university's two recently founded service organizations, the Cowboys and the Orange Jackets; and a crowd of UT coeds and young women representing A&M, who waved to fans from opposite ends of a tractor-trailer rig.[130] Even the uniforms of the Texas band were almost new—another of Lutcher Stark's contributions.[131]

The extravaganza and the signal victory over A&M provided a capital conclusion to what had been an essentially mediocre football season for the Longhorns. Austin merchants who had contributed to the building fund were doubtless delighted with their foresight, and for those who were still attempting to collect pledges or who had given up trying, the promise of income from the games offered hope of retiring the debt.

The stadium, constructed to accommodate both football and track, helped boost the University of Texas to a higher level in intercollegiate sports. It also sparked renewed loyalty among the Texas Exes, very few of whom had helped finance the project but most of whom were properly impressed by such a massive achievement accomplished by so many. Two additional years were required to finish construction, but by 1926 the north end zone completed the horseshoe, bringing the total number of seats to 40,500.[132]

The Memorial Stadium project constituted a monumental accomplishment, funded by neither the university nor the state but entirely with private money raised in all manner of creative ways. In that day, securing $500,000 in pledges represented no small challenge, and collecting them an even greater one. It had been Lutcher Stark's initial suggestion that the project represent a tribute to those university students, faculty, and staff who had served and died on the battlefields of Europe in World War I,[133] but before its completion, it broadened into a memorial to all Texans who had served in the war. The stadium was rededicated on September 18, 1948, to honor Texans who had died in World War II, and in 1977, a third dedication included American veterans of all wars.[134] The colossal structure stands as of this writing, a source of pride through the years for students, alumni, administration, faculty, and any associated with the University of Texas.

At the same time the stadium was being planned and built, Lutcher Stark involved himself in another major project at the university, which took form in 1923 and 1924 with plans for much-needed construction of academic buildings. Even though the Santa Rita discovery held promise of an immense financial windfall, the actual funds would not make their way through the various necessary channels for some time. But a Master Plan began to emerge through the work of two talented architects—Cass Gilbert, the university's architect from 1910 to 1922, and Herbert M. Greene, who held the post from 1922 to 1930. It was they who were most deeply involved in its actual design and implementation.[135]

Gilbert, an award-winning architect from New York, "imagined a campus for the University of Texas that was grand and monumental." He actually designed and constructed only two buildings: the elegant Old Library (today's Battle Hall) and the Education Building (now Sutton Hall). But he also contributed an essential element to the university's development—a comprehensive plan for the layout of the campus. Envisioning an "urban" campus with access to the surrounding neighborhoods on all four sides of the Forty Acres, he recommended replacing the Main Building with a multistory skyscraper, retaining the rest of the buildings but blending them with well-planned new construction and laying out four malls that intersected at the new Main Building. As author Lawrence Speck notes, "Gilbert helped the University administration and regents make the leap from seeing their institution as a small-town college to envisioning it as a sophisticated institution 'of the first class.'" Greene continued to design largely in line with Gilbert's plan, his major innovation being to incorporate ornamentation into the design of each building that reflected the discipline housed in it.[136]

Lutcher Stark served on the Board of Regents during the terms of both these architects as well as that of their successor, Paul Cret, whose term ran from 1930 to 1942. From the first, Lutcher showed a real interest in the design and construction of the campus. In 1919 he was named chairman of the Building and Grounds Committee, and he maintained that interest throughout his service on the board.[137] He involved himself in campus landscaping and, being an aficionado of the iconic coastal live oak trees of his native region, worked with Southeast Texas nurseries to prepare bids and place orders for a number of the majestic trees, many of which still shade the campus today. (The order for the first four coastal live oaks to be planted on campus was placed with Griffing Nurseries of Beaumont, undoubtedly at his instigation.)[138]

He also understood the need to ensure that the various bidding processes were kept within the rules.[139] He paid a great deal of attention to the details of campus design and construction, as he did to every aspect of his life. Herbert Greene, while drawing the plans for Memorial Stadium, reported that he received input from Lutcher, "who was himself trained as a civil engineer," and as the Anna Hiss Women's Gymnasium was being built in 1930, Lutcher arrived at regents' meetings prepared to discuss the tile he meant to recommend for the edges of the swimming pool.[140]

L utcher's first six-year term as regent ended in 1925. Serving a second term necessitated his reappointment, this time by a new governor, since William P. Hobby, who had initially appointed him, had left office in 1920, and Pat Neff was nearing the end of his second two-year term (although the state constitution placed no limits on gubernatorial terms, a strong two-term tradition still held sway in Texas at that time). Thus, any future appointment of Lutcher to the Board of Regents depended on the outcome of the 1924 gubernatorial election.

Essentially, Texas remained a one-party state: after Reconstruction, the political careers of few Republicans had survived, so a victory in the Democratic primary was tantamount to winning the general election. Four major Democratic candidates entered the 1924 primary: Miriam A. "Ma" Ferguson, the wife of the impeached and convicted former governor James E. Ferguson and the first woman to seek the Texas governorship, who had entered the gubernatorial primary at her husband's instigation;[141] two anti–Ku Klux Klan candidates who, unfortunately for their respective aspirations, were saddled with the same surname of Davidson; and one prominent Klan supporter, Felix Robertson.

Texas was in all probability the strongest pro-Klan state in the country; since its resurgence in the South in the early 1920s as a reaction to social and economic changes, the organization had spread throughout the state like an infectious disease.[142] The Klan claimed that citizens who obeyed the law need not fear it and also that it cared for widows and orphans, helping many when they were "down and out." (In 1924, the Austin chapter of the Klan even contributed to the Memorial Stadium building fund.)[143]

Notwithstanding the Klan's peaceful protestations, along with its hostility toward African Americans it also assumed an anti-immigrant, anti-Jewish, anti-Catholic stance, and it was often found at the root of lynchings and other episodes of violence. The conflicting concerns generated an atmosphere of increasing intolerance, based largely on fear and reflected in the behavior of many Texans. In 1922, Earle B. Mayfield had won the Democratic primary and then the general election to the US Senate with open backing from the Klan, and by 1923 the organization was riding high in the state, its power bolstered by the election of Senator Mayfield.[144]

By the time of the 1924 election, however, resistance to the Texas Klan had begun to grow. It had come under attack through the courts for its central role in the increasing incidents of violence, and its power had rapidly begun to decline.[145] The path to victory for "Ma" Ferguson would necessarily lie in campaigning against the Klan.[146]

Lutcher Stark, by his own description "born a Democrat," actively endorsed "Ma" against Robertson, the strongest Klan candidate in the Democratic primary.[147] Although Texas alumni predominantly supported Robertson, not all did; when conservative, staunch Texas Ex D.A. Frank of Dallas sent a notice to university ex-students urging them to vote for Robertson rather than Ferguson, who had caused such turmoil at the university, Edward Crane, a prominent Texas Democrat, ex-student, and future regent, took issue with him, declaring that a militant Klan majority on the Board of Regents would see to it that "the professors at the University will bow their knees in allegiance to the invisible empire, or go elsewhere. The ablest, the independent thinking members of the faculty will resign, and there will only remain and be added thereto second-rate, cowardly time-serving salary takers." Although Robertson placed first in the primary to "Ma" Ferguson's second, she won the Democratic nomination in the run-off—a strong sign of the Klan's diminishing strength.[148]

It was with difficulty that the minority Republican Party found a candidate to oppose her in the general election. Their ultimate choice, George C. Butte, dean of the University of Texas Law School, resigned his post to oppose Ferguson and then proceeded to run the strongest race that any Republican had run in the preceding fifty years. But "Ma" Ferguson won the election, meanwhile having offered Lutcher Stark a means of returning to the Board of Regents. During her campaign, she had announced that ex-students against Lutcher's reappointment could suggest names for two places on the board; if she named two of those individuals, she promised, she would appoint Lutcher Stark, thus both sides would be represented.[149] (Rhodes S. Baker of Dallas, then president of the Ex-Students' Association, was proposed as a candidate to fill one of the spots but promptly declined. "Many ex-students, including myself, believe that Mr. Stark . . . is responsible for a disturbing factional division in the ranks of ex-students and for great unrest in the faculty," Baker asserted, "and that his continuance on the board, however worthy he may be personally, is not in the interest of the University.")[150]

When Ferguson sent her nominations to the Senate, members of the

Figure 8.9. Lutcher Stark (*third from left*) and Governor Miriam A. "Ma" Ferguson (*center*) at dedication of the new Neches River bridge in Beaumont, Texas, May 9, 1925. Governor Ferguson had recently reappointed Lutcher Stark to the UT Board of Regents. Stark Foundation Archives.

Ex-Students Association fought vigorously against Lutcher's appointment in the hearings, but his defenders spoke up for him. Three former governors attended the hearings in his support, along with William "Bill" Lea, ex-mayor of Orange and soon-to-be administrative assistant to Ferguson. (Lutcher apparently did not defend himself, seemingly following his own often-declared rule: "Never admit, never explain, never deny.")[151]

Newspaper accounts of the proceedings reported that "it was charged that [Lutcher Stark] was a Ku Kluxer; that in the city of Orange he had given a hall for a meeting place to the local Klan; that he was obnoxious to the anti-Klansmen of Texas and the ex-students of the University." Lutcher's supporters riposted that "he was utterly hostile to any proscription on men and women in Texas on account of religious or racial prejudices" and that "he had quit the Klan on account of its proscription of Catholics and Jews."[152] If Lutcher had indeed belonged to the Klan at one time, as is reasonable to suppose from his supporters' testimony, he was certainly no longer a member by the time of the Senate hearings.

Lutcher's was the only nomination debated in a three-hour closed executive session, but after Governor Ferguson sent a "strong plea" for his confirmation, the Senate granted it 24-6, and Lutcher was duly reappointed to the Board of Regents in February 1925.[153] "So many rumors have been floating around town regarding this matter," commented Ben Woodhead in the *Beaumont Enterprise*, "that it would be folly to attempt to separate the wheat from the chaff and to find out the truth about this whole matter."[154] With Lutcher's confirmation, Will Hogg declined to serve as a regent, even though he had been a leader of the ex-student faction. One fact was certain: no love would ever be lost between Lutcher Stark and Will Hogg. There had been none to lose.

When Lutcher returned to the Board of Regents, he operated from a powerful position. He was reelected as its chairman, and in spite of his damaged relationship with the Ex-Students Association and particularly with Will Hogg, he still enjoyed broad support on campus. After all, in the eyes of the students, it had been Lutcher who had pushed for the construction of Memorial Stadium as well as for the expansion of athletic facilities for the student body, both for intramural competition and for their own personal use. And the fact remained that he had also supported student activities in myriad other ways, including financing many of their college costs. In fact, the staff of the *Cactus* yearbook dedicated the 1926 publication to "H. J. Lutcher Stark, the spirit of whose pioneer ancestors has been shown in his constructive patronage of the University of Texas."

Such was Lutcher Stark's total immersion in the Austin–University of Texas universe that several years later, he and Nita bought 15.66 acres in Pemberton Heights, an exclusive subdivision on a bluff above Shoal Creek, and began landscaping the spacious lot with plans to build a home.[155] Notably, however, many of the trees, shrubs, and plants they chose—coastal live oaks, dogwood, redbud, holly, grancy graybeard, yaupon, honeysuckle, wisteria, trumpet vine—were native to East Texas.[156]

That eventful year of 1924 also saw a presidential election, and in the midst of it all, Lutcher served as a delegate to the Democratic National Convention in New York City. Toward the end of the convention, he received a telegram from F.H. Farwell, reporting on business matters at home. "For the love of Mike," Farwell ended the telegram, "nominate somebody and come home. . . . We are all going to vote for Coolidge anyhow."[157] Farwell was right: amid the wave of conservatism sweeping the nation—even in some of the states of the "Solid South," including Texas—Republican Calvin Coolidge was duly elected president of the United States.[158] Later, Lutcher and William Lea attended Coolidge's inauguration as representatives of Governor Miriam A. Ferguson and Texas.[159]

CHAPTER NINE

Old Man Depression

From our knowledge of the yellow pine timber belt, we are led to the conclusion that there is no available supply for the Orange mills.
—F. H. FARWELL, FEBRUARY 1927[1]

The first signs began to surface in the late 1910s and early 1920s. As it had in the Susquehanna River Valley so many years ago, the handwriting on the wall loomed ever more clearly, this time in the timber regions of the South. After decades of being subjected to the "cut-out-and-get-out" practices common to the lumber companies of the time, the virgin timberlands had been laid bare, and the great southern lumber boom—the "bonanza era" of lumbering, as some historians have called it—was drawing to a close. The end was brought on more abruptly by the nationwide building explosion of 1922–1925 (which, ironically, gave the industry its most profitable years while simultaneously hastening its decline) and, later, by the onset of the Great Depression.[2]

And as Henry Jacob Lutcher had known it must, the timber supply for Lutcher & Moore itself was beginning to run out. Some even retroactively placed part of the blame on Henry Lutcher's shoulders, speculating that he had been "shortsighted"—that in the beginning of the company's operations, he had cut too much timber from his own lands instead of purchasing more from other logging companies, thus leaving more of his own timber in reserve for later availability.[3] But speculation remained an exercise in futility; whether sooner or later, the first-growth timber was fast disappearing throughout the entire region, and the second growth had not yet reached sufficient maturity to harvest. In the following years, the signs coalesced into reality: by 1927, Lutcher & Moore's timber supply was entirely exhausted. In the face of the impending shortage, the company garnered enough to operate for the next two years with purchased timber from local sources, but those proved scarce as well, and by 1929 they too had dried up, forcing the company to extend the search much farther afield.[4]

Figure 9.1. Lutcher & Moore group with guides in Nicaragua in 1920s in search of timber sources: Doug Pruter (*second from right*) and Lutcher Stark (*third from right*). Stark Foundation Archives.

As early as 1921, Lutcher & Moore had begun to explore options for timber prospects as far away as Oregon, Mexico, Nicaragua, and British Honduras (modern-day Belize), among other locales.[5] By 1926, they were considering "a fir project of some magnitude" that would involve "either Honduras timber or fir, in order to continue the Orange mills," as Farwell informed H.M. Spain, one of the company's "cruisers," or timber scouts, but the project came to nothing.[6] A few years later, they even investigated sources in California for redwood logs to be brought in to the Orange mills and made into squares and flitches but quickly came to understand that it would not be cost-effective to bring the logs all the way to Orange for manufacture.[7]

As company officials were planning a timber investigation to Portland, Oregon, in 1926, Farwell briefed William Stark, by now seventy-six and increasingly troubled by poor vision, on the details of the property they were considering buying. Falwell reported to Lutcher Stark:

Told [your father] I should like to have him come out with you and thought he would enjoy it, but he said he wouldn't be of any use, for he couldn't see. I told him that was foolish, for I knew he would enjoy going into the timber and we would be more than glad to show him around and introduce him, and it would create a better impression than anything you or I could do. After a moment, he said, "go on," and I think I am leaving with his passive approval, but I also think . . . he personally would prefer we do nothing. I did tell him, however, all we ask . . . [is] for the company to go on, and he said that was all right.[8]

In a memo dated February 16, 1927, Farwell summarized the bare truth:

From our knowledge of the yellow pine timber belt, we are led to the conclusion that there is no available supply for the Orange mills. West Louisiana is practically cut out. In Texas, the remaining timber lies west and north . . . and is controlled principally by [John Henry] Kirby and Temple and the Lufkin interests. South of the block, Kirby controls for his Evadale, Call, Voth, and Silsbee plants. There is, therefore, little use in our exploring this field for anything like a timber supply.[9]

Even so, the company itself continued to show a profit through most of the 1920s, and by 1928, its financial footing still rested on solid ground. Farwell wrote Lutcher Stark that September: "We have been paying out money pretty fast, and had to laugh the other day when George [Colburn] concluded it was about all gone. . . . With all we have paid out, there is an approximate million and half dollars that we could convert tomorrow morning, with probably three hundred thousand more in foreign and domestic acceptances. I still have hopes of holding on to enough to continue in the lumber business," he added optimistically.[10]

Notwithstanding the shortage of timber sources, in an era of national prosperity many of the related family interests flourished.[11] One of the most successful, the Wier Long Leaf Lumber Company, continued its lucrative production—for the time being, at least—as did the ventures in Louisiana, the Lutcher & Moore Cypress Lumber Company and Dibert, Stark and Brown. The Yellow Pine Paper Mill, dependent as it was on Orange's lumber mills to supply it with shavings and sawdust used in its paper-manufacturing process, continued to show profits as long as the mills were still operating. The Texas Creosoting Company, founded in 1923 with William Stark as president, Farwell as vice president, and Lutcher Stark as secretary-treasurer, showed a loss for the year 1925 but profit in 1926 and 1927.[12]

The Vinton Petroleum Company, a perennial success, also showed a profit during those years, paying handsome dividends.[13] In the flurry of drilling following the massive new oil discovery on Beaumont's Spindletop Hill in 1925,[14] Vinton Petroleum and its principals received substantial income from wells drilled on their various mineral interests.[15] In September 1929, a large new well, the Stark No. 1, was brought in on family land in Orange County, heralding the birth of the new Stark field, and Doug Pruter estimated that the amount of William's royalty check for the next month alone would be between $9,000 and $10,000.[16] "I never saw the future look so bright and I believe by this time next year we will be kept busy looking for good investments, as by that time we will have everything worked out and behind us," Pruter wrote William with what would shortly prove to be supreme irony.[17]

William Stark, ever the farmer at heart, instituted a forest management program—replanting, managing, and protecting the forestlands—that he had actually begun on Lutcher & Moore lands soon after the turn of the century, when he had assumed command of the Lutcher & Moore family interests.[18] (In the future, the program became a model for the entire industry.)[19] But he harbored another longtime dream as well: from his lifelong, intimate knowledge of the Southeast Texas terrain, animal husbandry, crops, and farming methods, he envisioned setting the region on a path toward the development of cattle raising and diversified agriculture, which he believed was a reasonable solution to the problem of cutover timberlands—his own and those of other lumber companies.[20] Since the area's other source of livelihood, the rice industry, was seasonal and the fields needed to be rotated over three years, he believed diversification was the key to economic improvement, and given Orange County's rich soil and mild climate, it would be possible to grow some crops year-round.[21]

To further his vision, William helped establish two companies. In 1926 he, Lutcher Stark, and another investor, A.G. Wilkins, incorporated the Sabine Packing Company, with the purpose of "constructing and maintaining establishments for slaughtering, refrigerating, canning, curing and packing meat." The plant, built west of Orange on the south side of the Orangefield Road (present-day FM 105), contained stock pens, a slaughter floor, refrigeration, a sausage kitchen, and a so-called gut room for processing entrails, thus furnishing a local venue for processing the region's cattle and hogs from start to finished product.[22]

The following year, William and Lutcher also established the Orange Products Company, located on Dayton (Gum) Street in West Orange. This project embodied the kind of diversified farming close to William's heart, the plan being that the plant would furnish an outlet where fully five hundred truck farms could sell their produce. Additional produce was also brought in by rail to be processed at the plant, which canned green beans, okra and tomatoes, turnip and mustard greens, spinach, limas, kidney beans, black-eyed peas and pork, and sweet, sour, and dill pickles, as well as the Texas Magnolia figs William loved.[23] ("Have the cook put up about five or six dozen pints of fig preserves," he had written Pruter one summer

Figure 9.2. William Stark on horseback, dressed as if for church or other formal occasion. He enjoyed riding for most of his life. Stark Foundation Archives.

from the Samoset, then had thought better of it. "Better make it six dozen for I am wild about them.")[24] In light of hard times to come, many of the companies created by the Starks, especially the Sabine Packing Company and the Orange Products Company, afforded vital assistance to the people of Orange County.[25]

During the 1920s, William Stark also developed a fine herd of Brahman cattle.[26] "I must say that you have a wonderful herd," Pruter wrote him in 1927 in Cologne, Germany, where he was touring Europe with the family. "At the present rate I would be will[ing] to wager that your Brahma herd will be worth at least $250,000 within the next three years."[27] At one time the herd was the "best source of Brahman blood in the country," according to one source, and at the time of William's death it was reputed to be the largest.[28]

Lutcher Stark, now in his vigorous thirties, continued to blaze his own high-profile, ever-broadening trail, immersed primarily in University of Texas affairs but also entering increasingly into the family's business concerns. During the 1920s, he held office or a directorship in the Lutcher & Moore Lumber Company, Yellow Pine Paper Mill, Sabine Supply Company, Vinton Petroleum Company, Lutcher Memorial Hospital, Orange Cameron Land Company, Lutcher & Moore Cypress Lumber Company, and San Jacinto Life Insurance Company, among several other ventures in the process of being developed. In answer to an inquiry proposing that either Farwell or Lutcher serve as an officer with a projected new East Texas Chamber of Commerce, the former replied, "I just have a little hunch that [Lutcher's] own interests are taking all of his time, particularly as he is giving unselfishly to the State University."[29] "Lutcher Stark's holdings are enormous," one writer concluded, "a little too big to get hold of in a single picture."[30]

In the mid-1920s, Lutcher became the darling of the press, which pounced on the novel idea of someone of his young years possessing such wealth; articles lionizing him and deliberately exaggerating his worth appeared in local and some national newspapers. "How Texas' Richest Young Man Spends His Money" appeared in the *Beaumont Enterprise* on March 7, 1926. Interviewing Lutcher at his home in Orange, the writer described him as "athletic," "muscled," and "active," adding that "the term nervously active might be applied, though he can sit comfortably still in a chair" and predicting—accurately, as it happened—that "he was born in Orange . . . has always lived in Orange, and probably always will. . . . He is always closely in touch with Orange and [its] affairs." According to the reporter, Lutcher gave full credit for what he was to his father and mother, "mincing no words about it." "Living for others is one of the first and one of the last things about the man that ones very close to him will tell you," the writer concluded, then quoted Lutcher as declaring that "no man is my boss."[31]

Several other articles appeared contemporaneously, among them "The Small Town Texan Who Has 75 Million Dollars," published in the *Kansas City Star* on July 31, 1927, which rhapsodized that Lutcher Stark was "said to be the wealthiest young man in Texas" and owned "a controlling inter-

Figure 9.3. Lutcher Stark portrayed with his various interests, 1920s.
Stark Foundation Archives.

est in the city of Orange," with "millions at his command, with his finger
in almost every commercial and industrial project in his part of the state."
"The little city hangs on his every move, and yet it hasn't quite figured
him out," the article declared, a little obscurely. It went on to assert that

Stark owns a large cattle ranch in Colorado, a coal mine in New Mexico. He
has part interest in one of Texas's greatest pine sawmills, a paper mill, one of

the largest creosoting plants in the state, a cannery, a great car and steel plant and he recently sold an electrical power plant for several million. He controls a bank and has a large interest in a Texas life insurance company. . . . He has an interest in the third largest oil field in South Texas, and recently brought in a field of his own in Louisiana. . . . He owns much virgin timber on the Pacific Coast, besides one of the largest pieces of virgin yellow pine in his own state, and has been negotiating for a mahogany forest in South America.[32]

Such wildly extravagant claims, aiming for effect, contained some kernels of fact but also many oversimplifications and deliberate exaggerations, as well as outright falsifications. But because of his wealth and position, Lutcher Stark remained the subject of such speculation throughout his life.

A short doggerel poem he penned in 1926 affords a glimpse of his daily routine as well as his sense of humor:

18 callers waiting since 11—
Phone Willard to have boat ready at 7—
Check up gas and fur tags—
Get a bottle of Scotch at Babb's.
Ask Mrs. H. to phone my pilot
Memo: Order 12 gross of violets???
Byron: Be sure to write
Mrs. O'Hair that letter
Why can't the rat ranch [the Orange Cameron Land Company venture] do
    much better?
Have Murray look at trailer
2 P.M.—call on the tailor
3 P.M.—call Dr. Foster
Tell Byron to give me Rotary Roster
Take Nita home some toffy
Phone Willard to get butter, eggs and coffee.
Endless memos, terse and clever—
Do I ever read them? NEVER![33]

Through his father and Farwell, Lutcher developed an intense interest in golf. Farwell encouraged him to follow his father's example. "I want to see you get into the game," he urged, "for it is wonderful."[34] "I'm sure that you have taught Lutcher how to play golf by this time," Pruter wrote William at the Samoset in Maine in August 1923.[35] "We have been playing golf all the time since we arrived," Lutcher reported to Frances Ann from the Samoset. "All my life I've said I'd never do this but on account

Figure 9.4. Sunset Grove Country Club, Donald Ross golf course and clubhouse.
Stark Foundation Archives.

of Nita's loss [the death of her father the previous month] and Pop's health I'm doing it."[36] "Lutcher is putting in his time at golf," William replied to Pruter.[37]

True to form, Lutcher progressed quickly from simply playing the game to the idea of building a golf course in Orange, in large part for his father. The reason could simply have been for William's health, but two tales persist. One holds that, for unknown reasons, Lutcher's then-estranged cousin, Edgar Brown Jr., who owned the Pinehurst Country Club a little west of Orange, had denied William access to play. Lutcher, angry at the slight to his father, decided to build his own course, where the older man could play at will. The other story maintains that at a Christmas party at the Pinehurst club, Lutcher requested the band to play a particular selection, but Edgar Brown refused to allow it to be played, spurring Lutcher to build his own club.[38]

Whatever the reason, Lutcher began laying plans for the new course and country club to be constructed on a spacious acreage of pine and hardwood forest just west of downtown Orange on the east side of Adams Bayou.[39] As always for Lutcher Stark, nothing but the best would do: he proceeded to hire the Scotsman Donald J. Ross, at that time the most famous golf course architect in the world, to design it. Ross completed the design in 1923, and construction commenced that year.[40] Play began in December 1925 on Lutcher's $750,000 course, the first in Texas to be designed by Ross. Initially Lutcher named the course "Peavine" after a nearby farm, but Nita Stark disliked the name. One evening when she was at the course, observing the red sun setting behind a grove of pines, she pronounced its name to be "Sunset Grove."[41] In time, Nita herself became an ardent golfer.[42]

William derived much enjoyment from play at Sunset Grove. Although in his later years he became almost blind, he remained an intrepid golfer, playing with specially made bright yellow balls. Longtime Orange resident Julius H. "Jules" David, who frequently caddied for William, remembered that his caddies always carried a piece of yellow-painted broomstick for him to use as a guide in aiming the ball. By this time, Lutcher himself had grown into an avid if not stellar golfer, approaching the game as he did everything he tackled in life—with total energy and focus. On one occasion, he began play before daybreak and played 104 holes, walking with a caddy the entire time and finishing after dark by auto headlights. "He wore out his partner and a couple of caddies," David recalled.[43]

In 1927, Lutcher built a two-story white frame clubhouse for $35,000, complete with ballroom, weight-lifting room, and handball court.[44] He had become quite proficient at the game of handball, playing with characteristic ferocity. Sportswriter Lloyd Gregory once commented that Lutcher and one of the latter's favorite Austin opponents, former Varsity athlete Walter Fisher,

> would make a big hit on any vaudeville program with their handball playing. Many University students would rather "hear" the two play than go to any movie. The two men are evenly matched, and the winner is usually the one who talks the other out of the largest number of points. During the games, each makes dire threats of physical violence on the other, but after each has been cooled off by a bath, they shake hands; each admits that he "cheated rottenly," and they are the best of friends in the world until they get on the handball court again.[45]

As Hubert D. "Buddy" Cox, Lutcher's frequent handball partner in Orange, declared, "He was tough to handle. He was a good player . . . [and] a tough competitor."[46]

With Lutcher himself carrying the bulk of the club's expenses, Sunset Grove became a hub for Orange's social life, furnishing recreation to area residents for several generations.[47] He built a lake, complete with diving tower, and stocked its waters with bass, but Homer Stark later

Figure 9.5. William Stark (*left*) at Sunset Grove Country Club with George Colburn, auditor at Lutcher & Moore. Stark Foundation Archives.

remembered that his father allowed no fishing except with barbless hooks and ruled that fish must be returned to the lake.[48] Through the years, the Starks and others utilized the club to host lavish parties, teas, Christmas dances, graduation galas, and other special occasions.[49] "I wished for you to be at the dance at the Country Club the other night," Pruter wrote William Stark in Maine, describing an extraordinary scene during one dance number:

> You know Lutcher has a young gangling aviator, that is about 6 feet 4 inches tall, and I think the same urge that impels him to fly impels him to dance. He slipped, nose dived, glided and tail-spinned around the floor. In fact, he did everything but loop-the-loop. Watching that boy do his stuff is worth all I have ever paid to the Country Club in dues. I know you would have enjoyed it.[50]

Lutcher had indeed employed a pilot—for his recently purchased airplane. In 1928, deciding that an airplane was needed for the Frances Ann Lutcher Hospital, he engineered the purchase of a WACO-10 biplane through the Lutcher & Moore Lumber Company.[51] That August, the plane duly arrived at the municipal airport in Beaumont from Troy, Ohio, where it had been manufactured. It was flown by that same "young gangling aviator," Bledsoe Payne. The plane, "of the latest design," was equipped with a nine-cylinder "whirlwind" motor, parachutes, and navigation devices, including those needed for night flying.[52] Lutcher began at once to take flying lessons from Payne.[53] He also sent I.B. Murray, his and Nita's chauffeur, to Beaumont and paid for his flying lessons.[54]

Murray's son, Laurence, later recalled that Lutcher often wing-walked without benefit of parachute or safety belt, simply holding on to the struts of the biplane. Laurence Murray also recalled that, if wind conditions permitted, his father could actually suspend the plane in one spot. Seeing the plane hanging almost motionless in midair, local residents, believing he was in trouble, frequently called the fire department or the Murray home. "Murray's stuck up there, you know," they would report. "What the hell do you expect us to do about it?" one family member was heard to snap on one of those occasions. "We don't have a ladder that long."[55] The WACO biplane met its end on the runway of the Municipal Airport in Beaumont, when another plane swung into its path as Murray was taking off. According to Laurence Murray, his father "hauled it all away in a pickup truck."[56]

Since the late fall of 1923, Lutcher and Nita Stark had been playing the role of new parents to their adopted twins, now called "Homer" and "Bill." Although the Starks employed ample household staff, some directly responsible for the boys, the presence of two small one-year-olds undoubtedly accelerated the rhythm of life in the ten-room Stark home on the corner of Tenth and Pine, and happily so; in fact, Nita expressed the hope that if they were able to find twin girls eligible for adoption, they would enlarge their family further.[57] That opportunity never materialized, but as soon as Homer and Bill grew old enough to understand, Lutcher informed them that they were adopted. "Most people have to take what they get," he told them, "but we looked all over the world for you."[58]

Perhaps it was Lutcher's new parenthood that spurred him to undertake another enterprise, one that would amplify his work with youth and eventually evolved into a major interest. In 1923, he was invited to teach a Sunday School class at his home church, the First Presbyterian Church of Orange, consisting of seven lively young boys other teachers had not been able to control. The first time he met with the class, one of them asked with spurious innocence, "Mr. Stark, just tell us what the devil looks like." "I'm not much up on the devil," Lutcher shot back, "but I'll find out, and next Sunday I'll give you the devil." The class understood his meaning perfectly—and gave him no more trouble.[59]

That original Sunday School class grew past all imagining. In 1926, Lutcher, recognizing the need for organized activities to fill the active youngsters' leisure time, incorporated his own boys' club, "Lutch Stark's Boys Inc.," its purpose to "support, foster and develop the spiritual, moral, mental, and physical education and welfare of boyhood."[60] Members were required to attend Sunday School and church regularly, and membership was contingent on a strict set of rules; if a boy broke them, he was required to drop himself from the group.[61]

Lutcher formed the group into a baseball team, a Boy Scout troop, then a band he christened "Lutcher Stark's Boys' Band," administering it and the club's other activities through the parent corporation.[62] He opened the membership to boys of all creeds and even expanded it to include three girls,[63] engaging the church's assistant pastor, S.E. Ayers, a former band director, to lead the group.[64] (An honor guard of "Lutcher's Loyals," their initial moniker, served as escort for the coffin of Frances Ann Lutcher as her remains were conveyed to and from the Presbyterian Church and to the family mausoleum in Evergreen Cemetery.)[65]

At first, band members were required to furnish their own instruments, uniforms, and music lessons, but later, Lutch Stark's Boys, Inc., bought and retained ownership of the instruments and provided class lessons, each member still furnishing his own uniform. The group provided music for all of Orange High School's football games and played for local events such as banquets and commencements. Each summer, Lutcher loaded them into special passenger buses and took them on tours throughout Texas and other states.[66] In June 1926, the band was photographed in

Figure 9.6. Miriam Stark reading to her adopted grandsons, Bill (*left*) and Homer (*right*). Stark Foundation Archives.

Figure 9.7. The Lutcher Stark family, from left, Nita, Homer, Bill, and Lutcher, undated. Stark Foundation Archives.

Figure 9.8. Lutcher Stark's Boys' Band at the First Presbyterian Church,
Orange, mid-1920s. Note Nelda Childers (*bottom row, seventh from right*),
at that time the only female member of the group. Stark Foundation Archives.

uniform, giving a concert atop Pike's Peak amid the snow, playing "I'm
Sitting on Top of the World" and inevitably, "The Eyes of Texas."[67]

Arguably, the wide participation in the club's activities resulted in a decline in incidents of juvenile delinquency in Orange County, from seventy in 1924 to three in 1925, and an *Austin American-Statesman* article
published in May 1926 announced that no incidents had yet occurred that
year. By 1926, Lutcher's Sunday School class had grown to eighty or ninety
members.[68]

In 1927, Nita and Lutcher Stark planned an epic three-month tour to eastern and western Europe, the Middle East, and North Africa, taking William, Miriam, and four-year-old Homer and Bill with them. Accompanying the party were Maria "Ria" Kiefer, a German national who served as
governess to the twins, and Margaret Wilber, a young Lutcher cousin from
South Williamsport who lived for a time with Miriam and William, serving as a companion and part-time secretary.[69] On this particular journey,
Margaret also assisted Ria with the boys.

The group embarked from New York in late February 1927, arriving on
the French coast at Cherbourg in early March, then traveling by train to
Paris, Venice, Florence, and Rome. Nita faithfully kept a journal of the
entire trip, and her entries reveal her as a clear-eyed observer and an interesting individual. Like her mother-in-law before her, she loved traveling and devoured the various sights, scenes, and treasures she was seeing, revealing an extensive knowledge of the history and culture of the

places they visited and writing of them with style and enthusiasm. She also displayed a sharp wit; after attending a musical at the Moulin Rouge in Paris, she opined that it was "disgusting" because of the physical condition of some of the dancers. "When I grow old and unmoral," she wrote, tongue firmly in cheek, "I know that I can get a job in the chorus—operation scars, et al."[70]

She eloquently expressed her sense of romance, evoked by the beauty of

Figure 9.9. Homer (*left*) and Bill Stark, at around four or five years of age, late 1920s. Stark Foundation Archives.

the places they saw. In Naples, she noted, "From the balcony . . . I see Vesuvius, rising majestically above the Bay of Naples, the smoke a silver cloud lighted by the clear moon, the view romantic. . . . This beauty enchants."[71]

Her disgust and wry amusement at primitive, unsanitary conditions they frequently encountered were also apparent:

> I could write for hours on the water closets I have seen. There were crude ones behind prickly pears, some a long cement groove with gourd wash, some a bit more refined—a rectangular hole with a pitcher and a barrel at its side, some a bit more modern, excepting you pull a cord twenty to thirty minutes and maybe some water will come down, and sometimes you hold on to the cord and suddenly all the water is on you instead of going into the hole. I . . . must conclude with the statement that there is no sex to toilets over here. One other thing I have learned is that the users of toilet paper in this Country are heroes.[72]

Predictably, the twins were thoroughly intrigued by the W.C.s and were delighted to use them.[73]

The Stark entourage spent extended time in the Holy Land, particularly in Jerusalem and Bethlehem. Nita, deeply religious and an avid student of biblical history, delighted in visiting the sacred places she had studied. She and Lutcher celebrated their sixteenth wedding anniversary by walking through Jerusalem's Jaffa Gate. "By now we are soaked," she exulted as they struggled through a downpour in the Old City. "But what care we! We are living in the past."[74]

In Egypt, they visited Cairo, then Aswan (which William dubbed "Ass Warm" for the 113 degrees that the thermometer registered when they arrived). "I have found no living thing to have quite the bed of ease that these old sacred bulls had," Nita mused on seeing the tombs of the sacred bulls at Sakkara. "[They] did not even have to switch the flies off," she noted. "The Persians broke up bull worship, and ever since, the bull has had to take on a real job."[75]

When the party trekked to the Valley of the Kings, they spotted the approach of a troop of armed soldiers and were told that they were escorting treasures from the tomb of Pharaoh Tutankhamen to the Egyptian Museum in Cairo.[76] The party rode by camel (Nita, Margaret, Ria, and the twins), donkey (Lutcher), and two-wheeled sand cart (Miriam and William) to the pyramids at Giza, where Lutcher climbed the Great Pyramid in twenty-five minutes (he was bested by one of the locals, who, for $2.50, climbed up and down the pyramid in seven minutes flat).[77]

Homer and Bill were fascinated with everything they saw. They fell into malodorous mud puddles in Jerusalem; adopted flea-infested stray

Figure 9.10. William Stark awaits Miriam in a lace shop in Brittany, ca. 1927.
Stark Foundation Archives.

kittens; galloped full tilt on donkeys and camels in the Egyptian desert (presumably accompanied by attendants); watched, entranced, as a snake charmer enticed a cobra into his basket; and learned a few choice expletives in Arabic and German. Even so, their mother pronounced them to be very well behaved. Nita quoted their Grandmother Stark as saying that she thought Homer "would make an extraordinary choir boy—but is a bit doubtful about Bill's behavior."[78]

William Stark, who at best regarded foreign travel with a jaundiced eye, sometimes looked after the twins while everyone else shopped or saw the sights. On one occasion the three "played hookey," in Nita's words, while the rest visited the Egyptian Museum in Cairo. When she returned to the hotel, she found that "havoc took place at home. Dad was to have looked after the children and instead, he let them run wild—hairbrushes, combs, bottles, etc., all over the garden, etc. Some things we will never find. Why didn't Dad make them behave? Homer explains he's too old, but Bill adds that he's just lazy."[79]

Homer came much closer to a correct, if undiplomatic, analysis: William Stark had never been lazy for a moment in his life, but he was certainly facing advancing age and increasingly serious health issues, chief among which was his failing eyesight. Perhaps the choice of another sitter would have averted most of the havoc. (Considering his own austere youth in the house in Burkeville as he helped bring up his numerous siblings, one is tempted to speculate on his private thoughts regarding the lavish manner in which his grandsons were being reared.)

After leaving Egypt, the travelers journeyed through Yugoslavia to Hungary and Austria, entering Germany to deliver Ria and the boys to her parents in Berlin for a visit and a rest while the remainder of the party toured extensively in Germany, northern Italy, and Switzerland. They reunited with Ria, Homer, and Bill in Berlin, headed for Belgium, and joined their ship in Ostend for the return trip to New York—then southward toward home.[80] The lengthy global jaunt was the family's last extended journey together.

Not all of the family interests prospered. In addition to the growing shortage of timber, other worries began appearing on the horizon. Lutcher Stark operated in large part on inherited capital, at the heart of which lay the parent company, Lutcher & Moore; when he launched concerns of his own, he sometimes encountered major surprises, not all of them pleasant. In 1923, he and eight others formed the Orange Cameron Land Company, a Texas-based corporation that purchased two tracts of land known as the "Joyce Tract" and the "Texas Tract" in Cameron Parish, Louisiana—some 170,000 acres in all.[81] The land was described by a

Figure 9.11. Orange Cameron Land Company headquarters. Stark Foundation Archives.

visitor as being "as flat as a floor, hasn't a tree on it, is a jungle of marsh grasses, has only small patches of dry ground and to all outward appearances is an utter wasteland."[82] But the group's purpose was to trap mink, muskrat, raccoon, otter, and alligators, and at the time of purchase, it teemed with wildlife.

From the beginning, the corporation encountered misfortune, mainly in the form of an unscrupulous shareholder who defaulted on his part of the loan and who had, before the land was purchased, signed a long-term trapping lease with another company. Subsequent litigation went against Orange Cameron, leaving the group unable to trap either tract. Additionally, saltwater intrusion from the Intracoastal Canal and the network of canals cut by Orange Cameron for trappers' use blighted the freshwater plants, diminishing the number of fur-bearing animals. The problems were eventually alleviated by litigation and William Stark's 1925 purchase of the Joyce Tract at a sheriff's sale, enabling him to lease it back to Orange Cameron for trapping purposes, but the overall result was that the company suffered severe financial losses.[83]

Ultimately, through buyouts to rescue his friends, Lutcher came to own most of the property.[84] He never made a profit from the trapping operations but fell under the spell of the marsh itself, and through the

Figure 9.12. George Raborn, manager of Orange Cameron Land Company, seated near fur bailer. Stark Foundation Archives.

years it became an integral part of his and his sons' lives. He built a spacious camp complex on an artificial hill in the marsh to which he invited coaches, players, newspapermen, politicians, sportswriters, dignitaries, family members, and friends to enjoy the abundant fishing and waterfowl hunting. "The shooting . . . was secondary to the sights, the fun and the eating," sportswriter Flem Hall, present at one hunt in 1934, wrote, noting that, by Lutcher's orders, all shooting ceased at noon in order to leave the birds alone in the afternoons to allow them to rest.[85]

The Orange Cameron Land Company venture produced at least one positive result: Lutcher's interest in the comparatively new concept of conservation grew, and he developed a reputation among Louisiana government officials as someone who knew and cared for his land.[86] "At the risk of an unbecomingness which I hate to assume," he declared in August 1928, writing to an official in the Louisiana Department of Conservation, "there are few single persons in the US today who are doing more for the spirit and result of conservation than I am."[87] A year later, he wrote, "May I say . . . that this whole subject of conservation is . . . a tremendously interesting subject, and, I think you will admit, one about which none of us have sounded the full depth." But he could not resist adding, "As a conservationist of wild life, I personally take my hat off to no man, not even your department."[88] He retained a lifelong commitment to sound conservation practices—vindicating, in a way, the early, doomed efforts of his grandfather Lutcher in timber conservation.

Lutcher Stark was not alone in his problems. In 1922, when the old

Southern Shipbuilding and Drydock Company had been reincarnated as the Orange Car and Steel Company, both William and Miriam Stark had also purchased large amounts of capital stock.[89] After several years of losses, Orange Car and Steel stood heavily in debt to Lutcher & Moore, and a 1929 auditor's report revealed that it would not survive without other sources of income.[90]

At about the same time, another of William's investments went sour. Sometime after 1923, he had become a majority stockholder in the San Jacinto Life Insurance Company, which had built a handsome multistory office building in downtown Beaumont. The company never attained sound financial ground, however, in spite of the infusion of large sums of William's money, and in 1928 the stockholders sold him the building.[91] In turn, he sold it to Lutcher, who created a separate company, the San Jacinto Building, Inc.[92] But both companies were left in debt, and William lost the money he had invested. In 1932 San Jacinto Life was sold to the Great Southern Life Insurance Company at a loss.[93] At William's death, his stock was listed as worthless. Lutcher & Moore ultimately came into possession of the notes on the building and foreclosed on it at a loss.[94]

By the late 1920s, the ill-starred Hagan Coal Mines was spiraling toward its doom. In the spring of 1926, a business associate of the family, E.S. Simms, visited the site and afterward wrote Pruter a searing assessment, citing an overshot budget, scant production, and widespread mis-

Figure 9.13. Lutcher Stark at Orange Cameron Land Company duck hunt.
Stark Foundation Archives.

management. He warned that Hagan was not filling existing coal orders and stood in danger of being sued by companies that had not received shipments. "The probability [is] that it can never be made to pay expenses," he warned. "All that has been spent . . . will be a total loss except for the small amount of salvage."[95]

Nor did Simms spare the investors. "I wish that I could find some rich man who even tho I gypped him out of two or three millions would still have confidence in me and keep me on the payroll at a princely salary," he fumed. But he saved the worst of his criticisms for John de Praslin, the promoter of the project, charging him with blithely spending William's money even though he knew there was no "workable coal" to be found. "Unless Mr. [William] Stark has suddenly lost his reason I know he is not going to give this fakir another opportunity to make a fool of him. . . . Doc [de Praslin] is still sitting pretty," Simms concluded, "but I know that you [Pruter] feel just as I do about him and if you were free to act as your judgement dictated you would tie a can to him quicker than Hell would scorch a feather."[96] The investors eventually cut their losses. In 1932, William Stark leased the mine and property,[97] and de Praslin and his wife, Margaret, executed a quitclaim deed for the Sandoval County holdings.[98] The company was eventually liquidated, though the land remained in the Stark family until after Lutcher Stark's death.[99]

The Hagan Coal Mines, San Jacinto Life, and Orange Car and Steel figured, along with several others, in the only clash ever recorded between William and Lutcher Stark. William had remained away from home for almost the entire year of 1927. After the family's odyssey the previous spring, they returned to New York that June. From New York, they apparently traveled to Maine, where he and Miriam remained for the summer.[100] In the fall, they returned to New York and were going to return to Orange by October 20, but their plans were thwarted by William's health, an unspecified problem that necessitated a stay in the hospital.[101] As the autumn wore on, he began to improve. "We have all been glad to learn the good news regarding your condition," Pruter wrote November 19, "[and] . . . to learn that you will be able to return home next week."[102] But by mid-December, William was still convalescing, and Pruter reassured him that there was "nothing to worry about but to get well and be welcomed back home."[103] Presumably, the Starks arrived home in time for Christmas.

In William's absence, it was natural that Lutcher Stark would assume an increasingly prominent role in the family interests, and he undoubtedly grew accustomed to making many of the day-to-day decisions. Given his quicksilver nature and innate penchant for assuming command and doubtless having in mind his father's failing health, perhaps it also followed naturally that he would make an increasing number of unilateral decisions. But in some instances, he apparently overstepped his boundaries. After all, his father had not yet abdicated his sovereignty.

That October, while William and Miriam still remained in New York, a rumor sprang up in Orange that the Starks had withdrawn their financial support from the First National Bank. In an expansive gesture, Lutcher promptly ordered $500,000 in hard cash to be shipped into the bank. (It was said to have been hauled in a pickup truck and displayed in the lobby.) Lutcher declared the rumor that they had withdrawn their money to be "utterly false": "Our interests, and we personally, have approximately a million and one half dollars on deposit. As the best answer to the rumor we decided to put in the additional funds. . . . We wanted only to show our confidence in the bank and that every dollar of Stark money is solidly behind the First National."[104] Pruter wrote William enigmatically a few days after the incident: "When you get back we will all have to get together and have a big pow-wow and make plans for the future, which I think should be firm and positive as personal feelings and business will not mix very well."[105]

The next year, in August 1928, Pruter reported to William at the Samoset that Dave Nelson, who managed the Stark land and cattle interests, planned to drill several water wells, two on the Joyce Tract at Orange Cameron Land Company and one at the Sunset Grove golf course.[106] Nelson had also informed Pruter that, since William was now the owner of the Joyce Tract, having recently bought it from Lutcher and his investors, Lutcher wanted the new wells charged to William's account. When questioned, Nelson agreed that the wells on the Joyce Tract were unnecessary, since William was running only a small number of cattle on it.

In light of William's recent extensive losses, the proposition rang warning bells with Pruter, who directed Nelson to "hold up" drilling until he secured William's approval. Pruter then informed William that Lutcher and Nelson had discussed drilling a much larger number of wells on another tract of land, presumably to enhance its marketability. Pruter pronounced the investment to be "unwise at this time." He added, "I do not want you to think that I am criticizing Lutcher or Dave in their plans but I do want you to know what is contemplated for your account and the expenditure of your money, therefore I will thank you to advise whether or not the contemplated well drilling program meets with your approval."[107] "I am opposed to having any water wells drilled for my account this year," William tersely wired back.[108] No wells were drilled; William Stark still stood firmly at the helm of his world.

But three months later, a similar situation involving Vinton Petroleum Company erupted into open dissension and wounded feelings. In February 1927, the Vinton Petroleum Company, with William Stark serving as president, had evidently granted Stark family attorney George Hill a twelve-month option to purchase the company's production in the Vinton-Ged field for a ten-year term.[109] In turn, Hill had assigned the option to the Sabine Terminal Oil Corporation, run by Houston oilmen Stephen P. and Robert D. Farish, to purchase "all of the pipeline oil belonging to the Vinton Petroleum Company . . . and produced by it in the Vinton-Ged field" for the ten-year time period.[110] The undertaking was apparently engineered by Hill and Lutcher Stark.[111]

In January 1928, Hill sent the signed contract to William, at the same time asking Lutcher to "look over it and confer with Mr. W.H. Stark about the matter."[112] In the meantime, that October, the Sun Oil Company, under contract with Vinton Petroleum since 1925 to buy production from several tracts in the Vinton-Ged field, notified the company that it wished to extend its existing contract to November of the next year.[113]

The situation broke open in November, when Hill and the Farishes received a written notice on behalf of the board of Vinton Petroleum that they had lately learned that William had signed both the February 1927 option and the contract with the Farishes "without the knowledge of or conference with the board."[114] In a called board meeting, held November 13, 1928, the contract was termed "a secret proceeding, conducted entirely by and known only to William and Lutcher Stark.[115] Hill promptly contacted the Farishes, who agreed to return the document to William.[116] It was then returned to the board at a subsequent meeting on November 27.[117] At the meeting, William announced that he believed the contract to be "a bad one" and that he wished it canceled. The board voted accordingly.[118]

Lutcher Stark felt betrayed by his father. In the aftermath of the meeting, Lutcher, in the grip of a full-blown case of frayed temper and wounded feelings, wrote to both William and Hill, as well as to various of the Starks' business ventures, resigning his offices in them. Evidently, none of the letters were sent; the originals were found in the files unsigned, and the accompanying envelopes bore no postmarks.

"Dear George," Lutcher wrote to Hill,

> It finally came out, unintentionally, that the objection to your and my making this contract in secret was the trouble. Of course, you know and I know that such was not the case and we had no intention of its formation being kept a secret. . . . But . . . Pop finally said that he thought it was a bad contract and . . . it ought to be cancelled. . . . After Pop's publicly expressed opinion that we had "put over a deal on him," I saw no reason to do anything other than to present the contract to the Vinton Petroleum Company.
>
> This thing pretty well breaks up our playhouse, and I see no way in which

I can continue doing the many things that—unasked by Pop—I have taken upon my shoulders to do, making the many decisions in which I have spent tremendous sums of his money . . . and having to have Pop admit, publicly, that, personally, I had gotten him in a box. . . . The thing I can never forget is the fact that *Pop made this contract and then had a guilty feeling that he hadn't done the right thing*—that is the thing that crushed me. . . . [You and I] would never do anything which would cause him one moment's regret and the fact that we did . . . was the most damning thing of my experience.[119]

The letter of apology Lutcher wrote to his father—spurious, melodramatic, meant to wound—nevertheless contained a world of genuine hurt as well as possibly some awareness of his own faults. "Dear Dad," he wrote,

I can't in any way express to you my appreciation for your thoughtfulness and care with which you have sought to instruct me in the course of business training . . . but the circumstances which have arisen of late have brought to my consideration that, perhaps, I have bungled things tremendously all down the line.

I have merely sought . . . to take from your honored shoulders some of the responsibilities . . . which have called for untiring work, thought and consideration. . . . To be your representative has been more than I had ever hoped to be at this stage of the game. . . . In looking over the decisions that I felt called upon to make . . . I can see where I have made many serious errors.

The San Jacinto Life has called for a tremendous expenditure of money and you are not through yet. . . . I permitted you, knowingly, to become mixed up with the Orange Car and Steel. . . . The Orange Cameron Land Company could have been sold at a high profit, but I thought it was meager in comparison to what I hoped the future might prove in return. The Sabine Supply company is another mistake, coupled with the Golf Course and high living on my part, which has no excuse under the shining sun except that I wanted to do [it].

I frankly say to you that I am at my wit's end and I hereby . . . absolve you of any responsibility in the mistakes that I have made. . . . Worse than anything, I have spent your money. The position that you now find yourself in I blame myself for.[120]

"I know that this [resigning his business responsibilities] is a cruel thing to do," he continued, "and I know that you did not realize the position that I was placed in, but that is the second time that this has happened and there will never be a third. All in all," he could not resist reminding William, "there are a few bright spots in my career, which could repay you for the blunders I have made."[121]

Questions remained. In their November 14, 1928, letter to Hill and the Farishes, Vinton Petroleum board members L.J. Benckenstein (also the company's attorney) and W.D. Gordon confirmed that William, acting as president of the company, had indeed signed both documents—Hill's original option as well as the contract with Sabine Terminal. Did Lutcher confer with his father prior to William's signing, as Hill had requested? Did William sign the documents at Lutcher and Hill's directive without understanding the deal? (It would have been unlike him.) Or, as Lutcher believed, did William make the deal, then begin to regret it? The entire truth may never be known.

At the time of the Vinton Petroleum incident, Lutcher was also receiving insistent letters from former US attorney general Thomas Watt Gregory, chairman of the fund-raising committee for construction of the new Student Union building at the University of Texas, urging him to send his promised subscription of $25,000 on behalf the Stark family.[122] After a long silence, during which Gregory grew increasingly impatient and then irate, Lutcher finally pledged $25,000 worth of Lutcher & Moore lumber at wholesale value. "I say to you confidentially," Lutcher explained to Gregory, "that my family has found it necessary to make very substantial advances . . . [and] unforeseen contributions to enterprises in which we are heavy investors, that have made it . . . inadvisable to bring this matter to a head."[123] Perhaps Lutcher, like Icarus, had not heeded the warnings of his father and had been flying too near the sun. Perhaps he realized it, and therein might be found the reason the letter to his father was probably never sent.

L utcher and William apparently resolved their difficulties in the best Stark father-son tradition; all appeared well at a surprise seventy-eighth birthday party for William—hosted by Lutcher on the actual anniversary itself, March 19, 1929, in the ballroom of the Sunset Grove Country Club.[124] William, who that day had shot a score of 49 on nine holes of golf at the Sunset Grove course, had "no inkling" of the surprise, but as he entered the darkened room, the lights went up and eighty-five distinguished guests stood and cheered.[125]

The room was decorated with dozens of Star and Crescent emblems, the enduring symbol of Lutcher & Moore, and as he took his place at the front of the room, before him stood an enormous birthday cake, weighing over a hundred pounds and lit by seventy-eight candles. "With the stride of a much younger man and a steady voice," according to an article in the *Beaumont Enterprise*, William, "a gray, quiet man, unobtrusive always but

Figure 9.14. William Stark's surprise seventy-eighth birthday party,
Sunset Grove Country Club (*William in center*). Stark Foundation Archives.

the most powerful financial figure in this part of the state," took his place
at the front of the room and thanked the assemblage.[126]

Farwell served as toastmaster for the occasion, and Jack Dionne of
Houston, editor of the *Gulf Coast Lumberman*, as the principal speaker. According to Dionne, "Uncle Bill," as he called him, "constantly preached the
gospel of quality in lumber. . . . He put the integrity of his company into
his lumber product." At the end of the evening, William, smiling broadly,
thanked the assembled company. "I did not know," he ended, "that I would
hear my funeral oration preached by my friends while I was here."[127]

Later that year, a feature writer for the *Beaumont Enterprise* interviewed
William at his Front Street office, affording another glimpse of him for
posterity: "The dinginess of the morning fell away . . . in the welcoming
smile of William H. Stark—Southeast Texas' grandest old man—who will
soon be 79 years old. . . . That smile lingers and always will and I [pray]
that I could describe it as it is. Here is a man who commands attention but
never demands it."[128]

William maintained his custom of fastidiousness in dress and person throughout his life and permitted himself at least one small conces-
sion to vanity: every morning, the Starks' gardener, George Grinstead, attached an orchid from the family's greenhouses to the steering wheel of
William's car. He always tucked it into his buttonhole, as he liked wearing
a fresh flower in his lapel.[129]

Figure 9.15. William Stark, relaxing at home. Note orchid adorning his buttonhole. Stark Foundation Archives.

In the meantime, the problem of the declining timber sources grew more acute. In July 1928, William, on vacation at the Samoset, faced reality. "Dear Lutcher," he wrote,

> I wired you Saturday night was not willing to sign notes to keep the mill going. She lost nearly $9,000 operating in June and as the operating has eaten up the $124,000 that we had in the surplus account think about time we shut it down. . . . Even I realize that it will throw quite a few out of employment but I cannot afford to throw away what I have. . . . We stand a chance to lose our stock but we won't have notes to take up if we do not sign them[.] Wrote you Saturday am leaving that letter in this envelope and returning the notes unsigned.[130]

On September 19, 1929, Lutcher & Moore duly closed the Lower Mill.[131]

And in a textbook example of bad timing, the company launched another misadventure in New Mexico that coincided almost exactly with the onset of the worst economic catastrophe of all—the Great Depression. That August, in what at first appeared to be a heaven-sent solution to the looming problem of timber shortage, Lutcher & Moore purchased the contract of a New Mexico lumber concern, the A.B. McGaffey Company, to log approximately a billion feet of Arizona western yellow pine timber (also known as ponderosa or "bull" pine) on 150,000 acres of the Defiance Plateau, a huge geological formation located northwest of Gallup, New Mexico, and a part of the Navajo Nation.[132] The contract (originally made in 1928 between the McGaffey Company and the Southern Navajo Indian Agency) was executed under the auspices of the Bureau of Indian Affairs of the US Department of the Interior.[133]

Farwell, who had investigated the deal, urged William and Lutcher Stark to go ahead with it. "Our judgment is if we are to continue in the lumber business," he opined, "this is the best opportunity in good timber with minimum investment and will yield a profit." He added a caveat: "We fear that continued delay on our part may cause us loss of [the] timber."[134] John de Praslin also figured in this ill-fated venture, having apparently instigated the contact between the McGaffey Company and Lutcher & Moore. Originally McGaffey was to pay de Praslin a 5 percent commission, but during negotiations, he agreed to waive it.[135] In the end, Lutcher & Moore paid McGaffey $354,764.[136]

Lutcher & Moore went immediately to work on the project, which was known as the Defiance Plateau Timber Unit, pushing ahead with plans even in the face of increasingly ominous signs that the American economy was in trouble.[137] Only eleven weeks later, on October 29, 1929—the infamous "Black Tuesday," the most disastrous day in the history of the stock market—the New York Stock Exchange dissolved in chaos and stock prices collapsed. In the wake of the crash, the US economy hurtled downward at a rate that only a few prosperous years before would have been unthinkable, and the Great Depression engulfed the country in a great dark wave. Industries laid off workers or shut down completely. Crop prices plummeted, unemployment skyrocketed, and construction slammed to a halt. Hunger grew widespread, and numbers at soup kitchens and bread lines swelled. President Herbert Hoover's measures proved inadequate to the crisis, and public confidence in him evaporated.[138]

The effects of the Depression on Southeast Texas were profound. As Orange native, longtime resident, and former Orange County district attorney Roy Wingate put it, "[Any]one who was not here during those bad years can never imagine how bad it really was." Cash was scarce; many lost their land for lack of funds to pay the taxes. (Terms of a chattel mortgage signed to the Orange Furniture Company for a heater costing $3 and a hose for 25 cents called for the customer to pay installments—by the week.)[139] Those who were able kept cows, pigs, and chickens. Many fished and trapped small game—rabbits, squirrels, opossums, armadillos—which was cheaper than hunting them; ammunition for guns cost money. But many families simply went hungry. The prevailing mood was one of fear and despair.[140] (Pruter reported in September 1931 that of the $78,000 the San Jacinto Life Insurance Company had paid in mortality claims, $28,000 had been for suicides.)[141]

In Orange, unemployment was rife. Gone were the ample opportunities of the earlier decade; many business concerns simply closed their doors, and those that managed to stay open cut personnel and salaries. Town leaders met periodically to discuss efforts for unemployment relief. Lutcher Stark attended one such meeting in May 1932 at the First Baptist Church of Orange, at which the pastor of the church, Edgar Eskridge, for reasons unknown, struck Lutcher with his fist. Eskridge was charged with aggravated assault, to which he entered a plea of guilty. He was fined $25 and ordered to pay court costs.[142]

Even in the face of their declining lumber operations, Lutcher and William Stark made valiant efforts to keep their other business concerns open, but they were often forced to scale them down. Some believed they ran many of the concerns at a loss simply to keep friends and neighbors employed.[143] Two of their companies actively assisted the desperate community: the Orange Products Company employed a large number of workers and bought produce from many of the area's truck farmers to process in the company's canning plant.[144] Since figs ripened in late June and early July, the company even offered summer jobs picking figs to area schoolchildren. The other, the Sabine Packing Company, fed the hungry. One

Figure 9.16. The last crew working at the Upper Mill when Lutcher & Moore
shut it down in 1930. Stark Foundation Archives.

of the federal relief agencies installed a large kitchen in the old Orange
County Fair building at First and Cypress Streets, buying cattle from local ranchers and directing them to deliver the animals to Sabine Packing Company. They were then butchered and transported to the kitchen,
where the meat was cooked and canned. The cans of meat were placed in
bags containing flour, sugar, dried beans, and other food items and given
to those on relief (i.e., those receiving government assistance because
of need).[145]

On December 16, 1930, after over five decades of operation, Lutcher &
Moore cut its last log and closed the doors of its venerable Upper Mill for
good.[146] As Farwell put it, "It was not a happy day for those who had been
associated with the Company throughout the years."[147] The following June
1931, the company also shut down its mill at Lunita, Louisiana.[148] That November, Lutcher & Moore sold "its entire stock of lumber, timbers, posts,
molding, lumber stack foundations, stripping sticks and dry kiln sticks
. . . at the upper and lower plants or mills . . . at Orange, Texas, and at its
plant at Lunita, La." to the South Texas Lumber Company for the sum of
$106,000.[149]

Lutcher & Moore's lumber future in New Mexico was doomed as well;
by the summer of 1930, the company was forced to abandon preliminary
work on the Defiance Plateau Timber Unit. In March 1931, "due to the de-
plorable conditions of business in general and the lumber trade in partic-

ular," as Farwell put it, Lutcher & Moore officials were forced to request a year's extension of time, which the Department of the Interior readily granted—with the condition that the company pay $12,500 in advance stumpage.[150]

That October, Lutcher & Moore requested further relief from the Department's superintendent of the Southern Navajo Indian Agency, declaring that "the continued depression made construction of logging roads and large sawmills, calling for a large investment, impossible." They suggested that Lutcher & Moore install portable bandsaw units on the timber acreage and gradually increase production as supply and demand justified. In February 1932 the department granted another year's extension, waiving further payment of advance stumpage, and modifying cutting requirements.[151] But the project's future remained unknown.

B y that time, the Depression was quickly growing to mammoth proportions. To make matters worse, a severe drought afflicted the American Great Plains throughout the 1930s, causing huge dust storms—"black blizzards"—to rage over multistate areas, depositing displaced topsoil over a vast part of the country. The so-called Dust Bowl forced many farmers to pick up stakes and migrate to other parts of the country in search of better conditions.

The election of November 1932 mirrored the country's growing desperation. "Politics is the chief topic of conversation down this way," Lutcher wrote Leo Becker in New York, first updating him on the situation in Texas:

> "Ma" Ferguson finally won out, after a most bitter campaign, both in the primaries and through the courts, Governor Sterling having contested her nomination but the Supreme Court of Texas on last Saturday unanimously ruled that she was the nominee, and that no power, courts or otherwise, could prevent her name being printed on the official ballot in the general election of November 8th. Governor Sterling of course has bolted, and says that he will support the Republican candidate, and this means we are in for another hectic campaign, but I feel safe in saying that Mrs. Ferguson will win out. And don't let anybody kid you into believing that Texas will go Republican again. Roosevelt and Garner will sweep the state.[152]

Lutcher was right on both counts; "Ma" Ferguson trounced Republican Orville Bullington in the general election, and in a landslide of epic proportions, voters not only in Texas but the entire country repudiated Herbert Hoover and all he stood for in favor of the Democratic nominee, New York governor Franklin Delano Roosevelt. The new president would immediately begin implementing extensive measures—his so-called New Deal—designed to bring relief to the beleaguered country, but at the time of his inauguration in March 1933—the low point of the Depression, the "winter of despair"—fully a quarter of the workforce remained without work, and the number of home foreclosures stood terrifyingly high. Banks were failing. Agriculture lay at low ebb, and hunger marches were being staged in larger cities.[153] Consumption in the lumber industry, in large part residential building, had dropped drastically, creating a glut in the market, and prices had plunged.[154]

Officials at Lutcher & Moore, realizing that "it would be suicide to . . . put more lumber on an unwilling market,"[155] were yet again forced to appeal to the Department of the Interior. In May 1933, Roosevelt's newly appointed commissioner of Indian affairs, John Collier, consented to modify their contract with the Navajo, providing temporary relief from payments and certain timber-cutting conditions. This relief was rescinded in August when it was found that the Department of the Interior lacked the authority to grant it without the Navajos' consent.[156]

That October, Farwell wrote directly to the Navajo Tribal Council, requesting modifications or cancellation of the contract retroactive to March 1, 1933.[157] "With no desire to shirk our duty, but facing conditions as they are, and desiring to conserve our remaining funds to ultimately manufacture this timber at a profit, we respectfully ask [that] terms and conditions of said contract . . . be held in abeyance until market conditions justify economical operation on a profitable basis."[158] Farwell also requested a refund of the company's investment from the US Treasury. "We believe we have a moral claim for refund of our tremendous loss, and . . . we respectfully ask your assistance in securing said refund."[159] He also reiterated Lutcher & Moore's previous proposal to install portable sawmills on the Navajos' timber tracts in return for an agreed-upon amount per thousand feet of lumber cut monthly, reminding the council of how much Lutcher and Moore stood to lose—approximately $475,000 already sunk into the project—"for no neglect of ours, or anyone else's . . . and over which no one had any control."[160]

But soon afterward, Farwell attended a tribal council meeting in Arizona, at which Commissioner Collier declared Lutcher & Moore in default of the original contract. Following his recommendation, the council voted to kill the contract but to retain $32,000 in advance stumpage that Lutcher & Moore had already paid in and to allow the department to decide whether to file suit for $25,000 (that Collier had previously absolved them from owing) and damages.[161]

Farwell's arguments—that all delays and time extensions had been authorized and that the company had not cut a single tree but had already spent enormous sums of money for the contract and preparatory work—were to no avail, as were his appeals to US Representative Martin Dies and Senators Tom Connally and Morris Sheppard for "advice and assistance" in requesting that a bill be introduced in Congress reimbursing the amount Lutcher & Moore had expended.[162] All efforts were useless.

The Defiance Plateau debacle crept along for several years. In May 1934, George Colburn traveled to Washington, met with all concerned, and concluded that Commissioner Collier had never had any intention to approach the matter in a cooperative spirit, instead demanding "the last pound of flesh" from Lutcher & Moore. "I am of the opinion," he wrote, "that we should . . . get completely free of this contract, regardless of whether we ever recover a penny, having in mind primarily that we don't get called upon to pay a lot more."[163]

As of June 1935, however, the Defiance Plateau Timber Unit affair still remained unresolved. No resolution of the problem has been found to date in the records, but in all probability it died a natural death, thwarting the company's recovery of the enormous sum they had expended. Added to the other adverse effects of the Depression, the overall negative economic impact of the Defiance Plateau episode on the company is incalculable.[164] The scarcity of available timber and the Great Depression constituted a one-two punch that rang the death knell for the milling operations of Lutcher & Moore. (In a domino effect, the Yellow Pine Paper Mill, deprived of the sawdust and shavings from the mills, also closed its doors, although briefly; it reopened in 1935 after being acquired by Orange's Equitable Bag Company.)[165]

Notwithstanding its huge losses and reduced operations, Lutcher & Moore as a business entity was still able to survive the worst of the Depression because of its wide financial base and its diversification into other business concerns, although its resources were vastly depleted.[166] By 1936, Farwell was able to write that "the company is holding itself together as no other so-called 'cut-out' mill in the South has ever done and still has opportunity in new fields, not only to make history, but to be of service to its community."[167] For many years thereafter, Lutcher & Moore confined itself to managing its vast tracts of timberland and mineral properties in Texas and Louisiana, running a limited wholesale and retail lumber concern in Orange and, as Lutcher Stark is purported to have allowed, "raising alligators."[168]

Even in the depths of the Depression, the Stark family enjoyed one festive occasion. On December 22, 1931, Miriam and William Stark, at the respective ages of seventy-two and eighty, celebrated their golden wedding anniversary with a reception held at the Sunset Grove Country Club.

The couple did not send invitations for the event and requested that no gifts or flowers be brought, but all family and friends were invited, and according to a newspaper account, the event was attended by "scores." The club rooms were "elaborately decorated" with gold and yellow roses and evergreens, refreshments were served, and an orchestra played throughout the afternoon and evening. For the occasion, Nita Stark wore the wedding dress that Miriam herself had worn fifty years before,[169] and William whimsically recalled that on the day of their wedding, the weather had been "freezing cold."

Throughout the prosperity of the 1920s and the difficult years of the 1930s, Lutcher Stark's submersion in the world of the University of Texas never abated. The 1920s constituted his years of greatest influence on the board: he retained the chairmanship from 1921 until stepping down in early 1930.[170] In January 1931, in the only hiatus in the nearly twenty-four years he served on the Board of Regents, he was removed from the board by Texas governor Ross Sterling, who replaced him with wealthy Beaumont oilman Miles Frank Yount, one of the masterminds of the 1925 Spindletop oil discovery.[171] Lutcher stayed off the board only until February 1933, however, when incoming governor Miriam A. Ferguson, his old political associate, reappointed him to serve a third six-year term, and on March 30, 1935, he was reelected chairman.[172]

For much of his time as a regent, Lutcher was periodically embroiled in controversy surrounding his old friend and one of his most powerful allies, L. Theo Bellmont, then the athletic director for intercollegiate sports. One controversy centered around William Disch, popularly known as "Uncle Billy," the highly successful and widely respected baseball coach at the university, who had won twelve conference championships in his thirteen years as coach. Bellmont closely supervised the athletic programs—perhaps too closely for Disch, who preferred running his own program without outside interference.

The inevitable conflict began in the summer of 1924, when Disch scouted for the New York Yankees during a vacation, for which service he was paid $500. By early 1925, the issue of the coach's acceptance of the fee had come to the attention of the university's Athletic Council, of which Bellmont was an outspoken member. On April 30, 1925, the *Daily Texan* ran a front-page story reporting that "the majority of the faculty members on the Athletic Council upheld Bellmont in his stand that 'Disch had taken steps that were opposed to the general spirit of amateur athletics.'" Disch, insulted and incensed, maintained that he had done nothing wrong, since he had scouted for the Yankees at a time when he was not working for the university. Announcing that he could no longer work with

Figure 9.17. UT baseball coach Billy Disch (*fourth from left*) and
athletic director L. Theodore Bellmont (*center*). Stark Foundation Archives.

Bellmont, he resigned his position and accepted a job coaching baseball at
Southern Methodist University.[173] Many, including Lutcher Stark, worked
diligently to establish peace between him and Bellmont. Ultimately, SMU
released Disch, and he returned to the university. The crisis was resolved,
but resentment remained.

In April 1927, while Lutcher and his family were vacationing in the
Middle East, Bellmont plunged into another controversy, this time involving the Longhorn football coach, E.J. "Doc" Stewart. Bellmont, disillusioned with Stewart, especially after a mediocre football season in 1926,
successfully led a charge to fire him.[174] The subsequent backlash against
Bellmont, fed by Disch and Stewart, who openly lobbied for his dismissal,
resulted in a faculty investigation. He was ultimately exonerated, but
Harry Y. Benedict, then president of the university, placed him on probation.[175] At its April meeting, the Board of Regents appointed a special committee of three regents to hold an independent investigation of the Athletic Department.[176]

Lutcher returned from his travels in time to preside at the July regents'
meeting, when the committee presented its recommendations. Two of
the three recommended that Bellmont be removed as athletic director;
the third member, Sam Neathery, issued a minority report and a motion
to retain him. Ultimately, the board decided to retain Bellmont, instructing him to deal more diplomatically with employees teaching and coaching under him. "If he can do this," wrote Neathery, "he should prove a
valuable man with his energy and ability. If he is unable to accomplish
this, then his usefulness will cease."[177] Bellmont would thenceforth be
carefully watched by regents, some of whom were already questioning his
effectiveness.

The Bellmont conflict came to a head in late 1928. Only fifteen months
after Bellmont was admonished to tread more lightly with colleagues and

subordinates, the regents removed him as athletic director by an 8-1 vote (Lutcher Stark being his lone supporter) with little public discussion of the decision.[178] In the words of President Benedict, "Mr. Bellmont is so deeply involved in personal controversies that he would not be able to contribute to the harmony of the University."[179] In December 1928, his title was changed to professor of physical training for men, and he remained a faculty member at the university until his retirement in 1957.[180]

One unfortunate aspect of the controversy was that, though both Lutcher and Bellmont firmly advocated intercollegiate athletics in all of the major sports, they also supported a strong intramural program—a rigorous physical training program and recreational sports facilities—for the university's general student body. This intramural program, funded almost entirely by income from the new stadium's football program, provided for a much larger group of students, both male and female, than did intercollegiate athletics. The loss of Theo Bellmont as athletic director resulted in less consistent support for facilities and programs for the general student body. When Lutcher Stark left the Board of Regents in 1931, he offered the following resolution at the last meeting he attended, which passed unanimously:

> The Board of Regents of The University of Texas looks with disfavor upon the over emphasis and the commercialization of intercollegiate contests, and especially in regard to intercollegiate football as compared to other intercollegiate sports. It regrets that the Southwest Conference has seen fit to reduce the importance of baseball, track, and other athletic activities participated in by large numbers of young men attending the Southwest Conference schools. The Board of Regents feels that the purpose of athletics is to develop physically as many young men of the University as is possible, and desires to promote and encourage those athletic contests in which the largest number of students can participate, such as baseball, tennis, swimming, track, and other intramural games.[181]

During the late 1920s, Lutcher Stark focused on two additional issues at the university—one of long standing, the other of recent origin and great interest. The long-standing issue lay in the need for new buildings and the money to pay for them, as the infamous shacks continued to reign supreme on the campus of the "university of the first class." The regents worked toward resolving the problem, however, and in March 1926 approved a massive building program for construction of twenty to twenty-five buildings in the various disciplines, many to be funded with loans to be repaid with interest from the Permanent University Fund that had then been paid into the Available University Fund. The remainder of the

Figure 9.18. The infamous "shacks" on the University of Texas campus. They survived until the 1940s. Dolph Briscoe Center for American History, University of Texas at Austin, Prints and Photographs Collection, UT Buildings, Temporary, di_05236.

Figure 9.19. Time capsule from the cornerstone of Old Main on the University of Texas campus, demolished in 1934. Left to right: President H.Y. Benedict and Regents Edward Randall, Beauford H. Jester, and Lutcher Stark. Dolph Briscoe Center for American History, University of Texas at Austin, Prints and Photographs Collection, Richard Fleming, University Writings, di_01055, also Box 3Y609 and CN9378.

Figure 9.20. Aerial view, University of Texas, as the Master Plan is gradually implemented, undated but in the 1930s. Stark Foundation Archives.

funding would come from government programs and private fund drives. By 1933, according to historian David Prindle, "ten new structures [among them buildings to house classes in history, engineering, chemistry, physics, geology, home economics, and architecture, as well as Hogg Memorial Auditorium, Gregory Gymnasium for men, Anna Hiss women's gymnasium, and a Student Union, in addition to the partially-completed new Main (Tower) Building], stood on the main campus, and the shacks had almost disappeared."[182] By 1935, $4.5 million had been spent for construction of buildings on the university's properties.[183]

The new development, occurring in 1926, came as a complete surprise—the entry of the University of Texas into the field of astronomy. On February 6, William Johnson McDonald, a retired banker and lifelong bachelor from Paris, Texas, died, leaving no direct descendants. After bequeathing a token amount of $120,000 to a few relatives, he left the bulk of his estate—over $1 million—in trust to the Board of Regents of the University of Texas for the sole purpose of building and operating an astronomical observatory. McDonald had no direct connection with the University of Texas; the staff and administration first heard of him and his gift from a reporter, who read the wire service report on the will in a telephone call to them.[184]

Stunned family members sued to break the will, tying up the estate for years and giving the university time to hope for victory—and to initiate planning. The university employed no astronomer on the full-time teaching faculty; the only person on campus with any experience in astronomy was Harry Y. Benedict, then dean of the College of Arts and Sciences, who had worked as an assistant at the McCormick Observatory at the University of Virginia and had received his PhD in mathematical astronomy from Harvard University.[185] "Thus, President Walter Splawn designated him [Dean Benedict] to be the principal activist on the academic side."[186] By the next year, Benedict had become president of the university and an even more dominant force in the project.

Five court proceedings later, a 1929 out-of-court settlement granted family members $250,000, leaving the university, after expenses, $840,000 for the future McDonald Observatory.[187] Several immediate decisions needed to be made, among them a choice of location and a method of operation, since there were no astronomers on the university's faculty. Those decisions were ultimately addressed satisfactorily in late November 1932, when the parties agreed on a proposal to make the observatory a joint project of the University of Texas and the Yerkes Observatory at the University of Chicago.[188]

The idea was a radical innovation born of necessity; Texas possessed funds and no astronomers; Chicago had an excellent faculty and staff but antiquated equipment and much less money to invest. The project was principally the work of Chicago professor Otto Struve, scion of a family of prominent astronomers, who ultimately became director of both observatories. Struve also served as the driving force behind the choice of location, settling on one where ambient light was minimal: Mount Locke in remote West Texas, some eighteen miles from Fort Davis in the Davis Mountains, near the Big Bend region of the state.[189]

During the litigation regarding McDonald's estate, Lutcher Stark had played only the role of interested observer, and before the project could gain momentum, his second six-year term as regent drew to a close. After his two-year hiatus from the board, Lutcher served as vice chairman of the board from 1933 to 1935, as chairman from 1935 to 1937, and as an active member of the Building and Grounds Committee throughout the massive campus building and landscaping projects of the 1930s.[190]

He returned to the Board of Regents while planning was already in progress for construction of the eighty-two-inch telescope for the McDonald Observatory and the sturdy building in which to house it. When he became chair of the Building and Grounds Committee after his return to the board, he characteristically took a deep personal interest in the construction of the observatory. Ironically, one of his first acts was to vote

Figure 9.21. The McDonald Observatory near Fort Davis, Jeff Davis County, Texas.
Stark Foundation Archives.

"no" on the type of telescope that Otto Struve had chosen. Lutcher, with his usual obsession with detail, had already consulted with the director of the National Naval Observatory in Washington, D.C., concerning the telescope in use at its facility—one quite different from the one Struve had in mind.

Lutcher also disagreed with other choices made on the observatory project. As authors David Evans and J. Derral Mulholland have pointed out,

> He hadn't liked the idea of collaborating with Chicago to start with. He didn't think much of Warner and Swasey [the company chosen to make the concave primary mirror]. The use of Pyrex glass was too radical for him, as was the new technique for coating mirrors.[191] It appears that none of these objections came from blind prejudice, and some of them were based on reasonable grounds. He just carried them to extremes.[192]

To anyone who knew Lutcher, his raising these issues was just business as usual, but his timing was unfortunate; much of the groundwork for the observatory had already been laid. When he asked that experts be consulted, he gave the impression that he had little faith in those at

Figure 9.22. Lutcher Stark (*center*) and Byron Simmons (*right*) at the dedication of the McDonald Observatory. Stark Foundation Archives.

the University of Chicago, who had already considered and answered the questions he raised. For a time Lutcher delayed board approval of Struve's choice of telescopes, but ultimately, after the professor explained his reasons, Lutcher changed his mind. As Evans and Mulholland concluded, "In the end, Otto Struve got the design he wanted. Lutcher Stark was converted to being a staunch supporter of the project, later becoming a very helpful chairman of the Board of Regents."[193] Struve proved to be a successful administrator, and the joint project between the two universities endured for the entire thirty years of the original agreement.[194]

Even after all differences were resolved, however, the large reflector telescope suffered numerous installation problems, large and small, that periodically slowed and nearly halted the process of grinding and polishing. In the meantime, other types of smaller telescopes were installed on Mount Locke, allowing research projects to begin as early as 1935.[195]

When dedication day finally arrived on May 5, 1939, Lutcher, who by then was serving as chairman of the Observatory Visiting Committee for the Board of Regents, stood proudly present. Also invited to the celebration were "nearly all of the astronomers of any standing in the world." In spite of global economic problems, a looming world war, and the geographic isolation of the Davis Mountains, an extraordinary number attended (renowned astronomer Edwin Hubble among them). According to Evans and Mulholland, "They probably represented the most remarkable galaxy of astronomical talent gathered together in any one place in the years between the two world wars." Following the dedication, the group stayed another week for a symposium on galactic and extragalactic structure. At its conclusion, "the savants dispersed, having baptized the telescope and initiated the formal life of the observatory. They were going back to a world of increasing troubles that would soon shatter true international cooperation in science for most of a decade."[196]

Before the world plunged into another global conflict, Lutcher helped achieve one more major milestone in the history of the University of Texas, this time in more familiar territory, the sports program—the hiring of a new football coach. In the 1930s, the process of hiring coaches for UT sports began with a search by the Athletic Council, which was composed primarily of faculty members, at times including members of the regents and the Ex-Students Association. The final step was approval by the Board of Regents, of which Lutcher was chairman in early 1937.

As chairman of the board, Lutcher would have been involved in the search for a new football coach in any case, but in 1936–1937 he took a position front and center very early. In the late fall of 1936 he was serving, along with Chairman H.H. Weinert and Regent J.R. Parten, as a member of the regents' three-man Committee on Athletics.[197] Lutcher's longtime connection with the football program was well known, and he was often accused of attempting to meddle with their coaching or to influence their hiring or firing. When Clyde Littlefield left the football coaching job in 1933, after seven generally successful years and two Southwest Conference championships, in order to return to his first love of coaching track, he was quoted as saying that Lutcher had been after him to resign.[198] Lutcher had also reportedly tried to get Littlefield's line coach, Bill James, fired and had clashed with another Littlefield assistant, Marty Karow.[199]

Littlefield's replacement was Jack Chevigny, a former Notre Dame football player and graduate who came to the University of Texas in 1933 from St. Edward's University in Austin. His first year as coach seemed promising, especially with the Longhorn victory over Notre Dame on the latter school's home field, but the next two years proved less successful, and Chevigny resigned at the conclusion of the 1936 season.[200] It seemed as though the university was destined to field a losing team under a series of short-term coaches.

The search for Jack Chevigny's replacement led Lutcher Stark to begin campaigning for the most capable football coach available. "The University of Texas deserves the best in everything," he announced. In early December 1936, Lutcher, dubbed "the super-powerful Texas booster" by the *Austin American-Statesman*, again asserted: "We've tried cheaper salaries and had continual troubles. The only thing they've done is to unite the 60,000 ex-students in demanding a solution to the athletics situation. If we're going to have athletics, let's have the best possible coach."[201] Two weeks later, in Austin as a presidential elector to cast his vote for a second term for Franklin Roosevelt, Stark declared to the United Press that "the University of Texas can afford the best coach in the country."[202]

The *Daily Texan* quoted Lutcher as mentioning $15,000 a year to be the salary necessary to attract a "big time" coach.[203] At the time, the highest-paid college coach in the country was making $12,000, the president of the University of Texas was making $8,000, and the highest-paid faculty member at the university was making less than $5,000. Even the governor of Texas was paid only $4,000.[204] These salary discrepancies resulted in controversy at the university and in other athletic programs around the country. But Lutcher informed the regents that he failed to see a necessary correlation between salaries of teaching staff and coaches because they were paid from different funds— coaches from income from athletic programs and professors from state funds. Besides, he went on, the Texas legislature should raise salaries of the university's teaching staff and administrators, and he believed a successful football program might actually help with this issue.[205]

To find a new coach, the Athletic Council, chaired by Professor J.C. Dolley, considered three highly placed college coaches, among them those at Vanderbilt and Southern California. Neither was interested.[206] When the council reported to the regents in early 1937, they recommended the coach of the University of Nebraska, Dana Xenophon Bible,[207] who had already coached successfully at Texas A&M from 1919 to 1929, where he won five conference championships in ten seasons. During those same years, the University of Texas had won only two.

At A&M, Bible had been known as "a snarling perfectionist, much given to cuffing forgetful halfbacks and kicking lazy tackles." He had also gained notice for initiating the famed "Twelfth Man" tradition in 1922, however, when injuries had reduced the Aggie squad to fifteen players: He had instructed "a reserve halfback who was working in the press box to put on a uniform and be ready to play if necessary."[208] When Bible left A&M in 1929 to accept the head coaching job at Nebraska, "the University of Texas Athletic Council passed a resolution of regret that such 'an exemplary sportsman both in victory and defeat' should be leaving the conference."[209]

In December 1936 Dolley held an off-the-record meeting at his home with D.X. Bible, including members of the Athletic Council and a number of other interested individuals. Bible believed he had been invited strictly to play an advisory role, but Dolley, Stark, and Parten aimed to convince him to accept the two UT positions of head football coach and athletic director. The meeting evolved into a negotiating session, with Bible placing his own demands on the table. At its end, the members of the Athletic Council, which had become convinced that he was the man for the job, recommended him to the regents.[210]

From Bible's perspective, in the event that he accepted the offer, he would be leaving a secure position and a highly successful team for the poorly organized and generally unsuccessful program at the University of Texas—a real challenge, regardless of how well the job paid. Fortunately for him, Lutcher Stark stated publicly that, even if Bible won no championships at Texas, his presence on the campus would be a benefit to all, especially to the young men who played for him.[211]

During negotiations, Bible added several conditions to the unheard-of $15,000 yearly salary he requested, stipulating a ten-year commitment for his term as a coach as well, after which he would stay on as athletic director. He also required that the president, the Athletic Council, and the Board of Regents accept his hiring unanimously: that if even one of the fifteen voted "no," he would not accept the job. Major interest groups on campus also had to agree to accept him and his "Bible Plan," which included using ex-students as recruiting scouts and hiring the best Texas high school coaches as his assistants.[212] He acknowledged that implementation of his plan would take time, cautioning all concerned against expecting championships for at least four or five years.[213]

The $15,000 annual salary figure was, of course, the most controversial of Bible's requirements. Some who had initially harbored reservations, among them president Harry Benedict, were swayed by the inevitability of the situation and by Lutcher Stark's argument that high pay for a coach might convince the legislature to raise other salaries on campus. And in a relatively short time, the legislature duly raised the president's salary to $17,500, and faculty salaries began to edge upward. Others justified the expensive coach by echoing Lutcher's assertion that coaches' salaries came from sources other than state tax revenues.[214] Support came from unexpected quarters: the Houston area ex-students, represented by Mike Hogg, raised $5,000 in private contributions to supplement Bible's salary, to which Lutcher added $100, to cover losses on the sale of the Bible family's newly completed home in Lincoln, Nebraska.[215]

From the beginning of his tenure, Bible made it clear that he was bringing a new philosophy—and a new authority—to University of Texas sports. *Houston Post* sportswriter Lloyd Gregory quoted him as saying, "I am interested in college men who want to play football, not in football players who are incidentally going to college. If a boy is not interested in an education, we should not be interested in him. We need boys on our squad who

Figure 9.23. University of Texas football coach Dana X. Bible, conducting "skull practice" with his team in preparation for a game against Southern Methodist University, undated. Dolph Briscoe Center for American History, University of Texas at Austin, Prints and Photographs Collection, di_02806.

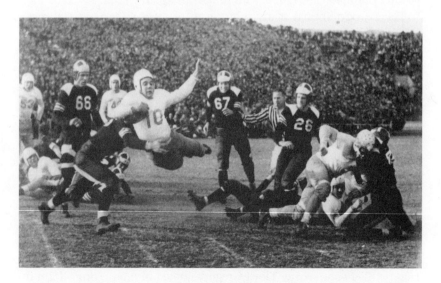

Figure 9.24. Nelson Pruett makes the winning touchdown for a UT victory over Texas A&M, 7-6, Texas Memorial Stadium, 1938. After two losing seasons for new UT coach D.X. Bible, this game marked the beginning of future success. Dolph Briscoe Center for American History, University of Texas at Austin, Prints and Photographs Collection, UT, Football after 1931, CN01649a, CN01649b.

want to make a contribution, not boys who are looking for a handout."[216] Even though Bible's coaching methods had matured since the 1920s and he now motivated teams with psychology and organization rather than snarls, cuffs, and kicks, his first two years of coaching produced only three Longhorn victories. After the second losing year, disgruntled fans began calling Bible and his team "Ali Bible and his Forty Sieves," a reference to what they considered a leaky defense.[217] But the last game of the 1938 season saw a 7-6 Texas victory over Texas A&M, saving Bible from an 0-9 season and heralding successes to come.

In the fall of 1939, however, the tide turned with a single play during the conference opener against Arkansas. With the Longhorns trailing 13-7 and only seconds remaining, a surprise Texas victory came with a sixty-seven-yard pass play and touchdown run by "Cowboy" Jack Crain, who also kicked the winning extra point. "That play and that victory changed our outlook, mine, the players', the student body's and the ex-students'," Bible later exulted. "The way was still long, but we had tasted the fruits of victory and we were on our way."[218] That game led to seven winning seasons and national status for the Longhorns.

Through those first difficult years, Lutcher Stark's support of Bible remained strong in spite of an early encounter that might have threatened their friendship. Since his years as assistant manager, Lutcher had sat on the benches with the team during the games, continuing the custom even after he became a regent. When Bible was hired, however, the new coach put a stop to it. In relating the incident, both Lutcher and Bible depicted the scene humorously, Bible declaring that, as coach, he was having a difficult time explaining why no one else could sit on the bench, and both later remembered that Lutcher responded by promising to obtain the best seats available in the stands.[219] Some held afterward that Bible had informed Lutcher that a team really could not have more than one head coach.[220] Others said that, although Lutcher accepted the edict gracefully, in fact, he was hurt by it.[221] The story goes that when the 1937 Thanksgiving game with A&M approached, the Aggies offered Lutcher the opportunity to sit on their bench, since he had been ejected from his own.

In 1941, after five years with no Southwest Conference championship yet in hand, Lutcher Stark wrote Bible:

My dear D. X.: Yesterday at noon, I phoned you to tell you exactly how I felt about your problem, you, and your future. I am sure I expressed the feelings that were in my heart at the time, but I still feel that perhaps in the years to come I should like to have in your files and mine an expression of our conversation.

About five years ago, or maybe longer, I made the following public expression: "If Mr. D. X. Bible and his teams never win a game for The University of

Texas I will still be satisfied that we have selected one of the finest coaches & Christian gentlemen of the nation, and one whose influence I am glad to have had a hand in bringing to the campus of the University of Texas."

I have never changed my opinion, and I merely want to say that I feel today as I did five years ago and that I would like to add to that statement that I hope you and your influence remain in The University of Texas throughout the rest of your and my natural life.[222]

The very next day, Bible responded:

Dear Lutcher: I think so much of your letter that I am going to take it home in order to have it in my possession. It just warmed and encouraged so much and just when I need a tonic. I hope that my services will be such that I can always have your confidence and support. . . . I will put my "fighting togs" on again to-day, and I am expecting everyone to follow suit. If we can make a strong finish, we will end up, not with a great record, but with a good record.[223]

The next year, Bible's Longhorns won their first Southwest Conference championship, doing so again in 1943 and 1945. After his ten-year contract expired in 1947, Bible retired from coaching but, as per his previous agreement, retained the position of athletic director. Sportswriter Lou Maysel said of Coach Bible's accomplishments: "Most of all, Bible lifted the Longhorns from the league patsy to one of the respected football powers of the country. But perhaps Bible's most outstanding contribution at Texas was the order, stability and prosperity he brought to the entire athletic program, which was in a state of disarray when he assumed the reins."[224]

In the years that followed, Bible continued to be honored for his coaching skills. A charter member of the National Football Hall of Fame and the 1954 recipient of the Amos Alonzo Stagg Award, he was elected to the Texas Sports Hall of Fame in 1959. In the 1960s he was placed in the Halls of Fame at the University of Texas, the University of Nebraska, and Texas A&M University.[225]

At the time of Bible's retirement, Lutcher Stark had been absent from the Board of Regents for two years, his fourth six-year term having ended in 1945. Even so, the two men stayed in close touch. The Bibles were frequently invited to Orange and Roslyn Ranch as house guests. Nita, in particular, wrote to Bible quite often. As her health failed, necessitating her absence from more games than she was able to attend, she sent frequent notes congratulating or commiserating with him, as the occasion dictated. To her encouraging wire, sent before the university's loss against Oklahoma in 1938, he responded: "I was so in hopes that I could send you a wire after the game that might enable you to feel a little better. . . . I

Figure 9.25. Nita Hill Stark, 1930s. Stark Foundation Archives.

just know how it does hurt you to miss a football game and I hope it will not be very long now before you will be feeling like a 'three-year old' and ready to see us in action again."[226] But that was not to be. In 1939, as Nita's health continued to deteriorate, Bible sent her a complimentary thank-you note for her successful efforts in furnishing the lounge in Hill Hall (now Moore-Hill Hall), named for her father, Longhorn team physician Homer Barksdale Hill.[227]

On May 31, 1933, in recognition of his interest in and contributions to education in Texas, Lutcher received an honorary doctor of laws degree from Baylor University. Three years later, on June 4, 1936, Baylor also awarded the same degree to Nita Stark in recognition of her interest in young womanhood, making the Starks the first couple in the state's academic history to receive identical degrees from the same institution.[228]

In the meantime, the adopted Stark twins, Homer and Bill, had reached school age. Lutcher Stark's aim for his boys was a normal, no-frills upbringing (he is rumored to have declared that, for them, "it'll be public school and no curls"[229]). True to his word, he sent them to Orange public schools. But being Lutcher Stark, he still wanted the best for them—and by extension, for all the young people of Orange, taking every opportunity to enrich their lives.

Sometime in 1935, a chance meeting at a cocktail party in Orange presented him with a new idea and the venue for his next great obsession. At the party, he met Elizabeth Smith "Smitty" Hustmyre, a trim, brunette, dark-eyed woman from Whiteville, Tennessee, who had come to Port Arthur in the 1920s to teach physical education at Thomas Jefferson High School. She had established a girls' drum and bugle corps at Thomas Jefferson named the Red Hussars, with a reputation for fast marching and crack precision drills. When she married Orange native Laurence W. Hustmyre, the young couple set up housekeeping in his hometown.[230]

That fall, Stark hired Smitty Hustmyre away from Thomas Jefferson to develop a similar girls' drum and bugle corps at Orange High School. She initially recruited forty-five members, and that charter group practiced for many months, learning "left foot from right foot" and the basics of cadence marching.[231] In February 1936 Stark bought two sets of the finest instruments obtainable—one for practice, the other for performance—and their musical training began.[232] He bought them orange-and-white uniforms, and with the 1936 football season, the Bengal Guards, as he named them—flag bearers, drummers, buglers, bass drummers, and cymbal players—stood ready to perform. "Just to be good isn't good enough," Stark declared. "We've got to be the best."[233]

With their first drum major, Mary Murray (daughter of the Starks' chauffeur, I.B. Murray), leading the corps, they made their debut October 2, 1936, at the halftime of the football game between Orange and Jasper, marching at the fearsome cadence of 180 steps per minute.[234] That year, they also performed in Beaumont at the Lamar College–Schreiner Institute game and in Austin at Memorial Stadium for the Thanksgiving Day game between the University of Texas and Texas A&M—the first time in the history of the field that a high school group had been asked to give an entire halftime performance.[235]

The Bengal Guards worked hard, practicing early mornings and late afternoons in the summers, "raking the mosquitoes off of us," according to Smitty's younger sister, Celeste. In summers, they also attended music clinics or related activities.[236] Throughout the school year, they took music classes in school, practicing in the gymnasium in their off-periods as well as after school for two to three hours daily.[237] They received an intangible additional benefit; in addition to her teaching skills, energy, and musical ability—she could play every instrument—Smitty Hustmyre instilled in her charges a measure of gentility: good etiquette, refinement, the cultural niceties.[238] (Alexine Boudreaux Adams recalled that they practiced table manners with actual settings of silver.)[239]

Smitty not only inspired their love but also their respect, and she stood rock firm as far as performing standards were concerned. One member remembered that, during one performance, the Guards' "pivot point," at which every girl was required to turn at exactly the same spot, was located squarely in the middle of a mud hole. They all gamely pivoted at the exact required spot, coming away with muddy boots but a perfectly straight line.[240] "She had a megaphone that was bigger than she was," another observed, "and if somebody was the least bit—an inch—out of line, *whack!* She would whack you with it."[241]

Lutcher believed that martial drilling was good for the health since it developed such benefits as better posture and carriage; he also believed that music, "a great coordinator," was good for youth because, unlike team sports, it was not seasonal.[242] He bought them two sets of uniforms and four pairs of travel uniforms (white coveralls with "Bengal Guards, Orange, Texas," emblazoned across the backs).[243] For their travels, he furnished them with identical aluminum luggage and even gave them spending money, so no one would have more than another.[244] He issued cod-liver-oil pills to them after practices—and made sure they took them. Before a performance, he inspected them. "If somebody needed a perm," Adams recalled, "he sent them to the beauty shop. [If] somebody . . . needed dental work, he'd call the dentist and have them go in and have their teeth fixed. He took care of us in every kind of way."[245] The Guards called him "Pop" or "Pops."[246]

He was strict but fair. "I saw him a couple of times take out his hankie and wipe lipstick off a girl's mouth," one Guard remembered. "We were to be clean girls, and we were ladies!"[247] Many recalled an incident when Lutcher, tiring of the girls' careless treatment of their fine instruments, assembled the group and spread several watches and other pieces of fine jewelry on a table in front of them. He called various ones to the table, picked up a watch or other item, and asked her if she wanted it. When she predictably responded, "Oh, yes," he picked up a hammer and smashed the piece, effectively making the point that his treatment of the watch amounted to the same as their treatment of the instruments and that the cost of the watch was tantamount to the cost of a bugle. Apparently, he drove the lesson home: from then on, the group took better care of their instruments.[248]

Lutcher attended every practice, viewing the proceedings from a tall structure similar to a deer blind that the girls called the "crow's nest." If someone made a mistake, he corrected her through a bullhorn he always brought. (One Guard's mother once remarked to her, as she returned home after a practice, "I know you made a mistake today; I heard Mr. Stark yelling at you through the bull horn.")[249] At the beginning of every performance, he himself introduced them, always with the same words: "We give you now, America's own—the Bengal Guards."[250]

The Guards were thus launched on their storied career, their formidable skill—and their legend—growing by the season and affording hundreds of young Depression-era women the adventure of a lifetime. And throughout, the entire operation was founded, funded, and lovingly overseen by one man—Lutcher Stark.

In 1937, just as the nation had begun to gain traction in its long climb toward recovery from the Depression, the economy took another sudden downturn, plunging the country into a recession. Stock prices fell, industrial production diminished, and unemployment increased. Many blamed this new adversity, so unpleasantly reminiscent of the recent hard times, on President Franklin D. Roosevelt's curtailment of funds for federal programs. The situation worsened throughout the remainder of the year and into the spring of 1938, when Congress appropriated $33 billion for increased federal spending, beginning a reversal of recession conditions.[251]

In the ranks of Texas Democrats, the 1937 recession contributed to a split between the party's liberal and conservative factions. Predictably, the New Deal had provoked a negative reaction from the wealthy, conservative establishment, who were innately suspicious of its reforms and particularly of Roosevelt's ill-received scheme to enlarge the US Supreme Court in 1937.[252] That year, a group of conservative senators, predominantly southerners and including Texans, formed a coalition with Republicans that effectively blocked many amplifications of Roosevelt's New Deal.[253] Although Lutcher Stark had supported the president by virtue of being a lifelong Democrat, he was still a man of his times—a wealthy, conservative, self-confessed fundamentalist who remained above all a product of his background and socioeconomic stratum, by temperament a proponent of the establishment and the status quo.[254] Thus, by definition, in those times of radical change, Lutcher Stark found himself aligned with the conservative establishment in the state as well as on the University of Texas Board of Regents.

CHAPTER TEN

Change and Loss

In the chorus of praise sung by their own good works, to the memory of [Miriam and William Stark], their services to the State through their gifts to the University rises [sic] strong and clear and exquisitely lovely above all others.

—FANNIE RATCHFORD, "UNIVERSITY'S GREATEST WOMAN BENEFACTOR DIES"[1]

A s the 1930s wore on, the Stark family began to be stalked by illness and death. Both Miriam and William continued to suffer the vicissitudes of advancing age. "Bless her [Miriam], and Mr. Stark too," Fannie Ratchford wrote Nita in 1933; "it hurts me to see their interests and enjoyments curtailed by physical limitations."[2] Nita wrote Ratchford the next year, "Mrs. Stark is far from well. Mrs. Achenbach, one of her girlhood friends, has been visiting her for the past few weeks and she has been a Godsend to the dear."[3]

The year 1936 began auspiciously enough; on April 6, Nita and Lutcher Stark celebrated their silver wedding anniversary, and for the occasion, a group of their friends in Orange presented them with an engraved silver vase.[4] They traveled to Austin to attend the "pig dinner," the annual banquet held by his fraternity, Phi Gamma Delta, held on the very night of their anniversary. At the previous year's dinner, Lutcher had presented the chapter with a challenge: if they won either first or second place in scholarship the next year, he would tear up the $30,000 mortgage on the house, "Buen Retiro," held by his mother. At this year's dinner, it was announced that the chapter had tied for first place in scholarship among all the fraternities on campus, whereupon Lutcher, true to his word, tore up the mortgage and forgave the debt. (Not to be outdone, Nita forgave the Pi Beta Phi debt the university chapter owed her.)[5]

But the specter of the older Starks' ill health increasingly reared its head.

Figure 10.1. William Stark in later life. Stark Foundation Archives.

"The folks are getting very old," Nita wrote Lutcher cousin Lana Smith in Williamsport. "As you know, Dad is eighty-five now and Mrs. Stark is seventy-seven. She has broken more than Dad has. He is practically blind and very deaf, but they seem to be contented with each other." She added, "Of course, he worries because he has been hit so hard financially."[6]

William Stark's race was nearly run. His unspecified "trouble," as he called it, or his failing health in general, had continued to plague him, and

Figure 10.2. Miriam Stark in later life. Stark Foundation Archives.

as Nita had remarked, his eyesight was nearly gone.[7] He chafed at his increasingly limited capacity, wanting to conduct his normal business affairs, but as early as 1928, his health problems had become chronic,[8] and in 1934, a letter from Lutcher to Leo Becker had revealed that William's mental faculties were deteriorating as well. The incident had occurred when he and Miriam were visiting in New York, probably on their way home from the Samoset. "My dear Leo," Lutcher wrote,

I was shocked and terribly heartsore to find that Pop had had another, shall we call it hallucination, and this time instead of hurting Nita's feelings, he hurt yours. I just cannot put into words how much it grieved Nita and me to have had him misunderstand the altogether thoughtful and unselfish sacrifice that you were making in order to bring some little part of joy into their . . . lives. . . . Unfortunately you and I know that that is the characteristic of advancing age.[9]

In an answering letter, Becker observed that "it is awfully difficult to understand how the human mind works at times . . . whether it be hallucination, senile decay, or old age, unfortunately, the wounds so inflicted seem to hurt."[10] Each party expressed sincere regrets for the incident, and their friendship apparently survived, but the fact remained that, inexorably, William and Miriam were confronting their mortality.

For some time, the Starks had employed Ollie Drake, a young woman from Starks, Louisiana, to live at their home and serve as a companion and nurse for Miriam, who had developed diabetes and whose memory had begun to fade.[11] In September 1935, Drake informed Byron Simmons that she was suffering from exhaustion—"just worn out," as she put it—and that she needed a vacation and, afterward, a lighter work schedule. "[Ollie] is mentally exhausted," Simmons in turn reported to Lutcher, "and she just cannot and will not be confined in the future as she has in the past."[12] The Starks' family physician, Dr. Henry Wynne Pearce (the son of Dr. A.G. Pearce, who had also been their family doctor), recommended that they hire an assistant for Drake, and arrangements were duly made to hire a night nurse to enable Drake to return to her own home at night.[13]

It was William, however, who first made the final journey. On Tuesday, October 6, 1936, he began his regular routine, visiting his barbershop around ten o'clock that morning, but complained to friends that he was not feeling well. Instead of attending the weekly Rotary luncheon, he sent word to Lutcher that he would instead return home to listen to a radio broadcast of that week's ball game.[14] His condition worsened throughout the day and night, and Wednesday night he lapsed into a coma. Thursday night, October 8, Lutcher wired Leo Becker, "Dad sinking just matter of moments it would be great comfort to all of us especially Mama if you could arrange to come now to spend the winter with her thanks for message all join in love Lutcher."[15] William died at 9:30 that evening, surrounded by his immediate family and several close friends and employees.[16] The cause of death was reported as "complications of the heart aggravated by a deep-seated cold."[17]

His funeral services were conducted in the Lutcher Memorial Building of the First Presbyterian Church two days later, led by Rev. E.T. Drake, longtime minister of the church and the Starks' close family friend. The choir sang the old hymns that William loved, including "O God, Our Help in Ages Past," "Rock of Ages," and "The Sweet By and By." Floral tributes were sent in a variety of forms, prominent among them William's stock brand—the letter "Y"—and the Star and Crescent emblem.[18] Among those serving as active pallbearers were Doug Pruter and other friends and long-time employees, as well as William's nephews-in-law, Edgar and Lutcher Brown and Rucie Moore.[19]

"[William Stark] was one man whose extensive means never in any instance alienated a single friend," asserted the *Orange Leader*. "[Those] who knew Mr. Stark before he had great [wealth] declared there was not the slightest change in his demeanor brought about by his wealth or social standing. He appreciated the old-time friends and enjoyed being called by his universal name, 'Uncle Bill.' Scores of men of all walks of life in Orange [were] heard to remark, 'There will never be another Bill Stark for Orange.'"[20] Every business establishment, municipal and county office, as well as the US Post Office, closed in his honor, and flags flew at half-mast throughout Orange, while "thousands" attended William's services, according to the *Leader*.[21] The Friday after he died, the Texas Senate adjourned in his honor, and Senator Allan Shivers of Port Arthur introduced a resolution praising him for his work in "developing the resources of Southeast Texas and his contributions to the good of man."[22]

William's will, like the man himself, was spare, direct, and precisely to the point. He left his property, real and personal, equally to his "adored wife," Miriam, and his "beloved son," Lutcher. Following family custom, he authorized payment of monthly stipends to two of his sisters, Mary Stark Kelly and Eugenia Stark Ford, and to his sister-in-law, Serena Stark, the wife of his brother Jerry.[23] He added a final, noteworthy clause:

> I repose great confidence and trust in my now private secretary, D. A. Pruter, who has long served me honestly, cheerfully and faithfully; therefore it is my earnest desire and request that my executor do hereafter retain my said secretary in his service and employ; and I respectfully suggest that my executor seek the counsel and consider well the advice of my very good friend, comrade and confidant, the said D. A. Pruter, in the management of his said estate.[24]

The segment was doubtless William's way of providing continuity to Lutcher, affording his son the benefit of his own expertise and experience through his trusted friend and lieutenant, Doug Pruter. William was only too well acquainted with the pitfalls inherent in dealing with such vast wealth, and he was probably hoping that Pruter would act as a check to the more impulsive aspects of Lutcher's nature.

Seven weeks later, on November 27, 1936, Miriam followed her husband in death. Although she had been unwell for years and especially since William's demise, her own was comparatively unexpected. As Nita put it in a letter to several relatives, "Her death coming so close to Dad's has been such a shock that it has been hard for me to talk about it." Nita reported that for a week before her death, Miriam had been sleeping most of the time but that her sugar count had dropped to normal without insulin and her system seemed to be holding its own. Even so, she had developed a palsy, which made it dangerous for her to walk down the stairs, and was consequently confined to her bedroom. The shaking of her hands made it difficult for her to hold a fork, making it necessary for Ollie Drake to feed her.[25]

The day before Thanksgiving, however, Nita reported that Miriam was "brighter and clearer" than she had been for some time, and on Thanksgiving Day, she seemed perfectly happy for Nita and Lutcher to leave town to attend the Texas–Texas A&M football game, played that year in College Station. At three o'clock the next morning, however, Dr. Wynne Pearce called to inform them that Miriam was "quite ill"; the night nurse, whose bed was beside Miriam's, had heard her stirring and had asked her if anything was wrong. "No," Miriam replied, "but I feel funny."[26] "Are you suffering?" the nurse asked.

"No," Miriam answered, but the nurse immediately called Dr. Pearce, who, after assessing her condition, placed the call to Nita and Lutcher. Before departing College Station for home, they called back to instruct the nurse and Dr. Pearce to call Ollie Drake. Nelda Childers, the administrator of the Frances Ann Lutcher Hospital, answered the phone. She informed Nita and Lutcher that Ollie was already present but that Miriam looked "mighty bad," and her death seemed "just a matter of minutes." The Starks then asked the group to call Annie Lucas, a dear friend of Miriam's, in order that, in their absence, an old friend could be with her.[27] A few minutes later, the Starks received the call from Nelda Childers that Miriam had died. According to Nita, Miriam appeared beautiful in death. "Whenever I looked at the dear soul, I expected her to breathe," she wrote. "I never saw such a peaceful sleep. We buried her in a pale blue dress with beautiful lace around the neck, a dress which she had worn last summer. It was her favorite dress."[28]

Miriam's funeral service was held the following Sunday in the Lutcher Memorial Building at First Presbyterian in place of the regular church service. The family had requested charitable donations in lieu of flowers, but myriad floral offerings poured in to create a mass of flowers in the church's front hall. As per their custom, Lutcher & Moore sent an easel in the shape of a Star and Crescent. Tributes to her philanthropies came from many, chiefly praising her gifts to the University of Texas, but some remembering her personally. "We shall not soon forget Mrs. Stark, her gentle low voice, her charming graciousness of manner, her dignified, aristocratic bearing," promised the *Orange Leader*.[29] "It was all simple and beautiful," Nita declared, "as was her life." She admitted that, although Miriam's death was difficult for them, they knew it was best. "She would look up into our faces in a most pitiful way," Nita ended, "and say, 'I want to go to William.'"[30]

Amid the stress and difficult timing of his parents' deaths so near to each other, Lutcher Stark could perhaps have been pardoned for occasionally giving free rein to his temper. The next spring, his office engaged a firm from Lafayette, Louisiana, to clean and repair the Lutcher-Stark mausoleum. They apparently overstepped their boundaries, at least as far as Lutcher was concerned, by entering the building and recaulking the crypts with a substance that stained the marble. The incident prompted an irate memo from Lutcher. "My understanding was that the contract was made to clean the outside of the vault, to re-point the seams in the granite, and to re-set the curb and re-point it," he fumed.

> Today is the first time I have ever heard it suggested that anyone should go inside and re-point the crypts at all. If this had even been contemplated, I would have had nothing whatever done. It is the height of carelessness, degenerating into imbecility, to turn loose a corps of men, about whom we know nothing, without any bond whatsoever, to play with at least $12,000 worth of caskets and the bones of my own ancestors.[31] I must have in my hands tomorrow a signed report from someone in my employ who has actually seen all of the caskets within the crypts. I want all of the daubing removed from the marble. I want this report in my hands before the crew now doing repairs leaves the city. . . . I . . . see no reason why any of this memorandum should become public and disclaim any responsibility . . . but I wish it complied with.[32]

No doubt it was—and quickly.

In the meantime, the estate of Frances Ann Lutcher remained unsettled; the litigation had forced it into limbo for the intervening years. The onset of the Depression had infinitely complicated the matter; according to Lutcher Stark, as executor of her estate, he had been forced to expend large sums of money to preserve it. Notwithstanding, losses had occurred.[33] That December 1936, twelve years after Frances Ann Lutcher's death and exactly five years after the last Stark-Brown lawsuit over her will had been dismissed, Carrie Lutcher Brown decided that matters had gone on long enough. "Dear Lutcher," she wrote her nephew:

I am sorry that it is necessary for me to write you in a formal manner and request that you furnish me on or before the first of the coming year a complete
and itemized account of the estate of my Mother; and also what you intend doing with her estate. You have been acting as executor of her estate for more
than ten years but during that period have not made an accounting to anyone
that I know of, and I am completely in the dark as to what you have done. . . .
You will readily agree, I am sure, that such procedure is quite unusual. I also
wish to request that you return to me my pictures which I painted and which I
left with my Father and Mother as they desired me to do as long as they lived.
You recognize that I am getting along in years and that it would be well for
these things to be disposed of as soon as possible.[34]

"This is what my father said to me one day," she informed Byron Simmons. "'Carrie, what about all these things you painted in this house? I
would like to have them as long as I live.' Then I said, 'all right, Papa, you
can have them as long as you live and as long as Mama lives.' Now, that
is what I said to my father." Of two paintings that Carrie had previously
given Miriam, Lutcher Stark informed the Brown family that Miriam had
hoped that they could be a part of the collection she had donated to the
University of Texas, but Carrie demurred; she wanted them all returned
to her.[35]

Once his aunt had identified the paintings, Lutcher promptly returned
them, and both parties seemed to enter the proceedings in a new spirit of
cooperation—or determination, at least—to bring the decades-long estate
dispute to a close.[36] An undated draft of a memo in Lutcher Stark's papers,
unsigned but obviously written by him, expresses his hope for closure on
that "rather painful subject," as he called it:[37]

Through the passage of generations covering an extensive period of time,
questions, problems, and counter-claims have developed among the Stark and
Brown family representatives which, for some reason or other, have never been
solved by separation, agreement, or otherwise.

It seems to me that we have now arrived at the accepted time where a just,
friendly, and legal separation of all of these things may be arrived at.

In view of the above, I now wish to dedicate my time and that of my associates looking towards the consummation of this desired result in the speediest
possible time.[38]

From that point on, both contingents—Lutcher Stark on the one hand
and Carrie and her sons on the other—began the lengthy procedure of dividing the vast, complex network of their family's joint holdings.[39] Carrie
had achieved one aim—she had acquired possession of her paintings—

Figure 10.3. Carrie Lutcher Brown in later life. Stark Foundation Archives.

but she died October 3, 1941, over a year before the final settlement of her mother's estate was reached on July 7, 1943, nearly twenty years after Frances Ann's death.[40] At a concluding meeting of the Stark and Brown groups the following July 23, copies of the Settlement Agreement were handed to both contingents, and Lutcher Stark delivered the jewelry Frances Ann had willed to individual members of the Brown family.[41] He explained that some of the pieces could not be located but that he had substituted like articles. "Well, Babette," Edgar Brown said to his niece after some discussion, "I think it is all right for us to accept the substitutions." "Whatever you say, Edgar," Babette Moore Odom replied, "is all right with me."[42] With that, the terms of Frances Ann Lutcher's will, so long a source of family strife, were brought to completion.

On February 5, 1937, Lutcher Stark announced that he was giving Miriam's collection of rare books and manuscripts, art, and art objects, now valued at $5 million, to the University of Texas.[43] Although Miriam herself had actually donated the collection to the university in December 1925 and many of the books had in fact already been brought to the campus as needed by faculty and graduate students, the bulk of the collection had remained in Orange awaiting construction of a museum to house the contents.[44] At his parents' deaths, Lutcher Stark had inherited the collection along with the rest of their estates.

During Lutcher's two-year absence (1931–1933) from the Board of Regents, the board had authorized the dismantling and removal of the walnut-paneled John Henry Wrenn Library, a group of rooms housing the Wrenn collection of rare books in English literature, from the existing University Library to the back of the third floor in the new Main, or Tower, Building, where the school's library would be located in the future.[45] The move would have included the university's other two so-called English libraries, the Miriam Lutcher Stark and the George Atherton Aitkin collections, at that time housed within the Wrenn Library.[46]

Lutcher had bitterly opposed—and publicly protested—the plan; according to him, one of the conditions of the gift dictated that it be permanently housed in the old University Library building, and to move it would possibly place the gift in danger of forfeiture. Moreover, he believed that leaving it in isolation in the University Library while the other two collections were moved away from it would reduce its usefulness.[47] He had strenuously urged the Board of Regents to leave all three collections in the old library building, adding that members of the Littlefield family, who had donated the Wrenn Library, were equally opposed to moving it.[48] Bowing to the wishes of such major donors, the board had voted to retain the libraries in their existing location in the old University Library building.[49]

Figure 10.4. The Miriam Lutcher Stark Library in its new quarters, the fourth floor of the new Main (Tower) Building at the University of Texas at Austin. Note the August Benziger portrait of Miriam Stark (*on left*), provided by Lutcher Stark. Dolph Briscoe Center for American History, University of Texas at Austin, Prints and Photographs Collection, Creator Guerrero, UT Libraries, Rare Books, di_00613.

That February 5, 1937, accompanied by much publicity, Lutcher "formally presented" Miriam's collection to Governor James Allred, reaffirming that his mother had "always intended for her things to go to the University and the people of Texas."[50] (It is possible that Lutcher, never above using publicity to gain an end, purposely "regave" Miriam's gift in order to garner public notice to further his aim of keeping the collection in the old University Library.)[51] He attached certain conditions to the gift, chief among them that the state furnish $400,000 to prepare the library building to house the collection, including installing an air-conditioning system to protect the rare pieces. Governor Allred duly responded that he planned to request the needed funds from the legislature as soon as possible.[52]

In the end, however, the parties reached a compromise: the rare books and manuscripts of Miriam's collection would indeed be moved to the newly completed Main Building but in a more favorable location than had previously been planned—a special room on the fourth floor, with the Wrenn and Aitken collections placed near it. Some of the furniture and objets d'art from Miriam's collection would be used to appoint the newly christened Miriam Lutcher Stark Library and the adjacent roof garden, but most would remain in Orange, still awaiting the university's promised construction of a museum to house them.[53] In December 1938, Lutcher presented to the university the full-length portrait of his mother, painted by August Benziger, to be hung in the library bearing her name.[54]

On June 7, 1938, Lutcher Stark's growing list of honors was augmented by Southwestern University at Memphis, Tennessee, when the school awarded him an honorary doctorate of laws, his second such degree, for "scholarship, eminent distinction and attainments."[55]

In the meantime, Nita's own health, which had troubled her for years, gradually grew worse.[56] "Someday Lutcher and I are going to get up there to see you all," she wrote to Lillie Esslinger, another Lutcher cousin in Williamsport, in 1937, "but I have been in such miserable health for so many years that I could not make the trip."[57] "Lutcher has really taken good care of me," she wrote to a well-wisher the following year. "Had he not, with ill health, I would probably not be alive today."[58]

Nita's chief complaint—the one that ultimately took her life—was urological in nature.[59] In September 1938, she was issued a diet by Turner Urological Institute in Houston, the regimen dictating that she eat plainly prepared meats, vegetables, and fruits but forbade her to eat salty, fried, rich, or greasy foods, condiments, spices, and alcohol, among other items. "First, it requires will power and judgment to eat properly," the directions admonished her. "Drink at least two quarts of fluid daily (all but one glass at each meal) between meals. Eat slowly, chew thoroughly."[60]

"Nita has been ill all summer, and is still confined to her bed in Orange," Lutcher wrote another Williamsport cousin, Arthur Smith, in October 1938. "I am in hopes we can get her on her feet sometime in the near future. There just doesn't seem to be any particular thing that has gone bad," he wrote sadly, "and yet I don't know of anything about her that hasn't gone bad." In early November, she was still suffering. "Since returning home [from Roslyn Ranch] Miss Nita has been very much under the weather, and has been confined to her bed," Lutcher confided to Hans Holmes, a Roslyn Ranch employee. "I am happy to announce now that we have reduced her blood pressure and swelling, gotten rid of the headaches and she is now walking around upstairs," he wrote hopefully. "This is more improvement than we accomplished all summer, and needless to say we are very much delighted."[61]

On November 17, Nita herself wrote her old sparring partner, sportswriter Lloyd Gregory, "I read your column very carefully every morning to see if there is anything I can get mad about. Lying in bed all fall has given my brain time to be more active." (In an aside, she wrote that Lutcher was listening to her dictation. "At it again," he commented.) "I wanted so badly to see Bill and Homer play [football at the latest Orange High School

Figure 10.5. Nita Hill Stark, toward the end of her life. Stark Foundation Archives.

game] that the doctor let them carry me to the car and drive me there," she confessed to Gregory. "Everything happened right at the goal line in front of me."[62] From her vantage point, she was able to see her son Bill make two touchdowns.[63] That year, because of her ill health, she resigned her national office in Pi Beta Phi.[64]

In June 1939 she made her will, and the following July, while she and Lutcher were at Roslyn Ranch, she again grew worse.[65] By July 31, she was in a hotel in Denver, presumably receiving treatment. She wrote Lutcher's secretary, Ruby Childers, and Ruby's sister, Nelda (the hospital superintendent): "My Dear Nelda and Ruby, you blessed darlings, sending me that . . . beautiful bouquet. You never saw such an exquisite one in all your lives. . . . I love each blossom. . . . I have been so worried over my condition," she confessed. "I guess I cannot go back to the ranch. I shall keep Clemmie [Rosenthal, a Stark employee] down here and get an apartment until we leave." She signed it, "My dear love—Nita."[66]

In early August, her condition became critical, and on August 6, accompanied by a nurse, she left Colorado and traveled to Orange by special coach, where Dr. Wynne Pearce assumed her care.[67] Nita's nurse wired back to the ranch, "We had hard trip but arrived home all right. . . . Miss Nita is holding her own stop Garrett and the boys reached here last night and okeh."[68] Lutcher, wiring a ranch employee, admitted, "Miss Nita very much weaker."[69] Byron Simmons wrote the university's Board of Regents to decline his employer's attendance at the next meeting: "Mrs. Stark's continued illness precludes any definite engagements or plans, and at present her condition is such that a prediction of the future is impossible. She was given her eighth blood transfusion this morning. . . . During the past seven weeks he has not even been to his office, but spends his entire time at his home."[70]

On October 2, Simmons wrote Lutcher's cousin, Alford Stark: "Mrs. Stark's condition remains unchanged and for eight weeks Lutcher has stayed very close at home. He has not been to the office since their return home from Colorado."[71] Throughout her illness, the Bengal Guards and the Boys' Band sent Nita notes and dedicated special numbers to her during their performances.[72]

Nita Stark died at home October 11, 1939, some weeks shy of her forty-ninth birthday, of uremia and acute nephritis, accompanied by myocarditis and pulmonary edema.[73] Lutcher, Homer, and Bill were with her at the end, as well as immediate family and friends.[74] Knowing her death was imminent, she had requested shortly before she died that no flowers be sent to her service but that the donations be given instead to charity.[75] The *Daily Texan* recapped her contributions to the school: her support, both monetary and moral, for the Longhorn Band and for her sorority, Pi Beta Phi; her gift of an added 10 percent of funds to all students' pledges to build Memorial Stadium; furnishing the lobby of the new dormitory for university athletes, Hill Hall, named for her father, Homer Hill (completed the summer before she died); and for her many other philanthropies to the university throughout her life. "The University flags were flying at half-mast Thursday, and few students failed to know the reason why," the *Texan* concluded. "They realized that they, the University, and the State of Texas have lost a true friend."[76]

"The University has lost one of its most loyal ex-students; the State, one of education's staunchest friends," pronounced the school's new president, Homer Rainey. "The university, as well as all of us who knew Mrs. Stark personally, has lost a loyal supporter, a valuable friend and a faithful follower," Coach D.X. Bible lamented. "We shall always cherish the memory of her fine friendship."[77] In respect to her, Orange schools were dismissed for the rest of that week, and the afternoon of her funeral, October 13, the Orange County courthouse and the city hall were closed, as were all other municipal offices.[78] The Bengal Guards and the Boys' Band formed an honor guard at the Starks' home, as they did at her funeral service and afterward at the cemetery for her interment.[79] Her service, like those of all the family, was held in the Lutcher Memorial Building of the First Presbyterian Church with Rev. E.T. Drake officiating, as always, and she was interred in the Lutcher mausoleum with the other members of the family.

After Nita's death, Lutcher, Homer, and Bill were left to sort out their lives. According to Ann Raborn, a family friend, "Lutcher was so terribly lonely. . . . He occupied himself by working on the grounds in that property [his house at the corner of Tenth and Pine Streets]. . . . My family and I would go over there at night and sit around the fish pond and talk, or else we would go into his kitchen and eat supper with [him], just for him to have somebody to be with."[80] "We are getting along fairly well," Lutcher wrote in answer to a query from Hans Holmes. "Hunting season has opened here, and the boys have been on a couple of hunts."[81] Arno "Shorty" Nowotny, then the university's assistant dean of men, wrote, "I was shocked to learn of the tragic loss of your wife. . . . It seems to me that you have had more than your share of sorrow in recent years."[82]

A few weeks later, Lutcher began preparations to move the bodies of Nita's parents, Ella and Homer Hill, to the Lutcher-Stark mausoleum in Evergreen Cemetery.[83] He proposed the plan to Dr. Hill's sister, Lucy Hill Jones, and others in the Hill family. "Dear Lutcher," she wrote,

> The family here . . . all readily agree to your proposal to remove the remains of Nita's parents from Austin to the mausoleum where her body rests, which undoubtedly also would be her wish. . . . Since Nita's passing the wish had come to me most persistently . . . that the caskets of her father and mother could rest with hers. . . . It was indeed a most loving thought on your part and I deeply appreciate the motive that prompted it.[84]

Lutcher duly carried out his plan; on or about December 16, 1939, the Hills were reinterred in the mausoleum with their daughter.[85] The next year, he also disinterred the bodies of the Hills' two infants, Herbert and Mary Creola, from their graves in Oakrest Cemetery, north of Brenham, and moved them into the mausoleum.[86]

In a letter to Lucy Jones in mid-December, in response to her request for a Hill family portrait, he reflected on his new circumstances and the inevitably altered family dynamics for him and his boys in the aftermath of Nita's death:

> For thirty-four years my thoughts have revolved around Nita and her kin, and the fact that we might not continue to think the same thoughts had never entered into my mind. While I have a large and prolific kin, somehow or other they have dropped completely from my life and I have grown to look upon myself as a Hill connection, and perhaps the repository of the Hill history and tradition. The more I think of it though, the less I am sure of what the future holds for you and yours and the boys and myself. I am sure that my boys will never become part of the Stark family as we know it here in Orange, but by the same token I am not so sure that they may continue as part of the Hills in Austin, although I am very positive that they will naturally gravitate to you and yours with deepest affection. . . . Certainly . . . our boys will continue to be members of the fold in Austin, but they will of course be lacking the main driving influence for its continuance, their mother.[87]

Lutcher Stark's speculations on the future of his sons' connections to the Austin world might just as logically have been applied to his own. At the time of Nita's death, he was beginning his fourth and final term as a University of Texas regent, and his interactions with Austin and the university might understandably have been affected as he faced this major transition in his life. And more changes were to come.

When he had first returned to the Board of Regents in 1933 as vice chairman, his life had still been following a fairly predictable course. He had continued his chairmanship of the Building and Grounds Committee, remaining deeply involved in the massive building program in progress on the campus, raising funds for part of the new construction through federal New Deal building programs and pursuing more federal dollars to build the infrastructure for the university. He had also continued to add books and collections to the Stark Library, among them a first edition of the King James Bible, as well as to the Latin American Collection and the Littlefield Fund for Southern History.[88]

With his reelection to the chairmanship of the board in 1935, Lutcher's major concerns had lain in construction of dormitories for men and women at the main campus in Austin, the School of Mines at El Paso, and Galveston's University of Texas Medical Branch; a carillon for the tower; a children's hospital and a "colored" hospital, as it was then termed, in Galveston; and a retirement plan for faculty and staff. In addition, in preparation for the 1936 Centennial Celebration of Texas' Independence from

Figure 10.6. The University of Texas Board of Regents, 1939. Chairman J.R. Parten is on left and Lutcher Stark, third from left. *Cactus*, 1939, yearly publication of Texas Student Publications (now Texas Student Media), University of Texas.

Mexico, plans for a Texas Memorial Museum in Austin were placed under the auspices of the Board of Regents, who were appointed its board of directors. The US Congress appropriated $3 million to the Texas Centennial Commission, which in turn provided $300,000 for construction of the museum. The groundbreaking for the Paul Cret–designed building was held June 11, 1936, with President Franklin Roosevelt in attendance.[89]

Lutcher had long since established a reputation as a confrontational regent whose penchant was to demand rather than to negotiate and whose intent was to control every situation within his sphere. Texas oilman and retired US Army major J.R. Parten, a newly appointed regent chosen by Governor James Allred in 1935, quickly learned of his new colleague's propensities; when Parten, realizing that he himself held little concept of a university regent's role, made an appointment with President Benedict to discuss the matter, "he learned from Benedict that the person he should not emulate was Lutcher Stark."[90]

Parten apparently took the lesson to heart; when Lutcher asked for his vote for the chairmanship of the board, Parten agreed to support him only after extracting a promise from him that he would treat his fellow regents and President Benedict with respect and that he would not "meddle in administrative affairs." Parten was approached by several other regents, requesting that he run for chairman, predicting—correctly, as it happened—that "[Lutcher's] habit of interfering in the daily affairs of the university would cause no end of trouble." Parten refused the offer, and Lutcher assumed the chairmanship in March of that year.[91] Benedict, knowing Lutcher's bent only too well, requested publicly that instead of attempting to control every minor issue, the regents "cut the Texas Union Board some slack" by setting general parameters and allowing the Union Board to run their own operation, indicating that that perennial problem had not disappeared.[92]

In January 1939, as Allred reached the end of his second term of office, he appointed new regents to replace two who were nearing the end of their six-year terms, including Lutcher Stark. Allred placed him on the list for reappointment; the incoming governor, W. Lee O'Daniel, with the choice either to endorse Allred's nominations or to drop them from the roster in favor of other nominees, elected to support Lutcher's appointment, referring it to the Senate for approval. Thus, Lutcher, by this time an eighteen-year veteran, began his fourth and final six-year term on the Board of Regents. This term would be marred by strife on the board, turbulence in his business ventures, and additional personal tragedy.

And all the while, Texas' political climate was undergoing major changes, making for tumultuous years on the state's political scene. In addition to the recession in the late 1930s, its metamorphosis into an urban, increasingly industrial state with an expanding middle class, a halting integration movement, and New Deal economic innovations had resulted in the Democratic Party's contentious split into conservative and pro–New Deal factions.

Texas' new governor represented a wild card in Texas politics.[93] W. Lee "Pappy" O'Daniel had come to Texas in 1925 and had gained employment in Fort Worth with the Burrus Mill and Elevator Company before setting out on his own to establish the Hillbilly Flour Company. He excelled at utilizing radio to advertise the Burrus Mill's Light Crust Flour brand, then later his own, Hillbilly Flour, entertaining his listeners with the music of Bob Wills and the Light Crust Dough Boys and offering poetry and homespun advice to the audiences enthralled by his noon-hour show on Fort Worth, San Antonio, and Houston radio stations.[94]

O'Daniel had never been active in Texas politics, but he had hinted on his radio program that various people had at times urged him to run for office, and in 1938, he threw his hat into the ring. Since he had failed to pay the state poll tax required at that time, he was unable even to vote for himself, but with thirteen candidates from whom to choose, he still won the Democratic nomination without a runoff, astounding the state's political leaders, who had paid him little attention. Apparently, Texas voters enjoyed his music—and his political shenanigans.[95]

During his three years in the governor's office, O'Daniel proved to be simultaneously ultraconservative and erratic, refusing to reappoint J.R. Parten, a moderately liberal Democrat, and another independent oilman, George Morgan, to the University of Texas Board of Regents. He and his successor in office, Coke Stevenson, replaced them with conservatives such as Orville Bullington of Wichita Falls, Dan Harrison of Houston, D. Frank Strickland of Mission, and Scott Schreiner of Kerrville. The new board members joined the two conservatives already serving on the board, Lutcher Stark and Hilmar H. Weinert, thereby altering its makeup—and its character. As historian Don E. Carleton has put it, "Led by Orville Bullington, this new board majority believed that the university was overrun by politically subversive undesirables who advocated such dangerous ideas as labor unionism, civil rights for blacks, federal fair labor standards and antitrust laws, and corporate and personal income taxes."[96] It was inevitable that this more conservative new board would clash with the university's administration and faculty, who expected to teach, conduct research, and write with the protection of academic freedom, a right already guaranteed in the official policies of the Board of Regents.[97]

On May 10, 1937, stunning the entire university, its much-loved president, Harry Yandell Benedict, had collapsed while heading to the Capitol Building to lobby the legislature for the school. Several hours later, he died of a cerebral hemorrhage.[98] Following the sudden loss of Benedict, who had served as president for the past decade, the Board of Regents appointed the university's comptroller, John Calhoun, as acting president and launched a national search for a new leader. Their eventual choice was the native Texan and educator Homer Price Rainey.

Rainey was seemingly a perfect fit for the presidency of the University of Texas. Other candidates were added or removed from consideration, but ultimately Rainey emerged as the regents' choice. A former president of Indiana's Franklin College and Pennsylvania's Bucknell University and previous director of the American Youth Commission in Washington, D.C., he was also an ordained Baptist minister and, briefly, a professional baseball player.[99] When Rainey was approved in early 1939, at the beginning of Lutcher Stark's last term on the board, prospects seemed auspicious for both the new president and the school. The latest legislative session under Allred's administration had provided one of the most positive responses to the school's financial needs in its history—raising salaries, increasing general appropriations, and designating funds to purchase a new rare-book collection on Mexican history. In addition, the preceding

Board of Regents had taken progressive stands on a number of matters (although their censorship of the *Daily Texan* was not among them).[100]

Lutcher Stark, along with regents Weinert and Edward Randall, was initially unenthusiastic regarding Rainey, who was much more the choice of Regent Parten (who served on the board 1939–1941), then chairman of the board and the driving force behind the presidential search committee. But the final vote came down unanimously in favor of Rainey. He accepted the position on December 28, 1938, and reported for work in midsummer of 1939. And unfortunately, as one historian has noted, "a period of bitter conflict rather than peace and harmony lay ahead." Rainey was inaugurated December 9, 1939, a bright, sunny day in Austin, but storm clouds were already gathering on the university's horizon—a growing crisis at the University of Texas Medical Branch in Galveston. The problem had developed long before the beginning of Rainey's tenure in office, but it bedeviled him for the next five years and exacerbated tensions between him and the Board of Regents.[101]

From its earliest history, the Medical Branch, whose location in Galveston had been originally determined by a statewide vote, had enjoyed much independence and little oversight because of its distance from the main campus. Consequently, attendant problems had been building for decades. The major issue lay in the fact that the university did not exercise total control of the medical school's operation but shared it, by contract, with three other entities: the Galveston city government, the Sealy & Smith Foundation (benefiting Galveston's John Sealy Hospital, a charity hospital established in conjunction with the medical school), and the hospital's board of managers.[102] In reality, however, it was the Medical Branch's elected faculty council that made most decisions, and individual departments enjoyed a great deal of autonomy. The medical staff were generally comfortable with this system, but it remained essentially a decentralized structure that made it difficult for university leaders in Austin and deans of the medical school in Galveston to govern the Medical Branch.[103]

In 1939, the Board of Regents, led by Edward Randall, chair of the selection committee, chose a new dean for the Medical Branch—John Spies, to whom they gave the authority to strengthen the university's control over the Medical Branch.[104] Spies soon discovered, however, that he could do little within the existing system without running afoul of the faculty council, perennially controlled by most of the same members, among them his former advocate, Randall, who would soon become his intractable adversary.[105] Since Randall also wielded power in the city of Galveston, Spies constantly ran into the opposition of the local power structure when he proposed changes in the Medical Branch, particularly when he suggested moving some of the school's facilities to Houston. To top it all, Spies was no diplomat, disinclined to compromise or sometimes even to discuss problems with the faculty council and department heads, many of whom wanted him removed and the old system restored in its entirety.[106]

These and other issues developed into regents' hearings from October 7 to 9, 1939, just before Rainey was inaugurated.[107] By this time Nita Stark was terminally ill, and that fall, Lutcher seldom left her side; thus, he failed to attend the hearings, none of which resolved the problems.[108] And the regents faced one inescapable fact: the existing structure, with its issues of divided authority, could not stand. Accordingly, they increased the university's jurisdiction over the medical school's policies and its operation. Another fact was becoming obvious as well, however: Spies was becoming a lightning rod for the various factions' dissent. By 1940, Lutcher moved that Spies be given "a perpetual leave of absence."[109] His motion died for lack of a second, but the medical school fight continued to intensify.

In the meantime, President Rainey studied the situation and made a range of recommendations to ameliorate the situation, but the regents largely ignored them. Throughout the controversy, however, he continued to defend Spies, considering it his responsibility as president of the university. A second round of hearings was held in 1942, reiterating the earlier complaints regarding Spies. By that time, World War II was raging, and America needed doctors, but at the medical school, morale was plummeting, students were suffering, and the adverse conditions were driving away potential newcomers.

In the midst of the controversy, with fear of communism and fascism rampant throughout the country, the chairman of the House Un-American Activities Committee, Martin Dies Jr., a US representative for East Texas, leveled charges that a communist "cell" existed among students at the University of Texas, and Dies Committee investigators arrived on the campus to search for evidence. After interviews with a small number of students, the investigators announced to Rainey that they found "no evidence of subversive activities."[110]

At the same time, a committee from the Texas House of Representatives investigated the same issue at the Medical Branch, delivering their findings to the regents at a meeting in Galveston on February 28, 1942: they found *no* un-American activities at the medical school other than the fact that it was wartime and the administrators and faculty were failing to perform their responsibilities while the country needed doctors so desperately. They also offered three recommendations: first, that Dean Spies be removed from his position; second, that some faculty members who had continually defied Spies also be removed; and third, that full power over the Medical Branch be vested in the president of the university. The com-

mittee also found that the regents themselves had been negligent in allowing the problems to develop to that point.[111]

At the regents' meeting in February 1942, a petition signed by fifty-
one members of the Medical Branch's faculty, requesting that Spies be re-
lieved of his office, was also presented to the regents, but as of their meeting in March, they still had leveled no formal charges against him.[112] In
the meantime, however, the school was investigated and ultimately placed
on probation by both the American Association of Medical Colleges and
the American Medical Association.[113] In spite of Spies's many positive accomplishments, among them plans for establishment of the M.D. Anderson Cancer Center in Houston, the sentence of probation jarred the regents into action, numbering his days.[114] The board held hearings on the
issue in Galveston in late May and early June 1942. Lutcher Stark was present at only one of those meetings.[115]

At the Board's August 1, 1942, meeting, the regents finally dealt directly
with the Spies issue, expressing "the definite belief that Dean Spies's usefulness to the School had reached an end." Spies was called into the room
and presented with the board's conclusion. He declined the opportunity to
make a statement except to express the hope that "the Board would prefer
charges against him and give him the opportunity of a hearing in view of
the attitude of the Board." After Spies's departure, Lutcher moved that "a
grave emergency" existed, thus entitling the board to remove Spies as of
that day, with no charges levied against him and therefore with no hearing.[116] The motion passed.

When the regents restructured the university's relationship to the Medical Branch, they named a university vice president, Chauncey D. Leake, to
serve simultaneously as dean of the medical school. Under the newly revised system, Leake would answer directly to the regents, bypassing the
president completely and taking him out of the chain of command—an
odd administrative structure in itself but a slap to Rainey and an ominous
indication of the growing animosity between him and a majority of the regents. The probationary status of the Medical Branch was removed in November 1943 by both the American Medical Association and the Association of American Medical Colleges, vastly improving the outlook for the
school's future, but as the makeup of the board became more and more
conservative, its relations with Rainey grew even more strained.[117]

In the aftermath of Nita's death, Lutcher Stark became bitterly angry
with Homer Rainey regarding, improbably, changes in the rules of high
school football. Lutcher's personal feud with Rainey actually began in May
1940, during a controversy involving repeated attempts of the University
Interscholastic League (UIL) to establish equitable rules governing the el-

igibility of high school students to play football. The rules potentially affected nine Orange High School players slated to become seniors for the school year of 1940–1941. Among them were Lutcher's adopted sons, Homer and Bill.

The UIL had been created in 1910 under the auspices of the University of Texas Extension Bureau as an outreach program, first staging debate competitions.[118] It had later added some sports, beginning with track and field in 1912, and still later had developed divisions for its member schools in academics, music, and athletics, including football. (It was ultimately touted as "unsurpassed anywhere in the nation for its efficiency in coordinating the curricula of rural and city schools in . . . Texas.")[119] Lutcher, following a tradition established by his mother, had provided awards for winners in debate competitions, both while he was a student at the university and thereafter, when he "remained active in promoting and maintaining the Interscholastic League."[120]

In the UIL's early stages, with few rules in place, developing the structure to govern statewide competitions in all three major divisions—academics, music, and athletics—proved to be a complex matter. The UIL suffered growing pains as it developed, especially in the late 1930s in the popular sport of football. "Each new rule brought a ripple of complaints," reported a later history of the organization. "At times, the ripple turned into a wave."[121] This was the arena in which Lutcher Stark, the UIL's leaders, and Rainey clashed in the spring of 1940, spawning a ripple that in Lutcher's case ultimately became a tidal wave.

During the 1930s, football attracted the largest participation of any sport in the athletic division of the UIL, and state leaders of the organization became increasingly concerned with the rising number of serious injuries inflicted on players.[122] The UIL's athletic director, Rodney J. Kidd, writing in the September 1938 issue of the *Interscholastic Leaguer*, the UIL's monthly newsletter, called for "safety first in Interscholastic football," including medical exams for each player, complete and adequate uniforms, sufficient training and conditioning, and restricting injured or ill players from playing.[123]

Concerns also surfaced regarding the differing ages, weight, and strength among students playing on the various teams. Some school districts operated with ten grades, others with eleven, and still others with twelve. The State Board of Education ultimately aimed to establish twelve grades in all Texas member high schools but had not yet achieved that goal. Moreover, as Roy Bedichek, a folklorist and naturalist who was then president of the UIL, noted, "We know that there will be pupils who will fail deliberately of graduation in order to be eligible for play the following fall. This is no new thing."[124] Twelfth-grade students, or those who deliberately stayed over in order to play football an additional year, were much older—that is, potentially taller and heavier—than freshman players on opposing teams, thus capable of inflicting serious injury on the younger ones.

It was actually Bedichek, the best known of the presidents of the UIL, at whom Lutcher Stark initially aimed his wrath. In the early days of Lutcher's stint as a regent, relations between the two had been civil, if not cordial; they had occasionally even played handball together.[125] But increasingly, Lutcher's assumptions and actions regarding the role and power of the Board of Regents had incurred Bedichek's ire, and he held his own opinion of Lutcher's involvement in the UIL. In his view, "what Lutcher had actually contributed was about $400 per year to buy medals with. . . . When I got charge of the League, I dragged the same contribution out of Lutcher for a year or two, but my gorge rose at the flattery necessary, and finally I simply quit, and he quit, and we were both quits, and relations, even in our occasional handball games, became strained."[126]

The catalyst that precipitated their quarrel, however, was a controversy over the so-called eight-semester rule—a policy that, regardless of a student's grade level, banned him or her from further participation in sports after playing for eight semesters. It is fair to say that, considering the differing sizes and structures of the schools then participating in UIL football, it would have been nearly impossible to craft a policy to fit the criteria of every member school. The result was that the schools were simply unable to come to an agreement on establishing age limits for participants or the number of semesters in which they would be allowed to play.[127] In the UIL's continual efforts to find common ground, there ensued a period of constantly changing policies, and the disagreement seethed for years. Throughout the 1930s, revisions swung back and forth.

In 1938, the UIL again modified the policy, directing that a student be required to be under the age of eighteen on September 1 of a given year of play but abolishing the eight-semester rule.[128] The new policy was slated to go into effect in the fall of 1940. This latest version served Lutcher Stark's interests quite well: Homer and Bill, who had turned seventeen the previous April, would still be under eighteen years of age as of September 1940, and if the policy were not challenged, they would be allowed to play football their senior year in Orange High School. But if a challenge were made and the eight-semester rule reinstated, then the possibility existed that Homer and Bill, along with seven of their teammates, might potentially be barred from play during their twelfth-grade year, since they had begun play in their eighth-grade year (even though they all had played on Orange High School's "C" team against only three local elementary schools, in non-UIL play).[129]

The first signs of discontent with the new policy surfaced from member schools in December 1939 and grew into "considerable agitation," as Roy Bedichek later described it, to hold a referendum ballot on the question of changing it. Lutcher, getting wind of the growing dissatisfaction, paid Bedichek an office visit and quizzed him on the possibility of a change in the rules. According to Bedichek, he informed Lutcher that he felt a change was unlikely, and Lutcher took his statement as a promise. But just as Lutcher and his secretary were leaving his office, Bedichek warned him that "there might be a revolution and anything could happen in a revolution." Lutcher either did not hear his words or paid no attention to them. And as Bedichek stated later, "What happened was, there was a revolution." Letters began pouring into the UIL office, and a straw vote conducted by a coach at one of the member schools showed that by 3-1, they favored holding a referendum.[130]

The referendum was duly announced in early April 1940. The possibility that, if the referendum vote came in for reinstatement of the eight-semester rule, his sons and their teammates might be barred from play at such a late date, as well as the UIL's vacillations, enraged Lutcher Stark, who was in the process of helping build a new football stadium at Orange High, reseeding the field, and buying new uniforms for the team in preparation for his sons' senior year. Claiming that Bedichek and his UIL colleagues, Athletic Director Rodney Kidd and Extension Division Dean Thomas Shelby, had broken their promise to him, he set out to have all three discharged from the university. He first called Shelby and threatened to reduce his salary, then rang up Kidd and threatened him with dismissal for breaking his word. Bedichek, Shelby, and Kidd, in fear for their jobs, subsequently held a conference with President Rainey, who assured the three that they would not be discharged without a hearing.[131]

The referendum's official ballot held a key specification that, since such a wide divergence of opinion existed among the schools, the results of the vote "would become effective in each Conference as the majority of the schools in the respective Conferences may vote"—in effect granting each conference the autonomy to decide and implement the issues for itself. Although the AA Conference voted to abolish the eight-semester rule,[132] the other conferences—A (including Orange), B, and the Six-Man Conference—all voted to reinstate it.[133] Subsequently, the State Executive Committee, deciding that enough was enough, announced in May that no further referendum would be submitted.

The new rules, instituted so hastily, gave coaches and players little time to readjust their plans for the upcoming season. Lutcher Stark remained irate at the prospect of his sons' being denied play, the back-and-forth waffling of the UIL, and the trio of UIL officials for what he perceived as their inability to have arrived at a workable solution to the eligibility issue. At the regents' meeting of May 31, 1940, Lutcher, citing "certain promises" that had been made to him by members of the State Executive Committee, introduced a resolution containing his own compromise proposal, giving as his reasons that

> there has been such general dissatisfaction with the eligibility rules submitted by the Executive Committee of the University Interscholastic League, and . . . the Interscholastic League . . . adopted an eligibility rule [in 1938] which should serve for the year 1940–41, and . . . all were informed that this rule would apply during 1940–41 with no possibility of change, and . . . the High School participants in athletics had prepared over the course of twelve months for the acceptance of this rule, and . . . without proper notice, due consideration of plans, and in absolute disagreement with the accepted rule, a referendum vote *was* submitted by the Directors of the Interscholastic League, and . . . the terms of this referendum please few members and individuals in the state, and . . . the results have thrown the Interscholastic participation into a turmoil, and . . . I believe that seventy-five per cent of the troubles of the University and the lack of confidence displayed throughout the state are directly traceable to this dictatorial vacillating policy.[134]

Lutcher's compromise featured an age limit of nineteen on the September 1 preceding a given contest for students who had already participated in sports for four years and an age limit of eighteen for others, with the added proviso that "any and all teams can invoke both rules for their participants for the year 1940–41." "The essence of this suggestion," he added, "is the fairness to the coaches, parents, and the boys themselves, and to give the Interscholastic League members a chance to determine a universally acceptable rule which shall apply to all classes and all participants for governing the session 1941–42."[135] (His proposed rules, of course, allowed his sons and their teammates to play their senior year.) The resolution failed to carry.

But he still aimed to rid the university of Bedichek, Shelby, and Kidd. At the same meeting, he then moved that charges be preferred against Bedichek and Kidd and that they be "removed from the University staff." (The motion received a second, but Regent Kenneth H. Aynesworth presented a substitute motion providing that their reappointments be held up until the next meeting of the board. Aynesworth's motion was adopted, with Lutcher voting "no.") Lutcher then moved that Shelby be given notice that the board would seek a new dean for the Extension Division, in effect replacing him, but this motion died for lack of a second.[136] Lutcher availed himself of another avenue as well. He stormed into Rainey's office and demanded that the president summarily discharge Bedichek, Shelby, and Kidd. When Rainey requested that he go through regular channels so that they be allowed a hearing, Lutcher purposely refused to bring formal charges, thus denying them the hearing.[137] Rainey refused to fire them. "I'm going to fight you like hell," Lutcher shot back.[138]

The entire issue was rendered moot that summer by a change of policy, when the seniors at Orange High School were allowed to compete legally in UIL football.[139] But Lutcher Stark still harbored his grudge against Bedichek, later telling him at a chance meeting in a local sporting goods store, "I'm going to clean you out; I gave you your chance and President Rainey, too."[140] And he would make good his threat to fight Homer Rainey and Bedichek.

In the wake of Nita Stark's last illness and death, Lutcher's temper had grown more uncertain, without doubt fueling his widening conflict with the University of Texas.[141] And with the lack of Nita's leveling presence to anchor him to the school and the city of Austin, his focus inevitably veered more and more toward his home region. Since Homer and Bill would remain students in Orange public schools for the next year and a half, he continued to enhance and enrich the city's schools.

And his pride and joy, the Bengal Guards, were garnering national recognition.[142] He had spared no expense in their training. During the summer of 1938, he imported Col. George E. Hurt, director of the University of Texas Longhorn Band, to conduct a clinic for the Guards and the boys' band (soon to be renamed the Bengal Lancers), and at the end of the summer Colonel Hurt recommended his assistant director, a young man named Frank Hubert, to serve as band director for both groups.[143] Hubert began work that September. He later explained the arrangement:

> The position was an unusual one in that it was two dimensional in nature. I was employed by Lutch Stark Boys, Inc., and served at the pleasure of Mr. Stark. At the same time, I was a full-time member of the high school faculty, responsible to the school principal (Helen Carr) for my teaching schedule and for complying fully with the rules and regulations of the Orange School District. . . . My salary, however, was paid directly to me by Lutch Stark Boys, Inc.[144]

Lutcher hired Lewis Gay, an employee of the *Port Arthur News*, as drillmaster for both groups. Gay boasted a strong military background, enabling him to teach them strictly military marching and formations from the US Army drill manual.[145] Harry "Doc" Bishop assumed charge of instrument maintenance, and the quartermaster for the corps, Jimmy Dartez, assisted with care of the instruments and equipment. University of

Figure 10.7. Lutcher Stark in Orange High School letter jacket, observing the
Bengal Guards at practice. Stark Foundation Archives, Bengal Guards Collections.

Figure 10.8. Lutcher Stark addressing the Bengal Guards. Trubbie, Eunice Benckenstein's golden cocker spaniel adopted by the Starks, lounges on the floor.
Stark Foundation Archives, Bengal Guards Collections.

Texas student "Jiggs" Walston taught the Guards baton-twirling and drum-majoring techniques, and Jack Hamby transported equipment—uniforms, instruments, and so on—on the huge customized bus Lutcher had purchased and outfitted.[146]

Lutcher periodically added other instruments, such as herald trumpets and helicon basses, to the original ensemble.[147] He also established an off-shoot of the Guards, a small orchestra called the Bengalaires, featuring bell lyres, accordions, and herald trumpets and, later, marimbas and vibra-harps.[148] (The task of composing and arranging music that incorporated the "voices" of the new instruments fell to Frank Hubert.) If a girl finished in the upper fourth of her class, Lutcher promised a year's tuition to a Texas college of her choice.[149]

In 1938, the number of Guards was increased to ninety-five, and the corps was led by drum major Rebecca "Becky" Havens, who won state and national awards for her astonishing skill in baton twirling. The group's junior drum major, Patsy Levingston, won the national twirling championship the following year at the young age of eleven. In 1939, with Havens as twirling drum major, Carol Jo "Frodie" Colburn performed as

Figure 10.9. Bengal Guards form their famous company front.
Stark Foundation Archives, Bengal Guards Collections.

Figure 10.10. Bengal Guards and Bengal Lancers, heart-and-arrow formation, practice at
Orange football field. Stark Foundation Archives, Bengal Guards Collections.

signal drum major, issuing her commands with shots from a pair of pistols worn at her belt instead of the usual whistle. That year, the Guards also incorporated Swiss flag twirling into their routines and initiated their famous "company front"—the entire corps abreast, marching the length of the field.[150] (To ensure their precision as they practiced the company front, Lutcher placed ropes in front and behind the line, held by a Guard at each end as they marched. As Billie Jeanne DeLane [Wright], a Guard and future Stark employee, recalled, "Mr. Stark didn't want to see anybody's fanny sticking out behind that rope, or anybody's stomach sticking out in front of it.")[151]

In late December 1939, the Guards, accompanied by their directors, chaperones, and even a pair of Texas highway patrolmen, traveled by special Pullman train to New Orleans to perform at the 1940 New Year's Day Sugar Bowl game between Tulane University and Texas A&M. They participated in an afternoon parade and made an appearance at City Park before presenting an impeccable fifteen-minute performance to the seventy thousand fans at the game, which performance lasted the entire halftime.[152]

"The Bengal Guards of Orange, Texas High School put on the greatest show I ever saw in a stadium," wrote a reporter from the *New Orleans Item*. "They made most college bands look like they lost all their horns."[153] Another New Orleans newspaper reported that "the lovely young brunette miss out front with the smart strut and the flashing baton will be Becky Havens. . . . Her magic fingers can make a baton do everything up to and including the Lambeth Walk."[154] That year's Official Sugar Bowl Program billed them as "Orange High School Bengal Guards—America's finest marching organization." The Guards gave repeat performances at the Sugar Bowl for the next two years.[155] In May 1940, they also traveled to Waco to perform at the National School Music Competition Festival (possibly at the instigation of Lutcher's old friend, former governor Pat M. Neff, who at that time was serving as president of Baylor University.)[156]

That September, the new $50,000 Tiger Stadium was dedicated, replacing the old Howell Stadium.[157] The venture was funded for the most part by Lutcher through the Lutcher & Moore Lumber Company.[158] He also furnished practice halls on the Orange High School campus for the Guards and the Lancers. The Guards' hall contained hardwood floors and was hung with paintings by noted southwestern artists from the Starks' collection.[159] Since both Homer and Bill played football, Bill as captain of the team (Homer served as captain of the basketball team), Lutcher built a clubhouse at the high school for the players, as well as a cinder track. He arranged for—and probably supplemented the salaries of—excellent

Figure 10.11. Interior of practice hall at Orange High School, built by Lutcher Stark.
Note three paintings of southwestern art by William Herbert Dunton. From left to right:
Lady on Horseback; *McMullin, Guide*; and *The Hunter*, all presently housed in the Stark
Museum of Art in Orange. Stark Foundation Archives, Bengal Guards Collections.

teachers and staff, including an exceptional superintendent, J.W. Edgar,
who was later appointed state commissioner of education.[160]

In August 1940, Lutcher chartered an entire special Southern Pacific
train to convey the Guards, now consisting of over a hundred regulars and
twenty-two substitutes, to the Eleventh Annual Chicagoland Music Festival, sponsored by the *Chicago Tribune* and held at Chicago's Soldier Field.
For the occasion, he purchased new uniforms for the corps, including
"cowgirl" outfits for the drum majors.[161] He also added twin innovations in
the persons of mascots, Cecil Moses and Helen McDonald, both six years
old. (Cecil had tried out for the position by twirling a sawed-off broomstick
her father had made her, but Lutcher ordered a small-size baton made especially for her.)[162] Their assigned tasks were twirling and tumbling—
splits, headstands, and cartwheels—and blowing kisses to the audience.
Lutcher ordered uniforms custom-made for them and, given their young
years, provided them with chaperones.[163]

In Chicago, the Guards stunned an audience of eighty thousand at
the Chicagoland Festival with their crack precision drills and continuous fifteen-minute musical performance.[164] "The greatest exhibition of
grace and precision marching ever seen in Chicago," the *Chicago Tribune*

raved. "The throng that filled the amphitheater apparently had never seen anything quite like this amazing spectacle. . . . It was better than a West Point parade."[165] Signal drum major Frodie Colburn was lauded by one reporter, who dubbed her "the greatest little field general I have ever seen in my life."[166]

When Lutcher was informed that the Guards were allowed a maximum of only twelve minutes to perform their routine, he "rebelled," according to one newspaper account. "When Lutcher Stark rebels, it's a first-class, roaring revolution," the article went on. "'Listen,' he said, 'we can't do it. It's impossible. Tell you what I'll do, though; give us three more minutes; that will make fifteen, and for every minute over fifteen, I'll give you $1,000.'" The officials agreed. Lutcher knew his Guards; they finished in fifteen minutes flat.[167] After the festival, they returned to Orange in triumph to find a large crowd waiting at the Southern Pacific station to welcome them home.[168]

For the Guards, many of whom had never traveled outside the state and

Figure 10.12. Bengal Guards mascots Helen McDonald (*third from left*) and Cecil Moses (*second from right*) with the "Redbug," a small electric car in which they were driven around the stadiums before football games. Twirler Patsy Ruth Levingston, who drove them, is third from right, and Lutcher Stark is at right.
Stark Foundation Archives, Bengal Guards Collections.

Figure 10.13. The Bengal Guards' performance before a crowd of 80,000
at the Chicagoland Festival, 1940. Stark Foundation Archives.

had never even ridden a train, the extended journeys by rail presented
their own set of adventures. On the way to Chicago, they practiced their
music in the baggage car, where the instruments were stowed.[169] They
slept in the Pullman bunks and ate in the dining car, which was complete with table linens, flowers, crystal and silver, and their own printed
menus.[170] When they were served English peas, they were at first wary of
eating them, thinking they were chinaberries (the toxic fruit of a tree common in Southeast Texas), and when the waiters set bowls of a clear liquid
in front of them, they took spoons and tasted it, thinking it was a clear
soup. "Girls," Lutcher laughingly explained, "these are finger bowls."[171]
One girl looked out the window of the train and saw that they were traveling through a huge peach orchard. "Look at the peaches," she exclaimed.
"Oh, I wish I was a worm!"[172]

After their triumph in 1940, they were ensconced on the train, homeward bound, when it slowed, then stopped. Soon, Smitty Hustmyre appeared in one car after the other. "The hotel has called us," she reported,
"and told us that 'half of the Stevens Hotel must be on this train, because
your girls have taken it and put it in their suitcases.' Now, I'm going to tell
you this," she went on; "there will be a box at the beginning of each car.
Nobody will watch; if you've taken anything out of that hotel, you get it out
and put it in that box, and no questions will be asked. But be sure you do
it." "Well," as one Guard remembered, "when Mrs. Hustmyre said something, you did it. Every box was filled."[173]

The Guards performed at an ever-increasing number of regional public
events—bridge openings, festivals, and political conventions—and served

as honor guards for visits of public officials, including Governor W. Lee O'Daniel and First Lady Eleanor Roosevelt.[174] Frank Hubert later opined, "I believe strongly that the Bengal Guards were the most outstanding and unique all-girls' high school instrumental musical organization in America during the twentieth century." He further added, "[The Bengal Guards and the Bengal Lancers program] was begun by the creative mind of a benevolent philanthropist who was totally dedicated to providing unusual educational opportunities to the children and youth of [the] community through two unique musical organizations."[175] And to Bengal Guards, most of whose families had had little or nothing during those bleak Depression years, it remained the most rewarding experience of their lives.[176] (Lutcher Stark's command of the Bengal Guards ended in 1944, when he relinquished the program to the Orange school system.)[177]

That October, near the first anniversary of Nita's death, Lutcher Stark stunned the school and the community by firing the head coach of the Orange High School football team, former University of Texas football star Dexter Shelley.[178] The reason—or reasons—remained unclear. "A considerable portion of this community [Orange] appeared late Saturday to have gone 'stark mad,' and all [of it] over pants. Or was it grass?" the Port Arthur News queried, tongue firmly in cheek.[179]

> Not just ordinary pants, of course. Nor ordinary grass. Whichever it was, the simple facts appear to be these: there was a heated discussion over either the Orange football squad's new uniforms—or new field—between Coach Dexter Shelley and H. J. Lutcher Stark, Orange millionaire who furnished both uniforms and field. Whereupon Coach Shelley, whether fired or resigned, left town, and Stark, to the disappointment of football fans . . . ordered a "no show" by his famed Bengal Guards between halves of Friday night's football game.[180]

The "pants" version held that, when the team had practiced in one set of the new uniforms, they had soiled them; hence, Coach Shelley planned for them to wear the second set for the game. Lutcher vetoed the plan, maintaining that Shelley had failed to ask his permission and that the team should not have practiced in either of the new sets. "Shelley then, according to reports, handed Stark one of the said uniforms—from about 10 feet away," the article went on. "Whereupon Stark said something to the effect that 'Shelley doesn't work here anymore.'" Shelley asserted that his resignation had occurred as he was "returning" one of the uniforms to Lutcher.[181]

The "grass" version maintained that, according to Shelley, Lutcher was displeased that the coach allowed his team to practice on the new field, where the game was to be held, that he had been afraid the team's cleats would mar its surface. Lutcher himself refused to throw light on the controversy, one way or the other. "We have a definite policy . . . in our organization," he declared. "We never explain, we never admit, we never deny. All I have to say is, I believe Shelley pulled a blade of grass."[182] (Homer Stark later stated that his father had fired Shelley because the coach had allowed the team to play on the practice field after Lutcher had recently had it planted with grass.) "Will the Bengal Guards march again?" the *Port Arthur News* wondered waggishly. "Will they stay benched, or will some good fairy persuade their godfather to relent? Will the blade of grass Shelley pulled ever grow back? Will he be rehired? Were any pants torn? Will the Marines never land?"[183]

The team promptly went on strike, refusing to attend class until Shelley was rehired. "It will either be Coach Dexter Shelley or no football and no school," said a spokesman for the team, and the strikers paraded in downtown Orange until nearly midnight, carrying placards that read, "No Shelley, no team. No team, no school." (The *Beaumont Journal* noted that two members of the team did not participate in the strike: Homer and Bill Stark.) In a conference with the team and Superintendent J.W. Edgar, Shelley expressed his wish that they resume play and return to their classes. All but about a dozen players did as he asked, and Charles Quinn, a former Sam Houston Teachers College player, became the new coach.[184]

An editorial in the *Port Arthur News* added a cautionary postscript: "It's all a pity the matter broke open as it did—for . . . Stark [is not] the kind of character the situation has painted him. His gifts are real benevolences, and he honestly has the welfare of these school kids at heart. So much so in fact that it doubtless hurt him the more when he learned they were needlessly spoiling the new uniforms or scarring the playing turf."[185] "But we cannot at all follow the logic that benches the Bengal Guards because of circumstances in which they weren't even involved," the editorial added, echoing the bewilderment of the community.

A final act remained. In what an *Austin-Statesman* article termed "a split in Orange's little colony of millionaires," Lutcher's cousin, Edgar Brown, weighed in on the side of Dexter Shelley. Brown, who had also contributed funds toward construction of the new stadium, offered to donate the portion of Shelley's salary that Lutcher had been paying—which was over and above the amount paid him by the school board. The offer was made, Brown further allowed, "with the understanding that I would attempt to exercise no authority over the team. . . . No one should have the authority to dictate the policy of the school."[186]

The *Houston Post* reported that Brown had told the school board that "I had rather have those children wear calico dresses and beat tin drums than have our whole town disgraced by unfavorable publicity. While

Lutcher is to be commended for what he has done for the boys and girls of Orange High School . . . I still contend that these things should come under the definite authority of the school." The *Post* also noted that Superintendent J.W. Edgar had announced that, with the apologies and return to school of the protesting students, "peace reigned" in the schools. "They said they had found out the truth before they apologized," Superintendent Edgar continued. "I didn't ask them what the truth was or how they found it out."[187] Whatever "the truth" might have been, it never publicly surfaced, and the furor subsided and rapidly died a natural death.

And in spite of momentary fears, the Bengal Guards continued to perform. A week after the Dexter Shelley incident, the group was favored with a three-page pictorial write-up in *Life* magazine:

> The Orange school band is the creation of Mr. Lutcher Stark who inherited a lumber fortune and spends a lot of it now on the band. The school has a boys' band of 100 pieces but Orange's pride and Lutcher Stark's joy is the girls' band, the "Bengal Guards." . . . He makes the players keep up in their studies, behave themselves, practice eleven months a year. When they graduate he gives them a $50 scholarship for college. While in the band he gives them medical attention and crams them with vitamins. "Why last year," he beams, "I put 3,000 lb. on my corps."[188]

Lutcher had, in fact, placed the Guards, the boys' band, and the entire Orange Tiger football team on a regimen of three cod-liver-oil pills per day, distributed to each group at their respective practices from small tin-lined wooden troughs.[189]

Later that same month, however, the Guards were stunned by the sudden resignation of their director, Smitty Hustmyre. A few days before, a disagreement had erupted between her and Lutcher over the Guards' routines that had apparently ended when Lutcher lost his temper. In a rare gesture, he apologized to her for his "exhibition," but added, "after the return from Chicago, I thought I had made it perfectly clear that there *must* be *no* changes in the performance without first receiving my personal okeh. . . . One of the privileges of being a sponsor means paying a tremendous expense account, therefore I think I should have some say as to the performance."[190] Hustmyre fired back a spirited reply, then offered her resignation. "Dear Mr. Stark," she wrote,

> My understanding . . . was that it would be satisfactory for me to change the stunt. . . . You could easily have told me Monday that you did not want to change [it]. . . . I have tried in every way possible to please you, keeping in mind at all times that you paid a "tremendous expense" and [were] most certainly en-

Figure 10.14. Bengal Guards members received cod-liver-oil pills after each practice, at Lutcher Stark's direction. Stark Foundation Archives, Bengal Guards Collections.

titled to have some say as to the performance. But I did think that I was supposed to attend to some of the details without worrying you. Since it seems impossible for me to please you or anticipate your wishes, and having the interest
of you and the Bengal Guards at heart, I deem it necessary to tender my resignation effective today. . . . Thanking you for present and past favors, and wishing for you and the girls continued success, and I want you to know there are
no hard feelings on my part.[191]

She added a postscript: "You have tried to teach me, 'Never admit,
never explain, and never deny,' but I did want you to have some idea of my
feelings. I have never deliberately done anything which I thought you ob-
jected to. When I haven't pleased you, it was due to a misunderstanding
on my part."[192]

Hustmyre's primary concern was for the Guards. She wrote them some
days later to inform them of her resignation:

I want you to know how tremendously I have enjoyed my five and one half
years of association with you, you have been the dearest group of girls in the

world, and at times when you have thought me hard, please try to think that I had your interest at heart all the time. . . . YOU GIRLS have made the Bengal Guards what they are today. . . . For all the spirit of determination and loyalty which you have always shown . . . you all are very near and dear to me, and . . . I wish for each and every one of you all the joy and happiness possible . . . for remember that you get out of anything just what you put into it.[193]

Figure 10.15. Director Elizabeth "Smitty" Hustmyre at work in her office on Bengal Guards routines, ca. early 1940s. Stark Foundation Archives, Bengal Guards Collections.

Sadly, the Guards went on without their beloved "Mrs. Hustmyre," as they unfailingly called her, spending the summer of 1941 in practice for their encore appearance in August at the Twelfth Chicagoland Music Festival. For that occasion, Lutcher, doubtless with the dire worldwide situation in mind, purchased new red, white, and blue uniforms for the Guards,[194] and he gave each mascot a surprise. "Mr. Stark had a little gift for us," Cecil Moses (Broom) remembered. "He did not give it to us until after we left, and the train was gone a few hours. Then they brought us these little suitcases; each one of us had one with our name on it, and we opened it up, and inside was a doll for each of us, with all the clothes and everything. Now, how thoughtful was that of him to think of us?"[195]

The *Chicago Tribune* offered its readers a preview of the Guards' upcoming performance: "They can hardly be called a band, yet they are a great deal more than a drum and bugle corps. They are hardly a musical show chorus, yet in many ways they outshine the greatest precision choruses in the world. And no drill team ever has been able to compete with them." The newspaper went on to list a dazzling array of elements comprising their routines: "the double revolving wheel, the interlocking wheel, the moving divided diamond, the telescope, the accordion, the figure eight"—not to mention their famous company front. "They do everything listed in the infantry drill manual," the article went on. "Their white booted feet keep up a steady twinkling against the green of the arena."[196]

For reasons unknown, Lutcher had long ago chosen the number thirteen as his lifelong lucky number,[197] and many of his automobile license plates sported the number.[198] One story holds that, for the Guards' stay at the Stevens Hotel in Chicago, he booked an entire floor, specially requesting the thirteenth. The hotel, like most, did not offer a thirteenth floor, skipping directly from the twelfth to the fourteenth, but, on discovering Lutcher's numerical preference, the management housed the group on the fourteenth floor and changed out all the numbers to read "13" instead.[199] Or so the story goes. The morning of August 16 the Guards were the featured guests at the festival's luncheon, held in the grand ballroom of the hotel. That evening, at the festival itself on Soldier Field, they executed a smashing follow-up of their previous year's performance—this time for a crowd of one hundred thousand.[200]

Accompanying Lutcher and his entourage to Chicago that year was his new bride—his former secretary, née Ruby Childers.[201] At Thanksgiving in 1940, just a little over a year after Nita's death, Lutcher and Ruby, fifteen years his junior, a slight, brown-haired young woman with a quiet, sweet nature and a wide, friendly smile, had announced their engagement.[202] Their family and friends were delighted. "Raymond and I have long been admirers of yours," Frankie Hill wrote to Ruby, "and wish for you both all

Figure 10.16. Ruby Belle Childers Stark, undated. Stark Foundation Archives.

the happiness in the world."[203] Theo Bellmont's wife, Freda, extended "the very warmest, heartiest welcome possible into our family & friendship." She confessed their worry over Lutcher: "Knowing him so well we have realized how restless & lonely he is, and have been so afraid that he might fall into the hands of someone designing. . . . You have everything that means much to Lutcher—character & charm & a sincerity that is perfect, and you both love the same things & will be happy in Orange which needs you and where you both belong & love to be."[204]

Freda Bellmont added a few words of counsel, artless but sincere:

> Ruby, I want you to have perfect confidence in yourself. You come from a home of splendid people far ahead of all the important people with whom he associates or ever has here in Austin. In addition to that you have an ability and competence and training superior to 99% of the people he knows; & when you've been to Neiman's a trip or two you with your trim build, carriage, etc. are going to look better than anyone you ever laid your eyes on. Which really is a small matter, but it does give a woman satisfaction & confidence. . . . Lutcher is one of the finest men we ever expect to know & so sweet and kind we all just love him like he belonged to us which he almost does. All that gruffness just serves as a cover to keep too many people from finding out what he is really like—but of course you know all this. Ruby, be sweet & kind to him he deserves it so richly & has had too little of it in his life.[205]

Fannie Ratchford wrote to Ruby, "You have much to give Mr. Stark that he needs; you will make him happy, I know. I am deeply glad you are marrying him. And there is every reason to hope that you yourself will be as happy as you deserve to be."[206]

Ruby Childers and Lutcher Stark were married the following April 6, 1941. The wedding ceremony took place in the Lutcher Memorial Building of the First Presbyterian Church, the site of all the family's solemn occasions, following "reports of many months' standing which have been circulating," according to the newspapers. Rev. E.T. Drake performed the ceremony. The church was decorated with calla lilies and white stock, arranged against a background of palm leaves and other green foliage. The bride wore "a smart *poudre* blue ensemble," one writer noted, "with rose accessories and a shoulder corsage of orchids. "It was an excited Orange when the hometown millionaire and his level-headed, tailor-dressed former employee said 'I do,'" the writer rhapsodized. "Immediately following the ceremony, the 53-year-old capitalist and his 38-year-old bride left the church for their one-room houseboat which will take them on their moneymoon on the Sabine River," the writer added.[207]

A large crowd gathered at Lutcher's boathouse to see the couple off, including both the Lancers and the Guards. The girls serenaded the newlyweds and pinned a corsage of carnations to Ruby's lapel. "I've warned him. I can't cook," Ruby answered a reporter's query. "He can cook, though. I promised to wash the dishes." After the crowd showered them with rice, they headed down the Sabine in Lutcher's speedboat, waving to the crowd,

Figure 10.17. Ruby and Lutcher Stark in the kitchen of the houseboat *Ruby*.
Stark Foundation Archives.

Figure 10.18. Ruby and Lutcher Stark, honeymooners. Stark Foundation Archives.

en route to a short honeymoon on the houseboat, which he had christened the *Ruby* in her honor.[208] Following the honeymoon, they came home to live in Lutcher's house on Pine Street but departed shortly thereafter for an extended stay at Roslyn Ranch.[209]

Lutcher knew his bride well. Ruby Belle Childers had come from pioneer East Texas stock on both the paternal and maternal sides of her family and had lived in Orange since birth. She was born August 25, 1902, the second child of James Patton "Jim" Childers, a sawmill worker who later became foreman at the Miller-Link Lumber Company in Orange, and his wife, née Mary Martha "Mamie" Litchfield. An older brother, Oscar Pruitt Childers, had been born December 20, 1899, but died October 4, 1906, shortly before his seventh birthday. A little over two years after Oscar's death, on February 19, 1909, another daughter, Nelda, was born to Jim and Mamie Childers.[210] The two sisters, Ruby and Nelda, six and a half years apart and complete opposites in looks, temperament, and every other way, nevertheless remained close to each other for all of their lives.

Ruby attended Orange public schools, graduating May 21, 1920, from Orange High School.[211] That fall she entered Ward-Belmont, a women's college in Nashville, Tennessee.[212] A diary she kept during the spring

Figure 10.19. Ruby and Lutcher Stark at Roslyn Ranch,
where they traveled after their honeymoon. Stark Foundation Archives.

Figure 10.20 and 10.21. Mamie and James Patton "Jim" Childers, dressed for the wedding of their daughter, Ruby, to Lutcher Stark. Stark Foundation Archives.

semester, from January 1 to June 3, 1921, reveals that she lived in a girls' dormitory and spent much time studying—as befitted the serious young woman that she was—enjoying her subjects (even trigonometry, as she herself admitted) and making A's and B's.[213] She also took a class in basketball and played right center on the beginners' basketball team. Her friends made up a group of other young women who spent plenty of time at their books but who also held bull sessions in dorm rooms and attended movies, concerts, basketball games, and dances.[214]

Her diary reflects the everyday details of her life as a student in an all-female college. The diary is filled with references to home—letters, food, and gifts received from her family in Orange: her mother, her father (who sent her mayhaw jelly that spring), "Dub" (her younger sister, Nelda), and various friends.[215] "Went to math; heard from home," a typical entry reads. "Had Miss Morrison as a teacher and she worked us to a peanut. We were sent to hear Mr. Johnson, the famous tenor, at the Ryman [Auditorium; later the home of the 'Grand Ole Opry']. He was fine."[216] "Washington's birthday," she reported on February 22. "Someone talked in chapel. Went to see Miss Morris about dropping math; she said no. Colonial dinner. I went with Audrey, and Marjorie went with Fay. We went over to the dance for a few minutes. Went up to Fay's room and brushed powder out of our hair." On May 28, she reported, "Math exam—terrible; English exam—hard; Spanish exam—not so bad." (She later reported that she made a "B" in math.)

Figure 10.22. Nelda (*left*) and Ruby Childers as children. Stark Foundation Archives.

Figure 10.23. Ruby (*left*) and Nelda Childers. Stark Foundation Archives, Anita Cowan.

At the end of the school year she left Nashville and headed homeward, arriving in Beaumont on June 3, where Nelda and a friend met her and conveyed her back to Orange.[217] She possibly returned to Ward-Belmont the following year—at that time the school offered a two-year secretarial degree—but no diary survives, and decades later, Nelda stated in an interview that Ruby did not finish college.[218] More likely, she stayed at home in Orange and began working for the Stark family interests, serving as secretary to William Stark. (William called Ruby his "jewel," a double play on her name and capability.)[219] After William's death, Lutcher Stark employed her as his own secretary.[220] By the time of her marriage, she had been employed by the Stark interests "in a confidential capacity," as the newspapers termed it, for a full twenty years.[221]

The newspaper accounts of Ruby and Lutcher's wedding festivities reflected no sign of a private drama—lacking a happy ending. It had begun the previous April when Nelda Childers had discovered a lump in one of her breasts. She immediately took herself to a doctor, and Beaumont pathologist H.B. Williford, after performing a biopsy, reported that the tumor was benign.[222] The incident prompted Ruby, who in the meantime had discovered a lump in her own breast, to pay Dr. Williford a visit. Her visit to the doctor brought unwelcome news—the lump was malignant.[223] A telegram from an unnamed laboratory in Rochester, Minnesota, dated December 2, 1940—only a few days after she and Lutcher had announced their engagement—confirmed the grim diagnosis: "Tissue breast shows grade 2 adenocarcinoma."[224] Dr. Williford's follow-up report to Dr. Pearce confirmed the diagnosis but noted that the tumor, one centimeter in diameter, was actually a stage three. Dr. Williford's final comment was hopeful: "I believe the prognosis in this case better than the average."[225] Ruby offered to call off the wedding, but Lutcher remained adamant.

But all hopes came to naught. Ruby and Lutcher enjoyed seven months of married life—happy, to all appearances—before the ravages of the disease began to defeat her. By November 1941, she had become bedridden.[226] The following spring, she made her will. "Keep up your courage," a friend wrote, "as it requires a lot on an uphill pull."[227] That June, Herbert Kerr wrote Lutcher, "I am just sick to hear of Miss Ruby's sickness, I . . . had no idea she was so bad until lately, was so in hopes it was a mistake. . . . I just can't tell you how bad I feel, we all thot so much of her."[228] On June 24, 1942, in an eerie echo of Nita's illness, Byron Simmons notified the secretary to the University of Texas Board of Regents, "Due to the continued illness of Mrs. Stark, I regret to advise you that it will be impossible for Mr. Stark to be present [for the upcoming regents' meeting]."[229]

That July, Ruby began sinking rapidly.[230] Lutcher kept registered nurses with her twenty-four hours a day, but Nelda stayed every night with her sister also, sleeping in the room with her and nursing her.[231] Ruby died at 6:50 a.m. on July 12, 1942, at the Starks' home on Pine Street. She was thirty-nine years of age. Private funeral services were held the next evening at the Orange Avenue home of her surviving parents, Jim and Mamie Childers, and were conducted by the family's pastor and friend, Rev. E.T. Drake, who had married Ruby and Lutcher such a short time before. Ruby was buried in Evergreen Cemetery in the Childers plot on the cemetery's eastern edge, near her older brother.[232]

Letters and telegrams arrived in abundance, praising Ruby and expressing sympathy for her widower, Lutcher, and her sister, Nelda.[233] "Bless her precious life," Frankie Hill wrote Nelda, "she was goodness on this earth and we can feel our lives have been blessed [in] knowing her."[234] "To have her as a friend," wrote another of their friends, "was like having an extra bit of sunshine in your life."[235] The *Orange Leader* asserted, "Her passing brings deep grief to a host of friends."[236] Ruby and Lutcher had been married a bare fifteen months, and her death marked Lutcher's fourth major loss in six years.

Ruby left two portraits of Lutcher, one a miniature, to her mother; a gold wristwatch to their longtime family friend, Eunice Robinson; various pieces of silver and two lots on West Park Avenue in Orange to Nelda, as well as the residue of her estate; and her two wedding rings, her charm bracelet, her Ford convertible, and her white mink coat to Lutcher, specifying that the latter was to be "kept by him and in its present style, never to be altered nor permitted by him to be worn by any other person."[237] To her stepsons, she willed a loving message:

> Inasmuch as I have no material thing that will show the affection I have for two wonderfully fine boys, Homer Stark and Bill Stark, I can only give them my love and my wishes that they may enjoy all of the happiness that life may bring to them, and I can hope for nothing better for them than that they follow the example and advice of their father, whom I have always found to be a just, fair and fine gentleman.[238]

CHAPTER ELEVEN

Kiss the Boys Good-Bye: World War II

It was hard to realize what was going on at first, and then when you did
realize it, why, it was pretty shocking . . . because we were sitting there, and we
couldn't do nothing.
—JOE ROUGEAU, PEARL HARBOR, DECEMBER 7, 1941[1]

Exactly eight months after Ruby and Lutcher's wedding, on the morning of December 7, 1941, Japanese planes bombed the US naval base at Pearl Harbor, Hawaii, in a surprise attack. The horror of Pearl Harbor abruptly changed the rules, dispelled the last traces of American isolationism, and united the country behind a new war effort. The day after the bombing, Roosevelt successfully petitioned Congress to declare war on Japan, and on December 11, Germany and Italy in turn declared war on the United States.[2]

As it had in the Great War, the shipbuilding industry in Orange again proved vital to the war effort. The city already hosted two major shipbuilding companies, Weaver and Sons and the Levingston Shipbuilding Company, and a third was on its way; in January 1940, amid the escalating war in Europe, the Consolidated Western Steel Corporation had bought the Orange Car and Steel Company, renaming it Consolidated Steel, Shipbuilding Division, and had established a steel-fabrication plant.[3] The following September, the government awarded Consolidated Steel an $82 million government contract to build an immense new shipyard and to construct twelve Fletcher-class destroyers.[4]

The news produced a maelstrom of activity in Orange and launched a boom the likes of which the city had not known since the glory days of Lutcher & Moore or the shipbuilding explosion during World War I. Excitement—and hope—ran high; the new shipyard at Consolidated would create jobs aplenty, a welcome prospect for those still suffering from the Depression. Workers in search of jobs began pouring into town by the

Figure 11.1. Levingston Shipbuilding Company in Orange, undated.
Stark Foundation Archives.

hundreds and thousands, necessitating training and housing for them and their families. City officials scrambled to extend and enlarge facilities to accommodate the anticipated onrush, and construction of government housing rapidly began.[5]

On May 14, 1941, keels were laid at Consolidated for the first two destroyers, the USS *Aulick* and the USS *Charles Ausburne*.[6] Weaver Shipyards began manufacturing submarine chasers and wooden minesweepers, which were impervious to German magnetic mines. Levingston built barges, tankers, and steel tugboats—many of them huge, powerful seagoing vessels, frequently employed as rescue ships by the British.[7] And in the flurry of such massive construction projects, some vestiges of the past became casualties in the name of progress: the remnants of the abandoned Lutcher & Moore sawmill, once the "nucleus of the vast fortunes of the Stark and Brown families," was razed to make room for the burgeoning shipbuilding concerns.[8]

Although the crowds had been expected, no resident or city official of drowsy prewar Orange could possibly have imagined the reality. Suddenly the town was crammed with humanity; its population, a modest seven thousand at the beginning of the war, mushroomed to over sixty thousand, and at its peak, Consolidated alone employed a workforce of twenty-seven thousand.[9] As historian Louis Fairchild has noted, "Goldbrickers, firefighters, nurses, cooks, teenagers, ex-convicts, bankers, aspiring actors, wrestlers, shell-shocked veterans, draft dodgers, movie stars, ropers and riders—they were all there."[10] Since the US Navy maintained an active naval base at Orange, servicemen added their numbers to the crush.[11]

In 1942, a shuttle train was instituted among the region's communities to better manage the throngs daily flooding in and out of Orange. Longtime Orange resident Roy Wingate remembered that

> the train would make up in Port Arthur every morning, a long passenger train, and it would pick up people . . . and come right on through Beaumont and stop . . . and [it] would come into Orange back down the Front Street railroad track to the front gate of the shipyard. And the back car would be at the front gate of the shipyard down at the end of Front Street, and the front car would be way up around Seventh Street. And all the workers for that shift would get off and check in, and the ones who were getting off shift would get on the train and go back home, and that was two times a day, the morning shift and the night shift. So that's one way to give you an idea of how crowded it was.[12]

The government built hundreds of units of temporary housing—barracks and two subdivisions, the Navy Addition and Riverside, the latter built on the riverbank on sand and mud pumped from the bottom of the Sabine. Many lived in government-issued trailers or tents erected on vacant lots. Brownwood, a little distance upriver from the shipyards, comprised a regular tent city. People found housing where they could, or they improvised, setting up housekeeping in barns, garages, boxcars, even bunks in the city jail if cells were vacant. Many rented rooms from residents; others simply slept in makeshift tarpaper lean-tos or in eight-hour shifts on army cots in vacant buildings. According to Wingate, "[The workers] would sleep in flophouses and trucks. They had trucks parked . . . in the field next to our house, with an extension cord to our house, with a hotplate and one light bulb for each one."[13] Conditions were unsanitary; temporary and permanent residents alike fought rats, mosquitoes, roaches, fleas, and other vermin.

Orange schools faced their own set of hardships. Haskell Monroe, at the time a student in Orange schools, remembered that one of the school buildings, which had been designed for five hundred students in four grades, now accommodated nearly three thousand sixth-graders alone. "All the classes were packed, and it was not at all unusual for students to be standing up in the back of the room," Monroe recalled. "There were classes held in the hallway; you literally had to stand in line to get to the restrooms and . . . there were classes going on in the cafeteria . . . while there were people eating."[14]

Few of the workers were familiar with heavy steel construction, and many had come from jobs on farms or in sawmills in rural East Texas and Louisiana. Many could not read rulers or blueprints; some could not even read. Schools were set up, operating twenty-four hours a day, to train workers in welding, riveting, shipfitting, and other specialized jobs in the shipyards. Because Wingate had taken a high school course in mechanical drawing, he was assigned to make layouts for cutting bulkheads, portholes, and manholes.[15]

Work in the shipyards was difficult, dirty, and dangerous. Workers labored in twelve-hour shifts for the duration of the war.[16] Accidents abounded: burns and other injuries from explosions, falls from scaffolding, eye burns from welders' arcs, broken limbs, electrocutions, lung injuries from the noxious welding fumes, and drownings. In the summers, workers sweltered in the interiors of the metal ships; in the winters, they froze. Dr. Wynne Pearce worked far past the point of exhaustion, rising at six o'clock in the morning to work a long day and often called out again in the middle of the night.[17] Wingate remembered that once, when Dr. Pearce made a house call at their residence, he fell asleep in the porch swing afterward, practically in midsentence. Wingate's father instructed the family to allow him to sleep.[18]

Women entered the workforce at the shipyards as secretaries, bookkeepers, and typists, but as male workers were drafted, they took the men's places as riveters, welders, or shipfitters. Those who did not work at paying jobs at the shipyards rolled bandages and took first-aid courses. "There wasn't any monotony," another resident asserted. "We were busy. . . . Of course, we were proud of that shipyard," she went on. "We felt like that was what was winning the war."[19]

Ordinary citizens contributed in other ways. In 1942, a USO recreation center was built in Orange, where dances, teas, and other activities, generally hosted by the young women of the town, were held for the sailors' benefit.[20] The Orange County Red Cross organized a Disaster Planning Committee, its headquarters at Pinehurst Country Club. Hal Carter, an employee of the Brown interests, headed the committee, and his wife, Deru, formerly the chief surgical nurse for the Frances Ann Lutcher Hospital, taught classes for preparing surgical dressings. Smitty Hustmyre directed the Red Cross Motor Corps, training female drivers to carry out necessary tasks for the Red Cross—evacuations, emergency transportation of personnel, and other jobs as needed.[21]

Drives to sell war bonds and stamps were held constantly, with high school students conducting spirited contests. The Bengal Guards performed at football games and other occasions in their new red, white, and blue uniforms. Lutcher Stark bought caps for his Bengal Lancers in red, white, blue, and the colors representing the other Allied nations, and for every home football game, the band donned the caps displaying the colors of one of those nations, played its national anthem, then formed its flag on the field.[22]

Consolidated launched the first of its destroyers, the two thousand–ton *Aulick*, on Texas Independence Day, March 2, 1942, amid the universal trepidation of the crowd of six thousand spectators; heretofore, Orange's long shipbuilding tradition had lain in wooden ship construction, and steel construction was unfamiliar territory.[23] Their fears came to nothing; the launch went flawlessly as the destroyer glided down the shipway and into the Sabine to the Bengal Guards' lively tunes and the cheers of the assembled crowd.[24]

Many from Orange served in the military. Joe Rougeau, a young Orange native who had joined the US Navy in January 1941, was sent directly to Pearl Harbor and was assigned to a fleet repair ship that was anchored near the destroyers, where he worked during that year. As it happened, their ship was required to change locations in early December 1941, just before the sounding of the General Quarters alarm—the signal to all hands to prepare to join battle—early in the morning of December 7. Rougeau reached his station in time to see the USS *Utah* in the process of capsizing. His own ship suffered heavy bombing and strafing attacks while the men helplessly watched the destruction. "We could see sailors trying to swim through that [burning] oil," Rougeau remembered, "and of course we couldn't do nothing about that because our lifeboats were made out of wood, and they'd 'a caught fire."[25]

Roy Wingate came ashore with US Army troops at Omaha Beach during the Allied invasion on D-Day, June 6, 1944, and later saw action at the Battle of the Bulge. "I was not in actual frontline combat at any time," he recalled, "[but] I was close enough to be strafed a little bit. And Bedcheck Charlie would come over when we were on Omaha Beach; the Germans would send Bedcheck Charlie over to see what kind of pictures he could get for what happened during the day, and everybody would be shooting at him, and that shrapnel would be coming down."[26]

Howard Williams went into the army in January 1944, the day after he got out of high school, and he was sent to Europe the following June to land on the beaches of Normandy. He too saw action at the Battle of the Bulge.[27] In March 1944, Frank Hubert left Orange to enter the military.[28] Leon Parish, who was stationed in England with the army, remembered that, throughout the night before the D-Day invasion, a constant thunder roared from the skies from planes of every description, flying into Normandy for Operation Overlord. "You've never heard the like," Parish remembered. He was hit once at the Battle of Bastogne in December 1944; then, pushing eastward the following February, twenty-five miles inside the German border, he caught a piece of shrapnel from an artillery shell. "So the war was over for me," Parish observed. "I was headed for Orange."[29]

Homer and Bill Stark, both of whom had entered college in the fall of 1941—Homer at Texas A&M and Bill at Washington and Lee University—dropped out of school to enlist in the US Navy.[30] "You know Uncle [Raymond] is proud that you volunteered and didn't wait for the draft," Frankie Hill wrote Bill, who became a flying cadet in the US Naval Reserve, Aviation Branch, taking flight training in Dallas, then becoming a bomber pilot for the US Marine Corps, in which he would attain the rank of 1st Lieutenant.[31] Homer became a third-class gunner's mate on the cruiser USS *Richmond*, shipping out of Bremerton, Washington.[32] Both twins saw combat in the Pacific.[33] "I hear of Homer and Bill through friends," Fannie Ratchford wrote Lutcher Stark, "and I pray always for their safety."[34]

Above all loomed the shadow of human loss—husbands, fathers, sons, brothers, sweethearts. Families hung a blue star in a front window of their house for every family member in the service and a gold one for those whose lives had been lost. Blue stars hung in the windows of many houses in Orange—sometimes multiple stars for each household—and more than a few gold ones. Of their five draft-age sons, Roy Wingate's parents, Claude and Lumea Bonin Wingate, sent four to war (the fifth son was in divinity school and thus exempt), and the family hung four blue stars in the front window of their house. A sister, Julia, declared that everyone was "scared to death" to get a telegram: "To this day I hate to see a telegram come," she said years later.[35]

Lutcher Stark did his part. In 1940, the National Defense Act had authorized the organization of independent defense units to serve in place of the National Guard while the latter was engaged in government service, and on February 10, 1941, the Texas legislature authorized the creation of the Texas Defense Guard to encompass these independent units.[36] Many of the men of Orange were eager to join the local Company D, 43rd Battalion, of the Defense Guard, among them Laurence W. Hustmyre, the captain of the group; Lieutenants Charles Cottle and V.T. Bolton; Henry Lee Woodworth, an employee of the Stark interests; music director Frank Hubert; county commissioner Sid Caillavet; Howard S. Peterson, vice president of the Texas Creosoting Company; R.C. Terry, manager of United Gas Corporation; and Lutcher Stark.[37] When he joined the unit as a private first class on April 21, 1941, just after his and Ruby's marriage, he was fifty-three years old.[38]

The members of Company D took their duties seriously. With esprit de corps running high, they engaged in combat drill and infantry drill; civil disturbance practice; riot duty; use of the rifle, bayonet, and gas; patrol and guard duty; and battalion maneuvers. They even practiced with real tear gas, returning home to their wives with reddened, weeping eyes. A contemporary news article noted irreverently that their combat drill "looked like a bunch of boys playing Indians . . . with hats that should have belonged to the yardmen and saggy sweat shirts." The writer had the grace to add that their effort was earnest and their mood serious and that each man wanted to make the company "the best in 43rd Battalion so that 43rd Battalion can be the best in Texas." The article noted that "in [Company D] . . . there is one millionaire, a private, who one night wore to practice a jacket admired by men of his platoon. They asked where he got it. The reply: 'Ruby got it with cigaret coupons.'"[39]

A little over a year later, Lutcher requested a discharge from Company D, citing "late conditions in America" as his reason. (More probably, the real one was Ruby's rapidly advancing illness; she died two months later.) Captain Hustmyre duly sent papers for an honorable discharge May 12, 1942,[40] and Lutcher returned his uniforms and his Reising submachine gun to the unit. In granting the discharge, Hustmyre noted, "I consider . . . that you have made one of the best soldiers in Company D. . . . When given an assignment you have always fulfilled it in the manner of a good soldier, many times taking the most undesirable one, and you have won for yourself the comradeship and admiration of all the men."[41]

The next year, to aid in easing the manpower shortage in Orange, Lutcher took a job, at least for a night, driving a dump truck at a federal housing construction project. His pay: seventy cents an hour. "Why not?" he was reported to have asked. "My time is mine."[42] When Dallas investment analyst R.H. Moodie saw the article, he wrote Lutcher: "Damned if that is not as fine a patriotic act as I have heard of anywhere, and I can but say if the entire thinking population took this war as seriously as you evidently have, we would be much farther along with it."[43]

Although the situation of most African Americans in military service remained essentially one of segregated circumstances and menial jobs, the war saw some improvement; officer candidate schools (except that of the air force) were desegregated, and the Tuskegee Institute flight school produced around six hundred black pilots, many of whom distinguished themselves in combat missions.[44] In Orange, a product of the culture of the Old South, prejudice and discrimination still predominated, but some steps, even if small, were taken toward equality. "If the war did not change things, it certainly set change in motion," observed historian Louis Fairchild. African Americans in Orange received government housing, better job opportunities, and improved education.[45]

When race riots occurred in Beaumont and Port Arthur in 1943, it was

Lutcher Stark who made Orange's African American community feel that no harm would come to them. "They castrated some young black men" in Port Arthur, Elizabeth Washington remembered, "and burned down a shop in Beaumont. . . . And Mr. Stark just did everything to make everybody comfortable." "Okay, they [the troublemakers] are not invited," Lutcher told the workers who were building the houses in the Navy Addition. "But if they want to come, let them come on, but [just let them] try what they did in Beaumont and Port Arthur."[46]

The treatment of Japanese, German, and Italian Americans marked a dark chapter in the history of the war and a blot on the American ideal, and Japanese Americans were victims of the worst treatment. Many Americans fell prey to irrational fears, assuming that all people of Japanese descent remained loyal to Japan and thus constituted a potential threat. In response, Roosevelt ordered the creation of the War Relocation Authority, which forced 120,000 Japanese Americans to abandon their homes and work and to move into "relocation" camps. There they lived and worked behind barbed wire in shacks or flimsy, barracks-like structures under the watchful eyes of armed guards.[47]

One such Japanese American group who suffered innocently as a result of their heritage was the Kishi family, longtime, highly respected residents of the Orange area. The patriarch, Kichimatsu Kishi, a college-educated factory supervisor who was the son of a Tokyo banker, had immigrated to the United States in 1906 to farm rice, choosing to live in Southeast Texas because of its flat terrain, abundant water supply, and the "welcoming attitude" of its local residents.[48] Kishi had settled on a thirty-five hundred–acre tract near Terry, a small settlement just west of Orange, and had established a rice farm and a colony of Japanese expatriates that eventually numbered around forty.

Over the years, the Kishi family and other members of the colony became established members of the community.[49] Hard times struck, however, with crop disease and the onset of the Great Depression, and in 1931, Kishi lost his farmland.[50] The Stark interests (William Stark, Lutcher & Moore, and the San Jacinto Life Insurance Company), Kishi's major creditors, repeatedly adjusted their terms in an attempt to assist him (at a late date in the proceedings, Kishi's son, Taro, wired his father, who was in Tokyo attempting to raise capital, "Mister Stark says will not take profit from you").[51] But by that time, the Starks themselves were in financial straits; in spite of Kishi's strenuous, sustained efforts, the outcome was inevitable: the Starks were forced to foreclose in September 1931.[52] The foreclosure marked the end of the colony; most returned to Japan, but Kishi and his family remained in Texas.[53]

Immediately following the Japanese attack at Pearl Harbor, Kishi turned himself in to the Port Arthur offices of the Federal Bureau of Investigation. For two months, he was detained at the Kenedy Alien Detention Camp in Kenedy, Texas. He gained a hearing before a board chaired by Steve M. King, the US attorney for the Eastern District of Texas.[54] "If you were ordered by the Emperor to bomb the oil refinery in Port Arthur, would you do so?" a member of the board asked. "Suppose I was adopted into another family and my biological parent ordered me to harm my adopted family?" Kishi replied. "I cannot do so."[55] Although his radios, guns, and cameras were confiscated, he was released after two months' confinement.[56]

In March 1942, the Stark family had been surprised by the news that Homer Stark, aged eighteen, had eloped with Becky Havens, the Bengal Guards' former champion twirling drum major, the previous January 22. At the time of the marriage, the nineteen-year-old Becky was a sophomore at the University of Texas; Homer, at Texas A&M. "The announcement climaxed a high school romance of several years' standing," reported the *Beaumont Enterprise*, "but news of the ceremony came as an apparent surprise, both to Mrs. Havens [Becky's mother] and to the Starks."[57] The next year, Bill Stark, then stationed in Dallas, announced similar news of his own: his engagement and upcoming marriage to Ida Marie Dickens of Walden and Longmont, Colorado, the daughter of ranch owner John Henry Dickens.[58] The two were married in Dallas on June 27, 1943.[59]

Later that year, Lutcher, not to be outdone by his sons, remarried on December 16, 1943, sixteen months after Ruby's death—this time to her younger sister, Nelda Childers. Yet again, the Lutcher Memorial Building of the First Presbyterian Church was the scene of the rites, where Rev. E.T. Drake performed the ceremony, reprising his often-played role.[60] Guests at the wedding, a small affair, consisted of immediate family members. Serving as the bride's only attendant was the Childers' close friend and boarder Eunice Robinson, who had recently become the bride of Charles Haight Benckenstein, the manager of Vinton Petroleum Company.[61] The bride, like her sister before her, wore a powder-blue suit, but with brown and white accessories and a corsage of white camellias. (Eunice Benckenstein, the newspaper noted, "was attired in black and wore a red camellia corsage.")[62] At the time of their marriage, Nelda was thirty-four years old; Lutcher, fifty-six.

In every way, Nelda Childers Stark stood in diametric opposition to her sister, Ruby—and for that matter, to Nita Stark. A tall, slender, no-nonsense medical technician who had wanted to be a doctor, she presented a direct, often abrupt front to the world but held deep feelings of loyalty and affection toward her family, close friends, and employees, feel-

Figure 11.2. Nelda Childers, engagement photograph, 1943. Stark Foundation Archives.

ings reciprocated in large part by those who worked for and with her.[63] Her marriage to Lutcher, like William Stark's to Miriam, would prove to be another of the family's fortuitous unions: she was blessed with a brilliant mind and a strong aptitude for business that in the future came into play in her careful stewardship of her husband's interests.[64] "Except for the management of the money . . . I don't think the money made one bit of difference to her," asserted Stark employee Billie Jeanne DeLane Wright. "I don't think it made her happy or unhappy. I think it was just a job to take care of the money and increase it."[65]

In many ways, Nelda Stark was a woman ahead of her time, following her own dictates even though they were often at odds with the norms of the day. She cared not at all for traditional female pursuits and scorned social occasions of all kinds, dismissing such activities with a succinct "I didn't have time."[66] If she perceived her way to be clear, she proceeded directly, regardless of conventional mores or the opinions of others. "[Nelda] was not introverted at all," Eunice Benckenstein observed, "and she was not reclusive at all; she was just pretty self-assured, and really, Mr. [Lutcher] Stark used her as a general manager. I think he expected her to see that he did this and that and the other."[67]

"[Lutcher Stark], recognizing Nelda's keen mind and management skills, had turned much of the management of assets over to Nelda," Anita Cowan, Eunice Benckenstein's niece, commented. "[He] always had women managing for him. That's how he obtained the leeway to follow his hobbies and passions. There was his mother, then his first wife, then Nelda."[68]

Born February 2, 1909, in Orange, Nelda made her appearance in the Childers family only a little over two years after her parents had lost their

Figure 11.3. Nelda (left) and Ruby Childers climbing a tree, while their mother, Mamie, reaches up to catch them, undated. Stark Foundation Archives.

Figure 11.4. Nelda Childers and four-legged friend, undated, but probably ca. 1920. She owned dogs all her life. Stark Foundation Archives.

only son. According to Anita Cowan, "Dub," as Nelda's father always called her, took her deceased older brother's place as his "son," at least in his eyes.[69] (Cowan remembered that Jim Childers owned an ancient parrot who imitated him, periodically screaming "Du-u-u-b! Du-u-u-b!" from his perch on the back porch.)[70] Nelda grew up in the house on Orange Avenue that her father had built, playing typical games and putting on skits and plays with Ruby, who indulged her, and other neighborhood children and doting on the family's wire-haired fox terriers, which numbered half a dozen through the years.[71]

At the age of six, while crossing a street near Anderson School where she was a student, Nelda was run over by an automobile, its wheels crushing her abdomen. She recovered, but she was troubled with adhesions and other intestinal problems for the rest of her life. As Eunice Benckenstein later remarked, "She was never a hundred per cent well."[72]

Attending Orange High School, Nelda acquired a reputation as a good dancer; in her junior year, the 1925 *Orange Peel* yearbook, listing traits for "the Ideal High School Girl," proclaimed that she would "dance like Nelda Childers." She also developed a love of music, and during her school years, she learned to play the cornet. In 1924, following the dictates of her independent nature, she joined Lutcher Stark's Boys' Band as a charter member. "Nelda Childers . . . the only young lady in the band," the *Beaumont Enterprise* reported, "has been playing cornet since its organization." (At one time, three young women were members of the band, including Nelda.)[73] When the group trekked to Colorado in June 1926, shortly after Nelda's graduation from Orange High School, she played with them amid the snow during their concert atop Pike's Peak. In a photograph of the event, two lone skirts—one of them Nelda's—are discernible among the forest of boys' trousers.[74]

After her graduation from high school in 1926 at the age of sixteen, she entered the College of Industrial Arts (CIA, now Texas Woman's University) in Denton, Texas. During her college years, "Miss Nelda Childers, perhaps better known as 'Blossom,'" according to the campus newspaper, continued playing cornet and served as the director of the school's small freshman orchestra.[75] At CIA, she studied bacteriology and received a bachelor of science degree in June 1930. The following August, she found employment in Houston as a laboratory technician and also taught bacteriology and nursing training at Jefferson Davis Hospital.[76] (According to Nelda herself, she also took a course at the University of Texas in preparation for attending medical school, a plan that did not materialize.)[77]

In June 1932, a vacancy occurred in the staff of the Frances Ann Lutcher Hospital in Orange when the previous administrator resigned. Nita Stark called Nelda in Houston to persuade her to come to Orange to

Figure 11.5. Nelda Childers as a member of Lutcher Stark's Boys' Band, holding what appears to be a trumpet rather than her usual instrument, the cornet. Stark Foundation Archives.

Figure 11.6. Lutcher Stark's Boys' Band playing atop Pike's Peak.
Nelda Childers stands third to the right of the director. Stark Foundation Archives.

Figure 11.7. Nelda Childers with one of the family's wire-haired fox terriers, undated.
Stark Foundation Archives.

interview for the position. Nelda agreed to take the job, and Lutcher hired
her as the superintendent of the hospital. She occupied the position for the
next eleven years, placing the hospital "on a more than satisfactory operating basis."[78] As she put it in a later interview, "It was a small hospital. I
did it all. Blood transfusions, all lab work and all office work. There were
no other hospitals in town." At the same time, she also owned a part of

Figure 11.8. Nelda Childers, probably high school age, ca. 1922–1926.
Stark Foundation Archives.

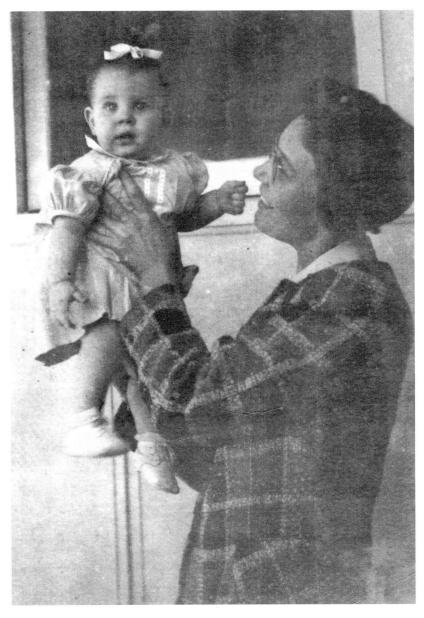

Figure 11.9. Nelda Childers holding baby Ben Irene McDonough, daughter of longtime Lutcher & Moore official Ben McDonough, undated. Stark Foundation Archives.

Service Drug Company in Orange. Seemingly, she was set on her chosen career path.[79]

In the fall of 1942, however, shortly after Ruby's death, Lutcher, already acquainted with Nelda's administrative abilities and having observed first-hand the excellent care she had given to her sister, asked her to marry him. She flatly turned him down.[80] Being unaccustomed to being told no, he persisted. In his efforts to persuade her, he lobbied her mother, Mamie Childers, to the point of annoying her, finally prompting an exasperated Eunice Benckenstein to type an "anonymous" note to him, signing it "Dorothea [Dorothy] Dix," a noted advice columnist of the day. "No. 1," the memo read, "Let Mom alone, No. 2, If Mom calls, just be nice to her, but don't go near her, No. 3, Don't talk about Nelda, No. 4, Marry Nelda, or SHUT UP!" "I now accept the above suggestions," he wrote meekly across the bottom of the list, signed it, and sent it back to Eunice.[81]

But he incurred Nelda's anger one day as she was assisting a doctor in the hospital's emergency room by wanting her to stop what she was doing and talk to *him*. She promptly resigned as administrator of the hospital, and the two did not see each other for an entire year.[82] "I quit," she declared. "I went home. I opened a lab. I was independent."[83] She joined two Beaumont doctors in organizing an Orange branch of the Williford-Furey Laboratories of Beaumont, also serving as part owner and director.[84] Then, when Eunice Benckenstein married in October 1943, she asked Lutcher to bring Nelda to the wedding, and afterward they began seeing each other again. Two months later, they were married.[85]

After the wedding, the newlyweds departed immediately by auto for Santa Barbara, California, to spend their honeymoon over Christmas with Ida Marie and Bill Stark and close friends of Lutcher's, Helen and Tommy Hughes (née Helen Milam, Nita Stark's cousin[86]). Bill was due to leave Santa Barbara for active duty immediately after Christmas Day. Early in the morning of December 28, he came by the Starks' hotel room amid pouring rain to say good-bye before leaving from San Francisco with other servicemen to report back to active duty. "There certainly are a lot of unhappy wives around," Nelda wrote Eunice. "Bill will be a 1st Lieut. Jan. 1st," she added. "It really gives one the idea that there is a war when you are around these people out here."[87]

"Happy New Year," she wrote Eunice January 1, 1944, from Flagstaff, Arizona, as the couple headed for Albuquerque. She reported that Lutcher had developed pain in the right sacroiliac joint. "The worst is," she went on, "he has decided he has Sister's [Ruby's] trouble and is terribly worried. He always looks for the worst I know."[88] Nelda had made the decision that she would insist on the shortest route homeward. "This is an early start for us today," she went on, "but we have been doing . . . that since the back

Figure 11.10. Eunice Robinson Benckenstein, undated.
Stark Foundation Archives, Anita Cowan.

won't let us stay in bed. He . . . said he would be in for a lot of kidding if he doesn't get the back well before we get home," she added. "I hope we don't get snowed in," she ended.

Her fears were well founded; they encountered snow aplenty on the way back to Texas, necessitating a change of their route. When they left California, they bypassed their planned jaunt through Yosemite, where the roads were closed, rerouting their travels instead through Arizona, New

Mexico, and Oklahoma back to Texas. "We hit a nice day at Grand Canyon and enjoyed the view, also the Painted Desert and the Petrified Forest," Lutcher wrote to Tommy Hughes. From Albuquerque, the newlyweds attempted to head northward to Santa Fe and Taos, doubtless to visit artists and shop for art. When they reached Santa Fe, however, Lutcher reported that "the snow and ice were so terrible we immediately went back to Albuquerque and travelled our route from there."[89]

Even before they left California, they had encountered the wartime gasoline shortages. "I hasten to assure you . . . from our experience in California," Lutcher declared, "that rating B gasoline cards and having money to pay for the gas does not mean that you are going to get the gasoline."[90] They had encountered a "complete vacuum of gasoline" near Needles, California. "We were able to coast down hill about twelve miles into Needles or we would not have been able to have stretched our quarter of a tank that far," Lutcher wrote. "We kidded around for about one hour until the filling station man received his next months' supply. . . . For the life of me, I cannot see why they permit the coupon holders to get as many gallons of gas per coupon as they do out on the Pacific coast. I believe I would rather have less coupons and be assured that I might get gasoline."[91]

Winter blizzards and gasoline shortages notwithstanding, Lutcher Stark showed himself to be a happy man. "What with being married to a wonderful woman," he wrote Tommy exuberantly, "spending Christmas with Butch [Ida Marie] and Bill, you and Helen, having a wonderful trip, I would say that that season ranks with any other Christmas that I have ever known. We are continuing to find happiness each day as our lives go on."[92] When they reached home, Lutcher and Nelda found Orange still teeming with wartime activity.

> The shipyards are busy as they can be turning out war materials and I saw more LCI's or landing craft on the ways the other day. They are continuing to finish and occupy more houses daily, and I have no way of knowing just how many people we will have here;—although Doug [Pruter] shakes his head regularly and says they will never fill up all the houses, we still have no vacancies nor do we seem to have any in sight.[93]

They also found that Mamie and Jim Childers had been ill with influenza during their entire absence. "Nelda and I . . . found that her mother and father had been sick the entire Christmas holidays, and we, of course, moved in with them. We had intended to move home when Butch arrived but she got here before Mrs. Childers was able to be left and . . . we just continued to stay at 602 Orange Avenue [the Childers' home] during Mrs. Childers' convalescence."[94] Mamie, perhaps worn down by her bout of flu as well as her lingering grief over the loss of Ruby, died three months later, April 6, 1944. Nelda and Lutcher soon made their permanent residence with Jim Childers in the home on Orange Avenue, there to remain for the duration of their lives. "[Lutcher] was well satisfied to live in my home on Orange Avenue," Nelda said later, "and he told me at one time he enjoyed living there because it was a one story home and that he had always lived in two story homes before. He offered to build me a home with gold door handles and I asked him if he wanted to build a home and he said no, that the house on Orange Avenue was fine with him."[95]

After their arrival in Orange, Lutcher wrote Homer, confirming his marriage to Nelda. "This is to acknowledge your frank letter to me," he wrote.

> My communications to you have never been in the sense of an explanation, an apology or a request. I do not believe that I have ever taken a step in my life or yours without giving due consideration to the future happiness of all concerned. After five weeks of a very happy life with Miss Nelda, I can only say that I am more sure than when I first wrote you that her presence in our family will bring happiness to all and as I have looked for and confessed to you the wisdom of your choice, knowing you as well as I do, I know that you will be as free to acknowledge any mistake that you have made through any misunderstanding.[96]

Lutcher closed with the constant, heartfelt wish of them all: that Homer, Bill, and all of the boys in the service would return safely. "We fervently hope when you come home, that you will love us as much as you did when you left," he added. "That we will all be changed goes without saying, but that we will be different is not necessarily true. That we can understand each other is possible if we will only try, and there can be no doubt that we can bear for one another all of the love, honor, and respect that we each are due."[97] Lutcher wrote him again in August, giving him the latest home news. "I think I have pretty well covered the water front," he ended,

> and can only say in closing . . . Years ago your Mother and I adopted two small boys and into them and their lives we put all of our lives, our love, our thought and our efforts. . . . There is nothing in this world that can come between us which can erase the love and affection I hold for you, and nothing ever will. . . . I do not care to thrust ourselves into your lives, nor do we require any recognition other than that you choose to give. . . . I remember distinctly that I did not want my Father to interfere. I also remember that a 21 year old boy always wonders how anybody as dumb as their Dad could have lived as long as he had, and

Figure 11.11. Nelda and Lutcher Stark, undated. Stark Foundation Archives.

at 25 we are surprised how much the old man had learned in the last 4 years. When you get to be 25 I hope I will still be here, and as long as I live remember that you are my boy. Love, Dad.[98]

While the war played out on the world stage, Lutcher Stark was waging a battle of his own. His grudge against Homer Rainey, engendered when the president had refused to fire Bedichek, Shelby, and Kidd over the UIL football rules controversy, had continued to fester, accompanied by his growing disillusionment with the elemental social and cultural changes occurring in his world and the alma mater he loved. Perhaps he was also foreseeing that his power in the school's affairs, which had previously been all but absolute, was beginning to erode.

Lutcher had frequently been absent from regents' meetings, necessitated in part by the lingering illnesses and deaths of both Nita and Ruby and in part because he and Rainey "never did gee," as he put it, constantly squabbling during the meetings, and he hoped that by his staying away, "the rest would get along better."[99] But his alliance with the ultraconservative majority of regents[100]—Weinert, Bullington, Strickland, Harrison, and Schreiner—who opposed Rainey, remained unshakable and undeniable, and he ultimately played a supporting but pivotal role in the conflagration to come.

In the meantime, a major controversy was brewing between Rainey and the Board of Regents. Rainey found himself on a collision course with the board's majority, who still operated from the mandate of the original

Texas statutes, which had granted extensive powers to the Board of Regents in the absence of a president. They believed that they held the responsibility to strictly exercise those powers given to them in the statutes, as Bullington stated,

> to establish departments, determine the officers and professorships of the University, appoint persons to fill all positions it creates, prescribe their duties, fix their salaries, regulate the courses of instruction, and with the advice of the faculty prescribe the books and authorities to be used in the several departments. The Board is charged with the responsibility of conducting all the business affairs of the University and authorizing and ordering all expenditures.[101]

The regents also held the power to remove any professor, tutor, or officer when in their view the interests of the university required it. As Lutcher Stark put it, in the board's eyes, "the president of the University of Texas occupies the same position to the Board of Regents as a general manager of a corporation does to its Board of Directors."[102]

Over the years, limitations were placed on these statutory powers by rules and regulations enacted by the board itself, but often the statutes dictated one policy and the rules and regulations contradicted them. Consequently, Rainey often questioned whether the regents' actions reflected appropriate administrative procedure. It made for a confusing and potentially explosive situation, especially when the president and the Board of Regents disagreed, which was quite often. As objective an account of the series of incidents following Rainey's assumption of the presidency as is available may be found in a paper presented at the request of the Student Committee for Academic Freedom on August 13, 1945, by Henry Nash Smith, professor of American history and English at the university, titled "The Controversy at the University of Texas, 1939–1945: A Documentary History."[103]

Some of the controversies between Rainey and the regents had originated before he took office, such as the situation at the Medical Branch in Galveston, which had developed over several decades. As early as 1940, "it was common gossip," as former regent J.R. Parten later testified in Senate Education Committee hearings, "that if Dr. Rainey did not cease to give support to Dean Spies, there were certain forces that would get his, Dr. Rainey's, job as well because he was considered a little 'pink' [communistic] anyway."[104] The discharge of Spies and the sidelining of Rainey in favor of Dean Chauncey Leake had added fuel to that particular rumor.

Other issues arose between Rainey and the board as well. Shortly after he assumed the presidency of the university in 1939, he was approached by Regent Weinert, requesting that he refrain from reappointing the chairman of the university's Faculty Athletic Council, James C. Dolley, whose offense in Weinert's eyes was the manner in which he had discharged former football coach Jack Chevigny.[105] "The only basis of [Weinert's] request, as I understood it, was that Dr. Dolley was personally unsatisfactory to him," Rainey later stated, and refused Weinert's request.[106] Dolley was reappointed by the regents at their next meeting, but Rainey had earned Weinert's enmity.[107] (Another account holds that it was Major Parten who asked Dolley to resign in the interests of unanimity on the board, whereupon Dolley refused.)[108]

At the same May 31, 1940, meeting in which Lutcher Stark had unsuccessfully moved to fire Bedichek, Shelby, and Kidd, Regent Fred Branson, a recent O'Daniel appointee, moved to strike from the budget the salary of Robert H. Montgomery, a tenured economics professor, liberal New Dealer, and one of the most popular teachers on campus, effectively discharging him without a hearing. (Branson had privately confessed to Parten that his employer, Galveston insurance magnate Maco Stewart, had ordered him to fire Montgomery because he was a "dangerous subversive.") The motion was seconded by Lutcher Stark. Rainey defended Montgomery, reminding the regents that they were clearly violating their own rules of tenure by the approach they were taking.[109] Parten, at that time chairman of the board, ruled the motion out of order on those grounds.[110]

In 1942, Governor O'Daniel failed to reappoint Parten and George Morgan to the board. When O'Daniel's appointees, Bullington and Harrison, and, after O'Daniel's election to the Senate in 1941, Coke Stevenson's appointees, Strickland and Schreiner, joined the board, the conservative faction gained reinforcements, coalescing with Stark and Weinert into a solid majority. In March 1942, the regents summarily dismissed three untenured economics instructors who had attended an "open" meeting purporting to discuss the Fair Labor Standards Act. The chairman of the meeting, Dallas tycoon Karl Hoblitzelle, maintained that "the main object of the meeting is to offer every citizen an opportunity to express his sentiments concerning the important issues now before Congress."[111]

When the three instructors attended the meeting,[112] they heard misrepresentations of the act that claimed it limited laborers to only forty working hours a week, thereby decreasing production, depriving the armed forces of needed equipment, and costing American lives. The instructors requested two minutes' speaking time to correct the misapprehensions and to explain that the act "simply required the payment of overtime wages for hours of work in excess of forty hours a week." But they were denied a time to speak. The instructors then made a statement to the *Dallas Morning News* to the effect that "the meeting was not spontaneous but was well organized. . . . Volunteer speakers were refused permission to address

The Board of Regents

JOHN H. BICKETT, JR., Dallas

K. Y. AYNESWORTH, Waco

H. H. WEINERT, Seguin

W. S. SCHREINER, Kerrville

H. J. LUTCHER STARK, Orange

D. F. STRICKLAND, Mission

ORVILLE BULLINGTON, Wichita Falls

MRS. I. D. FAIRCHILD, Lufkin

D. J. HARRISON, Houston

Figure 11.12. The University of Texas Board of Regents, 1944. This board effected the dismissal of President Homer P. Rainey in October of that year. *Cactus,* 1944, yearly publication of Texas Student Publications (now Texas Student Media), University of Texas.

the meeting. . . . The speakers were . . . selected on the basis of their particular viewpoints . . . [and] Organized Labor was the object of particular and consistent condemnation by speakers."[113]

On review, the Budget Council of the Department of Economics found that the instructors acted "strictly in accordance with their rights and privileges as citizens and as teachers as . . . described in . . . the rules and Regulations of the Board of Regents for the Government of the University of Texas."[114] At their board meeting in June 1942, in defiance of recommendations from the Budget Council, the dean of the College of Arts and Sciences, the vice president, and president, the regents refused to rehire them.[115] After that month's regents' meeting, they issued a statement that the instructors "have violated the Rules and Regulations of the Board of Regents for the Government of the University of Texas. They were not re-employed."[116] Only full and associate professors were entitled to a hearing when terminated against their will, and these men were instructors and assistant professors. Having no recourse, they left the university. At that point, the American Association of University Professors, suspecting that the instructors' academic freedoms had been violated, began an investigation into the goings-on at the university.[117]

The regents' meeting of January 1943 was fraught with drama and conflict. Judge D.F. Strickland introduced a resolution requiring all faculty and staff to complete a questionnaire designed to determine "whether any members of the university community cherished unpatriotic or subversive attitudes," but the board declined to adopt it.[118] Then, in the most blatant threat to academic freedom yet proposed, Strickland introduced another resolution, this one aimed at crippling the rule of tenure itself—"a long established and recognized policy in all first-class educational institutions," as Rainey described it.[119] Strickland's resolution proposed to eliminate the section delineating the conditions of faculty tenure and the right of faculty members to a hearing of charges made against them before they were dismissed. The changes also removed the nonteaching staff, including Rainey, from tenure's protection.[120]

When Rainey requested that Strickland withdraw his resolution, the latter shot back: "I doubt the wisdom and propriety of you, as President of the University, urging or suggesting that a member of the Board of Regents refrain from doing anything whatsoever that such Regent might think proper in connection of the performance of his official duties."[121] The matter was referred to the state attorney general's office, which upheld the university's right to employ the rule of tenure.[122] At Rainey's request, the resolution was tabled until a faculty committee, in consultation with the board, drew up a revised version of the tenure rule, which the board adopted. Rainey himself congratulated the faculty committee on a job well done: "I think the final adjustment of this matter is satisfactory, and preserves the fundamental principle of our tenure system." (Later, he criticized the revised rule as being weaker than the original but explained his conflicting attitudes by maintaining that, although it was inferior to the previous rule, it was preferable to Strickland's resolution, and at least a tenure rule of sorts had been instituted.)[123]

By far the most infamous incident to arise during that meeting of January 1943 concerned *The Big Money*, the final work in *U.S.A.*, a trilogy by American writer John Dos Passos, listed as supplementary reading for a course in sophomore English. The regents took upon themselves the role of censors qualified to determine proper reading for sophomore "boys and girls," as Bullington termed them.[124] (Actually, many were newly returned war veterans who had resumed their education.) "About 1,400 or 1,500 pages of that book are filled with filth and obscenity," Bullington declared. "No teacher who would put that book in for a sophomore to read is fit to teach in a penitentiary or reform school—let alone the university. . . . As long as I'm a regent I'm going to repress that book and put out any teacher who teaches it."[125]

In a statement to the press, Bullington pointed out that in a poll conducted by the *Saturday Review of Literature,* Rainey had called the *U.S.A.* trilogy among the best American novels of the previous twenty years. "I am so profoundly and deeply concerned and disappointed in [Rainey's] attitude," Bullington declared, "that this alone, in my judgment, renders him unfit to be President of the University."[126] An account issued by members of the university's English Department maintained, however, that

> *The Big Money* is a serious book dealing specifically with the disintegration of character resulting from life lived on a level of brutality, without standards and without idealism. . . . *U.S.A.* is generally regarded, by teachers and critics of contemporary literature, as among the great novels of our generation. It is generally regarded, by these teachers and critics, as a highly moral book in which immorality is introduced only to show its hideousness.[127]

Because of the escalating controversy, a faculty committee in the English Department decided to drop the book from the course. But Bullington persisted, subjecting the committee and the chairman of the English Department to a two-hour examination that ended with the question, "Do you know what person was responsible for the proposing of *The Big Money?*"[128] Throughout, Strickland kept repeating that "he wanted to fire someone," but members of the committee never revealed the name or names of the persons responsible.[129] (In fact, the work had actually been chosen by joint decision of a committee of English faculty.) Deprived of a scapegoat, the regents were left with no choice but to pass a resolution banning the book from the reading list of any course taught at the university.[130]

In actuality, according to the committee's report, the regents' action made the work the most popular book in Texas, and within a short time it could not be found in any bookstore in the state.[131] Supposedly, Lutcher Stark bought out the stock of many bookstores and then distributed the book to any and all takers to demonstrate its moral depravity.[132] (At the time, the *U.S.A.* trilogy was widely taught in other American colleges, and in 1998, the Modern Library ranked it as one of the one hundred best English-language novels of the twentieth century.)

Tensions between Rainey and the board continued to escalate during the remainder of 1943 and into 1944. On July 15, 1944, the president submitted a plan for the university's future development, among his recommendations relocating the University Medical Branch from Galveston to Austin, an action generally regarded unfavorably by the regents, who postponed action on the motion.[133] That fall, Strickland, after conferring with Schreiner and chairman of the board Judge John H. Bickett (who had joined the board in 1942), sent word to Rainey through Vice President Alton Burdine that "he [Rainey] was making too many speeches that did not concern university business. He's running all over the country making speeches to religious groups." The *Austin American* published a report of the episode, although Strickland later denied mentioning the subject of religion.[134]

The publicized incident proved to be the catalyst that triggered the final crisis. On October 12, 1944, Rainey called a meeting of the faculty and presented a dramatic sixteen-point catalog of instances wherein he accused the regents, either individually or as a board, of improprieties in carrying out their official duties.[135] "A critical situation has developed between the University Administration and the Board of Regents," he began. "Matters have developed to the point . . . where I believe that only a statement from me will bring the facts and issues underlying the current situation into the open. . . . I regard it as my duty and obligation."[136]

He went on to state that the fundamental issues at stake were freedom of thought, research and investigation, and expression at the university, "without which it is not a university and can never become a university of the first class." He pointed out that "for centuries, universities worthy of the name have been the meeting place for conflicting ideas. It is well that this is true, for conflicts in ideas when resolved through the orderly processes of society lead to human progress. An idea, if contrary to prevailing opinions, usually gains more momentum when forced into subterranean channels through repression. I believe that history proves that the strength of democracy lies in tolerance."[137]

He proceeded to enumerate what he believed to be the regents' violations of these tenets, including the previously discussed issues as well as the regents' refusal to grant financial assistance for various research projects, mainly in the social sciences, and rejecting establishment of a new School of Social Work (apparently out of the fear that such a school would produce "bureaucrats and socialists"). He also gave full attention to Lutcher Stark's demand for the dismissal of Bedichek, Shelby, and Kidd without benefit of charges or a hearing.[138] The faculty responded with a prolonged ovation and an official vote of confidence for Rainey.[139] An editor for the *Dallas Morning News* declared that Rainey's statement "rocked [the regents] back on their heels."[140] (When later queried regarding just what he had told Rainey in their UIL confrontation, Lutcher Stark snapped, "I don't admit, explain, or deny. Why don't you ask him?")[141]

When Rainey publicly made the statement to the faculty, he threw down the proverbial gauntlet, and all efforts on his behalf would thereafter be to no avail. The Board of Regents met at the Rice Hotel in Houston October 27–28, 1944, recessed because of the death of one of the regents, Kenneth Aynesworth, one of Rainey's two supporters on the board (the other being Lufkin civic leader Marguerite Shearer Fairchild), then reconvened October 30.[142] In executive session, the regents demanded that Rainey retract his entire sixteen-point statement, and when he refused, Lutcher Stark, who had not attended a regents' meeting for the previous eleven months (except for partial attendance at one hearing), made the motion to discharge him.[143] His motion was seconded by Scott Schreiner.

The count came in at six votes to two to terminate Rainey's employment at the university, with Bickett and Fairchild casting the dissenting votes.[144] (When Lutcher was asked during later Senate Education Committee hearings if he would have voted to retain Rainey as president even if he had not made the public charges against the board, Lutcher answered simply, "No.")[145] At the regents' request, a committee of the Ex-Students' Council had traveled to the Houston meeting to attend an executive session of the board, their purpose to try to persuade both parties to "wipe the slate clean, start over, and run a university of the first class," according to its president, W.H. Francis. They appointed one of their number, Judge J.C. Hutcheson of Houston, to be their spokesperson during the meeting, but afterward, at the regents' executive session, the Ex-Students were excluded, and it was that session at which the regents fired Rainey.[146]

Late in the evening of November 1, 1944, the Board of Regents announced Rainey's dismissal on grounds that "the sixteen-point statement

. . . reflected upon the motives and good faith of the board in exercising and discharging their official duties"; that the attack on the board was "unprovoked and unexpected and calculated to discredit the Board and its members"; and that Rainey had failed to "abide by orders, rules, regulations, and policies of the Board."[147]

At the same time, the regents named Theophilus S. Painter, a faculty member specializing in genetics, as president, Lutcher Stark making the motion to hire him. Painter accepted as acting president after promising the faculty that he would not accept a position as permanent president.[148] (He later reneged on that promise by accepting the permanent position.)[149] Surprisingly, three of the regents—Bickett, Weinert, and Harrison—resigned as the meeting adjourned, and the next day Bullington and two other regents announced their own impending resignations.[150]

Word of Rainey's dismissal reached Austin late that night of November 1. The next morning a large contingent of the student body gathered in front of the Tower Building. Led by Student Association President Mac Wallace, they marched to the Capitol to demand of Governor Coke Stevenson that he invite the regents to meet with them.[151] They then set a mass meeting at Gregory Gymnasium and sent telegrams to each regent, inviting them to attend, but none accepted; the sizable crowd of students waited two hours, but no regents appeared.[152] Many of the students went on strike for the remainder of the week, refusing to attend classes. Chaos reigned among the entire university community.

After the meetings in Houston, the Ex-Students' Committee traveled on to Austin and found "the University Faculty and student body and the city of Austin in a turmoil and . . . a crisis in existence and tension terrific." On November 2, the Ex-Students met with Governor Stevenson and recommended that he accept the resignations of the six regents who had either resigned or were promising to resign and that he refrain from reappointing them. In fact, the committee recommended that in the best interests of the university, the entire board resign, advising the governor to appoint in their stead persons who possessed "character, cultivated minds, openmindedness, thoughtfulness, broadness of viewpoint, without prejudice, non-political in approach, capable of acting on the facts after deliberation and of reaching sound and objective conclusions, and deeply interested in building and maintaining in the University of Texas a University of the first class." "As I view it," Francis concluded, "you can't settle issues between factions by the same men who created them." Nevertheless, the three regents who had promised to resign did not, nor did the remaining board members.[153]

On November 3, 1944, an estimated five thousand students (some estimates run as high as eight thousand) paraded through downtown Austin

Figure 11.13. University of Texas students rally in front of the Tower on November 3, 1944, to support recently dismissed president Homer P. Rainey. Dolph Briscoe Center for American History, University of Texas at Austin, Prints and Photographs Collection, UT-Rainey Controversy, di_04254l

to the slow beat of muffled drums and the mournful strains of Chopin's "Funeral March," played by the Longhorn Band, following a black-draped coffin figuratively containing the corpse of Academic Freedom. That day, the faculty passed a resolution requesting the reinstatement of Rainey to the presidency.[154] Not surprisingly, on November 9, the Southern Association of Colleges and Secondary Schools appointed a committee to probe the emergency at the university.[155]

The board as a whole never issued a statement regarding the matter, but Regent Orville Bullington released his own lengthy individual statement, "Reasons for My Vote," in which he attempted to refute each of Rainey's "complaints," as he termed them. His statement was also endorsed by Regents Stark, Strickland, and Schreiner.[156] Regarding Strickland's telephone call to Burdine, Bullington hastened to point out that "no order from any individual regent is valid and binding on the Board"; therefore, whatever Strickland had said to Burdine was irrelevant to the actions of the entire board.[157]

Bullington gave as a reason for the board's refusal to rehire the three economics faculty members that they had violated one of the university's rules by showing a lack of proper respect for "rights, feelings, and opinions of others," calling their conduct "discourteous and disrespectful" and going "far beyond the bounds of propriety." He defended the revised tenure rule and maintained that the board had not violated academic freedom in removing Dos Passos's *The Big Money*, that "obscene and filthy volume," from the sophomore English reading list.[158] He went on to dispute the remainder of Rainey's points and raised new charges as well: that the former president had recommended several teachers for employment at the university "who were unworthy of their high profession," including a conscientious objector and two accused homosexuals.[159]

Bullington concluded by stating the board's generally held principles, among them that the president "has a responsibility as the hired executive of the Board of Regents." "There can be little doubt that powerful forces in and outside of Texas have inspired and are directing this attack upon the freedom and independence of the University," he hinted darkly, "and the right of the people to guide and direct and develop it into a University of the first class, through their own lawfully chosen Trustees and Representatives, the Board of Regents." Bullington later named those "outside forces" as the American Association of University Professors and the American Civil Liberties Union. "The AAUP is behind it," he declared. "That attack on the board was planned like a military campaign."[160]

In the meantime, Senator Penrose Metcalfe, the chairman of the Senate Committee on Education, convened his committee on November 16–28, 1944, to hold an investigation of the crisis at the university. The hearings were conducted over an eight-day period, with some sessions lasting ten hours a day.[161] Testifying were the remaining regents, including Lutcher Stark; Rainey; Vice President Burdine; several faculty members, including Bedichek and his two longtime friends, historian Walter Prescott Webb and writer J. Frank Dobie; Ralph Himstead, the secretary general of the American Association of University Professors; and Col. Homer Garrison, chief of the Texas Department of Public Safety (who had been brought into the controversy when the charges against homosexuality, at that time by law a criminal offense, had been levied against the two accused faculty members).[162]

During the hearing, new charges were brought into play by some of the regents. Bullington addressed the issue of the supposed immorality at the university, "the sordid and tedious details . . . [of which]," Henry Nash Smith declared in his report, "I shall pass over without further comment." (After Bullington had completed his testimony, one senator asked him in revulsion, "Any other dirty thing about the university you want to volunteer?")[163] Homer Garrison, however, testified that "Dr. Rainey had followed the best possible course in the matter." Strickland charged that communism was being taught and made a "rather vague contention that Dr. Rainey's views on the Negro race question were 'too liberal' for a Southern university president."[164] To that charge, Rainey replied prophetically, "I am a friend of the negroes and happy to be called a friend of theirs. We ought to be working to give them better existence. The racial problem is one of the greatest facing us. It cannot be solved by extremes on either point of view but by people with tolerant attitudes." Two economics professors who had been accused of teaching communism summarized their remarks on the questioned occasions, and Smith commented, "I believe I am warranted in saying that the issue proved, on examination, to be fictitious . . . [and] the same is true of Judge Strickland's criticisms of President Rainey's attitudes toward the Negro."[165]

In his testimony to the Senate Committee's direct questioning regarding his issues with the UIL, Lutcher Stark stated that his sons' eligibility to play football their senior year had not been affected by the April 1940 change in rules. Subsequently, in his own testimony, Bedichek accused Lutcher of lying to the committee, declaring that he, Bedichek, supported then-President Rainey's statement in his October 12, 1944, address to the faculty, in which Rainey stated, "Mr. Stark's reason for urging their [Bedichek's, Shelby's, and Kidd's] removal was *due, as he [Lutcher Stark] said, to the part which they had played in changing the rules of the Interscholastic League which affected the eligibility of his two sons who were then Seniors in Orange High School.*"[166] Bedichek himself attended the hearings for the express purpose of backing Rainey's statement and contradicting Lutcher's testimony.[167] (As Bedichek wrote later, "I am mean enough to take some pleasure in proving that he [Lutcher Stark] lied on the witness stand.")[168]

There is a possibility that Lutcher could have been telling the truth. Notwithstanding the A Conference's vote to reinstate the eight-semester rule, the eligibility of the Orange High School seniors could still have been preserved because, in their eighth-grade year, their "C" team had played only the three local elementary schools and had participated in no UIL play whatsoever.[169] It is possible that UIL officials had ruled this to be a mitigating circumstance and had thus allowed the Orange seniors to play football during their twelfth-grade year. No record of such a ruling, if indeed there was one, has been found to date, and the true sequence of events may never be known. But for whatever reason, Homer, Bill, and the other seven Orange High School seniors did in fact play football their senior year. And as was his custom, Lutcher did not admit, explain, or deny.

Figure 11.14. Lutcher Stark with his adopted twins, Homer (*left*) and Bill (*right*), both Orange High School football stars who played the 1940 season their senior year. Stark Foundation Archives.

Homer Rainey himself stated afterward that in the course of the hearing, Lutcher Stark "summarized the [entire] problem succinctly":

Now, all this controversy stems from one fundamental thing. . . . It started when Dr. Rainey came . . . to the University as President. And simply stated, it's just this: The Board of Regents . . . take an oath of office in which they swear to uphold the statutes and the laws. . . . Those laws are very plain. . . . Here and now I should like to adopt Orville Bullington's statement of the situation as he made it very lengthily today. I concur in every word he said, but those are just instances of the problem. On the other hand, Dr. Rainey came to the University thoroughly imbued with the idea of making a great university *under the generally accepted academic practices.* Well, now, those two things clash, that's where we got into trouble and that's where we will always get into trouble. That's the meat in the whole cocoanut.[170]

During the course of the entire debacle, it was made abundantly clear that the group of regents then in the majority at the University of Texas paid little homage to the established principles of academic tradition as observed by the great universities. As Lutcher had put it, the ideas of Rainey and the majority of the regents, including Lutcher himself, differed diametrically regarding the very concept of the University of Texas and the tenets by which it should be governed—what in fact constituted the essence of that elusive Holy Grail, that "university of the first class" envisioned by the makers of the 1876 Texas Constitution, and each faction in the conflict had repeatedly invoked that vision in defense of its own ground. Yet at that low point in the university's history, never had it seemed so unattainable.

"I hope the people and forces now at work trying to solve the situation will be successful," Vice President Burdine warned, "so that the dishonor of being censured and blacklisted by all of the nationally recognized educational associations may be avoided in view of the fact that an institution so censured generally cannot recover its prestige short of a generation."[171] Nevertheless, the Senate Committee failed to make a report on the hearing, which has been variously described as "the most dramatic incident in the history of the University of Texas," and none was made during the following session of the legislature.[172]

During the January 26, 1945, board meeting, a faculty committee as well as members of the Students' Association and the Ex-Students' Association petitioned the regents to reinstate Rainey when they hired a permanent president, but their efforts were unsuccessful; Regent Schreiner moved that all the petitions be denied. The motion carried, even though several members of the board had not yet received Senate confirmation.[173] Rainey's career at the University of Texas was officially—and finally—ended. After an unsuccessful run for governor in 1946, he became president of Stephens College in Missouri, then joined the faculty in the Department of Education at the University of Colorado at Boulder. He died in 1985.[174]

The conservative block on the university's Board of Regents had won the battle; they had accomplished their aim of ridding the university of Homer Rainey. But it proved to be a Pyrrhic victory; following Rainey's dismissal, on July 22, 1945, the Southern Association of Colleges and Secondary Schools placed the university on probation "until such time as the Association is assured of full observance of its principles and standards."[175] The association lifted the probation after a year's time, but Phi Beta Kappa condemned the actions of the regents, and in the spring of 1946, the American Association of University Professors, described as one of the "highest-ranking educational associations in the United States," took punitive action as well, placing the school on its list of censured colleges and universities, where it remained for a full nine years.[176] As Burdine had feared, the damage done to the university by the entire controversy—to the school's reputation among academic institutions, to its ability to recruit and retain the highest-quality professors, and in many other ways—would be felt for years.[177]

Lutcher Stark, disillusioned and embittered by the fight and the repercussions of the Rainey controversy and perhaps foreseeing the waning of his power at the university in the face of the drastic changes taking place at the school and in the world, was present at the January 1945 regents' meeting to cast his vote to deny reinstatement to Rainey. When his term expired on January 10 of that year, he was not reappointed, nor did he campaign for a spot on the new board.[178] In the Senate hearings, he had already stated his belief that "I doubt I'd get by the senate [for confirmation]."[179] And as he approached the end of his career as a regent, he began curtailing his customary gifts to the university.[180]

"I have been very much distressed by recent events, because through the years you have been my friend and the friend of this office," Arno "Shorty" Nowotny, then acting dean of student life, wrote Lutcher. "I hate to see that you are not at present officially connected with our Board of Regents. I hope the time comes when things will return to normal, and you can serve us once more." Nowotny added a handwritten note: "You are to me one of the finest Regents the University of Texas has ever had. We have not always agreed, but I know your actions are always what you believe to be to the best interests of the University."[181]

Although Lutcher Stark had once been described by university history professor Joe Frantz as a man who "seemed likely to outlast the university," his life was shortly to turn in new directions.[182] He continued supporting the educations of individual students, but much of his attention turned toward home.

In 1944, President Franklin Roosevelt won election to an unprecedented fourth term, but he would not stand at the nation's helm through the war's climax and resolution: on April 12, 1945, he died, stunning the nation. It fell to the new president, the unassuming, plain-spoken Harry S. Truman, to make the final decision to drop the newly developed atomic bomb, first on Hiroshima on August 6, then, when Japan still refused to surrender, on Nagasaki on August 9. Five days later, on August 14, Impe-

US NAVAL STATION AND RESERVE
FLEET AT ORANGE, TEXAS.

Figure 11.15. US Naval Station and Reserve Fleet at Orange, Texas, undated. At war's end, the US Navy expanded its base in Orange to house the fleet. Stark Foundation Archives.

rial Japan surrendered unconditionally, and on September 2, 1945, Japan signed a formal surrender to Allied forces. America's Greatest Generation had triumphed; the deadliest war in world history was over for good, and the nation—and the world—rejoiced.[183]

When the news was received in Orange, all the whistles blew and horns of every kind sounded in celebration as people poured into the streets in their joy and relief.[184] Homer and Bill Stark, Howard Williams, Roy Wingate, Leon Parish, Joe Rougeau, and Red Moore, among others, received honorable discharges and returned safely home to live out their lives in their hometown, their memories forever alive with their experiences in the greatest, deadliest war in world history and their comrades-in-arms who did not return.[185] Tommy Hughes, writing Lutcher late in August 1945, doubtless expressed the feelings of the entire Stark family when he declared, "It is impossible for me to say just how thankful I am that both [Homer and Bill Stark] came through this thing in good shape."[186]

After the war's end, Eri Kull, a young German woman who had formerly been employed as a governess for Homer and Bill Stark during their childhood, wrote to "Mrs. and Mr. Stark," apparently unaware of Nita's death. "[I] should very much like to know where Bill and Homer are, what they were doing and if they had been soldiers in this terrible war," she wrote. "It was highest time, that the war came to an end. Everybody was happy, when the Americans arrived in our town. They came just in time. We couldn't have endure any longer all those awful things, we had to go through. It was like in hell. We hated [Hitler] from the beginning," she went on, "and my father and [I] had been announced [denounced] by the Gestapo, because we had Jewish friends and heard the American Radio and didn't give our vote to that murderer."[187]

After the war, America slowly settled into a new norm, different from the old in many ways, for life would never be quite the same again; faces were missing from family circles, and permanent injuries, not all of them physical, haunted victims and their families for the rest of their lives. In postwar Orange, the pace of daily life slowed after the war's frenzied activity, and the population decreased by half.[188]

Lutcher Stark stepped in to assist when and where he was able. In 1942, he donated $250,000 in real estate to the Orange Independent School District for new junior and senior high schools. And in the face of a diminishing postwar shipbuilding industry, he and his cousin Edgar Brown, in a rare spirit of cooperation, collaborated on taking a leading role on the Industrial Development Committee, formed by a group of Orange citizens aiming to attract new industry to the city—within the realm of possibility, since the area offered land, water, transportation, and natural gas. Lutcher Stark and Edgar Brown, as the area's largest landowners, assumed the responsibility of ensuring that land for industrial development was attainable at affordable prices.[189]

In 1944, negotiations were completed with E.I. DuPont de Nemours and Company, which built the first of several chemical plants in Orange— a huge economic boost for the city—and the $22 million DuPont Sabine River Works at Orange entered its planning stages. (In January of that year, Lutcher received another gratifying piece of news, this one personal to him: the Orange School Board had renamed Orange High School after him; henceforth it would be known as Lutcher Stark Senior High School. "I was more than pleased," he wrote Homer, "and hope you will be likewise.")[190]

Construction of the DuPont plant began in 1945, and it commenced operations in July 1946, manufacturing "intermediates," a component of nylon, which was a highly desired commodity during the war, not least for the manufacture of women's hosiery.[191] DuPont's construction marked the genesis of a complex of petrochemical plants located just outside Orange that became known as "Chemical Row."[192]

Lutcher was commended years later by Robert W. Akers, then editor of

Figure 11.16. Edgar W. Brown Jr. (*left*) and Lutcher Stark (*right*) collaborated on Orange's Industrial Development Committee, formed to attract new industry in the face of dwindling shipbuilding, undated. Stark Foundation Archives.

the neighboring *Beaumont Enterprise*, for his policy of offering fair land prices to the various chemical companies to encourage them to build the plants in Orange. Akers also praised him for offering reasonable deals for city rights-of-way and development for new commercial and residential areas. "To say it plainly," Akers went on to state, "Lutcher Stark has in this past decade made a fine record of enlightened capitalism. One definition

Figure 11.17. E.I. DuPont de Nemours Sabine River Works, Orange, Texas. Stark Foundation Archives.

of capitalism is 'the use of wealth to create more wealth.' In Mr. Stark's case, wealth is being used to assist everyone in his home community to create more wealth." Akers concluded, "An orchid for Mr. Orange."[193] In May 1954, Lutcher donated land for Orange's new $2.5 million, 160-bed Memorial Hospital, with groundbreaking ceremonies held November 1 of that year.[194]

CHAPTER TWELVE

Shangri-La

Ever since I was a boy I've wanted to develop this particular garden area.
I'm working with nature, trying to paint this scene with the most beautiful
colors nature will give me.
—LUTCHER STARK, ON BUILDING SHANGRI-LA[1]

O n December 8, 1947, Lutcher Stark marked his sixtieth birthday. Throughout the hardships and chaos of the Great Depression and the Second World War, he had survived successive rapid-fire personal traumas—the illnesses and deaths of his parents and two wives in a span of only six years. His involvement with the University of Texas had ended in estrangement and bitterness, and, although the university continued to court him periodically, he could not—or would not—return to its fold. He had relinquished his sponsorship of the Bengal Guards, another all-consuming interest that had lain close to his heart.

Although his physical vitality was diminishing, his enormous store of native mental energy continued to drive him in his perennial efforts to perfect his world—or, as one editorial more kindly put it, "his never-ceasing quest for ways in which he might make things better for his fellow men."[2] Perhaps, in view of such fundamental changes in his life, it was natural that he retreated to the one element that had been a constant from his childhood: the natural world.

It is probable that the seed of his idea for creating his own personal Utopia grew from a 1933 best-selling sensation by English novelist James Hilton called *Lost Horizon*. Written as escalating frictions were propelling the outside world ever closer to another global war, Hilton's book spun a tale of Shangri-La, a fabled Himalayan paradise ruled by Tibetan lamas, where time stood still and peace, beauty, and kindness reigned supreme. The book, a smashing success, was followed in 1937 by a movie directed by legendary director Frank Capra and starring Ronald Coleman, Jane Wyatt, and Sam Jaffe. (Unlike the book, the movie was not well received at first, but as time went on, it became a cult favorite.)[3]

Lutcher had certainly read *Lost Horizon* and had probably seen the movie, prompting him to name his garden retreat after the mythic land featured in both.[4] He had viewed the great gardens of Europe as well and had doubtless seen two of the most famous estate gardens in the South, Bellingrath Gardens in Alabama and Hodges Gardens in Louisiana, both of which lay within easy drives from Orange.[5] Perhaps the idea of building a Shangri-La of his own offered welcome solace to him, and, significantly, it would be a world of his own creation, where, excepting only the vagaries of nature, he could exercise total control.

It is impossible to determine exactly when Lutcher first solidified his intent. In the late 1930s, he and Nita had planned to build a house on a choice wooded tract of Stark family land on Adams Bayou, just west of downtown Orange, where he had spent many of his childhood hours.[6] Noted Houston architect John Staub had already drawn up plans for the house, but the project had been brought to an abrupt halt by Nita's death in October 1939. "I had so long looked forward to collaboration with you and Mrs. Stark in the building of a house," Staub wrote Lutcher shortly after her death, "and you, no doubt, understand that in addition to the great sorrow, there is the keen regret that the house may never materialize."[7]

"I want to . . . thank you for your many courtesies, kindness and patience with Nita during the time she was planning this home," Lutcher wrote in reply.[8] As Staub had predicted, the house was never built, but ultimately it was this tract of land, a mixed pine-hardwood forest abutting a cypress-tupelo swamp, where Lutcher decided to build his Shangri-La.[9]

He launched actual construction of the gardens in early 1942, with planting implemented that fall.[10] He himself designed and supervised road and path building through the moss-shrouded woods, buying up waste concrete and bricks from demolished buildings in Orange to use as material.[11] ("Look at those roads," Michael Hoke, the first managing director of present-day Shangri La Botanical Gardens and Nature Center, declared sixty years later. "They're as well-engineered as they could possibly be—no one could have built them better than Lutcher Stark. They're still flat as tables. And the drainage is wonderful—it retains the wetlands.")[12]

Lutcher dredged the site of a natural spring, where normal drainage already collected, to form a twenty-acre lake. He named the new body of water "Ruby Lake" after the quiet, smiling woman who was then his wife and who was at that time in the throes of her final illness.[13] (She died before the lake was finished.) Later that summer, he stocked the lake with black bass, perch, and crappie he had hauled in from Louisiana.[14] Above

Figure 12.1. Frog ponds being constructed at Lutcher Stark's Shangri-La in Orange, undated. He pitched in to assist in the construction. The cobblestones were imported from Bordeaux, France. Stark Foundation Archives.

all, he particularly instructed his employees to avoid harming the existing trees.[15]

He labored alongside his workers, always lending a hand where it was needed, even pitching in to help build the frog ponds.[16] As Roy Wingate passed by the gardens in the mornings on his way to work, he often saw Lutcher "on his hands and knees, pulling grass from the plants, raising Cain with the guys that they hadn't done it right the first time."[17] Ann Raborn remembered that "Lutcher was always there in his khaki trousers, talking about the ducks or the new plants he had planted, or commenting that 'this azalea is named this; this camellia is named this'—he knew the names of all the plants."[18] Every day found him working at the site. After their marriage, he and Nelda ate dinner almost every night with Eunice Benckenstein, widowed in 1946, who had moved into a house only a block away from the gardens and who employed a live-in cook.[19]

Lutcher proceeded to stock Shangri-La with myriad flora and fauna, buying giant patriarch azaleas, camellias, and magnolia trees during automobile forays to Louisiana and Mississippi and as far away as Alabama, Florida, and Georgia, then hauling them into the gardens by truck or rail. Several of the 'Alba Plena' camellias he brought from Woodville, Mississippi, were over a hundred years old, one with a trunk over four feet in circumference.[20] He dug no holes for the massive trees, some weighing into the tons; he simply placed them on the level ground, stacked rotted oak firewood around the bases, and mounded earth around them, sloping it gradually, then extending the lawn to cover them, "giv[ing] the garden the effect of being on gently rolling land," according to one writer.[21]

He planted sweet olive, snowflakes, jonquils, and narcissus by the thousands throughout the gardens and lined Ruby Lake with water-loving Louisiana iris. Near the lake, he created an area he dubbed the "hanging gardens," featuring varied collections of crinum, daylilies, iris, and amaryllis, which he planted in huge, ancient sugar kettles he brought in from Louisiana sugarcane plantations.[22] He transplanted several thousand young dogwood trees into a wooded tract adjoining the formal gardens.[23]

Shangri-La soon teemed with countless species of wildlife—herons, egrets, roseate spoonbills, ducks of all varieties, water turkeys, squirrels, opossums, raccoons, rabbits, foxes, otters—most of them native species that simply took up residence in the gardens. Some he imported: swans, Canada geese, and even 250 white squirrels from Mexico that he had bought from a nurseryman in Fredericksburg, Texas.[24] (For years af-

Figure 12.2. Lutcher Stark with a patriarch camellia he is transplanting into Shangri-La, early 1940s. Stark Foundation Archives.

Figure 12.3. Workers installing sugar kettles purchased by Lutcher Stark in Louisiana.
Stark Foundation Archives.

terward, their descendants could be spotted in Orange.)[25] He later established a herd of Texas Longhorn cattle, initially numbering thirteen but
later growing to as many as thirty, which he kept in a pen in Shangri-
La.[26] He regarded them as his pets, frequently visiting their pen, talking
or singing to them (one of the songs he sang was "Down in the Valley," according to one witness) and sometimes even strolling among them.[27]

Stark employee Felix Anderson, who helped build the gardens, remembered driving with Lutcher past the barn where the Longhorns were kept
and seeing two of them fighting. "I've got to break them up," Lutcher declared. "They'll fight to the death." He drove close to the herd and parked,
telling Anderson, "You stay in the car." "Trust me," Anderson promised,
"I'll be right here." Pulling out a .30-30 pistol, Lutcher walked into the
herd, firing repeatedly into the air. It took a few minutes, but the gun's reports finally succeeded in breaking up the fight. "What's going on?" another employee asked Anderson afterward. "Sounded like a small army
out there."[28]

From Louisiana, Lutcher trucked in lemna, or duckweed—minuscule
three-leaf floating water plants—as food for the flocks of ducks, geese, and
swans that made Shangri-La their home. Anderson remembered that, as
they dumped the lemna into the lake, the waterfowl came crowding up to
eat it. "They would eat half a load, seems like, before we could get it unloaded," he recalled. "Those little old beaks on top of the water, you could
hear them just a-flapping." Lutcher paid Anderson for catching bullfrogs
to relocate into the lake. "He would count every one of them," Anderson
said. "He'd take them out one at a time and set them on the bank; they'd
hop off in the water. . . . [He] gave me fifty cents apiece." Lutcher inquired

Figure 12.4. Lutcher Stark's Longhorn cattle in Shangri-La. He treated them as pets, often walking among them and sometimes even singing to them. Stark Foundation Archives.

Figure 12.5. Lutcher Stark brought swans into Shangri-La, among many other species of wildlife, undated. Stark Foundation Archives.

Figure 12.6. Lutcher Stark purchased huge logs of petrified wood from the
East Texas Piney Woods and hauled them into Shangri-La, undated but ca. early 1940s.
Stark Foundation Archives.

of Anderson if he could obtain alligators. Anderson bought seven small
gators from a man in Bridge City, and Lutcher gave him a hundred-dollar
bill for the lot.[29]

He installed greenhouses and bought and transported giant four
hundred–pound Philippine bivalve shells, "looking like the teeth of some
prehistoric monster," as one observer said, into Shangri-La, as well as
massive trunks of petrified trees from the East Texas forests.[30] "You probably realize that I do not care to argue about the price," he informed the
owner of one petrified stump. "If it is too high, it is still your stump. . . . If
it comes within what I would think it [would be] worth to me, you would
make a deal."[31] He imported the stones bordering the frog ponds from
Bordeaux, France; they were said to have been walked on by Joan of Arc.[32]

Taking his cue from the movie version of *Lost Horizon*, which featured
bells ringing as the lost travelers emerged into the Shangri-La Valley, he
purchased bells for his own gardens.[33] He bought the largest, an iron giant
dubbed the "Great Bell," from a Catholic church in Duson, Louisiana. It
was duly delivered at Shangri-La and unloaded at a temporary spot. When

workers prepared to move it into its permanent spot, they found that a mother duck had nested under it; Lutcher issued orders that the bell remain in place until the duck had hatched her eggs and removed her ducklings to safety.[34] A story is told that, when it was installed in its permanent spot, Lutcher struck it to make it ring. As might be imagined, its sheer size made a deafening peal, frightening all the birds in the gardens. "This," Lutcher declared, "is the first and last time this bell will ever ring."[35] As he had decreed, the bell remained silent for the next six decades.[36]

He built a swimming pool in the gardens and an enormous multistory birdhouse "estate" at the entrance that even sported a miniature television antenna on its roof. He daily provided the birds with a hundred pounds of food.[37] He bought century-old cypress fencing in Louisiana and installed it throughout the gardens. He retrieved the old millstones from the site of the Joe Mattox Mill, an old grain mill near the Stark family homestead in Burkeville, where, during the early days, John Thomas Stark had taken his grain to be ground for the family's bread making.[38]

Lutcher installed a "Dr. Campbell's Malaria-Eradicating-Guano-Producing Bat Roost," a fifty-foot shingle-covered tower, one side vented

Figure 12.7. Aerial view of Shangri-La, undated. Stark Foundation Archives.

Figure 12.8. From 1946, when Lutcher Stark opened the gardens, until 1958,
when he closed them, thousands visited Shangri-La, undated but ca. late 1940s.
Stark Foundation Archives.

with a series of louvered slats and an entrance/exit hole located midway on
the structure.[39] Shangri-La's "bat house," as it was locally known, was built
according to the design of physician Charles Campbell, San Antonio's
one-time health director, who had invented and built such structures in
the early 1900s in the hope of attracting bats to devour malaria-carrying
mosquitoes.[40] But Lutcher's own efforts might have been in vain; according to Michael Hoke, no evidence exists that bats ever lived in Shangri-La's
bat house, at least not in great numbers, probably because it stood among
trees, which are known to interfere with bats' internal sonar and navigation patterns.[41]

   Lutcher opened Shangri-La to the public in 1946, and for the next
twelve years, tens of thousands of visitors streamed through its gates on
weekends at no cost to see his phenomenal creation for themselves. Both
Lutcher and Nelda went often to the gardens to admit and greet incoming
visitors. One guest commented, "Many persons entering the gates never
learn that the smiling, white-haired man and tall, quietly tailored woman
directing visitors through the turnstiles are the owners of Shangri-La."[42]
Lutcher moved the houseboat *Ruby* into Ruby Lake and anchored it there,

and he and Nelda frequently sat on its diminutive back porch to greet passersby.

"They really loved having people come to see Shangri-La," remembered Mary Louise McKee, the wife of Clyde V. McKee, Jr., the former business manager and general counsel for the Stark interests.[43] "They would talk to them and welcome them. . . . They would go out late in the afternoon every day and watch the egrets come into Shangri-La." She added, "And that was really something."[44] A story was told that visitors could always tell if Lutcher was "in residence" on the houseboat: if he were, smoke from his cigarette would rise from the boat.[45] He remained a smoker for most of his adult life, failing early on to maintain the tobacco-free regimen for which his parents and grandparents had initially rewarded him.

At one time, according to some sources, Lutcher and Nelda actually contemplated building a home in Shangri-La.[46] As the story goes, Nelda realized that she had the prettiest view of the gardens from the vantage point of the houseboat, so they decided to build their house on a spot on the lakeshore near where the houseboat was anchored. Lutcher planned to construct a hill "taller than the cypress out there" on which to build the house, according to Felix Anderson. "At the top," Anderson recalled, "he wanted to build a half-acre dream house."[47] Lutcher and Nelda never constructed their dream house, and he only made a start on building the hill;

Figure 12.9. Nelda and Lutcher Stark on the houseboat *Ruby,* brought into Shangri-La and anchored in Ruby Lake, undated. Stark Foundation Archives, Anita Cowan.

Anderson remembered that workers later came back and capped the rise with three or four feet of clay.[48]

Anderson also recalled that Lutcher frequently pointed out the old pond cypress tree, telling him that, in roaming over the area, the local privateer Jean Lafitte had likely passed the tree, which by Lutcher's estimation was "three or four hundred years old." (In fact, at the venerable age of twelve hundred years, the tree proved to be three times that age.) "He liked teaching," Anderson said.[49] One Orange resident remembered that Lutcher invited youngsters to go with him into Shangri-La. When he wanted them to learn something, he placed a boy on each side of him as they walked through the gardens, holding their attention while he talked with first one, then the other about that day's lesson.[50] "He was a great teacher of children," Anita Cowan stated, "an explainer and a patient man."[51]

"[Lutcher Stark] always said there was nothing that couldn't be done," Anderson asserted. "Anything he went at, he did it with full intensity. He felt that that's what he needed to do; he was going to give it his best. That was one of the . . . things he tried to put across. . . . I'd like to come back and work for the Old Man," Anderson added. "Oh, I know he's not here, but it would still be like I was working for him. . . . He was quite a man."[52]

In 1949, artist Lorentz Kleiser and his wife, Constance, came to live in a secluded, wooded spot in Shangri-La in a four-room cabin that Lutcher had built for them.[53] The tiny dwelling was christened "Blue Moon Cottage" after the Valley of the Blue Moon, another name for Shangri-La in Hilton's *Lost Horizon*.[54] Kleiser, a tall, quiet man who was an internationally recognized artist and tapestry designer, had met Lutcher when a mutual friend in Houston, an admirer of Kleiser's work, introduced them.[55]

Kleiser had been born in Elgin, Illinois, of Norwegian parents, but at age five had returned with them to Norway. He spent his boyhood and young adulthood studying in Norway and Munich, then began his painting career. At twenty-one years of age he returned to America and New York, where he became interested in the art of tapestry design and weaving, and in 1913 he founded Edgewater Tapestry Looms, Inc., which won him an international reputation; thereafter, many of his tapestries were purchased for hanging in the permanent collections of museums. He continued to paint, however, and beginning in 1935 held a series of one-man shows of tapestries and paintings in art galleries throughout the United States. Finally he began devoting his entire time to painting.[56]

During the sojourn in Shangri-La, Kleiser painted landscapes of various scenes in the gardens as well as a series of images featuring the various camellia species, always in combination with a small art object—"a small vase from an Egyptian tomb or a gem-studded necklace worn by

Figure 12.10. Artist Lorentz Kleiser at Blue Moon Cottage, the small home Lutcher Stark
had built for Kleiser and his wife, Connie, within the grounds of Shangri-La,
undated but after 1949. Stark Foundation Archives.

Figure 12.11. Lorentz Kleiser, painting a scene in Shangri-La, undated. The Kleisers lived in Blue Moon Cottage at Shangri-La for thirteen years, from 1949 to 1962.
Stark Foundation Archives.

some famous *femme fatale* of several centuries past"—from the Starks' collections.[57] Lutcher did not sponsor Kleiser or retain a business interest in his work, according to one writer, but he did give him complete access to the gardens and furnish him with prize specimens of camellias that he used as the subjects of his paintings.[58] The Kleisers lived in Blue Moon Cottage in Shangri-La for the next thirteen years.

In the meantime, a fragment of unfinished business with the University of Texas remained to be settled. Although for some years Miriam Lutcher Stark's collection of rare books and manuscripts had been safely ensconced in the library bearing her name at the University of Texas, the school had so far failed to live up to its end of the bargain with, first, Miriam, then Lutcher to build a suitable museum to house the residue of the collection, consisting of Miriam's art, art objects, furnishings, and other items. Through the intervening years, the objects had remained in the elder Starks' Orange home on Green Avenue at Sixth Street, which had remained unoccupied since their deaths in 1936.[59]

Even as early as 1946, Lutcher had considered building his own museum to house the priceless artifacts, commissioning Herbert W. Winkelman, the longtime accountant for the family interests, to research the feasibility of such a project. Winkelman reported: "I have given your question considerable thought with reference to your desire to transfer 'The W.H. Stark Home' and site to a charitable literary or educational organization to be organized and operated exclusively for the purpose of establishing a museum to house certain valuable painting and art objects as a permanent public memorial for your father and mother in Orange." With the painstaking expertise for which he was noted, Winkelman proceeded to outline Lutcher's various options, but the latter did not initially move forward on any such project.[60]

He grew increasingly impatient, however, with the university's failure to act, especially in view of his damaged relationship with the school, and in 1953, he finally reclaimed the collection. He and Nelda then announced that they intended to sell the vacant Stark residence and construct a museum for the collection where the house had stood. The chancellor of the university, James Pinckney Hart, responded that the school's reason for failing to build the museum had been that, in the period of time that had lapsed since the offer had been made, it had not had available the necessary funds, and the Board of Regents had decided that "other building needs, especially classroom space, was more urgently needed." Hart went on to state that "the University is still looking into the matter, but all they can find is that Stark's offer was on condition that we would construct a suitable building to house the exhibit," in effect admitting that, for whatever reasons, the university's failure to build the museum had been the cause of its losing the collection.[61]

"There were hints here and there on the University campus . . . that the lack of suitable housing was only one reason for the loss of the collection," reported the *Austin Statesman*. "It is known that the Starks and University officials haven't exactly been achieving mental rapport during the past few years." University officials made no comment regarding that aspect of the situation; Hart said only that "we, of course, regret very much the loss of the Stark Collection—however, we are immensely grateful for everything else Mr. and Mrs. Stark have done for the University."[62] Eight months later, the Starks gave a $25,000 gift to Nelda's alma mater, formerly the College of Industrial Arts, at that time Texas State College for Women.[63]

Miriam's collection of books and manuscripts remained in her library at the university, unaffected by the various tugs-of-war being fought over the rest of her treasures. "I've wanted to build a suitable place where the public could see these things for a long time," Lutcher was quoted as saying, "but heavy federal taxes have kept me from doing it."[64] The collection remained in the otherwise unoccupied house on Green Avenue, heavily guarded and equipped with an elaborate burglar alarm system, its future and that of the house as yet undetermined. Perhaps the "heavy federal taxes" continued to deter Lutcher from carrying out his plan; in any event, he never built his own museum. But it is tempting to speculate that perhaps he retained a trace of residual reluctance to tear down his boyhood home.

L ife in Lutcher Stark's sphere was apparently never dull. According to Eunice Benckenstein, he was a "smart, smart man. He was the smartest man I believe I ever knew. He was planning and organizing . . . something all the time, all the time." Benckenstein remembered that he was capable of terrific focus—and whatever his project, it must be a hundred percent perfect. "And he saw that it was," she added. "[He was] very outgoing and very noisy; not quiet at all; never quiet. . . . He was a positive person, [with] an active mind that just worked lickety-split all the time." She also remembered his generosity, one of his lifelong defining characteristics. "He was opinionated," she added, "and ninety-nine times out of a hundred, he was right."[65]

And his world was not without its humor, intentional on Lutcher's part or not. In the 1950s, he purchased a new Cadillac, a particularly expensive model. On one of the Stark family's treks to Colorado, the radio went out. Lutcher found the nearest Cadillac dealership and asked to buy a new radio. The dealer told him that they had none in stock, that it would be necessary to order it. But Lutcher wanted a new radio on the spot. Spying another Cadillac of the same model on the showroom floor, he requested that they remove the radio and install it in his vehicle. The dealer refused, whereupon Lutcher bought the second automobile, then demanded that they remove the radio and install it in his own. Since he then owned both vehicles, the dealer had no choice but to comply. The radio was duly installed in Lutcher's original auto, and the family continued on their journey.[66]

And a story still circulates that once Lutcher was driving home from Roslyn Ranch in Colorado with his usual caravan, and Stark employee Jack Hamby was at the wheel of a station wagon following behind him, carrying employees, the art the Starks had purchased, and miscellaneous items. Coming through an intersection in Beaumont, Lutcher hit a yellow light and accelerated in order to go through it. Seeing him increase his speed, Hamby, behind him, also accelerated.

At that point, Lutcher glanced to the side of the street and saw a police car waiting there. He slammed on his brakes. Hamby, failing to see that Lutcher had stopped abruptly, crashed his vehicle into the rear end of Lutcher's auto. Lutcher's hair-trigger temper flared and he jumped out, swinging his fists, ready to fight his own employee. The policeman, seeing

Figure 12.12. Nelda and Lutcher Stark at home, undated. Stark Foundation Archives.

Figure 12.13. Nelda and Lutcher Stark admire Trubbie, charmingly framed in a car window, undated. Trubbie accompanied the Starks everywhere. Stark Foundation Archives.

a potential altercation, jumped out of his car and slapped a pair of hand-cuffs on Lutcher. "No, no, no," Hamby yelled. "It's all a mistake!" It apparently took some time for him to convince the policeman that it was an in-house problem.[67]

Lutcher himself was blessed with a lively sense of humor, and he was an indefatigable practical joker. He and James Kirby "Jimmy" Conn, the owner of an Orange furniture store and a friend of Lutcher's, played elaborate jokes on each other. Once, when Lutcher traveled to Washington, "half the town" came to the train station to see him off, including Jimmy Conn. As he was boarding the train, Conn called out, "Hey, Mr. Stark, if you need any money while you're gone, just draft on me." "And he didn't have fifty cents in the bank," Conn's wife, Charlotte, recalled. As a joke, Lutcher did draw on Conn's account—and the joke was on Lutcher himself; there were no funds in the account. Luckily, however, he owned a con-trolling interest in the bank, so Conn's lack of funds made no difference.[68]

Perhaps the best-known prank Lutcher and Jimmy Conn played on each other concerned the latter's truck, which carried the name and logo of his furniture store. Conn and his crew habitually parked the truck on West Park Avenue, across from the main entrance of Shangri-La, probably to take advantage of the free advertising afforded by the crowds going to and from the gardens. Lutcher soon tired of the truck's being parked there and called Clyde McKee. He explained the situation to McKee. "What can we do about it?" he asked. "We can put a fence around it," McKee replied, tongue firmly in cheek. Lutcher promptly called his fence crew, instructing them to go out to the truck that night and build a fence around it— with no gate. "A picture of the truck was in all the newspapers," recalled McKee's son, Clyde V. "Tad" McKee III. A week lapsed before Lutcher took down the fence, and Conn never parked the truck there again.[69]

Stories abounded concerning "Trubbie," a magnificent male golden cocker spaniel. Trubbie, whose real name was "Trouble-Go-Ferdinand," was actually owned by Eunice Benckenstein, but the dog spent most of his time with Nelda and Lutcher, who adored him and pampered him shamelessly. Nelda ordered him decorative collars from Tiffany's in New York,

Figure 12.14. Lutcher Stark and Trubbie taking in some fresh air at Roslyn Ranch, undated. Stark Foundation Archives.

and every afternoon at four o'clock, he was fed a Coca-Cola. At the annual
meetings of the Lutcher & Moore Lumber Company, he ensconced himself in the middle of the conference table until the meeting was over.[70]
And when Lutcher addressed the Bengal Guards at practices, Trubbie
could be seen sprawled at his leisure on the floor in front of the assembled—and intently listening—Guards. Since Lutcher disliked driving,
Nelda usually drove and Trubbie rode in Lutcher's lap, hanging his head
out the window.[71]

Opinions varied regarding Trubbie's disposition. Eunice Benckenstein
maintained that he was "sweet as sugar candy."[72] Mary Louise McKee, on
the other hand, declared that he was a "beautiful dog, but he bit nearly
everybody. . . . I stayed out of his way. . . . [He] was infamous. . . . You dare
not try to be friendly to him, because that was a sure invitation. He wanted
to approach you; he didn't want you to approach him."[73] "Trubbie bit me
one time," Billie Jeanne DeLane Wright remembered. "I didn't want any
part of that dog."[74]

Trubbie enjoyed a privileged position in the Stark household. Lutcher
and Nelda went frequently to Little Mexico restaurant in Orange (located
in the home on Green Avenue previously owned by the Farwell family),
and they often brought shrimp home for Trubbie. On those occasions,
Leona "Leonie" Batchan, a Stark employee, sat in the kitchen with Trubbie and fed him the shrimp by hand—the only way he would eat them.
Batchan frequently traveled with the Starks to the ranch in Colorado,
her assignment to ride in the back seat with Trubbie. At the beginning
of one trip, only a short distance out of Orange, Trubbie went to sleep
on Batchan's arm. Lutcher, glancing around, observed that Trubbie was
asleep: "Don't disturb Trubbie," he instructed her firmly. "My arm was
paralyzed," Batchan said later. "I didn't dare move, because I knew that
Mr. Stark would be mad if I disturbed Trubbie. I *never* forgot that trip."[75]

James Kirby Conn's wife, Charlotte, told the story that Lutcher, accompanied as usual by Trubbie, was considering buying a special Cadillac at a
dealership in Orange—a one-of-a-kind, enormously expensive vehicle. "I'll
buy it if Trubbie can jump up in it," Lutcher told the dealer. *Go on, Trubbie, jump up in the car*, the dealer mentally urged the dog. To no avail; Trubbie refused to jump into the car. "I won't buy anything that Trubbie can't,
or won't, get into," Lutcher declared, and the dealer lost the sale. As he
told it later, "I never wanted to kill a dog so bad in my life." A story is told
that when Trubbie died, the Starks purchased a coffin designed for a baby,
placed the dog in it, and buried him in the shady reaches of Shangri-La.[76]

CHAPTER THIRTEEN

The Cypress Tree

I am happy in a small town, and I expect to die here.
—LUTCHER STARK, SEPTEMBER 22, 1940[1]

In 1958, Southeast Texas was hit by a rare snowstorm, accompanied by a hard freeze. The harsh weather heavily damaged the region's vegetation and wreaked havoc with the plantings in Shangri-La.[2] Lutcher Stark, nothing if not a perfectionist, closed the gardens, unwilling to allow visitors to view them in their damaged state. The story persists that he was also disenchanted with the public, who often pinched and tore the plants, littered, strayed from the paths, and generally abused the gardens. His decision was probably the result of a combination of both.[3]

For the duration of his life, Lutcher never opened Shangri-La to the public again, but as he aged, he began to use it as his own personal retreat, spending more and more time in the gardens and largely leaving the family business interests in Nelda's capable hands.[4] He reserved for his own an untouched spot in Shangri-La, an area with no roads where no one else was allowed to enter, and by the hour, he sat on the bench he had placed near the ancient pond cypress, enjoying the panoply of nature so abundant in his own private kingdom.[5]

When he had built Shangri-La, Lutcher's intent had been to reclaim it from its natural state and reshape it into a cultivated, controlled garden. Shangri-La's official booklet described his aim: "Once upon a time there was a homely little frog that was transformed by love into a Prince Charming. Remember? A modern version of the fable is the story of Shangri-La of Orange, Texas. Shangri-La was born a nondescript swampland like other swamplands—but this one was loved. And like the little frog, was transformed by it."[6]

But as Lutcher's years advanced, his thinking gradually veered from the outer world of meticulously designed landscapes and show gardens to-

Figure 13.1. Lutcher Stark seated in Shangri-La, contemplating his private paradise, undated. Stark Foundation Archives.

ward nature in its purest form. He came to realize that the "homely little frog," the seemingly nondescript woods and marsh, was instead a wonderland of nature, a place of beauty in its own untouched state. "He was always a naturalist," Michael Hoke said. "I think it's . . . interesting that he preserved those areas that were really, really pristine."[7]

Lutcher's early bent toward conservation also emerged into a realization of the dangers of chemical sprays to the natural environment. "Sprays and poison are indiscriminate and they kill the good with the bad," he wrote in 1959. "[They] merely unbalance nature and in the vacuum created by them, some other plague rises up to bite us."[8] Once he refused to donate to the Orange Jaycees' plan to spray the entire county with DDT.[9] (Clyde McKee hastily resigned his membership in the Jaycees.)[10] In 1964, the year before his death, Lutcher became a founding member of the Big Thicket Association, an organization founded with the purpose of preserving the flora, fauna, and diverse ecosystems of the Big Thicket of Texas, that impenetrable but biologically significant region a little northwest of Orange through which Henry Lutcher and Bedell Moore once trekked in 1877 in search of timber.

Lutcher Stark's love of the natural world also influenced and pervaded his acquisitions in art, which he continued to collect for the duration of his life. "Though a businessman and philanthropist, he was above all a natural historian," wrote Julie Schimmel, the first curator of collections at the Stark Museum of Art. "His enthusiasm for nature focused particularly on the wildlife and vegetation of Texas and the West, but extended to art, particularly works which represented the wildlife and natural landscapes he knew firsthand."[11]

Lutcher's affinity for all things natural did indeed extend well beyond his native habitat. He had first become enamored of the vast landscapes and native flora and fauna of the American Southwest in the 1920s on the family's journeys to and from Roslyn Ranch, and in the 1940s he grew serious about collecting artworks by the American Indian and New Mexican artists of Taos and Santa Fe who depicted that world.[12] According to Sarah Boehme, current curator of the Stark Museum of Art, he acquired many works by W. Herbert Dunton in 1942, during the terminal illness of his second wife, Ruby.[13] "Very early in his art collecting, Lutcher Stark planned to have a museum," commented Boehme. "I think his idea of a museum then fueled his approach to collecting. He wanted major works of art, but he also wanted to collect artists in depth and to be able to show a range of their works."[14]

On their yearly summer treks to the ranch, Nelda and Lutcher Stark regularly steered their route through Santa Fe and Taos to meet artists and shop for art. The daughter of one artist remembered their arriving in two "chauffeur-driven touring cars," the lead car carrying passengers and the following vehicle designated for the art they acquired. "It would take us one and a half to two days to drive from Orange to Taos," Nelda remembered. "I didn't know a thing about art and didn't care. But when we went to Taos, we went to buy art. We stayed for more than a day because we couldn't get Lutcher out in a day."[15]

The Starks visited various artists' studios, often accompanied by Jane Hiatt, a Taos art dealer who was also a personal friend. "When we saw a

Figure 13.2. Lutcher and Nelda Stark at Roslyn Ranch, undated. Nelda Stark
is holding Tiny and Tim, the Starks' two Chihuahuas, wrapped up against the cold.
Stark Foundation Archives.

painting we liked, we bought it," Nelda commented later. "Lutcher did not
haggle over the price of a painting. He didn't ask for a discount or a deal. If
we wanted it, it was bought." One of the artists, Ernest Martin Hennings,
brought a carload of his paintings from Taos to Orange. Lutcher asked his
staff to name their favorites, then bought all of the paintings Hennings
had brought, directing the employees to hang them over their desks. As
authors Dean A. Porter, Teresa Ebie, and Suzan Campbell noted, "it surely
must have been a happy artist who headed back home to Taos, the back
seat and trunk of his car empty."[16] Hennings later confirmed that sentiment, writing Nelda and Lutcher: "The way you arranged my showing of
paintings in the office, with the entire staff force casting their votes for
their preferences was delightful and then your buying all five paintings
was just too wonderful for words. I certainly am happy to be represented
in your collection," he added.[17]

All told, Nelda and Lutcher Stark amassed one of the most significant
collections of nineteenth- and twentieth-century American western art
in the country by the classic masters of the genre—Frederic Remington,
Charles Russell, Albert Bierstadt, over two hundred works by Paul Kane,
some four hundred paintings and illustrations by Herbert Dunton (the latter works constituting the largest such collection in America), and many
more—as well as a large group of American Indian art, including rugs,

beadwork, baskets, and other objects.[18] They also enlarged their holdings in the 1950s and 1960s to include works by painters not yet represented in their collections, either from the artists themselves or, after their deaths, from their dealers or surviving families. These included works by Ernest Blumenschein, Oscar Berninghaus, Joseph Henry Sharp, Victor Higgins, John Young-Hunter, and Nicolai Fechin (Nelda Stark's favorite Taos artist).[19]

In a signal acquisition in 1954, Lutcher pursued his interest in the natural world in art by purchasing a five-volume set of John James Audubon's double elephant folio *The Birds of America*, which had been the artist's

Figure 13.3. Lutcher Stark relaxing in pajamas and robe, Roslyn Ranch, undated. Stark Foundation Archives.

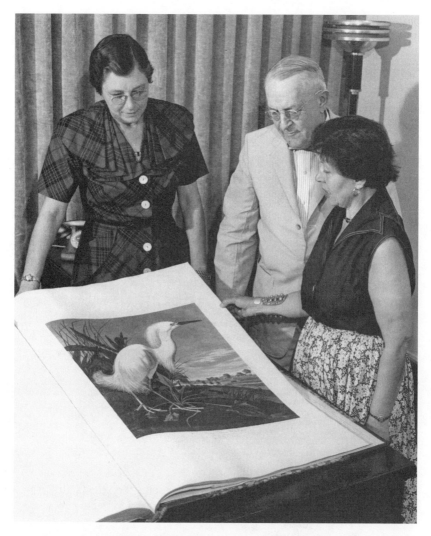

Figure 13.4. Nelda (*left*) and Lutcher Stark in 1954, admiring their purchase of the
five-volume set of John James Audubon's double elephant folio *The Birds of America*,
formerly the artist's personal property. Stark Foundation Archives.

personal property.[20] In addition to acquiring the only complete set of *The
United States in Crystal* by Steuben Glass Works, Lutcher also purchased
engraved crystal plates featuring images from Audubon's *Birds of America*,
some of which were commissioned by Lutcher himself.[21] The exquisitely wrought porcelain birds of Dorothy Doughty and Edward Marshall
Boehm reflect nature at her most beautiful, and Lutcher's love of the natural world even figured in his acquisition of seven medieval illuminated

Books of Hours, not least because he was interested in the depictions of flora in the borders of the illustrations.[22]

On June 29, 1956, Lutcher and Nelda concluded a mammoth land sale to the Largo Company, a venture of Houston oil operator John W. Mecom, for approximately $15 million. The sale constituted virtually all the Starks' holdings in South Louisiana: 213,590 acres of land, which included 142,590 acres of mineral interest, in nine parishes—Calcasieu, Cameron, Assumption, Terrebonne, Lafourche, St. Martin, St. John the Baptist, Ascension, and St. James—as well as 1,409.5 shares of common stock in the Lutcher & Moore Cypress Lumber Company.[23] The sold lands consisted mainly of cutover cypress swamp and marshland, excepting only the timberlands and acreage being developed by Lutcher & Moore's ongoing reforestation program. Also excluded from the sale were the oil- and sulfur-producing properties near Starks, Louisiana. Lutcher's net profit from the deal amounted to approximately $13.5 million.[24] The contract with Largo stipulated that in return, the Starks be granted a twenty-year exclusive lease and hunting rights on a sixteen-square-mile tract of land in Cameron Parish, bordering the Gulf of Mexico. The sheer enormity of the transaction was noted by an article in the *Orange Leader* announcing the sale: "Considerable legal work was necessary[,] covering tedious examination of titles and deeds to complete the transaction. Included were 30,000 pages of abstracts."[25] (The first well Mecom drilled on the newly acquired land came in a dry hole.)[26]

In the late 1950s, Lutcher made a last foray into the lumber manufacturing business. He built a new Lutcher & Moore mill on a 5.5-acre tract on the Sabine River at the corner of Georgia and Border Streets in Orange.[27] Including sales and administrative headquarters, the facility occupied 56 acres.[28] Its location lay within easy reach of the company's timber holdings in East Texas and Louisiana, much of which, thanks to their pioneering reforestation program, was now ready to harvest. The mill was also well situated to supply lumber to Southeast Texas retail and wholesale consumers.[29]

Slated to begin production in October 1958, the facility was touted to cut sixty thousand board feet of dry rough lumber per eight-hour day. It boasted state-of-the-art, automatic equipment, operated mainly by push-button control—an automatic debarker, a six-foot vertical bandsaw with a preselection setting device, an automatic flat-board sorter, and more. Everything in the entire facility, including the dry kiln, was mechanized.[30]

Unfortunately, the ultramodern project, built at enormous cost, was ill fated from the start. Primarily, its engineers failed to install conveyor belts to dispose of the sawdust. In addition, they had installed electric eyes throughout the facility to operate the system, but they were forced to hire a journeyman electrician to prevent sawdust from accumulating on the lenses. One thing after another went wrong with the new mill, and it never manufactured any quantity of lumber. "So Mr. Stark just shut it down," recalled Ernest Hammond "Ernie" Willey, a longtime Brown family employee and friend.[31]

Figure 13.5. Lutcher Stark, portrait by Gittings, undated. Stark Foundation Archives.

Figure 13.6. Lutcher Stark shakes hands with John Simmons (the son of Byron Simmons, Stark's longtime private secretary) at the opening of the Interstate Highway 10 Sabine River bridge, as Nelda Stark looks on, early 1950s. Stark Foundation Archives.

On June 3, 1957, with Lutcher in the audience, Texas State College for Women awarded Nelda Stark, then serving on the college's Board of Regents, an honorary doctor of laws degree—the first such award that the school had ever given—for "singularly and exceptionally high civic and humanitarian achievements."[32] And the following year, Lutcher finally returned to his alma mater. In November 1958, he was inducted into the University of Texas Longhorn Hall of Honor, then in the second year of its existence, given "in recognition of those qualities that brought credit and renown to the University of Texas."[33] Receiving the honor with him were three of the university's former football stars: Gus "Pig" Dittmar; Wilson H. (Bull) Elkins, at that time president of the University of Maryland; and the deceased Arnold Kirkpatrick, halfback of the 1910 football team at the time Lutcher had been manager.[34]

Attending the ceremony at Austin's Driskill Hotel were "two hundred Longhorn partisans and a few lonely Aggies," according to the *Austin American.* Two principal speeches were given, one an "impromptu crowd-pleaser" by the "outspoken" Lutcher Stark. Making the presentation to Lutcher was his old friend Theo Bellmont, one of the first year's inductees.

Figure 13.7. Nelda Stark (*right*) receives an honorary doctor of laws degree from the
Texas State College for Women (now Texas Woman's University), June 3, 1957.
Lady Bird Johnson is in center. Stark Foundation Archives.

Figure 13.8. Lutcher Stark (*right*) is inducted into the Longhorn Hall of Honor
at the University of Texas, Austin, Texas, November 1958. Handing him the award
is his old friend L. Theodore Bellmont. Stark Foundation Archives.

The "salty Stark," as the newspaper described him, tacitly acknowledged his differences with the university, claiming to have been kicked out of the school twice—"in fact, I don't know of anything I wasn't kicked out of," he declared to the assembled crowd—"so you can understand how surprised I was when they gave me the greatest award I could ever want."[35]

"I don't believe in any of these moral victories," he ended his unscripted talk. "I want to win! And when you say the other fellow ought to win sometimes, I say that's hooey!" Not surprisingly, with that declaration, he brought down the house. When the keynote speaker rose to make his scheduled speech, he confessed, "In case you don't know it, you've already heard the principal speaker." Lutcher's many university friends were understandably delighted. "Lutcher, I feel you've come home tonight," toastmaster Lloyd Gregory exulted. "There ought to be as much rejoicing here tonight as in a revival tent when a sinner hits the sawdust trail."[36]

"I do not know of anybody who has stood by the University of Texas more consistently, who has by personal service and financial assistance done more than you have for the progress of the University," wrote one supporter, M.L. Graves. "You have been an inspiration."[37] Texas Woman's University president John A. Guinn added his plaudits: "The people of the State of Texas will forever owe you a debt of gratitude for your fruitful dreams and labors in behalf of the University of Texas, as well as for the material support which you have bestowed upon the institution in exceedingly generous measure," he wrote. "The recognition which you were accorded . . . was more than richly deserved and I wish to offer you my heartiest congratulations."[38]

"Nothing has made me any happier than to learn of your election to the Longhorn Hall of Honor," added Lutcher's old friend Arno "Shorty" Nowotny, dean of student life, who had long hoped for the latter's reconciliation with the school. "I join a host of your friends, who congratulate you and The University of Texas for this great honor that has come to you."[39]

At that point, however, Lutcher's reconciliation with his school remained incomplete; the following January 1959, when Logan Wilson, then president of the university, invited him to join a group of ten leading alumni for a luncheon meeting for the purpose of advising the Ex-Students Association on obtaining necessary support for the university, he declined the invitation. "You have crossed the Rubicon," Lutcher responded for reasons he did not make clear in the letter. "Until you fill up that river, we will never have lasting peace and sufficient monies for the state-supported colleges and Universities. Thank you for the invitation, which of course I cannot accept."[40]

Three years later, however, he received another such overture, this one from Harry Huntt Ransom, then serving as chancellor, who requested an appointment to visit with Lutcher at his office in Orange. "I am eager to seek counsel from former regents who are an essential source of good sense about the University," Ransom wrote.[41] This time, Lutcher found himself able to accept.

In 1961, in an act rife with portent for the economic, cultural, and educational future of the entire Southeast Texas region, Nelda and Lutcher Stark established a nonprofit corporation, the Nelda C. and H.J. Lutcher Stark Foundation, its purpose to operate as a private foundation and to "encourage and assist education and to improve and enrich the quality of life in Southeast Texas." Since its establishment in 1961, the Stark Foundation has served to enrich the quality of life in Southeast Texas, in part through the continued operations of its venues—Shangri La, the Stark Museum of Art, the W.H. Stark House, and the Lutcher Theater. To date, as part of its mission, the foundation has expended more than $165 million for its various charitable purposes, assisting, improving, and enhancing the lives of countless individuals.

Two years later, in 1963, Lorentz Kleiser, aged and critically ill, and his wife, Constance, left Shangri-La and Orange for good, publishing an "Au Revoir" in the *Orange Leader*. "Dear Orange," Constance wrote,

> Sharing Shangri-La with the birds has been a soul-satisfying experience. Add hospitality and friendships and you have ideal ingredients for transplanting. . . . Comes a time, however, when health, family and long distances make it necessary to stay put in one place or the other, and after all, New York City is home town. So dear friends in Orange, we thank you for showing us how big a small town can become and is. . . . And know that "shadows appear only when you let something come between you and the Light." May we meet again.[42]

Although Constance later wrote Lutcher, Nelda, and Eunice that their trip to New York was a "miracle of good luck" in that they managed to find assistance all along the way, in reality it must have been a nightmare journey—Kleiser almost totally disabled and Constance driving the entire distance, searching every night for hotels or hospitals to accommodate his desperate condition. They arrived at the home of Kleiser's daughter in East Chatham, New York, on May 26, 1963, his eighty-fourth birthday, and two days later, he died in his sleep. "Ever has it been," Constance wrote the Starks and Eunice, quoting Kahlil Gibran, "that love knows not its own depth until the hour of separation."[43]

I nevitably, Lutcher Stark's health began to fail. He suffered from a variety of health issues, chiefly arteriosclerosis, which was diagnosed in June 1960, and from that point over the next five years, his physical and mental faculties slowly but steadily deteriorated.[44] He began to suffer from a series of small strokes, depression, some memory loss, and periods of agitation, and as he aged, he became more difficult.[45]

At home, he walked incessantly. "I've got to have some rest; come and get him and take him riding," Nelda sometimes requested of Billie Jeanne DeLane Wright. "He's restless." Wright would "ride him around, and around, and around—wherever he wanted to go."[46] During the last two years of his life, according to Clyde McKee, Lutcher felt protected by Nelda, who would not permit him to go to his office without her. His condition was made worse by stress relating to the lingering illness and death of Nelda's father, Jim Childers, who lived with them, and who, by the time of his death on May 21, 1964, was ninety-two years of age and had become "completely senile."[47]

"Mr. Stark had a slight stroke about a month ago," Eunice Benckenstein wrote Anita Cowan that August.

> There was no paralysis, no impairment of speech or anything of that sort, but his current memory is affected a little. His hearing has become very much worse too, but I don't know whether that is from the stroke or not. The doctor is giving him a vascular dilator (a pill), has urged him to drink more whiskey (which dilates the blood vessels to a helpful extent they say), and has told him not to drive. That no-drive order is a little galling to him.[48]

On June 14, 1965, Lutcher was admitted to John Sealy Hospital in Galveston under the care of his and Nelda's personal physician, Dr. Raymond L. Gregory, for treatment for congestive heart failure and emphysema.[49] He also suffered from extreme confusion and agitation, apparently complicated by his various medical issues and numerous medications.[50] Nelda and Eunice stayed at a nearby hotel for the duration. He never left the hospital.[51] Ruth Robinson Murphy, Eunice's sister, wrote Anita Cowan,

> Eunice and all the Starks are all in Galveston. . . . Mr. Stark is *very* ill—many things—circulatory trouble—breaking capillaries in the brain (causing extreme confusion and non-awareness)—prostate gland and kidney trouble, diabetes, a heart condition—emphysema (*very* bad)—They had no idea how long he might be in the hospital when I left there a week ago—the doctors call it a *terminal* illness—he *can't* improve much—he could go in 5 minutes—or five years—they just don't know—but it really *is* serious.[52]

Lutcher's condition continued to worsen, and he died at 1:20 p.m., September 2, 1965, in John Sealy Hospital of respiratory and cardiac arrest.[53] His last rites were held at 5:00 p.m. on September 3, the day following his death, at Claybar Funeral Home in Orange.[54] By this time, Reverend

Drake, having retired, was not at hand to lead his service; it was conducted instead by the First Presbyterian Church's current pastor, Rev. Ben Gillespie.[55] "Mr. Stark's funeral was the shortest one I have ever attended," Mary Robinson Cowan, Anita's mother, wrote her later. "No music, no eulogy, only scripture, a few scripture-related words and a prayer or two. Mr. Stark's name was never mentioned and of course the casket was never opened. The flowers were very, very beautiful. Telegrams came from everywhere—Governor [John B.] Connally, former Governor Allan Shivers, artists of Taos and S[anta] F[e] and many many more."[56] Following the service, Lutcher was entombed with his family in the Lutcher-Stark Mausoleum in Evergreen Cemetery.[57]

Lutcher Stark was seen as a hero by some, a villain by others, but the fact remains that he was human in the fullest sense of that word, possessed of human virtues and weaknesses that, because of his wealth and power, were necessarily magnified a hundredfold. Being accustomed from birth to exercise complete control over his domain, he was not in the habit of having his will thwarted, and undoubtedly, some of his viewpoints, actions, and reactions were hasty and ill advised, some misguided, such as his quarrel with Bedichek and the UIL, or ultimately harmful, such as his part in the regents' firing of Homer Rainey. But unquestionably, he acted according to the dictates of his own conscience regarding what he believed to be the best for those entities he loved, were they the University of Texas or his own family, even if he sometimes erred in the execution. And there remains no question that the good he did for a great many was vast and immeasurable. Whether he was viewed for good or ill, his passing was monumental.

"The last years when he was not well are times to be forgotten," Ruth Murphy wrote. "There are so many good things to remember about him and the things he did for Orange and others."[58] Tributes to him flooded in from all directions—from friends and colleagues, in editorials in many of the state's leading newspapers. With the Rainey dispute more than twenty years in the past, an editorial in the *Austin American-Statesman* felt able to give him credit for the good he accomplished for the university: "One of the most ardent friends and devoted benefactors of the University of Texas . . . his efforts, his interest and financial support of the education of youth will be reflected in the lives of many persons through the years."[59] "The Orange philanthropist, in the finest Texas tradition, shared his great wealth with others," the *Houston Post* noted, "with particular emphasis on contributions to the University of Texas."[60] Declared the *Dallas Morning News:* "It was a measure of the philanthropy of H.J. Lutcher Stark that much of what he gave was given anonymously. It is the test of a big man."[61]

In Southeast Texas, support for him had never flagged throughout the years. "In the death Thursday of H. J. Lutcher Stark," the neighboring *Beaumont Journal* wrote, "Southeast Texas lost one of its most prominent and respected citizens."[62] "Lutcher Stark was an empire builder in the best Texas tradition," wrote the *Enterprise*.

> Blessed with the brainpower, imagination and courage so long associated with great industrial figures of the Southwest . . . he directed a great deal of his time and talents and financial resources to satisfying a deep interest in the plants and wildlife of his beloved Gulf coast and in the masterpieces of renowned artists. More important to the people of his community and state, [he] gave unstinting support to character-building agencies for youth, and to a large number of cultural programs and educational institutions.[63]

"Felling of the industrial giant gives an especially keen sense of loss to our good neighbors in Orange, which was home to Lutcher Stark in the most meaningful and heartwarming sense of the word," continued the *Enterprise*. "All Texas feels some of their sorrow."[64]

Perhaps an editorial in the *Orange Leader*, Lutcher's home newspaper, spoke most eloquently of his home region's veneration of him: "A man of means who is possessed of a strong conscience is a double blessing to his community, the nation and the world. . . . Suffice it to say that few men who have been blessed as he was have found as many avenues for being a blessing to others."[65]

True to his long-ago prophecy, Lutcher Stark indeed found himself happiest spending his entire life in his small hometown of Orange. Even if he did not die within its physical boundaries, his heart had always remained there, and when his life ended, he returned to his lifelong home, where the old cypress tree still grows in solitary splendor on the banks of Adams Bayou.

Figure 13.9. The ancient pond cypress, "the Survivor," still casts its long shadow across the waters of Adams Bayou in the new incarnation of Lutcher Stark's Shangri-La, now the Shangri La Botanical Gardens and Nature Center, Orange, Texas. Stark Foundation Archives.

Nelda

I didn't marry him for his money. We were happy.
—NELDA CHILDERS STARK[1]

O n September 9, 1965, eight days after his death, Lutcher Stark's
will was filed for probate. The will was dated February 23, 1961—
the same day he and Nelda had created the Stark Foundation. He
left specific tax-free bequests of $1 million each to Homer and Bill, but
the remainder of his estate—the corpus of one of the nation's great lumber fortunes—he left to Nelda and the foundation they had created.[2] Conducting an inventory of the estate required over a year's efforts, but on November 22, 1966, an official inventory was filed, listing Lutcher's holdings
at $78.2 million.[3] At his death, Nelda became chief executive officer of the
Stark Foundation, which she managed together with a board of directors
composed primarily of independent individuals.

Nelda remained at the helm of the Stark Foundation for thirty-four
years, serving as a careful steward of her husband's wealth and making
numerous grants and charitable contributions, both from the foundation
and from her personal funds, and often, in her husband's tradition, anonymously. "She didn't like for people to know that she gave a great deal of
money to different things . . . and a lot of it was done anonymously," Joan
Cummings, a Stark Foundation employee, remembered. "We weren't supposed to tell," she added. "And we didn't."[4]

On September 17, 1970, per instructions she had received from Lutcher
Stark shortly before his death, Nelda negotiated the sale of the entire assets of the Lutcher & Moore Lumber Company. ("I'm not going to sell
now," he had told her. "You sell first thing when I die.")[5] She complied,
selling Lutcher & Moore—by that time one of the nation's oldest lumber
companies—to Boise Southern, a joint venture of Boise Cascade, Inc., of
Boise, Idaho, and the Southern Natural Gas Company of Birmingham, Al-

Figure E.1. Nelda Stark in later life, undated. Stark Foundation Archives.

abama, which was at the time of the sale operating a kraft paper and news-print mill in DeRidder, Louisiana.[6]

Over two hundred thousand acres of timberland in East Texas and Southwest Louisiana, as well as mineral rights, including producing wells, changed ownership in the sale.[7] The price was not disclosed, but the *Orange Leader* reported that the revenue generated by the sale went to the Stark Foundation, speculating that it would possibly be utilized to build the long-hoped-for art museum.[8] Because the forest management program originally initiated by William Stark and carried on by Lutcher had made the properties more valuable, most of the country's major lumber concerns were among the bidders.[9] Articles of Dissolution marking the end of the old company's existence were executed two months later on November 5, 1970.[10]

Through the years, Nelda continued to aid her alma mater, Texas Woman's University (TWU), donating equipment for the Laboratories for Human Nutrition Research on campus (which was afterward named for her), providing funds for air-conditioning the main auditorium, and establishing and equipping the TWU Lass-O Band.[11] In early 1966, construction began on a thirty-one-story dormitory on campus to be named for her. At that time she was serving as vice chairman of the school's Board of Regents and had been a member of the board since 1955. Nelda C. Stark

Hall was dedicated on December 11, 1967.[12] In 1974, TWU again honored her by awarding her a special citation for rendering "distinguished service to her alma mater."[13]

Under Nelda's guidance, the Stark Foundation continued sponsorship of the Miriam Lutcher Stark Contest in Reading and Declamation, which had been held annually since its inception in 1904. In 1976, it became a qualified scholarship program of the Stark Foundation, observing its centennial in 2004.

The Foundation also established several world-class cultural venues in Orange. In 1978, in a realization of both Miriam's and Lutcher's longtime dream, the Stark Museum of Art opened as a venue to share the family's vast art collections with the public. Two years later, on February 7, 1980, a premier performance featuring world-renowned pianist and entertainer Liberace celebrated the opening of the Frances Ann Lutcher Theater for the Performing Arts, a nonprofit state-of-the-art performing arts venue honoring the matriarch of the family and evoking recollection of her early venture with the Lutcher Opera House. The theater features Broadway shows, performances by stellar names in the entertainment world, and a children's theater series.[14]

In 1981, the Stark Foundation completed a project begun a decade earlier: the restoration of the fourteen thousand–square-foot Queen Anne residence of Miriam and William Stark, which had remained closed and

Figure E.2. Stark Museum of Art, Orange, Texas. Image by Will France.
Stark Foundation Archives.

Figure E.3. Frances Ann Lutcher Theater for the Performing Arts, Orange, Texas.
Stark Foundation Archives.

uninhabited since the time of their deaths in 1936 and had been used as
storage for the family's collections. During his lifetime, Lutcher Stark had
made one attempt to renovate the house, but when he discovered that it
was infested with termites, he lost patience with the project. ("Tear the
damn thing down!" he was reported to have roared.) Nelda, perhaps thinking that it might eventually be saved, talked him out of dismantling it, but
he nevertheless insisted on closing it again. After his death, when the restoration finally began in 1971, Eunice Benckenstein, working in tandem
with Nelda, contributed greatly to its successful completion.[15]

The restored W.H. Stark House, as it is officially called, depicts the domestic life of the W.H. Stark family around the turn of the twentieth century and features their personal effects and collections of rich furnishings, art, and art objects, including antique rugs, silver, Meissen and
Dresden porcelain, glassware, and a particularly significant collection of
American Brilliant cut glass. The house is unusual among historic house
restorations in that neither it nor its contents were ever owned by anyone
other than the Stark family. The W.H. Stark House is listed in the National Register of Historic Places and is designated as a recorded Texas
Historic Landmark by the Texas Historical Commission.

Throughout, and in spite of the wealth and power she commanded,
Nelda remained essentially the same person she had always been—direct,

Figure E.4. The W.H. Stark House, Orange, Texas. Image by Will France.
Stark Foundation Archives.

Figure E.5. Music Room at The W.H. Stark House, Orange, Texas, 2015.
Stark Foundation Archives

no-nonsense, brusque in manner but quietly generous, liking her own way, unpretentious in the extreme, plain in her dress and in every other aspect of her life. It was true that she owned various suits and dresses she had purchased from Neiman Marcus, Sakowitz, or other upscale clothing stores, which she wore for formal occasions, but even these were invariably tailored in style. For daily wear, she habitually donned slacks and cotton shirts.[16] "She didn't like food, she didn't like to travel, she didn't like clothes, she didn't like diamonds," recalled Odeen Martindill, a longtime friend of Nelda's. "She didn't spend [her money] on herself."[17]

Nelda's spartan habits extended to her taste in food. Although she employed a cook, she herself sometimes cooked for friends on Sundays at noon or dined at local restaurants on weekend nights, frequently inviting several friends to accompany her.[18] Bacon and rice were staples in her diet, and her favorite foods included homegrown tomatoes, rice pudding, and homemade fudge.[19] Many remembered that, throughout her life, she preferred drinking Coca-Cola from the original small green bottles, maintaining that the beverage tasted better from the bottles than from any other kind of container. She nearly always wrapped them neatly in a napkin in a particular manner that Anita Cowan, Eunice Benckenstein's niece and a frequent visitor to Nelda's home, called the "Nelda Wrap."[20]

Even after Lutcher's death, Nelda continued to make yearly trips in the summers to Roslyn Ranch. In his lifetime, guests at the ranch had frequently traveled to nearby Cheyenne, Wyoming, to attend the rodeo held there every summer. Nelda herself actually disliked rodeos, but since Lutcher enjoyed them, she went along with him. (At one of the last Cheyenne rodeos they attended together, he bought her a belt, which she kept for the rest of her life.)[21] In all likelihood, her treks to the rodeos stopped after Lutcher's death, although she possibly returned to Cheyenne to visit friends who owned a hotel there.[22]

When Nelda traveled to the ranch in the years after Lutcher's death, usually for a two-week stay, she entertained a select group—Eunice Benckenstein and her sisters; her personal physician, Fred Gregory, and his wife, Joan; Edgar Poth, a surgeon with the University of Texas Medical Branch at Galveston; his wife, ophthalmologist Gaynelle Robertson; a favorite nurse, Jackie Rudberg Leake, who had cared for both Nelda and Lutcher; and others of Nelda's inner circle.[23] The group was always accompanied by Nelda's private security detail, which had provided her with twenty-four-hour personal security ever since an unsuccessful kidnapping attempt had been made on her in the late 1970s.

On their treks westward, made after the snow melted in late June or early July, the party often traveled in a Ford Aerostar van, which Nelda's guards drove in two-hour shifts. (If they exceeded the hours of their shift,

Figure E.6. Nelda Stark and Fred Gregory showing off the results of his fishing expedition during a stay at Roslyn Ranch, undated. Stark Foundation Archives.

Nelda, fearing they would tire, announced that it was time to change drivers.) Usually, the travelers spent two nights on the road before they reached the ranch, taking various routes, sometimes through Tulsa, sometimes Amarillo, sometimes via other cities.[24]

During their stay at the ranch, visitors hiked, explored the countryside,

Figure E.7. A scenic view across the Roslyn Ranch property, undated,
but prior to 1990. Stark Foundation Archives.

rode horses, made exploratory forays into nearby towns, and fished for
rainbow trout in the thirty-five-acre artificial Roslyn Lake (which Lutcher
Stark had created by damming up two creeks).[25] A grove of aspens grew
on the property, and visitors were invited to carve their initials into the
trunks of the trees. (When the Gregorys went to the grove to carve their
initials, they found those of Fred's parents, carved some forty years be-

fore.)[26] Nelda herself spent much of her time outdoors, trimming trees and working at other tasks. "She was happiest when she was outside doing something," recalled Robert Risinger, one of the guards who also shared in driving duties.[27]

Nelda insisted on keeping a strict schedule, and not surprisingly, meal-times were set at the times she preferred. At the designated hours, every-one gathered in the dining hall for meals—all of them substantial—pre-pared by Nelda's cook, Marie Salter, and served punctually. (Dr. Gregory remembered that Marie was a wonderful cook and that the food was al-ways delicious.) The company seldom saw Nelda herself at the breakfast hour; she sometimes ate half a piece of toast or a banana but more often skipped breakfast altogether. She invariably drank a Coca-Cola shortly af-ter she rose, however, even in the early mornings, always from the small green bottle. She preferred eating dinner between 5:00 and 5:30 p.m., and although she herself never drank alcohol, she never hesitated to offer it to her guests, both at the ranch and at her home.[28]

The two-week sojourns at the ranch were timed between the founda-tion's payroll dates (Nelda herself signed the checks), but the party seldom stayed the entire time.[29] The guards never knew exactly when the return trip was planned; Nelda simply announced at dinner that "we're leaving in the morning." The travels homeward were often of shorter duration than those going to the ranch; many times, when the party was returning, they spent one night in Lamar, Colorado, and then drove straight through, leav-ing early one morning and arriving in Orange at daybreak the next morn-ing. Risinger remembered that once, as they were traveling home, they re-ceived word that a hurricane was threatening to hit Southeast Texas. "We had to try to get [to Orange] before it hit," he remembered. "She had to make sure that everybody had done what they were supposed to do to pre-pare for it, you know."[30]

Toward the end of her life, Nelda, never fond of travel, became ill nearly every time she traveled to Colorado, seldom if ever emerging from her cabin. Once, the party turned around and returned to Orange even before reaching the ranch.[31]

In the years after Nelda and Lutcher married, relations between her and Lutcher's adopted sons—which had never been on the best of foot-ings—had grown more and more strained. In the beginning, Lutcher had informed Homer and Bill, who had been accustomed to treating their fa-ther's house as their own, that from then on, certain rules were to be ob-served, and further, that he and Nelda were not to be expected to babysit the grandchildren.[32] "Nelda did not like having a lot of children around," Anita Cowan remembered, "especially if they were rowdy. They made her nervous and disrupted the kind of atmosphere that worked best for her, which was quiet, orderly, and controlled."[33]

Both Homer and Bill appeared to feel that, after the marriage, their father not only grew distant from them but saw very little of his grandchildren. The distance between father and sons may also have widened because neither Homer nor Bill showed interest or acumen in following the footsteps of the three generations before them, preferring instead to pursue their own concerns.[34] (Homer managed the Sabine Yacht Basin for a time, and Bill served as the longtime golf professional at the Sunset Grove Country Club.) Compounding the difficulty was Lutcher's advancing age, failing health, and increasing dependency on Nelda. Thus, the groundwork had already been laid for future trouble.

Long-festering resentments came to a head in March 1988 when Ida Marie Stark, by then a widow (Bill had died of lung cancer on September 25, 1979, at age fifty-six), and her children filed suit in the 260th District Court in Orange County against Nelda Stark and the Stark Foundation, charging that Lutcher Stark "negligently failed to include as part of the estate of Nita Hill Stark, deceased, substantial assets, including community property, community rights of reimbursement, and other assets, which should have been included in the Inventory and subsequently duly transmitted to his sons, W.H. Stark II, and Homer B.H. Stark."[35] Since, by the terms of her will, Nita had left her half of the couple's community property to her sons on her death in 1939, the allegations of the 1988 suit were that, by failing to include those assets, Lutcher, nearly a half century ago, had cheated Homer and Bill out of property that should have been part of Nita's share of the community estate.

The lawsuit further alleged that Nelda, as the executrix of Lutcher's will, had participated in and perpetrated the fraud by "negligently" including assets in Lutcher's inventory that, decades before, had belonged to Nita's estate. The suit also sought to require Nelda to make an accounting of the manner in which the Nita Hill Stark estate had been handled.[36] (In all, the claims of the family members of Homer and Bill Stark against Lutcher's widow and the Stark Foundation were ironically reminiscent of the Brown family's challenge to Lutcher Stark and the Estate of Frances Ann Lutcher so many decades ago.)

Nelda's attorneys argued that in 1948, Lutcher, as Nita's executor, had previously furnished detailed accounts of the distribution of the estate to the proper parties at the time that the estate had been closed, and further, that Homer and Bill had signed receipts and releases in the 1940s acknowledging various distributions made to them during the administration of Nita's estate, including a Full and Final Release signed by both on May 4 of that year. Homer Stark, who was still living at the time of the filing of the 1988 lawsuit, declined to participate in the suit, but it was soon joined by one of his children.[37]

It was not until March 1991 that, after almost three years of litigation, the Homer and Bill Stark family members and Nelda Stark settled out of court for $5 million. Each family's portion of the settlement amounted to $2.5 million, which was paid by Nelda, personally. Ultimately, in the final amended petition, all the family members—Ida Marie and her three children and Homer and his four children—had joined the lawsuit as plaintiffs, and Homer, who initially had refused to participate in the suit, eventually did so and thus received a share of the settlement proceeds.[38]

As a condition of the settlement, the family members signed a "Full, Final, and Complete Release," which barred them from bringing any further litigation against Nelda or the Foundation.[39] (After the conclusion of the 1988 litigation, the attorney for the plaintiffs admitted that, in spite of examining more than four hundred thousand pages of documents, he had found no evidence of fraudulent intent.)[40] In the end, Nelda Stark successfully defended her husband's estate and legacy, just as he had prevailed many decades before against the challenges in the Brown family litigation. Lutcher's plans and directives—like those of his grandmother, Frances Ann Lutcher—remained intact, in spite of the attempts of others to effect changes through the courts.

Contemporaneously, the Texas Attorney General's office, an intervenor in the suit (by virtue of the fact that the bulk of Lutcher's estate went to the Stark Foundation, a charitable organization), opined in a 1991 letter that Homer Stark should be asked to resign from the Stark Foundation Board, since his participation as a party in the lawsuit while also serving as a Foundation director created a conflict of interest and demonstrated "a direct breach of his duty of loyalty to the Foundation." The letter went on to provide that, if Homer failed to resign, he should be removed from the Board of Directors of the Stark Foundation pursuant to the Foundation's bylaws.[41] Because Homer refused to resign, he was subsequently removed by the remaining members of the board.[42]

The other line of descent from Frances Ann and Henry Jacob Lutcher had made their own mark in the world—in vastly divergent directions. After the Brown family's interest in Lutcher-Stark business ventures had been bought out by the Starks in 1919–1920, the two surviving children of Carrie and Edgar Brown—Edgar Jr. and Henry Lutcher Brown—went their separate ways, one to live his life in Orange, the other to end his days in South America. Edgar Brown remained in his native town, becoming a financier, industrialist, and dominant force in city and regional business affairs, at one time serving as chairman of the board of Orange National

Bank and, in 1933, becoming the major owner of two large Orange business concerns, Levingston Shipbuilding Company and Higman Towing Company.[43]

Edgar and his wife, Gladys Slade Brown, whom he had married in 1915, established the two hundred–acre farm of Pinehurst just west of Orange, built a stately home called "Linden," and established a ranch and stables, where they raised American Saddlebred horses and Hackney ponies.[44] The farm, "one of the real showplaces of the South," as it was described, was also used as an experimental ground in the production of new types of grain and hay for stock feed.[45] Edgar Brown, in the tradition of his grandmother, Frances Ann Lutcher, became a philanthropist for many local charities, particularly the churches of Orange, including the First Presbyterian Church.[46]

Gladys Brown died on September 17, 1959. The next year, in a curious turn of events, the newly widowed Edgar married Elizabeth Smith "Smitty" Hustmyre, the former director of Lutcher Stark's Bengal Guards, who, after her first husband's death, had worked as registrar for the city of Orange. The two were able to spend some pleasurable years together.[47] "He enjoyed life," his sister-in-law, Celeste Smith Hart, allowed, "if ever anybody did."[48] He died January 8, 1976, and was buried in the Brown family mausoleum in Evergreen Cemetery.

Henry Lutcher Brown, the youngest of Carrie and Edgar's brood, married Emily Katherine Wells in 1917. Lutcher Brown, as he was known, moved the machinery of the defunct Yellow Pine Paper Mill to Monroe, Louisiana; bought hundreds of thousands of acres of forestlands; and organized the Brown Container Corporation, consisting of a paper mill, bag factory, and box factory.[49] Lutcher, Carrie, and Edgar Brown Jr. served as the three principals in the enterprise, but Lutcher Brown was the driving force, developing a process for utilizing southern pine to make pulp, thus paving the way for the establishment of the pulp industry in the South.[50]

Around 1930, Emily and Lutcher Brown moved to San Antonio, where they built a Georgian-style mansion they called Oak Court.[51] He later developed business interests in Uruguay, where he eventually became a citizen.[52] In the 1950s, the Browns sold their interest in the Brown Container Corporation to Olin Mathieson Chemical Corporation. "Mr. Lutcher Brown [was] a very good businessman," Ben McDonough, the treasurer of Lutcher & Moore Lumber Company, remembered, "and extremely hard to deal with."[53] Lutcher Brown died on December 7, 1970.

Sometime in 1997, Nelda Stark's health began to decline in earnest. In 1999, shortly before her death, she made a gift of $1 million to the University of Texas Medical Branch at Galveston to establish and endow a distinguished professorship in internal medicine. The gift, she explained, was given in gratitude for the care she and Lutcher Stark had received there during the 1950s and 1960s.[54] In early December 1999, she collapsed at her home and was flown by air ambulance to the Diagnostic Center Hospital in Houston, where Dr. Fred Gregory attended her.[55] This event marked the first time Nelda, who was afraid of flying, had ever flown, although, mercifully, she was apparently unaware of making her first—and last—flight.[56]

Nelda Stark died on December 13, 1999, the date perhaps a nod to Lutcher's lucky number, which, during the course of their marriage, had become hers as well. At age ninety, she had outlived her husband by nearly twenty-five years. Her will stipulated several specific monetary bequests, including $1 million in cash to her stepson, Homer Stark (whom Nelda included as a beneficiary in her will despite his involvement in the prior litigation against her and his receipt of monies from the subsequent settlement). Other specific gifts went to friends, associates, and employees. She bequeathed the remainder of her estate in its entirety, including cash, real property, and museum-quality art and art objects, to the Stark Foundation.[57]

Vilified in some quarters though she might have been, Nelda Stark was liked, respected, even loved in others. "I admired her," asserted Dr. Gregory. "She was a very kind person, very quiet and private, very generous."[58] Besides her philanthropy to public institutions, numerous individuals also found themselves the recipients of her generosity throughout the years. "If you needed something," Billie Jeanne DeLane Wright asserted, "she saw that you had it. And she always told me that my children came first."[59]

According to Odeen Martindill, who served for many years as chief X-ray technician at Orange Memorial Hospital, "She took good care of Bill [Stark] when he was sick. She would call me and I would open [the] back door to the hospital and she would bring him in." Martindill observed that very few people knew how many houses Nelda had bought and remodeled, then rented to friends and business associates at a low rate. "She was [a caretaker]," Martindill went on. "I think she took care of half of the people in town. . . . She gave most of [her money] away."[60]

"She was a grand lady," Stark Foundation board member Ruby Wimberley declared, "who was under-appreciated by most people."[61] Betty Em Wall Giarratano, an Orange neighbor of Nelda's and a victim of polio, recalled that Nelda's generosity extended to old friends:

In 1950 my parents traveled to and from Houston in an old Chevrolet. They would visit me once or twice a week during the several years I stayed at a polio rehabilitation clinic. One weekend when I was home on a visit to Orange, Miss Nelda came to our house with the keys to a new Ford—and very little comment. She allowed us to thank her and she was gone. She was a wonder. Since she has been such a positive light among so many lives for 90 years, I just thought she was going to stay with us forever. Her generosity to the citizens of Orange was remarkable.[62]

"Few of us, it's true, were afforded the opportunity to know her," an editorial in the *Orange Leader* reflected, "yet each of us in Orange was influenced by her, and we all have a lesson to learn from her." The editorial went on:

Nelda C. Stark could simply have retired to a secluded estate and lived out her life in comfort. Yet she chose instead to live in a plain white house built by her father in an unassuming Orange neighborhood, remaining a vibrant business-woman who refused to turn her back on her community. . . . She invested some of [her fortune] in construction of a park, a museum and a beautiful theater which, over time, have helped anchor the revitalization of the city and give it a future as a center of culture and learning.

Through it all, she remained unassuming and publicity-shy. . . . Her quiet donations to charitable organizations and to fund scholarships left a stamp on virtually every life in Orange and the surrounding communities. God bless you, Nelda Stark.[63]

After Nelda's death, the Board of Directors of the Stark Foundation continued its founders' philanthropic efforts, awarding grants to various health-care institutions, including the Stark Diabetes Center at the University of Texas Medical Branch Health Science Center in Galveston. In 2006, aided by a major grant from the Stark Foundation, Texas Woman's University constructed a new school of nursing at its Institute of Health Sciences in the Texas Medical Center in Houston. It was christened the Nelda C. Stark College of Nursing.[64]

And in recent years, thanks in large part to a major grant from the foundation, Lutcher Stark received a posthumous honor from his alma mater with the establishment of the H.J. Lutcher Stark Center for Physical Culture and Sports in the north end zone of UT's Darrell K. Royal–Texas Memorial Stadium in Austin. The Stark Center museum and archive, founded by university faculty members Terry and Jan Todd, houses the Todd-McLean Library, the largest collection of material relating to physical culture and sports in the world. The museum, displaying various memorabilia from the world of physical culture and sports, honors the memory

Figure E.8. Lifelong friends Nelda Stark and Eunice Benckenstein
at a Stark Foundation Christmas Party. Stark Foundation Archives.

Figure E.9. Nelda C. Stark College of Nursing at Texas Woman's University
Institute of Health Sciences–Houston Center, Houston, Texas, undated.
Courtesy of Texas Woman's University.

Figure E.10. The elevator lobby of the H.J. Lutcher Stark Center for
Physical Culture and Sports, University of Texas at Austin, 2015.
Courtesy of the H.J. Lutcher Stark Center for Physical Culture and Sports.

of Lutcher Stark, the man who long stood as one of the most generous phi-
lanthropists in the history of the University of Texas, both for his years of
largesse to the school and his lifelong advocacy of physical fitness.[65]

Final acts in the melodrama created by legal proceedings between various Stark family descendants and the Stark Foundation still remained
to be played out. In spring 2000, only a few months after Nelda Stark's
death (and in spite of the Final Release prohibiting any further claims
that had been signed by Stark family litigants as part of the settlement
of their 1988 lawsuit), foundation officials received notice from an attorney for Stark descendants, threatening more lawsuits. The attorney indicated that the aim of additional litigation by his clients was to reopen the
1988 lawsuit, seek to set aside the prior settlement and release, and re-
assert the same claims of mismanagement regarding the 1939 estate of
Nita Hill Stark that had previously been adjudicated.[66]

The attorney stated his plan for lawsuits to be filed, this time in Louisi-
ana, against the Foundation; Nelda's estate; its co-executors, Roy Wingate,
Eunice Benckenstein, and Stark Foundation chief executive officer Walter
Riedel; and Wingate, Benckenstein, and Riedel, individually.

On July 14, 2000, the Foundation and the three co-executors of Nelda
Stark's estate preemptively filed a Petition for Declaratory Judgment in

the 260th Judicial District Court of Orange County, Texas, requesting that the court interpret the 1991 release, declare its validity, and uphold it as a bar to any further litigation by Stark descendants.[67] Before a ruling could be handed down, however, Stark family litigants filed a $200 million counterclaim in Calcasieu Parish, Louisiana, against Nelda's estate as well as a countersuit in the Texas Declaratory Judgment case to set aside the 1991 release and to ask for additional damages.[68]

The following year, on March 6, 2001, Homer Stark also filed suit in the Orange County Court-at-Law against Nelda's estate and its co-executors—Wingate, Benckenstein, and Riedel—asking for damages, lost fees, cash, property, and assets Homer maintained were owed him as a result of what he alleged to be a conspiracy by Nelda and others to remove him as trustee of the Stark Foundation following the 1988 litigation. Homer also petitioned for ownership of Roslyn Ranch, contending that before her death, Nelda had promised to give him the property plus funds sufficient to run it.[69]

On July 8, 2002, however, the various issues in the Texas Declaratory Judgment case were resolved by Visiting Judge Lee Duggan Jr. from Houston, who was appointed to hear the case in place of local judge Buddie J. Hahn, who had recused himself. Judge Duggan granted a Summary Judgment in favor of the Stark Foundation and executors of the estate of Nelda C. Stark (and also the Texas attorney general, who once again intervened in the litigation on behalf of the State of Texas), upholding the 1991 release as valid and binding against the Stark family litigants.[70]

The Summary Judgment issued by the court prohibited the litigants from making any further claims or filing any more lawsuits that involved matters they had released when they signed the 1991 release. (This included claims pertaining to the Stark Foundation, to Nelda Stark or her estate, to the prior estates of H.J. Lutcher Stark and Nita Hill Stark, and any of the other allegations that had been part of the 1988 lawsuit and 1991 release.) The Order Granting Summary Judgment also dismissed with prejudice (i.e., permanently, without future recourse) all counterclaims that had been filed by the Stark family litigants.[71]

On February 13, 2003, Judge Duggan also ruled that the family of Bill Stark must pay more than $500,000 in attorneys' fees and court costs to the executors of Nelda Stark's estate, with the Texas attorney general to receive nearly $20,000 of that amount, also in attorneys' fees and court costs.[72] The judge's order also provided for additional monetary awards to the co-executors of Nelda Stark's estate and to the Texas attorney general in the event subsequent appeals were pursued by the Stark family litigants at the Texas Court of Civil Appeals and the Texas Supreme Court.[73]

The following October 28, Judge Robert L. Wyatt of the 14th Judicial

District Court of Calcasieu Parish, Louisiana, ruled in the petition of the plaintiffs (the Homer and Bill Stark families) for an administration of the H. J. Lutcher Stark Ancillary Succession that "any and all claims filed herein on behalf of the plaintiffs are barred and hereby dismissed . . . [and] all costs of proceedings are taxed to plaintiffs."[74] On September 29, 2004, a unanimous three-judge panel of the 3rd Circuit Court of Appeals for the State of Louisiana affirmed Judge Wyatt's decision. In the Louisiana appellate court's written ruling, Judge Oswald A. DeCuir noted, "Suggestions of misdeeds the plaintiffs already knew about, sued upon, and accepted a settlement on do not create a new cause of action or resurrect one that has [expired]."[75]

In the meantime, Texas appellate courts were in the process of making similar determinations, as the Stark family litigants had elected to pursue appeals of the Texas Declaratory Judgment case despite significant fees and costs that would apply in the event such appeals were rejected. Indeed, on December 30, 2004, in a published opinion, the 9th Court of Appeals, sitting in Beaumont, unanimously affirmed the Summary Judgment that had been granted by Judge Duggan in 2002 in the Texas Declaratory Judgment case. The Texas Supreme Court twice denied further review of the Texas appellate court's ruling (on June 10, 2005, and September 2, 2005), meaning that the original ruling of Judge Duggan at the trial court level in favor of the Stark Foundation and estate of Nelda Stark was upheld as rendered.[76]

In addition to the conflicts and controversies perpetuated by the various claims filed in Texas and Louisiana courts in the years after Nelda Stark's death, matters took a strange, dark turn in March 2001 when Homer Stark and his four children made an ex parte filing in Orange County of a document titled "Petition to Obtain Genetic Samples."[77] In their filing, Homer and his children sought an ex parte court order—without opportunity for response or objection by any other interested parties—for the exhumation of the remains of both William and Lutcher Stark from the Stark Family Mausoleum in Evergreen Cemetery, so that technicians "may remove tissue samples for testing small quantities of tissue."[78] The court granted the petition, and family members unilaterally arranged for the exhumation of the bodies.

It is unknown what any tissue sampling or testing may have involved or what, if anything, it may have revealed, as no further allegations were asserted by the Homer Stark petitioners in the years following the incident, and evidence was never made public due to the ex parte nature of the petitioners' filing and the court's similar order. In the end, this bizarre episode did not seem to advance any agenda of the Stark family litigants. One point, however, is clear: Lutcher Stark himself would have adamantly opposed such actions. Decades earlier, after an actual prior intrusion that had taken place in the family mausoleum without his express permission, Lutcher had been so incensed by the thought of any person's entering his family's crypts that he had written a memo describing such action as "the height of carelessness, degenerating into imbecility" and had threatened reprisal against anyone who ever "play[ed] with . . . the bones of my own ancestors."[79]

An equally bizarre, although less macabre, series of events involving Homer Stark and his children occurred several years later. In March 2006, in an effort to resolve the separate, remaining lawsuit that had been filed by Homer in Orange County, the co-executors of the estate of Nelda Stark agreed to give Homer the right of first refusal in connection with any sale of Roslyn Ranch, the longtime summer gathering place for Stark family members in the years since Frances Ann Lutcher had acquired it in 1907. Homer informed Nelda's co-executors that he considered the ranch to be his "legacy, part of the family story," according to Walter Riedel, one of the co-executors, and as such, Homer indicated it was important to him that the ranch remain "in the family."[80]

After requesting and receiving approval from the Internal Revenue Service in a private letter ruling, the co-executors entered into an agreement with Homer Stark that permitted him to purchase Roslyn Ranch at fair market value. Accordingly, the estate of Nelda Stark ultimately sold the ranch to Stark Ranch, LP, a Texas limited partnership established and controlled by one of Homer Stark's grandsons and to which Homer assigned his interest in purchasing Roslyn Ranch.[81]

The sale of Roslyn Ranch to the Homer Stark family partnership occurred on March 23, 2006, at the appraised value of $3.927 million.[82] Less than twenty-four hours later, after dividing the ranch into two tracts, Stark Ranch, LP, sold the long-sought ranch to two unrelated buyers for $4.725 million.[83] While the deeds for conveyance of the ranch from the family partnership to the buyers were dated March 24, 2006, all other documentation pertaining to the sales by Stark Ranch, LP, was completed a full week before Stark Ranch, LP, had legally acquired the property. Thus, the Homer Stark family's instantaneous financial gain resulted in the permanent loss of Roslyn Ranch to the Lutcher-Stark family legacy.

In the years since Lutcher Stark had closed and locked the gates of his Shangri-La in 1958, the 252-acre gardens had slumbered in solitude except for his and Nelda's own visits with their selected guests and intermittent upkeep by maintenance workers. Consequently, the garden areas had gradually reverted to nature. But the mystique of the place loomed perennially in the collective consciousness of Southeast Texas, fueled by the memories of those who had visited it in the days when Lutcher had greeted them at the gates. (In fact, many of the area's youth considered it a rite of passage to paddle their canoes or jon boats along Adams Bayou into Shangri-La's forbidden reaches.)

And they all remembered the old pond cypress. In 1998, a communitywide contest for area students was held to choose a name for the ancient tree. Each contestant chose a name and wrote an accompanying essay, after which a committee chose the winner—"the Survivor," the name submitted by a West Orange–Stark Middle School student named Timothy Smith.[84] "For at least twelve hundred years this old tree has been nurtured by the waters of Adams Bayou," wrote Michael Hoke, a local award-winning science teacher who, in an effort to expand his students' knowledge of the natural world, had established a "Nature Classroom" on cypress swampland adjoining Shangri-La and who knew its ecosystems intimately.[85] "For twelve hundred years it has dodged fires, storms, axes and disease," Hoke went on. "Like any old living thing, it has earned our respect, and it is up to us to protect it."[86] That year, the Texas Forest Service crowned the old tree as a state champion, the largest known of its species in Texas. (As of the time it was named, its circumference measured 213 inches, its height 46 feet, and its average crown spread 90 feet.)[87]

In 2002, the Stark Foundation launched plans for reopening Shangri-La, soon to be renamed the Shangri La Botanical Gardens and Nature Center (sans hyphen). The Foundation engaged three firms: landscape architect Jeffrey Carbo of Alexandria, Louisiana; the MESA Design Group of Dallas; and Lake|Flato, a San Antonio design concern specializing in sustainable architecture, to create a master plan, incorporating the property's natural features into the overall design. The Foundation also hired Hoke—whose energy, creativity, dedication to the environment, and wide knowledge of the Southeast Texas natural world made him a perfect choice—as Shangri La's first managing director.[88]

A full restoration of Lutcher Stark's Shangri-La was not possible; the property had undergone too much change in the decades it had lain dormant. Maintenance had simply consisted of periodic mowing, and the garden areas had long ago reverted to nature. Yet some vestiges of his old gardens remained: several greenhouses, including a section of a 1917 Lord & Burnham conservatory once belonging to Lutcher's parents; the millstones that had ground the grain for his grandfather's family; the bells he had found in churches, schools, and other widespread locations; a few of the Bordeaux cobblestones he himself had helped to place around the frog ponds; the old sugar kettles; a cast-iron birdbath; the petrified East Texas logs; and the Philippine bivalve shells. Ruby Lake remained as a memento

Figure E.11. The Lord & Burnham conservatory belonging to Miriam and William Stark was moved from The W.H. Stark House into Shangri-La by Lutcher Stark in the 1940s and still stands in the present-day Shangri La Botanical Gardens and Nature Center. Stark Foundation Archives.

of Lutcher's tribute to his dying wife Ruby but had evolved into a cypress-studded rookery hosting more than five thousand waterbirds—a bonus for the environmental thrust of the plan.[89]

All these remnants of Lutcher Stark's Shangri-La were incorporated into the new design—and perhaps recognized by those visitors who had first viewed them in the gardens more than fifty years before. Not only Lutcher's collected objects but his ideas were considered; Carbo, whose main focus lay in planning the botanical gardens, brought into his design Lutcher's longtime interest in the connection between art and nature, incorporating artistic elements that would reflect and interpret natural forms.[90]

April 23, 2005, marked the formal groundbreaking for the project.[91] But Mother Nature had other plans, and the following September, she revealed them in a particularly brutal manner. Work had just been under way for a short time when, in the early morning hours of September 24, 2005, a monster Category 5 hurricane dubbed Rita, armed with 180-mile-per-hour winds and "a mean swirl of clouds about the size of Brazil," quickly bore down on the Texas coast.[92] By the time it savaged the Southeast Texas coast just east of Sabine Pass, Hurricane Rita had weakened to

Figure E.12. Lutcher Stark's bells still hang in the new Shangri La Botanical Gardens and Nature Center. Stark Foundation Archives.

Figure E.13. The old sugar kettles that Lutcher Stark purchased in Louisiana take their proper place in the new Shangri La. Stark Foundation Archives.

a high Category 3 storm, but its winds, still raging in excess of 120 miles per hour, caused several deaths and incalculable wind damage throughout Southeast Texas and beyond.

In the aftermath of the storm, dazed personnel at Shangri La surveyed the wreckage. It had lost fifty-five thousand trees—nearly all of its pine, cedar, and cypress—which would necessitate a reorganization of the entire project.[93] "The challenge before the storm was that there was no sunlight [in the garden]," Carbo remarked. "Then the pendulum swung in the other direction."[94] But a miracle had occurred. When workers made their way through the fallen timber and debris to the edge of Adams Bayou, they found the old pond cypress, battered but still standing, having lost only a lower branch—and living up to its newly acquired name.[95]

The Stark Foundation decided to press on with the restoration. In keeping with their original intent to make the project as sustainable as possible, all salvageable material was either reused or repurposed.[96] The gardens finally opened the morning of March 11, 2008, in their new incarnation; opening ceremonies were conducted with fanfare, and the Great Bell, now mounted at the front gate of the gardens, was rung for the first time in more than sixty years. (In an eerie coincidence, Homer Stark, who had opposed the restoration, claiming that his father would have preferred that the funds expended for it be applied to other projects, died at a

Figure E.14. On March 11, 2008, Stark Foundation officials cut a "ribbon" of fresh flowers to mark the grand opening of the Shangri La Botanical Gardens and Nature Center. From left: Clyde V. "Tad" McKee III; John Cash "Jack" Smith; Ruby M. Wimberley; James R. Dunaway; Walter G. Riedel III, president and chief executive officer of the Stark Foundation; Michael Hoke, the first managing director of Shangri La; Laurence R. David; Deborah L. Hughes; and R. Frederick Gregory. Stark Foundation Archives.

hospice facility in the very moments the opening ceremonies were being conducted.)[97]

The newly reopened Shangri La revealed natural wonders—and the fruits of years of labor and innovative design. The botanical gardens featured nine formal theme gardens. The Nature Center offered Adams Bayou excursions, several nature "outposts"—each with an open-air classroom—and a greatly expanded teaching program with certified educators for area high school and college students. Shangri La garnered national and international notice; on February 8, 2008, the gardens received the US Green Building Council's Platinum certification for LEED-NC, confirming that its design and construction had attained the highest "green" building and performance criteria—the first project in Texas and the fiftieth in the world to attain such distinction. And in March 2009, the American Institute of Architects named it one of the ten most earth-friendly projects in the world.

As ill luck—and Mother Nature—would have it, Shangri La's debut to the public was short-lived. Five months and two days after its triumphant opening, in a scenario straight from a recurring nightmare, a high

Category 2 hurricane by the name of Ike hit Southeast Texas on September 13, 2008, like Rita in the hours just before dawn. Unlike Rita, this colossal cyclone, its size abnormally large, carried a lethal twenty-two-foot storm surge to Southeast Texas, made more calamitous by a high Gulf tide that peaked just as the hurricane's 110-mile-per-hour winds and giant waves crashed ashore on Galveston Island. When day broke to widespread destruction and reports of dead and missing, much of coastal Southeast Texas found itself under many feet of water, and floodwaters inundated much of the city of Orange. This time, the new buildings at Shangri La were flooded, as were the gardens, but luckily the salt water brought by the storm surge, which would have been deadly to the plantings, had stopped a mile short of Adams Bayou.[98]

Particularly disheartening to all concerned was the overriding fact that, although Southeast Texas had not been hit by a major storm for the last half century, it had been struck by not one but two within the space of three years, bringing home the fact that the entire Gulf Coast—and thus Shangri La—would always remain vulnerable to the vagaries of extreme weather. Even so, to Stark Foundation officials, abandoning a project offering so much to the community and the world was out of the question. "We had too much invested to walk away," asserted Foundation CEO Walter Riedel. "We couldn't just lock the gates."[99] The extensive damage necessitated another six-month cleanup before the gardens could resume oper-

Figure E.15. Shangri La Botanical Gardens and Nature Center, Orange, Texas.
Stark Foundation Archives.

Figure E.16. Adams Bayou winds its shadowed way through Shangri La and Southeast Texas. Stark Foundation Archives.

ation, but the Shangri La Botanical Gardens and Nature Center duly re-opened once more on March 7, 2009, almost exactly a year after its initial reopening.

In the wake of the second major hurricane, fears again ran high for the Survivor, but when the waters receded and workers were able to make their way into the interior of the gardens, they again found it standing strong—as it had done for twelve hundred years.

As of this writing, after the depredations of just over a millennium and the destruction wrought by the two known major hurricanes, not to mention other unnamed horrors through the years, the ancient cypress, that "majestic veteran of nature's wars," as one poet was inspired to call it,[100] still casts its long shadow across the muddy waters of Adams Bayou, deep in the heart of Lutcher Stark's private, now public, paradise—just as the shadow of his grandfather, Henry Jacob Lutcher, still casts its benign length over the works his vision made possible well over a century ago.

The extraordinary triumvirate of Lutcher and Stark generations now rest together for eternity in the family mausoleum in Orange's Evergreen Cemetery.[101] As the tree survives, their legacy lives on through their ultimate successor, the Stark Foundation, which serves as a current manifestation of the collective history of that singular trio of generations—on which the Foundation is based and by which it thrives.

Notes

Chapter 1

1. "G. Bedell Moore's Personal Account of 15-Day Trek through Texas January 11–February 13, 1877," *Las Sabinas* 2, no. 1 (Winter 1976): 14–39 (Orange, Texas, Orange County Heritage Society).

2. "Pennsylvania Lumber History," Timber! Pennsylvania Lumber Museum, 6 January 2012, http://www.lumbermuseum.org/history.html, 2.

3. Ludwig Friedrich (later Lewis Frederick) Lutscher was born September 22, 1803, and Maria Barbara (Mary Barbara) Beerweiler Lutscher, February 28, 1811. They were married (date unknown) in Germany before their immigration to the United States. *The Holy Bible*, 4th ed. (New York: American Bible Society, 1860), Lutscher family Bible, family records section, no pagination, gift of Charles Robert and Jeannette Lutscher, Williamsport, Pennsylvania, to the Nelda C. and H.J. Lutcher Stark Foundation, Orange, Texas. Also see Henry Jacob Lutcher, US passport application, 5 January 1898, and Frances A. Lutcher, US passport application, 9 May 1921, Stark Foundation Archives.

4. Lutscher family Bible. The Bible gives the German version of Henry Jacob Lutcher's name as "Jacob Heinrich." Whether the inversion of the two names was accidental or deliberate is unknown.

5. Court of Common Pleas, Records, Lycoming County Courthouse, Williamsport, Pennsylvania; Lutscher family Bible; *Daily Gazette and Bulletin* (Williamsport, Pennsylvania), 9 April 1883, clipping, Stark Foundation Archives; H.J.L. Stark to Lawrence J. Lutcher, 10 July 1961, Stark Foundation Archives.

6. Andrew Boyd and W. Harry Boyd, *Boyd's Williamsport City Directory* (Williamsport, PA: Thomas T. Taber Museum of Lycoming County Historical Society), 1869–70, 170; 1871–72, 207.

7. Lutscher family Bible; headstones of Lewis and Barbara Lutscher in Wildwood Cemetery, Williamsport, displaying their last names with the spelling of "Lutscher."

8. Court of Common Pleas, Lycoming County Courthouse: "And now to wit. Feby 13 1844. Petition read and the court admit Lewis Lutscher a Citizen of the United States of America." A younger relative, Frederick Lutscher, also emigrated from Wurttemberg to Williamsport in May 1868, declaring his intention to become a US citizen in 1893.

9. Thomas T. Taber III, *Williamsport: Lumber Capital* (Muncy, PA: Thomas T. Taber III, 1995), 5.

10. Barry L. Stocker, "The Repasz Band in the Civil War," Repasz Band 1831, September 2014, http://www.lycoming.org/repaszband/Main/civilwarhistory.htm. In 1859 the band

voted to name itself after one of its gifted conductors, Daniel Repasz. The band still exists, the oldest nonmilitary band in continuous existence in the United States.

11. Robin Van Auken, Timeline of Historic Events, 18 January 2012, http://www.news ofyesteryear.com/resources/timeline/.

12. "Pennsylvania Lumber History."

13. Lou Hunsinger Jr., "James H. Perkins: Father of the Susquehanna Boom," News of Yesteryear: Historic Pennsylvania, 3 November 2008, https://newsofyesteryear.wordpress .com/2008/11/03/james-h-perkins-father-of-the-susquehanna-boom/; "The Susquehanna Boom," Lumbering Industry Exhibit, Thomas T. Taber Museum of the Lycoming County Historical Society, Williamsport, Pennsylvania; Thad Stephen Meckley, *Williamsport*, Post-card History Series (Charleston, SC: Arcadia Publishing, 2006), 107; John F. Meginness, ed., *History of Lycoming County, Pennsylvania*, A Heritage Classic (Evansville, IN: Heritage Books, sponsored by Lycoming County Genealogical Society, 1996), 356–362.

14. Meginness, *History of Lycoming County*, 341.

15. A cant hook is a logging tool consisting of a wooden pole with a blunt, movable metal hook on the end, used to maneuver logs. A peavey is a similar tool but with a rigid spike on the end.

16. Lumbering Industry Exhibit, Thomas T. Taber Museum; "Williamsport, Pennsyl-vania-History," City of Williamsport, 17 January 2012, http://www.cityofwilliamsport.org /History.php.

17. Meginness, *History of Lycoming County*, 371–372.

18. "Millionaire's Row—Williamsport, PA," Historic Houses, 17 July 2008, http:// historichouses.wordpress.com/2008/07/17/mi.

19. Thad Stephen Meckley, *Williamsport's Millionaires' Row*, Postcard History Series (Charleston, SC: Arcadia Publishing, 2005), 9–11, 16–22, 24–36, 63–66, 69–71, 74, 76. In 1853, the lure of the lumber boom brought New Yorker Peter Herdic to Williamsport, where he became one of the greatest of the lumber tycoons and builders. In 1854 he constructed a palatial mansion in the Italian Villa style on West Fourth Street and went into partnership with architect Eber Culver to build many of the other grand homes on Millionaire's Row. "Peter Herdic (1824–1888) Historical Marker: Behind the Marker," Historical Markers, Ex-plorePAhistory.com, http://explorepahistory.com/hmarker.php?markerId=1-A-334 (accessed 18 November 2015).

20. Boyd and Boyd, *Boyd's Williamsport City Directory*, 1875–76, 99.

21. Alexander Fletcher, *A Guide to Family Devotion* (London: Virtue, 1836), book of devo-tions belonging to Lewis and Mary Lutscher, Stark Foundation Archives, containing an en-graving of the English Lutheran Church in Williamsport. On the back of the engraving is written in ink, "Lewis Lutscher, Williamsport, PA."

22. "St. Mark's Lutheran Church [Williamsport]," Rootsweb, http://freepages.geneal ogy.rootsweb.ancestry.com (accessed 5 October 2015); Fletcher, *A Guide to Family Devotion*; Bible belonging to Henry Jacob Lutscher, inscribed "Reward No. 1. For bringing the largest number of children into the Lutheran Sabbath School," Stark Foundation Archives.

23. "Henry J. Lutcher, Esq.," *St. Louis Lumberman*, March 1880, clipping, Stark Founda-tion Archives.

24. *Eighth Annual Catalogue of the Officers and Students of Dickinson Seminary for the Academical Year of June 10, 1855, to June 10, 1856* (Williamsport, PA: Barrett & Butt, Print-ers, 1856), 25, Records of Lycoming College (formerly Dickinson Seminary), Williamsport, Pennsylvania; advertisement for Dickinson Seminary, *Lycoming Weekly Gazette* (Williams-port, Pennsylvania), 21 July 1858.

25. *Seventh Annual Catalogue of the Officers and Students of Dickinson Seminary for the*

Academical Year of June 10, 1854, to June 10, 1855 (Elmira, NY: Fairman Brothers, Printers and Binders, 1855), 14, Records of Lycoming College (formerly Dickinson Seminary), Williamsport, Pennsylvania; *Eighth Annual Catalogue*, 14.

26. *Seventh Annual Catalogue*, 14; *Eighth Annual Catalogue*, 14. On many early deed records, Lutcher's name retains the German spelling; the change could possibly have occurred in his adulthood.

27. *Eighth Annual Catalogue*, 25–26.

28. *Seventh Annual Catalogue*, 31, 14. Fall term began in August, winter term in December, and spring term in early March; and the academic year ended in June. *Eighth Annual Catalogue*, 30.

29. Sometimes spelled "Snavel." "Henry J. Lutcher, Esq."

30. Earl E. Brown, "Rafts on the West Branch," in *Commerce on Early American Waterways: The Transport of Goods by Arks, Rafts, and Log Drives* (Jefferson, NC: McFarland, 2010), 107.

31. Meginness, *History of Lycoming County*, 530; "Henry J. Lutcher, Esq."

32. Van Auken, "Timeline of Historic Events."

33. Deed Records, Lycoming County, 42:351, Williamsport, Pennsylvania.

34. Lutscher family Bible. Charles Robert and Jeannette Lutcher, descendants of Albert William Lutcher, Henry Jacob Lutcher's brother, lived in the South Williamsport area near the old mill site until 2010.

35. Boyd and Boyd, *Boyd's Williamsport City Directory*, 1869–70, 170; 1871–72, 207.

36. Robin Van Auken and Louis E. Hunsinger Jr., *Williamsport: The Grit Photograph Collection*, Images of America Series (Charleston, SC: Arcadia Publishing, 2004), 26; Meckley, *Williamsport*, 50.

37. Meckley, *Williamsport*, 50.

38. "At Rest in Wildwood," Lewis Lutscher obituary, undated clipping from a Williamsport newspaper, Stark Foundation Archives.

39. H.J.L. Stark to Lawrence J. Lutcher, 10 July 1961, Stark Foundation Archives. *Note: All letters cited are located in the Stark Foundation Archives unless otherwise indicated.*

40. L.E. Daniell, "Henry J. Lutcher, Orange," in *Texas—the Country and Its Men* (Austin: L.E. Daniell, 1917), 470; "Henry J. Lutcher," typescript of interview (the article refers to him as "in the prime of a vigorous mental and physical manhood and approaching the meridian of the unusually successful and brilliant career"), no author, undated, unattributed, Stark Foundation Archives, 1; "Henry J. Lutcher Died Yesterday," *Daily Gazette and Bulletin*, 2 October 1912; "Henry Jacob Lutcher Thrived as Wealthy Sawmill Operator," *Orange Leader*, 25 July 1985.

41. Matilda Roulon Wilson Robinson obituary, clipping, undated and unattributed but probably a Lincoln, Kansas, newspaper, copy in Stark Foundation Archives; Kyle Hood, "Remembrances of Mrs. Lutcher, 1966–2008," collected stories of Frances Ann Lutcher from members of First (Lutcher Memorial) Presbyterian Church, Orange, Texas, unpublished typescript 1966–2008.

42. H.J.L. Stark to Lawrence J. Lutcher, 10 July 1961; Hood, "Remembrances of Mrs. Lutcher"; Frances A. Lutcher obituary, typescript, Williamsport newspaper, 12 November 1924, Stark Foundation Archives. Records of both Frances Ann's birthplace and the year of her birth are contradictory. In the aforementioned 1961 letter, Lutcher Stark refers to his grandmother as "a little French Canadian girl from Windsor, Canada" and Kyle Hood's record of the oral traditions of the church Frances Ann built and attended, First (Lutcher Memorial) Presbyterian in Orange, indicates she was born in Windsor, as does the typescript of her obituary. Her passport application dated May 9, 1921, however, lists her birthplace as

Philadelphia and her birth date as 1840. The most convincing evidence seems to indicate that she was born in Windsor.

43. H.J.L. Stark to Lawrence J. Lutcher, 10 July 1961; Hood, "Remembrances of Mrs. Lutcher"; family Bible belonging to H.J. and Frances A. Lutcher, family records section, no pagination, Stark Foundation Archives. This record states that David Robinson was born June 8, 1811, in Amherstburg.

44. Robinson petitioned for citizenship in 1857. Court of Common Pleas, 16 October 1857.

45. Matilda Roulon Wilson Robinson obituary; Hood, "Remembrances of Mrs. Lutcher." Matilda Robinson's obituary gives the following information on her: "She was born August 30, 1824, in Gloucester County, New Jersey. She was of Revolutionary ancestry, as her father was a patriot soldier against the British red-coat much more than a hundred years ago. When yet a child Matilda Roulon removed with her parents 'out west,' to Potter county, Penna., which was then a vast wilderness inhabited by wild beasts and a few hardy pioneers. Tiring of frontier life and its dangers, the Roulons removed to Jersey Shore, Lycoming County, Penna."

46. Matilda Roulon Wilson Robinson obituary.

47. Ida Nichols [Achenbach] (childhood friend of Frances Ann's older daughter, Miriam Lutcher [Stark] and later companion and amanuensis to Frances Ann Lutcher) to Miriam "Minie" Lutcher, 17 May 1880, asking Miriam to "tell your ma to tell your grandma [Matilda] hello," indicating at least a measure of family solidarity; "How Henry Lutcher Courted His Bride," handwritten poem, undated, possibly written by Frances Ann herself, calling Matilda "her mother," Stark Foundation Archives; Frances A. Lutcher's will, County Court, Orange County, Texas, leaving to her older daughter, Miriam, "the portraits of my father and mother now in my residence at Orange."

48. Matilda Roulon Wilson Robinson obituary.

49. Boyd and Boyd, *Boyd's Williamsport City Directory*, 1866–67, 72, lists David Robinson as a "merchant tailor"; Frances A. Lutcher obituary, typescript; Deed Records, Lycoming County, 79:203. In Boyd and Boyd, *Boyd's Williamsport City Directory*, 1875–76, 229, he is listed as having a shop at 59 West Fourth Street, probably the same property. Frances Ann's stepbrother, George Wilson, also became a tailor, remaining in the Robinson household through their final move to Kansas. Matilda Roulon Wilson Robinson obituary.

50. Deed Records, Lycoming County, 79:203.

51. Frances A. Lutcher, photograph and passport, Stark Foundation Archives.

52. Genealogy chart, *Las Sabinas* 6, no. 4 (1980): 42.

53. The author of this poem uses both spellings of the surname, the Americanized spelling in the first stanza and the old German spelling in the fifth.

54. Bible probably belonging to Frances Ann Lutcher in the later years of her life, containing pressed flowers, snapshots of family groups, and other memorabilia, Stark Foundation Archives.

55. Matilda had married David Robinson when Frances Ann was twelve years old. The poem was written *after* Frances Ann's marriage to Henry Jacob Lutcher, when she was seventeen; hence, Matilda Robinson was the "mother" to whom Frances Ann confesses the elopement.

56. Kenneth Foree Jr., "Archangel and His Bible," *Saturday Evening Post*, 9 October 1937; H.J.L. Stark to Lawrence J. Lutcher, 25 June 1961.

57. Boyd and Boyd, *Boyd's Williamsport City Directory*, 1866–67, 54.

58. Genealogy chart, *Las Sabinas*, 42.

59. H.J.L. Stark to Lawrence J. Lutcher, 10 July 1961.

60. Meginness, *History of Lycoming County*, 431.

61. Van Auken, "Timeline of Historic Events." Amherstburg, Ontario, the birthplace of David Robinson, served as a port of entry for runaway slaves coming into Canada.

62. Meginness, *History of Lycoming County*, 432.

63. Randall B. Woods and Willard D. Gatewood, *America Interpreted* (Fort Worth: Harcourt Brace College Publishers, 1998), 486.

64. Meginness, *History of Lycoming County*, 432.

65. Christian B. Keller, "Pennsylvania and Virginia Germans during the Civil War: A Brief History and Comparative Analysis," *Virginia Magazine of History and Biography*, Virginia Historical Society, http://www.vahistorical.org/publications/Abstract_1091_Keller.htm (site discontinued).

66. "Henry Jacob Lutcher Thrived as Wealthy Sawmill Operator," *Orange Leader*, 25 July 1985; "Henry J. Lutcher," typescript of interview, 3.

67. "Henry J. Lutcher," typescript of interview, 3; Foree, "Archangel and His Bible," 96; Robert Wooster, "Lutcher, Henry Jacob," *Handbook of Texas Online*, accessed 12 February 2010, http://www.tshaonline.org/handbook/online/articles/flu13, uploaded 15 June 2010, published by the Texas State Historical Association.

68. Van Auken, "Timeline of Historic Events"; Meginness, *History of Lycoming County*, 432–433, 435.

69. Meginness, *History of Lycoming County*, 456.

70. "Antietam," Civil War Trust, http://www.civilwar.org/battlefields/antietam.html (accessed 5 October 2015).

71. Foree, "Archangel and His Bible," 96.

72. "American Civil War Soldiers," ancestry.com, http://search.ancestry.com/cgi-bin/sse.dll?rank=1&new=1&MSAV=0&msT=1&gss=angs-... (site discontinued).

73. *Eighth Annual Catalogue*, 9; *Ninth Annual Catalogue for the Academical Year of June 10, 1856, to June 10, 1857* (Elmira, NY: Fairman & Co.'s Steam Printing Establishment, 1857), 9, Records of Lycoming College (formerly Dickinson Seminary), Williamsport, Pennsylvania.

Chapter 2

1. "Lumbering in the Lone Star State," *Weekly Sun and Banner* (Williamsport, Pennsylvania), 13 October 1881, clipping, Stark Foundation Archives.

2. "Appomattox Court House," National Park Service, US Department of the Interior, http://www.nps.gov/apco/index.htm (accessed 5 October 2015).

3. Stocker, "The Repasz Band in the Civil War."

4. Daniell, "Henry J. Lutcher, Orange," 470; "Henry Jacob Lutcher Thrived as Wealthy Sawmill Operator," *Orange Leader*, 25 July 1985; "Henry J. Lutcher," typescript of interview, Stark Foundation Archives. For the month of September 1862, Lutcher was taxed for owning eighteen head of cattle and one calf. Tax Rolls, State of Pennsylvania, Division No. 7, Collection District No. 18.

5. Deed Records, Lycoming County, 50:232; Frances A. Lutcher obituary, typescript, Williamsport newspaper, 12 November 1924; interviews with Charles Robert Lutcher, descendant of Henry Jacob Lutcher's brother, Albert William Lutcher, by Patsy Herrington, Jo Ann Stiles, and Ellen Rienstra, South Williamsport, Pennsylvania, 7 April 2010.

6. Deed Records, Lycoming County, 50:232, 58:175.

7. Meginness, *History of Lycoming County*, 290.

8. Deed Records, Lycoming County, 54:369–370.

9. Ibid., 369.

10. Meginness, *History of Lycoming County*, 530.

11. "The Jobbing Mill, Establishment of Lutscher and Moore on the South Side—Its Size and Capacity Fully Described—a Successful Enterprise—What Pluck Will Do," *Daily Gazette and Bulletin* (Williamsport, Pennsylvania), 20 November 1872, 4; Meginness, *History of Lycoming County*, 530; Taber, *Williamsport: Lumber Capital*, 71. A muley saw is built into a framework resembling a window frame, using an up-and-down motion to cut lumber.

12. "The Jobbing Mill," 4; Taber, *Williamsport: Lumber Capital*, 71; Elizabeth Blasdel [Mrs. G. Bedell] Moore, "Sketch of the Life of Gregory Bedell Moore," vols. 1 and 2, handwritten manuscript provided to Eric Steinfeldt by Elizabeth Moore, November 1986, originals in G. Bedell Moore Collection, Stephen F. Austin University, Nacogdoches, Texas; "Henry J. Lutcher," typescript of interview, 1; Daniell, "Henry J. Lutcher, Orange," 470; "Henry Jacob Lutcher Thrived as Wealthy Sawmill Operator." As previously noted, Henry Lutcher and Bedell Moore were students at Dickinson Academy during different years, and both were members of the Militia of 1862, 3rd Regiment, Company K (consisting of Williamsport men), Lutcher as a corporal, Moore as a private.

13. Moore, "Sketch of the Life of Gregory Bedell Moore," vol. 1.

14. Ibid.

15. Some sources give Rev. Richard Channing Moore's term as rector of Christ Church as 1855–1865. See *Christ Church Parish: A Tour*, pamphlet, Christ Episcopal Church, Williamsport, Pennsylvania.

16. *Seventh Annual Catalogue*, 14; *Eighth Annual Catalogue*, 9; *Ninth Annual Catalogue*, 9.

17. *Ninth Annual Catalogue*, 9.

18. Moore, "Sketch of the Life of Gregory Bedell Moore," vol. 1.

19. Boyd and Boyd, *Boyd's Williamsport City Directory*, 1866–67, 55.

20. Moore, "Sketch of the Life of Gregory Bedell Moore," vol. 1.

21. Ibid.; "Brief History of Lutcher & Moore Lumber Company and G. Bedell Moore," *Las Sabinas* 2, no. 1 (Winter 1976): 9, citing information given by Ernest Hammond "Ernie" Willey obtained from the Moore family Bible, courtesy of Mrs. G. Bedell Moore Jr. of San Antonio, Texas. The Moores married September 1, 1864.

22. Moore, "Sketch of the Life of Gregory Bedell Moore, 1:11; "Brief History of Lutcher & Moore Lumber Company," 9.

23. Boyd and Boyd, *Boyd's Williamsport City Directory*, 1866–67, 55; "Peter Herdic (1824–1881) Historical Marker."

24. The house still stands, although the original turret has been removed. In the 1880s, the houses were renumbered, and the address of the Moore house is now 918 West Fourth Street. Boyd and Boyd, *Boyd's Williamsport City Directory*, 1875–76.

25. Moore, "Sketch of the Life of Gregory Bedell Moore," 1:7.

26. Deed Records, Lycoming County, 55:404–405.

27. Boyd and Boyd, *Boyd's Williamsport City Directory*, 1879–80, 205.

28. Interview with Charles Robert Lutcher, 7 April 2010; H.J.L. Stark to Lawrence J. Lutcher, 10 July 1961, 2; headstones of Lutcher family, Wildwood Cemetery, Williamsport.

29. Deed Records, Lycoming County, 64:7, 65:435.

30. "The Jobbing Mill."

31. Ibid., 4.

32. Ibid., 5, 6.

33. Taber, *Williamsport: Lumber Capital*, 41, 71.

34. "The Jobbing Mill."

35. Meginness, *History of Lycoming County*, 362.

36. *Daily Gazette and Bulletin*, 9 August 1875.

37. Deed Records, Lycoming County, 64:7, 1 March 1871; 65:435, 1 June 1871; 68:629–630, 9 October 1872; 68:57–58, 14 December 1872; 70:209, 29 November 1873; 72:271, 3 October 1874; 74:38, 17 July 1875; 79:519–521, 27 August 1877; 94:140–141, 8 August 1882; 117:19–20, 9 November 1886. On November 2, 1899, they sold the eight hundred acres that had been their first purchase on April 22, 1868. They paid $450 for the land and sold it for $1,500.

38. "Henry J. Lutcher," typescript of interview, 1; Daniell, "Henry J. Lutcher, Orange," 470; "Henry Jacob Lutcher Thrived as Wealthy Sawmill Operator."

39. Both Frances Ann and Henry Lutcher had apparently received only limited educations. The daughter of portraitist August Benziger quoted her father as saying that Frances Ann had never learned to write. Although she could certainly read, the few existing examples of her writing are spare, laborious, and difficult to decipher, especially in her later years, and she utilized the services of her companion and amanuensis, Williamsport family friend Ida Nichols Achenbach, or family members for her correspondence. Marieli Benziger, *August Benziger: International Portrait Painter*, ed. Janet Reberdy (Kansas City, MO: Society of the Sacred Heart by Sheed & Ward, 1993), 245.

40. Weldon Scheel, "Stark Donations Increase Library Value," *Daily Texan*, 28 May 1933.

41. *Miss Wilson's School for Young Ladies and Children*, pamphlet (Williamsport, PA: Gazette & Bulletin Printing House, 1879), Stark Foundation Archives; Scheel, "Stark Donations Increase Library Value"; Meginness, *History of Lycoming County*, 414.

42. Scheel, "Stark Donations Increase Library Value."

43. Ibid.

44. She signed a notebook into which she had copied poems, quotations, and essays "Miriam M. Lutscher, Rocktown, Pa." The earliest date in the notebook is September 6, 1870. Stark Foundation Archives.

45. "Orange Citizens Mourn Death of Mrs. Stark," *Orange Leader*, 29 November 1936.

46. Meckley, *Williamsport's Millionaires' Row*, 104; Meckley, *Williamsport*, 51; "Severin Roesen (ca. 1816–after 1872): Artist Biography," MME Fine Art, http://www.mmefineart.com/artist/bio/index.php?aid=274 (accessed 3 December 2015).

47. Ida [Nichols Achenbach] to Miriam Lutcher, 17 May 1880; Moore, "Sketch of the Life of Gregory Bedell Moore."

48. Helen Breese Weidman, *A History of Messiah's Evangelical Lutheran Church, South Williamsport, Penna.*, booklet (Williamsport, PA: Messiah's Evangelical Lutheran Church, 1943), 7.

49. Meginness, *History of Lycoming County*, 529; Deed Records, Lycoming County, 60:174. The congregation purchased the land from Michael McDonough.

50. Deed Records, Lycoming County, 60:174.

51. Charles Robert Lutcher to Nelda Stark, 19 December 1986.

52. Weidman, *A History of Messiah's Evangelical Lutheran Church*, 10.

53. Messiah's Evangelical Lutheran Church, Records, South Williamsport, Pennsylvania.

54. Woods and Gatewood, *America Interpreted*, 535–536.

55. "Pennsylvania Lumber History," 2.

56. *Daily Sun and Banner*, 25 January 1882, clipping in Stark Foundation Archives.

57. Taber, *Williamsport: Lumber Capital*, 7.

58. F.H. Farwell, "Saw Mill Industry Plays Major Part in Texas History: Orange Center of Early Day Development," *Orange Leader*, 29 May 1936.

59. "G. Bedell Moore's Personal Account of 15-Day Trek through Texas January 11–February 13, 1877," *Las Sabinas* 2, no. 1 (Winter 1976): 14; Robert S. Maxwell and Robert D. Baker, *Sawdust Empire: The Texas Lumber Industry, 1830–1940* (Austin: Texas A&M University Press, 1983), 22–23.

60. "G. Bedell Moore's Personal Account," 14, 16.

61. Ibid., 17.

62. Ibid., 18.

63. Ibid., 20.

64. Ibid., 21. Coincidentally, William Hooks was author Rienstra's great-grandfather.

65. Ibid., 22.

66. Ibid., 21.

67. Ibid., 22.

68. William Seale, *Texas Riverman: The Life and Times of Captain Andrew Farney Smyth* (Austin: University of Texas Press, 1966), 145–154.

69. Ibid., 12, 26; Diana J. Kleiner, "Bevilport, TX," *Handbook of Texas Online*, accessed 16 April 2012, http://www.tshaonline.org/handbook/online/articles/hrb29, uploaded 12 June 2010, published by the Texas State Historical Association. The town of Bevilport had been named in 1830 for a John Bevil, probably either this man or his father.

70. "G. Bedell Moore's Personal Account," 23.

71. Ibid., 24.

72. "Lumbering in the Lone Star State: Our Reporter Interviews Mr. H.J. Lutcher of Orange, Texas—What Eastern Enterprise Has Done in That Country, &c. &c.," *Weekly Sun and Banner*, 13 October 1881.

73. "G. Bedell Moore's Personal Account," 26, 25.

74. Ibid.

75. Lutcher and Moore also learned of a potential impediment to operations: "the narrows," a constricted spot approximately fifteen miles upriver from Orange, where the Sabine was only 75 to 125 feet wide and was choked with stumps and fallen trees. Luckily, the river had formed an oxbow at that point, and Lutcher and Moore determined that the problem could be surmounted by cutting a ditch straight across the oxbow, thus allowing logs to be floated through without difficulty. Ibid., 26.

76. Ibid., 29, 7. Specifically, Moore related a conversation between himself and two lumbermen who owned lumber yards in Columbus, Texas. They believed that eighteen to twenty million feet of lumber could be sold annually between Columbus and San Antonio inclusive. One owner was paying $11 to $12 per million to Long & Company, a Beaumont lumber mill.

77. Ibid., 30, 29, 31.

78. Ibid., 32.

79. Ibid., 34.

80. Maxwell and Baker, *Sawdust Empire*, 29–30.

81. "G. Bedell Moore's Personal Account," 35–36; Maxwell and Baker, *Sawdust Empire*, 30.

82. "G. Bedell Moore's Personal Account," 39.

83. Donald R. Walker, "Harvesting the Forest: Henry Jacob Lutcher, G. Bedell Moore, and the Advent of Commercial Lumbering in Texas," *Journal of the West* 35, no. 3 (July 1996): 14.

84. When annexed in 1845, Texas had retained its own public lands that remained after it had discharged its debts and liabilities and after it had ceded public edifices and "all property pertaining to the public defence." The Annexation of Texas Joint Resolution of Congress 1 March 1845 (US Statutes at Large, 5797–5798).

85. Frances A. Lutcher obituary, typescript. Lutcher Stark told a family story that credited Frances Ann Lutcher with the decision to relocate: "My grandmother sent my grandfather down to [East Texas] because she had heard there was a lots of timber down in Texas and Louisiana. . . . She saw an opportunity to put him into the sawmill business with what money they had amassed. . . . She had all the drive in the world." H.J.L. Stark to Lawrence Lutcher, 10 July 1961.

86. Robert S. Weddle, "La Salle, René Robert Cavelier, Sieur de," *Handbook of Texas Online*, accessed 1 July 2011, http://www.tshaonline.org/handbook/online/articles/fla04, uploaded 15 June 2010, published by the Texas State Historical Association.

87. Howard C. Williams, *Gateway to Texas: The History of Orange and Orange County* (Orange, TX: Heritage House Museum of Orange, 1986), 21–23; Judith Walker Linsley and Ellen Walker Rienstra, *Beaumont: A Chronicle of Progress* (Woodland Hills, CA: Windsor Publications, 1982), 19.

88. Linsley and Rienstra, *Beaumont*, 17.

89. John V. Haggard, "Neutral Ground," *Handbook of Texas Online*, accessed 1 July 2011, http://www.tshaonline.org/handbook/online/articles/nbn02, uploaded 15 June 2010, published by the Texas State Historical Association.

90. Ibid., 27.

91. Sarah Moore, "River Decided for Settlers," *Beaumont Enterprise*, 6 June 2011; H. Williams, *Gateway to Texas*, 37–39; *Earliest Records and Census Abstracts of Nineteenth Century Orange County Texas (1836–1880)* (Orange, TX: A Sesquicentennial Project Compiled and Published by the Orange County Historical Society, 1986), 6–11.

92. Rupert Norval Richardson, Adrian Anderson, Cary D. Wintz, and Ernest Wallace, *Texas: The Lone Star State*, 10th ed. (Boston: Prentice Hall, 2010), 67–80, 88–89; H. Williams, *Gateway to Texas*, 33. On November 12, 1835, Claiborne West attended the Consultation as a delegate from the Liberty Municipality. (The Consultation was a group that purported to serve as the provisional government of Mexican Texas from November 1835 through March 1836 during the Texas Revolution, although there was a lack of accord on the extent of the power of this group.) In his role as Consultation delegate, West effected the creation of the new Municipality of Jefferson, formed from the portion of the Liberty district east of the Neches River. On December 21, 1837, the First Congress of the Republic of Texas established the county system, extending the boundaries of Claiborne West's existing Municipality of Jefferson to the west, across the Neches River, to encompass the town of Beaumont.

93. H. Williams, *Gateway to Texas*, 36.

94. Ibid.

95. Richardson et al., *Texas*, 122–123.

96. H. Williams, *Gateway to Texas*, 38–39.

97. Ibid., 97.

98. Ibid., 79.

99. *Beaumont: A Guide to the City and Its Environs*, Work Projects Administration, in the State of Texas, Federal Writers' Project, American Guide Series (Houston: Anson Jones Press, 1938), 67.

100. Ibid., 68; H. Williams, *Gateway to Texas*, 81.

101. *Beaumont: A Guide to the City*, 69–72.

102. Robert E. Russell, *A History of Orange*, ed. Loren LeBlanc, booklet (Orange, TX: Orange County Historical Society, n.d.), 7–8.

103. Hamilton Pratt Easton, "The History of the Texas Lumbering Industry" (PhD diss., University of Texas at Austin, 1947).

104. Deed Records, Orange County, Orange, Texas, F:384–385, 386–387, 427–428. Ac-

cording to some accounts, a small sawmill already existed on one of these tracts; hence, instead of building a new mill, Lutcher simply improved, enlarged, and modernized the existing one. It is also possible that Lutcher and Moore operated the existing mill until they could complete a separate, larger one. Maxwell and Baker, *Sawdust Empire*, 31, citing interview with B.C. McDonough, general manager, retired, Lutcher & Moore Lumber Company, 13 August 1963, and with Robert P. Turpin, secretary, retired, Lutcher & Moore Lumber Company, 13 August 1963, Oral History Collections, Forest History Collections, Stephen F. Austin State University, Nacogdoches, Texas; Walker, "Harvesting the Forest," 13.

105. H.J. Lutcher to G.B. Moore, 19 March 1877; H. Williams, *Gateway to Texas*, 149. The name of the shipyard is unknown; small shipyards had sprung up on the riverbank throughout the last half of the nineteenth century and then had disappeared.

106. Deed Records, Orange County, F:386.

107. In his letters to Moore, Lutcher spells his name "Rinehart"; in the Lutcher family Bible and in the history of Messiah's Lutheran Church in Williamsport, the name is spelled "Reinhart." H.J. Lutcher to G.B. Moore, 19 March, 11 April, and 28 May 1877.

108. "An Orange Mill," *Beaumont Enterprise*, 10 October 1905; W. T. Block, "The Lutcher & Moore Lumber Company," in *East Texas Mill Towns and Ghost Towns* (Lufkin, TX: Best of East Texas Publishers, 1994), 1:261–266; W. T. Block, *Cotton Bales, Keelboats, and Sternwheelers: A History of the Sabine River and Trinity River Cotton Trades, 1837–1900* (Woodville, TX: Dogwood Press, 1996), 54. See list of Block's books online at http://www.wtblock.com/wtblockjr/Books.htm.

109. The whistle blew for fifteen minutes at 4:30 a.m. At 5:45 a.m., it blew two short blasts to signify the commencement of work in fifteen minutes, then at 6:00 a.m. one short blast to signal the beginning of the workday. It blew again at noon to begin the lunch hour, then again at 6:00 p.m. to proclaim the end of Lutcher & Moore's eleven-hour workday. When the mill was dismantled, Lutcher Stark gave the whistle to a "local pickle factory" (possibly the Orange Products Company), but so much steam was required to blow it that it interfered with the canning process. It was then given to the DuPont Sabine River Works petrochemical plant in Orange, which in turn donated it to the Orange County Heritage House Museum. Its distinctive whistle has been recorded. "Pertinent Facts concerning the Lutcher & Moore Lumber Company Whistle Now in Use at the DuPont Plant," typescript, Stark Foundation Archives; Bob McGuffin, "Lutcher Whistle on DuPont Plant Refuses to Be Quiet," *Port Arthur News*, 15 November 1959; Margaret Toal, "Old Whistle Loses Steam," *Beaumont Enterprise*, 9 September 1993.

110. H.J. Lutcher to G.B. Moore, 19 March and 6 April 1877.

111. Ibid., 21 March, 6 April, 11 April, and 6 April 1877.

112. Ibid., 26 March 1877.

113. Ibid., 28 March and 11 April 1877.

114. Ibid., 12 April, 28 March, 11 April, 16 April, 23 April, 11 May, 1 May, and 14 May 1877.

115. Ibid., 23 May 1877.

116. Tyler E. Bagwell, "Brunswick and the Mallory Line Steamship Company," Jekyll Island History, http://www.jekyllislandhistory.com/malloryline.shtml (accessed 2 November 2015).

117. H.J. Lutcher to G.B. Moore, 30 May 1877.

118. George Britenbach to G.B. Moore, 1 June 1877.

119. "The Mills at Orange, Lutcher & Moore," clipping, undated, Stark Foundation Archives.

120. "The Lutcher & Moore Lumber Company," undated, unattributed article, probably written around 1892, G. Bedell Moore Collection, Stephen F. Austin University, Nacogdo-

ches, Texas; Maxwell and Baker, *Sawdust Empire*, 31; Walker, "Harvesting the Forest," 10–17; Block, "The Lutcher & Moore Lumber Company," 33.

121. "William Henry Stark," *Las Sabinas* 6, no. 4 (1980): 27.

Chapter 3

1. A longer version of the same poem was found in the Newton County Historical Commission, *Glimpses of Newton County History* (Burnet, TX: Nortex Press, 1982), 218. In that source, it was also listed as an unidentified clipping.

2. Naming the firstborn son "John" was a Stark family tradition. Archibald was an oldest son, but his father broke with tradition and named him after his wife's family.

3. Jane Harter Abbott, "A Stark Genealogy: Some Descendants of John Stark from Scotland to the United States about 1710 and His Son, James Stark, Born in Scotland in 1695, Settled in Overwharton Parish, Stafford, Virginia, Prior to 1730," unpublished manuscript, compiled between 1928 and 1931 for Mrs. William Henry (Miriam Lutcher) Stark, Rare Books Room, Library of Congress, Scotland Section, Stark Foundation Archives; *The Name and Family of Stark(e) or Starks*, pt. 2 (Washington, DC: Media Research Bureau, 1938), Stark Foundation Archives.

4. "John Stark, Soldier," Celebrate Boston, http://www.celebrateboston.com/biography /john-stark.htm (accessed 7 October 2015); John Spargo, *The Bennington Battle Monument* (Rutland, VT: Tuttle, 1925), 32–62, Stark Foundation Archives.

5. Abbott, "A Stark Genealogy," citing James Clark to Miss Mary Fanny Clark, secretary of the Stark Family Association of New London, Connecticut, 26 October 1921. In this letter James Clark speculates that John Stark, the father of the three boys who immigrated, and a Dr. Richard Stark who moved to York County, Virginia, in 1700 were brothers and business partners. Clark reasons that Richard brought James to Virginia with him when the boy was five years old to serve as a student preparatory to becoming a doctor. However, the physician Dr. Richard Stark, who came to Virginia with *two* dependents named James Stark, died when the James in question was only nine years old, at which point James disappears from Virginia records, to reappear long after and to die there. Other sources say that James came to New Hampshire with his brothers. The authors do not know which version, if either, is correct.

6. Will of James Stark, Clerk's Office, Stafford Circuit Court, Stafford, Virginia, O:27, 2 September 1753, Stark Foundation Archives. James had fifteen children, eight female and seven male.

7. Abbott, "A Stark Genealogy," Fourth Generation, Thomas Stark.

8. Stark family Bible, Stark Foundation Archives.

9. The major political factions in the Republic of Texas, whether supporters or opponents of Sam Houston, the hero of San Jacinto, twice president of the Republic of Texas, and implacable advocate of annexation, fought bitterly over the republic's best course, but one truth became increasingly evident: stability and prosperity would not be at hand until after Texas joined the Union, and even then, improved conditions would not last. The situation posed difficulties enough, but to add to the fledgling republic's woes, Mexican forces reinvaded Texas twice in the early 1840s, although unsuccessfully. Richardson et al., *Texas*, 104–123.

10. Land Commissioner's Office, minutes, 1837, San Augustine County, Texas, 208.

11. In 1848, Jeremiah served as constable of Precinct 6 of San Augustine County.

12. Marriage Records, 1:93, San Augustine County, Texas. Justice of the Peace John N.

Lewis performed the ceremony. It is possible that they eloped; years later, John Thomas, away at war, wrote Martha: "You are still the same sweet girl who one dark night left home to cast her fortunes and her all in with a boy who had nothing but an invincible determination to make a living for himself and the fond girl who marched by his side." John Thomas Stark to Martha Stark, 10 February 1863.

13. Abbott, "A Stark Genealogy," Seventh Generation, William Henry Stark.

14. William Seale, *San Augustine in the Texas Republic* (Austin: Encino Press, 1969), 10–15, reprinted through the courtesy of the Texas State Historical Association and Lelia Wynn, originally published in the January 1969 issue of *Southwestern Historical Quarterly*; Gilbert M. Cuthbertson, "Regulator-Moderator War," *Handbook of Texas Online*, accessed 26 March 2014, http://www.tshaonline.org/handbook/online/articles/jcr01, uploaded 15 June 2010, published by the Texas State Historical Association.

15. Eugenia Rebecca Stark Ford, handwritten family history donated to Stark Foundation Archives by Madge Channing Luquette, a descendant of Eugenia Ford, undated, no pagination; Robert Wooster, "Burkeville, TX," *Handbook of Texas Online*, accessed 20 January 2012, http://tshaonline.org/handbook/online/articles/hlb64, uploaded 12 June 2010, published by the Texas State Historical Association; Robert Wooster, "Newton, TX," *Handbook of Texas Online*, accessed 20 January 2012, http://tshaonline.org/handbook/online /articles/hjn05, uploaded 15 June 2010, published by the Texas State Historical Association. Newton did offer a mail service briefly in 1847 but did not acquire a post office until 1853. Newton County was carved from Jasper County by the legislature of the new state of Texas on April 22, 1846. Originally, the location of the county seat was planned for the center of the county; no town existed in that vicinity, only a small stream called Quicksand Creek. In 1848, the citizens of Burkeville had successfully petitioned the legislature to make their town the county seat; however, even as John Thomas and Martha prepared their move to Burkeville in 1853, the seat was in the process of being moved to Newton, a newer town more centrally located. See Wooster, "Newton, TX."

16. Inventory & Appraisement of Common Property, Estate of M.A. Stark, Dec'd, Stark Foundation Archives. At Martha's death in September 1863, she and John Thomas had acquired a considerable amount of property. J.T. Stark to Martha Ann Stark, 25 May 1853.

17. Rebecca's first husband, Martha's biological father, had died on a trip to New Orleans before she was born. Her second husband, John B. Wofford, Martha's stepfather, had headed for the California gold fields and never returned. He was presumed dead. John B. Wofford to Rebecca Wofford, 22 April 1854, from Chinese Camp, Trolumne County, California; Ford, handwritten family history. The letter stated that he was starting for home, but he never arrived, and no further word was ever received.

18. John Thomas Stark carried a piece of paper folded into a small square, on which were handwritten the words to the wedding ceremony. Stark Foundation Archives.

19. Horatio King, first assistant postmaster general, to J.T. Stark, 12 July 1860.

20. Evans was a relative of the Starks' neighbors, the Triplett family.

21. A.H. Evans to J.T. Stark, 18 March 1860 (emphasis added).

22. Extract from a letter from Col. A.H. Evans to [?] (perhaps to Evans's sister, Mrs. Triplett), 21 October 1860.

23. J.T. Stark to postmaster general of the United States, 6 November 1860; A.H. Evans to J.T. Stark, 28 January 1861, Washington City, D.C.

24. J.T. Stark to John A. Kapon, first assistant postmaster general, Washington City, D.C., 30 April 1861 (emphasis added).

25. J.T. Stark to Rebecca Wofford, August 1864.

26. J.T. Stark to Dr. David Ford, 10 March 1873.

27. Testimony of Col. A.F. Crawford before the Retiring Board of Forney's Division,

Co. H, 13th Texas Cavalry, regarding Capt. John T. Stark, 13 November 1864, Stark Foundation Archives.

28. Photo of William Stark and his son, Lutcher, playing violins, and his wife, Miriam Lutcher Stark, playing piano, Stark Foundation Archives; Ford, handwritten family history.

29. Ford, handwritten family history.

30. J.T. Stark Jr. to Donna J. Stark, 12 February 1895; Dr. N.P. West to J.T. Stark, 5 September 1863.

31. Violins made by the Amati family, a violin-making dynasty living in Cremona, Italy, during the sixteenth to the eighteenth centuries. Amati violins were considered to be almost of equal quality as those made by the Stradivari and Guarneri families. "Violin Makers of the Amati family," Smithsonian Seriously Amazing, http://www.si.edu/encyclopedia_si/nmah/amati.htm (accessed 3 December 2015).

32. J.T. Stark Jr. to Donna J. Stark, 12 February 1895. This story came from Donna Stark to Hobby Stark and his wife, Mae; then to their son, Mitchell Stark (who ultimately inherited the violin); and finally to Lilly Rose Stark, Hobby's youngest sister. Lilly Rose told this story to a nephew, the late Jeremiah Milton Stark, who told the story to the authors on or around May 2, 2012. Jeremiah Stark transcribed all of these early letters; his transcriber's note in the typed copy of the letter in the Stark Foundation Archives contains this story. The authors owe a debt of gratitude to him for his donation of, and work with, these letters.

33. Richardson et al., *Texas*, 130–133. The immediate result of annexation had been the Mexican War, fought 1846 to 1848 and ending with the Treaty of Guadalupe Hidalgo, which awarded Texans a boundary they had never possessed under Spanish or Mexican control but had claimed for themselves during the time of the republic. But the treaty also gave a significant amount of land to the United States—all the way to the Pacific Ocean—leading to internal conflict between Texas and New Mexico. Texas Rangers were actually sent to New Mexico twice to organize much of it under Texas control, but they were driven away by New Mexico citizens with threats of being tarred and feathered. A dispute between Texas and the US government arose, culminating in Texas' threatened secession in 1849, barely four years into statehood. Ultimately, the Compromise of 1850 established the present boundary between Texas, New Mexico, and the Indian Territory (later Oklahoma). To placate Texans, the treaty also made provision to pay the state $10 million to give up its claim to land that it had never owned, committing the money to paying the existing debt incurred during the Texas Revolution and the republic and quieting the cries for secession.

34. Ibid., 141–143. The Indian issue had begun to fade in East Texas after President Mirabeau B. Lamar sent an army to drive out the Cherokee in 1839. The situation had become so serious on the frontier in the 1850s, however, that the government moved federal troops to Texas and built a sizable number of forts. Predictably, this problem grew worse as federal troops were removed. The first complaint listed in Texas' Declaration of Secession was the failure of the US government to provide protection from Indian depredations.

35. When gold was discovered in California in 1848, that territory gained enough population almost overnight to qualify for statehood. California's admission as a free state in 1850 destroyed the previously balanced number of slave and free states in the Senate, giving the free states control in both houses of Congress, thus threatening the institution of slavery.

36. Sam Houston, at that time a US senator from Texas (serving from 1846 to 1859) and a staunch supporter of the Union, spoke out against the concept of states' rights. His stance caused passions to rise even higher in Texas.

37. Texas' secession convention also removed Sam Houston, by then governor of the state (1859–1861), from office because of his refusal to take a loyalty oath to the Confederacy.

38. Richardson et al., *Texas*, 169–174.

39. Martha Stark to J.T. Stark, 17–21 August 1862.

40. John H. Reagan, postmaster general of the Confederate States of America, to the Burkeville postmaster, 20 May 1861.

41. Ibid.; "William Henry Stark," *Las Sabinas* 6, no. 4 (1980): 25–26.

42. "Orange Pays Final Tribute to W.H. Stark," *Orange Leader*, 9 October 1936.

43. Foree, "Archangel and His Bible."

44. J.P. Blessington, *The Campaigns of Walker's Texas Division* (Austin: Pemberton Press, 1968), 48–49; Thomas Reid, *Spartan Band: Burnett's 13th Texas Cavalry in the Civil War* (Denton: University of North Texas Press, 2005), 27–34; Richard Lowe, *Walker's Texas Division, C.S.A.: Greyhounds of the Trans-Mississippi* (Baton Rouge: Louisiana State University Press, 2004), 5–7; J.T. Stark, draft of letter outlining his military career, 22 July 1864, Stark Foundation Archives.

45. Lester Newton Fitzhugh, "Walker's Texas Division," *Handbook of Texas Online*, accessed 28 February 2012, http://www.tshaonline.org/handbook/online/articles/qkwo1, uploaded 15 June 2010, published by the Texas State Historical Association.

46. Reid, *Spartan Band*, 37, 46–82.

47. They fought with "dismounted" tactics, "which meant that they threw all their infantry training out the window and did what they darned well pleased." Clipping, "The Civil War Comes to Orange County," in *The Record Archives: From the Pages of Orange County History*, 22 April 1998, 10B, Stark Foundation Archives.

48. Fitzhugh, "Walker's Texas Division."

49. Eugenia Stark to J.T. Stark, 24 September 1862.

50. J.T. Stark to Martha Stark, 20 August 1862.

51. Martha Stark to J.T. Stark, 1 March 1862–1 August 1863.

52. Abbott, "A Stark Genealogy," Seventh Generation, William Henry Stark; "William H. Stark," 25.

53. Martha Stark to J.T. Stark, 20 July 1862; J.T. Stark to Martha Stark, 9 August 1862. Stark mentioned in the letter that he had been revaccinated; since no vaccine for typhoid yet existed, he was probably revaccinated for smallpox; Martha Stark to J.T. Stark, 17 July 1863; W.H. Stark to J.T. Stark, 21 August 1863.

54. Abbott, "A Stark Genealogy," Sixth Generation, John Thomas Stark.

55. Martha Stark to J.T. Stark, 22 May 1862.

56. Ibid., 22 May, 20 July, and 17–21 August 1862.

57. Martha was now thirty-two years old but had borne nine children, with seven still living. She did not name the woman in her letter, but she knew her identity.

58. Martha Stark to J.T. Stark, 22 July 1862.

59. J.T. Stark to Martha Stark, undated.

60. W.H. Stark to J.T. Stark, 6 August 1862. Spelling and punctuation have been left as written.

61. Martha Stark to J.T. Stark, 11 August 1862.

62. W.H. Stark to J.T. Stark, 21 August 1863.

63. Martha Stark to J.T. Stark, 26 August 1863; Dr. N.P. West to J.T. Stark, 20–30 April 1864.

64. Martha Stark to J.T. Stark, 24–25 October 1862.

65. Maj. C.R. Beaty to Nancy Blewett, 24 September 1862; J.T. Stark to Martha Stark, 9 August and 24 September 1862.

66. Lowe, *Walker's Texas Division*, 71–78, 115; Reid, *Spartan Band*, 90.

67. J.T. Stark to Martha Stark, 3 August 1863; Martha Stark to J.T. Stark, 1 August, 26 July, and 11 August 1863; W.H. Stark to J.T. Stark, 21 August 1863.

68. Madge Channing Luquette, conversation with Jo Ann Stiles and Ellen Rienstra, 4 May 2004, Stark Foundation Archives.

69. J.T. Stark to Rebecca Wofford, 26 August 1863.

70. Accounts differ regarding the location of Martha Stark's grave; it has been variously identified as Pleasant Hill Church near Bayou Bucoff in Rapides Parish, Louisiana; Pine Hill Cemetery on Bayou Bucoff; and Springhill Church, also in the same area. Luquette, conversation with Stiles and Rienstra. Abbott, "A Stark Genealogy," Sixth Generation, John Thomas Stark (there are many errors in this sketch); Ford, handwritten family history.

71. J.T. Stark to Rebecca Wofford, 3 November 1863.

72. John Thomas's description should settle the location of her burial. Martha Stark is not listed on the inventory of marked graves in Springhill Cemetery, but it mentions two hundred unmarked graves and a part of the cemetery that had fallen into a ravine.

73. Ford, handwritten family history. Ford named Springhill Church as the burial site of her mother. Springhill Cemetery is still on the Louisiana maps today as an African American cemetery, with the aforementioned unmarked graves.

74. Rebecca Wofford to J.T. Stark, 31 December 1863.

75. Ibid.; Eugenia Stark (Ford) to J.T. Stark, November 1863; Ford, handwritten family history.

76. "Orange Pays Final Tribute to W.H. Stark."

77. Rebecca Wofford to J.T. Stark, 31 December 1863.

78. Eugenia Stark (Ford) to J.T. Stark, 3 May 1864.

79. Ibid., 20 May 1864; Rebecca Wofford to J. T. Stark, 5 May 1864.

80. Fitzhugh, "Walker's Texas Division"; Lowe, *Walker's Texas Division*, 255.

81. A rank Stark never attained.

82. Confederate general John Bankhead Magruder, who successfully defended Galveston in 1863 against the Union army and navy.

83. William R. Blackshear to J.T. Stark, 1 February 1864; Stark's response on same sheet, undated.

84. Reid, *Spartan Band*, 121.

85. Ibid., 126.

86. Alonzo H. Plummer, *Confederate Victory at Mansfield* (Mansfield, LA: Ideal Printing, 1969), 6.

87. Lowe, *Walker's Texas Division*, 133.

88. J.T. Stark, "His Diary: 25 September 1863 to 13 October 1864," typed transcript, 5, Stark Foundation Archives.

89. Ibid., 6, 8; Reid, *Spartan Band*, 130–134.

90. The Texas and Louisiana Confederates had easier access to water and the advantage of the supplies captured the day before; water for the Union forces was located at more than twice the distance, and to avoid capture of more supplies, Banks's forces destroyed what they could not carry with them in their retreat.

91. Reid, *Spartan Band*, 126, 136–144.

92. Plummer, *Confederate Victory at Mansfield*, 34–37.

93. Eugenia Stark (Ford) to John Thomas Stark, 27 May 1864.

94. Stark, "His Diary," 17.

95. Abbott, "A Stark Genealogy," Sixth Generation, J.T. Stark.

96. Eugenia Stark (Ford) to J.T. Stark, 16 September 1864; J.T. Stark to Rebecca Wofford, August 1864; W.H. Stark to J.T. Stark, 31 October 1864.

97. J.T. Stark, draft of letter not addressed and/or possibly not sent, 22 July 1864, summary of Stark's military career and that of Capt. Elias Seale; F.B. Sexton to J.T. Stark, 28 July 1864, letter from the Confederate congressman who recommended Captain Seale for promotion.

98. Appeal from J.T. Stark to the secretary of war of the Confederacy, 22 July 1864.

99. Reid, *Spartan Band*, 109, 200. Company F was later redesignated as Company G.

100. Recommendation in support of Capt. John T. Stark, signed by twelve officers of the 13th Texas Cavalry Regiment, 13 November 1864, Stark Foundation Archives.

101. Testimony of Col. A.F. Crawford and Lt. Col. C.R. Beaty before the Retiring Board of Forney's Division, Company H, 13th Texas Cavalry Regiment, regarding Capt. John T. Stark, 13 November 1864, Stark Foundation Archives.

102. Spargo, *The Bennington Battle Monument*, 33, Stark Foundation Archives.

103. Headquarters, Trans-Mississippi Department, Shreveport, Louisiana, Special Orders No. 296, 26 November 1864, Stark Foundation Archives.

104. Dr. N.P. West to the Board of Examining Surgeons, 14 February 1865.

105. Eliza Wooderson to J.T. Stark, 8 March 1865.

106. Headquarters of Confederate Service, Department of Texas, Rusk, Special Order No. 50, 7 March 1865, extract, Stark Foundation Archives.

107. James Donaho to J.T. Stark, 27 April 1865; Eliza Wooderson to J.T. Stark, 8 March 1865.

108. Richardson et al., *Texas*, 193.

109. Promissory note written by David Ford, in which J.T. Stark agrees to pay $500 in quarterly payments, 1 February 1865, Stark Foundation Archives.

110. Office of Hobby & Post to J.T. Stark, 20 November 1872; Hobby & Post to J.T. Stark, 2 July 1873; E.J. Hart & Co. to J.T. Stark, 9 July 1873.

111. J.T. Stark, pocket-size leather notebook containing a few business records, poems, acrostics, and miscellaneous notes, 1859–1865, Stark Foundation Archives.

112. Richardson et al., *Texas*, 192–208.

113. Some federal troops remained in Texas to deal with American Indian unrest.

114. Richardson et al., *Texas*, 192–208.

115. John Thomas was certified to practice in Texas in June 1868 and set up an office as a lawyer and notary public in Newton County. Certificate of John Thomas Stark's confirmation as Notary Public of Newton County, 25 March 1874, Stark Foundation Archives. It was signed by Governor Richard Coke.

116. Nida A. Marshall, *The Jasper Journal* (Austin: Nortex Press, 1993), 1:24–29. Nancy's parents were Abel and Elizabeth Ann Paramore Adams; Elizabeth was the sister of John Blewett's wife, Sarah Paramore Adams, and the two families moved to Texas together, along with a number of other Thomasville families. The two oldest Blewett children, William and his sister, Nancy, wrote a series of letters between 1849 and 1852 to relatives and friends back in Georgia, filled with information about early Jasper. Both married in 1852, Nancy to Charles R. Beaty and William to his first cousin, Nancy Adams.

117. Blewett family papers, Heritage Village, Woodville, Texas.

118. Marshall, *The Jasper Journal*, 1:24–29; Blewett family papers.

119. "1860 U.S. Federal Census-Slave Schedules," ancestry.com, 2010, http://search .ancestry.com/search/db.aspx?dbid=7668; "U.S., Civil War Soldiers and Records, 1861–1865," ancestry.com, 2007, http://search.ancestry.com/search/db.aspx?dbid=1555; "1860 United States Federal Census," ancestry.com, 2009, http://search.ancestry.com/search/db .aspx?dbid=7667. William Snell was the owner of one slave at the time of their marriage (when William Blewett died, Nancy had inherited twelve slaves).

120. Blewett family papers.

121. There is no direct evidence that they moved to the Blewett house, but there are no letters from Martha's children to John Thomas after the latter's marriage. When they were apart, they wrote one another.

122. Stark family genealogical information, Stark Foundation Archives.

123. Blewett family material; "U.S. Federal Census Mortality Schedules, 1850–1885," ancestry.com, 2010, http://search.ancestry.com/search/db.aspx?dbid=8756.

124. Dr. Jeremiah Milton Stark to authors, on or around 2 May 2012. John Thomas administered Nancy's estate, as well as those of her two previous husbands, William Blewett and William Snell.

125. J.T. Stark to A. and P.C. Gilmer, 17 May 1869.

126. Stark family Bible.

127. Legislative Reference Library of Texas, sessions, http://www.lrl.state.tx.us/sessions /sessionsnapshot.cfm?page=members&legSession (accessed 7 October 2015). Ford was later elected to the House.

128. Stark family Bible.

129. Abbott, "A Stark Genealogy," Seventh Generation, William Henry Stark; N. Dean Tevis, "W.H. Stark of Orange Helps Remake East Texas as Lumber Industry Passes Out," *Beaumont Enterprise*, 15 December 1929.

130. Abbott, "A Stark Genealogy," Seventh Generation, William Henry Stark; Tevis, "W.H. Stark of Orange."

131. Tevis, "W.H. Stark of Orange." The actual distance from Newton to Orange by modern transportation methods is approximately sixty miles.

132. Ibid.; Tevis, "W.H. Stark of Orange"; "William Henry Stark," 27.

133. Tevis, "W.H. Stark of Orange."

134. Ibid.

135. Records of Trips Made and of Failures en Route, Hardy sworn in 19 August 1869; "John Thomas Stark: His Life Letters and Papers, Somewhat of His Ancestors, Relatives, and Friends, vol. 2, 1868–1905," Stark Foundation Archives. Hardy was the son of J.T. Stark's sister Elizabeth Sarah Stark Hardy and her husband, Madison Hardy.

136. J.T. Stark to Susannah Mitchell, 17 March 1870.

137. Susannah Mitchell to J.T. Stark, 7 April 1870.

138. Abbott, "A Stark Genealogy," Sixth Generation, John Thomas Stark.

139. J.T. Stark to W.H. Stark, 19 October 1871.

140. Ibid.

141. Tevis, "W.H. Stark of Orange"; Abbott, "A Stark Genealogy," Seventh Generation, William Henry Stark; D.A. Pruter to W.H. Stark, 21 July 1925.

Chapter 4

1. Abbott, "A Stark Genealogy," Seventh Generation, William Henry Stark; Howard Williams, "William H. Stark," *Las Sabinas* 6, no. 4 (1980): 27.

2. R.B. Russell to J.T. Starks [sic], 12 November 1871.

3. W.H. Stark to Miriam Lutcher, 9 September, 5 October, and 24 November 1878.

4. Jeremiah Milton Stark to W.H. Stark, 2 February 1873.

5. William J. Phillips, US marshal, Eastern District of Texas, to J.T. Stark, 5 June 1876. Includes Stark's commission and oath of office. In 1871 he had been named a deputy US marshal in the Eastern District of Texas, and in 1873 he served as president and acting secretary of the Newton County Board of School Directors, with the responsibility of finding teachers for the county's schools. J.C. De Gress, superintendent of public instruction, to J.T. Stark, 10 March 1873.

6. Dan Triplett to J.T. Stark, 26 January 1873.

7. Ibid.

8. Nina Hardin, "Lily Rose Stark's House," *Opportunity Valley News*, 21 February 1973. "Pleasant View" was located west of town, across Adams Bayou from present-day Shangri La Botanical Gardens.

9. Jeremiah Stark Sr. to J.T. Stark, 11 December 1875. John Thomas apparently resolved his differences with his "Pap," as he called him; in 1877 he invited his sister Eliza to visit his family in their "Prairie home" two miles west of Orange and to travel with him to Newton to visit their father, then in poor health, and other relatives who lived in the vicinity. J.T. Stark to Eliza (Mrs. E.J.) Wooderson, 29 April 1877.

10. J.T. Stark to Jeremiah Stark Sr., 21 December 1875.

11. E.J. Hart & Company to J.T. Stark & Son, 9 July 1873.

12. Donna J. Stark to H.J. Hall & Co., 18 February 1876; Ledger, 1877–1881, transcribed by Jeremiah Stark, original in Stark Foundation Archives. Entries begin in 1877 in John Thomas Stark's handwriting, but most were written by Donna Stark when he was away on legal business.

13. W.H. Stark to Miriam Lutcher, 23 May 1879.

14. H. Williams, *Gateway to Texas*, 121; *Orange Weekly Tribune*, 12 September 1879, Rosenberg Library, Galveston, Texas. A transcription of excerpts from that paper, now located in the Stark Foundation Archives, is a gift from Jeremiah Stark, who accessed the material 26 August 1969.

15. J.T. Stark to Mrs. E.J. Wooderson, 29 April 1877.

16. Tevis, "W.H. Stark of Orange," *Beaumont Enterprise*, 15 December 1929.

17. J.T. Stark to Mrs. E.J. Wooderson, 25 August 1877.

18. H.J. Lutcher to G.B. Moore, 26 March 1877.

19. The town boasted its own Hanging Tree, a huge old oak standing at the corner of Fourth and Front Streets. H. Williams, *Gateway to Texas*, 58.

20. Lewis was apparently in financial straits, as he was frequently; Henry also reported that he had that day sent $117 to one of his father's creditors to pay the older man's interest on a note. "It was a very bad time for me to pay it," Henry added, "but it had to be done." H.J. Lutcher to Lewis Lutscher, 29 July 1879.

21. "Henry J. Lutcher, Esq.," *St. Louis Lumberman*, March 1880.

22. Arlene Turkel, "Growing Orchids and Affection for the Stark Family," *Orange County Record* 37, no. 17 (8 August 1995): 1A.

23. W.H. Stark to Miriam Lutcher, 25 August 1878.

24. W.H. Stark to H.J.L. Stark, 7 December 1908.

25. W.H. Stark to Miriam Lutcher, 8 September 1878.

26. Ibid., 25 October and 24 November 1878.

27. Ibid., 29 September and 5 October 1878; 9 March, 13 April, and 23 May 1879; 25 August 1878–8 October 1881.

28. Ibid., 8 September, 5 October, and 8 September 1878.

29. Ibid., 25 October 1878. This was cause for celebration indeed, since the mosquito was the culprit that transmitted the deadly yellow fever virus, although William—as well as the rest of the world—did not yet know it; it was not until the Spanish-American War that US Army pathologist Walter Reed discovered that yellow fever is transmitted through the bite of the mosquito. "Walter Reed, Medical Professional, Doctor, Scientist (1851–1902)," Biography.com, http://www.biography.com/people/walter-reed-9454083?page=1 (accessed 12 October 2015).

30. W.H. Stark to Miriam Lutcher, 5 February 1879.

31. Ibid., 5 October 1881 and 30 March 1879.

32. *A Century for Christ, 1878–1978: A Brief History of First Presbyterian Church of Orange, Texas, in Commemoration of the 100th Anniversary of Our Church*, pamphlet (Orange: First Presbyterian Church), 4–5, photocopy in Stark Foundation Archives.

33. The Baptist and Methodist congregations seemed to hold the most frequent revivals. They also constructed the first permanent structures in the county in which to hold services—Baptists by 1857, Methodists in 1873. "A Brief History of the First United Methodist Church," *Las Sabinas* 2, no. 3 (Summer 1976): 18–20.

34. W.H. Stark to Miriam Lutcher, 5 October, 13 October, and 25 August 1878; 19 January and 5 February 1879.

35. The border was set in the middle of the Sabine River in the Adams-Onís, or Transcontinental, Treaty of 1821, so the Neutral Ground went to the United States.

36. Richardson et al., *Texas*, 53.

37. W.H. Stark to Miriam Lutcher, 25 October 1878.

38. Ibid., 27 July 1881.

39. H.J. Lutcher to G.B. Moore, 19 March–1 June 1877, passim. In October 1885, R.B. Flick of Williamsport was hired at $115 per month "to man engine & take care machinery lower part of mill." That month, Emmet Buehler of Williamsport was to "get ready and go at once to Orange, Texas, as foreman of Mill of Lutcher & Moore at that place and remain with them one year . . . at the rate of thirteen thousand dollars per annum, payable monthly." Stark Foundation Archives.

40. H. Williams, *Gateway to Texas*, 60–61; W.H. Stark to Miriam Lutcher, 1 September 1881.

41. W.H. Stark to Miriam Lutcher, 26 September 1881; Judith Walker Linsley, Ellen Walker Rienstra, and Jo Ann Stiles, *Giant under the Hill: A History of the Spindletop Oil Discovery in Beaumont, Texas, in 1901* (Austin: Texas State Historical Association, 2002), 28–29, 32–34, 37–66.

42. Earlier 1856 and 1858 incorporations had lapsed during the Civil War.

43. W.H. Stark to Miriam Lutcher, 5 October and 8 October 1881.

44. "Lumbering in the Lone Star State," *Weekly Sun and Banner* (Williamsport, Pennsylvania), 13 October 1881.

45. W.H. Stark to Miriam Lutcher, 25 August 1878.

46. Ibid., 5 October and 29 September 1878, 30 March 1879.

47. Ibid., 19 January and 23 May 1879.

48. Ibid., 29 September 1878.

49. Ibid., 13 October 1878.

50. Ibid., 5 October 1878 and 19 January 1879.

51. Ibid., 23 May 1879.

52. Abbott, "A Stark Genealogy," Seventh Generation, William Henry Stark; William Stark to Miriam Lutcher, 23 May 1879; page from receipt book of "W.H. Stark, Dealer in Staple and Fancy Groceries, Grain and Feed a Specialty," Stark Foundation Archives. The page is dated 1881, the year that William and Miriam were married. Also, Prohibition was becoming an increasingly serious reform movement in East Texas in the late nineteenth and early twentieth centuries.

53. W.H. Stark to Miriam Lutcher, 29 September 1878; 10 August and 27 July 1881.

54. No known connection to Frances Ann Robinson Lutcher.

55. Wilbur was married to Henry Lutcher's sister Louisa. He designed Holly Home as well as the future homes of Miriam and William Stark and Carrie and her future husband, Edgar Brown, in the same style of architecture.

56. Sanborn Fire Maps, Perry-Castañeda Library, Map Collection, University of Texas

Online, 1896, http://www.lib.utexas.edu/maps/sanborn/m-o/txu-sanborn-orange-1896-03 .jpg.

57. W.H. Stark to Miriam Lutcher, 1 September 1881.

58. Ibid.; Sanborn Fire Maps; *Orange Leader*, "Orange, the City Beautiful: A Splendid Record of Improvement," 18 December 1908. The marsh was bordered roughly by Main, Fifth, Front, and Sixth Streets, leading east toward the Sabine River. The marsh was filled in by the city of Orange in 1908.

59. With the expansion of the town, that did not remain the case; in the 1890s, both Miriam's and Carrie's families built homes north of the marsh, along Green Avenue, and the Lutcher neighborhood faded. Nothing remains of the Lutcher house, and the lot has been absorbed into an industrial complex.

60. W.H. Stark to Miriam Lutcher, 26 September 1881.

61. Marriage license, Miriam Lutcher and William Stark, Stark Foundation Archives; "Starks Observe Golden Wedding," *Beaumont Enterprise*, 22 December 1931.

62. H. Williams, "William H. Stark," 28.

63. "Starks Observe Golden Wedding."

64. Wedding invitation, Miriam Lutcher to William Stark, 22 December 1881, Stark Foundation Archives.

65. W.H. Stark to Miriam Lutcher, 19 January 1879.

66. William's early photos show him with a mid-chest-length black beard, but at least one of his letters indicates that, before his marriage to Miriam, he was apparently clean-shaven; he wrote her on September 1, 1881, that he "had forgotten to shave and I could not go without."

67. W.H. Stark to Miriam Lutcher, 27 July and 1 September 1881.

68. Ibid., 25 August 1878–8 October 1881.

69. Ibid., 8 September 1878.

70. Ibid., 13 April 1879; H. Williams, *Gateway to Texas*, 15.

71. W.H. Stark to Miriam Lutcher, 26 September, 5 October, and 8 October 1881. The one time William mentioned a Will Byrd, the reference had nothing to do with Carrie.

72. Ibid., 9 March 1879.

73. Howard Williams, "Dr. Samuel M. Brown," and "Dr. Edgar M. Brown," *Las Sabinas* 6, no. 4 (October 1980): 21–22, 36.

74. Louis Dugas, "Orange County History," *Opportunity Valley News*, 3 March 1972, Stark Foundation Archives, gift of the James Pruter family; H. Williams, "Dr. Samuel M. Brown," 21.

75. H. Williams, "Dr. Samuel M. Brown," 21.

76. Dan Triplett to J.T. Stark, 29 August 1875. See transcriber's notes attached.

77. Winifred Arndt Duffy, *John Wiley Link* (Houston: D. Armstrong, 1974), 24; W.H. Stark to Miriam Lutcher, 25 October 1878. One event held in the hall on November 18, 1879, featured a lecture by Professor T.W. Neville on "the character of the Human Family, as Taught by the Science of Phrenology." The flyer boasted that "the whole proceedings will be interesting and instructive to all." It further admonished, "Do not fail to attend." Flyer, "Notice! To the Public, Lecture by Prof. T.W. Neville, at Dr. Brown's Hall," Stark Foundation Archives.

78. Dugas, "Orange County History"; H. Williams, "Dr. Samuel M. Brown," 22.

79. W.H. Stark to Miriam Lutcher, 26 September 1881.

80. H. Williams, "Dr. Edgar William Brown," 36; Abbott, "Stark Genealogy," Seventh Generation, William Henry Stark and Miriam Lutcher Stark. Both of these resources, as well as *The Handbook of Texas Online*, give the wedding date as November 28, 1888, but the

wedding invitation states that the date is Thursday, November 29, 1888. The authors have chosen to use that date. Wedding invitation for Carrie L. Lutcher and Dr. Edgar W. Brown, Stark Foundation Archives.

81. Henry J. Lutcher, family Bible, family records section, Stark Foundation Archives.

82. John Miller Horger of Newton, who moved to Orange that year to find sawmill work. Newton County Historical Commission, *Glimpses of Newton County History*, 174.

83. Donna Stark to J.T. Stark, 8 August 1884.

84. List of burials in Stark mausoleum, Evergreen Cemetery, Orange, Texas; H.J.L. Stark to Lucy Hill Jones, 17 January 1951; checks to Otto Zirkel for building the mausoleum 3 January and 9 July 1908; ledger, containing Account of the Estate of Frances Ann Lutcher, 1898–1924, and George S. Colburn, Deposition, Answers to Direct and Cross Interrogatories in Carrie L. Brown vs. H.J.L. Stark, No. 5203, District Court of Orange County, Texas, Stark Foundation Archives.

85. Howard Williams, "William H. Stark," *Las Sabinas* 6, no. 4 (October 1980): 44.

86. Lutscher family Bible, family records section.

87. "Lewis Lutcher [sic]," obituary, Williamsport, *Gazette and Bulletin* (Williamsport, Pennsylvania), 9 April 1883.

88. Rocktown was soon to be known as South Williamsport; with several other small towns, it was incorporated as the Borough of South Williamsport on November 29, 1886.

89. "Mrs. Mary B. Lutcher," *Town and Country* (Williamsport, Pennsylvania), 22–25 March 1883; "Lewis Lutcher," obituary; "At Rest in Wildwood: Funeral of the Late Lewis Lutcher," undated clipping, Stark Foundation Archives.

90. Conversation with Robert Lutcher, by Ellen Walker Rienstra, Jo Ann Stiles, and Patsy Herrington, 7 April 2009.

91. John G. Bastian, sheriff, to H.H. Blair and George S. Eves, Deed Records, Lycoming County, 82:98.

92. H.J. Lutcher to G.B. Moore, 16 May 1877.

93. "Mrs. David Robinson," Williamsport *Gazette and Bulletin*, 15 February 1898; Kansas State Census, 1885, Battle Creek, Lincoln, Kansas, http://search.ancestrylibrary.com/Browse/print_u.aspx?dbid=1088&iid=ks1885_75-0018 (accessed 26 June 2010; site discontinued). There is an inconsistency between the obituary of Matilda and the 1885 Kansas state census. The obituary states that the couple moved to Lincoln Avenue in Lincoln in 1883; the census states that they still lived in Battle Creek in Lincoln in 1885.

94. Ida [Nichols] Achenbach to Miriam Lutcher, 17 May 1880.

95. "Mrs. David Robinson"; "The Death Record," *Lincoln County Sentinel*, February 1898 (probably between 9 and 12 February; it was quoted in the Williamsport newspaper on 15 February 1898).

96. "The Death Record"; headstones for David and Matilda Robinson and George Wilson, Lincoln, Kansas.

97. H. Williams, "Dr. Edgar William Brown," 36, 40n, 44. This article spells their daughter's name as "Fannye," as does her death certificate. In most other sources the name is spelled "Fannie," although in a few instances it is spelled "Fanny." In his handwritten will, her father, E.W. Brown, spells the name "Fannie"; consequently, the authors are accepting that source as definitive. Edgar W. Brown, holographic will, 17 September 1916, proved 11 February 1925, A:377 et seq., Probate Records, Orange County, Texas.

98. Deposition of William Stark, filed 30 May 1930, 124:176, Orange County Records, outlining the organizational structure of the Lutcher & Moore Lumber Company, 1878–1930.

99. "Among the Millmen," *Galveston Daily News*, 20 December 1887.

100. "Henry J. Lutcher Esq."

101. The right to cut and remove timber from other landowners' property.

102. "The Lutcher & Moore Lumber Company," G. Bedell Moore Collection; H.J. Lutcher to G.B. Moore, 19 March 1877.

103. Easton, "History of the Texas Lumbering Industry," 122; Walker, "Harvesting the Forest," 16.

104. "Lumbering in the Lone Star State"; Walker, "Harvesting the Forest," 15.

105. "Lumbering in the Lone Star State"; A.J. Miller, "Manufacturing Industries," in *Where the Port of Orange Is Located on the World's Map* (Orange, TX: Stark Foundation Archives and Heritage House, 1916); Walker, "Harvesting the Forest," 14–15. Accounts differ as to the boom's storage capacity; "The Lutcher & Moore Lumber Company" article states it as eight million board feet, while the *Weekly Sun and Banner* interview of Lutcher states it as fifty million board feet.

106. Tevis, "W.H. Stark of Orange."

107. "Henry J. Lutcher Died Yesterday," Williamsport *Gazette and Bulletin*, 2 October 1912; Meginness, *History of Lycoming County*, 367.

108. Easton, "History of the Texas Lumbering Industry," 125; Walker, "Harvesting the Forest," 15.

109. Easton, "History of the Texas Lumbering Industry," 124; Farwell, "Saw Mill Industry Plays Major Part in Texas History," *Orange Leader*, 29 May 1936.

110. Michael L. Lanza, *Agrarianism and Reconstruction Politics: The Southern Homestead Act* (Baton Rouge: Louisiana State University Press, 1990), 113–124; Walker, "Harvesting the Forest," 11.

111. Lutcher & Moore eventually owned land in Beauregard Parish that they had initially bought in Calcasieu Parish after the former was created from land in what was originally known as Imperial Calcasieu Parish. "Beauregard Parish," http://www.library.beau .org/history/bphistory/ (accessed 12 October 2015); Easton, "History of the Texas Lumbering Industry," 122; Walker, "Harvesting the Forest," 11. The five states affected by the act were Louisiana, Arkansas, Alabama, Florida, and Mississippi. Much of the land in question was heavily wooded, consequently desired by the lumber interests.

112. Tevis, "W.H. Stark of Orange."

113. F.H. Farwell wrote later that Lutcher would buy only fully wooded tracts of land, and that others bought up the partially wooded tracts and made a bigger profit because they did not cut their timber until the market price was higher than in Lutcher's time. Easton, "History of the Texas Lumbering Industry," 124, citing interview with F.H. Farwell, 6 December 1940.

114. Maxwell and Baker, *Sawdust Empire*, 31.

115. "Henry J. Lutcher, Esq."

116. H.P.N. Gammel, *Gammel's Laws of Texas, 1822–1897*, vol. 8, *1881–1882* (Austin: Gammel Book Company, 1898).

117. Scott Sager, a researcher with the Lycoming County Historical Society in Williamsport, could find no trace of Lutcher & Moore's having used the Star and Crescent emblem in their operations in Pennsylvania; neither could the authors, who made two research trips to Williamsport.

118. W.T. Block, "Henry Jacob Lutcher, Sawmiller and Architect of Orange, Texas," *Beaumont Enterprise*, 15 June 2002; Lutcher & Moore Lumber Company, 1877–1930, Sawmill Database, Texas Forestry Museum, http://www.treetexas.com/research/sawmill/?action =view&cid=49 (accessed 12 October 2015).

119. Photographs and stationery displaying the Star and Crescent symbol are located

in the Stark Foundation Archives. *Nelda C. and H.J. Lutcher Stark Foundation, 1961–2011: A Golden Anniversary of Giving*, booklet published by the Nelda C. and H.J. Lutcher Stark Foundation, 2011, 1–2. The third Lutcher & Moore office building now houses offices for the Port of Orange.

120. The Star and Crescent symbol of the Lutcher & Moore Lumber Company was adopted as the insignia for the Nelda C. and H.J. Lutcher Stark Foundation, a nonprofit organization established in 1961 by Lutcher Stark, in tribute to his heritage. In the twenty-first century, the symbol is often connected with Islam, used on the national flags of several Islamic states; however, the origin of the star and crescent predates the rise of Islam by several thousand years. See "The Crescent Moon—a Symbol of Islam?," aboutreligion.com, http://islam.about.com/od/history/a/crescent_moon.htm (accessed 28 November 2015). See also *Stark Foundation 1961–2011*, 1–2.

121. "The Lutcher & Moore Lumber Company," G. Bedell Moore Collection; *Orange Leader*, 18 December 1908.

122. Marcus E. Sperry, "The Port of Orange, Texas," in *Where the Port of Orange Is Located on the World's Map*, 1916, pamphlet, no pagination, copies in Stark Foundation Archives, Forest History Collections, Stephen F. Austin State University Library, Nacogdoches, Texas; and Heritage House, Orange, Texas.

123. Tevis, "W.H. Stark of Orange"; "The Lutcher & Moore Lumber Company." In the early 1900s, in two other departures from the East Texas norm, Lutcher & Moore became the first company in the region to abandon the notorious "commissary-scrip" system that kept employees in debt for years. The company instead paid its employees in cash every Saturday night and helped them purchase homes. In spite of universal objections from the lumber industry, which considered circular saws to be superior in cutting lumber, Lutcher ultimately added a bandsaw mill to the plant in Orange, thus altering the concept of lumber-manufacturing methods in the region and becoming "the father of economical, well-manufactured lumber in the South." Farwell, "Saw Mill Industry Plays Major Part in Texas History."

124. In 1901 the tram was chartered as a common carrier to applicants W.H. Stark, G. Bedell Moore, and other Orange lumbermen. By 1905 it had changed hands but continued to serve East Texas as a passenger and freight carrier until 1956. Robert Wooster and Nancy Beck Young, "Orange and Northwestern Railroad," *Handbook of Texas Online*, accessed 19 January 2015, http://www.tshaonline.org/handbook/online/articles/eqoo2, uploaded 15 June 2010, published by the Texas State Historical Association; Texas Forestry Museum, Research: Tram & Railroad Database, "Orange & Northwestern Railway Company," http://www.treetexas.com/research/railroad/?action=view&cid=13 (accessed 12 October 2015); W.T. Block, "Tram Roads Preceded Railroads, Towns," *Big Thicket Bulletin* 65 (Winter 1980–1981): 6–7, Saratoga, Texas. Some of the locomotives the company purchased were "Shay" engines, which utilized a vertical arrangement of pistons and cylinders and were said to have been used previously in the construction of the Panama Canal.

125. Walker, "Harvesting the Forest," 16.

126. Agreement between Lutcher & Moore, W.H. Stark, and Frank J. Drick, 19 May 1886, Stark Foundation Archives.

127. "Death of Frank J. Drick," Williamsport *Gazette and Bulletin*, 19 March 1890; "The Sabine Country—a Reminiscence," *Northwestern Lumberman*, 18 April 1896.

128. Taber, *Williamsport: Lumber Capital*, 71.

129. "Track of the Flood: A Boat Ride Down to the Loyalsock," Williamsport *Gazette and Bulletin*, 17 June 1889.

130. The company was first listed as the San Antonio Lumber Company, with Lutcher

Stark as president and William Stark as vice president. Between 1885 and 1890, Moore's name appears as an officer in the company, and in 1890 the name was changed to the Lutcher & Moore Lumber Company, located at Commerce and Walnut Streets. Moore's name appears in city directories as living first in a hotel, then a flat, then a residence address. Correspondence between Michael Idrogo, San Antonio, Texas, and Walter G. Riedel, chief executive officer of the Nelda C. and H.J. Lutcher Stark Foundation, Orange, Texas, 31 January and 4 February 1998, Stark Foundation Archives. The correspondence cites material found in the Texana Department of the Central Library in San Antonio, city directories, and Sanborn Fire Maps.

131. Moore, "Sketch of the Life of Gregory Bedell Moore," 1:20, handwritten manuscript provided to Eric Steinfeldt by Elizabeth Moore, November 1986. Originals in G. Bedell Moore Collection, Stephen F. Austin University, Nacogdoches, Texas.

132. Sperry, "The Port of Orange, Texas"; "Prospects of Orange," *Galveston Weekly News*, 9 February 1888.

133. Deposition of William Stark, filed 30 May 1930, 124:176, Orange County Records, 176–177; Lutcher & Moore Lumber Co., Articles of Incorporation, 12 November 1890, certified copy in Stark Foundation Archives.

134. "Henry J. Lutcher, Esq."

135. "Texas' First Lumber Tycoons," *Crosscut*, Texas Forestry Museum Society (fourth quarter, 1990).

136. The Lutcher & Moore Cypress Lumber Company was incorporated July 13, 1891. "Henry J. Lutcher," typescript of interview made during Lutcher's lifetime, Stark Foundation Archives; Roy Wingate, "A Summary of Some of the Business Enterprises of the Lutcher and the Stark Families of Orange, Texas," compiled 2006–2007, 27–28, Stark Foundation Archives.

137. Wingate, "Summary," 9.

138. According to William Stark, when Lutcher and Moore applied for a loan from the First National Bank of Houston, the bank "put [Dibert, an experienced lumberman,] into the woods" to aid the partners in choosing timberlands in Louisiana. "W.H. Stark of Orange."

139. Wingate, "Summary," 9.

140. Henry Jacob Lutcher, Inventory, Stark Foundation Archives; Ledger, Account of Estate of Frances Ann Lutcher; George S. Colburn, Deposition, Answers to Direct and Cross Interrogatories in Carrie L. Brown vs. H.J.L. Stark, No. 5203, District Court of Orange County, Texas, Stark Foundation Archives.

141. Sperry, "The Port of Orange, Texas"; Laurie Haynes, "Making of the Port of Orange," *Penny Record and the County Record Newspapers of Orange County, Texas*, 19 January 2000; W.C. Averill, "Some Early Waterway History," letter to the editor, *Beaumont Enterprise*, clipping, undated but sometime after 1912, Stark Foundation Archives.

142. Sperry, "The Port of Orange, Texas."

143. "Lutcher & Moore Lbr. Co., City's Pioneer Industry," *Orange Leader*, undated article from Woman's Club Scrapbook, donated to Heritage House, Orange, Texas, June 2004; Sperry, "The Port of Orange, Texas."

144. "Lutcher & Moore Lbr. Co., City's Pioneer Industry" ; Sperry, "The Port of Orange, Texas."

145. Sperry, "The Port of Orange, Texas."

146. Averill, "Some Early Waterway History."

147. Sperry, "The Port of Orange, Texas."

148. Ibid.

149. "The Democrats Ratify. Big Time in the Ranks Last Night. The Court House Crowded with the Enthusiastic Shouters for Cleveland and Stevenson—Interesting Speeches and Street Demonstration," Williamsport *Gazette and Bulletin*, 29 June 1892.

150. Texas instituted a poll tax and a white primary but never adopted a literacy test.

151. "A Southern Speech," Williamsport *Gazette and Bulletin*, 29 June 1892.

152. *Daily Sun* of Williamsport, Pennsylvania, 14 November 1892. The South then remained solidly Democratic until the turmoil of the 1960s, when the Southern Democratic Party shattered—with racial issues, again, a central factor.

153. H.J. Lutcher, *A Stronger and More Permanent Union*, booklet (Orange, TX: Leader Steam Print, 1896), 6–7, Stark Foundation Archives; Lutcher & Moore Lumber Company Papers, Forest History Collection, Stephen F. Austin State University, Nacogdoches, Texas.

154. Ibid., 7–12.

155. Ibid., 12–13 (emphasis added).

156. Walker, "Harvesting the Forest," 10.

157. "The Sabine Country: A Reminiscence," *Northwestern Lumberman*, 18 April 1896, Stark Foundation Archives.

158. "Henry J. Lutcher," typescript of interview.

159. H.J. Lutcher to Frances A. Lutcher, 24 March 1894.

Chapter 5

1. The Lutcher & Moore Cypress Lumber Company was founded in Lutcher, Louisiana, by Henry J. Lutcher and G. Bedell Moore for the manufacture of cypress products and formally incorporated July 13, 1891. The original stockholders were Lutcher, Moore, D.H. McEwen, A.S. Moore (G. Bedell Moore's wife, Alice), and John Dibert. Wingate, "Summary," 27–28.

2. "A Big Mill at Orange Tallies One More Success," unattributed clipping hand-dated 13 March 1895, Orange newspaper, probably the *Orange Leader*, pasted inside the flyleaf of Lutcher Stark's book *Menagerie of Animals, or Natural History Made Easy for Boys and Girls* (Monarch Publishing, 1894), inscribed to him as a Christmas gift in 1894, Stark Foundation Archives.

3. A frequently fatal form of gastroenteritis, indigenous to the central and southern United States, with symptoms similar to those of cholera, affecting infants. "Cholera Infantum," http://medical-dictionary.thefreedictionary.com/cholera+infantum (accessed 28 November 2015); Foree, "Archangel and His Bible," 94.

4. Foree, "Archangel and His Bible," 94.

5. "Yester-Year," *Opportunity Valley News*, 27 June 1973, 10.

6. Howard C. Williams, ed., *Picturing Orange: A Pictorial History of Orange County* (Orange, TX: Heritage House of Orange County Association, 2000), 127, 128.

7. "Orange Notes," *Galveston Daily News*, 11 August 1893.

8. Joint Committee on Ceremonies of World's Columbian Commission and Exposition, ed., *Memorial Volume, Dedicatory and Opening Ceremonies of the World's Columbian Exposition* (Chicago: Stone, Kastler & Painter, 1893), 272, Stark Foundation Archives; *The White City: The Historical, Biographical and Philanthropical Record of Illinois* (Chicago: Chicago World Book, 1893), 71, https://archive.org/details/cihm_25316, in which "Mrs. W.H. Stark" is listed as an exhibitor in the Woman's Building of the Columbian Exposition, her exhibit a lace bedspread and pillow shams, but no proof exists that the woman listed is Miriam Lutcher Stark of Orange.

9. *Lutcher Memorial Building, First Presbyterian Congregation of the Church in Orange*, pamphlet (Orange, TX: First Presbyterian Church); Rosemary Williams, "Luxurious Legacy: A Trio of Buildings in Orange Reflects a Prominent Family's Eye For Beauty," *Texas Highways*, March 1990, 19.

10. R. Williams, "Luxurious Legacy," 19.

11. In 1896, the group changed the name to the Shakespeare Reading Club and in 1899 to the Ladies' Reading Club.

12. Minutes, Shakespeare Reading Club, 1896–1897, Stark Foundation Archives; Mrs. W. O. Brice, "History of the Reading Club," clipping, undated and unattributed but probably from *Orange Leader*, Stark Foundation Archives.

13. Brice, "History of the Reading Club."

14. Minutes, Ladies' Study Club, 1906–1908, Stark Foundation Archives.

15. Jeannette Heard Robinson, Elizabeth Q. Williams, and Linda B. Farris, "Orange Comes of Age," in H. Williams, *Picturing Orange*, 128.

16. *Lycoming Weekly Gazette*, 28 February 1827.

17. Founded in 1904 by Miriam Stark and continued at her death in 1936 by H.J.L. Stark, the contest became a qualified scholarship program of the Nelda C. and H.J. Lutcher Stark Foundation in 1976. *Nelda C. and H.J. Lutcher Stark Foundation 1961–2011: A Golden Anniversary of Giving*, 30.

18. Photograph, W.H. Stark and H.J.L. Stark, playing violins, and Miriam Stark playing piano, Stark Foundation Archives.

19. Cynthia Carter Leedy Horn, conversation with Jo Ann Stiles, Richard H. Dickerson, and Ellen Rienstra, Burnet, Texas, 9 May 2012.

20. "Lumbering in the Lone Star State," *Weekly Sun and Banner* (Williamsport, Pennsylvania), 13 October 1881.

21. John Thomas Stark, obituary, *Orange Weekly Tribune*, 29 September 1893.

22. Donna Stark to Jay C. Snell, son of Donna's sister, Jane Snell, 4 December 1894, Stark Foundation Archives.

23. Dr. Jeremiah Stark, conversation with Jo Ann Stiles, 17 May 2010, Woodville, Texas.

24. John Thomas Stark, obituary, *Orange Weekly Tribune*, 29 September 1893.

25. Ibid.

26. Donna Stark to Jay C. Snell, 4 December 1894. Donna died in late September 1923, outliving her husband by three decades.

27. Undated newspaper clipping, *Houston Post*, ca. 1893–1894, Stark Foundation Archives.

28. Ibid.

29. Ibid. The house still stands today as the W.H. Stark House, a program of the Nelda C. and H.J. Lutcher Stark Foundation, and is listed in the National Register of Historic Places.

30. "Henry J. Lutcher," typescript of interview.

31. "Yester-Year," 10.

32. Robinson, Williams, and Farris, "Orange Comes of Age," 132; Elizabeth Williams, ed., "Entertaining Orange Style—1904," *Las Sabinas* 8, no. 1 (January 1982): 6–7.

33. Will, Estate of H.J. Lutcher, Deceased, filed 11 January 1913, Orange County Probate Court, Case No. 345; Affidavit, signed by Frances A. Lutcher as executrix of the estate of Henry Jacob Lutcher and in her own right, W.H. Stark, Miriam M. Stark, Carrie L. Brown, and E.W. Brown, 15 October 1912 and notarized 8 May 1913, ratifying the power of attorney H.J. Lutcher gave to W.H. Stark 6 January 1898 and all acts done by Stark as attorney in

fact for H.J. Lutcher between the dates of 6 January 1898 and 3 October 1912, copy in Stark Foundation Archives.

34. *Souvenir List of Members of Clark's Cruise to the Orient, by Specially Chartered North German Lloyd Express Steamer* Aller, pamphlet, Stark Foundation Archives.

35. Frances A. Lutcher to Miriam Stark and family, 21 February 1898.

36. H.J. Lutcher to Miriam Stark and family, 24 February 1898.

37. Ibid., 12 March 1898.

38. Frances A. Lutcher to Miriam Stark and family, 6 March 1898.

39. Frances A. Lutcher to H.J.L. Stark, 18 March 1898.

40. H.J. Lutcher to Miriam Stark and family, 29 March 1898.

41. Frances A. Lutcher to Miriam Stark and family, 15 April 1898.

42. H.J. Lutcher to Miriam Stark and family, 21 April 1898.

43. Frances A. Lutcher to H.J.L. Stark, 18 March 1898.

44. H.J. Lutcher to Miriam Stark, 21 April 1898.

45. Horn, conversation with Stiles, Dickerson, and Rienstra, 9 May 2012.

46. Moore, "Sketch of the Life of Gregory Bedell Moore."

47. Deed Records, Lycoming County, 175:170–172, 1901 (no day or month given); 200:76, 23 January 1907. The deed stated that the Episcopal Church was to use the land to build "a church, rectory, and other parochial buildings."

48. "In Memoriam," typescript, resolution of directors of the First National Bank Orange on death of Henry J. Lutcher, including W.H. Stark, H.J.L. Stark, E.W. Brown, and F.H. Farwell, Stark Foundation Archives.

49. Horn, conversation with Stiles, Rienstra, and Dickerson, 9 April 2012; deposition, Rosa Hamilton, in re Carrie L. Brown vs. H.J.L. Stark, Orange County District Court, 19 November 1925.

50. Memorandum, "Summary of a Conversation with Mr. McKee [Clyde McKee, business manager and general counsel for the Stark interests] May 30, 1990," Stark Foundation Archives. According to McKee, Lutcher Stark "from time to time" expressed to him concerns that "he would turn out like his grandfather, Mr. Lutcher, who spent the last years of his life in an asylum."

51. Horn, conversation with Stiles, Rienstra, and Dickerson, 9 April 2012.

52. A check from the Lutchers' joint checking account, written 21 October 1902 for $500, was marked "H.J. Lutcher trip to Cincinnati." Lutcher and Stark family records indicate the family's periodic presence in Cincinnati. Ledger, Account of Estate of Frances Ann Lutcher; and George S. Colburn, Deposition, Answers to Direct and Cross Interrogatories. Expenditures from H.J. and Frances Ann Lutcher's joint account include a check dated 26 September 1901 in the amount of $1,000 to H.J. Lutcher for "Cincinnati trip"; $1,000 on 4 February 1902 to Frances Ann for "Check on Cincinnati"; $55 on 8 April 1902 to "Williams Dentist Cincinnati"; $500 on 21 October 1902 to H.J. Lutcher for "trip to Cincinnati"; $42 on 11 March 1905 to C.A. Russell for "Drayage By Refund Cincinnati." The US Census of 1910 shows Lutcher as a patient at the Cincinnati Sanitarium.

53. US Census, 1910; "A History of the Children's Hospital College Hill Campus," College Hill eNewsletter Archive, 17 January 2007, http://chenewsletter.blogspot.com/2007/01/history-of-children-hospitale-college.html. Also, an invitation to the wedding of Nita Hill and H.J.L. Stark was sent to Henry Jacob Lutcher in care of "College Hill Sanitarium, Cincinnati, Ohio."

54. "A History of the Children's Hospital."

55. Moore, "Sketch of the Life of Gregory Bedell Moore," 21.

56. Wingate, "Summary," 27; "Change in the Lutcher & Moore Company," *American Lumberman*, 10 March 1900; "For $550,000: G. Bedell Moore Retires from the Lutcher & Moore Cypress Co.," clipping, undated, unattributed, Stark Foundation Archives.

57. Moore, "Sketch of the Life of Gregory Bedell Moore."

58. Ibid., 21; Lutcher & Moore Lumber Company records, 1 April and 2 July 1901, Stark Foundation Archives; "F.H. Farwell Brought First Ships to Docks," *Orange Leader*, 29 May 1936.

59. Deed Records, Orange County, Z:1–102.

60. Minutes, Lutcher & Moore Lumber Company, 31 December 1901, Stark Foundation Archives; report, *Timber Lands, Mill Property, etc., Purchases from G. Bedell Moore*, 4/1/01, Stark Foundation Archives.

61. Minute Book, Lutcher & Moore Lumber Company, 2 July 1901. After the redistribution of Moore's stock, Lutcher owned 2,474 shares; Brown, 392; Stark, 627; Dibert, 392; and Farwell, 100 (Mrs. H.L. Field and E.M. Hammond also held small amounts of stock).

62. "F.H. Farwell Brought First Ships to Docks." Farwell was later promoted to general manager, and on January 1, 1920, was elected vice president of the company. He played a significant role in Lutcher & Moore's affairs for many years to come.

63. Ibid.; Minute Book, Lutcher & Moore Lumber Company, 2 July 1901.

64. Deed Records, Orange County, Z:1–102.

65. *Gazette and Bulletin* (Williamsport, Pennsylvania), 7 May 1901.

66. Jeanette Heard Robinson, "Brown, Edgar William, Sr.," *Handbook of Texas Online*, accessed 11 August 2012, http://www.tshaonline.org/handbook/online/articles/fbrdr, uploaded 12 June 2010, published by the Texas State Historical Association.

67. Advertisement for Dibert, Stark and Brown Cypress Company, *Orange Leader*, 17 December 1909.

68. Ernest Hammond "Ernie" Willey, interview with Jo Ann Stiles, 18 April 2007, Stark Foundation offices, Stark Foundation Archives.

69. "The Lutcher Moore Lumber Company Headquarters Office," *Las Sabinas* 24, no. 2 (1997): 1; "The Lutcher & Moore Lumber Company," clipping, Orange newspaper, in Moore, "Sketch of the Life of Gregory Bedell Moore."

70. F.H. Farwell, "Orange Center of Early Day Development," *Orange Leader*, 29 May 1936.

71. Ibid.; "The Lutcher & Moore Lumber Company," *Orange Leader*, 18 December 1908; "Practical Optimists: The Story of a Lumber Firm Which Refused to Let Recent Business Depression 'Phase 'em,'" in *The Port of Orange, Texas, U.S.A.*, booklet, undated but probably published 1921 or 1922, no pagination, Stark Foundation Archives.

72. "The Lutcher & Moore Lumber Company," *Orange Leader*, 17 December 1909; "The Lutcher & Moore Lumber Company."

73. Walker, "Harvesting the Forest," 15; W.H. Stark Historic House Museum, Genealogical Records; W.T. Block, "Henry J. Lutcher: Sawmiller and Architect of Orange, Texas," *Beaumont Enterprise*, 15 June 2002.

74. "The Lutcher & Moore Lumber Company."

75. Block, "Henry J. Lutcher."

76. Easton, "History of the Texas Lumbering Industry," 123.

77. Robinson, "Brown, Edgar William, Sr."; "Dr. Edgar William Brown," *Las Sabinas* 6, no. 4 (1980): 40n4.

78. "An Orange Mill: One of the Big Ones and the Men Who Run It," *Beaumont Enterprise*, 15 October 1905.

79. Tevis, "W.H. Stark of Orange," 15 December 1929.

80. Roy S. Wingate, Address to the Orange County Historical Society, Orange, Texas, 9 November 2004, 1, copy in Stark Foundation Archives.

81. H. Williams, *Gateway to Texas*, 101, 103.

82. Wingate, "Summary," 53. Other directors were W.W. Reid, G.W. Curtis, A.T. Chenault, and W.D. Bettis.

83. Ibid.; "Dr. Edgar William Brown," 40n5, 41n10; Cynthia Horn, phone interview with Ellen Rienstra, 17 April 2012; H. Williams, *Picturing Orange*, 118. The Browns' daughter, Fannie, had eloped with Moore (no relation to G. Bedell Moore) to New Orleans, and they were married on June 11, 1909. Edgar Brown was said to have been so enraged that he chartered a Southern Pacific locomotive in which he could pursue them. Apparently, Brown soon became reconciled to the situation; he purchased the palatial Greek Revival mansion on Green Avenue formerly belonging to the John Wiley Link family and gave it to the newly-weds as a wedding present. According to Cynthia Horn, it was actually Frances Ann Lutcher who bought the Link home and gave it to Fannie and Rucie Moore as a wedding present.

84. Wingate, address to the Orange County Historical Society, 4–5.

85. Nina Hardin, "The Yellow Pine Paper Mill, and the Orange Box Manufacturing Co.," *Opportunity Valley News*, 19 February 1975; *A Condensed History of Paper Making, Compliments of the Yellow Pine Paper Mill Co., Orange, Texas*, pamphlet, Stark Foundation Archives.

86. "Yellow Pine Paper Mill Company," *Orange Leader*, 17 December 1909.

87. Wingate, "Summary," 75; Hardin, "The Yellow Pine Paper Mill."

88. "The Orange Ice, Light and Water Company," *Orange Leader*, 23 December 1910.

89. Wingate, "Summary," 46, 44, 70.

90. H. Williams, *Gateway to Texas*, 189–195, 196.

91. Typescript, information from scrapbook containing newspaper clippings from the *Orange Weekly Tribune*, Stark Foundation Archives. According to the typescript, the first building burned in 1889, and a two-story building, the "Henderson School," was erected by the school system on the same site.

92. H.J.L. Stark, riddle book, 4, Stark Foundation Archives.

93. "Oliver Goldsmith," tenth-grade essay by H.J.L. Stark for literature class, Stark Foundation Archives.

94. High school diploma, H.J.L. Stark, Stark Foundation Archives; "Stark Awards Presented to H. S. Winners," *Orange Leader*, 17 May 1928.

95. Draft, Lutcher Stark's high school graduation speech as salutatorian of his class, given 19 May 1905, Stark Foundation Archives.

96. Foree, "Archangel and His Bible," 94.

97. Information given to Stark offices by R.P. Turpin, director and secretary of Lutcher & Moore Lumber Company, 24 August 1970, Stark Foundation Archives.

98. Rex Byerley Shaw, "Stark, Who Makes Texas Triumph Possible," *Houston Post*, undated but probably around October 1923, clipping, scrapbook on H.J.L. Stark kept by Byron Simmons, ca. 1921–ca. 1928, Stark Foundation Archives.

99. "1904 Pope-Toledo Type IV," Conceptcarz, conceptcarz.com/vehicle/z10298/Pope-Toledo-Type-IV.aspx (accessed 15 October 2015), photographs in Stark Foundation Archives. Both the Pope-Toledo, "the pinnacle of Pope automobiles," as one authority called it, and the Pope-Hartford were made by the Pope Manufacturing Company of Hartford, Connecticut, and Toledo, Ohio. Photographs of Lutcher Stark's car more closely match those of the Pope-Toledo, the Pope-Hartford being a sportier model.

100. Photo of H.J.L. Stark's college room, Stark Foundation Archives; Dean A. Porter, Teresa Hayes Ebie, and Suzan Campbell, "Lutcher and Nelda Stark," in *Taos Artists*

and Their Patrons, 1898–1950 (Notre Dame, IN: Snite Museum of Art, University of Notre Dame, 1999), 129; "The Stark Legacy," *American Art Review* 18, no. 3 (May–June 2006): 152.

101. H.J.L. Stark, college essay, undated, Stark Foundation Archives.

102. Ibid.

103. Harold W. Brooms, "And Next We Have Lutcher Stark: Texas Alumnus, Whose Gifts to University and Fraternity Have Been Unstinted, Is Loyalty Epitomized," *Phi Gamma Delta* (April 1928): 598.

104. Shaw, "Stark, Who Makes Texas Triumph Possible."

105. Foree, "Archangel and His Bible," 96.

106. Ibid.

107. Brooms, "And Next We Have Lutcher Stark," 598.

108. Dale Miller, "Wins $30,000 Scholarship Prize: Challenge of H.J. Lutcher Stark to Lead Fraternities on Texas Campus Is Met by Tau Deuteron Chapter," *Phi Gamma Delta* 10, no. 6 (April 1937): 590.

109. *Cactus*, University of Texas Yearbook, 1910, 72; 1911, 110–111; Minutes, University of Texas Board of Regents, 13 June 1910, http://www.utsystem.edu/sites/utsfiles/offices/board -of-regents/board-meetings/board-minutes/1910minutes.pdf, 61–65. H.J.L. Stark graduated from the university in June 1910, before he served as manager, a job normally held by a student.

110. Shaw, "Stark, Who Makes Texas Triumph Possible."

111. E.C.H. Bantel, chairman of the Athletic Council of the University of Texas, to H.J.L. Stark, 16 December 1910.

112. Brooms, "And Next We Have Lutcher Stark," 598.

113. Charles E. Green, clipping, untitled, undated article, Stark Foundation Archives.

114. *Cactus*, 1911, 111.

115. "He Talks about Forest Country of 70 Years Ago," *Beaumont Journal*, 15 December 1929.

116. Felix Anderson, conversation with Jo Ann Stiles and Ellen Rienstra, Stark Foundation offices, 17 November 2004, Stark Foundation Archives.

117. "Aeroplane to Fly from Clark Field," *The Texan*, 29 October 1910, article courtesy of the H.J. Lutcher Stark Center for Physical Culture and Sports, the University of Texas, Austin, Texas.

118. Shaw, "Stark, Who Makes Texas Triumph Possible."

119. Foree, "Archangel and His Bible," 16.

120. "Death Takes Wife of Lutcher Stark," *Dallas Morning News*, 12 October 1939.

121. "Doctor Homer Hill," typescript of obituary, 1, Stark Foundation Archives; "Recollections of James Monroe Hill: Written by His Own Hand," 19 October 1897, typescript by one of his children, L.A. Hill, Austin History Center/Austin Public Library, Austin, Texas. In his recollections, Hill vividly describes the battle and the aftermath, in which the captured general Antonio López de Santa Anna is brought before the wounded general Sam Houston.

122. "Dormitory to House University Athletes," *The Alcalde* 27, no. 6 (March 1939): 131; historical marker, "Homer Barksdale Hill, Physician," at Moore-Hill Hall, University of Texas, 204 E. 21st St., Austin, Texas; "New Dorm Named for Hill," *Daily Texan*, 5 February 1939, 1; Benckenstein Papers.

123. Benckenstein Papers; Stark family records, Stark Foundation Archives. After Nita Hill Stark's death on October 11, 1939, Lutcher Stark moved the remains of Dr. and Mrs. Hill and their first two children to the Lutcher-Stark mausoleum in Evergreen Cemetery in Orange on April 23, 1940.

124. Ibid.

125. "Granny's Boys," *The Alcalde* 8, no. 8 (March 1921): 373–375.

126. Ibid.; Nita Hill Stark, postcard album, 1907–1908, Stark Foundation Archives. The postcards are addressed to "2007 Whitis."

127. Arthur Gray Jones, *Thornton Rogers Sampson, D.D., LL.D: A Biographical Sketch* (San Antonio: Richmond Press, 1917), 86. Dr. Sampson was the father of Mrs. E.T. Drake, wife of the longtime minister at First Presbyterian Church in Orange. In 1915, while hiking alone in Colorado, Sampson was lost in a snowstorm. His body was found by other hikers after a spring thaw ten years later. "Body of Texan Missing 10 Years Believed Found," *Orange Leader*, 18 September 1925.

128. H.J.L. Stark to Nita Hill, 23 July 1907, postcard album.

129. Ibid., 7 August and 25 August 1907.

130. Ibid., 14 August 1907.

131. Nita Hill to H.J.L. Stark, 10 July, no year noted, but probably 1907.

132. Ibid.

133. Ibid., 26 July 1907.

134. "Mrs. H.J. Lutcher Stark Dies in Orange," *Daily Texan*, 12 October 1939; Nita Hill to H.J.L. Stark, 14 July 1908–23 August 1908.

135. Nita Hill to H.J.L. Stark, 14 June and 17 June 1908.

136. "In Memoriam: Mrs. Lutcher (Nita Hill) Stark," *Delta Kappa Gamma Bulletin* (January 1940): 15, clipping, Stark Foundation Archives.

137. "Texas College Boy Has Valet and Three Autos," *Mountain Democrat* (Placerville, California), 28 January 1911, courtesy of the H.J. Lutcher Stark Center for Physical Culture and Sports.

138. "A Brilliant Entertainment: Mr. and Mrs. W.H. Stark Celebrate Twenty-Fifth Anniversary," clipping, hand-dated 1906 but no month, day, or name of newspaper given, Stark Foundation Archives.

139. Russell, *A History of Orange*, 2.

140. Ibid.

141. A sticky substance applied in a band around tree trunks to protect trees from crawling insects.

142. H.J.L. Stark, "My Father," essay, undated but probably written 1907 or 1908.

143. Ibid.

144. Ibid.

145. Ledger, Account of Estate of Frances Ann Lutcher; and Colburn, Deposition.

146. Warranty deed, 15 August 1907, Lizzie K. Howd to Mrs. H.J. Lutcher, 235:515, Larimer County, Colorado.

147. Moore, "Sketch of the Life of Gregory Bedell Moore."

148. "G. Bedell Moore, Former Resident, Who Carved Success out of Life," *Williamsport Sun*, 2 July 1906.

149. "In the Harness Again," clipping, undated and unattributed, included in Moore, "Sketch of the Life of Gregory Bedell Moore."

150. Moore, "Sketch of the Life of Gregory Bedell Moore."

151. Ibid.

152. Ibid.

153. "Funeral Tomorrow Morning: Services for G. Bedell Moore at St. Mark's Episcopal Church," clipping, undated, unattributed, included in ibid.

154. "Funeral of G. Bedell Moore at Wildwood," clipping, 24 October 1908, unattributed, included in Moore, "Sketch of the Life of Gregory Bedell Moore."

155. Telegram, 24 October 1908, Dr. S. Grant Moore to Elizabeth Blasdel Moore, included in Moore, "Sketch of the Life of Gregory Bedell Moore."

156. Moore, "Sketch of the Life of Gregory Bedell Moore."

157. "Funeral of G. Bedell Moore at Wildwood," clipping, Williamsport newspaper, included in ibid.

158. "Large Gathering Pays Its Final Tribute," clipping, San Antonio newspaper, included in Moore, "Sketch of the Life of Gregory Bedell Moore."

159. W.H. Stark to H.J.L. Stark, 7 December 1908.

160. Ibid.

161. Ibid.

162. Ibid.

163. Ibid., 24 December 1908.

164. Lutcher & Moore Lumber Co., Notes on Requests for Admissions and Interrogatories No. 27, Stark Foundation Archives.

165. Illustrative of the economic power the lumber industry then wielded in the state, Houston lumberman John Henry Kirby was appointed a regent at the University of Texas in the same year, 1911. Regarding Kirby's stature, a story is told that an African American porter in Beaumont, when asked the identity of a certain "distinguished gentleman," replied, "Cap, that's John Henry Kirby . . . and when he crows, it's daylight in East Texas." Maxwell and Baker, *Sawdust Empire*, 103, 104.

166. "William H. Stark," *Las Sabinas* 6, no. 4 (1980): 29.

167. Wedding invitation, Nita Hill to H.J.L. Stark, Stark Foundation Archives.

168. Invitation lists to Hill-Stark wedding and reception, 5 April 1911, Stark Foundation Archives; "Pujo, Arsène Paulin," Biographical Directory of the United States Congress, http://bioguide.congress.gov/scripts/biodisplay.pl?index=p000567 (accessed 1 October 2015); "Dr. S. M. Brown," *Las Sabinas* 6, no. 4 (1980): 22.

169. Nita Hill and H.J.L. Stark, wedding and reception invitation lists, Stark Foundation Archives.

170. Brooms, "And Next We Have Lutcher Stark," 598. Stark's habit of carrying pliers is corroborated by many other sources.

171. Ray E. Lee, "Lutcher Stark's Wealth Used in Good for Others," *Austin American-Statesman*, 16 May 1926.

172. Engraved invitation, "Mrs. Henry J. Lutcher requests the pleasure of your company at a reception and dance at the Holland Hotel Tuesday, May the Eighth, Eight-Thirty O'Clock, Orange, Texas, Mr. and Mrs. Lutcher Stark," Stark Foundation Archives.

173. Sanborn Fire Insurance Map, 1914, Dolph Briscoe Center for American History, University of Texas at Austin (hereafter DBCAH); Howard C. Williams, "The Lutcher & Moore Lumber Company Headquarters Office," *Las Sabinas* 23, no. 2 (1997): 2, citing *Beaumont Enterprise*, 26 December 1912.

174. H. Williams, "The Lutcher & Moore Lumber Company Headquarters Office."

175. Ibid., citing a report by architectural historian Peter Flagg Maxson. Both the Stark office building on Front Street and the Lutcher & Moore office building still stand, the latter now owned by the Port of Orange.

176. "Lutcher Dies in Cincinnati," *Beaumont Enterprise*, 3 October 1912; "Henry J. Lutcher Died Yesterday," *Gazette and Bulletin*, 3 October 1912, clipping, Stark Foundation Archives.

177. State of Ohio, Bureau of Vital Statistics, death certificate of Henry J. Lutcher.

178. Daniell, "Henry J. Lutcher, Orange," 472.

179. *A Century for Christ.*

180. Daniell, "Henry J. Lutcher, Orange," 472.

181. Ibid.

182. The mausoleum was built in 1908. Checks to Otto Zirkel for building it, 3 January and 9 July 1908, Ledger, Account of Estate of Frances Ann Lutcher; and Colburn, Deposition.

183. Daniell, "Henry J. Lutcher, Orange," 473.

184. Ibid., 472, 471.

185. "In Memoriam," resolution signed by directors of the First National Bank, Orange, Stark Foundation Archives.

186. "Henry J. Lutcher Died Yesterday," *Gazette and Bulletin*, 3 October 1912, clipping, Stark Foundation Archives.

187. Farwell, "Orange Center of Early Day Development."

188. Miriam Stark to W.H. Stark, 1 October 1917.

189. H.J. Lutcher, will; Ledger, Account of Estate of Frances Ann Lutcher; Colburn, Deposition.

190. Ratification of H.J. Lutcher, power of attorney to W.H. Stark, 15 October 1912, Stark Foundation Archives.

191. Minute Book, Lutcher & Moore Lumber Company, 20 January 1913.

Chapter 6

1. "Texas College Boy Has Valet and Three Autos," *Mountain Democrat* (Placerville, California), 28 January 1911.

2. "In Memoriam: Mrs. Lutcher (Nita Hill) Stark," 15.

3. Foree, "Archangel and His Bible," 96.

4. Appraisal Report, H.J.L. Stark and Estate of Nita Hill Stark, Orange, Texas, 11 October 1939, by the American Appraisal Company, Milwaukee, Wisconsin, Stark Foundation Archives.

5. Nita Stark to W.H. Stark, 9 October 1913, signed "Devotedly, Nita"; Nita Stark to Miriam and William Stark, 25 February 1914; Nita Stark to Frances A. Lutcher, no date, signed "My dearest love, your ever devoted Nita"; Miriam Stark to Nita Stark, 8 November, no year, signed "oceans of love to you, I am yours lovingly, Miriam L. Stark."

6. Bill, Best & Co. to Mrs. H.J.L. Stark, Waldorf Astoria, New York.

7. Cora P. Bishop to Miriam Stark, 30 October 1913.

8. E.A. Howd to Frances A. Lutcher, 25 May 1913.

9. Miriam Stark to W.H. Stark, 16 November 1913.

10. Jessie Andrews was the first female to complete the entrance examinations and enter the University of Texas in 1883, and the school's first female graduate. Margaret C. Berry, "Andrews, Jessie," *Handbook of Texas Online*, accessed 27 November 2012, http://www.tsha online.org/handbook/online/articles/fan20, uploaded 9 June 2010, published by the Texas State Historical Association; "Jessie Andrews, Scholar and Poet, 1867–1919," Great Texas Women, University of Texas at Austin, http://www.utexas.edu/gtw/andrews.php. (accessed 19 November 2015).

11. "Little Mother Longing," handwritten poem by Jessie Andrews, undated, addressed to "Mrs. Lutcher Stark, Austin, Texas," signed "Sincerely yours, Jessie Andrews," Stark Foundation Archives.

12. Mary Murray Weber, the daughter of I.B. Murray, chauffeur for the Stark families, remembered that "Miss Nita . . . would be in labor for days; it would nearly kill her, and then she had nothing to show for it; the baby would be dead." Oral History Interview, Mary Murray Weber by Ellen Rienstra, 1 March 2004, Stark Foundation Archives.

13. Stark family records, Stark Foundation Archives.

14. Rex Byerley Shaw, "Stark, Who Makes Texas Triumph Possible," *Houston Post*, undated but probably around October 1923.

15. James L. Bowie, "Longhorn Logo Turns 50," *The Alcalde*, September/October 2011, 46; Pat Bomar, "UT Longhorns Given Handle by H.J. [sic] Stark," *Daily Texan*, 31 March 1950.

16. Foree, "Archangel and His Bible."

17. Shaw, "Stark, Who Makes Texas Triumph Possible."

18. H.J.L. Stark to L. Theo Bellmont, 28 May 1922.

19. Foree, "Archangel and His Bible," 94.

20. Shaw, "Stark, Who Makes Texas Triumph Possible."

21. Foree, "Archangel and His Bible," 94; Helen Hargrave, Office of the President, the University of Texas, to Byron Simmons, 28 January 1932; note dated 2 February 1932 from Byron Simmons: "Upon instructions of H.J.L. Stark this letter is not answered. HJLS said let them find out all they can and whatever they desire or want to use okeh but we are not to give them any details."

22. Passport, H.J.L. Stark, 9 May 1921, Stark Foundation Archives.

23. Terry Todd, "The History of Strength Training for Athletes at the University of Texas," *Iron Game History* 2, no. 5 (January 1993): 7.

24. Ibid.; Terry Todd, "History: Message from the Director: The Legacy of Lutcher Stark," H.J. Lutcher Stark Center for Physical Culture and Sports, University of Texas at Austin, http://www.starkcenter.org/about/history (accessed 21 October 2015).

25. "A Short Life Story of Lionel Strongfort, 1878–1970," Iron Game Collectors Series, http://www.sandowplus.co.uk/Competition/Strongfort/stronfortindex.html (accessed 21 October 2015); Lionel Strongfort to H.J.L. Stark, 28 November 1914, Stark Foundation Archives and H.J. Lutcher Stark Center.

26. Lionel Strongfort to H.J.L. Stark, 28 November 1914.

27. D.A. Pruter to W.H. Stark, 15 April 1922, Stark Foundation Archives.

28. Todd, "The History of Strength Training," 7; "In Memoriam: L. Theo Bellmont, September 24, 1881–December 27, 1967," http://www.utexas.edu/faculty/council/2000-2001/memorials/SCANNED/bellmont.pdf (accessed 1 October 2015), no pagination; Margaret C. Berry, "Bellmont, L. Theodore," *Handbook of Texas Online*, accessed 16 September 2012, http://www.tshaonline.org/handbook/online/articles/fbeaa, uploaded 12 June 2010, published by the Texas State Historical Association.

29. "In Memoriam: L. Theo Bellmont."

30. Ibid.; Berry, "Bellmont, L. Theodore."

31. "In Memoriam: L. Theo Bellmont."

32. Todd, "The History of Strength Training," 8. As Todd reports, "It was certainly true that throughout the first half of the 20th century, weight training was disapproved of by almost all coaches and physical educators." Nowadays, resistance training is a widely accepted element in athletic programs of all kinds. Ibid., 12.

33. Ibid., 8.

34. Will Temple, "UT's Hall of Honor Adds 4 More Figures," *Austin American*, 27 November 1958.

35. Photos of the team of the Orange Gray Eagles and the game between the Eagles and the Philadelphia Athletics (managed and partially owned by Connie Mack), West End Park, Orange, 1907, Stark Foundation Archives.

36. M.J. Huggins, manager of the St. Louis National League Ball Club, to H.J.L. Stark, 2 July 1914; K.N. Hempstead, president of the New York Base Ball Club, to H.J.L. Stark, 20 May 1914; Cincinnati Exhibition Company, Operating the Cincinnati Base Ball Club, to

H.J.L. Stark, 1 July 1914; Charles A. Comiskey, Chicago White Sox Base Ball Club, to H.J.L. Stark, 2 July 1914; C.A. Thomas, president of the Chicago National League Baseball Club, to H.J.L. Stark, 6 July 1914.

37. Among the portraits Frances Ann commissioned were of herself with her infant great-granddaughter, Brownie Babette Moore (born August 20, 1911, to Rucie and Fannie Brown Moore); her granddaughter, Fannie Brown Moore; and her two daughters, Miriam Stark and Carrie Brown.

38. Benziger, *August Benziger*, 246; invoice, August Benziger to Frances A. Lutcher, 24 October 1913.

39. Benziger, *August Benziger*, 244.

40. Ibid., 245.

41. Ibid., 245, 245–246.

42. Neiman Marcus was founded in 1907 by Herbert Marcus and his sister, Carrie Marcus Neiman, and brother-in-law, A.L. Neiman.

43. Stanley Marcus, quoting August Benziger in letter to Marieli Benziger and her niece, published in the *Dallas Morning News*, 30 November 1970, Stark Foundation Archives.

44. Benziger, *August Benziger*, 244.

45. In 1913, as a mark of their friendship, the Benzigers gave "Smoky," their female Boston bull terrier, to Miriam and William Stark. Gertrude Benziger to Miriam Stark, 10 November 1913; Benziger, *August Benziger*, 245.

46. Benziger, *August Benziger*, 354.

47. "Seeing America First: An Account of One of the Recent Lutcher Tours," *Pierce-Arrow Salesman*, clipping, no date, 29–31, Texas Energy Museum and Tyrrell Historical Library, Beaumont, copy in Stark Foundation Archives.

48. "From the *Journal* 1910," clipping, *Beaumont Journal*, no date but probably around 29 July 1940, Stark Foundation Archives.

49. "Seeing America First," 29–31; Benziger, *August Benziger*, 244, 246; Hood, "Remembrances of Mrs. Lutcher."

50. "Seeing America First," 29–31.

51. Ledger, Account of Estate of Frances Ann Lutcher, entries for October 1902, November–December 1903, May 1904, January–February 1905, March 1906, July 1906, June 1908, October 1908, July 1909, September 1909, August 1910, February 1911, April 1913, October–November 1914, November 1915, January 1916, July 1917, October–November 1917, June 1918, July 1920, June 1921, October 1921, July 1922, October 1922, November 1923, passim.

52. Billie Jeanne DeLane Stephenson Wright, conversation with Jo Ann Stiles and Ellen Rienstra, Lake Rayburn, 18 April 2005.

53. Miriam Stark to W.H. Stark, 7 October and 17 October 1913.

54. Ibid., 5 October 1913.

55. Ibid., 7, 5, 17, and 18 October 1913.

56. Ibid., 7 October 1913; 8 September 1914; 5 December and 6 December 1918; 26 July, 17 August, 18 August, and 21 August 1921; 2 April 1930.

57. "Just Because," floral card from Miriam to W.H. Stark, undated.

58. Miriam Stark to W.H. Stark, 17 and 24 October 1913.

59. Ibid.

60. Ibid., 16 November 1913.

61. Ibid., 6 October, 16 November, and 17 November 1913.

62. Miriam Stark, Travel Diary, 27 May–27 August 1913, her trip to Europe with Frances Ann Lutcher, Ida Achenbach, and August and Gertrude Benziger.

63. Ibid., entries for 31 May and 5 June 1913.

64. Ibid., entries for 19 July, 14 June, and 3 July 1913.

65. Ibid., entry for 22 June 1913.

66. Benziger, *August Benziger*, 205–207.

67. Ibid., 211; Miriam Stark, Travel Diary, entry for 16 June 1913.

68. Miriam Stark, Travel Diary, entry for 16 June 1913.

69. Ibid., entries for 29, 30, and 31 July 1913.

70. Ibid., entry for 5 August 1913.

71. Benziger, *August Benziger*, 246.

72. Miriam Stark, Travel Diary, second entry for 27 August 1913. Gerrit Dou was Rembrandt's first pupil.

73. *A Sleeping Dog beside a Terra-Cotta Jug, a Basket and a Pile of Kindling Wood* was acquired by Mrs. H.J.L. (Nita) Stark December 7, 1927, according to Christie's official description of its provenance. The painting was bought during Miriam's lifetime, and it is possible that she was influential in the purchase, since, according to the diary, she already knew and liked Dou's work. In the division of Nita Stark's estate, the painting passed to her surviving spouse, Lutcher Stark, who later left it to the Nelda C. and H.J. Lutcher Stark Foundation, along with the remainder of his residuary estate. In 2005, the painting was sold at auction at Christie's for the Stark Foundation for $4.72 million. http://www.artnet.com /magazineus/features/jeromack/jeromack7-29-05_detail.asp?picnum=2 (accessed 19 November 2015); Jamie Reid, "Dog Fetches $4.72 Million," *Beaumont Enterprise*, 3 June 2005.

74. Miriam Stark, Travel Diary, entry for 21 August 1913.

75. Linsley, Rienstra, and Stiles, *Giant under the Hill*, 1–4, 56, 3–4. A salt dome is a geologic anomaly formed by a narrow plug of salt thrusting upward from deep salt beds and piercing the overlying sedimentary rock to form a dome. Oil, sulfur, and gas are frequently found associated with salt domes.

76. Jeff A. Spencer, "The Vinton (Ged) Oil Field, Calcasieu Parish, Louisiana," Petroleum History Institute, *Oil-Industry History* 11, no. 1 (December 2010): 15–27, abstract available at http://www.petroleumhistory.org/journal/vol_11.html#spencer.

77. Howard C. Williams, "Leonard Frederick Benckenstein," *Las Sabinas* 26, no. 4 (2000): 41.

78. "Petroleum Second Only to Lumber as Natural Resource in Orange Area," *Orange Leader*, 25 July 1985, reprinting an article by Leonard F. Benckenstein, originally published in the *Orange Leader* in 1916.

79. Howard Williams, "A Promise of Prosperity: The Oil Boom," in H. Williams, *Gateway to Texas*, 129–130; Nina Harden, "Boom Began in 1922 after 1912 Discovery," *Orange Leader*, 25 July 1985.

80. Wingate, "Summary," 70–71.

81. "Petroleum Second Only to Lumber"; Minute Book and Stockholders' Book, Rescue Oil Co., 1912–1928, Stark Foundation Archives.

82. Linsley, Rienstra, and Stiles, *Giant under the Hill*, 4.

83. Woods and Gatewood, *America Interpreted*, 686, 689.

84. H.J.L. Stark to W.H. Stark, 11 August 1915; Block, "The Lutcher & Moore Lumber Company."

85. "Quarter Million Loss by Fire in Lutcher & Moore Company's Yards," *Orange Leader*, 22 October 1909.

86. H.J.L. Stark to W.H. Stark, 11 August 1915.

87. Farwell, "Orange Center of Early Day Development."

88. Maxwell and Baker, *Sawdust Empire*, 182.

89. Sperry, "The Port of Orange, Texas," 1916.

90. Farwell, "Orange Center of Early Day Development."

91. Ibid.

92. Sperry, "Port of Orange, Texas."

93. In April 1901, when the Lutcher, Stark, and Brown interests had bought Bedell Moore out of their holdings, Moore had deeded his undivided half interest in this Texas property to the Lutcher & Moore Lumber Company, leaving Henry Lutcher to own one-half and the company one-half. On September 22, 1902, Lutcher & Moore conveyed its half interest to Henry Lutcher, Edgar Brown, and William Stark in equal shares; Lutcher then owned two-thirds of the property, and Brown and Stark owned one-sixth each. At Lutcher's death, Frances Ann inherited one-third as her half of their community property, and Miriam and Carrie each inherited one-sixth. Wingate, "Summary," 72; Deed Records, Orange County, Z:1; Deed Records, Jasper County, Jasper, Texas, 44:241.

94. Maxwell and Baker, *Sawdust Empire*, 196, 195.

95. Deed Records, Jasper County, 25:455.

96. Ibid.; Maxwell and Baker, *Sawdust Empire*, 195, 195n, citing contract between R.W. Wier and Lutcher-Stark-Brown interests, 12 February 1918 [*sic*], Lutcher & Moore Lumber Company Papers, East Texas History Center, Stephen F. Austin State University, Nacogdoches, Texas.

97. Affidavit, H.J.L. Stark, 24 November 1924, Stark Foundation Archives.

98. Woods and Gatewood, *America Interpreted*, 691, 695.

99. Ibid., 696.

100. Maxwell and Baker, *Sawdust Empire*, 185, 188.

101. Richard W. Bricker, *Wooden Ships from Texas* (College Station: Texas A&M University Press, 1998), 3; Frank Karppi, "Shipbuilding in Two Wars: Masters of the Sea," in H. Williams, *Gateway to Texas*, 151, 153. After the war's end, the unfinished ships were left to rot, and many of the new shipyards were forced to adapt to the manufacture of new products.

102. Bricker, *Wooden Ships from Texas*, 4; Linda B. Farris, "Making the World Safe for Democracy," in H. Williams, *Picturing Orange*, 157.

103. Farris, "Making the World Safe for Democracy," 151.

104. Bricker, *Wooden Ships from Texas*, 3, 20; Maxwell and Baker, *Sawdust Empire*, 183–184, citing *American Lumberman*, 20 May 1916, 30; 8 July 1916, 53; 9 September 1916, 51; 23 December 1916, 51.

105. Bricker, *Wooden ships from Texas*, 163–166; Maxwell and Baker, *Sawdust Empire*, 192.

106. Maxwell and Baker, *Sawdust Empire*, 192.

107. Jean Nudd, "U.S. World War I Draft Registrations," *Eastman's Online Genealogy Newsletter* 9, no. 3 (19 January 2004), http://www.eogn.com/archives/news0403.htm#WorldWarIDraftRegistrations.

108. Frances A. Lutcher, Petition to the Orange County Draft Board, 22 February 1918.

109. Ibid.

110. Miriam Stark to W.H. Stark, 5 December 1918.

111. Farwell, "Orange Center of Early Day Development." Farwell did not name the company or the shipyard.

112. Telegram, J.W. Hoopes, deputy governor, Federal Reserve Bank, to Luther [*sic*] Stark, 11 June 1917.

113. Jeannette Heard Robinson, Elizabeth Q. Williams, and Linda B. Farris, "Orange Comes of Age," in H. Williams, *Gateway to Texas*, 132.

114. Clipping, *The Alcalde*, March 1918, University of Texas System Regents' Files, Austin, Texas.

115. Ledger, Account of Estate of Frances Ann Lutcher, entries for 30 May 1917, her check to Lord & Burnham, an American manufacturer of conservatories and greenhouses, for $842.95; 29 August 1917 for $7,337.50; 18 September 1917 for $3,643.75; and 2 October 1917 for $3,643.75, totaling $15,467.95; Orange, 1909, Sanborn Fire Maps, Perry-Castañeda Library, Map Collection, University of Texas Online, www.lib.utexas.edu/maps/sanborn /m-o/txu-sanborn-orange-1919-09.jpg, showing the footprint of a greenhouse behind the Lutcher mansion with a characteristic hexagonal Lord & Burnham shape (top row, middle). In addition, Frances Ann owned a conventionally built greenhouse in back of the Lord & Burnham conservatory as well as two additional ones across the street. Miriam owned Lord & Burnham conservatories as well.

116. "Henry Jacob Lutcher," *Las Sabinas* 6, no. 4 (1980): 17; "Colorful Experience," *Opportunity Valley News*, 22 October 1997.

117. President Woodrow Wilson to Frances A. Lutcher, 3 January 1922.

118. Edith Bolling Wilson to Frances A. Lutcher, 14 February 1922.

119. Florence Kling Harding to Frances A. Lutcher, 23 February 1922.

120. Hood, "Remembrances of Mrs. Lutcher"; Frances A. Lutcher to Cpl. Malcolm W. Pearce, 4 October 1915, Stark Foundation Archives.

121. Citation of Mrs. H.J. Lutcher from the US Department of the Navy, for participation in "Eyes for the Navy," Stark Foundation Archives.

122. Miriam Stark to W.H. Stark, 3 October 1917.

123. *The Alcalde*, March 1918. The "Kishi Colony" was settled by the illustrious Kishi family and others who came from Japan with patriarch Kichimatsu Kishi in 1907 to settle a nine thousand–acre tract west of Orange and engage in rice farming. Kishi later helped found the Orange Petroleum Company and donated acreage for the original Orange-field High School. See "Japanese Settler Left Mark on Area," *Orange Leader*, 25 July 1985; and George J. Hirasaki, Thomas K. Walls, and Kazuhiko Orii, "The Kishi Colony," http:// hirasaki.net/Family_Stories/Kishi_Colony/Kishi.htm (accessed 21 October 2015).

124. Certificates to "Mrs. Lutcher Stark," Stark Foundation Archives.

125. Nita Stark (and Frances A. Lutcher) to Miriam and W.H. Stark, 25 February 1914.

126. "Handsome New Houseboat," *Gossip: Once a Month*, Austin, Texas, 31 August 1917, clipping in Stark Foundation Archives.

127. Robinson, "Brown, Edgar, Sr."; "Dr. Edgar Brown," *Las Sabinas* 6, no. 4 (1980): 38; H. Williams, *Picturing Orange*, 129. One story holds that Dr. Brown died of throat cancer, the malignancy having developed after he was hit in the throat by a flame from a Roman candle. Horn, conversation with Dickerson, Stiles, and Rienstra, 9 May 2012.

128. "Dr. E.W. Brown Was Community Builder," *Orange Leader*, 29 May 1936.

129. "Dr. Edgar Brown," *Las Sabinas*, 38.

130. Edgar W. Brown, Will, A:377 et seq., Probate Records, County Court, Orange County, Texas.

131. "Dr. Edgar Brown," *Las Sabinas*, 36, 38.

132. "Dr. E.W. Brown Was Community Builder."

133. John M. Barry, *The Great Influenza: The Epic Story of the Deadliest Plague in History* (New York: Penguin Books, 2005), 169–173, 192–193.

134. Ibid., 92.

135. "The Influenza Pandemic of 1918," http://virus.stanford.edu/uda/ (accessed 1 October 2015); "Pandemic Flu History, 1918–1919," FLU.gov, http://www.flu.gov/pandemic /history (accessed 1 October 2015).

136. "1918 Flu Pandemic," http://www.history.com/search?q=1918%20flu%20pandemic (accessed 19 November 2015).

137. Memorabilia from the family of James Pruter, whose father, D.A. Pruter, was a longtime employee of the Lutcher & Moore Lumber Company, serving as executive secretary to W.H. Stark and an assistant to H.J.L. Stark. Donated by the Pruter family to the Stark Foundation Archives.

138. Molly Brown, daughter of Edgar W. Brown III, conversation with Jo Ann Stiles and Ellen Rienstra, Houston, 11 May 2006, Stark Foundation Archives.

139. Frances A. Lutcher to Cpl. Malcolm W. Pearce, 24 October 1918, Stark Foundation Archives; "Dr. Edgar Brown," *Las Sabinas*, 40n; Brown Family Tree, *Las Sabinas* 6, no. 4 (1980): 44; "The Influenza Pandemic of 1918," citing N.R. Grist, "A Letter from Camp Devens 1918," *British Medical Journal* (22–29 December 1979). In her letter to Corporal Pearce, Frances Ann gives Fannie's death date as October 12, 1918; other records show it as October 13.

140. Frances A. Lutcher to Cpl. Malcolm W. Pearce, 24 October 1918.

141. Ibid. This letter, as was much of Frances Ann's correspondence, was written by her companion and amanuensis, Ida Achenbach.

142. Ibid.

143. Ibid.

144. Ledger, Account of Estate of Frances Ann Lutcher; and George S. Colburn, Answers to Direct and Cross Interrogatories in Carrie L. Brown vs. H.J.L. Stark, No. 5203, District Court of Orange County, Texas; Frances A. Lutcher's Will, County Clerk's Office, Orange County, Texas, P665.

145. H. Williams, *Picturing Orange*, 133.

146. Carrie Joiner Woliver, *The Train Stopped in Orange* (Orange, TX: Carrie Joiner Woliver, 2012), 41; Robinson, Williams, and Farris, "Orange Comes of Age," 132.

147. Farris, "Making the World Safe for Democracy," 157.

148. Wingate, "Summary," 22, 37, 52, 64, 67.

149. "Rotary Club of Orange, Texas," Yearbook, 1951–52, copy in Stark Foundation Archives.

150. Ray E. Lee, "Lutcher Stark's Wealth Used in Good for Others," *Austin American-Statesman*, 16 May 1926; Proceedings: Twelfth Annual Rotary Convention, Edinburgh, Scotland, 13–16 June 1921, International Association of Rotary Clubs, Eighteenth District, report by H.J. Lutcher Stark, District Governor, 444.

151. Board of Regents, Former Regents, The University of Texas System, http://www.utsystem.edu/bor/former_regents/name.htm (accessed 15 October 2015).

Chapter 7

1. Horn, conversation with Stiles, Dickerson, and Rienstra, 17 April 2012. Cynthia Horn is the daughter of Hal Grafton Carter and Ruth DeRieux Carter. Hal Carter was hired as an office boy in 1913 by Edgar Brown and, aside from a stint in World War I, continued to work for the Browns as secretary and general troubleshooter for many years. Ruth was hired by Frances Ann Lutcher to work as the first surgical nurse at the Frances Ann Lutcher Hospital and became her friend and confidante. After Ruth's marriage to Carter she ceased to work as a nurse but held the post of organist at the Presbyterian Church in Orange for many years. Cynthia Horn was married first to Arthur Leedy, then, after his death, to Cleo Horn.

2. W.H. Stark to H.J.L. Stark, 7 December 1908; Henry Lutcher Brown to H.J.L. Stark, 27 March 1960.

3. Benziger, *Benziger*, 245.

4. Ibid.

5. Ibid.

6. R. Williams, "Luxurious Legacy," 20; *Lutcher Memorial Building*.

7. R. Williams, "Luxurious Legacy," 20.

8. Ibid.; *Lutcher Memorial Building*; *The Building in Which You Worship, Something of Its Art Background*, pamphlet, First Presbyterian Church, Orange, Texas, copy in Stark Foundation Archives.

9. The glass dome was encased by a copper dome in the mid-1950s. See architect's plans, 23 November 1956, First Presbyterian (Lutcher Memorial) Church, Orange, copy in church archives, and interviews with several church members by Kyle Hood.

10. R. Williams, "Luxurious Legacy," 23.

11. The original Hope-Jones organ was replaced in 1953 by a three-manual Casavant pipe organ made by the Casavant Freres Company of Saint-Hyacinthe, Quebec. Edgar and Lutcher Brown gave the new organ in memory of their mother, Carrie Lutcher Brown. *A Century For Christ*; *Lutcher Memorial Building*.

12. R. Williams, "Luxurious Legacy," 23.

13. Ibid., 21; *Lutcher Memorial Building*.

14. The *Orange Leader* issue of 17 December 1909 gives a cost of $225,000 for the church, but the 23 December 1910 issue gives the figure at $300,000. The final construction figure was probably even higher.

15. *Lutcher Memorial Building*.

16. General Warranty Deed, Frances Ann Lutcher to F.H. Farwell, George W. Curtis, and H.J.L. Stark, trustees of the First Presbyterian Church of Orange, Texas, County Court, Orange County, Texas, 15:179, Deed Records, Orange County.

17. *Orange Leader*, 23 December 1910; R. Williams, "Luxurious Legacy," 20.

18. *A Century for Christ*.

19. Frances Ann Lutcher's Account, 1914–1924 (one of several listed), Ledger, Account of Estate of Frances Ann Lutcher, entry for April 1914, her check to "Opera House Account" for $8,120.17; journal voucher noting check from Mrs. H.J. Lutcher, 25 May 1914, "Lutcher Building a/c, to close Lutcher Opera House a/c into Mrs. Lutcher's personal a/c," for $8,120.17.

20. A.F. Burns, "Lutcher Model Farm Is Largest Venture of Kind in Country," *Beaumont Enterprise*, undated clipping, probably late July or early August 1913, Stark Foundation Archives.

21. This tract was part of a larger parcel that Henry Lutcher and Bedell Moore had purchased from J. Minnick Williams in 1889. Deed Records, Orange County, M:65. Frances Ann then bought Moore's undivided half interest in 1907 (the same year she purchased Roslyn Ranch).

22. Burns, "Lutcher Model Farm Is Largest Venture."

23. Ibid.

24. Ibid.

25. Commemorative Booklet, Frances Ann Lutcher Hospital, dedicated 15 May 1921, Stark Foundation Archives, 3.

26. "Orange Is to Have Its Own Hospital," *Orange Leader*, undated clipping, probably around 1916. The article named the house as "the Filson Home."

27. Program, Service of Dedication, Frances Ann Lutcher Hospital, 15 May 1921, Stark Foundation Archives.

28. Program, Service of Dedication; Commemorative Booklet, Frances Ann Lutcher Hospital, 9.

29. Commemorative Booklet, Frances Ann Lutcher Hospital, 3.

30. Ibid., 9, 12, 21.

31. Ibid., 16, 21.

32. Griffing Nurseries, in its day one of the largest nurseries in the country, was originally located in Port Arthur but relocated to a site north of Beaumont circa 1920, around the time of the hospital's construction. The nursery shipped trees and plants all over the United States, including to the 1939 New York World's Fair. As one columnist put it, "[Griffing Nurseries] was more than petunias in the spring; it was a major industry." Frances Ann's ledger entries reflect her checks to Griffing Nurseries during 1920–1921 totaling $14,100. Don Streater, "Another Day," *Beaumont Enterprise*, undated clipping, courtesy of Gloria Griffing Graham, copies in Stark Foundation Archives; Ledger, Account of Estate of Frances Ann Lutcher, entries for 10 and 27 January, 12 February, 20 and 30 March, 4 May 1920; and 26 February 1921.

33. She was possibly referring to Nita and Lutcher Stark's second baby, Henry, born June 8, 1916, who lived only a few hours.

34. Commemorative Booklet, Frances Ann Lutcher Hospital, 21, 16.

35. Ibid., 39.

36. Handwritten note by R.F. Miller, M.D., on Program, Service of Dedication.

37. Deed Records, Newton County, 19:560 et seq., 11 July 1919; Deed Records, Jasper County, 30:551 et seq., 12 July 1919; Deed Records, Sabine County, 15:266–270, 14 July 1919; Affidavit, H.J.L. Stark, 24 November 1924, Stark Foundation Archives.

38. George Holland to Lutcher Brown, 12 August 1917.

39. Miriam Stark to W.H. Stark, 23 September 1917.

40. Affidavit, J.O. Sims, 24 November 1924, Stark Foundation Archives; Affidavit, Dr. A.G. Pearce, 24 November 1924, Stark Foundation Archives.

41. Ledger, Account of Estate of Frances Ann Lutcher, entries beginning 24 December 1907 et seq.

42. Photo, August 1898, Cheyenne Canyon, Colorado, Frances A. Lutcher and H.J.L. Stark, age eleven, Stark Foundation Archives.

43. Ledger, Account of Estate of Frances Ann Lutcher, and George S. Colburn, Deposition, Answers to Direct and Cross Interrogatories in Carrie L. Brown vs. H.J.L. Stark, No. 5203, District Court of Orange County, Texas.

44. Horn, conversation with Stiles, Dickerson, and Rienstra, 17 April 2012. Rosa Hamilton, Frances Ann's housekeeper from September 17, 1900, until February 1925, stated, "Mr. H.J.L. Stark and wife and Mr. & Mrs. W.H. Stark were very regular visitors. Mrs. Brown was a frequent visitor, but the [Brown] children did not come very often." Deposition, Rosa Hamilton, in re Carrie L. Brown vs. H.J.L. Stark, Orange County District Court, 19 November 1925. Frances Ann had befriended Ruth DeRieux "Deru" Carter when she was serving as the Frances Ann Lutcher Hospital's first surgical nurse. Later Carter assisted as caregiver for both Frances Ann and Carrie Lutcher Brown.

45. Affidavit, H.J.L. Stark, 24 November 1924.

46. N. Dean Tevis, "How Texas' Richest Young Man Spends His Money," *Beaumont Enterprise*, 7 March 1926; Lee, "Lutcher Stark's Wealth Used in Good for Others," *Austin American-Statesman*, 16 May 1926; "The Small Town Texan Who Has 75 Million Dollars," *Kansas City Star*, 31 July 1927.

47. Affidavit, H.J.L. Stark, 24 November 1924.

48. Ibid.

49. "Mrs. C.L. Brown Proves Talents in Many Lines," *Orange Leader*, Centennial Edition, 29 May 1936.

50. Deed Records, Orange County, 32:581; Brown group's final offer to Lutcher/Stark group, $2,914,600, signed by Dr. E.W. Brown Estate by Mrs. E.W. Brown, H.L. Brown, and E.W. Brown Jr., dated 10 November 1919 and accepted and signed by F.H. Farwell 17 November 1919, Stark Foundation Archives.

51. Minute Book, Lutcher & Moore Lumber Company, 30 December 1919, 55.

52. Ibid., 55–56; Brown group's final offer to Lutcher/Stark group of $2,914,600, 10 November 1919 and 17 November 1919, Stark Foundation Archives; check, $500,000 to the First National Bank, Orange, from Lutcher & Moore Lumber Company, signed by H.J.L. Stark (initial cash payment to Brown group), 1 December 1919, Stark Foundation Archives; seven promissory notes of $344,942.86 each, dated 25 November 1919, from the Lutcher and Stark group to the Brown group, to be paid each year from that date for seven years, Stark Foundation Archives.

53. Minute Book, Lutcher & Moore Lumber Company, 30 December 1919, 55–56; Deed Records, Orange County, 32:593.

54. Minute Book, Lutcher & Moore Lumber Company, 20 January 1920, 59.

55. Ibid., 19 February 1920, 61.

56. Stark Family Records, Stark Foundation Archives; "Granny Hill," *The Alcalde* 8, no. 8 (March 1921): 379.

57. Miriam Stark to Nita Stark, undated but after Ella's and Dr. Hill's deaths, Samoset letterhead, Stark Foundation Archives.

58. Ella Hill to Frances A. Lutcher, 8 April and 21 October 1919.

59. Ibid., 21 October 1919.

60. "Granny's Boys" and "Granny Hill," *The Alcalde* (March 1921): 369–371, 371–385.

61. "Granny's Boys," *The Alcalde* (March 1920): 369.

62. "Granny Hill," *The Alcalde* (March 1920): 376, 380.

63. W.B. Simmons to Thurlow Weed, 1 December 1939.

64. "Granny Hill," *The Alcalde* (March 1920): 385.

65. *Practical Optimists: The Story of a Lumber Firm Which Refused to Let Recent Business Depression "Phase 'Em,"* Port of Orange, Texas, USA, booklet, undated but probably 1921 or 1922, Stark Foundation Archives.

66. Report, Assets of the Lutcher & Moore Lumber Company, 1 July 1921, Stark Foundation Archives.

67. Bob Axelson, "Milestone Marked in Lutcher & Moore's 108-Year History," *Orange Leader,* 17 September 1970; *Practical Optimists.* One story holds that the name "Lunita" was formed as a combination of the Starks' first names, "Lutcher" and "Nita." T.J. Ratliff, "History of Lutcher-Moore," *DeQuincy News* (DeQuincy, Louisiana), 1 October 1970.

68. *Practical Optimists.*

69. *The Story of Grade Marked Yellow Pine Lumber,* booklet, Lutcher & Moore Lumber Company, 1 January 1926, Stark Foundation Archives.

70. Farwell, "Saw Mill Industry Plays Major Part in Texas History," *Orange Leader,* 29 May 1936; Maxwell and Baker, *Sawdust Empire,* 97n; Howard Williams, "Stark, Henry Jacob Lutcher," *Handbook of Texas Online,* accessed 22 February 2013, http://www.tshaonline.org/handbook/online/articles/fst16, uploaded 15 June 2010, published by the Texas State Historical Association.

71. *Story of Grade Marked Yellow Pine Lumber.*

72. Proposed Labor Agreement from Federal Labor Union No. 16124, approved by the American Federation of Labor 6 December 1918 and presented to Miller-Link Lumber Co. of Orange and Lutcher & Moore Lumber Co. 2 January 1919, Stark Foundation Archives.

73. W.H. Stark to J.E. Crain, 21 January 1919.

74. J.E. Crain, secretary of Orange Central Labor Union, to W.H. Stark, 21 January 1919; W.H. Stark to J.E. Crain, 21 January 1919; J.E. Crain to W.H. Stark, 24 January 1919.

75. "Negroes Walk out of Lumber Mills," *Orange Daily Leader*, 28 January 1919.

76. F.H. Farwell, memorandum on meeting with committee from the AFL Central Labor Body, 7 April 1919.

77. James C. Maroney, "Organized Labor in Texas, 1900–1930" (PhD diss., University of Houston, 1975), 204–206.

78. Stock certificate for twenty-five thousand shares of stock in Hagan Coal Mines, Inc., to W.H. Stark, 4 August 1920, Stark Foundation Archives; Wingate, "Summary," 22.

79. "John de Praslin," All 1930 United States Federal Census Results, http://www.swla history.org/newsletter.htm, http://search.ancestry.com/cgi-bin/sse.dll?indir=1&db=1930us fedcen&h=107927408&tid=&pid=&usePUB=true&rhsource=2442 (accessed 29 November 2015); Wingate, "Summary," 22.

80. Wingate, "Summary," 23.

81. D.A. Pruter to W.H. Stark, 5 June 1922.

82. Wingate, "Summary," 22.

83. F.H. Farwell, memorandum, 26 October 1923.

84. D.A. Pruter to W.H. Stark, 3 May, 21 June, 12 July, 1 August, 11 August, 14 August, 23 August, 24 September, 2 October, 17 October, and 29 November 1924; 2 May and 2 September 1925; 16 March 1927; 14 August, 23 August, and 17 October 1924; 2 May 1925; 8 August 1924.

85. Lutcher Stark's cousin, Alford Stark, went to work at the Hagan mine in an attempt to sell the coal in Denver, Colorado, where he was told that the coal was "too powdery, and had too much sulfur in it." Alford's son, Dr. Jeremiah Stark, described Dr. de Praslin as "a real personality, a promoter." Jeremiah Stark, conversation with Jo Ann Stiles, 17 May 2010, Woodville, Texas.

86. Lee, "Lutcher Stark's Wealth Used in Good for Others."

87. W.H. Stark from Samoset, Rockland, Maine, to D.A. Pruter, 1 July 1924; W.H. Stark to D.A. Pruter, 12 July 1924; F.H. Farwell to W.H. Stark, 24 July 1925; D.A. Pruter to W.H. Stark, 21 June 1924.

88. Nita Stark to Frances A. Lutcher, undated but probably late summer or early fall of 1923.

89. Wingate, "Summary," 6–76.

90. Tevis, "How Texas' Richest Young Man Spends His Money"; Lee, "Lutcher Stark's Wealth Used in Good for Others"; "The Small Town Texan Who Has 75 Million Dollars."

91. "Henry Jacob Lutcher Stark," Former Regents, University of Texas System, http:// www.utsystem.edu/bor/former_regents/regents/StarkHenry (accessed 29 November 2015).

92. Clipping, undated, unattributed, scrapbook on H.J.L. Stark by W.B. Simmons, ca. 1921–1928, Stark Foundation Archives.

93. Foree, "Archangel and His Bible," 97, 95.

94. Nita Stark to Fannie Ratchford, 6 January 1936.

95. Clipping, scrapbook on H.J.L. Stark by W.B. Simmons.

96. Ida Elisabeth Roos, called "Fraulein" by family members, was a Swiss national who met Miriam and William Stark while they were traveling with August and Gertrude Benziger in Switzerland. Roos lived with Miriam and William from 1914 to 1923. In 1923, she met her future husband, a man with the surname of Jackson, in New York, and was married in 1924 at the Waldorf Astoria in New York City. The wedding was financed by Miriam and William Stark. Roos died in 1938. Stark Foundation Archives, information courtesy Jeffry Harris, W.H. Stark House.

97. F.H. Farwell to W.H. Stark, 28 June 1921; "W.B. Simmons, Orange Civic Leader, Is Dead," *Beaumont Enterprise*, 12 January 1961.

98. W.B. Simmons to F.H. Farwell, 18 May 1921; Nita Stark to Frankie and Raymond Hill, Edinburgh, 14 June 1921; London, 27 June 1921; London, 30 June 1921; Barcelona, 10 July 1921; letters of introduction 10 and 21 May 1921 from US senator Morris Sheppard and Texas governor Pat Neff carried by H.J.L. Stark.

99. W.B. Simmons to F.H. Farwell, 18 May 1921.

100. Letter of introduction for H.J.L. Stark to Col. George Harvey, US ambassador to Great Britain, from Governor Pat M. Neff, 21 May 1921, and general letter of introduction from Morris Sheppard, 10 May 1921.

101. Nita Stark to Raymond and Frankie Hill, 14 and 27 June 1921.

102. Frankie Cochran Hill was also a childhood friend of Nita's and her sorority sister in Pi Beta Phi at the University of Texas.

103. Nita Stark to Raymond and Frankie Hill, 14 and 27 June 1921.

104. Ibid., 14 June 1921.

105. Ibid., 30 June and 10 July 1921.

106. Ibid.

107. F.H. Farwell to H.J.L. Stark, 21 July 1921.

108. Abbott, "A Stark Genealogy," Seventh Generation, William Henry Stark.

109. F.H. Farwell to H.J.L. Stark, 21 July 1921.

110. Miriam Stark to W.H. Stark, 23 August 1921.

111. Ibid., 28 August 1921.

112. Ibid., 10 and 30 July 1921.

113. Nita Stark to Raymond and Frankie Hill, 10 July 1921.

114. Ibid.

115. F.H. Farwell to W.H. Stark, 21 July 1921.

116. Carlos Alzugaray to H.J.L. Stark, 28 September 1921; telegram, H.J.L. Stark to Carlos Alzugaray, 6 February 1922.

117. F.H. Farwell to H.J.L. Stark, 9 March 1922.

118. W.B. Simmons to Senator Morris Sheppard, 15 May 1922.

119. Clipping, scrapbook on H.J.L. Stark by W.B. Simmons.

120. Clipping, *Orange Leader*, scrapbook on H.J.L. Stark by W.B. Simmons, 21 October 1922.

121. F.H. Farwell to H.J.L. Stark, 21 July 1921.

122. Memo of a statement by Ben McDonough, general manager of Lutcher & Moore Lumber Company, who stated that William Stark was blind, or very nearly so, as early as 1930. Memo, 12 August 1959.

123. Telegram, W.H. Stark to D.A. Pruter, 9 April 1922; letter, W.H. Stark to D.A. Pruter, June 1922.

124. Telegram, F.H. Farwell to H.J.L. Stark, 11 April 1922.

125. "William H. Stark," *Las Sabinas* 6, no. 4 (1980): 29–30; W.H. Stark to H.J.L. Stark, 2 July 1928; W.H. Stark to D.A. Pruter, 1 July 1924.

126. W.H. Stark to D.A. Pruter, June 1922.

127. Telegram, Miriam Stark to Douglas Pruter, 27 June 1923.

128. F.H. Farwell to H.J.L. Stark, 29 June 1923.

129. H.J.L. Stark to Frances A. Lutcher, 27 August 1923.

130. W.H. Stark to D.A. Pruter, 29 September 1923.

131. Henry San, D.D.S., bill for services rendered to Mr. and Mrs. Stark, marked "Paid in Full," 14 November 1923.

132. Nita Stark to Frances A. Lutcher, undated but probably late summer or fall of 1923.

133. Telegram, W.H. Stark to D.A. Pruter, 1 December 1924.

134. Ibid., 1 and 6 December 1924.

135. D.A. Pruter to W.H. Stark, 13 December 1924.

136. W.H. Stark to D.A. Pruter, 5 August 1925 (emphasis added).

137. Miriam Stark to Nita Stark, undated but after the death in 1923 of Homer Hill.

138. "Mrs. Stark Is Active Officer of Pi Beta Phi," clipping, *Orange Leader*, undated but probably around 1935, Stark Foundation Archives; H.J.L. Stark to Frances A. Lutcher, 27 August 1923.

139. Certificate, Special Commission, State of Texas, Governor's Office, appointing Nita Stark as Texas delegate to Illiteracy Conference, Little Rock, Arkansas, 10 and 11 April 1923, Stark Foundation Archives.

140. H.J.L. Stark to Nita Stark, 20 September 1924.

141. H.J.L. Stark to Frances A. Lutcher, 27 August 1925.

142. F.H. Farwell to W.H. Stark, 21 July 1921.

143. Family Records, Stark Foundation Archives.

144. Clipping, 18 July but no year listed, scrapbook on H.J.L. Stark by W.B. Simmons.

145. Ibid.

146. "Dr. Hill Buried," clipping, undated, unattributed, scrapbook on H.J.L. Stark by W.B. Simmons; W.B. Simmons to Thurlow Weed, 1 December 1939, Stark Foundation Archives.

147. Dr. Homer Hill, typescript of obituary, Stark Foundation Archives.

148. R. Barton to Nita Stark, 10 September 1923.

149. Dr. Homer Hill, typescript of obituary.

150. H.J.L. Stark to Frances A. Lutcher, 27 August 1923.

151. Nita Stark to Frances A. Lutcher, undated but after Dr. Hill's death, probably late summer or early fall 1923.

152. Frank Mills was born 26 April 1923, at 11:30 a.m., and William Mills at 11:55 a.m. See Children's Home Society of Virginia to Nita Stark, 31 October 1923.

153. Statement by J.A. Noblin, M.D., re background information on Mills twins, Frank and William, 14 October 1923, enclosed in letter from the Children's Home Society of Virginia to Mrs. J. Lester [sic] Stark, 31 October 1923; Consent to Adoption, Children's Home Society of Virginia, 29 January 1925.

154. Statement of J.A. Noblin; commitment, William and Frank Mills, to State Board of Public Welfare, Judge W.M. Delp, Juvenile and Domestic Relations Court, Radford, Virginia, 28 September 1923.

155. "Howe/Mills, Radford, Virginia," Genealogy.com, 3 October 2000, http://genforum.genealogy.com/howe/messages/2077.html.

156. Commitment, William and Frank Mills to State Board of Public Welfare; correspondence of Children's Home Society of Virginia re Frank and William Mills, 12 October 1923–24 March 1925.

157. DeVault's headstone, Monte Vista Cemetery, Johnson City, Tennessee; Children's Home Society of Virginia to DeVault, 12 October 1923.

158. Children's Home Society of Virginia to Mrs. H.J.L. Stark, 19 December 1924.

159. Clipping, undated but probably January or February 1924, scrapbook on H.J.L. Stark by W.B. Simmons.

160. Statement of J.A. Noblin.

161. Ibid.

162. Children's Home Society of Virginia to Mrs. J. Lester [sic] Stark, 31 October 1923.

163. Children's Home Society of Virginia, Certificate of Consent to Adoption of Frank and William Mills by J. Lester Stark [corrected to read H.J.L. Stark] and Nita Hill Stark, 29 January 1925.

164. Adoption, Frank and William Mills, Deed Records, Orange County, signed by Lutcher and Nita Stark 24 March 1925 and filed 30 March 1925, 41:50, 51.

165. "Death of Mrs. Henry J. Lutcher," clipping, undated but shortly after Frances Ann's death, unattributed but possibly from a lumbering publication, Stark Foundation Archives.

166. "Funeral of Mrs. H.J. Lutcher to Be Held Here Saturday," clipping, *Orange Leader*, undated but probably 22 or 23 October 1924, Stark Foundation Archives.

167. In September, Miriam and William were in Maine, and from there they came straight to New York. Lutcher, who had come through Orange October 11 on his way to Austin, must have traveled directly from the latter city. See telegram, W.H. Stark to D.A. Pruter, 19 September 1924; and D.A. Pruter to W.H. Stark, 11 October 1924.

168. D.A. Pruter to W.H. Stark, 11 October 1926.

169. "Death of Mrs. Henry J. Lutcher," clipping, Stark Foundation Archives; "Funeral of Mrs. H.J. Lutcher to Be Held Here Saturday."

170. "Industries to Close for Funeral of Mrs. Lutcher at 3 P.M. Saturday," clipping, *Orange Leader*, undated but probably 22 or 23 October 1924, Stark Foundation Archives; "Simple Service Marks Funeral of Mrs. Lutcher; Friend of Flowers in Life, Surrounded by Them in Death," *Orange Leader*, 26 October 1924.

171. "Simple Service Marks Funeral of Mrs. Lutcher."

172. Proclamation by Orange mayor S.M. White, clipping, *Orange Leader*, undated but 22, 23, or 24 October 1924, Stark Foundation Archives.

173. "Industries to Close for Funeral of Mrs. Lutcher."

174. "Simple Service Marks Funeral of Mrs. Lutcher."

175. "Memorial Church and Hospital Are Leading Gifts to Orange of Mrs. Frances Ann Lutcher: City's Philanthropist Was Lover of Flowers, and of Humanity," *Beaumont Enterprise*, 25 October 1924.

176. Ibid.

177. "A Tribute," clipping, *Orange Leader*, undated, Stark Foundation Archives.

178. "Death of Mrs. Henry J. Lutcher," Stark Foundation Archives.

179. Frances A. Lutcher, typescript of obituary, undated, probably Williamsport newspaper, 12 November 1924, Stark Foundation Archives; "Mrs. Henry Lutcher Highly Praised," clipping, undated, probably Williamsport newspaper, Stark Foundation Archives.

180. "A Tribute."

181. Envelope fragment addressed to "Mrs. H.J. Lutcher, Waldorf-Astoria, New York City," Stark Foundation Archives.

182. Frances A. Lutcher, will, 17 February 1919, admitted to probate 12 January 1925, J:294, Orange County Probate Minutes.

183. Ibid.

184. Ibid.; "The Small Town Texan Who Has 75 Million Dollars."

185. Frances A. Lutcher, will.

186. Orange County Probate Court, in re Estate of Mrs. Frances A. Lutcher, 31 October 1924; Orange County Probate Court, in re Estate of Mrs. Frances A. Lutcher, Deceased, Probate Docket, Cause #666, ordered by County Judge Ed. S. McCarver, 3 November 1924.

187. Orange County Probate Court, in re Estate of Francis [*sic*] Ann Lutcher, Deceased, Contest of Will by Brownie Babette Moore by Her Guardian R.A. Moore, 3 November 1924.

188. Orange County Probate Court, in re Estate of F.A. Lutcher, Deceased, R.A. Moore, Contest of Application of H.J.L. Stark to be appointed as Temporary Administrator of Estate of F.A. Lutcher, 3 November 1924.

189. H.J.L. Stark, Sworn Statement as Temporary Administrator of Estate of Frances Ann Lutcher, Stark Foundation Archives.

190. Orange County Probate Court, Petition of Carrie Lutcher Brown, Estate of Mrs. Frances A. Lutcher, Deceased, in re Cause #666, 2 December 1924.

191. Ibid.

192. Ibid.

193. Orange County Probate Court, in re Estate of F.A. Lutcher, Deceased, 20 December 1924, 5 January 1925.

194. Orange County Court, in re Estate of Frances A. Lutcher, Deceased, Case #665, 12 January 1925.

195. Frances A. Lutcher, will, Orange County Probate Minutes.

196. Orange County Probate Court, Case #665, Oath of Office, H.J.L. Stark, as Independent Executor of Estate of Frances A. Lutcher, Deceased, 12 January 1925.

197. Orange County Probate Court, Decree Admitting Will to Probate, in re Estate of Frances A. Lutcher, Deceased, Case #665, 2 January 1925; Orange County Probate Court, Probate Docket, Case #665, in re Estate of Mrs. F.A. Lutcher, Deceased, 12 January 1925; Orange County District Court, R.A. Moore, Guardian of Brownie Babette Moore, vs. H.J.L. Stark, #5202, Postponement of Case until 23 November 1925, 10 November 1925.

198. Victor Hoy Stark, the oldest child of John Thomas Stark and his third wife, Donna Jerusha Smith, was William Stark's half brother.

199. Orange County District Court, R.A. Moore, Guardian of Brownie Babette Moore, vs. H.J.L. Stark, #5202, Postponement of Case until 23 November 1925, 10 November 1925.

200. Orange County District Court, Brownie Babette Moore vs. H.J.L. Stark, #5202, Judgment in Favor of Defendant, 1 December 1925.

201. Opinion of Commission of Appeals of Texas, Section B, 12 June 1929, 17:1037, *Southwestern Reporter*, 2nd ser.; Opinion of Commission of Appeals of Texas, Section B, 13 November 1929, 21:296, *Southwestern Reporter*, 2nd ser.

202. H.J.L. Stark, Deposition, 15 February 1939, copy in Stark Foundation Archives; Mandate, 22 February 1930, P:124, District Court Minutes of Orange County, Texas.

203. Jasper County District Court, Carrie L. Brown vs. H.J.L. Stark, Cause #2641, Plaintiff's Original Petition, filed 29 May 1926.

204. Ibid.

205. H.J.L. Stark, Deposition, 15 February 1939.

206. Rosa Hamilton, Deposition, in re Carrie L. Brown vs. H.J.L. Stark, Orange County District Court, 19 November 1925.

207. Clinton B. Glasgow, Deposition, in re Carrie L. Brown vs. H.J.L. Stark, Orange County District Court, 14 November 1925.

208. Ledger, Account of Estate of Frances Ann Lutcher; and George S. Colburn, Deposition, Answers to Direct and Cross Interrogatories in Carrie L. Brown vs. H.J.L. Stark, No. 5203, District Court of Orange County, Texas.

209. Ibid.

210. B.M. Hammond to H.J.L. Stark, 14 June 1926.

211. H.J.L. Stark, Affidavit, 15 February 1939, Stark Foundation Archives.

212. Leo Becker to Raymond M. Hill, 21 April 1931; deed, H.J.L. Stark as Executor of Estate of F.A. Lutcher to Mary E. Deacon, 22 May 1931, Stark Foundation Archives.

Chapter 8

1. "City of Austin Population History, 1840 to 2015," http://www.austintexas.gov/sites
/default/files/files/Planning/Demographics/population_history_pub.pdf (accessed 16 December 2015); Austin Postcard Collection, http://www.austinpostcard.com/pclist.php (accessed 28 October 2015).

2. Austin's growth continued to accelerate during the 1920s, and by 1945, when Lutcher
Stark left the Board of Regents, the city boasted a population of over one hundred thousand.
Austin Postcard Collection; "City of Austin Population History, 1840 to 2015."

3. *Gammel's Laws of Texas* (1898), Vol. IX, 1876 Constitution, Article VII, sec. 10–15, 811–
813. The much-amended Constitution of 1876 remains in effect in Texas as of this writing.

4. Elizabeth Silverthorne, *Ashbel Smith of Texas: Pioneer, Patriot, Statesman, 1805–1886*
(College Station: Texas A&M University Press, 1982), 214–225.

5. Kenneth Hafertepe, *Abner Cook: Master Builder on the Texas Frontier* (Austin: Texas
State Historical Association, 1992), 184–189; Margaret C. Berry, *The University of Texas: A
Pictorial Account of Its First Century* (Austin: University of Texas Press, 1980), 6–7.

6. Berry, *The University of Texas*, 95–98.

7. Lutcher Stark served on the Board of Regents from 1919 to 1945, with one hiatus: Governor Ross Sterling did not reappoint him in 1931. He was reappointed in 1933 by Governor
Miriam A. "Ma" Ferguson. He held the position of chairman from 1921 to 1930 and again
from 1935 to 1937.

8. *Gammel's Laws of Texas* (1881), Vol. IX, "An Act to Establish the University of Texas,"
chap. LXXV, 171–174.

9. Berry, *The University of Texas*, 288.

10. Ibid.; Jenna Hays McEachern, *100 Things Longhorn Fans Should Know & Do before
They Die* (Chicago: Triumph Books, 2008), 181.

11. Alvin Johnson, *Pioneer's Progress* (New York: Viking Press, 1952), 196–197.

12. Miller, "Wins $30,000 Scholarship Prize," *Phi Gamma Delta* 10, no. 6 (April 1937):
590; Nugent E. Brown, *B Hall, Texas: Old Stories and Incidents of This Famous Dormitory*
(San Antonio: Naylor, 1938), 1–10.

13. David B. Gracy II, "Brackenridge, George Washington," *Handbook of Texas Online*,
accessed 2 March 2014, http://www.tshaonline.org/handbook/online/articles/fbro2, uploaded 12 June 2010, published by the Texas State Historical Association; Marilyn McAdams Sibley, *George W. Brackenridge: Maverick Philanthropist* (Austin: University of Texas
Press, 1973), 182–185; Joe B. Frantz, *The Forty-Acre Follies: An Opinionated History of the University of Texas* (Austin: Texas Monthly Press, 1983), 95–109; Berry, *The University of Texas*,
65.

14. Lewis Gould, *Progressives and Prohibitionists: Texas Democrats in the Wilson Era*, Fred
and Ella Mae Moore Texas History Reprint Series (Austin: Texas State Historical Association, 1992), 185–221; Frantz, *Forty-Acre Follies*, 78; Richardson et al., 300–303.

15. Gould, *Progressives and Prohibitionists*, 185–221; Frantz, *Forty-Acre Follies*, 78; Richardson et al., 300–303. Jim Ferguson was also restricted from ever holding an office of
honor, trust, or profit in Texas again, but that did not prevent him from running for governor in 1918, for US president in 1920, and for the US Senate in 1922, all unsuccessfully.

16. Berry, *The University of Texas*, 212.

17. Regents' Minutes, 9 June 1919.

18. Pennington, *"For Texas, I Will,"* 8–9.

19. Richard A. Holland, "Brackenridge, Littlefield, and the Shadow of the Past," in *The*

Texas Book: Profiles, History, and Reminiscences of the University (Austin: University of Texas Press, 2006), 88.

20. Margaret Berry, associate dean in the UT Office of Student Affairs, referred to this style of architecture as "shack-o'tecture." Berry, *The University of Texas*, 69.

21. Regents' Minutes, 24 May 1921; Martin W. Schwettmann, *Santa Rita: The University of Texas Oil Discovery* (Austin: Texas State Historical Association, 1943), xv; Berry, *The University of Texas*, 69.

22. Pennington, *"For Texas, I Will,"* 9.

23. Matthew D. Tippins, *Turning Germans into Texans: World War I and the Assimilation and Survival of German Culture in Texas, 1900–1930* (Austin: Kleingarten Press, 2010), 171.

24. Regents' Minutes, 10 June 1918.

25. Tippens, *Turning Germans into Texans*, 172.

26. Eduard Prokosch to President Robert Vinson, 1 July 1919, printed in Regents' Minutes, 7 July 1919, 302–303.

27. Regents' Minutes, 7 July 1919.

28. Ibid.

29. Leonard Bloomfield, "Eduard Prokosch," *Language* 14, no. 4 (October–December 1938): 310–313.

30. Fannie Ratchford, correspondence, 1923–1936, passim.

31. Carol Palaima, *From a Shared Border to Western Hemisphere Concerns: The History of Latin American Studies at the University of Texas at Austin*, report presented at the Title VI 50th Anniversary Conference, March 2009, Washington, DC, http://www.utexas.edu/cola /llilas/_files/pdf/about/LLILAS_History.pdf.

32. J.L. Mecham, E.C. Barker, C.E. Castañeda, M.R. Gutsch, and J.R. Spell, "In Memoriam: Charles Wilson Hackett," filed with the Secretary of the General Faculty by the Special C.W. Hackett Memorial Resolution Committee, University of Texas, 30 April 1951; Christopher Minster, "Biography of Álvaro Obregón," Latin American History, About.com, http://www.latinamericanhistory.about.com/od/thehistoryofmexico/a/obregon.htm; luncheon invitation from El Presidente de la Republica, President Obregón of Mexico, 1 December 1920, Stark Foundation Archives. Hackett had trained under Herbert Eugene Bolton at the University of Texas, Stanford University, and the University of California, and he, like many of Bolton's students, had followed the eminent professor.

33. "The Nettie Lee Benson Latin American Collection, University of Texas Libraries," Celebrating Research, http://www.celebratingresearch.org/libraries/texas/benson~print .shtml (accessed 3 November 2015). The volume remains in the Latin American Collection, adorned with a small sticker from the Mexico City bookstore where it was purchased and a bookplate indicating that it was a gift from Lutcher Stark to the university.

34. Bettye Turner, "Latin American Collection," *The Alcalde* (October 1962): 13–17.

35. Jane Haun, "University's Latin American Collection Considered to Be One of Nation's Best," *Daily Texan*, 11 August 1964; "A Library for Latin America: Nettie Lee Benson Latin American Collection," http://www.conocimientoenlinea.com/content/view/556/ (site discontinued); Turner, "Latin American Collection," 13–17.

36. Palaima, *From a Shared Border to Western Hemisphere Concerns*.

37. W.D. Blunk to H.J.L. Stark, 9 November 1964.

38. "The Stark Library: A Survey of This Rare Collection of Books," *Dartmouth Alumni Magazine*, January 1931, clipping in Stark Foundation Archives.

39. "Stark Room in University of Texas Library Completed," *San Antonio Express*, 8 May 1938.

40. Fannie Ratchford, "University's Greatest Woman Benefactor Dies," *The Alcalde* (December 1936): 54–55; "The Gift with the Giver," *The Alcalde* (October 1929): 6; Fannie Ratchford, correspondence with Miriam, Nita, and Lutcher Stark, 1923–1936, passim.

41. Regents' Minutes, 8 December 1925.

42. "Orange Woman Gives $650,000 to State University," undated, unattributed clipping; "The Gift with the Giver," 6.

43. "Orange Woman Gives $650,000 to State University."

44. Fannie Ratchford to Nita Stark, 1 June 1928.

45. Fannie Ratchford, correspondence with Miriam, Nita, and Lutcher Stark, 1923–1936, passim; "The Miriam Stark Library," Harry Ransom Center, University of Texas at Austin, http://www.hrc.utexas.edu/collections/books/holdings/stark (accessed 28 October 2015).

46. "Stark Is Chosen Head of U. of T. Regents," *Houston Post*, 24 May 1921; "Orange Man Head of U.T. Regents," *Beaumont Enterprise*, 24 May 1921. Not only did the regents choose Stark, the youngest board chairman to that date, but the new board also included a woman, Mrs. J.H. O'Hair of Coleman, recently appointed by Governor Neff. She was the first woman in UT history to serve on the board.

47. Regents' Minutes, 24 May 1921.

48. Brackenridge served as a regent for a little over twenty-six years, even longer than Lutcher Stark ultimately served, almost twenty-four years.

49. Sibley, *George W. Brackenridge*, 238–239.

50. Gracy, "Littlefield, George Washington."

51. Walter E. Long, *For All Time to Come* (Austin: Steck, 1964), 47; memorial adopted by the regents of the University of Texas for removal of the university to the Brackenridge land, Regents' Minutes, 5 January 1921.

52. Sibley, *George W. Brackenridge*, 244–256; Long, *For All Time to Come*, 33–77.

53. Sibley, *George W. Brackenridge*, 245–249.

54. Ibid., 244–246. The arch was never built, but Littlefield Fountain was subsequently constructed, surrounded by statues of prominent Confederate figures and President Woodrow Wilson. (In the face of increased public pressure, the statue of Confederate president Jefferson Davis was moved August 30, 2015, to the Dolph Briscoe Center for American History.)

55. Senate Bill No. 111 passed in both the House and Senate on 12 March 1921, providing $1.35 million for purchase of 135 acres of land adjacent to the Forty Acres.

56. Long, *For All Time to Come*, 74–82; Sibley, *George W. Brackenridge*, 238–254; memorial adopted by the regents of the University of Texas for removal of the university to the Brackenridge land; Regents' Minutes, 5 January 1921.

57. H.J.L. Stark to E.J. Mathews, registrar, 12 October 1921, UT President's Office Records, VF4/E b, DBCAH.

58. Holland, "Brackenridge, Littlefield, and the Shadow of the Past," 88.

59. David Prindle, "Oil and the Permanent University Fund: The Early Years," *Southwestern Historical Quarterly* 86 (October 1982): 280–282; Schwettmann, *Santa Rita*, 3–9; Julia Cauble Smith, "Santa Rita Oil Well," *Handbook of Texas Online*, accessed 19 January 2015, http://www.tshaonline.org/handbook/online/articles/dos01, uploaded 15 June 2010, published by the Texas State Historical Association.

60. Prindle, "Oil and the Permanent University Fund," 282; Schwettmann, *Santa Rita*, 1–9, 37.

61. Prindle, "Oil and the Permanent University Fund," 283.

62. Ibid., 287, 296.

63. Ibid., 296–298.

64. F.M. Law to H.J.L. Stark, 27 April 1929; UT Presidents' Office Records, photocopy, Box VF4/E.b, DBCAH.

65. Prindle, "Oil and the Permanent University Fund," 294.

66. The other institutions did seek a part of the Available Fund, but their requests were denied. Some of them gained access to its revenue after the University of Texas system was expanded in 1950. Prindle, *Santa Rita*, 294.

67. Richardson et al., *Texas*, 315–321.

68. Regents' Minutes, 24 May 1921.

69. The reason this issue came before the board is unknown; there is no mention of it in earlier minutes. It possibly reflected the religious fundamentalism prevalent in the 1920s, brought to public notice in 1925 with the Scopes Monkey Trial. One critic suggested a possible connection between the search for a new president for the university and the controversy aroused by the abortive attempt to appoint Governor Pat Neff, who was a strong Baptist and whose background was not academic but political. Brother "Railroad" Smith, *A Little Preachment and a Short Epistle to the Bigots of Texas* (Jourdanton, TX: Atascosa News-Monitor, 1925), DBCAH, 36–37, copy in Stark Foundation Archives. This booklet, which Smith dedicated to Lutcher Stark, contains a series of articles and editorials from the *Alcalde*, expressing the author's opinions against the resolution.

70. Regents' Minutes, 10 July, 1923.

71. Senate Bill 98, "An Act to Establish the University of Texas," Sec. 20, 17th Texas Legislature, Regular Called Session, 11 January to 1 April 1881, quoted in H.Y. Benedict, "A Source Book Relating to the History of the University of Texas: Legislative, Legal, Bibliographical, and Statistical," *University of Texas Bulletin* 1757 (10 October 1917): 263.

72. B. Smith, *A Little Preachment*.

73. William Seneca Sutton was appointed ad interim president when President Vinson resigned in 1923 after losing the battle over the permanent site of the university. Sutton served in 1923–1924 until incoming president Walter Splawn replaced him.

74. Norman D. Brown, *Hood, Bonnet, and Little Brown Jug: Texas Politics, 1921–1928* (College Station: Texas A&M University Press, 1984), 164–165. Brown noted that the Orange County Ku Klux Klan endorsed the resolution, as did D.A. Frank, editor in chief of the *Alcalde*.

75. Brown, *Hood, Bonnet, and Little Brown Jug*, 164; Ronnie Dugger, *Our Invaded Universities: Form, Reform and New Starts* (New York: W.W. Norton, 1974), 22–23; David Dettmer, "Benedicere Benedictus: A Profile of H.Y. Benedict," in *The Texas Book Two: More Profiles, History and Reminiscences of the University*, ed. David Dettmer (Austin: University of Texas Press, 2012), 53–55; Anonymous, *Texas Merry-Go-Round* (Houston: Sun Publishing, 1933), 77–78.

76. A later version of this story involves a member of the Texas legislature talking to another faculty member, using the exact words.

77. "'No Apology from Board,' Says Stark," *Dallas Texas News*, 21 May 1924, clipping, undated, unattributed, scrapbook on Lutcher Stark by W.B. Simmons, ca. 1921–1928.

78. "The Small Town Texan Who Has 75 Million Dollars."

79. Tevis, "How Texas' Richest Young Man Spends His Money"; Lee, "Stark's Wealth Used in Good for Others," *Austin American-Statesman*, 16 May 1926.

80. *The Alcalde* 5, no. 3 (January 1917): 226.

81. Nita Stark to Lloyd Gregory, 27 November 1933, 24 October and 1 November 1934, 17 November 1938; telegram, 16 May 1935, 10 and 30 November 1937, draft of letter, undated

and never sent (on instructions from Lutcher Stark). As Nita's health worsened, her letters grew aggressive and angry, and her husband chose not to send all of them.

82. Nita Stark to Lloyd Gregory, 10 November 1937 and 27 November 1933.

83. Lloyd Gregory to Nita Stark, 12 December 1933.

84. Flem R. Hall, "The Sport Tide," *Fort Worth Star-Telegram*, 8 January 1934.

85. "A History of Longhorn Athletics," unfinished scrapbook begun in 1936 or later, Stark Foundation Archives; Berry, *The University of Texas*, 341. Berry writes that the McLane brothers attended Cornell, not Yale, where the *Daily Texan* sportswriter Harry Moore had placed them.

86. Harry E. Moore, "McLane Brothers Here from Yale and Organized First Football Squad: U.T. Was First School in State to Kick Pigskin," *Daily Texan*, 26 November 1922. Harry Moore, sportswriter for the *Daily Texan* in 1922, was later a professor of sociology at UT until his death in the summer of 1966.

87. Ibid.; Pennington, *"For Texas, I Will,"* 1–2; "A History of Longhorn Athletics" scrapbook.

88. Moore, "McLane Brothers."

89. Ibid. Dave Furman's father was a successful Dallas lawyer.

90. Robert L. Sutherland, Warner Gettys, and Paul White, "In Memoriam: Harry E. Moore," filed with the Secretary of the General Faculty by Robert L. Sutherland, chairman of the Special Harry E. Moore Memorial Resolution Committee, University of Texas, Austin, 9 January 1967.

91. In 1905, eighteen deaths and over 180 serious injuries occurred nationwide.

92. Ronald Smith, *Sports and Freedom: The Rise of Big-Time College Athletics* (New York: Oxford University Press, 1988), 198–205; "In the Arena: The NCAA's First Century," http://www.ncaapublications.com/p-4039-in-the-arena-ncaas-first-century.aspx (accessed 9 December 2015); John J. Miller, "How Teddy Roosevelt Saved Football," *New York Post*, 22 January 2012.

93. L. Theo Bellmont to H.J.L. Stark, 19 December 1925 and 24 February 1927.

94. Pennington, *"For Texas, I Will,"* 6–7.

95. Regents' Minutes, 19 April 1927. The Longhorn community continued to debate the role that athletics should play on a college campus, a debate that had not concluded in 2016.

96. "'UT Can Afford Best Coach,' Regent Stark Says," *Daily Texan*, 12 December 1936.

97. Elizabeth Washington, conversation with Jo Ann Stiles, Dallas, Texas, 28 February 2013.

98. Steve Wray to H.J.L. Stark, 5 May 1926.

99. Alexine Boudreaux Adams, Oral History Interview, conducted by Jo Ann Stiles and Ellen Rienstra, Stark Foundation Offices, 14 April 2004, 1, Stark Foundation Archives.

100. Ibid., 1–2.

101. Pennington, *"For Texas, I Will,"* 2, 3.

102. Ibid., 11.

103. Ibid., 11, 11–12, 17.

104. The stadium was not actually completed until 1926, although enough of it was finished by Thanksgiving Day 1924 that the game could be played. It has been further enlarged through the years and continues in use today.

105. Pennington, *"For Texas, I Will,"* 16–17.

106. Ibid., 18–19.

107. Ibid., 22–23.

108. Ibid., 24; Lou Maysel, *Here Come the Texas Longhorns, 1893–1970* (Fort Worth: Stadium Publishing, 1970), 86.

109. H.J.L. Stark, "The $500,000 Memorial Stadium Campaign, How and Why It Is to Be Put Over," *The Alcalde* 1 (April 1924): 1, 3.

110. Pennington, *"For Texas, I Will,"* 16.

111. Vinson had been isolated by the failure of the campaign to move the campus to the Brackenridge tract on the Colorado River; with his position thus untenable, he resigned to assume the presidency of Case Western Reserve University in Cleveland, Ohio. Walter Long described him as "the last lone player on the offensive, facing the defensive team. . . . He had played the game as a gentleman for all it was worth, gallantly and with fortitude." Thus, construction of the stadium began under the administration of acting president Sutton. Long, *For All Time to Come*, 75.

112. Clipping, scrapbook by W.B. Simmons.

113. Brown, *Hood, Bonnet, and Little Brown Jug*, 165.

114. Ibid., 162–163.

115. Kate Sayen Kirkland, *The Hogg Family and Houston: Philanthropy and the Civic Ideal* (Austin: University of Texas Press, 2009), 129–131; Brown, *Hood, Bonnet, and Little Brown Jug*, 162–163.

116. Brown, *Hood, Bonnet, and Little Brown Jug*, 166–167. Most of this material is derived from an oral history interview with Richard T. Fleming, 30 July 1968, provided to Brown by L. Tuffly Ellis, former executive director of the Texas State Historical Association. Ronnie Dugger also cited this interview in *Our Invaded Universities*. It is impossible to determine from regents' minutes for 15 and 16 May 1924 that the ex-students' delegation even attended the meeting. No lunch break is mentioned on 16 May. The minutes report the vote on Neff for the presidency and the immediate resignation of Regents Cochran and Jones was followed an hour or so later by Governor Neff's refusal to accept the offer of the office.

117. *"Texan* Reporter Hid," *Daily Texan*, 30 November 1940, DBCAH.

118. Regents' Minutes, 16 May 1924.

119. Brown, *Hood, Bonnet, and Little Brown Jug*, 167.

120. Telegram, Carltons [*sic*], Dickson, Fleming, et al., 16 May 1924, 6:30 p.m., to H.J.L. Stark. It is difficult to determine if the position to which they referred was the presidency of the university or the chairmanship of the regents.

121. Ibid. The wording of the telegram indicates the senders' extreme anger and at times makes little sense.

122. "'No Apology from Board.'"

123. Pennington, *"For Texas, I Will,"* 28.

124. Ibid.; Kirkland, *The Hogg Family and Houston*, 132.

125. John A. Lomax, *Will Hogg, Texan* (Austin: University of Texas Press, 1956), 48.

126. Pennington, *"For Texas, I Will,"* 28.

127. Ibid., 29.

128. Ibid., 34, 56; telegrams, F.H. Farwell to H.J.L. Stark, Plaza Hotel, New York City, 1 and 3 July 1924. This sum included donations, the lumber sold at cost, and "loans" that had failed to be repaid.

129. Pennington, *"For Texas, I Will,"* 46, 47.

130. Ibid., 49.

131. The previous year Stark had given $1,000 for the band to be fitted with uniforms. Regents' Minutes, 19 December 1923. In 1937, with Stark again serving as chairman of the board, the regents voted to donate $2,500 for new uniforms for the band to wear to the Thanksgiving Day game against the Aggies in Austin. Pennington, *"For Texas I Will,"* 46.

132. Pennington, *"For Texas I Will,"* 7.

133. Stark made the suggestion at a meeting in President Sutton's office on January 14, 1924. Regents' Minutes, 24 January 1924; Pennington, *"For Texas, I Will,"* 18.

134. Richard Pennington, "Darrell K. Royal–Texas Memorial Stadium," *Handbook of Texas Online*, accessed 30 May 2013, http://www.tshaonline.org/handbook/online/articles /xvdo1, uploaded 12 June 2010, published by the Texas State Historical Association.

135. For additional information on the work of these two architects, see Lawrence Speck, "Campus Architecture: The Heroic Decades," in *The Texas Book: Profiles, History and Reminiscences of the University*, ed. Richard A. Holland (Austin: University of Texas Press, 2006), 125–138.

136. Ibid., 126–127, 127, 128, 129–130.

137. Regents' Minutes, 9 June 1919. Lutcher Stark was also named to the Finance Committee and the Committee on the Medical Department in Galveston.

138. The coastal live oak (*Quercus virginiana*) is known as the "aristocrat of oaks." "I've got documentation that says the first . . . trial they did were four [coastal live oak] trees brought from Griffing Nurseries from Beaumont, Texas," according to Larry Maginnis, University of Texas arborist. Conversation with Stiles and Rienstra, Austin, 4 February 2010, Stark Foundation Archives.

139. Regents' Minutes, 10 February 1934.

140. Ibid.; Pennington, *"For Texas, I Will,"* 16; Regents' Minutes, 21 April 1930.

141. May Nell Paulissen and Carl McQueary, *Miriam: The Southern Belle Who Became the First Woman Governor of Texas* (Austin: Eakin Press, 1995), 94–116; Richardson et al., *Texas*, 311; Brown, *Hood, Bonnet, and Little Brown Jug*, 229.

142. In Orange, a local chapter, Klan No. 51, staged a parade on July 2, 1921, with over three hundred hooded horsemen riding in solemn procession through the streets, distributing circulars proclaiming that "law-abiding citizens had no reason to fear" the Klan. "Ku Klux Clan Formed Here; Law Breakers Are Warned to Leave," *Orange Leader*, 3 July 1921.

143. Pennington, *"For Texas, I Will,"* 25.

144. Brown, *Hood, Bonnet, and Little Brown Jug*, 128; Charles Alexander, *Crusade for Conformity: The Ku Klux Klan in the Southwest, 1920–1930* (Houston: Texas Gulf Coast Historical Association, 1962), 126–127; Richardson et al., *Texas*, 310–312.

145. Brown, *Hood, Bonnet, and Little Brown Jug*, 128; Alexander, *Crusade for Conformity*, 126–127.

146. Paulison and McQueary, *Miriam*, 102; Richardson et al., *Texas*, 311.

147. Lee, "Stark's Wealth Used in Good for Others."

148. Brown, *Hood, Bonnet, and Little Brown Jug*, 230, citing Edward Crane to Judge Victor Brooks, 12 August 1924, Martin M. Crane papers, 238–239.

149. Ibid., 246, 235, 256–257.

150. "Baker Rejects Post as Regent: Dallas Lawyer Opposes Stark for Place," clipping, undated, unattributed, scrapbook by W.B. Simmons.

151. Lutcher Stark makes this statement in several letters in the Stark Foundation Archives. It is also part of oral tradition in Orange.

152. Partial column with subtitle "Ex Governors Back Him," clipping, undated, unattributed, scrapbook by W.B. Simmons; Hugh Nugent Fitzgerald, "Anti-Klan Fight Held Up Stark's Name in Senate: Former Membership in Secret Order Is Held against Member of Texas U. Regents," *News-Tribune*, no city or state given, clipping, scrapbook by W.B. Simmons.

153. Brown, *Hood, Bonnet, and Little Brown Jug*, 256–257.

154. Ben Woodhead Jr., "University of Texas Board of Regents Complete Again and Everything Is Roseate," *Beaumont Enterprise*, 14 February 1925.

155. Deed, Josephine Lucile Fisher to H.J.L. Stark, 12 November 1927, copy in Stark Foundation Archives.

156. Hugh Yantis to H.J.L. Stark, 15 April 1939.

157. Telegram, F.H. Farwell to J. L. [*sic*] Stark, 3 July 1924.

158. Robert A. Divine, ed., *America Past and Present*, vol. 2, *Since 1865*, 9th ed. (Boston: Longman Publishing, 2011), 642.

159. Clipping, undated, untitled, *Times Herald*, no city given, scrapbook by W.B. Simmons.

Chapter 9

1. F.H. Farwell, memorandum, 16 February 1927, Stark Foundation Archives.

2. William E. Leuchtenburg, *The Perils of Prosperity, 1914–1932*, 2nd ed. (Chicago: University of Chicago Press, 1993), 182; Maxwell and Baker, *Sawdust Empire*, 156–166; Walker, "Harvesting the Forest," 16; Donna Fricker, "Historic Context: The Louisiana Lumber Boom, c. 1880–1925," Fricker Historic Preservation Services LLC, http://www.crt.state.la.us/Assets/OCD/hp/nationalregister/historic_contexts/The_Louisiana_Lumber_Boom_c1880-1925.pdf, 1 (accessed 28 October 2015).

3. Easton, "History of the Texas Lumbering Industry," 126, citing Lutcher & Moore Lumber Company records and interview with F.H. Farwell, 5 December 1940.

4. Herbert W. Winkelman, Winkelman and Davies, Accountants, *Special Report: The Lutcher & Moore Lumber Company, Orange, Texas, 31 December 1936*, Stark Foundation Archives.

5. F.H. Farwell to Charles W. Davis, 7 April 1921; F.H. Farwell to Angel Caligaris, 22 April 1925; George A. Hill to F.H. Farwell, 5 February 1925; memorandum re "Nicaraguan Timber," F.H. Farwell, 7 February 1925; Bracher Timber Company to F.H. Farwell, 6 October 1925; memorandum, F.H. Farwell to H.J.L. Stark, 26 September 1928; F.H. Farwell to H.J.L. Stark, 6 November 1928; F.H. Farwell to Consolidated Tidewater Pine Co., 22 January 1929; correspondence, Lutcher & Moore Lumber Company papers, passim.

6. Memorandum re "Conference with Mr. Spain," F.H. Farwell, 13 January 1926.

7. Memorandum re "For Benefit of Mr. C.F. Flinn of the Albion Lumber Company and Mr. F.H. Farwell of the Lutcher & Moore Lumber Co.," 30 January 1930. Flitches are pieces of wood used as veneers.

8. F.H. Farwell to H.J.L. Stark, 18 May 1926.

9. F.H. Farwell, memorandum, 16 February 1927.

10. F.H. Farwell to H.J.L. Stark, 15 September 1928.

11. D.A. Pruter to W.H. and H.J.L. Stark, 1922–1926, passim.

12. Wingate, "Summary," 69.

13. Ibid., 70–71.

14. On November 13, 1925, oil was discovered on the flanks of the Spindletop dome, resulting in an even bigger field than the 1901 discovery.

15. D.A. Pruter to W.H. and H.J.L. Stark, 1922–1926, passim.

16. D.A. Pruter to W.H. Stark, 5 September 1929; George S. Colburn to H.J.L. Stark, 5 August 1937.

17. D.A. Pruter to W.H. Stark, 20 September 1929.

18. Axelson, "Milestone Marked in Lutcher & Moore's 108-Year History," *Orange Leader*, 17 September 1970.

19. Ibid.

20. Tevis, "W.H. Stark Helps Remake East Texas," *Beaumont Enterprise*, 15 December 1929; "William H. Stark," *Las Sabinas* 6, no. 4 (1980): 30.

21. Wingate, "Summary," 50.

22. Ibid., 58.

23. The Orange Products Company was long associated with the Del-Dixi brand. The records are unclear whether the Del-Dixi name originated with the Orange Products Company or whether it was acquired when the company merged in 1957 with the Best Maid Products in Fort Worth. The most probable explanation seems to be that the name originated with Orange Products; then, at the merger, the new company continued to market one of its lines of pickles under the name "Del-Dixi." A letter on Orange Products letterhead in the Stark Foundation Archives dated 18 December 1936 adds, "Packers of the famous Del-Dixi Brand." http://www.del-dixi.net (accessed 3 November 2015); Roy Wingate, address to the Orange County Historical Society, 9 November 2004.

24. W.H. Stark to D.A. Pruter, 14 August 1924.

25. Wingate, "Summary," 50, 58.

26. "William H. Stark," *Las Sabinas*, 30.

27. D.A. Pruter to W.H. Stark, 18 May 1927; "William H. Stark," *Las Sabinas*, 30.

28. Joe F. Combs, "Enterprise Farm Corner," column in *Beaumont Enterprise*, 12 February 1958.

29. F.H. Farwell to Homer D. Wade, 21 August 1925, in reply to Wade's invitation either to him or to Lutcher Stark to assist in organizing and/or serving as president of a proposed East Texas Chamber of Commerce.

30. Tevis, "How Texas' Richest Young Man Spends His Money," *Beaumont Enterprise*, 7 March 1926.

31. Ibid. Parts of this article later appeared in the *Austin American*, 16 May 1926, under a different title and byline: Ray E. Lee, "Lutcher Stark's Wealth Used in Good for Others."

32. "The Small Town Texan Who Has 75 Million Dollars."

33. H.J.L. Stark, typed card in program for 48th District Rotary Conference, 8–9 April 1926, Stark Foundation Archives.

34. F.H. Farwell to H.J.L. Stark, 21 July 1921.

35. D.A. Pruter to W.H. Stark, 25 August 1923.

36. H.J.L. Stark to Frances Ann Lutcher, 27 August 1923.

37. W.H. Stark to D.A. Pruter, 5 September 1923.

38. Louis Dugas, "Orange's Sunset Grove Country Club Founded over Feud," *County Record and the Penny Record: The Community Newspapers of Orange County, Texas*, 7 November 2001. One story holds that the song Lutcher requested was a "Paul Jones," or mixer, where dancers form concentric circles and change partners at a signal.

39. Ibid.; Glenda Dyer, "Stark Brothers Grew Up Playing at Sunset Grove," *Opportunity Valley News*, 12 August 1992.

40. Dugas, "Orange's Sunset Grove Country Club Founded over Feud"; D.A. Pruter to W.H. Stark, 10 August 1922.

41. Dugas, "Orange's Sunset Grove Country Club Founded over Feud."

42. Julius H. "Jules" David, Oral History Interview, conducted by Jo Ann Stiles and Ellen Rienstra, Stark Foundation Offices, 6 July 2004, 3, Stark Foundation Archives.

43. Ibid.

44. Clipping, undated but around 1924, unattributed, scrapbook by W.B. Simmons.

45. Lloyd Gregory, "Sports News and Comments," clipping, undated but around 1924, unattributed, scrapbook by W.B. Simmons.

46. Hubert D. "Buddy" Cox, Oral History Interview, conducted by Jo Ann Stiles and Ellen Rienstra, Orange, 9 February 2004, Stark Foundation Archives, 2.

47. Dugas, "Orange's Sunset Grove Country Club Founded over Feud"; Dyer, "Stark Brothers Grew Up Playing at Sunset Grove"; Wingate, Address to the Orange County Historical Society; W.B. Simmons to H.J.L. Stark, 29 August 1934.

48. Dyer, "Stark Brothers Grew Up Playing at Sunset Grove."

49. Dena Winn Cox, Oral History Interview, conducted by Jo Ann Stiles and Ellen Rienstra, Orange, 30 March 2004, n.p., Stark Foundation Archives; Hubert D. "Buddy" Cox, Oral History Interview, 2; Wingate, Address to the Orange County Historical Society; W.B. Simmons to H.J.L. Stark, 29 August 1934.

50. Copy of letter, unsigned but probably from Dave Nelson to W.H. Stark, 18 August 1928.

51. Laurence Bertrand "Larry" Murray, Oral History Interview, conducted by Ellen Rienstra, 8 October 2003, Stark Foundation offices, 25, Stark Foundation Archives; "Matters Pertaining to the Airplane, WACO, Owned by the Lutcher & Moore Lumber Company, Airplane License No. 7036," Stark Foundation Archives.

52. "Two Army Fliers and Lutcher Stark's Pilot Land at Field Here," undated, unattributed clipping, Stark Foundation Archives.

53. "Lutcher Stark Will Take Flying Lessons," unattributed clipping, 6 August 1928, Stark Foundation Archives.

54. Murray, Oral History Interview, 8 October 2003, 25.

55. Ibid., 26. Apparently, Lutcher Stark periodically "wing-walked"; a squib appeared in the *Beaumont Enterprise* on 23 September 1925, some three years before he acquired the *WACO*: "H.J. Lutcher Stark Thrilled Orange People Today When He Rode the Wings of an Aeroplane as It Flew over the Town with Capt. R.W. Mackey of Houston, as Pilot."

56. Murray, Oral History Interview, 8 October 2003, 27.

57. "The Small Town Texan Who Has 75 Million Dollars."

58. Foree, "Archangel and His Bible," 96.

59. "Lutch Stark's Boy's [sic] Inc. Has Splendid Band," *Orange Leader*, 29 May 1936.

60. Wingate, "Summary," 26. Lutcher Stark was only the second individual in the United States to incorporate his own boys' club.

61. "Lutch Stark's Boys Chartered," clipping, undated and unattributed, scrapbook by W.B. Simmons.

62. Ibid.

63. One of them was Nelda Childers, who in 1943 became Stark's third wife.

64. Tevis, "How Texas' Richest Young Man Spends His Money"; "Sunday School Has Fine Band," *Dallas Morning News*, 12 July 1925.

65. "Mrs. Lutcher Is Buried in Orange: Entire City Pays Last Respects to Pioneer and Beloved Citizen," undated but probably 24 October 1924, clipping, scrapbook by W.B. Simmons.

66. "Lutch Stark's Boy's Inc. Has Splendid Band"; "Stark Boys Band of Orange to Leave on Southwest Texas Tour Today," *Beaumont Enterprise*, 16 June 1925.

67. "Boys First to Play on Peak," *Orange Leader*, 17 June 1927.

68. Lee, "Stark's Wealth Used in Good for Others."

69. Although Margaret herself spelled her surname as "Wilber" on her passport documents and in signing letters, in many other sources the spelling is listed as "Wilbur." She was the daughter of Albert W. Wilbur (sometimes spelled "Wilber"), who was the son of Louisa and Frederick Wilbur, Henry Lutcher's sister and brother-in-law. The senior Wilburs, Louisa and Frederick, spelled their surname with a "u."

70. Nita Hill Stark, journal, March to early June 1927, 1–2, passim.

71. Ibid., 3.

72. Ibid., 20.

73. Ibid., 11.

74. Ibid., 15, 17.

75. Ibid., 22–37, 34–35.

76. Ibid., 27. Howard Carter's landmark discovery of the nearly intact tomb had occurred in November 1922, less than five years before the family's visit.

77. Ibid., 23.

78. Ibid., passim, 20.

79. Ibid.

80. Ibid., 43–54.

81. Wingate, "Summary," 31–36.

82. Hall, "The Sport Tide," *Fort Worth Star-Telegram*, 8 January 1934.

83. Wingate, "Summary," 31–36, 34–36. The Texas Tract was finally sold to the US Department of Agriculture in 1937, retiring most of that debt, but profit on the entire marsh was not realized until 1956, when the Joyce Tract was sold to oilman John Mecom and his Largo Company.

84. Wingate, "Summary," 33; Cameron Parish Conveyance Records, 5:197, 21 March 1925.

85. Hall, "The Sport Tide."

86. Wingate, "Summary," 31–36; Armand P. Daspit to H.J.L. Stark, 12 November 1930; Stanley C. Arthur to H.J.L. Stark, 8 December 1925; Stark to Daspit, 13 August 1928 and 29 October 1930.

87. H.J.L. Stark to Stanley C. Arthur, Department of Conservation, State of Louisiana, 13 August 1928.

88. H.J.L. Stark to Armand P. Daspit, Department of Conservation, State of Louisiana, 29 October 1930.

89. Wingate, "Summary," 37.

90. D.A. Pruter to W.H. Stark, 1922–1934, passim; Wingate, "Summary," 38.

91. Wingate, "Summary," 62; D.A. Pruter to W.H. Stark, 5 April 1927–19 May 1929, passim.

92. Wingate, "Summary," 65. William bought the building for $100 cash and a $1 million note and sold it to Lutcher on the same terms. William also gifted Lutcher with the consideration of the stock in the building company as well as lending him the purchase money for the building, which William in turn borrowed from Lutcher & Moore.

93. Paul Isaac, "Beaumont, Texas, the Great Depression, 1929–1933," *Texas Gulf Historical and Biographical Record* 14 (1978): 14–31.

94. Wingate, "Summary," 65.

95. E.S. Simms to D.A. Pruter, 16 April 1926.

96. Ibid.

97. Mining lease, W.H. Stark to Homer C. Hirsch of El Paso, El Paso County, Texas, 12 October 1932, Stark Foundation Archives.

98. Quitclaim deed, J.J. and Margaret S. de Praslin to W.H. Stark, 28 October 1932, Stark Foundation Archives.

99. Wingate, "Summary," 23.

100. W.H. Stark–D.A. Pruter correspondence, 1927, passim; D.A. Pruter to W.H. Stark, 27 May 1927. At the end of the European tour, William possibly returned to Orange for a brief time in June at Pruter's suggestion to investigate troubles at the San Jacinto Life Insurance Company between the board of directors and its president. But no evidence is on record that he made such a detour.

101. Telegram, W.H. Stark to D.A. Pruter, 5 October 1927.

102. D.A. Pruter to W.H. Stark, 19 and 26 November 1927.

103. Margaret Wilber, Miriam Stark's assistant, to D.A. Pruter, 13 December 1927; D.A. Pruter to W.H. Stark, 12 December 1927.

104. "Heavy Money Shipment Is Stark Answer to Reports Attacking First National," *Orange Leader*, 9 October 1927.

105. D.A. Pruter to W.H. Stark, 14 October 1927.

106. Ibid., 27 August 1928.

107. Ibid.

108. Telegram, W.H. Stark to D.A. Pruter, 31 August 1928.

109. W.D. Gordon and L.J. Benckenstein to George A. Hill Jr., Sabine Terminal Oil Corporation, and S.P. and R.D. Farish, 14 November 1928.

110. George A. Hill to W.H. Stark, 31 January 1928.

111. H.J. Lutcher Stark to George A. Hill, 28 November 1928 (unsent?).

112. Ibid.; George A. Hill to H.J.L. Stark, 31 January 1928.

113. Sun Oil Company by R.W. Pack, general agent, to Vinton Petroleum Company, 31 October 1928.

114. W.D. Gordon and L.F. Benckenstein to George A. Hill, Sabine Terminal Oil, and S.P. and R.D. Farish, 14 November 1928. The Vinton Petroleum Company board was composed of William Stark, Lutcher Stark, W.D. Gordon, L.F. Benckenstein, Charles H. Benckenstein, Edgar Brown Jr., and Lutcher Brown.

115. Ibid. In a memo dated November 19, 1928, Byron Simmons called Lutcher Stark's attention to the fact that none of the instruments involving the Sun Company contracts were attested by Vinton Petroleum's secretary, Charles Benckenstein; all had been handled solely by William Stark for Vinton Petroleum, as was apparently normal procedure.

116. George A. Hill to W.H. Stark, 16 November 1928.

117. Notice of Special Stockholders' Meeting, 16 November 1928; L.J. Benckenstein to Sabine Terminal Oil Corporation, 1 December 1928.

118. H.J.L. Stark to W.H. Stark, 28 November 1928 (probably unsent).

119. H.J.L. Stark to George A. Hill, 28 November 1928 (emphasis added).

120. H.J.L. Stark to W.H. Stark, 28 November 1928 (probably unsent).

121. Ibid.

122. T.W. Gregory to H.J. Lutcher Stark, 6, 16, and 26 November and 10 December 1928.

123. H.J.L. Stark to T.W. Gregory, 19 January 1929.

124. "William H. Stark of Orange Celebrates His 78th Birthday," *Beaumont Enterprise*, 20 March 1929.

125. Abbott, *A Stark Genealogy*, Seventh Generation, William Henry Stark; "William H. Stark of Orange Celebrates his 78th Birthday."

126. "William H. Stark of Orange Celebrates his 78th Birthday"; ingredients list, guest book, W.H. Stark 78th birthday, Stark Foundation Archives. The cake was made by the Stansbury Bakery of Orange and included twenty-one pounds of butter, four hundred eggs, fifteen pounds of pecans, and ten pounds of cherries.

127. "William H. Stark of Orange Celebrates his 78th Birthday."

128. Tevis, "W.H. Stark Helps Remake East Texas," *Beaumont Enterprise*, 15 December 1929; Arlene Turkel, "Growing Orchids and Affection for the Stark Family," *Orange County Record*, 8 August 1995.

129. Turkel, "Growing Orchids and Affection for the Stark Family."

130. W.H. Stark, Samoset, Rockland, Maine, to H.J.L. Stark, 2 July 1928.

131. Axelson, "Milestone Marked in Lutcher & Moore's 108-Year History."

132. "Buys Arizona Pine Timber," *American Lumberman*, 26 August 1930, clipping in Stark Foundation Archives; F.H. Farwell to H.J.L. Stark, 22 November 1929; F.H. Farwell to George Colburn, 10 March 1930.

133. Memorandum of contract between the McGaffey Company and Lutcher & Moore, 9 August 1929; F.H. Farwell to the Tribal Council of the Navajo Indians, 28 October 1933; Wingate, "Summary," 7–8.

134. Telegram, F.H. Farwell to W.H. Stark, 1 August 1929; telegram, F.H. Farwell to H.J.L. Stark, 6 August 1929; memorandum of contract between the McGaffey Company and Lutcher & Moore, 9 August 1929.

135. Agreement, A.B. McGaffey, president, McGaffey Company, and Dr. J.J. de Praslin, 9 January 1929, Stark Foundation Archives; F.H. Farwell to H.J.L. Stark, 22 November 1929.

136. Memo of contract, McGaffey Company and Lutcher & Moore; release, Dr. J.J. de Praslin to the McGaffey Company, 10 August 1929; F.H. Farwell to H.J.L. Stark, 22 November 1929. Indicating their lack of trust in de Praslin, the McGaffey Company demanded, and received, de Praslin's written release from his prior sales commission agreement with them. Even so, de Praslin later wrote Farwell that, because of medical bills from a daughter's recent surgery, he wanted to "get about $6,000 in cash on my commission." When reminded of the release he had signed, de Praslin acknowledged it but believed he was "entitled to something." Farwell replied that though de Praslin might be entitled to some consideration, he, Farwell, had no intention of discussing any commission.

Some months later, de Praslin, nothing if not persistent, made a further attempt to broker the sale of yet another New Mexico mill and lumber company to Lutcher & Moore. "I note Doc is writing Mr. [William] Stark," Farwell wrote to George Colburn, "and am convinced he is meddling purely to get another commission and misrepresenting us. I wish Mr. Stark or Lutcher would silence him . . . confirms me in not wanting anything to do with him. In the end, he will only make our path rougher." The Stark interests had no further dealings with de Praslin. F.H. Farwell to H.J.L. Stark, 22 November 1929; F.H. Farwell to George Colburn, 10 March 1930.

137. F.H. Farwell to William Stark, 29 April 1930; "Cost of Constructing Saw Mill Plant, Gallup, New Mexico," Stark Foundation Archives; Wingate, "Summary," 7.

138. Woods and Gatewood, *America Interpreted*, 734–736.

139. Wingate, "Summary," 48, 43.

140. H. Williams, *Gateway to Texas*, 160.

141. D.A. Pruter to W.H. Stark, 12 September 1931.

142. Orange County, Criminal Docket, The State of Texas vs. Edgar Eskridge, Orders of Court, 19 May 1932. A week earlier another charge of assault had been filed against Eskridge, and still another the day after he assaulted Lutcher Stark. He began carrying two guns, laying them on either side of the pulpit while he preached, and three years later, after a confrontation with police chief Ed J. O'Riley, Eskridge followed him to the corner of Main and Fifth Streets in Orange and shot him dead, for which he served two and one-half years in prison. In the 1960s, he returned to the First Baptist Church and, when the invitation was issued, asked to rejoin the church. The congregation voted to reinstate him as a member, and he died not long afterward. H. Williams, *Gateway to Texas*, 66–69.

143. Wingate, Address to the Orange County Historical Society.

144. Ibid.; Wingate, "Summary," 50.

145. Wingate, Address to the Orange County Historical Society.

146. Axelson, "Milestone Marked in Lutcher & Moore's 108-Year History"; Farwell, "Saw Mill Industry Plays Major Part in Texas History: Orange Center of Early Day Develop-

ment," *Orange Leader*, 29 May 1936, typescript draft of this article by Farwell titled "History of the Lutcher and Moore Lumber Company," Stark Foundation Archives.

147. Farwell, "Saw Mill Industry Plays Major Part in Texas History."

148. Axelson, "Milestone Marked in Lutcher & Moore's 108-Year History."

149. Deed, Lutcher & Moore Lumber Company to South Texas Lumber Company, November 1931, Stark Foundation Archives.

150. F.H. Farwell to Navajo Tribal Council, 28 October 1933.

151. Ibid.

152. H.J.L. Stark to Leo Becker, 12 October 1932.

153. Woods and Gatewood, *America Interpreted*, 749.

154. Farwell to Navajo Tribal Council.

155. F.H. Farwell to Senator Morris Sheppard, 15 January 1934.

156. Farwell to Navajo Tribal Council.

157. Ibid. In a letter to Senator Morris Sheppard dated January 15, 1934, Farwell explained that Lutcher & Moore had already investigated the possibility of receiving assistance from the Reconstruction Finance Corporation, formed by Congress in 1932 to facilitate economic activity by aiding state and local governments and lending to various business and industrial concerns. No federal funds were available.

158. Farwell to Navajo Tribal Council.

159. Ibid.; F.H. Farwell to H.J.L. Stark, 6 July 1933.

160. Farwell to Navajo Tribal Council.

161. F.H. Farwell to Congressman Martin Dies, 4 December 1933.

162. Ibid.; F.H. Farwell to Senator Tom Connally, 8 January 1934; F.H. Farwell to Senator Morris Sheppard, 15 January 1934.

163. George S. Colburn, memorandum, 21 May 1934.

164. Wingate, "Summary," 6–8.

165. Axelson, "Milestone Marked in Lutcher & Moore's 108-Year History."

166. Ben McDonough, Lutcher & Moore Lumber Company treasurer and general manager, note, 12 August 1959, Stark Foundation Archives.

167. Farwell, "Saw Mill Industry Plays Major Part in Texas History."

168. Maxwell and Baker, *Sawdust Empire*, 201.

169. Weldon Scheel, "Stark Donations Increase Library Value," *Daily Texan*, 28 May 1933; "Starks Observe Golden Wedding," *Beaumont Enterprise*, 23 December 1931.

170. Regents' Minutes, 1 January 1930.

171. Linsley, Rienstra, and Stiles, *Giant under the Hill*, 213–214; Berry, *The University of Texas*, 415; Regents' Minutes, 24 November 1933, 452; Ross S. Sterling and Ed Kilman, eds., *Ross Sterling, Texan: A Memoir by the Founder of Humble Oil and Refining Company*, rev. Don Carleton (Austin: Center for American History, University of Texas at Austin, 2007), 131. Frank Yount was an immensely wealthy oil man who in 1925 had brought in a second oil field on the flank of the old Spindletop salt dome near Beaumont. Not only had the discovery proved more productive than the first boom at that field in 1901, but Yount also controlled most of the producing area. He died suddenly on November 13, 1933, but by that time Lutcher Stark had been back on the Board of Regents for a year.

172. Regents' Minutes, 30 March 1935.

173. *Daily Texan*, 29 and 30 April 1925; "William J. Disch," *Daily Texan*, 1 May 1925; *Galveston News*, 28 April 1925; Sam Johnson, "Disch Will Resign as Baseball Coach," *Daily Texan*, 29 April 1925; Jumbo Haynes, "Disch Will Present Claims to Committee," *Daily Texan*, 30 April 1925; "William Disch," *Daily Texan* editorial, 1 May 1925; "Billy Disch, Famous Coach of Longhorn Baseball Team Resigns; Bellmont Is Cause," *Galveston News*,

29 April 1925; telegram, W.L. McGill to H.J.L. Stark, 28 April 1925, Stark Foundation Archives; telegram, W.B. Simmons to H.J.L. Stark, Waldorf Astoria Hotel, 28 April 1925, Stark Foundation Archives.

174. Bobby Hawthorne, *Longhorn Football: An Illustrated History* (Austin: University of Texas Press, 2007), 21; Maysel, *Here Come the Texas Longhorns*, 93–96.

175. Pennington, *"For Texas, I Will,"* 63.

176. Regents' Minutes, 19 April 1927. The faculty committee's report was sent to each regent before the April meeting but was never discussed by the board as a whole. Also, university president Splawn had delivered his resignation earlier in the meeting but stayed to voice his opposition to the Holliday motion for the new investigation. It was approved by the board nevertheless. The special committee was composed of Robert Holliday, Sam Neathery, and Edward Crane.

177. Ibid., 86.

178. L. Theo Bellmont to H.J.L. Stark, 15 May 1928; Pennington, *"For Texas, I Will,"* 63.

179. Maysel, *Here Come the Texas Longhorns*, 96.

180. Regents' Minutes, 1 October 1928, 328; Berry, "Bellmont, L. Theodore."

181. Regents' Minutes, 5 January 1931, 272–273.

182. Prindle, "Oil and the Permanent University Fund," 291; Speck, "Campus Architecture," 125–138.

183. Prindle, "Oil and the Permanent University Fund," 291. Littlefield Memorial Dormitory for Women was completed in 1927 with private funds provided in the will of Col. George Washington Littlefield and named in honor of his wife. Berry, *The University of Texas*, 90.

184. David S. Evans and J. Derral Mulholland, *Big and Bright: A History of the McDonald Observatory* (Austin: University of Texas Press, 1986), 9–11.

185. Margaret C. Berry, "Benedict, Harry Yandell," *Handbook of Texas Online*, accessed 10 January 2015, http://www.tshaonline.org/handbook/online/articles/fbe48, uploaded 12 June 2010, published by the Texas State Historical Association.

186. Evans and Mulholland, *Big and Bright*, 12.

187. Ibid., 17–20.

188. The observatory was actually located in Williams Bay, Wisconsin.

189. Evans and Mulholland, *Big and Bright*, 23–27.

190. Regents' Minutes, 30 March 1935.

191. The older method was to coat the mirror with a thin layer of silver. The newer—and it proved to be better—method was to coat it with a thin layer of aluminum. It did not tarnish and lasted indefinitely.

192. Evans and Mulholland, *Big and Bright*, 66.

193. Ibid.

194. Over the years, the McDonald Observatory has consistently demonstrated its value to the scientific community. In 2013, astronomers there announced the discovery of the largest known black hole in the universe, a black hole more than eleven times as wide as Neptune's orbit around the sun. According to Karl Gebhardt, UT astronomy professor, and a team of UT scientists, "This most recent breakthrough has the potential to upend current theories of how black holes and galaxies begin and evolve" (Jordan Schraeder, "Far-Out Discovery," *The Alcalde* [March/April 2013]: 24–25). The wildest dreams of William J. McDonald, the banker from Paris, and Lutcher Stark, the entrepreneur from Orange, would surely not have included this discovery, but they would most certainly have been proud.

195. Evans and Mulholland, *Big and Bright*, 54–59.

196. Ibid., 80–85, 88–89.

197. Regents' Minutes, 30 May 1936.

198. Margaret C. Berry, "Littlefield, Clyde," *Handbook of Texas Online*, accessed 9 January 2015, http://www.tshaonline.org/handbook/online/articles/fli32, uploaded 15 June 2010, published by the Texas State Historical Association; Maysel, *Here Come the Texas Longhorns*, 117. Littlefield stayed on as a successful track coach until 1961, a total of forty-one years' coaching at UT.

199. Maysel, *Here Come the Texas Longhorns*, 111, 119.

200. Ibid., 127–128. Chevigny was originally being considered to eventually replace Knute Rockne. At Rockne's untimely death in a plane crash in 1931, however, Chevigny was considered too young for the job and went instead to St. Edward's.

201. John Maher, "Two Powers with a Brief History," *Austin American-Statesman*, 2 December 1936.

202. "U.T. Can Afford Nation's Best Coach, Regent Stark Says," *Daily Texan*, 15 December 1936.

203. Ibid.

204. Joe B. Frantz, *Forty-Acre Follies*, 188.

205. Regents' Minutes, 9 January 1937, 439.

206. Maysel, *Here Come the Texas Longhorns*, 130.

207. Bible's father, Jonathan Bible, a Greek and Latin scholar, had named him for a famous historian of ancient Athens; his mother's name was Cleopatra.

208. Archie P. McDonald, "Dana X. Bible and the Twelfth Man," 20 November 2005, TexasEscapes.com, http://www.texasescapes.com/AllThingsHistorical/Dana-Xenophon-Bible-and-the-Twelfth-Man-AM1105.htm.

209. Joe Frantz, *Forty-Acre Follies*, 187.

210. Maysel, *Here Come the Longhorns*, 129–130.

211. Ibid.; H.J.L. Stark to D.X. Bible, 17 November 1941, Stark Foundation Archives.

212. "Bible Due Here for Conference: Nebraska Coach Will Talk Terms with Committee," *Austin American-Statesman*, 19 January 1937, copy in Stark Foundation Archives.

213. Don Carleton, *A Breed So Rare: The Life of J. R. Parten, Liberal Texas Oil Man, 1896–1992* (Austin: Texas State Historical Association in cooperation with the Center for American History, 1998), 178–179.

214. Ibid.; telegram from J.R. Parten to Dana X. Bible, 23 January 1937, copy in Stark Foundation Archives, original in the DBCAH, Vertical File on D.X. Bible.

215. Mike Hogg to the University of Texas Board of Regents, 12 January 1937, Stark Foundation Archives; George Heyer to H.J.L. Stark, 9 February 1937, Stark Foundation Archives; Mike Hogg to H.J. Lutcher Stark, 13 February 1937, Stark Foundation Archives.

216. Lloyd Gregory, "Looking 'Em Over: Southwest Conference Sport Dope: Is 'Bible Plan' Too Idealistic?," *Houston Post*, 27 February 1937 or 1938, clipping, Stark Foundation Archives.

217. "Bill Little Commentary: The Play That Changed the Face of Texas Football," 6 September 2003, http://www.texassports.com/news/2003/9/6/090603aaa_603.aspx.

218. Ibid.

219. Maysel, *Here Come the Longhorns*, 130; "Aggies Offer Lutcher Stark Seat on Bench," *Daily Texan*, 17 November 1940.

220. John Maher, "Showcase of Strength," *Austin American-Statesman*, 24 January 2007; John Maher and Kirk Bohls, "Lutcher Stark," in *Long Live the Longhorns! One Hundred Years of Texas Football* (New York: St. Martin's Press, 1993), 32.

221. Richard Pennington, *"For Texas, I Will,"* 72.

222. H.J.L. Stark to D.X. Bible, 17 November 1941, Stark Foundation Archives.

223. D.X. Bible to H.J. Lutcher Stark, 18 November 1941, Stark Foundation Archives.

224. Maysel, *Here Come the Longhorns*, 173. In 1956, nearly ten years after his retirement, Bible was a strong supporter of hiring Darrell Royal as head football coach. By the time Royal in turn became a supporter of Mack Brown in 1997, the Longhorns were well established in the top tier of teams in college football.

225. David S. Walkup, "Bible, Dana Xenophon," *Handbook of Texas Online*, accessed 19 January 2015, http://www.tshaonline.org/handbook/online/articles/fbi38, uploaded 12 June 2010, published by the Texas State Historical Association.

226. D.X. Bible to Nita Hill Stark, 11 October 1938, Stark Foundation Archives.

227. "Mrs. Stark's Funeral to Be This Afternoon," *Daily Texan*, 13 October 1939.

228. Nita and Lutcher Stark, honorary doctor of laws degrees, Baylor University, Stark Foundation Archives; "Stark Begins 18th Year as Regent," *Daily Texan*, 3 January 1939.

229. William T. Rives, "'Lutch' Stark Is Allergic to Money Idea, so He Gives It to School; and the Bengal Guards of Orange and the University Prosper," *Austin American-Statesman*, clipping, hand-dated 22 September 1940, Stark Foundation Archives.

230. Celeste Smith Hart, Oral History Interview, conducted by Jo Ann Stiles and Ellen Rienstra, Orange, 30 June 2004, 2, 26, 1, Stark Foundation Archives. Celeste Hart is Smitty Hustmyre's younger sister.

231. *The Lutcher Stark Bengal Guards, 1936–1944, Orange, Texas*, 25, pamphlet compiled by Virginia Mott Craig, Stark Foundation Archives.

232. Dorace McGill Ingram, Oral History Interview, conducted by Ellen Rienstra, Orange, 16 March 2004, 28, Stark Foundation Archives.

233. "Bengal Guards of Orange, Texas," *Southwestern Roundup* 1, no. 6 (December 1940): 14.

234. *The Lutcher Stark Bengal Guards*, 25; Frank W.R. Hubert, "My Experiences in the Orange School District: Teacher, Principal, and Superintendent of Schools," booklet, Stark Foundation Archives, 7.

235. *The Lutcher Stark Bengal Guards*, 26.

236. Hart, Oral History Interview, 30 June 2004, 18. Celeste Smith (later Hart) had moved from Whiteville, Tennessee, to live with Smitty for her years in high school. She was a member of the Bengal Guards.

237. Ingram, Oral History Interview, 16 March 2004, 31; Cecil Moses Broom, Oral History Interview, conducted by Ellen Rienstra, Frances Ann Lutcher Theater, 10 March 2004, Stark Foundation Archives.

238. Ingram, Oral History Interview, 33.

239. Adams, Oral History Interview, 14 April 2004, 20.

240. Vicki Parfait, "A Man and His Band," *Orange County Record*, 15 June 1999.

241. Ingram, Oral History Interview, 30.

242. "Building Living Monuments: Band and Drum Corps Training Is $165,000 Hobby to Lutch Stark," *Piano Trade Magazine* 37, no. 4 (April 1940): n.p.

243. Ingram, Oral History Interview, 13; Helen McDonald Reese, Oral History Interview, conducted by Jo Ann Stiles, Bridge City, Texas, 8 December 2003, 8, Stark Foundation Archives.

244. Adams, Oral History Interview, 6; photographs of Bengal Guards' identical luggage, Stark Foundation Archives, 6.

245. Adams, Oral History Interview, 5, 4.

246. Ibid., 1; Reese, Oral History Interview, 11.

247. Laurie D. Haynes, "A Man and His Band: Lutcher Stark and the Story of the Ben-

gal Guards," *Orange County Record*, 16 June 1999, quoting former Bengal Guard Dorothy Broussard Guidry.

248. Hart, Oral History Interview, 19; Broom, Oral History Interview, 8. Many other Bengal Guards furnished variations on the same story.

249. Wynne Edith Toney Winner, conversation with Ellen Rienstra, 18 April 2009, Auditorium, Shangri La Gardens, Orange, Texas.

250. Adams, Oral History Interview, 22.

251. Woods and Gatewood, *America Interpreted*, 766.

252. George Norris Green, *The Establishment in Texas Politics: The Primitive Years, 1938–1957* (Norman: University of Oklahoma Press, 1979), 14–16.

253. Woods and Gatewood, *Interpreting America*, 766; George Brown Tindall and David Emory Shi, *America: A Narrative History*, 9th ed. (New York: W.W. Norton, 2013), 1132–1133; Green, *The Establishment in Texas Politics*, 14–16.

254. "The Small Town Texan Who Has 75 Million Dollars."

Chapter 10

1. Fannie Ratchford, "University's Greatest Woman Benefactor Dies," *The Alcalde* (December 1936): 54.

2. Fannie Ratchford to Nita Stark, 10 May 1933.

3. Nita Stark to Fannie Ratchford, 5 February 1934.

4. F.H. Farwell to L. Lechenger, jeweler, 10 April 1936.

5. Miller, "Wins $30,000 Scholarship Prize," *Phi Gamma Delta* 10, no. 6 (April 1937): 587, 589, 595. After Miriam's death, Lutcher held the mortgage on "Buen Retiro."

6. Nita Stark to Lana A. Smith, 25 April 1936.

7. Nita Stark to Lillie Esslinger, 18 November 1936.

8. H.J.L. Stark to D.A. Pruter, 11 September 1928; telegram, H.J.L. Stark to D.A. Pruter, 18 September 1928; telegram, Miriam Stark to D.A. Pruter, 27 May 1929.

9. H.J.L. Stark to Leo Becker, 25 October 1934.

10. Leo Becker to H.J.L. Stark, 9 November 1934.

11. Fannie Ratchford to W.B. Simmons, 8 October 1933; Mary Murray Weber, Oral History Interview, conducted by Ellen Rienstra, Choupique, Louisiana, 1 March 2004, 22–23, Stark Foundation Archives.

12. W.B. Simmons to H.J.L. Stark, 20 September 1935.

13. Ibid.

14. "Final Tribute to W.H. Stark," *Orange Leader*, 9 October 1936.

15. Telegram, H.J.L. Stark to Leo Becker, 8 October 1936.

16. "Final Tribute to W.H. Stark."

17. "William H. Stark," *Las Sabinas* 6, no. 4 (1980): 30.

18. "Thousands Pay Final Homage to W.H. Stark," *Orange Leader*, 11 October 1936.

19. "Final Tribute to W.H. Stark."

20. Ibid.

21. "Thousands Pay Final Homage to W.H. Stark."

22. "Senate Pays Honor to W.H. Stark," *Houston Chronicle*, 9 October 1936.

23. W.H. Stark, will, 8 June 1933, filed 13 October 1936, Orange County Courthouse, Probate Records.

24. Ibid.

25. Nita Stark to Lillie Esslinger, Fannie Wilbur, Ida Achenbach, Mrs. E.S. Jackson Jr., and Ida Wilbur, 7 December 1936.

26. Ibid.

27. Annie Lucas was the wife of Joe Lucas, a prominent Orange jeweler and a longtime close friend of the Lutcher and Stark families.

28. Nita Stark to Lillie Esslinger, Fannie Wilbur, Ida Achenbach, Mrs. E.S. Jackson Jr., and Ida Wilbur, 7 December 1926.

29. "Orange Citizens Mourn Death of Mrs. Stark," *Orange Leader*, 29 November 1936.

30. Nita Stark to Lillie Esslinger, Fannie Wilbur, Ida Achenbach, Mrs. E.S. Jackson Jr., and Ida Wilbur, 7 December 1926.

31. H.J.L. Stark, office memorandum, 27 May 1937.

32. Ibid.

33. Affidavit, H.J.L. Stark, 24 November 1924.

34. Carrie Brown to H.J.L. Stark, 19 December 1936.

35. Conversation between W.B. Simmons and Mrs. Carrie L. Brown, 10 February 1937; memorandum, W.B. Simmons to H.J.L. Stark, 12 February 1937.

36. H.J.L. Stark, memorandum, undated but probably around 10 January 1937; memorandum, W.B. Simmons to H.J.L. Stark, 12 February 1937.

37. Memorandum, Alan B. Cameron, 12 January 1937.

38. Draft of memorandum, undated and unsigned but probably written by Lutcher Stark, Stark Foundation Archives.

39. H.J.L. Stark to H. Brown and Edgar W. Brown Jr., 15 January 1937; memorandum, conversation between E.W. Brown Jr. and W.B. Simmons, 20 January 1937; Carrie L. Brown to H.J.L. Stark, 25 January 1937; memorandum, H.J.L. Stark, 9 May 1938; W.B. Simmons to H.J.L. Stark, 8 August 1938; Irl F. Kennerly to H.J.L. Stark, 15 May 1943; Irl F. Kennerly to L.J. "Brub" Benckenstein, 26 May 1943.

40. Settlement agreement between Stark group and Brown group, 7 July 1943.

41. W.B. Simmons, memorandum, "To Whom It May Concern," final meeting of the Stark and Brown groups in E.W. Brown Jr.'s office, Orange National Bank Building, 23 July 1943, Stark Foundation Archives.

42. Ibid.

43. "$5,000,000 Fine Art Collection of Late Mrs. Miriam A. [sic] Stark Presented to Texas U by Son," undated, unattributed clipping, Stark Foundation Archives; Fannie Ratchford to H.J.L. Stark, 16 March 1933.

44. "The Gift with the Giver," *The Alcalde*, October 1929, 6; "Orange Woman Gives $650,000 to State University," undated, unattributed clipping; *The 1926 Cactus*, Yearbook, University of Texas, 94; Ratchford, "University's Greatest Woman Benefactor Dies," 53.

45. Regents' Minutes, 29 January 1932, 497–498. The 1909–1910 Cass Gilbert–designed "Old Library," as it became known, was first renamed the Eugene C. Barker Center for American History and, in 1973, Battle Hall after William James Battle, the sixth president of the university. The Tower Building was designed by the university's principal architect, Paul Philippe Cret. The John Henry Wrenn collection was acquired in 1918 when George W. Littlefield donated $225,000 toward its purchase. Gracy, "Littlefield, George Washington."

46. "U.T. Regents Face Library Question," clipping, *Austin American-Statesman*, 1933, Stark Foundation Archives.

47. Ibid.; Fannie Ratchford to H.J.L. Stark, 4 February 1932.

48. Regents' Minutes, 18 March 1933, 253–254.

49. Ibid.

50. "$5,000,000 Fine Art Collection of Late Mrs. Miriam Stark Presented to Texas U by Son."

51. Fannie Ratchford to H.J.L. Stark, 4 February 1932.

52. "$5,000,000 Fine Art Collection of Late Mrs. Miriam Stark Presented to Texas U by Son."

53. Fannie Ratchford to Nita Stark, 25 May 1936.

54. "Portrait of Miriam Stark Hung in Austin," *Orange Leader*, 4 December 1938.

55. H.J.L. Stark, certificate, Southwestern University, doctorate of laws, Stark Foundation Archives.

56. H.J.L. Stark to Nita Stark, 10 July 1930; D.A. Pruter to W.H. Stark, 8 August 1930; W.B. Simmons to H.J.L. Stark, 10 October 1934; memorandum, W.B. Simmons, 1 March 1937, Stark Foundation Archives.

57. Nita Stark to Lillie Esslinger, 18 November 1936.

58. Nita Stark to Lewis Johnson, 20 September 1938.

59. "General Diet List for Mrs. Lutcher Stark," from Turner Urological Institute, 506 Caroline Street, Houston, Texas, 27 September 1938, Stark Foundation Archives; Nita Hill Stark, death certificate, 11 October 1939. Eunice Benckenstein also stated that Nita died of "a kidney disease." Eunice Robinson Benckenstein, Oral History Interview, conducted by Ellen Rienstra, Stark Foundation offices, 8 October 2003, Stark Foundation Archives.

60. "General Diet List for Mrs. Lutcher Stark."

61. H.J.L. Stark to Hans Holmes, 2 November 1938.

62. Nita Stark to Lloyd Gregory, 17 November 1938.

63. "Stark Sparks Bengals with Steady Gains," undated clipping, *Orange Leader*, Stark Foundation Archives.

64. "Mrs. Nita H. Stark Rites Set Today," *Houston Post*, 13 October 1939.

65. "Long Illness Fatal to Alumna, Wife of Regent," *Daily Texan*, 18 October 1939.

66. Nita Stark to Nelda and Ruby Childers, 31 July 1939.

67. Ibid.; Ann Raborn Graves, Oral History Interview, by Jo Ann Stiles, Austin, 1 March 2004, 6, Stark Foundation Archives.

68. Telegram, "Miss Mary" to Julia and D.D. Wells, 11 August 1939. Garrett DeLaRue was a longtime Stark employee who cooked for the family and also owned a well-known barbecue stand on John Street in Orange.

69. Telegram, H.J.L. Stark to W.D. Smith, 22 September 1939.

70. W.B. Simmons to Leo Haynes, 26 September 1939.

71. W.B. Simmons to Alford Stark, 2 October 1939.

72. "Mrs. Nita Stark, Wife of Orange Capitalist, Dies," *Orange Leader*, 12 October 1939.

73. Nita Hill Stark, death certificate, 11 October 1939.

74. "Long Illness Fatal to Alumna, Wife of Regent."

75. "Mrs. Nita Stark, Wife of Orange Capitalist, Dies."

76. "Mrs. Nita Stark," editorial, *Daily Texan*, 13 October 1939.

77. "Mrs. Stark's Funeral to Be This Afternoon," *Daily Texan*, 13 October 1939.

78. "Mrs. Nita H. Stark Rites Set Today"; "City Closes for Funeral of Mrs. Nita Hill Stark," *Orange Leader*, 13 October 1939.

79. "City Closes for Funeral of Mrs. Nita Hill Stark."

80. Graves, Oral History Interview, 7.

81. H.J.L. Stark to Hans Holmes, 17 November 1939.

82. Arno Nowotny to H.J.L. Stark, 20 July 1942.

83. W.B. Simmons to Thurlow Weed, 1 December 1939; Lucy Amanda Hill Jones (Homer Hill's sister) to H.J.L. Stark, 3 December 1939.

84. Lucy Hill Jones to H.J.L. Stark, 3 December 1939.

85. Invoice, Wheeler Funeral Home, to H.J.L. Stark for "services rendered in depositing remains of Dr. Homer B. Hill and Mrs. Ella Rankin Hill in the Stark [sic] Mausoleum, Evergreen Cemetery, Orange, Texas."

86. Handwritten note with names and birth and death dates of Mary Creola Hill and Herbert Hill, "Placed in vault in Orange 4/23/40," Stark Foundation Archives; memo, "Stark Mausoleum at Evergreen Cemetery," listing Mary Creola Hill and Herbert Hill as located in the mausoleum, 17 January 1951, Stark Foundation Archives..

87. H.J.L. Stark to Lucy Hill Jones, 18 December 1939.

88. Regents' Minutes, 16 February, 1 June, and 28 October 1933. The Littlefield Fund for Southern History was established at the University of Texas in 1914 by Maj. George W. Littlefield "for the full and impartial study of the South and its part in American history."

89. Frederic F. Burchsted and P. Lynn Denton, "Texas Memorial Museum," *Handbook of Texas Online*, accessed 11 November 2014, http://www.tshaonline.org/handbook/online /articles/lbt02, uploaded 15 June 2010, published by the Texas State Historical Association.

90. Carleton, *A Breed So Rare*, 143. Parten served as a regent from March 1935 to February 1941 and as chairman from February 1939 to February 1941.

91. Ibid., 143–144.

92. Regents' Minutes, 30 March 1935. The Texas Union Board served as the governing body of the university's Student Union.

93. O'Daniel's nickname, "Pappy," came from the opening line of his daily radio program: "Pass the biscuits, Pappy."

94. Green, *The Establishment in Texas Politics*, 23. Bob Wills later left to establish his career with the Texas swing musical genre in the big-band era.

95. Ibid., 22–23, 24.

96. Carleton, *A Breed So Rare*, citing the *Austin American-Statesman*, 12 December 1971, J.R. Parten interview.

97. Carleton, *A Breed So Rare*, 300.

98. Benedict was walking on the "Drag," a section of Guadalupe Street bordering the western boundary of the university's campus, between the University Co-op and the YMCA when he collapsed.

99. Carleton, *A Breed So Rare*, 187–188.

100. Ibid., 164–166, 171–172.

101. Ibid., 211, 228, 236.

102. The Sealy & Smith Foundation was established in 1922 by John Sealy Jr., Jennie Sealy Smith, and her husband, R. Waverly Smith, members of a longtime prominent Galveston family, "to carry on the family tradition and concern for the health care of the people of Galveston." "The Sealy & Smith Foundation, Galveston, Texas," http://www.sealy -smith-foundation.org/about_us.html (accessed 21 October 2015).

103. Chester Burns, *Saving Lives, Training Caregivers, Making Discoveries: A Centennial History of the University of Texas Medical Branch at Galveston* (Austin: Texas State Historical Association, 2003), 46, 47.

104. When Spies, before he had been named dean of the medical school, came to Austin for an interview with the Board of Regents, he was introduced at a luncheon by Randall, chair of the search committee, as the new dean of the Medical Branch, to the surprise of the other regents (as well as Spies). They chose not to argue the point, but Randall quickly came to rue the day he pulled that end run on the board.

105. Although Dr. Randall held memberships on both the UT Board of Regents and the Medical Branch faculty council, he came to defend the independence of the latter. He resigned from the Board of Regents in January 1940. Berry, *The University of Texas*, 415.

106. Carleton, *A Breed So Rare*, 221–222.

107. Ibid., 227.

108. Nita Stark died on October 11, two days after the conclusion of the Galveston meeting.

109. Burns, *Saving Lives*, 51.

110. Carleton, *A Breed So Rare*, 241. Dies promised the university a formal report from his committee staff, but such a report somehow never materialized.

111. Regents' Minutes, 28 February 1942.

112. Ibid.

113. Ibid., 11 March 1942; Burns, *Saving Lives*, 53.

114. Burns, *Saving Lives*, 53.

115. Regents' Minutes, 23 May 1942.

116. Ibid., 1 August 1942.

117. Burns, *Saving Lives*, 55.

118. The league had first been known as the Debating League of Texas High Schools.

119. Christopher Long, "University Interscholastic League," *Handbook of Texas Online*, accessed 19 January 2015, http://www.tshaonline.org/handbook/online/articles/keu01, uploaded 15 June 2010, published by the Texas State Historical Association; Miller, "Wins $30,000 Scholarship Prize," 590.

120. Miller, "Wins $30,000 Scholarship Prize," 590.

121. University Interscholastic League, *A Brief History of the University Interscholastic League on the Occasion of the League's 75th Anniversary* (Austin: University Interscholastic League, 1985), 13.

122. *The Interscholastic Leaguer*, 1935–1941, passim, DBCAH. During the years, the *Leaguer* featured many articles and references to football safety.

123. Rodney J. Kidd, "Director Urges Safety First in Interscholastic Football," *Interscholastic Leaguer* 22, no. 2 (September 1938), DBCAH.

124. Roy Bedichek, "Editor's Column," *Interscholastic Leaguer* 23, no. 6 (February 1940).

125. Roy Bedichek to W.B. Simmons, 17 December 1950, Roy Bedichek Papers, Box 3Q13, DBCAH.

126. William A. Owens and Lyman Grant, eds., *Letters of Roy Bedichek* (Austin: University of Texas Press, 1985), 248.

127. "Brief of the 18-Year Age Rule Controversy," 2, unpublished typescript, Roy Bedichek Papers, DBCAH.

128. Ibid., 6.

129. *Orange Peel*, Yearbook, Orange High School, Orange, Texas, 1937.

130. Roy Bedichek, Testimony before the Senate Education Committee, 28 November 1944, 4:609, 610, State Legislative Library.

131. Ibid., 4:613.

132. In April 1940, the Orange District anticipated becoming a Conference AA school and building a new stadium and playing field, but it was still a Conference A school. "Permanent Grid Stadium Up for Approval Tonite," *Orange Leader*, 8 April 1940.

133. "Brief of the 18-Year Age Rule Controversy," 9–10.

134. Regents' Minutes, 31 May 1940.

135. Ibid.

136. Ibid.

137. Homer Price Rainey, *The Tower and the Dome* (Boulder, CO: Pruett Publishing, 1971), 42.

138. Texas Senate Education Committee, Investigation, Hearings, 16–28 November 1944, 1:136, Legislative Reference Library.

139. Henry Nash Smith, Horace Busby, and Rex D. Hopper, "The Controversy at the University of Texas, 1939–1946: A Documentary History," paper read 13 August 1945 by Henry Nash Smith at the request of the Student Committee for Academic Freedom (University of Texas: Student Committee for Academic Freedom), no publication date, Box 3L832, DBCAH, 7.

140. Bedichek, Testimony before the Senate Education Committee, 28 November 1944, 4:613.

141. Stephen C. Anderson, *J.W. Edgar: Educator for Texas* (Austin: Eakin Press, 1984), 27–28.

142. Hubert, *My Experiences in the Orange School District.*

143. Ibid., 3; Haskell Monroe, conversation with Jo Ann Stiles and Ellen Rienstra, College Station, 4 May 2004. Hubert later served as assistant principal, then principal of Lutcher Stark High School; superintendent of Schools for the Orange Independent School District; dean of the School of Arts and Sciences at Texas A&M University; and chancellor of the Texas A&M University System.

144. Lutch Stark Boys was a nonprofit corporation originally established by Lutcher Stark in 1926 for "supporting, fostering, and developing the spiritual, moral, mental and physical education and welfare of boyhood." It originally served as the parent corporation for Lutch Stark's Boys' Band, then the Bengal Guards and Bengal Lancers. Wingate, "Summary," 26, 3–4.

145. Ingram, Oral History Interview, 16 March 2004, 6; Hubert, *My Experiences in the Orange School District*, 6; Hart, Oral History Interview, 18, 18n.

146. Hubert, *My Experiences in the Orange School District,* 7.

147. Ibid., 5. The basses were custom-made by the Holton Instrument Company of Elkhart, Indiana.

148. *The Lutcher Stark Bengal Guards,* 28–29.

149. Clipping, undated, unattributed, William R. Frierson Scrapbook, Stark Foundation Archives.

150. *The Lutcher Stark Bengal Guards,* 28. Carol Jo "Frodie" Colburn was the daughter of Lutcher & Moore auditor George S. Colburn.

151. Wright, conversation with Stiles and Rienstra, 18 April 2005.

152. Ibid., 28.

153. "Bengal Guards Win Praise from Writers of 4 States," clipping from "Roundy's Column," *New Orleans Item*, series of undated, mainly unattributed clippings, Stark Foundation Archives.

154. "Beauteous Baton Twirler, Bengal Guards Will Lead Texas Show at Sugar Bowl Game," clipping, New Orleans newspaper, 1 January 1940, Stark Foundation Archives.

155. *The Lutcher Stark Bengal Guards,* 30, 31.

156. Photographs, 1940 National School Music Competition Festival, Waco, Texas, Stark Foundation Archives.

157. *The Lutcher Stark Bengal Guards,* 29; official souvenir program, Orange Tigers vs. Vinton Lions, 27 September 1940, copy courtesy of Celeste Smith Hart.

158. Winkelman and Davies, Accountants, Report, *Orange High School Stadium Fund Advanced by the Lutcher & Moore Lumber Company*, 24 July 1940–18 September 1941, Stark Foundation Archives. The cost of the stadium was touted as $50,000, but the actual sum advanced by Lutcher & Moore was $26,733.47. Others donated funds as well.

159. Reese, Oral History Interview, 8 December 2003, 20; photographs, Stark Foundation Archives.

160. Roy Wingate, Oral History Interview, conducted by Jo Ann Stiles and Ellen Rienstra, Orange, 13 February 2004, 4, Stark Foundation Archives; H. Williams, *Gateway to Texas,* 174.

161. *The Lutcher Stark Bengal Guards*, 29; photo caption, *Southern Pacific Bulletin*, September 1940, 11.

162. Belinda Gaudet, "Lutcher's Broom Recalls Bengal Days," *Orange Leader*, 30 April 1993.

163. Reese, Oral History Interview, 9; Broom, Oral History Interview, 10 March 2004. Cecil and Helen also rode in their own vehicle, the "Redbug," a miniature red car in which they made their entrance to a stadium, circling the field and waving to the crowd before joining the other Guards in the stands.

164. Hubert, *My Experiences in the Orange School District*, 7.

165. Excerpt from the *Chicago Tribune*, 18 August 1940, quoted in Diana Rinehart, "Bengal Guards 'Put Orange on the Map,' in 1940," *Orange Leader*, 9 June 1974.

166. Agnes Putnam, "Guards Wildly Welcomed Home after Leaving Chicago Gasping," clipping, probably *Port Arthur News*, 20 August 1940, Stark Foundation Archives.

167. Rives, "'Lutch' Stark Is Allergic to Money Idea," *Austin American-Statesman*, 22 September 1940.

168. Putnam, "Guards Wildly Welcomed Home after Leaving Chicago Gasping."

169. Ingram, Oral History Interview, 15.

170. Menu, "Bengal Guards Special," from Cecil Moses Broom, copy in Stark Foundation Archives; Adams, Oral History Interview, 14 April 2004, 9–10.

171. CD, recording of Bengal Guards' reunion, 14 May 2005, Stark Foundation Archives.

172. Adams, Oral History Interview, 5.

173. Ingram, Oral History Interview, 18–19.

174. *The Lutcher Stark Bengal Guards*, 27.

175. Hubert, *My Experiences in the Orange School District*, 2.

176. Adams, Oral History Interview, 23.

177. *The Lutcher Stark Bengal Guards*, 31–32.

178. Shelley, one of the all-time football greats at the University of Texas, lettered three years on the Varsity team and served as its captain in 1930. He played professional football before becoming Orange High School's head football coach in 1937. Official souvenir program, Orange Tigers vs. Vinton Lions.

179. "Will Bengal Guards March Again?—This Question Asked in Orange While Pants-Grass Issue Is Debated," *Port Arthur News*, 5 October 1940.

180. Ibid.

181. Ibid.

182. Ibid.

183. Glenda Dyer, "Stark Spark Exceeds 60 Years," clipping, *Orange County Record*, undated, Stark Foundation Archives.

184. "Orange Tigers Are on Strike: Football Row Reaches Climax," *Beaumont Journal*, 8 October 1940.

185. Editorial, *Port Arthur News*, 8 October 1940.

186. "Stark's Cousin Takes Up Shelley's Fight," *Austin American*, 9 October 1940.

187. "Brown Demands Showdown of Orange School Board: 'I Had Rather See the Band in Calico Than This,' He Says," *Houston Post*, 9 October 1940.

188. "The Pride and Joy of Orange, Texas, Is the Wonderful Girls' School Band," *Life*, 14 October 1940.

189. Agnes Putnam, "Stark Is Dosing Bengal Guards, Band and Football Team with 100,000 Cod Liver Oil Pills to Cure 'That Tired Feeling,'" *Port Arthur News*, 12 March 1940.

190. Memorandum, H.J.L. Stark to Elizabeth "Smitty" Hustmyre, 23 October 1940, from Celeste Smith Hart, copy in Stark Foundation Archives.

191. Elizabeth Hustmyre to H.J.L. Stark, 23 October 1940, courtesy of Celeste Smith Hart.

192. Ibid.

193. Elizabeth Hustmyre to Bengal Guards, 29 October 1940, courtesy of Celeste Smith Hart.

194. *The Lutcher Stark Bengal Guards*, 30.

195. Broom, Oral History Interview, 2.

196. "Bengal Guards to Be Back at Music Festival," *Chicago Sunday Tribune*, 27 July 1941.

197. A clipping in the scrapbook kept for Stark by W.B. Simmons, undated but probably around June 1923, reported that, for a convention that Stark attended, Texas Rotarians defied the jinx of the number thirteen: "The engine of the special train [conveying the Rotarians to the convention] was No. 413. The train consisted of thirteen cars and Texas is the thirteenth district in Rotary." Possibly this was the source of Stark's fixation with the number. H.J.L. Stark to "Old Main," ordering a publication by Walter Long, *For All Time to Come*, and requesting numbered copy "thirteen," Stark Foundation Archives.

198. Stark's automobile license plates, Stark Foundation Archives.

199. Reese, Oral History Interview, 9.

200. Ibid., 31.

201. Photographs of Bengal Guards' trip to Chicago, 1941, Stark Foundation Archives.

202. Frankie Cochran Hill to Ruby Childers, 3 December 1940; Freda Bellmont to Ruby Childers, 9 December 1940.

203. Frankie Cochran Hill to Ruby Childers, 3 December 1940.

204. Freda Bellmont to Ruby Childers, 7 December 1940.

205. Ibid.

206. Fannie Ratchford to Ruby Childers, 30 November 1940, Stark Foundation Archives.

207. Agnes Putnam, "Ruby Belle Childers and H.J.L. Stark Are Married Sunday Afternoon," clipping, unattributed but probably *Port Arthur News*, 7 April 1941.

208. Ibid.

209. "Mr. and Mrs. H.J.L. Stark," *Orange Leader*, 13 April 1941.

210. Childers family, genealogical material, Stark Foundation Archives.

211. Orange High School commencement program, School Friendship Book, belonging to Ruby Childers, 21 May 1920, Stark Foundation Archives.

212. "Mrs. H.J. Lutcher Stark Dies in Home at Orange after Lengthy Illness," *Beaumont Enterprise*, 13 July 1942.

213. Ruby Childers, report card, Ward-Belmont Scrapbook, Stark Foundation Archives.

214. Ruby Childers, diary, 1 January–3 June 1921, passim, Stark Foundation Archives.

215. Ibid., 1 January–3 June 1921, passim.

216. Ibid., 12 January 1921. Probably the "famous tenor" was Edward Johnson, a Canadian tenor who later became general manager of the Metropolitan Opera.

217. Ibid., 22 February and 3 June 1921.

218. The Childers family's close friend and sometime boarder Eunice Robinson (later Benckenstein) stated that Ruby had attended Ward-Belmont for two years. Benckenstein, Oral History Interview, 8 October 2003; summary of interview with Mrs. Nelda C. Stark, prepared by Harold Metts, 15 March 1990, 3, Stark Foundation Archives.

219. Summary of interview with Mrs. Nelda C. Stark, 3.

220. Benckenstein, Oral History Interview, 8 October 2003, 4, 7, and 29 March 2004, 2; H.J.L. Stark, Office Records, passim, Stark Foundation Archives.

221. Putnam, "Ruby Belle Childers and H.J.L. Stark Are Married."

222. H.B. Williford, M.D., to Nelda Childers, 8 April 1940; Benckenstein, Oral History Interview, 8 October 2003, 22.

223. Benckenstein, Oral History Interview, 8 October 2003, 22.

224. Telegram, unnamed laboratory in Rochester, Minnesota, to Dr. H.B. Williford, 2 December 1940, Stark Foundation Archives.

225. H.B. Williford, M.D., to Dr. H.W. Pearce, 3 December 1940.

226. "Mrs. Lutcher Stark Is Critically Ill," *Port Arthur News*, 12 July 1942.

227. Louise Benckenstein to Ruby Stark, 23 May 1942.

228. Herbert Kerr to H.J.L. Stark, 12 June 1942.

229. W.B. Simmons to Leo C. Haynes, secretary, University of Texas Board of Regents, 24 June 1942.

230. "Mrs. Lutcher Stark Is Critically Ill."

231. Benckenstein, Oral History Interview, 8 October 2003, 22.

232. "Mrs. H.J.L. Stark Dies in Home at Orange after Lengthy Illness."

233. H.J.L. Stark, correspondence, sympathy letters and telegrams, passim, following 12 July 1942.

234. Frankie Cochran Hill to Nelda Childers, 13 July 1942.

235. Mattie Johnson Beckham to Nelda Childers, 23 July 1942.

236. "Mrs. Ruby C. Stark Dies Sunday after Lingering Illness," *Orange Leader*, July 13, 1942.

237. Ruby Childers Stark, will, copy in Stark Foundation Archives.

238. Ibid.

Chapter 11

1. Joe Rougeau, navy veteran and later electrician for the Nelda C. and H.J. Lutcher Stark Foundation, conversation with Ellen Rienstra, Stark Foundation Offices, 10 February 2005.

2. Woods and Gatewood, *America Interpreted*, 787, 791, 789–793.

3. H. Williams, *Gateway to Texas*, 153; Louis Fairchild, *They Called It the War Effort: Oral Histories from WWII Orange, Texas*, 2nd ed. (Denton: Texas State Historical Association, 2012), xxviii–xxix.

4. H. Williams, *Picturing Orange*, 186–187; Fairchild, *They Called It the War Effort*, xxviii–xxix.

5. Fairchild, *They Called It the War Effort*, xxix.

6. Ibid.; H. Williams, *Picturing Orange*, 187.

7. H. Williams, *Picturing Orange*, 192, 195. During the war years, Edgar Brown was the majority stockholder in Levingston. In 1945, Ed Malloy, whom Brown had hired in 1939 as general manager and vice president, bought the controlling interest from him. Ibid., 192.

8. "Mill Which Founded Lutcher Fortune at Orange Razed as Defense Brings Modern Era to City," *Port Arthur News*, 26 January 1941.

9. H. Williams, *Gateway to Texas*, 165; H. Williams, *Picturing Orange*, 192.

10. Fairchild, *They Called It the War Effort*, 323.

11. H. Williams, *Gateway to Texas*, 165, 168.

12. Wingate, Oral History Interview, 13 February 2004, 26.

13. Fairchild, *They Called It the War Effort*, xxii–xxiv, xxxi–xxxii, 3, 28, 426, 441, 25.

14. Monroe, conversation with Stiles and Rienstra, 4 May 2004. Haskell Monroe served as history professor at Schreiner College and Texas A&M University; first dean of faculties at A&M; president, University of Texas at El Paso; chancellor, University of Missouri at Columbia; and is currently Dean of Faculties Emeritus, Texas A&M University.

15. Fairchild, *They Called It the War Effort*, 137; Wingate, Oral History Interview, 31.

16. H. Williams, *Gateway to Texas*, 166.

17. Fairchild, *They Called It the War Effort*, Fairchild interviewing Lanier C. Nantz, 244.

18. Roy Wingate, conversation with Jo Ann Stiles and Ellen Rienstra, 2006.

19. Fairchild, *They Called It the War Effort*, 163–164, 230, 317.

20. H. Williams, *Gateway to Texas*, 168–169.

21. Cynthia Carter Leedy Horn to Jo Ann Stiles, Richard Dickerson, and Ellen Rienstra, 6 July 2012, Stark Foundation Archives.

22. Monroe, conversation with Jo Ann Stiles and Ellen Rienstra, 4 May 2004.

23. Fairchild, *They Called It the War Effort*, xxxi.

24. H. Williams, *Picturing Orange*, 192.

25. Rougeau, conversation with Ellen Rienstra, 10 February 2005.

26. Wingate, Oral History Interview, 17.

27. Howard Williams, Oral History Interview, conducted by Jo Ann Stiles and Ellen Rienstra, Orange, 13 April 2005, Stark Foundation Archives.

28. *The Lutcher Stark Bengal Guards*, 31.

29. Leon Parish, conversation with Roy Wingate, Jo Ann Stiles, and Ellen Rienstra, Stark Foundation offices, 9 June 2005.

30. Dyer, "Stark Spark Exceeds 60 Years," clipping, *Orange County Record*, undated.

31. Ida Marie Dickens Stark, obituary, *Orange Leader*, 21 November 2008.

32. Dyer, "Stark Spark Exceeds 60 Years."

33. Fannie Ratchford to H.J.L. Stark, 23 July 1945; William H. Stark II, citation from secretary of the navy: "For meritorious achievement in aerial flight as Pilot of a Torpedo Bomber Plane in Marine Torpedo Bomber Squadron One Hundred Thirty-Four in action against enemy Japanese forces in the New Ireland Area, from 17 January to 2 March 1944; and in the Western Caroline Island Area, from 17 October 1944, to 7 March 1945. Flying on numerous missions against strongly defended enemy positions during this period, First Lieutenant Stark executed his bombing and strafing attacks on the targets with courage and determination despite heavy concentrations of hostile antiaircraft fire. By his skilled airmanship and courage, he contributed materially to the success of operations in both areas." Stark Foundation Archives.

34. Fannie Ratchford to H.J.L. Stark, 21 December 1944.

35. Fairchild, *They Called It the War Effort*, 113, xxxvii.

36. William C. Wilkes and Mary M. Standifer, "Texas State Guard," *Handbook of Texas Online*, accessed 18 September 2013, http://www.tshaonline.org/handbook/online/articles/qqto1, uploaded 15 June 2010, published by the Texas State Historical Association.

37. Agnes Putnam, "Orange Guardsmen Are Inspired by Good Leaders and Will to Succeed," *Port Arthur News*, clipping, 21 March, no year given but probably 1942, Stark Foundation Archives.

38. H.J. Lutcher Stark, honorable discharge from the Texas Defense Guard, 12 May 1942, Stark Foundation Archives.

39. Putnam, "Orange Guardsmen Are Inspired by Good Leaders and Will to Succeed."

40. H.J.L. Stark, honorable discharge, 12 May 1942.

41. Laurence W. Hustmyre to H.J.L. Stark, 12 May 1942.

42. "Lutcher Stark Gets Himself Job Driving Dump Truck," clipping, unattributed, 26 May 1943, Stark Foundation Archives; "Truck Driver," clipping, undated, unattributed, Stark Foundation Archives.

43. R.H. Moodie to H.J.L. Stark, 26 May 1943.

44. Woods and Gatewood, *America Interpreted*, 799.

45. Fairchild, *They Called It the War Effort*, 207, 236.

46. Washington, conversation with Stiles, 28 February 2013.

47. Woods and Gatewood, *America Interpreted*, 800.

48. Hirasaki, Walls, and Orii, "The Kishi Colony" http://hirasaki.net/ Family_Stories /Kishi_colony/kishi; "Japanese Settler Left Mark on Area," *Orange Leader*, 25 July 1985; Robert Lopez, "Recalling Kishi," *Beaumont Enterprise*, 10 October 2004.

49. Hirasaki, Walls, and Orii, "The Kishi Colony"; Lopez, "Recalling Kishi."

50. Correspondence re Kishi business affairs, 2 July 1923–2 October 1931, passim; Hirasaki, Walls, and Orii, "The Kishi Colony"; Lopez, "Recalling Kishi." Irrespective of their business dealings, the two families remained friendly through the years.

51. Hirasaki, Walls, and Orii, "The Kishi Colony"; correspondence re Kishi business affairs; telegram, Taro Kishi to Kichimatsu Kishi, 7 July 1931.

52. Hirasaki, Walls, and Orii, "The Kishi Colony."

53. Ibid.; "Japanese Settler Left Mark on Area."

54. Lopez, "Recalling Kishi."

55. Hirasaki, Walls, and Orii, "The Kishi Colony."

56. Lopez, "Recalling Kishi."

57. "Becky Havens, Noted Drum Major, Weds Homer Stark," *Beaumont Enterprise*, 28 March 1942.

58. "W.H. Stark II and Miss Dickens to Be Married," *Orange Leader*, 28 January 1943.

59. Stark Family Records, Stark Foundation Archives.

60. "Stark Weds Sister of Last Wife," *Austin American-Statesman*, 16 December 1943, Eugene C. Barker Texas History Collection (a division of the DBCAH).

61. Ibid.; "Miss Nelda Childers Becomes Bride of H.J.L. Stark at First Presbyterian Church," *Orange Leader*, 16 December 1943.

62. Eunice Robinson came to Orange in 1929 to teach school shortly after her graduation from the College of Industrial Arts. She met Nelda Childers at an alumni meeting and boarded with the Childers family, eventually becoming like a third sister to Nelda and Ruby. In 1936, the latter recommended her for the position of bookkeeper at the Vinton Petroleum Company, where she met her future husband, Charles Haight Benckenstein, manager of Vinton. (She also kept Lutcher Stark's personal accounts.) She married Benckenstein October 24, 1943. Ibid.; Eunice Robinson Benckenstein, Oral History Interview, by Ellen Rienstra, Stark Foundation Offices, 8 October 2003, 2–6, Stark Foundation Archives; "Miss Eunice Robinson and C.H. Benckenstein Marry," *Orange Leader*, clipping, no date, Stark Foundation Archives.

63. Nelda stood five feet, seven inches tall, with brown, wavy hair and hazel eyes, and favored tailored, understated clothing styles. Around the time of Ruby's death she had grown quite thin, according to family nurse and friend Ollie Drake, from nursing her sister throughout the last days of her illness. In writing to Nelda after Ruby's death, Drake scolded Nelda because her entire breakfast often consisted of a Coca-Cola, a drink she favored throughout her life. Drake also commented in the letter regarding Nelda's habit of writing her personal letters on gray stationery in green ink (green was her favorite color), another of her lifelong practices. Fred Gregory, conversation with Ellen Rienstra, Stark Foundation offices, 27 January 2005, Stark Foundation Archives; identification card issued to Nelda Childers by Port Capt. James H. Marsh, Port Arthur, Texas, 23 July 1942, Stark Foundation Archives; Ollie Drake O'Grady to Nelda Childers, 15 July 1942; summary of interview with Nelda C. Stark, 15 March 1990, Stark Foundation Archives.

64. Eunice Robinson Benckenstein, Oral History Interview, conducted by Jo Ann Stiles and Ellen Rienstra, Stark Foundation offices, 29 March 2004, Stark Foundation Archives.

65. Wright, conversation with Stiles and Rienstra, 18 April 2005.

66. Summary of interview with Nelda C. Stark.

67. Benckenstein, Oral History Interview, 9 October 2003.

68. Anita Cowan Papers, Stark Foundation Archives.

69. Some also called Nelda "Scout," and many called her "Blossom" or "Orange Blossom," a nickname given her during her college years. Anita Cowan Papers; Dr. Stanley Cox to Nelda Childers, 13 July 1942; Nelda Childers, correspondence, sympathy letters following Ruby Stark's death 12 July 1942, passim.

70. Anita Cowan Papers.

71. Ibid.; Stark family photos, Stark Foundation Archives.

72. Sometime shortly after Lutcher Stark's death, Nelda underwent major surgery to remove a substantial part of her colon, apparently a result of her childhood accident. "I certainly hope this clears up her trouble," Mary Cowan wrote Anita. Eunice Benckenstein, Oral History Interview, 8 October 2003; Mary Robinson Cowan to Anita Cowan, undated but soon after Lutcher Stark's death, 2 September 1965.

73. "Lutcher Stark Boys Band of Orange to Leave on Southwest Texas Tour Today," *Beaumont Enterprise*, 16 June 1925.

74. Photograph, Lutcher Stark's Boys Band on top of Pike's Peak, playing "On Top of the World," 15 June 1926, Stark Foundation Archives.

75. "'Fish' Organize Orchestra," clipping, undated and unattributed but probably from the CIA campus newspaper, Stark Foundation Archives. The orchestra consisted of the director and three other members, playing piano, saxophone, and violin.

76. Diploma, Nelda Childers, bachelor of science, College of Industrial Arts, 2 June 1930, Stark Foundation Archives; Mamie Litchfield Childers, diary, 1929–1941, Stark Foundation Archives; Benckenstein, Oral History Interview, 8 October 2003, 7; summary of interview with Nelda C. Stark; Gregory, conversation with Rienstra, 27 January 2005.

77. Summary of interview with Nelda C. Stark.

78. "Stark Weds Sister of Last Wife"; Benckenstein, Oral History Interview, 8 October 2003, 8; "Nelda Childers Married to H.J.L. Stark, Orange Capitalist, Today," *Port Arthur News*, 16 December 1943.

79. Summary of interview with Nelda C. Stark.

80. Ibid.

81. Memorandum, "Dorothea Dix" (Eunice Benckenstein) to H.J.L. Stark, "Subject: Behavior," Stark Foundation Archives.

82. Anita Cowan Papers; summary of interview with Nelda C. Stark.

83. Summary of interview with Nelda C. Stark.

84. "Miss Nelda Childers Becomes Bride of H.J.L. Stark at First Presbyterian Church."

85. Summary of interview with Nelda C. Stark.

86. Nita Hill Stark, will, 21 June 1939, filed 6 November 1939, Orange County Probate Court, copy in Stark Foundation Archives.

87. Nelda Stark to Eunice Benckenstein, 28 December 1943.

88. Shortly before her death, Ruby's malignancy had metastasized to her right pelvis and right femur. Anita Cowan Papers, citing Ruby Childers Stark's death certificate; Nelda Stark to Eunice Benckenstein, 1 January 1944.

89. H.J.L. Stark to Tommy Hughes, 21 January 1944.

90. "B" classification was issued for passenger cars that were allowed a supplemental ration.

91. H.J.L. Stark to Tommy Hughes, 21 January 1944.

92. Ibid.

93. Ibid.

94. Ibid.

95. Summary of interview with Nelda C. Stark.

96. H.J.L. Stark to Homer Stark, 12 January 1944.

97. Ibid.

98. Ibid., 8 August 1944.

99. Raymond Brooks and Margaret Mayer, "Charges, Accusations and Denials Fly in Long Probe before Senators," *Austin American*, 18 November 1944.

100. Historian George Norris Green has stated that "at least five of the regents were Texas Regulars"—extremely conservative Democrats opposed to Roosevelt and the New Deal. Green, *The Establishment in Texas Politics*, 87.

101. Orville Bullington, "Reasons for My Vote," in Rainey, *The Tower and the Dome*, 63.

102. Senate Education Committee, investigation, hearings, 2:571; Green, *The Establishment in Texas Politics*, 88.

103. Smith, Busby, and Hopper, "The Controversy at the University of Texas," 8, citing letter regarding two of the incidents between Rainey and the Board of Regents from Ralph Himstead, executive secretary of the American Association of University Professors, to Chairman John H. Bickett of the Board of Regents, 16 July 1943, stating that Himstead had submitted his letter to the Board of Regents asking for correction of errors and they had made no correction. Smith pronounced Himstead's account of the two incidents "as accurate as we are likely to have."

104. J.R. Parten, testimony, "An Educational Crisis: A Summary of Testimony before a Senate Committee Investigating the University of Texas Controversy," 15–28 November 1944, 11, DBCAH. Parten's complete testimony can be found in J.R. Parten, "The University of Texas Controversy: Statement," in Texas State Archives and DBCAH, Box 2-23/1079.

105. Carleton, *A Breed So Rare*, 232–233.

106. Homer P. Rainey, statement to UT faculty, 12 October 1944, draft, UT Presidents' Records, 4R126, DBCAH; Rainey, *The Tower and the Dome*, 39–54.

107. Carleton, *A Breed So Rare*, 233.

108. Smith, Busby, and Hopper, "The Controversy at the University of Texas," 6.

109. Carleton, *A Breed So Rare*, 236–237, 301.

110. Smith, Busby, and Hopper, "The Controversy at the University of Texas," 7.

111. Ibid., 5.

112. Actually, four economics instructors from the university were present at the meeting, but one, a visiting professor from Antioch College, left the university shortly after the incident.

113. Smith, Busby, and Hopper, "The Controversy at the University of Texas," 6, 9.

114. Ibid., 10, citing University of Texas System, Board of Regents, "Rules and Regulations of the Board of Regents for the Government of the University of Texas," *University of Texas Bulletin* 3631 (15 August 1936).

115. Carleton, *A Breed So Rare*, 10.

116. Smith, Busby, and Hopper, "The Controversy at the University of Texas," 10.

117. Ibid.; Rainey, *The Tower and the Dome*, 43.

118. Smith, Busby, and Hopper, "The Controversy at the University of Texas," 11.

119. Rainey, statement to UT faculty; Rainey, *The Tower and the Dome*, 44.

120. Smith, Busby, and Hopper, "The Controversy at the University of Texas," 12.

121. Rainey, statement to UT faculty; Rainey, *The Tower and the Dome*, 42; Rainey, testimony, Senate Education Committee, investigation, hearings, I:134.

122. Margaret Mayer, "Senate Investigation Goes into Dispelling Rumors on Rainey," *Austin American*, 17 November 1944.

123. Smith, Busby, and Hopper, "The Controversy at the University of Texas," 12, citing Rainey, letter to faculty committee on tenure, 13 July 1944.

124. Bullington, "Reasons for My Vote," 65, 72; Carleton, *A Breed So Rare*, 302.

125. Smith, Busby, and Hopper, "The Controversy at the University of Texas," 12.

126. Ibid., 13.

127. Ibid., 13–14.

128. Rainey, *The Tower and the Dome*, 92.

129. Smith, Busby, and Hopper, "The Controversy at the University of Texas," 14–15; Rainey, *The Tower and the Dome*, 43.

130. Rainey, *The Tower and the Dome*, 43.

131. Ibid., 92.

132. "2 High Groups Take Up UT Fight," *Austin American*, 11 November 1944.

133. Rainey, *The Tower and the Dome*, 52.

134. Smith, Busby, and Hopper, "The Controversy at the University of Texas," 16.

135. Carleton, *A Breed So Rare*, 304–305.

136. Rainey, statement to UT faculty.

137. Ibid.

138. Ibid.

139. Smith, Busby, and Hopper, "The Controversy at the University of Texas," 18.

140. Rainey, *The Tower and the Dome*, 55.

141. "'Won't Comment,' Says Stark," *Daily Texan*, 17 October 1944.

142. Carleton, *A Breed So Rare*, 306; Smith, Busby, and Hopper, "The Controversy at the University of Texas," 18.

143. Regents' Minutes, 1944, passim; Parten, testimony, "An Educational Crisis," 12; Carleton, *A Breed So Rare*, 306.

144. Carleton, *A Breed So Rare*, 306.

145. Parten, testimony, "An Educational Crisis," 12.

146. Rainey, *The Tower and the Dome*, 59–62, text of statement by W.H. Francis, chairman of the Texas Ex-Students Executive Council, and resolution by the council regarding the Rainey matter; Carleton, *A Breed So Rare*, 306–307.

147. Carleton, *A Breed So Rare*, 306–307; Smith, Busby, and Hopper, "The Controversy at the University of Texas," 19.

148. Carleton, *A Breed So Rare*, 306–307.

149. Ibid., 322; Green, *the Establishment in Texas Politics*, 88.

150. Smith, Busby, and Hopper, "The Controversy at the University of Texas," 18.

151. "Bullington Denies Charges," *Austin American*, 12 November 1944.

152. Rainey, *The Tower and the Dome*, 58.

153. Ibid., 60, 61, 62, 116.

154. Green, *The Establishment in Texas Politics*, 87; Rainey, *The Tower and the Dome*, 58; Smith, Busby, and Hopper, "The Controversy at the University of Texas," 19.

155. Smith, Busby, and Hopper, "The Controversy at the University of Texas," 20.

156. Rainey, *The Tower and the Dome*, 62, 77.

157. Smith, Busby, and Hopper, "The Controversy at the University of Texas," 20; Bullington, "Reasons for My Vote," 64.

158. Bullington, "Reasons for My Vote," 65, 72.

159. Smith, Busby, and Hopper, "Controversy at the University of Texas," 21.

160. Ibid., citing Bullington's testimony before the Senate Education Committee investigation hearings.

161. Ibid., 21–23; Rainey, *The Tower and the Dome*, 56.

162. Smith, Busby, and Hopper, "The Controversy at the University of Texas," 21–23; Rainey, *The Tower and the Dome*, 56; Carleton, *A Breed So Rare*, 311–313.

163. Carleton, *A Breed So Rare*, 312.

164. Smith, Busby, and Hopper, "The Controversy at the University of Texas," 22.

165. Mayer, "Senate Investigation Goes into Dispelling Rumors on Rainey."

166. Rainey, *The Tower and the Dome*, 42 (emphasis added).

167. Testimony of Roy Bedichek before the Senate Education Committee, 28 November 1944, 4:606–617; testimony of Homer Rainey before the Senate Education Committee, 28 November 1944, 1:156–245.

168. Owens and Grant, *Letters of Roy Bedichek*, 248.

169. *1937 Orange Peel*, Orange High School's yearbook, 52, Stark Foundation Archives.

170. Senate Education Committee, investigation, hearings, 1:554; Rainey, *The Tower and the Dome*, 81–82.

171. "2 High Groups Take Up UT Fight."

172. Smith, Busby, and Hopper, "The Controversy at the University of Texas," 23.

173. Ibid., 25; Carleton, *A Breed So Rare*, 321.

174. George N. Green, "Rainey, Homer Price," *Handbook of Texas Online*, accessed 14 December 2014, http://www.tshaonline.org/handbook/online/articles/fra54, uploaded on June 15, 2010, published by the Texas State Historical Association.

175. Smith, Busby, and Hopper, "The Controversy at the University of Texas," 31–32; Rainey, *The Tower and the Dome*, 135–136.

176. Rainey, *The Tower and the Dome*, 135–136; Green, *The Establishment in Texas Politics*, 89.

177. Rainey, *The Tower and the Dome*, 45–46.

178. "At Least 4 Coke Selectees Unavailable for Regent Posts; Exes Again Ask Consultation," *Austin American*, 14 November 1944.

179. Brooks and Mayer, "Charges, Accusations and Denials Fly in Long Probe before Senators," *Austin American*, 18 November 1944.

180. W.B. Simmons to Ed Olle, business manager for the Department of Athletics, 15 December 1944; Fannie Ratchford to H.J.L. Stark, 21 December 1944. In one instance, he had apparently been paying the salaries of the students who worked in the Miriam Lutcher Stark Library, delivering a regular check to the Department of Intercollegiate Athletics, but as of December 1944, he notified Ed Olle that the check authorized by him for August 1 through November 30, 1944, would be the final one.

181. Arno "Shorty" Nowotny to H.J.L. Stark, 23 April 1945.

182. Joe Frantz, *Forty-Acre Follies*, 82.

183. Ibid., 808–809.

184. H. Williams, *Gateway to Texas*, 171.

185. H. Williams, *Picturing Orange*, 207.

186. Tommy Hughes to H.J.L. Stark, 29 August 1945.

187. Eri Kull to Mrs. and Mr. Stark, 21 August 1946.

188. H. Williams, *Gateway to Texas*, 174.

189. H. Williams, *Picturing Orange*, 195, 198; "H.J.L. Stark Donates $250,000 in Real Estate to City Schools," *Orange Leader*, 24 December 1942; H. Williams, *Gateway to Texas*, 173. The three major shipyards—Weaver, Levingston, and Consolidated—survived the postwar decrease in demand for warships to turn out other types of ships—tugs, barges, offshore drilling rigs, shrimp boats, pilot boats, etc.—and other products.

190. H.J.L. Stark to Homer Stark, 21 January 1944.

191. E-mail, Rachel G. Harbuck, plant administration, DuPont Sabine River Works, to

Ellen Rienstra, October 2009; H. Williams, *Gateway to Texas*, 173; Don Hinga, "Orange: Industrial Giant on the Gulf," *Texas Parade*, October 1953, 16.

192. Not all business entities found Lutcher to be so cooperative; a September 1945 letter from P.A. Mattingly, vice president of Levingston Shipbuilding Company, refers to his previous meeting with Lutcher regarding Levingston's desire to purchase the former's stock in Sabine Supply Company. "It was our impression," Mattingly wrote, "that you have no particular desire to sell your stock in Sabine Supply. . . . This situation implies an attractive premium which we feel unwilling at this time to offer." P.A. Mattingly to H.J.L. Stark, 27 September 1945.

Mattingly's letter also reflects Lutcher's postwar fears regarding the future of the United States and the Southeast Texas region, which he had evidently aired during the meeting. Mattingly wrote: "We do not believe that our nation nor this community shall experience a revolution or even wild inflation. We truly believe in the American people. In many respects our views parallel your own, but apparently your view of the future and resulting ideas of values are a great deal different than our own." Apparently, the always-outspoken Lutcher was still holding forth on certain of his long-held conservative tenets.

193. Robert W. Akers, "It's like This . . . ," *Beaumont Enterprise*, 13 December 1952.

194. *Hospital Site Deed Signing*, photograph, *Orange Leader*, 23 May 1954; H. Williams, *Gateway to Texas*, 175–176.

Chapter 12

1. J.C. Watkins, "Shangri-La in the 'Jungle,'" *Houston Chronicle Rotogravure Magazine*, 29 May 1955.

2. Editorial, *Orange Leader*, 9 September 1965, on the occasion of Stark's death.

3. David Wallace, *Hollywoodland* (New York: St. Martin's Press, 2002), 131–132.

4. A paperback edition of *Lost Horizon*, which was published as Pocket Books No. 1, the first title launched by the company for its revolutionary new mass-market paperback line, was found in Lutcher's personal library. According to most sources, *Lost Horizon* introduced a new word to the language: "Shangri-La." In an article in the *American Camellia Yearbook 1953*, Lutcher Stark asserted that *his* Shangri-La had been named long before "a certain person [probably Franklin Roosevelt, who named his Maryland presidential retreat 'Shangri-La' in 1942] appropriated this name for a hideout." When that happened, according to the article, Lutcher "gave serious thought to the need for selecting another name. After serious consideration, it was decided that the name should be retained." Sam Harn, "Lutcher Stark, Shangri-La, Orange, Texas," *American Camellia Yearbook 1953*, 268, copy of article in Stark Foundation Archives.

5. Michael Hoke, first managing director of Shangri La Botanical Gardens and Nature Center, Orange, Texas, conversation with Ellen Rienstra and Roy Wingate, 25 February 2005, Stark Foundation Archives.

6. *Shangri-La*, official booklet, text by Constance Kleiser, reprinted in *Las Sabinas* 24, no. 4 (1998): 1, Stark Foundation Archives.

7. John Staub to H.J.L. Stark, 17 November 1939.

8. H.J.L. Stark to John Staub, 21 November 1939.

9. Amy Bria, "Assessing Eden," *Beaumont Enterprise*, interview with Michael Hoke, clipping, undated, Stark Foundation Archives.

10. Payroll lists for work in W.H. Stark Survey (Shangri-La), 1942, passim, Stark Foundation Archives; Lutcher Stark's "*Shangri-La*," official booklet; Vera Browning, "Over 11,000

Persons Visit Shangri-La, Famous Stark Garden, during Season," *Port Arthur News*, 5 April 1948.

11. Felix Anderson, conversation with Stiles and Rienstra, Stark Foundation offices, 17 November 2004; Hoke, conversation with Rienstra and Wingate, 25 February 2005. Much later, Lutcher Stark told Anderson, who worked on road construction in Shangri-La, that the "NL 13" on Lutcher's license plates, standing for "Nelda Lutcher 13" and displaying their lucky number, also represented the thirteen miles of road he had built in the gardens.

12. Ibid.

13. E-mail, Michael Hoke, Orange, Texas, 9 November 2013, to Ellen Rienstra, citing a conversation with Eunice Benckenstein, in which she told him that Ruby Lake was named for Ruby Childers Stark, Lutcher Stark's second wife, who died July 12, 1942, the year that formal construction began on Shangri-La and during the building of Ruby Lake.

14. Affidavit, H.J. Lutcher Stark, 24 July 1942, stating that he would use legal methods in hauling black bass, perch, and crappie from Louisiana for the purpose of stocking Lake Ruby. Stark Foundation Archives.

15. Anderson, conversation with Stiles and Rienstra.

16. Hoke, conversation with Rienstra and Wingate.

17. Wingate, Oral History Interview, 13 February 2004, 24.

18. Ann Raborn Graves, Oral History Interview, conducted by Jo Ann Stiles, Austin, 1 March 2004, Stark Foundation Archives. Graves was the daughter of George Raborn, long-time Stark family friend and manager of the Orange Cameron Land Company.

19. Benckenstein's husband, Charles Haight Benckenstein, died August 5, 1946. Eunice Robinson Benckenstein, Oral History Interview with Ellen Rienstra, Stark Foundation offices, 8 October 2003, 23, and 9 October 2003, 14, Stark Foundation Archives.

20. Harn, "Lutcher Stark, Shangri-La, Orange, Texas," 269. This azalea was featured in the 1934 historical novel *So Red the Rose*, by Stark Young, in which the bush was burned down by Union troops along with the plantation house where it was located. It then sprouted again from the roots. "New Plantings to Add Color to Texas' Most Famous Flower Gardens at Orange," clipping, undated, unattributed, Stark Foundation Archives.

21. Harn, "Lutcher Stark, Shangri-La, Orange, Texas," 269.

22. Ibid., 270; "This is Shangri-La," no author, *Home Gardening*, March 1950, clipping, Stark Foundation Archives.

23. "New Plantings to Add Color to Texas' Most Famous Flower Gardens at Orange."

24. Hoke, conversation with Rienstra, 25 February 2005; Arthur Black, "Memories of Shangri-La," *Las Sabinas* 25, no. 4 (1988): 67. The geese migrated to a spot behind Chemical Row, where they now nest. The colony is the only native population of snow geese in Texas.

25. Anderson, conversation with Stiles and Rienstra.

26. "City's Newest Attraction for Tourists Is Herd of 13 Genuine Longhorn Cattle," *Orange Leader*, 20 January 1952; Watkins, "Shangri-La in the 'Jungle'"; latter article also in *Las Sabinas* 25, no. 4 (1998): 17.

27. Sherri Lindsey Lee, conversation with Jo Ann Stiles and Ellen Rienstra, 22 November 2013.

28. Anderson, conversation with Stiles and Rienstra.

29. Ibid.

30. Harn, "Lutcher Stark, Shangri-La, Orange, Texas," 268.

31. H.J.L. Stark to A.B. Agan, 10 February 1956, Stark Foundation Archives.

32. Robert Hankins, "Rekindled Tranquility,"" *Beaumont Enterprise*, 11 March 2008.

33. Hoke, conversation with Rienstra and Wingate.

34. Browning, "Over 11,000 Persons Visit Shangri-La."

35. Howard Williams, "The Bell That Doesn't Ring," *Las Sabinas* 19, no. 3, cited in *Las Sabinas* 25, no. 4 (1988): 64.

36. The bell is now mounted near the entrance of the modern incarnation of the gardens, the Shangri La Botanical Gardens and Nature Center. It was rung at the new Shangri La's opening ceremonies in 2008. Robert Hankins, "Mossed Horizons," *Beaumont Enterprise*, 12 March 2008.

37. Harn, "Lutcher Stark, Shangri-La, Orange, Texas," 268.

38. Jeremiah "Jerry" Stark (son of Alford P. Stark) to H.J.L. Stark, 16 September 1951.

39. "The Rare Historical Hygieostatic Bat Roost—Orange Has One," *Las Sabinas* 25, no. 4 (1998): 55–62.

40. Mari Murphy, "Dr. Campbell's 'Malaria-Eradicating, Guano-Producing Bat Roosts,'" *Bats Magazine* 7, no. 2 (Summer 1989), Bat Conservation International, http://www.batcon.org/resources/media-education/bats-magazine/bat_article/386.

41. Kevin J. Dwyer, "Maybe They Were All at the Batcave," *Beaumont Enterprise*, clipping, undated, Stark Foundation Archives; Hoke, conversation with Rienstra and Wingate. Hoke tells the story that Lutcher Stark brought a number of bats into Shangri-La. Since the bats were lying immobile in the crates in which they arrived, the workers, believing they were dead, threw them into the lake.

42. "New Plantings to Add Color to Texas' Most Famous Flower Gardens at Orange."

43. In 1947, Clyde V. McKee Jr. and his wife, Mary Louise Bevil McKee, moved to Orange when he began work with Williams, Lee, Kennerly, and Cameron, a Houston law firm representing the Stark interests. In the 1950s he formed his own law firm with Frank Hustmyre, then shortly thereafter left the firm to become in-house business manager and general counsel for the Stark family enterprises.

44. Mary Louise McKee, Oral History Interview, conducted by Jo Ann Stiles and Ellen Rienstra, 19 December 2003, Orange, 11, Stark Foundation Archives.

45. Hoke, conversation with Rienstra and Wingate.

46. "This Is Shangri-La."

47. Browning, "Over 11,000 Persons Visit Shangri-La"; Anderson, conversation with Stiles and Rienstra, 17 November 2004.

48. Anderson, conversation with Stiles and Rienstra. Through time, according to Michael Hoke, the hill gradually became a lakeside island.

49. Ibid.

50. Louis Davis, conversation with Jo Ann Stiles, Shangri La Botanical Gardens and Nature Center, 2 May 2011. Davis later became a security guard at the modern Shangri La.

51. Anita Cowan, Oral History Interview, conducted by Ellen Rienstra, Stark Foundation offices, 12 December 2003, 4, Stark Foundation Archives.

52. Anderson, conversation with Stiles and Rienstra.

53. Lorentz Kafka, conversation with Jo Ann Stiles, Stark Foundation offices, 22 January 2010, Stark Foundation Archives.

54. *Shangri-La*, official booklet. In the book *Lost Horizon*, the enchanted valley of Shangri-La lay at the foot of a twenty-eight thousand–foot mountain called Karakal, which Hilton translated as "Blue Moon."

55. Kafka, conversation with Stiles.

56. "Lorentz Kleiser, Made Tapestries," *New York Times*, 31 May 1963; "L. Kleiser, Artist, Dies in New York," *Orange Leader*, 30 May 1963; *Shangri-La*, official booklet.

57. Harn, "Lutcher Stark, Shangri-La, Orange, Texas."

58. Ibid.

59. Bascom Nelson, "UT Loses $4 Million Art," *Daily Texan*, 20 February 1953.

60. Herbert W. Winkelman to H.J.L. Stark, 21 February 1946.

61. Nelson, "UT Loses $4 Million Art."

62. "UT Apparently Has Lost Valuable Stark Collection," *Austin American*, 20 February 1953.

63. "Lutcher Starks Give $25,000 to TSCA [sic]," *Austin American*, 10 October 1953.

64. Nelson, "UT Loses $4 Million Art."

65. Benckenstein, Oral History Interview, 29 March 2004, 15; 9 October 2003, 4; 8 October 2003, 17.

66. John Cash Smith, conversation with authors, 4 February 2004.

67. Brown Claybar, conversation with Ellen Rienstra, 19 June 2006, Orange, Stark Foundation Archives.

68. Charlotte Bushnell Conn, Oral History Interview, conducted by Jo Ann Stiles and Ellen Rienstra, 19 December 2003, Orange, Stark Foundation Archives.

69. McKee, Oral History Interview, 11n.

70. Conn, Oral History Interview, 12 February 2004, 12; Benckenstein, Oral History Interview, 8 October 2003, 13.

71. Benckenstein, Oral History Interview, 9 October 2003, 3.

72. Ibid., 8 October 2003, 13.

73. Mary Louise Bevil McKee, Oral History Interview, conducted by Jo Ann Stiles and Ellen Rienstra, Orange, 9 February 2004, 8–9, Stark Foundation Archives.

74. Wright, conversation with Stiles and Rienstra, 18 April 2005.

75. Conn, Oral History Interview, 12 February 2004, 12–13.

76. Ibid., 13, 12; Gregory, conversation with Rienstra, 27 January 2005.

Chapter 13

1. Rives, "'Lutch' Stark Is Allergic to Money Idea," *Austin American-Statesman*, 22 September 1940.

2. Daniel Jost, "Peaceful as a Hurricane's Eye," *Landscape Architecture* 99, no. 9 (September 2009): 143.

3. Hoke, Oral History Interview, 15 February 2005.

4. Benckenstein, Oral History Interview, 9 October 2003.

5. Anderson, conversation with Stiles and Rienstra, 17 November 2004; Hoke, conversation with Rienstra and Wingate, 15 February 2005.

6. *Shangri-La*, official booklet.

7. Hoke, conversation with Rienstra and Wingate.

8. H.J. Lutcher Stark to Cullen Browning, editor of the *Orange Leader*, 9 July 1959.

9. DDT (dichlorodiphenyltrichloroethane) is an insecticide that at first saw universal usage in the United States but was subsequently banned in the wake of the 1962 publication of Rachel Carson's history-changing *Silent Spring*, which documented its negative impact on the environment.

10. McKee, Oral History Interview, 19 December 2003.

11. Julie Schimmel, "A New Museum for the American West," *American West: The Magazine of Western History* 16, no. 1 (January–February 1979): 38.

12. Ibid.

13. Sarah Boehme, curator of the Stark Museum of Art, "Buckeroos, Birds, and Blan-

kets: H.J. Lutcher Stark as Art Collector," lecture to Orange County Historical Society, 5 August 2014; Julie Schimmel, *The Art and Life of W. Herbert Dunton, 1878–1935* (Austin: University of Texas Press for the Stark Museum of Art, 1984).

14. E-mail, Sarah Boehme, curator of the Stark Museum of Art, to Ellen Rienstra, 21 January 2015.

15. Porter, Ebie, and Campbell, "Nelda and Lutcher Stark," 129, 132.

16. Ibid., 133.

17. E. Martin Hennings to H.J.L. Stark, 10 June 1952.

18. Julie Schimmel, *Stark Museum of Art: The Western Collection 1978* (Orange, TX: Nelda C. and H.J. Lutcher Stark Foundation, 1978); "The Stark Legacy," 152–153; Porter, Ebie, and Campbell, "Nelda and Lutcher Stark," 131; Sarah E. Boehme, "The Stark Museum," *Journal of the West* 22, no. 1 (1983): 69–73; Sarah E. Boehme, "The Stark Collection," *Southwest Art* 9, no. 12 (1980): 132–139; Bobby D. Weaver, *First Artistic Traditions: The Native American Collection of the Stark Museum of Art* (Orange, TX: Nelda C. and H.J. Lutcher Stark Foundation, 1990); David W. Hunt with Richard Hunter, "The Stark Museum," *American Art Review* 13, no. 6 (2009): 210–221. Among the many other artists whose works Lutcher eventually collected were George Catlin, Alfred Jacob Miller, John Mix Stanley, Bert G. Phillips, E.I. Couse, Leon Gaspard, Thomas Moran, Frank Tenney Johnson, N.C. Wyeth, Walter Ufer, and Fremont Ellis. Additional titles and information on the collections are available through the Stark Museum of Art, Orange, Texas.

19. Porter, Ebie, and Campbell, "Nelda and Lutcher Stark," 133–140.

20. Edythe Capriol, "Stark Acquires Original Audubon Bird Folio Set," *Beaumont Journal*, 16 June 1954; Ron Tyler, *Nature's Classics: John James Audubon's Birds and Animals* (Orange, TX: Nelda C. and H.J. Lutcher Stark Foundation, 1992), 29.

21. Stark Museum of Art, *The Steuben Glass Collection* (Orange, TX: Nelda C. and H.J. Lutcher Stark Foundation and the Stark Museum of Art, 1978); Jim Wrenn and Joan Wrenn, "Bowling Them Over: The Institute and the 'Americana Series,'" *Uncommon Sense* 122, pt. 1 (Summer 2006): 18–24, and 123, pt. 2 (Winter 2006): 33–36. The latter article explores the collaboration of the Omohundro Institute of Early American History and Culture and Steuben Glass on a project resulting in the United States in Crystal series, of which the only known complete set resides in the Stark Museum of Art.

22. Stark Museum of Art, *The American and British Birds of Dorothy Doughty* (Orange, TX: Nelda C. and H.J. Lutcher Stark Foundation and the Stark Museum of Art, 1978); Boehme, "Buckeroos, Birds, and Blankets."

23. Records, Stark Foundation Archives; "Starks Close Huge Land Deal," *Orange Leader*, 29 June 1956.

24. Records, Stark Foundation Archives.

25. "Starks Close Huge Land Deal."

26. Roy Wingate, conversation with Jo Ann Stiles and Ellen Rienstra, 16 November 2005, Stark Foundation Archives.

27. Ernest Hammond "Ernie" Willey, Oral History Interview, conducted by Jo Ann Stiles (Roy Wingate also present), Stark Foundation offices, 27 April 2004, 7–8, Stark Foundation Archives.

28. "New Sawmill Built at Orange," *Texas Forest News* 35 (September–October 1958): 5.

29. Clyde Baser, "Feasibility of Scientific Forest Conservation Demonstrated in Experiment by Orange Lumber Firm," *Beaumont Enterprise*, 20 March 1949.

30. Ibid.

31. Willey, Oral History Interview, 19 December 2003, 8.

32. Nelda Stark served on the Texas Woman's University Board of Regents from 1955 to 1973, at which time she resigned. Texas Woman's University Archives.

33. "Men's Athletics Hall of Honor," http://texassports.com/sports/2013/7/30/GEN_0730134509.aspx?path=general (accessed 29 October 2015).

34. "4 to Be Enshrined Tonight in Longhorn Hall of Fame," *Austin American*, 26 November 1958.

35. Wick Temple, "UT's Hall of Honor Adds 4 More Figures," *Austin American*, 27 November 1958.

36. Ibid.

37. M.L. Graves, M.D., to Lutcher Stark, 10 March 1937.

38. John A. Guinn to H.J. Lutcher Stark, 16 December 1958.

39. Arno Nowotny to H.J. Lutcher Stark, 26 November, 1958. Almost to the end of his life, Lutcher continued to receive recognition for his philanthropy; in 1963, Texas Woman's University, in gratitude for his generosity to the school, honored him with a Distinguished Service Award. "Lutcher Stark, 77, UT Benefactor, Dies," *Dallas Morning News*, 3 September 1965.

40. Telegram, Logan Wilson to H.J.L. Stark, 14 January 1959; telegram, H.J.L. Stark to Logan Wilson, 15 January 1959.

41. Harry Huntt Ransom to H.J.L. Stark, 9 November 1962.

42. "Constance and Lorentz Kleiser Say Au Revoir to Orange," *Orange Leader*, 19 May 1963.

43. Constance Kleiser to Lutcher and Nelda Stark and Eunice Benckenstein, 8 June 1963.

44. Barbara Akers, RN, Medical Record Summary for Henry Jacob Luther [sic] Stark, 22 June 1989, Stark Foundation Archives; "Death Claims Lutcher Stark," *Orange Leader*, 2 September 1965; "Heir of Lumber Fortune Dies," *Galveston News*, 3 September 1965.

45. Anita Cowan Papers.

46. Wright, conversation with Stiles and Rienstra, 18 April 2005.

47. Memorandum, summary of a conversation with Clyde McKee, 1 June 1990, Stark Foundation Archives, 6.

48. Eunice Benckenstein to Anita Cowan, 11 August 1964.

49. Memorandum re medical record summary for H.J.L. Stark, Barbara Akers, RN, 22 June 1989; Gregory, conversation with Rienstra, 27 January 2005; "Heir of Lumber Fortune Dies."

50. Memorandum re medical record summary for H.J.L. Stark.

51. "Heir of Lumber Fortune Dies"; "Death Claims Lutcher Stark"; "Lutcher Stark, 77, UT Benefactor, Dies"; "Funeral Scheduled Today for H.J. Lutcher Stark," *Orange Leader*, 3 September 1965; "H.J.L. Stark Dies at Age 77; Services Today," *Beaumont Enterprise*, 3 September 1965.

52. Ruth Robinson Murphy, Eunice Benckenstein's sister, to Anita Cowan, their niece, undated but between 14 June and 2 September 1965.

53. Medical record summary for H.J.L. Stark, 11; "Death Claims Lutcher Stark"; "Funeral Scheduled Today for H.J. Lutcher Stark"; "Lutcher Stark, Orange Philanthropist, Is Dead," clipping, undated, unattributed, Stark Foundation Archives.

54. "H.J.L. Stark Dies at Age 77; Services Today."

55. "A Century for Christ," First Presbyterian Church, Orange, Texas; "Heir of Lumber Fortune Dies."

56. Mary Robinson Cowan to Anita Cowan, undated but marked "Sunday Afternoon."

57. "Funeral Scheduled Today for H.J. Lutcher Stark."

58. Ruth Murphy to Eunice Benckenstein, undated but shortly after Lutcher Stark's death, Stark Foundation Archives.

59. Editorial, "H.J. Lutcher Stark," *Austin American-Statesman*, 5 September 1965.

60. Editorial, "Lutcher Stark," *Houston Post*, 4 September 1965.

61. Editorial, "Lutcher Stark, Philanthropist," *Dallas Morning News*, 3 September 1965.

62. Editorial, "Lutcher Stark," *Beaumont Journal*, 4 September 1965.

63. Editorial, "Lutcher Stark," *Beaumont Enterprise*, 4 September 1965.

64. Ibid.

65. Editorial, *Orange Leader*, 3 September 1965.

Epilogue

1. Summary of interview with Nelda C. Stark, 9 July 1990, 2, Stark Foundation Archives.

2. "Bulk of Stark's Fortune Left to Widow, Foundation," *Orange Leader*, 10 September 1965.

3. Henry Holcomb, "$78.2 Million Is Listed in Stark Estate Inventory," *Orange Leader*, 22 November 1966.

4. Joan Cummings, Oral History Interview, conducted by Ellen Rienstra, Stark Foundation offices, 13 April 2004.

5. Summary of interview with Nelda C. Stark.

6. A paper with superior strength manufactured by the "kraft method"—treatment of wood chips with certain chemicals to produce wood pulp.

7. Bob Axelson, "Lutcher, Moore Lumber Empire Sold," *Orange Leader*, 17 September 1970.

8. Ibid.

9. "Boise Southern Is Joint Venture," *Orange Leader*, 17 September 1970; "Multimillion-Dollar Sale Involves Toledo Land," clipping, undated and unattributed, Stark Foundation Archives; Axelson, "Major Milestone Marked in Lutcher & Moore's 108-Year History," *Orange Leader*, 17 September 1970.

10. Stark Foundation Archives.

11. "TWU Dormitory Will Be Named for Mrs. Stark," clipping, undated but probably early 1966, unattributed, Stark Foundation Archives.

12. Invitation, dedication ceremonies for Nelda C. Stark Hall, 11 December 1967, Stark Foundation Archives; "TWU to Name Dorm for Mrs. Nelda Stark," *Dallas Morning News*, 30 December 1965.

13. "University Pays Tribute to Mrs. Stark," *Denton Record-Chronicle*, 17 February 1974; "Special Service Citation Presented Mrs. Stark," clipping, undated, unattributed, Stark Foundation Archives.

14. Stark Cultural Venues, http://starkculturalvenues.org (accessed 29 October 2015).

15. Walter Riedel, conversation with Ellen Rienstra, 11 August 2014. Nelda dealt with the construction and building aspects of the restoration; Eunice, with the placement of furnishings, art, and art objects from a historical standpoint.

16. Anita Cowan Papers.

17. Odeen Martindill, Oral History Interview, by Ellen Rienstra, Stark Foundation offices, 12 December 2003, 15, 17, Stark Foundation Archives.

18. Ibid., 17–18.

19. Joan Cummings, Oral History Interview, by Ellen Rienstra, Stark Foundation offices, 13 April 2004, 12; Martindill, Oral History Interview, 17–18; Ruby Wimberley, Oral History Interview, by Ellen Rienstra, Stark Foundation offices, 9 March 2004, 4, 12n; all Oral History Interviews in Stark Foundation Archives. Joan Cummings baked many rice puddings for Nelda Stark during her last illness, and Ruby Wimberley periodically prepared fudge for her.

20. Wimberley, Oral History Interview, 12; Anita Cowan Papers.

21. Norma Clark, conversation with Jo Ann Stiles and Ellen Rienstra, Stark Foundation offices, 11 April 2007, Stark Foundation Archives.

22. E-mail, Walter Riedel to Ellen Rienstra, 4 September 2014, Stark Foundation Archives.

23. Gregory, conversation with Rienstra, 27 January 2005; Jackie Rudberg Leake, Oral History Interview, by Ellen Rienstra, by telephone, 1 February 2005. Gregory is the son of the Starks' former physician, Raymond L. Gregory.

24. Robert Risinger, conversation with Jo Ann Stiles, Roy Wingate, and Ellen Rienstra, Stark Foundation offices, 13 April 2005.

25. Ibid.; Gregory, conversation with Rienstra; e-mail, Walter Riedel to Ellen Rienstra, 11 August 2014, Stark Foundation Archives. The 1938 and 1939 documents in the Stark Foundation offices refer to Lake Roslyn Dam, Lake Roslyn Project, and Lake Roslyn Reservoir. In a 1960 office memo, Lutcher Stark refers to it as Roslyn Lake. A few sources refer to it as Lake Ruby or Ruby Lake, but no explanation or corroboration of that name has been found to date. Stark Foundation Archives.

26. Gregory, conversation with Rienstra.

27. Risinger, conversation with Stiles, Wingate, and Rienstra, 13 April 2005.

28. Gregory, conversation with Rienstra, 27 January 2005.

29. E-mail, Riedel to Rienstra, 4 September 2014.

30. Risinger, conversation with Stiles, Wingate, and Rienstra, 13 April 2005.

31. E-mail, Riedel to Rienstra, 4 September 2014.

32. Summary of interview with Nelda C. Stark, 15 March 1990, 7.

33. Anita Cowan Papers.

34. E-mail, Riedel to Rienstra, 11 February 2015.

35. Death certificate, William Henry Stark II, 25 September 1979; Plaintiffs' Fifth Amended Original Petition, Ida Marie Stark et al. vs. Nelda Childers Stark et al., 260th District Court, Orange County, Texas, 4; Richard Stewart, "Land Baron's Heirs Take Battle to Court," *Houston Chronicle*, 16 July 1989; Andrew Kirtzman, "Dynasty Feud in Orange—Starks Fight over Fortune," *Houston Post*, 6 March 1989; Debi Derrick, "Heirs Take Stark Foundation to Court," *Orange Leader*, 5 March 1989.

36. Plantiffs' Fifth Amended Original Petition, Ida Marie Stark et al. vs. Nelda Childers Stark et al.; Stewart, "Land Baron's Heirs Take Battle to Court"; Kirtzman, "Dynasty Feud in Orange"; Derrick, "Heirs Take Stark Foundation to Court."

37. Plaintiffs' Fifth Amended Original Petition, Ida Marie Stark et al. vs. Nelda Childers Stark et al.

38. Ibid.

39. Full, Final, and Complete Release, 260th Judicial District Court, Orange County, Texas, Ida Marie Stark et al. vs. Nelda C. Stark et al., 25 February 1991.

40. "Stark Evidence," *Forbes*, 7 January 1991.

41. Rose Ann Reeser, assistant attorney general of the State of Texas, and chief of the Charitable Trust Section, to the board of the Nelda C. and H.J. Lutcher Stark Foundation, 5 March 1991.

42. Margaret Toal, "Legal Fees Costly in Stark Fight," *Orange Leader*, 15 February 2003; Callahan, "Homer Stark Asks for Day in Court."

43. "E.W. Brown Jr. Makes Wheels of Business Spin," *Orange Leader*, Centennial Edition, 29 May 1936; Robinson, "Brown, Edgar William, Jr."

44. The Browns donated their previous home, a handsome redbrick building on Green Avenue, to the city. It now serves as the Orange City Hall.

45. "Pinehurst Is Real Show Place of South," *Orange Leader*, Centennial Edition, 29 May 1936; "Industries Are Varied—Native Son of Orange," clipping, undated, unattributed, Woman's Club Scrapbook, Heritage House, Orange, Texas.

46. "E.W. Brown Jr. Makes Wheels of Business Spin"; Robinson, "Brown, Edgar William, Jr."

47. H. Williams, *Picturing Orange*, 117; Robinson, "Brown, Edgar William, Jr."

48. Hart, Oral History Interview, 30 June 2004, 30.

49. Statement of Ben C. McDonough to Lloyd Biskamp, 1 September 1959, Stark Foundation Archives; Jane Brown, conversation with Jo Ann Stiles and Ellen Rienstra, Orange, 4 May 2006, Stark Foundation Archives.

50. Molly Brown, Oral History Interview, conducted by Jo Ann Stiles and Ellen Rienstra, Houston, 11 May 2006, Stark Foundation Archives; obituary, "Mrs. H. Lutcher Brown," clipping, unattributed, 30 May 1985, Stark Foundation Archives.

51. The family later donated the house and grounds to the University of Texas at San Antonio. In the early twenty-first century, the university sold it to private owners. Obituary, "Mrs. H. Lutcher Brown."

52. Roy Wingate, conversation with Jo Ann Stiles, Stark Office Building, 13 December 2005; Cynthia Carter Leedy Horn to Richard Dickerson, 22 May 2012.

53. Statement of Ben C. McDonough to Lloyd Biskamp, 1 September 1959, Stark Foundation Archives; "Olin Mathieson Buys Brown Paper Mill Co.," *New York Journal-American*, 9 July 1955.

54. "UTMB Receives Donation from Former Patient," clipping, unattributed, 30 August 1999, Stark Foundation Archives.

55. Gregory, conversation with Rienstra.

56. Cummings, Oral History Interview, 13 April 2004, 11.

57. Nelda C. Stark, Last Will and Testament, 9 August 1996, Orange County Records, County Clerk's Office, Orange County Courthouse, 16 December 1999.

58. Gregory, conversation with Rienstra.

59. Wright, conversation with Stiles and Rienstra, 18 April 2005.

60. Martindill, Oral History Interview, 7, 4, 15, 17.

61. Wimberley, Oral History Interview, 12.

62. Betty Em Wall Giarratano to Eunice Benckenstein, 15 December 1999.

63. "Nelda Stark: A Role Model for Us All," clipping, editorial, *Orange Leader*, undated but probably 14–16 December 1999, Stark Foundation Archives.

64. Gregory, conversation with Rienstra.

65. The H.J. Lutcher Stark Center for Physical Culture and Sports, http://www.stark center.org (accessed 29 October 2015).

66. Benckenstein v. Stark, Cause No. D-000298-C, 260th Judicial District Court, Orange County, Texas, 14 July 2000; William P. Barrett, "How Lawyers Get Rich," *Forbes*, 2 April 2001; John Cash Smith, "Stark Foundation Executors Respond," clipping, *Orange Leader*, undated but sometime after the spring of 2002, Stark Foundation Archives.

67. Benckenstein v. Stark, Cause No. D-000298-C (Original Petition for Declaratory Relief, 14 July 2000).

68. Succession of No. 15,405 H.J. Lutcher Stark, 14th Judicial District Court, Parish of

Calcasieu, Louisiana; Benckenstein v. Stark, Cause No. D-000298-C; Smith, "Stark Foundation Executors Respond."

69. Estate of Nelda C. Stark, Deceased; Cause No. 11,627, Orange County Court-at-Law, Orange County, Texas, 6 March 2001. (Homer Stark also filed a separate action in the 128th Judicial District Court of Orange County, Texas, Cause No. A-010631-C, on December 13, 2001; because Homer Stark's second lawsuit involved the same claims and parties as the first, the district court transferred the second lawsuit and consolidated it with the County Court-at Law claim.) Also see Holly Callahan, "Homer Stark Asks for Day in Court," *Orange County Record* 41, no. 9 (11 April 2001).

70. Benckenstein v. Stark, Cause No. D-000298-C (Order Granting Summary Judgment, 8 July 2002). See also Tex.R.Civ.P. 166. According to the Texas Supreme Court, "The purpose of the summary judgment procedure is to permit the trial court to promptly dispose of cases that involve unmeritorious claims or untenable defenses." City of Houston v. Clear Creek Basin Auth., 539 S.W.2d.671, 678 n. 5 (Tex. 1979).

71. Benckenstein v. Stark, Cause No. D-000298-C, Order Granting Summary Judgment; Smith, "Stark Foundation Executors Respond"; Margaret Toal, "Judge Rules in Favor of Stark Estate Executors," *Orange Leader*, 11 May 2002.

72. Benckenstein v. Stark, Cause No. D-000298-C (Order Granting Recovery of Attorneys' Fees and Costs, 13 February 2003); Margaret Toal, "Legal Fees Costly in Stark Fight."

73. Benckenstein v. Stark, Cause No. D-000298-C (Order Granting Recovery of Attorneys' Fees and Costs, 13 February 2003); Margaret Toal, "Legal Fees Costly in Stark Fight."

74. Succession of No. 15,405 H.J. Lutcher Stark, 14th Judicial District Court, Parish of Calcasieu, Louisiana (Final Judgment, 28 October 2003).

75. Ancillary Succession of H.J. Lutcher Stark, No. 04-323, Court of Appeals, Third Circuit, State of Louisiana, re appeal from the 14th Judicial District Court, Parish of Calcasieu, No. 15,405 (29 September 2004).

76. Stark v. Benckenstein, 156 S.W.3d 112 (Tex. App.—Beaumont 2004), review denied (10 June 2005), rehearing of petition for review denied (September 2005).

77. According to *Black's Law Dictionary*, the term "ex parte" means "by or done for one party" or "on one side only." *Black's Law Dictionary*, 6th ed. (St. Paul, MN: West Publishing, 1991). "A judicial proceeding . . . is said to be *ex parte* when it is taken or granted at the instance and for the benefit of one party only, and without notice to, or contestation by, any person adversely interested."

78. Ex Parte: Rebecca Nugent, et al., Petitioners, Cause No. A-010145-C in the 128th District Court of Orange County, Texas (16 March 2001).

79. Memorandum, H.J. Lutcher Stark, 27 May 1937, Stark Archives.

80. E-mail, Walter Riedel to Ellen Rienstra, 11 February 2015.

81. Certificate of Limited Partnership of Stark Ranch, LP, filed 2 November 2005, with the Office of the Secretary of State of Texas.

82. Personal Representatives' Deed dated 23 March 2006 from the Estate of Nelda Stark (Grantor) to Stark Ranch, LP (Grantee) and conveying the total acreage of Roslyn Ranch, Colorado, of 1451.056 acres, more or less.

83. General Warranty Deed dated 24 March 2006 from Stark Ranch, LP (Grantor), to Roslyn Ranch, LLC (Grantee), and conveying 1,211.055 acres of Roslyn Ranch, Colorado, more or less; and General Warranty Deed dated 24 March 2006 from Stark Ranch, LP (Grantor), to Willow Creek Ranches, LLC (Grantee), of 240 acres of Roslyn Ranch, Colorado, more or less. Both named grantees of the sale by Stark Ranch, LP, are Colorado limited liability companies, the members of which are not related in any way to the Homer Stark family.

84. "Student Names Tree 'Survivor,'" *Orange Leader*, 10 May 1998.

85. Suzanne Labry, "The Way to Shangri La," *Texas Gardener*, September/October 2010, 21. Michael Hoke had previously received the Presidential Award for Excellence in Science Teaching from President George H.W. Bush. He used his award money to fund the "Nature's Classroom" project, spurring the Stark Foundation to consider restoring the gardens. Hoke's "Nature's Classroom" program was so successful that in 2002, the foundation made the facility permanent.

86. "Student Names Tree 'Survivor.'"

87. Certificate and press release from the Texas Forest Service, Stark Foundation Archives.

88. Jost, "Peaceful as a Hurricane's Eye," 144, 146–147; Labry, "The Way to Shangri La," 21.

89. Jost, "Peaceful as a Hurricane's Eye," 147.

90. Ibid., 147–148, 148.

91. Stark Foundation Archives; Labry, "The Way to Shangri La," 21.

92. Carol Christian, "8 Years Ago, Seemingly All of Houston Evacuated Ahead of Hurricane Rita," *Houston Chronicle*, 24 September 2013.

93. Jost, "Peaceful as a Hurricane's Eye," 144; Labry, "The Way to Shangri La," 21.

94. Jost, "Peaceful as a Hurricane's Eye," 155.

95. Jamie Reid, "Rebuilding Paradise," *Beaumont Enterprise*, 7 January 2006.

96. Labry, "The Way to Shangri La," 21.

97. Becky Stark had predeceased her husband by two years, dying, in another strange coincidence, on December 13, 2006, the seventh anniversary of Nelda's death. Bill's widow, Ida Marie, the last of the four, died on November 19, 2008. Robert Hankins, "Stark Dies as Gardens Reopen," *Beaumont Enterprise*, 12 March 2008; "Homer H. [*sic*] Stark," obituary, *Orange Leader*, 12 March 2008; "Becky Havens Stark," obituary, *Orange Leader*, 14 December 2006; "Ida Marie Dickens Stark," obituary, *Orange Leader*, 1 November 2008.

98. Labry, "The Way to Shangri La."

99. Jost, "Peaceful as a Hurricane's Eye," 156.

100. Joe F. Combs, "Farm Corner," quoting Francis E. Schiller, who wrote a poem on Shangri-La after a visit, clipping, undated but probably from the *Beaumont Enterprise*, Stark Foundation Archives.

101. Ruby Childers Stark and Nelda Childers Stark, the sisters who were Lutcher Stark's successive wives, lie side by side in the Childers family plot on the eastern edge of the cemetery.

Bibliography

Archival Sources

Austin History Center, Austin, Texas
East Texas History Center, Stephen F. Austin State University, Nacogdoches, Texas
Dolph Briscoe Center for American History, University of Texas at Austin
Heritage House Museum and Library and Archives, Orange, Texas
James V. Brown Library, Williamsport, Pennsylvania
Legislative Reference Library of Texas
Lorenzo de Zavala State Library and Archives
Lycoming College Library, Williamsport, Pennsylvania
Mary and John Gray Library, Lamar University, Beaumont, Texas
Messiah Lutheran Church Archives, Williamsport, Pennsylvania
Nelda C. and H.J. Lutcher Stark Foundation Archives, Orange, Texas
Nettie Lee Benson Latin American Collection, University of Texas at Austin
Newton County Historical Society Archives
Orange Public Library, Orange, Texas
Texas Legislative Reference Library, Austin, Texas
Thomas T. Taber Museum of the Lycoming County Historical Society, Williamsport, Pennsylvania
Tyrrell Historical Library, Beaumont, Texas
Woodville Pioneer House Museum Family Archives

Newspapers and Magazines

Alcalde
American Lumberman
Austin American
Austin American-Statesman
Beaumont Enterprise
Beaumont Journal
Chicago Tribune
Daily Gazette and Bulletin (Williamsport, Pennsylvania)
Daily Texan (Austin, Texas)
Daily/Weekly Sun and Banner (Williamsport, Pennsylvania)

Dallas Morning News
Fort Worth Star-Telegram
Galveston Daily News
Houston Chronicle
Houston Post
Interscholastic Leaguer
Kansas City Star
Las Sabinas (Orange, Texas, Orange County Historical Society)
Lincoln County Sentinel (Lincoln, Kansas)
Lycoming Weekly Gazette (Williamsport, Pennsylvania)
Mountain Democrat (Placerville, California)
New Orleans Item
Northwestern Lumberman
Opportunity Valley News (Orange, Texas)
Orange County Record
Orange Leader
Orange Weekly Tribune
Port Arthur News
Southern Pacific Bulletin
St. Louis Lumberman
Town and Country (Williamsport, Pennsylvania)

Publications

Adair, A. Garland, with E.H. Perry Sr. *Austin and Commodore Perry*. Austin: Texas Heritage Foundation, 1956.

Alexander, Charles. *Crusade for Conformity: The Ku Klux Klan in the Southwest, 1920–1930*. Houston: Texas Gulf Coast Historical Association, 1962.

American Lumbermen. Vol. 2, *The Personal History and Public and Business Achievements of One Hundred Eminent Lumbermen of the United States, Second Series, Chicago: The American Lumberman*. Memphis: RareBooksClub.com, General Books, 2012.

Anderson, Stephen C. *J.W. Edgar: Educator for Texas*. Austin: Eakin Press, 1984.

Anonymous. *Texas Merry-Go-Round*. Houston: Sun Publishing, 1933.

"Antietam." Civil War Trust. Accessed 1 October 2015. http://www.civilwar.org/battlefields/antietam.html.

"Appomattox Court House." National Park Service, US Department of the Interior. Accessed 1 October 2015. http://www.nps.gov/apco/index.htm.

Ashworth, Kenneth. *Horns of a Dilemma: Coping with Politics at the University of Texas*. Austin: Dolph Briscoe Center for American History, 2011.

Bagwell, Tyler E. "Brunswick and the Mallory Line Steamship Company." Jekyll Island History. Accessed 1 October 2015. http://www.jekyllislandhistory.com/malloryline.shtml.

Baker, James Graham. *Julian Onderdonk in New York: The Lost Years, the Lost Paintings*. Denton: Texas State Historical Association, 2014.

Barry, John M. *The Great Influenza: The Epic Story of the Deadliest Plague in History*. New York: Penguin Books, 2005.

Beaumont: A Guide to the City and Its Environs. Work Projects Administration in the State of Texas, Federal Writers' Project, American Guide Series. Houston: Anson Jones Press, 1938.

Bedichek, Roy. *Educational Competition: The Story of the University Interscholastic League of Texas.* Austin: University of Texas Press, 1956.

Benedict, H. Y. "A Source Book Relating to the History of the University of Texas: Legislative, Legal, Bibliographical, and Statistical." *University of Texas Bulletin* 1757 (10 October 1917): 263.

Benziger, Marieli. *August Benziger: International Portrait Painter.* Ed. Janet Reberdy. Kansas City, MO: Society of the Sacred Heart by Sheed & Ward, 1993.

Berry, Margaret C. "Andrews, Jessie." *Handbook of Texas Online.* Accessed 27 November 2012. http://www.tshaonline.org/handbook/online/articles/fan20. Uploaded 9 June 2010. Published by the Texas State Historical Association.

———. "Bellmont, L. Theodore." *Handbook of Texas Online.* Accessed 18 September 2012. http://www.tshaonline.org/handbook/online/articles/fbeaa. Uploaded 12 June 2010. Published by the Texas State Historical Association.

———. "Benedict, Harry Yandell." *Handbook of Texas Online.* Accessed 10 January 2015. http://www.tshaonline.org/handbook/online/articles/fbe48. Uploaded 12 June 2010. Published by the Texas State Historical Association.

———. "Littlefield, Clyde." *Handbook of Texas Online.* Accessed 9 January 2015. http://www.tshaonline.org/handbook/online/articles/fli32. Uploaded 15 June 2010. Published by the Texas State Historical Association.

———. *The University of Texas: A Pictorial Account of Its First Century.* Austin: University of Texas Press, 1980.

Black's Law Dictionary. 6th ed. St. Paul, MN: West Publishing, 1991.

Blessington, J.P. *The Campaigns of Walker's Texas Division.* Austin: Pemberton Press, 1968.

Block, W.T. *Cotton Bales, Keelboats, and Sternwheelers: A History of the Sabine River and Trinity River Cotton Trades, 1837–1900.* Woodville, TX: Dogwood Press, 1996.

———. "The Lutcher & Moore Lumber Company." In *East Texas Mill Towns and Ghost Towns,* 1:261–266. Lufkin: Best of East Texas Publishers, 1994.

Bloomfield, Leonard. "Eduard Prokosch." *Language* 14, no. 4 (October–December 1938): 310–313.

Boehme, Sarah E. "The Stark Collection." *Southwest Art* 9, no. 12 (1980): 132–139.

———. "The Stark Museum." *Journal of the West* 22, no. 1 (1983): 69–73.

"Brackenridge, George Washington." *Handbook of Texas Online.* Accessed 2 March 2014. http://www.tshaonline.org/handbook/online/articles/fbr02. Uploaded 12 June 2010. Published by the Texas State Historical Association.

Bricker, Richard W. *Wooden Ships from Texas.* College Station: Texas A&M University Press, 1998.

Brooms, Harold W. "And Next We Have Lutcher Stark: Texas Alumnus, Whose Gifts to University and Fraternity Have Been Unstinted, Is Loyalty Epitomized." *Phi Gamma Delta* (April 1928).

Brown, Earl E. "Rafts on the West Branch." In *Commerce on Early American Waterways: The Transport of Goods by Arks, Rafts, and Log Drives,* 105–122. Jefferson, NC: McFarland, 2010.

Brown, Norman D. *Hood, Bonnet, and Little Brown Jug: Texas Politics, 1921–1928.* College Station: Texas A&M University Press, 1984.

Brown, Nugent E. *B Hall, Texas: Old Stories and Incidents of This Famous Dormitory.* San Antonio: Naylor, 1938.

"Building Living Monuments: Band and Drum Corps Training Is $165,000 Hobby to Lutch Stark." *Piano Trade Magazine* 37, no. 4 (April 1940).

Bullington, Orville. "Reasons for My Vote." In *The Tower and the Dome*, by Homer Price Rainey. Boulder, CO: Pruett Publishing, 1971.

Burchstead, Frederic F., and P. Lynn Denton. "Texas Memorial Museum." *Handbook of Texas Online*. Accessed 11 November 2014. http://www.tshaonline.org/handbook /online/articles/lbt02. Uploaded 15 June 2010. Published by the Texas State Historical Association.

Burke, James, Jr. *Burke's Texas Almanac and Immigrant's Handbook, 1881*. Houston: Compiled, printed, and published by James Burke Jr., 1881.

Burns, Chester. *Saving Lives, Training Caregivers, Making Discoveries: A Centennial History of the University of Texas Medical Branch at Galveston*. Austin: Texas State Historical Association, 2003.

Carleton, Don. *A Breed So Rare: The Life of J. R. Parten, Liberal Texas Oil Man, 1896–1992*. Austin: Texas State Historical Association in cooperation with the Center for American History, 1998.

———. *Red Scare! Right-Wing Hysteria, Fifties Fanaticism, and Their Legacy in Texas*. Austin: Texas Monthly Press, 1985.

Copp, Tara, and Robert L. Rogers, eds. *The Daily Texan: The First 100 Years*. Austin: Eakin Press, 1999.

Cotner, Robert C. *James Stephen Hogg: A Biography*. Austin: University of Texas Press, 1959.

Cox, Patrick. *The First Texas News Barons*. Austin: University of Texas Press, 2005.

"The Crescent Moon—a Symbol of Islam?" Aboutreligion.com. Accessed 28 November 2015. http://islam.about.com/od/history/a/crescent_moon.htm.

Crowley, Joseph N. *In the Arena: The NCAA's First Century in the Arena*. NCAA Publications. com. Accessed 1 October 2015. http://www.ncaapublications.com/p-4039-in-the-arena -ncaas-first-century.aspx.

Cullen, David O'Donald, and Kyle G. Wilkison, eds. *The Texas Left: The Radical Roots of Lone Star Liberalism*. College Station: Texas A&M University Press, 2010.

———. *The Texas Right: The Radical Roots of Lone Star Conservatism*. College Station: Texas A&M University Press, 2014.

Cuthbertson, Gilbert M. "Regulator-Moderator War." *Handbook of Texas Online*. Accessed 26 March 2014. http://www.tshaonline.org/handbook/online/articles/jcr01. Uploaded 15 June 2010. Published by the Texas State Historical Association.

Daniell, L.E. "Henry J. Lutcher, Orange." In *Texas—the Country and Its Men*. Austin: L.E. Daniell, Publishers, 1917.

Dettmer, David. "Benedicere Benedictus: A Profile of H.Y. Benedict." In *The Texas Book Two: More Profiles, History and Reminiscence of the University*, David Dettmer, ed., 53–55. Austin: University of Texas Press, 2012.

Divine, Robert A., ed. *America Past and Present*. Vol. 2, *Since 1865*. 9th ed. Boston: Longman Publishing, 2011.

Dobbs, Ricky F. *Yellow Dogs and Republicans: Allan Shivers and Texas Two-Party Politics*. College Station: Texas A&M University Press, 2005.

Duffy, Winifred Arndt. *John Wiley Link*. Houston: D. Armstrong, 1974.

Dugger, Ronnie. *Our Invaded Universities: Form, Reform, and New Starts*. New York: W.W. Norton, 1974.

"An Educational Crisis: A Summary of Testimony before a Senate Committee Investigating the University of Texas Controversy 15–28 November 1944." Dolph Briscoe Center for American History, University of Texas at Austin.

Eighth Annual Catalogue of the Officers and Students of Dickinson Seminary from 10 June 1855 to 10 June 1856. Williamsport, PA: Barrett & Butt, Printers, 1856. [Lycoming College (formerly Dickinson Seminary), Williamsport, Pennsylvania]

Evans, David S., and J. Derral Mulholland. *Big and Bright: A History of the McDonald Observatory*. Austin: University of Texas Press, 1986.

Fairchild, Louis. *They Called It the War Effort: Oral Histories from WWII Orange, Texas*. 2nd ed. Denton: Texas State Historical Association, 2012.

Farris, Linda B. "Making the World Safe for Democracy." In *Gateway to Texas*, ed. Howard Williams. Orange, TX: Heritage House Museum of Orange, 1986.

Fickle, James E. *The New South and the "New Competition": Trade Association Development in the Southern Pine Industry*. Champaign: University of Illinois Press, 1980.

Fitzhugh, Lester Newton. "Walker's Texas Division." *Handbook of Texas Online*. Accessed 28 February 2012. http://www.tshaonline.org/handbook/online/articles/qkw01. Uploaded 15 June 2010. Published by the Texas State Historical Association.

Fletcher, Alexander. *A Guide to Family Devotion*. London: Virtue, 1836.

Foree, Kenneth, Jr. "Archangel and His Bible." *Saturday Evening Post*, 9 October 1937.

Frantz, Joe B. *The Forty-Acre Follies: An Opinionated History of the University of Texas*. Austin: Texas Monthly Press, 1983.

Fricker, Donna. "Historic Context: The Louisiana Lumber Boom, c. 1880–1925." Fricker Historic Preservation Services, LLC. Accessed 1 October 2015. http://www.crt.state.la.us/Assets/OCD/hp/nationalregister/historic_contexts/The_Louisiana_Lumber_Boom_c1880-1925.pdf.

Gammel, H.P.N. *Gammel's Laws of Texas, 1822–1897*. Austin: Gammel Book Company, 1898.

Gould, Lewis. *Progressives and Prohibitionists: Texas Democrats in the Wilson Era*. Fred H. and Ella Mae Moore Texas History Reprint Series. Austin: Texas State Historical Association, 1992.

Gracy, David B., II. "Littlefield, George Washington." *Handbook of Texas Online*. Accessed 21 January 2014. http://www.tshaonline.org/handbook/online/articles/fli18. Uploaded 15 June 2010. Published by the Texas State Historical Association.

Green, George Norris. *The Establishment in Texas Politics: The Primitive Years, 1938–1957*. Norman: University of Oklahoma Press, 1979.

———. "Rainey, Homer Price." *Handbook of Texas Online*. Accessed 14 December 2014. http://www.tshaonline.org/handbook/online/articles/fra54. Uploaded 15 June 2010. Published by the Texas State Historical Association.

Hafertepe, Kenneth. *Abner Cook: Master Builder on the Texas Frontier*. Austin: Texas State Historical Association, 1992.

Haggard, John V. "Neutral Ground." *Handbook of Texas Online*. Accessed 1 July 2011. http://www.tshaonline.org/handbook/online/articles/nbn02. Uploaded 15 June 2010. Published by the Texas State Historical Association.

Hawthorne, Bobby. *Longhorn Football: An Illustrated History*. Austin: University of Texas Press, 2007.

Hendrickson, Kenneth E., Jr. *The Chief Executives of Texas from Stephen F. Austin to John B. Connally, Jr.* Number Fifty-Five: Centennial Series of the Association of Former Students, Texas A&M University. College Station: Texas A&M University Press, 1995.

Hilton, James. *Lost Horizon*. New York: William Morrow and Sons, 1933.

Hines, Pauline, ed. *Newton County Nuggets: A Collection of Stories by Newton County Folk*. Newton, TX: Newton County Historical Commission, 1986.

Hirasaki, George, Thomas K. Walls, and Kazuhiko Orii. "The Kishi Colony." Accessed 21 October 2015. http://hirasaki.net/Family_Stories/Kishi_Colony/Kishi.htm.

"History of Williamsport." City of Williamsport, 17 January 2012. http://www.cityofwilliamsport.org/History.php.

"A History of the Children's Hospital College Hill Campus." College Hill [Ohio] eNews-

letter Archive, 17 January 2007. http://chenewsletter.blogspot.com/2007/01/history-of
-children-hospitale-college.html.

Holland, Richard A. "Brackenridge, Littlefield, and the Shadow of the Past." In *The Texas
Book: Profiles, History, and Reminiscences of the University*, ed. Richard A. Holland, 85–
104. Austin: University of Texas Press, 2006.

Horn, Stanley F. *This Fascinating Lumber Business.* New York: Bobbs-Merrill, 1951.

Hunsinger, Lou, Jr. "James H. Perkins: Father of the Susquehanna Boom." News of Yester-
year: Historic Pennsylvania, 3 November 2008. https://newsofyesteryear.wordpress.com
/2008/11/03/james-h-perkins-father-of-the-susquehanna-boom/.

Hunt, David W., with Richard Hunter. "The Stark Museum." *American Art Review* 13, no. 6
(2009): 210–221.

"In Memoriam: L. Theo Bellmont, September 24, 1881–December 27, 1967." Accessed 1 October 2015. http://www.utexas.edu/faculty/council/2000-2001/memorials/SCANNED
/bellmont.pdf.

"In Memoriam: Mrs. Lutcher (Nita Hill) Stark." *Delta Kappa Gamma Bulletin* (January
1940): 15.

"The Influenza Pandemic of 1918." Accessed 1 October 2015. http:// virus.stanford.edu/uda/.

Isaac, Paul. "Beaumont, Texas, the Great Depression, 1929–1933." *Texas Gulf Historical and
Biographical Record* 14 (1978): 14–31.

"Jessie Andrews, Scholar and Poet, 1867–1919." Great Texas Women, University of Texas at
Austin. Accessed 19 November 2015. http://www.utexas.edu/gtw/andrews.php.

"John Stark, Soldier." Celebrate Boston. Accessed 1 October 2015. http://www.celebrate
boston.com/biography/john-stark.htm.

Johnson, Alvin. *Pioneer's Progress.* New York: Viking Press, 1952.

Joint Committee on Ceremonies of World's Columbian Commission and World's Columbian Exposition, ed. *Memorial Volume, Dedicatory and Opening Ceremonies of the World's
Columbian Exposition.* Chicago: Stone, Kastler & Painter, 1893.

Joint Legislative Committee on Organization and Economy. *The Government of the State of
Texas.* Part XII, "Education; The University of Texas and Its Branches; the College of Industrial Arts, the Texas College of Arts and Industries, and the Texas Technological College." Austin: Von Boeckman Jones, 1933.

Jones, Arthur Gray. *Thornton Rogers Sampson, D.D., LL.D: A Biographical Sketch.* San Antonio: Richmond Press, 1917.

Jones, Joseph. *Life on Waller Creek: A Palaver about History as Pure and Applied Education.*
Austin: AAR/Tantalus, 1982.

Jost, Daniel. "Peaceful as a Hurricane's Eye." *Landscape Architecture Magazine* 99, no. 9
(September 2009): 143.

Karppi, Frank. "Shipbuilding in Two Wars: Masters of the Sea." In *Gateway to Texas*, ed.
Howard Williams, 149–158. Orange, TX: Heritage House Museum of Orange, 1986.

Keller, Christian B. "Pennsylvania and Virginia Germans during the Civil War: A Brief History and Comparative Analysis." *Virginia Magazine of History and Biography*, Virginia
Historical Society. http://www.vahistorical.org/publications/Abstract_2092_KKeller
.htm (site discontinued).

Kelley, Mary L. *The Foundations of Texan Philanthropy.* College Station: Texas A&M University Press, 2004.

Key, V.O. *Southern Politics in State and Nation.* Knoxville: University of Tennessee Press,
1977.

Kirkland, Kate Sayen. *The Hogg Family and Houston: Philanthropy and the Civic Ideal.* Austin: University of Texas Press, 2009.

Kleiner, Diana J. "Bevilport, TX." *Handbook of Texas Online*. Accessed 16 April 2012. http://www.tshaonline.org/handbook/online/articles/hrb29. Uploaded 12 June 2010. Published by the Texas State Historical Association.

Labry, Suzanne. "The Way to Shangri La." *Texas Gardener*, September–October, 2010.

Lanza, Michael L. *Agrarianism and Reconstruction Politics: The Southern Homestead Act*. Baton Rouge: Louisiana State University Press, 1990.

Leuchtenburg, William E. *The Perils of Prosperity, 1914–1932*. 2nd ed. Chicago: University of Chicago Press, 1993.

"A Library for Latin America, Nettie Lee Benson Latin American Collection." http://www.conocimientoenlinea.com/content/view/556/ (site discontinued).

Linklater, Patricia. "East Texas Pine Industry." In *Tracks on the Land: Stories of Immigrants, Outlaws, Artists, and Other Texans Who Left Their Mark on the Lone Star State*, ed. David C. DeBoe and Kenneth B. Ragsdale, 88–97. Austin: Texas State Historical Association, 1985.

Linsley, Judith Walker, and Ellen Walker Rienstra. *Beaumont: A Chronicle of Promise*. Woodland Hills, CA: Windsor Publications, 1982.

Linsley, Judith Walker, Ellen Walker Rienstra, and Jo Ann Stiles. *Giant under the Hill: A History of the Spindletop Oil Discovery at Beaumont, Texas, in 1901*. Austin: Texas State Historical Association, 2002.

Lomax, John A. *Will Hogg, Texan*. Austin: University of Texas Press, 1956.

Long, Christopher. "University Interscholastic League." *Handbook of Texas Online*. Accessed 19 January 2015. http://www.tshaonline.org/handbook/online/articles/keu01. Uploaded 15 June 2010. Published by the Texas State Historical Association.

Long, Walter E. *For All Time to Come*. Austin: Steck, 1964.

Louis, William Roger, ed. *Burnt Orange Britannia*. London: I.B. Tauris, 2005.

Lowe, Richard. *Walker's Texas Division, C.S.A.: Greyhounds of the Trans-Mississippi*. Baton Rouge: Louisiana State University Press, 2004.

Maher, John, and Kirk Bohls. "Lutcher Stark." In *Long Live the Longhorns! One Hundred Years of Texas Football*. New York: St. Martin's Press, 1993.

Marshall, Nida A. *The Jasper Journal*. Vol. 1. Austin: Nortex Press, 1993.

Maxwell, Robert S. *Whistle in the Piney Woods: Paul Bremond and the Houston, East and West Texas Railway*. Denton: East Texas Historical Association and University of North Texas Press, 1998.

Maxwell, Robert S., and Robert D. Baker. *Sawdust Empire: The Texas Lumber Industry, 1830–1940*. College Station: Texas A&M University Press, 1983.

Maysel, Lou. *Here Come the Texas Longhorns, 1893–1970*. Fort Worth: Stadium Publishing, 1970.

McEachern, Jenna Hays. *100 Things Longhorns Fans Should Know & Do before They Die*. Chicago: Triumph Books, 2008.

Mecham, J.L., E.C. Barker, C.E. Castañeda, M.R. Gutsch, and J.R. Spell. "In Memoriam: Charles Wilson Hackett." Filed with the Secretary of the General Faculty by the Special C.W. Hackett Memorial Resolution Committee, University of Texas, 30 April 1951.

Meckley, Thad Stephen. *Williamsport*. Postcard History Series. Charleston, SC: Arcadia Publishing, 2005.

———. *Williamsport's Millionaires' Row*. Postcard History Series. Charleston, SC: Arcadia Publishing, 2005.

Meginness, John F., ed. *History of Lycoming County, Pennsylvania*. A Heritage Classic. 1892. Reprint, Berwyn Heights, MD: Heritage Books, sponsored by Lycoming County Genealogical Society, 1996.

Miles, Bob. "McDonald Observatory." *Cenizo Journal* (Third Quarter 2013): 4, 21, 27.

Miller, A.J. "Manufacturing Industries." In *Where the Port of Orange Is Located on the World's Map*, n.p. Orange, TX: Stark Foundation Archives and Heritage House, 1916.

Miller, Dale. "Wins $30,000 Scholarship Prize: Challenge of H.J. Lutcher Stark to Lead Fraternities on Texas Campus Is Met by Tau Deuteron Chapter." *Phi Gamma Delta* 9 (April 1937): 587–595.

"Millionaire's Row—Williamsport, PA." Historic Houses, 17 July 2008. http://historic houses.wordpress.com/2008/07/17/mi.

Minster, Christopher. "Biography of Álvaro Obregón." Latin American History, About .com. Accessed 1 October 2015. http://www.latinamericanhistory.about.com/od/the historyofmexico/a/obregon.htm.

"Miriam Lutcher Stark Library." Harry Ransom Center, University of Texas at Austin. Accessed 1 October 2015. http://www.hrc.utexas.edu/collections/books/holdings/stark.

Murphy, Mari. "Dr. Campbell's 'Malaria-Eradicating, Guano-Producing Bat Roosts.'" *Bats* 7, no. 2 (Summer 1989). Bat Conservation International. http://www.batcon.org /resources/media-education/bats-magazine/bat_article/386.

The Name and Family of Stark(e) or Starks. Pt. 2. Washington, DC: Media Research Bureau, 1938.

Nelda C. and H.J. Lutcher Stark Foundation 1961–2011: A Golden Anniversary of Giving. Orange, TX: Nelda C. and H.J. Lutcher Stark Foundation, 2011.

"The Nettie Lee Benson Latin American Collection, University of Texas Libraries." Celebrating Research. Accessed 1 October 2015. http://www.celebratingresearch.org /libraries/texas/benson~print.shtml.

"New Sawmill Built at Orange." *Texas Forest News* 35 (September–October 1958): 4–5.

Newton County Historical Commission. *Glimpses of Newton County History.* Burnet, TX: Nortex Press, 1982.

"1918 Flu Pandemic." Accessed 19 November 2015. http://www.history.com/search?q =1918%20flu%20pandemic.

Ninth Annual Catalogue of the Officers and Students of Dickinson Seminary from 10 June 1856 to 10 June 1857. Elmira, NY: Fairman & Co.'s Steam Printing Establishment, 1857. [Lycoming College (formerly Dickinson Seminary), Williamsport, Pennsylvania.]

Nudd, Jean. "U.S. World War I Draft Registrations." *Eastman's Online Genealogy Newsletter* 9, no. 3 (19 January 2004). http://www.eogn.com/archives/news0403.htm#WorldWarI DraftRegistrations.

Owens, William A., and Lyman Grant, eds. *Letters of Roy Bedichek.* Austin: University of Texas Press, 1985.

Palaima, Carol. *From a Shared Border to Western Hemisphere Concerns: The History of Latin American Studies at the University of Texas at Austin.* Report presented at Title VI 50th Anniversary Conference, March 2009, Washington, DC. http://www.utexas.edu/cola /insts/llilas/about/history.php.

"Pandemic Flu History, 1918–1919." FLU.gov. Accessed 1 October 2015. http://www.flu.gov /pandemic/history.

Parten, J.R. "A Summary of Testimony before a Senate Committee Investigating the University of Texas Controversy, 15–28 November 1944." Dolph Briscoe Center for American History, University of Texas at Austin.

Paulissen, May Nell, and Carl McQueary. *Miriam: The Southern Belle Who Became the First Woman Governor of Texas.* Austin: Eakin Press, 1995.

Pennington, Richard. "Darrell K. Royal–Texas Memorial Stadium." *Handbook of Texas Online.* Accessed 30 May 2013. http://www.tshaonline.org/handbook/online/articles/xvd01. Uploaded 12 June 2010. Published by the Texas State Historical Association.

———. *"For Texas, I Will": The History of Memorial Stadium*. Austin: Historical Publications, 1992.

"Pennsylvania Lumber History." Timber! Pennsylvania Lumber Museum. Accessed 3 December 2015. http://www.lumbermuseum.org/history.html.

"Peter Herdic (1824–1888) Historical Marker: Behind the Marker." Historical Markers, ExplorePAhistory.com. Accessed 18 November 2015. http://explorepahistory.com/hmarker .php?markerId=1-A-334.

Plummer, Alonzo H. *Confederate Victory at Mansfield*. Mansfield, LA: Ideal Printing, 1969.

Polk, William R. *Polk's Folly: An American Family History*. New York: Anchor Books, 2000.

Porter, Dean A., Teresa Hayes Ebie, and Suzan Campbell. "Nelda and Lutcher Stark." In *Taos Artists and Their Patrons, 1898–1950*. Notre Dame, IN: Snite Museum of Art, University of Notre Dame, 1999.

Porterfield, Nolan. *Last Cavalier: The Life and Times of John A. Lomax, 1867–1948*. Urbana: University of Illinois Press, 1996.

Presthus, Robert Vance. *Men at the Top: A Study in Community Power*. Oxford: Oxford University Press, 1964.

"The Pride and Joy of Orange, Texas, Is the Wonderful Girls' School Band." *Life* magazine, 14 October 1940.

Prindle, David F. "Oil and the Permanent University Fund: The Early Years." *Southwestern Historical Quarterly* 86 (October 1982): 276–298.

"Pujo, Arsène Paulin." Biographical Directory of the United States Congress. Accessed 15 October 2015. http://bioguide.congress.gov/scripts/biodisplay.pl?index=p000567.

Rainey, Homer Price. *The Tower and the Dome*. Boulder, CO: Pruett Publishing, 1971.

Reid, Thomas. *Spartan Band: Burnett's 13th Texas Cavalry in the Civil War*. Denton: University of North Texas Press, 2005.

Richardson, Rupert Norval, Adrian Anderson, Cary D. Wintz, and Ernest Wallace. *Texas: The Lone Star State*. 10th ed. Englewood Cliffs, NJ: Prentice Hall, 2010.

Richardson, Steve. *Tales from the Texas Longhorns: A Collection of the Greatest Stories Ever Told*. Champaign, IL: Sports Publishing LLC, 2003.

Robbins, William G. *Lumberjacks and Legislators: Political Economy of the U.S. Lumber Industry, 1890–1941*. College Station: Texas A&M University Press, 1982.

Robinson, Jeanette Heard. "Brown, Edgar William, Sr." *Handbook of Texas Online*. Accessed 11 August 2012. http://www.tshaonline.org/handbook/online/articles/fbrdr. Uploaded 2 June 2010. Published by the Texas State Historical Association.

Robinson, Jeanette Heard, Elizabeth Q. Williams, and Linda B. Farris. "Orange Comes of Age." In *Picturing Orange: A Pictorial History of Orange County*, ed. Howard C. Williams, 127–134. Orange, TX: Heritage House of Orange County Association, 2000.

Schimmel, Julie. *The Art and Life of W. Herbert Dunton, 1878–1935*. Austin: University of Texas Press for the Stark Museum of Art, 1984.

———. "A New Museum for the American West." *American West: The Magazine of Western History* 16, no. 1 (January–February 1979): 38–45.

———. *Stark Museum of Art: The Western Collection 1978*. Orange, TX: Nelda C. and H.J. Lutcher Stark Foundation, 1978.

Schwettmann, Martin W. *Santa Rita: The University of Texas Oil Discovery*. Austin: Texas State Historical Association, 1943.

Seale, William. *San Augustine in the Texas Republic*. Austin: Encino Press, 1969. Reprinted through the courtesy of the Texas State Historical Association and Lelia Wynn; originally published in the January 1969 issue of *Southwestern Historical Quarterly*.

———. *Texas Riverman: The Life and Times of Captain Andrew Smyth*. Austin: University of Texas Press, 1966.

Seventh Annual Catalogue of the Officers and Students of Dickinson Seminary from 10 June 1854 to 10 June 1855. Elmira, NY: Fairman Brothers, Printers and Binders, 1855. [Lycoming College (formerly Dickinson Seminary), Williamsport, Pennsylvania.]

"Severin Roesen (ca. 1816–after 1872): Artist Biography." MME Fine Art. Accessed 27 November 2015. http://www.mmefineart.com/artist/bio/index.php?aid=274.

"A Short Life Story of Lionel Strongfort, 1878–1970." Iron Game Collectors Series. Accessed 21 October 2015. http://www.sandowplus.co.uk/Competition/Strongfort/stronfortindex .html.

Sibley, Marilyn McAdams. *George W. Brackenridge: Maverick Philanthropist.* Austin: University of Texas Press, 1973.

Silverthorne, Elizabeth. *Ashbel Smith of Texas: Pioneer, Patriot, Statesman, 1805–1886.* College Station: Texas A&M University Press, 1982.

Smith, Brother "Railroad." *A Little Preachment and a Short Epistle to the Bigots of Texas.* Jourdanton, TX: Atascosa News-Monitor, 1925.

Smith, Henry Nash, Horace Busby, and Rex D. Hopper. "The Controversy at the University of Texas, 1939–1946: A Documentary History." Paper read at the request of the Student Committee for Academic Freedom (University of Texas: Student Committee for Academic Freedom), no publication date. Box 3L832, Dolph Briscoe Center for American History.

Smith, Julia Cauble. "Santa Rita Oil Well." *Handbook of Texas Online.* Accessed 19 January 2015. http://www.tshaonline.org/handbook/online/articles/dos01. Uploaded 15 June 2010. Published by the Texas State Historical Association.

Smith, Ronald. *Sports and Freedom: The Rise of Big-Time College Athletics.* New York: Oxford University Press, 1988.

Spargo, John. *The Bennington Battle Monument.* Rutland, VT: Tuttle, 1925. [Stark Foundation Archives]

Speck, Lawrence. "Campus Architecture: The Heroic Decades." In *The Texas Book: Profiles, History and Reminiscences of the University,* ed. Richard A. Holland, 125–138. Austin: University of Texas Press, 2006.

Spencer, Jeff A. "The Vinton (Ged) Oil Field, Calcasieu Parish, Louisiana." Petroleum History Institute, *Oil-Industry History* 11, no. 1 (December 2010). http://www.petroleum history.org/journal/vol_11.html#spencer.

Sperry, Marcus E. "The Port of Orange, Texas." In *Where the Port of Orange Is Located on the World's Map,* n.p. Orange, TX: Stark Foundation Archives and Heritage House, 1916. Forest History Collections, Stephen F. Austin State University Library, Nacogdoches, Texas; and Heritage House, Orange, TX.

"St. Mark's Lutheran Church [Williamsport]." Rootsweb. Accessed 3 December 2015. http:// freepages.genealogy.rootsweb.ancestry.com/~stmarkswilliamsport/index.htm.

"The Stark Legacy." *American Art Review* 18 (May–June 2006): 152–153.

Stark Museum of Art. *The American and British Birds of Dorothy Doughty.* Orange, TX: Nelda C. and H.J. Lutcher Stark Foundation and the Stark Museum of Art, 1978.

———. *The Steuben Glass Collection.* Orange, TX: Nelda C. and H.J. Lutcher Stark Foundation and the Stark Museum of Art, 1978.

Sterling, Ross S., and Ed Kilman, eds. *Ross Sterling, Texan: A Memoir by the Founder of Humble Oil and Refining Company.* Rev. Don Carleton. Austin: Center for American History, University of Texas at Austin, 2007.

Stocker, Barry L. "The Repasz Band in the Civil War." Repasz Band 1831, September 2014. http://www.lycoming.org/repaszband/Main/civilwarhistory.htm.

Storey, John W., and Mary L. Kelley, eds. *Twentieth-Century Texas: A Social and Cultural History.* Denton: University of North Texas Press, 2008.

Taber, Thomas T., III. *Williamsport: Lumber Capital*. Muncy, PA: Thomas T. Taber III, 1995.

Thrall, Homer S. *A Pictorial History of Texas, from the Earliest Visits of European Adventurers, to A.D. 1883*. St. Louis, MO: N.D. Thompson, 1883.

Tindall, George Brown, and David Emory Shi. *America: A Narrative History*. 9th ed. New York: W.W. Norton, 2013.

Tippens, Matthew D. *Turning Germans into Texans: World War I and the Assimilation and Survival of German Culture in Texas, 1900–1930*. Austin: Kleingarten Press, 2010.

Toal, Margaret. *Stories of Orange: A Collection of Writings*. Orange, TX: n.p., n.d.

Todd, Terry. "The History of Strength Training for Athletes at the University of Texas." *Iron Game History* 2, no. 5 (January 1993): 6–13.

Tyler, Ron. *Nature's Classics: John James Audubon's Birds and Animals*. Orange, TX: Nelda C. and H.J. Lutcher Stark Foundation, 1992.

University of Texas System, Board of Regents. "Rules and Regulations of the Board of Regents for the Government of the University of Texas." *University of Texas Bulletin* 3631 (15 August 1936).

Van Auken, Robin. "Timeline of Historic Events." 18 January 2012. http://www.newsof yesteryear.com/resources/timeline.

Van Auken, Robin, and Louis E. Hunsinger Jr. *Williamsport: The Grit Photograph Collection*. Images of America Series. Charleston, SC: Arcadia Publishing, 2004.

"Violin Makers of the Amati Family." Smithsonian Seriously Amazing. Accessed 3 December 2015. http://www.si.edu/encyclopedia_si/nmah/amati.htm.

Walker, Donald R. "Harvesting the Forest: Henry Jacob Lutcher, G. Bedell Moore, and the Advent of Commercial Lumbering in Texas." *Journal of the West* 35 (July 1996): 10–17.

Walkup, David S. "Bible, Dana Xenophon." *Handbook of Texas Online*. Accessed 19 January 2015. http://www.tshaonline.org/handbook/online/articles/fbi38. Uploaded 12 June 2010. Published by the Texas State Historical Association.

Wallace, David. *Hollywoodland*. New York: St. Martin's Press, 2002.

"Walter Reed, Medical Professional, Doctor, Scientist (1851–1902)." Biography.com. Accessed 12 October 2015. http://www.biography.com/people/walter-reed-9454083?page=1.

Watkins, J.C. "Shangri-La in the 'Jungle.'" *Houston Chronicle Rotogravure Magazine*, 29 May 1955.

Weaver, Bobby D. *First Artistic Traditions: The Native American Collection of the Stark Museum of Art*. Orange, TX: Nelda C. and H.J. Lutcher Stark Foundation, 1990.

Webb, Jim. *Born Fighting: How the Scots-Irish Shaped America*. New York: Broadway Books, 2004.

Weddle, Robert S. "La Salle, René Robert Cavelier, Sieur de." *Handbook of Texas Online*. Accessed 1 July 2011. http://www.tshaonline.org/handbook/online/articles/fla04. Uploaded 15 June 2010. Published by the Texas State Historical Association.

The White City: The Historical, Biographical and Philanthropical Record of Illinois. Chicago: Chicago World Book, 1893. https://archive.org/details/cihm_25316.

Wilkes, William C., and Mary M. Standifer. "Texas State Guard." *Handbook of Texas Online*. Accessed 18 September 2013. http://www.tshaonline.org/handbook/online/articles /qqto1. Uploaded 15 June 2010. Published by the Texas State Historical Association.

Williams, Howard C., ed. *Gateway to Texas: The History of Orange and Orange County*. Orange, TX: Heritage House Museum of Orange, 1986.

———, ed. *Picturing Orange: A Pictorial History of Orange County*. Orange, TX: Heritage House of Orange County Association, 2000.

———. "Stark, Henry Jacob Lutcher." *Handbook of Texas Online*. Accessed 22 February

2013. http://www.tshaonline.org/handbook/online/articles/fst16. Uploaded 15 June 2010. Published by the Texas State Historical Association.

Williams, Rosemary. "Luxurious Legacy: A Trio of Buildings in Orange Reflects a Prominent Family's Eye for Beauty." *Texas Highways*, March 1990, 18–27.

Wilson, Carol O'Keefe. *In the Governor's Shadow: The True Story of Ma and Pa Ferguson.* Denton: University of North Texas Press, 2014.

Woliver, Carrie Joiner. *The Train Stopped in Orange.* Orange, TX: Carrie Joiner Woliver, 2012.

Woods, Randall B., and Willard B. Gatewood. *America Interpreted.* Fort Worth: Harcourt Brace College Publishers, 1998.

Wooster, Robert. "Burkeville, TX." *Handbook of Texas Online.* Accessed 20 January 2012. http://tshaonline.org/handbook/online/articles/hlb64. Uploaded 12 June 2010. Published by the Texas State Historical Association.

———. "Lutcher, Henry Jacob." *Handbook of Texas Online.* Accessed 12 February 2010. http://www.tshaonline.org/handbook/online/articles/flu13. Uploaded June 15, 2010. Published by the Texas State Historical Association.

———. "Newton, TX." *Handbook of Texas Online.* Accessed 20 January 2012. http://www.tshaonline.org/handbook/online/articles/hjn05. Uploaded 15 June 2010. Published by the Texas State Historical Association.

Wooster, Robert, and Nancy Beck Young. "Orange and Northwestern Railroad." *Handbook of Texas Online.* Accessed 19 January 2015. http://www.tshaonline.org/handbook/online/articles/eq002. Uploaded 15 June 2010. Published by the Texas State Historical Association.

Wrenn, Jim, and Joan Wrenn. "Bowling Them Over: The Institute and the 'Americana Series.'" *Uncommon Sense* 122, pt. 1 (Summer 2006): 18–24; 123, pt. 2 (Winter 2006): 33–36.

Other Sources

Abbott, Jane Harter. "A Stark Genealogy: Some Descendants of John Stark from Scotland to the United States about 1710 and His Son, James Stark, Born in Scotland in 1695, Settled in Overwharton Parish, Stafford, Virginia, Prior to 1730." Unpublished manuscript compiled between 1928 and 1931 for Mrs. William Henry (Miriam Lutcher) Stark. Rare Books Room, Library of Congress, Scotland Section, Stark Foundation Archives.

Annexation of Texas Joint Resolution of Congress, 1 March 1845 (U.S. Statutes at Large, 5, 797–798).

Bedichek, Roy. Testimony before the State Senate Education Committee Investigation, 28 November 1944, 4:606–617. Legislative Reference Library of Texas, Austin.

Benckenstein, Eunice Robinson. Papers, Stark Foundation Archives.

Bibles, Lutcher and Stark Families. Stark Foundation Archives.

Blewett Family Papers. Heritage Village, Woodville, TX.

Boehme, Sarah E. "Buckeroos, Birds, and Blankets: H.J. Lutcher Stark as Art Collector." Lecture to Orange County Historical Society, 5 August 2014.

Boyd, Andrew, and Harry Boyd. *Boyd's Williamsport City Directory.* Williamsport, Pennsylvania, office. Years 1866–1867, 1869–1870, 1871–1872, 1873–1874, 1875–1876, 1877–1878, 1879–1880, 1881–1882, 1883–1884. Thomas T. Taber Museum of the Lycoming County Historical Society, Williamsport, Pennsylvania.

Brief History of First Presbyterian Church of Orange, Texas: In Commemoration of the 100th Anniversary of Our Church. Pamphlet, First Presbyterian Church, Orange, Texas.

The Building in Which You Worship, Something of Its Art Background. Pamphlet, First Presbyterian Church, Orange, Texas. Copy in Stark Foundation Archives.

A Century for Christ, 1878–1978: A Brief History of First Presbyterian Church of Orange, Texas, in Commemoration of the 100th Anniversary of Our Church. Pamphlet, First Presbyterian Church, Orange, Texas.

Christ Church Parish: A Tour. Pamphlet, Christ Episcopal Church, Williamsport, Pennsylvania.

Commemorative Booklet, Frances Ann Lutcher Hospital, Dedicated May 15, 1921. Stark Foundation Archives.

A Condensed History of Paper Making, Compliments of the Yellow Pine Paper Mill Co., Orange, Texas. Pamphlet, Stark Foundation Archives.

Court of Common Pleas, Records. Lycoming County Courthouse, Williamsport, Pennsylvania.

Deed Records, Jasper County, Jasper, Texas.

Deed Records, Lycoming County, Williamsport, Pennsylvania.

Deed Records, Newton County, Newton, Texas

Deed Records, Orange County, Orange, Texas.

Deed Records, Sabine County, Hemphill, Texas.

Earliest Records and Census Abstracts of Nineteenth Century Orange County Texas (1836–1880). Booklet. Orange, TX: A Sesquicentennial Project compiled and published by the Orange County Historical Society, 1986.

Easton, Hamilton Pratt. "The History of the Texas Lumbering Industry." PhD diss., University of Texas at Austin, 1947.

"1860 United States Federal Census." Ancestry.com, 2009. http://search.ancestry.com/search/db.aspx?dbid=7667.

"1860 US Federal Census—Slave Schedules." Ancestry.com, 2010. http://search.ancestry.com/search/db.aspx?dbid=7668.

Farwell, Frederick Henry. "History of Lutcher and Moore Lumber Company." Typescript. Stark Foundation Archives. (Text for article "Saw Mill Industry Plays Major Part in Texas History: Orange Center of Early Day Development," *Orange Leader,* 29 May 1936.)

Ford, Eugenia Rebecca Stark. Handwritten family history donated to Stark Foundation Archives by Madge Channing Luquette. Undated, n.p.

Haydel, Leonce. *Stories from Blind River (Bayou Des Acadiens).* Booklet. Lutcher, LA: Leonce Haydel, 1998. Stark Foundation Archives.

Hearings, Texas State Senate Education Committee Investigation, 16–28 November 1944. Legislative Reference Library of Texas, Austin.

"Henry J. Lutcher." Unattributed, undated typescript of interview of Henry Jacob Lutcher during his lifetime. Stark Foundation Archives.

"A History of Longhorn Athletics." Unfinished scrapbook begun in 1936 or later. Stark Foundation Archives.

Hood, Kyle. "Remembrances of Mrs. Lutcher, 1966–2008." Memories of Frances Ann Lutcher collected from members of First (Lutcher Memorial) Presbyterian Church, Orange, Texas. Unpublished typescript.

Hubert, Frank W.R. "My Experiences in the Orange School District: Teacher, Principal, and Superintendent of Schools." Unpublished typescript, n.d. Stark Foundation Archives.

"In Memoriam." Typescript, Resolution of Directors of First National Bank, Orange, Texas, on Death of Henry J. Lutcher. Stark Foundation Archives.

"Information on History of Orange Public Schools." Typescript. Stark Foundation Archives.

Land Commissioner's Office. Minutes, 1837, San Augustine County, Texas.

Ledger, Account of Estate of Frances Ann Lutcher, 1898–1924. Stark Foundation Archives.

Ledger, J.T. Stark and Donna J. Stark, 1877–1881. Transcribed by Jeremiah Milton Stark. Stark Foundation Archives.

Lumbering Exhibit. Thomas T. Taber Museum of Lycoming County Historical Society, Williamsport, Pennsylvania.

Lutcher, Henry J. *A Stronger and More Permanent Union.* Booklet. Orange, TX: Leader Steam Print, 1896. Stark Foundation Archives; Lutcher & Moore Lumber Company Papers, Forest History Collection, Stephen F. Austin State University, Nacogdoches, Texas.

Lutcher Memorial Building, First Presbyterian Congregation of the Church in Orange. Pamphlet. First Presbyterian Church, Orange, Texas.

Maroney, James C. "Organized Labor in Texas, 1900–1930." PhD diss., University of Houston, 1975.

Marriage Records. San Augustine County, Texas, 1:93.

Messiah's Evangelical Lutheran Church. Records. South Williamsport, Pennsylvania.

Minute Book. Vol. 2, Lutcher & Moore Lumber Company, 1913–1935. Stark Foundation Archives.

Minute Book. Rescue Oil Company, 1912–1928. Stark Foundation Archives.

Minutes. Ladies' Study Club, 1906–1908, Orange, Texas. Stark Foundation Archives.

Minutes. Shakespeare Reading Club, 1896–1897, Orange, Texas. Stark Foundation Archives.

Miss Wilson's School for Young Ladies and Children. Pamphlet. Williamsport, PA: Gazette & Bulletin Printing House, 1879. Stark Foundation Archives.

Moore, Elizabeth Blasdel. "Sketch of the Life of Gregory Bedell Moore." 2 vols. Handwritten manuscript provided to Eric Steinfeldt by Elizabeth Moore, November 1986. Originals in G. Bedell Moore Collection, Stephen F. Austin University, Nacogdoches, Texas.

"Pertinent Facts Concerning the Lutcher & Moore Lumber Company Whistle Now in Use at the DuPont Plant." Typescript, n.d. Stark Foundation Archives.

Postcard Album belonging to Nita Hill, 1907–1908. Stark Foundation Archives.

Practical Optimists: The Story of a Lumber Firm Which Refused to Let Recent Business Depression "Phase 'Em." Port of Orange, Texas, USA. Booklet, undated, but probably 1921 or 1922. Stark Foundation Archives.

Rainey, Homer Price. Testimony before the Senate Education Committee Investigation, 15–28 November 1944, 1:156–245. Legislative Reference Library of Texas, Austin.

Regents' Minutes, 1919–1945. University of Texas at Austin.

Russell, Robert E. *A History of Orange.* Ed. Loren LeBlanc. Booklet. Orange, TX: Orange County Historical Society, n.d.

Sanborn Fire Maps. Perry-Castañeda Library, Map Collection, University of Texas Online, 1896. http://www.lib.utexas.edu/maps/sanborn/m-o/txu-sanborn-orange-1896-03.jpg.

Scrapbook. Clippings pertaining to H.J. Lutcher Stark, ca. 1921–ca. 1928. Compiled by Byron Simmons. Stark Foundation Archives.

Shangri-La. Official booklet, Lutcher Stark's Shangri-La. Stark Foundation Archives. Text by Constance Kleiser, reprinted in *Las Sabinas* 24, no. 4 (1998): 1.

Stark, H.J. Lutcher. Medical Records. Stark Foundation Archives.

Stark, John Thomas. "His Diary: 25 September 1863 to 13 October 1864." Typed transcript. Stark Foundation Archives.

———. "His Life Letters and Papers, Somewhat of His Ancestors, Relatives, and Friends." Vol. 1, 1835–1867; vol. 2, 1868–1905. Stark Foundation Archives.

Stark, Miriam Lutcher. Travel Diary, Europe, 27 May–27 August 1913. Stark Foundation Archives.

Stark, Nita Hill. Travel Diary, Europe, Egypt, and the Middle East, late February–early June 1927. Transcript. Stark Foundation Archives.

The Story of Grade Marked Yellow Pine Lumber. Booklet, compliments of Lutcher & Moore Lumber Company, 1 January 1926. Stark Foundation Archives.

Sutherland, Robert L. "In Memoriam: Harry E. Moore." Filed with the Secretary of the General Faculty by Robert L. Sutherland, Chairman of the Special Harry E. Moore Memorial Resolution Committee, University of Texas, Austin, Texas, 9 January 1967.

Tax Rolls. State of Pennsylvania, Division No. 7, Collection District No. 18.

"This Is Shangri-La." *Home Gardening*, March 1950. Typescript. Stark Foundation Archives.

"U.S., Civil War Soldiers and Records, 1861–1865." Ancestry.com, 2007. http://search .ancestry.com/search/db.aspx?dbid=1555.

"U.S. Federal Census Mortality Schedules, 1850–1885." Ancestry.com, 2010. http://search .ancestry.com/search/db.aspx?dbid=8756.

Weidman, Helen Breese. *A History of Messiah's Evangelical Lutheran Church, South Williamsport, Penna.* Booklet, Messiah's Evangelical Lutheran Church, 1943.

Wingate, Roy S. Address to the Orange County Historical Society, Orange, Texas, 9 November 2004. Stark Foundation Archives.

———. "A Summary of Some of the Business Enterprises of the Lutcher and Stark Families of Orange, Texas." Compiled 2006–2007. Stark Foundation Archives.

Winkelman, Herbert W., Winkelman and Davies, Accountants. *Special Report: The Lutcher & Moore Lumber Company, Orange, Texas, 31 December 1936*. Stark Foundation Archives.

Index

Page numbers followed by f indicate figures or photographs. HJL = Henry Jacob Lutcher. LS = Henry Jacob Lutcher Stark "Lutcher Stark." WHS = William Henry "Bud" Stark. L&M = Lutcher & Moore Lumber Co.